THE COMPANION GUIDE TO MAINLAND GREECE

THE COMPANION GUIDES

It is the aim of these guides to provide a Companion in the person of the author; who knows intimately the places and people of whom he writes, and is able to communicate this knowledge and affection to his readers. It is hoped that the text and pictures will aid them in their preparations and in their travels, and will help them remember on their return.

BURGUNDY · THE COUNTRY ROUND PARIS
DEVON · EDINBURGH AND THE BORDER COUNTRY
FLORENCE · GASCONY AND THE DORDOGNE
GREEK ISLANDS · ISTANBUL · KENT AND SUSSEX
LAKE DISTRICT · LONDON
MADRID AND CENTRAL SPAIN
NEW YORK · PARIS · ROME
SICILY · SOUTH OF SPAIN · VENICE

THE COMPANION GUIDE TO

MAINLAND GREECE

Brian de Jongh

Revised by

John Gandon and Geoffrey Graham-Bell

COMPANION GUIDES

First published in two volumes as
Southern Greece (1972)
and *Mainland Greece* (1979)
Revised one-volume edition 1989

Reissued 1996
Companion Guides, Woodbridge

New edition 2000

ISBN 1 900639 35 1

The publishers and author have done their best to ensure the accuracy and currency of all the information in The Companion Guide to Greece. *However, they can accept no responsibility for any loss, injury, or inconvenience sustained by any traveller as a result of information or advice contained in the guide.*

Companion Guides is an imprint of Boydell & Brewer Ltd
PO Box 9, Woodbridge, Suffolk IP12 3DF, UK
and of Boydell & Brewer Inc.
PO Box 41026, Rochester, NY 14604–4126, USA
website: http://www.companionguides.com

A catalogue record for this book is available
from the British Library

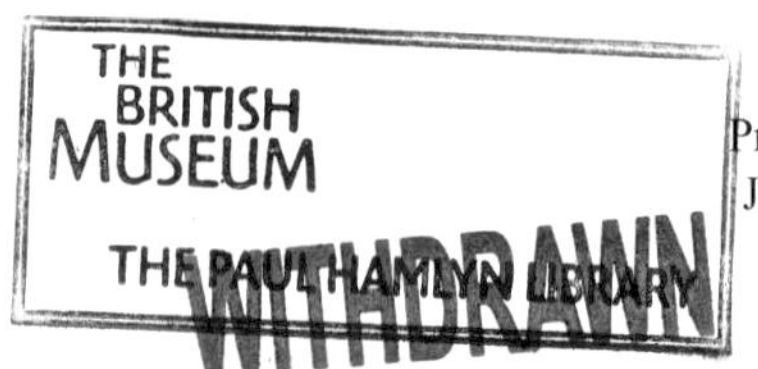

Printed in Great Britain by
J.W. Arrowsmith, Bristol

Contents

Maps and Plans

Illustrations

All illustrations by Topham Picturepoint; except Caryatid Portico and Tholos, Delphi which are by Axiom Photographic Agency, photographer James Morris.

Foreword

Robert Liddell in his Foreword to the First Edition wrote:

In this Companion Guide Brian shows himself equally at home in prehistoric and in Classical Greece, in the Byzantine world (whose fantastic history had a special appeal to him), and among the Franks and Catalans of the later Middle Ages. More than most Hellenic travellers he shows an interest in the local civilization that survived the long years of the Turkish occupation; and, of course, modern Greece was his home.

He is therefore an ideal guide to the ruins of Philippi, or to the Byzantine churches of Thessaloniki and Boeotia, as well as the lesser known painted houses of Kastoria and Siatista.

Of contemporary life he writes kindly and amusingly, without condescension, but also without the gush of the romantic philhellene for whom the sourest retsina is nectar and the toughest lump of charred octopus ambrosia, who will talk of the frescoes of Mystra in the same breath as Giotto, or compare bouzouki songs to Bach. Nevertheless Brian appreciated these Greek things, and saw that they had no need to be 'belied by false compare'. For he knew what it is about Greece that is beyond all comparison: the landscape. Travel writers from the time of Dodwell in the early nineteenth century have understood this, but too often guide-books ignore it. Their authors will tell the visitor to go and see a heap of stones interesting only to the professional archaeologist without indicating that the trouble is indeed worthwhile because of the Greek genius for choosing superb sites.

Brian was a patient and brave traveller, an amusing and unselfish companion - and Greek travel even now makes a demand on such virtues. I have travelled over much of the Aegean with him and remember, first and foremost, his rueful but humourous reactions to sea-sickness on that very rough sea - and all the delays and hazards of the journey, the dreadful food and comfortless lodgings that sometimes awaited the traveller. But he was aware that the very lack of amenities often protected lonely places from being swallowed up by tourism, and rejoiced in the fact that there are many hidden corners of Greece that can be discovered only at the expense of time and trouble.

Note on the New Edition

Brian de Jongh - my uncle - was originally commissioned to write the first edition of this book for publication in the early 1970s. In the event he could not include all the material that he had written in one volume and two were produced. The first, *Southern Greece*, covering the Peloponnese, Attica and Boeotia was published in 1972 and the second, *Mainland Greece*, covering the whole country apart from the Peloponnese, in 1979. Sadly, Brian died in 1977 when the second volume was in draft form and I took over and saw it through to publication.

When the time for a full revision arrived I felt that the advantages of having the whole Mainland covered in one volume outweighed the loss of some of Brian's original text - particularly as the original books had overlapped by several chapters covering the area from Athens to Delphi.

This edition is still essentially the book that Brian wrote; I have reduced its length by leaving out some of the mythological stories - which is a pity - and some of the more detailed descriptions of archaeological sites and artefacts in museums: information which is readily available in the excellent illustrated guide books now available in Greece. What I have tried to retain above all else is the evidence of Brian's love for Greece and the Greek people. There are some things he did not like - and of which he made no secret - but essentially he was a Hellenophile.

Brian was born in Smyrna, when it was a Greek city, to a family who, though originally of Dutch extraction, had lived in Greece arid Turkey for several generations. His mother was in fact of Greek and Irish parentage. He was educated in Switzerland and at Oxford, became a British citizen and served in the Intelligence Corps in the Greek Islands during the Second World War. Most of his adult life was spent in and around Athens where he earned his living as a writer. This background made him a natural choice when Vincent Cronin was looking for an author for this Companion Guide. This book was the culmination of Brian's writing career and the main preoccupation of the last ten years of his life.

As I live in England and have limited opportunity for travel in Greece, I have relied very heavily on my co-editor Geoffrey

Graham-Bell for the vast amount of detailed updating that has gone into this new edition. Geoffrey has lived in Athens, where he writes, paints and teaches, since 1949 and, in order to revise this book, has travelled to almost every corner of Mainland Greece.

One aspect that has given us considerable cause for deliberation has been how to present the spelling of modern Greek place-names. Anyone familiar with travel in Greece will know that many names can be spelt in a bewildering variety of ways on roadsigns, maps and in guide books. This is the result of many initiatives by a variety of people to provide suitable transliteration from modem Greek into English. In the previous editions of this book I tried to steer a course between these different spellings, using what I believed to be the most common version in use. In this edition we have moved away from this convention and tried to be as helpful as possible to English-speaking travellers by spelling names in a way that should allow pronounciation to be as close as possible to modern Greek, even though this spelling may differ somewhat from that which will be found on some maps or roadsigns.

John Gandon

1

Athens: The Acropolis

THE CENTRE OF ATHENS is **Syndagma Square**, midway between the hump of the Acropolis and the taller pinnacled crag of Lykavittos which overlooks the sprawling modern city. Lined with hotels, cafés and travel agencies, ablaze with illuminated signs by night, this is a typical twentieth-century square with little to recall the past. Streets and avenues branch out in all directions, their suburban tentacles encroaching on the foothills of the limestone mountains that enclose the city on three sides, with the sweep of the Saronic Gulf on the fourth.

Overlooking the square, the Grande Bretagne is the oldest and the most individual of Greece's luxury hotels, with a pleasant restaurant, the GB Corner. Café tables spread across the pavements of the square and the kiosks, which are focal points in the life of the shopper in Greece, are festooned with foreign newspapers, magazines and paperbacks; there is just enough room for the salesman to sit perched on a stool, smothered by stacks of airmail envelopes, films, soap, aspirin, after-shave lotion and other useful articles. At the eastern end of the square, beyond the orange trees and crowded benches, and above the new Metro station, is the austere war memorial, guarded by evzones. Behind it is a large, plain nineteenth-century building, once the royal palace, now the Parliament House. Politics are the breath of life to large sections of the population. Personalities are rated higher than policies, and loyalty to the man of the moment is sometimes so fanatical that the only outlet lies in acts of violence. Interim periods of dictatorship, repressive or otherwise and seldom generally accepted, form part of the pattern. On the right of the Parliament House is the National Garden, a pleasant refuge from the glare of the summer.

The Acropolis - an 'upper city' built on a natural outcrop whose sides have been strengthened with massive walls - and its immediate surroundings form a ragged ellipse. This is the 'city of Theseus'. Around it extends the 'city of Hadrian', which merges into modern residential Athens. One can therefore walk, in little more than half an hour, from Syndagma Square to any of the main archaeological sites, strung out like an irregular garland round the Acropolis.

Even leaving aside its associations - mythological, historical, artistic - the Acropolis is physically omnipresent. The walls and bastions dominate the apartment blocks on the periphery of its slopes and, consciously or not, one is always looking up to see if the colonnades of the Parthenon or the porches of the Erechtheion are still there, outlined against a sky which, for weeks on end, can be an astonishingly vivid blue when there is no air pollution. A sense of intimacy with this gleaming hump of limestone is quickly acquired; and equally quickly taken for granted. Athens without the Acropolis would be unthinkable; not only would the skyline be different, but also the entire town plan, ancient and modern, would probably have developed otherwise - if at all.

There are several approaches. An obvious one is to begin at Amalias Avenue, on the south-east corner of Syndagma Square. There is much on the way that is historically irrelevant, though not without charm. If you follow the avenue you will have the National Garden on the left; to the right, facing Filellinon Street, is the Church of the *Panayia* of Lykodemos, an attractive brick building, the first of several minor masterpieces of Byzantine architecture in Athens. Founded in the eleventh century, restored in the nineteenth, it is now the church of the Russian community. Further up Filellinon Street is the Anglican Church of St Paul, grey, austere and incongruously Gothic in the urban Mediterranean setting. Across the street from these two churches the narrow passage of Kydathenaion Street leads to two minute squares with struggling shrubbery. This is the crowded Plaka quarter, full of tavernas, snack-bars, churches and tourist shops.

At No. 17 Kydathenaion Street is the **Museum of Popular Arts**. The exhibits include elaborate and colourful national costumes and folk jewellery. Particularly striking is the work of the Epirot *terzides*, specialists in needlework with gold thread, who travelled across the country receiving orders for lavish embroideries whose designs were based on traditional regional patterns. On the far side of the second little square, Farmaki Street leads to the Byzantine Church of *Ayia Ekaterini* in a sunken square. Two ancient columns stand in front of a little garden. The building has unfortunately suffered from tasteless restoration.

A few yards away in another open space, surrounded by a

jumble of antique foundations, is the **Choregic Monument of Lysikrates**. The monument is a fantasy: a cylindrical drum of marble on a square stone base, with six Corinthian columns engaged under the architrave. The mutilated frieze of the monument represents the episode of Dionysos' capture by Tyrrhenian pirates and the tricks he played in order to confound them. A Franciscan monastery was built around it and this architectural extravaganza served as the monks' library. Byron lodged here in the winter of 1810-11; he read a great deal in the library, organized boxing matches between Catholic and Orthodox schoolboys and drank with the *Mufti* of Thebes and the *Kaimakam* of Athens. For the preservation of the monument much is owed to the French Government, which bought and restored it early in the nineteenth century.

From the Choregic Monument, Vyronos Street (named after Byron) leads into Dionysiou Areopayitou Avenue, which ascends towards the Acropolis. The Avenue is now closed to traffic as part of the plan to create a continuous walkway linking all the Classical sites between the Olympic Stadium and the Academy of Plato. On the other side, at the beginning of Makriyanni Street, is the Centre of Acropolis Studies, with an interesting Museum containing, among other things, plaster casts of the Parthenon frieze. The new Acropolis Museum, the construction of which has been seriously delayed by disagreements, will be here.

On the right of Dionysiou Areopayitou Avenue lie scattered marble slabs and truncated columns: fragments of the Sanctuary of Dionysos. A relative hush descends: the tremendous weight of antiquity, which has done so much to fashion the mind and character of modern Greeks, begins to impinge. Two slender unfluted Corinthian columns, once surmounted by votive gifts, stand above a grotto in the south side of the Acropolis behind the ruined **Theatre of Dionysos**. Hollowed out of the hillside, the auditorium consisted of seventy-eight semi-circular tiers, divided into three sectors by *diazômas*. Originally the auditorium had an earth surface, but it was remodelled in the fourth century BC into a stone structure by Lykurgos, an able financier and patron of the arts.

The theatre is a good example of the Greek practice of utilizing a natural declivity for carving out an amphitheatre in some dominant yet central position. Situated at the foot of the citadel, it once commanded a view of the shrubby groves and undulations of the country below Ymittos. Today nothing but an urban expanse meets the eye. Originally actors and chorus performed in the circular *orchestra*, surrounded in Roman times by a water conduit which enabled it to be flooded for the performance of mock naval battles. In the centre was the god's altar on a raised platform, marked by a large diamond-shaped paving stone, around which the chorus revolved in stately measures, chanting *dithyrambs* to the god. With the development of the art of the theatre, a proscenium - a narrow platform occupying a segment of the orchestra - was added as a stage for the main protagonists. The acoustics were improved by the placing of inverted bronze vessels on pedestals at various points in the auditorium where they redirected the voices of the actors. Painted scenic props were used and the actors wore large, grotesque masks.

The stage area was partly restored in 1985. Here the tragedies of Aeschylus, Sophocles and Euripides were performed for the first time and European drama was born. The throne of the high priest of Dionysos, with its decorations of lions, griffins and, very appropriately, satyrs and a bunch of grapes, is easily identified in the centre of the front row. The concave seats, reserved for archons and priests and once shaded with awnings, are extraordinarily comfortable. The earliest theatrical compositions were accompanied by dancing, mimed scenes and impassioned dialogues. The annual performances, which formed part of the Great Dionysia, were held with much pomp in the spring sunshine, to the accompaniment of flute-playing and the banging of cymbals and drums. The audience did not only seek entertainment; they were genuinely moved by religious exaltation and the desire to honour the licentious young god. During the festival all work in the city ceased, a general moratorium was declared, law courts were shut and prisoners released from jail. Abstinence from wine was considered a mark of disrespect to the god, and bawdy, colourful processions wound through the streets.

From the highest tier of the theatre a row of cypress trees leads westward between the ruins of the Asclepeion - a sheltered sanctuary for the sick, dedicated to the god of healing - and the *Stoa* of Eumenes, the work of a philhellenic king of Pergamum in the second century BC; the *stoa* consisted of a double colonnade and served as a foyer during the intervals between the trilogies of plays that lasted all day. From here one regains Dionysiou Areopayitou Avenue and mounts a broad marble stairway to the **Odeion of Herodes Atticus**, the gift of a wealthy public benefactor of the Antonine era to the people of Athens in about 162 AD. The cedar-wood roof has vanished and the thirty-two tiers have been restored with modern facings. When the arched stone façade of three stories is floodlit, it creates an effect of Roman splendour, the openings allowing for a glowing and mysterious interplay of light and shade, which is absent from the classical simplicity of the monuments on the Acropolis. The contrast is striking - yet the two styles complement each other, as Greek and Roman architecture often do. In front of the semi-circular orchestra, a chequer-board of dark blue and white marble, rises the stage and behind it the *skene* (the stone or marble background to a stage), consisting of a colonnade with niches for statues, surmounted by a narrow ledge reserved for actors who impersonate the gods.

A festival, very different from the Dionysia, is now held every summer (June - September) in the restored theatre. Apart from ancient drama, the festival includes performances by the world's leading orchestras and by opera, ballet and theatre companies. Acoustic imperfections are redeemed by the setting: especially the mellow glow of the arcaded *skene* and the slowly fading violet mass of Mount Ymittos beneath the summer evening sky. The trumpet solo in the *Leonora No. 3* overture echoing across the ruins could not be more dramatic.

Beyond the Odeion, a paved road ascends to the **Acropolis**, which has the shape of a flat-topped, elongated lozenge and is about a hundred metres high. 'There is but one entry,' says Pausanias, 'it affords no other, being precipitous throughout and having a strong wall.' As one climbs, one is conscious of a feeling of isolation, but at the same time of being at the heart of things; of one's proximity to the city and yet one's remoteness from it, of an atmosphere that has become unusually rarefied. The sheer sides of the Acropolis are honeycombed with grottoes and defended by strong walls, of which the earliest, below the Temple of Niké Apteros, are called Cyclopean, but are also attributed to the Pelasgi, the first inhabitants of the Attic plain.

On the left, as one ascends the restored ancient ramp, past the ticket office and crowds of tourists, touts and guides, stands a large pedestal of greyish-blue Ymittos marble, once surmounted by a statue of the Roman general Agrippa in a bronze chariot. In front rises the **Propylaia**, the entrance way to the citadel, one of the masterpieces of classical architecture. Commissioned by Pericles, it was built by Mnesikles, a fashionable fifth-century BC architect. Extending across the west side of the hill, the Propylaia, much of whose complexity of design is due to the asymmetrical slope of the

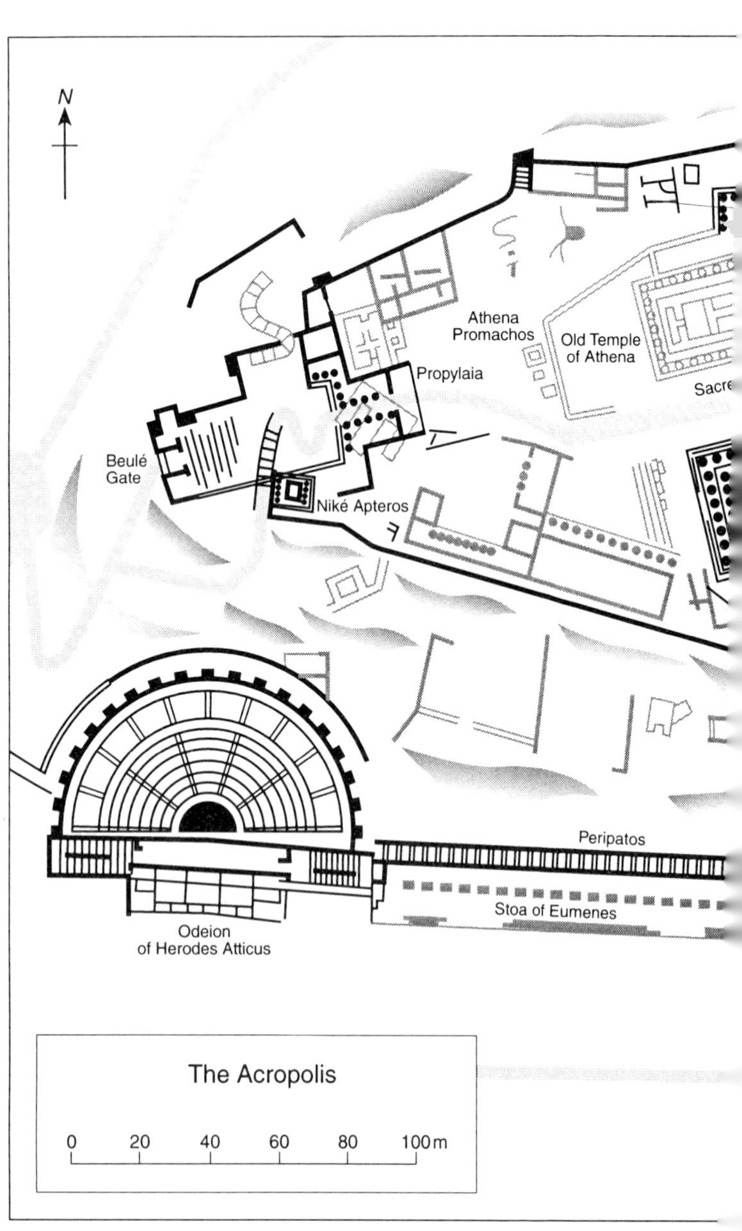

N
Athena
Promachos
Old Temple
of Athena
Propylaia
Beulé
Gate
Niké Apteros
Peripatos
Stoa of Eumenes
Odeion
of Herodes Atticus
The Acropolis
0 20 40 60 80 100m

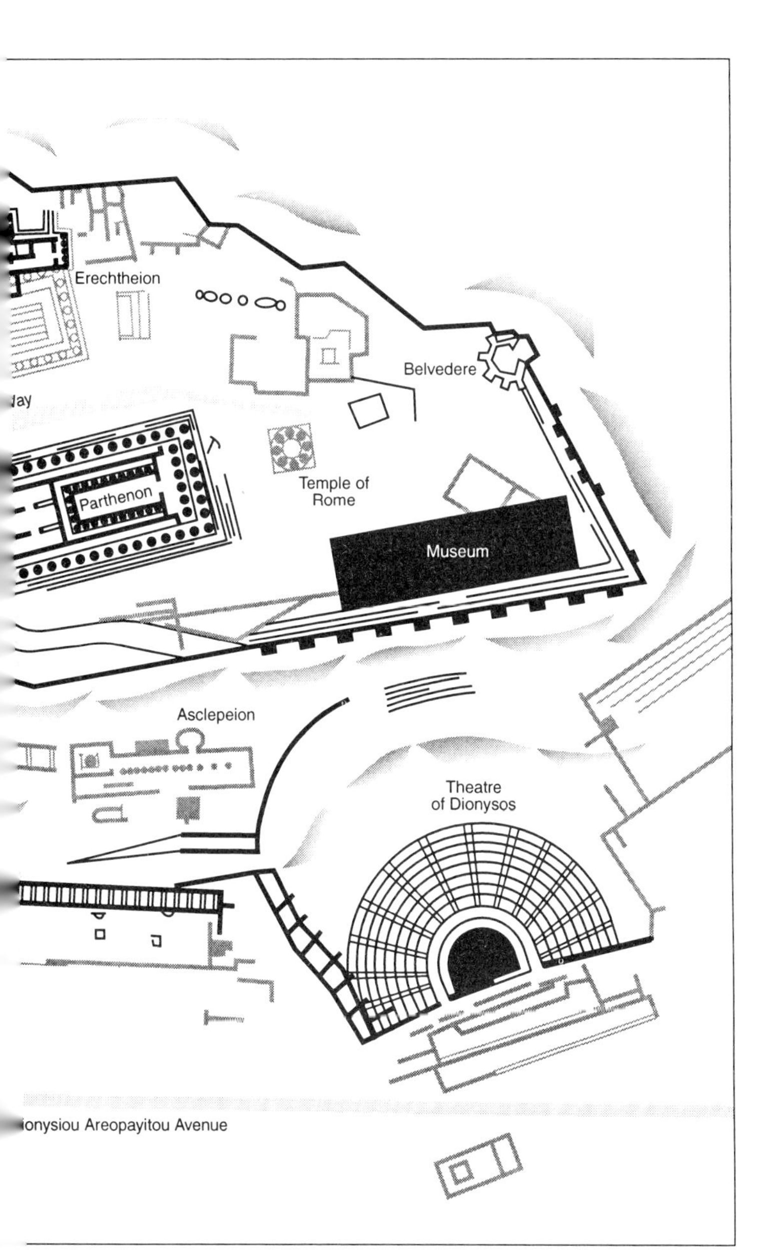

Erechtheion
Belvedere
Temple of Rome
Parthenon
Museum
Asclepeion
Theatre of Dionysos
ionysiou Areopayitou Avenue

ground, forms an entrance hall with five gates through which men and horses entered the precinct; the marks of chariot wheels are still visible. After climbing a flight of low steps, one enters the massive edifice of Pentelic marble, through the western façade of six Doric columns. In the west portico, two rows of three Ionic columns flank the main passage. The ceiling was coffered, each square having a gilt star in the centre. Towards the eastern end of the building there is a cross-wall in which are the five openings of the gateway. The gates, of different sizes, had huge doors made of wood faced with bronze; the loud grating noise they made when opened is mentioned by Aristophanes. On the eastern side of the wall there is another portico, also with a façade of six Doric columns, leading out onto the sacred area of the Acropolis. There are two projecting wings: one to the north, leading to the Pinakothiki, where paintings were exhibited on boards; the other, less well preserved, to the south (towards the Temple of Niké Apteros).

In the fourteenth century the Florentine Duke of Athens established his chancery in the Propylaia, adding a second storey, battlements and a tower. In the seventeenth century the Turks, with their customary disregard for historical monuments, turned the marble porticoes into a powder magazine; struck by lightning, the gunpowder ignited and blew the establishment sky-high and the central part of the building caved in. Much of what we now see standing is the result of laborious restoration by modern archaeologists. A more majestic entrance to a holy precinct can hardly be imagined.

Immediately to the right, the **Temple of Wingless Victory** (Niké Apteros) seems minuscule in comparison. Only five and a half metres by three and a half, it is a memorial to the Greek victories over the Persians. Pericles entrusted the plan to Kallikrates, who so constructed the temple, which rests on a stylobate of three steps, that its front pointed in the direction of the Parthenon: an effect probably designed to focus the eye on the more impressive building. This exquisitely-proportioned little monument, with its eight Ionic columns composed of monolithic shafts instead of the usual series of superimposed drums, was demolished by the Turks and the materials were used for the construction of a defence wall. A century and a half later King Othon commissioned the reconstruction of the temple. The original materials fortunately lay at hand, but the greater part of the frieze is so mutilated that it is difficult to identify the headless figures. The east frieze represented the assembly of the gods; the other three are believed to have depicted scenes from the Persian Wars, which was contrary to the usual practice of portraying mythical feats on the friezes of temples.

Returning to the Propylaia, one passes out of the east portico onto a large sloping area littered with the debris of centuries. To the left is the Erechtheion, to the right the Parthenon on a terrace dominating the entire precinct. There is no vegetation: nothing but rock and marble; and sky overhead. How often one has seen it all before - in paintings, drawings and photographs. However there is one thing not anticipated: the sheer physical dominance of the Parthenon over every other structure on the Acropolis. In the second century AD Pausanias described the Sacred Way, which led obliquely up the incline from the Propylaia to the east front of the Parthenon, as a jumble of statues, pedestals and votive offerings. Today nothing remains but the sun-baked bases, the ruts formed by ancient water-ducts, the sockets from which innumerable columns sprouted. At intervals faint incisions in the rock, intended to prevent horses and sacred animals from slipping on the hard, smooth surface, are noticeable. Here, as in the sanctuaries of Delphi and Olympia, buildings are seldom parallel to each other. The Greeks sought symmetry, but not parallelism, which they considered monotonous.

Stripped of its honey-coloured patina by acid rain to a pale cream not seen since the original paint disappeared centuries ago, the Temple of Athena Polias, tutelary goddess of Athens, or **Parthenon**, as it came to be known, stands on the site of an earlier temple burned by the Persians on the eve of the battle of Salamis. The new temple was the brain-child of Pericles; Iktinos, assisted by Kallikrates, was the principal architect; and Phidias, the greatest sculptor of the age, was in charge of the decoration. The plans were the most ambitious and architecturally daring ever attempted. Little wonder that the great building, primarily a place of worship, soon came to be regarded as a national treasury, containing bullion, archives and votive gifts of immense value. It is constructed entirely of Pentelic marble, but what is most remarkable is the architectural refinement employed to counteract unwanted optical effects. The forty-six Doric columns lean slightly inwards and have an outward curvature which prevents the eye from being carried upwards automatically; the columns acquire volume and elasticity and thus monotony is relieved. This all-important *entasis*, as it is called, was intended to correct an optical illusion, for a perfectly straight column invariably appears thinner in the middle when seen against a background of bright light. The resultant effect of strength and harmony is particularly evident from either end of the north and south colonnades. Another architectural refinement was the gradual rise of the stylobate to a point which is highest in the centre. There is, in fact, hardly a straight line in the building. The ultimate effect of all this *entasis*, almost invisible to the untrained eye, is to create an impression of a perfectly-proportioned edifice growing organically out of a natural eminence.

The sculptures, executed by Phidias and his pupils, and originally painted in bright hues of red, blue, yellow and green - the effect, it is thought, may have been rather gaudy - consisted of ninety-two *metopes*, a frieze five hundred and twenty-four feet long around the entire circumference of the outer walls of the *cella*, and two gigantic pediments, at each corner of which lions' heads projected. The decoration is arranged in three tiers - on, as it were, three different religious levels - embracing the entire cosmos in which the Greeks of the fifth century BC had their being. First came the Phidias frieze, representing the procession of the Great Panathenaia: a masterpiece of animation, with every section of the population depicted in motion, participating in the procession - on foot, on horseback, or in chariots. Recently evidence has been found that the frieze was not part of the original plan, and it has been suggested that it may not represent the Panathenaia procession. Parts of the frieze, though much damaged, may be glimpsed on the west end; in the equestrian groups the prancing horses seem to be defying the attempts of the young riders to control them. Visitors are unfortunately no longer allowed to enter the building; but anyway the angle of vision was always very awkward, for the frieze is twelve metres above the spectator, who had little room to manoeuvre in the narrow colonnade. Other slabs are in the Acropolis Museum and the remaining fifty-six in the British Museum.

From the human bustle of the frieze we move on to the *metopes*, which represent the gods and mythological heroes engaged in epic contests with giants, Centaurs and Amazons, symbolic of the victory of mind over matter. These are of inferior quality to the frieze. Thirty-two remain in their original position, between *triglyphs*, but they are mutilated almost beyond recognition. Other surviving *metopes* are in the British Museum and the Louvre; there is also one in the Acropolis Museum. Finally, on the highest level, the worshipper entered the realm of divine beings. The sculptures of the pediments represented two of the most venerable scenes in Athenian mythology: the birth of Athena, when she sprang fully armed from the head of Zeus 'with a mighty shout, while Heaven and Earth trembled before her', and her contest with Poseidon for possession of the city. The most important fragments are in the British Museum. Except for a cast of Dionysos, the superb heads of three horses from the chariots of the Sun and Moon at either end of the east front, and two headless figures in the west, the Parthenon pediments are now no more than two gaping wounds in a scarred and mutilated structure.

The huge *cella* of the Parthenon is now open to the sky. The interior arrangement can easily be traced: first (east to west), the *pronaos* (an outer porch), then the *naos*, the inner shrine which housed Phidias' great chryselephantine statue of Athena, over forty feet high and adorned with precious stones - probably as garish as it was awesome in the sombre glow of the sacred chamber; then the Parthenon proper, the chamber of the goddess' virgin priestesses, where the treasure and bullion were kept (a nice juxtaposition of god and mammon); finally the *opisthodomos*, a back porch corresponding to the *pronaos*.

In the fifth century the temple was converted into a Christian basilica consecrated to the Mother of God (there are traces of painting on the interior north-west wall) and Phidias' statue of the goddess was removed to Constantinople.

After the Frankish conquest of the Levant in 1204, the Parthenon became a Latin church. Two and a half centuries later, after the fall of Constantinople, Athens was visited by the conqueror Sultan Mehmet II, who could not resist converting the Parthenon into a mosque, to which a minaret was added. As such it remained until 1687 when a direct hit, during a siege by the Venetian army commanded by Morosini, set off a massive explosion in the temple which was being used as a Turkish powder magazine. Further damage was suffered during the War of Independence, and it was not until 1930 that the restoration of the north colonnade, with the drums, capitals and fragments of architrave left lying about since the seventeenth century, was completed by Greek archaeologists. Thus, in spite of siege, pillage and desecration, the bare bones of Pericles' brainchild, with the matchless subtlety of its proportions and its columns, which appear perfectly white in the brilliant sunshine, have survived the vicissitudes of centuries. Unfortunately the restoration caused unforeseen problems when the steel reinforcements corroded and started to expand, leading to splitting of the marble: it became necessary to replace the steel and repair the damage. The work proceeds.

The view from the Parthenon embraces the whole of Athens and its surrounding mountains. It is most spectacular at sunset, when the famous violet light spreads across the bare slopes of Ymittos and for one miraculous moment is reflected in the buildings of the entire city.

From the eastern front of the Parthenon you descend to the **Acropolis Museum**, a unique showcase of Archaic sculpture of the seventh, sixth and early fifth centuries BC. All the exhibits were found on the Acropolis. In Archaic sculpture the males, generally youths, are nude, whereas the females are fully clothed, for it is not until Hellenistic times that Eastern influences cause Greek modesty, with regard to the nude female figure, to be swept away in a wave of sensuous opulence. All Archaic statues, male and female, from the earliest to the latest, whether pleasing in a conventional sense or not, are based on the Greek concept of perfection in shape. The *kouroi*, narrow-waisted youths exulting in their beauty and athletic prowess, stand rigid, left leg slightly forward, head and neck very erect. The oblique eyes protrude and a faintly mocking smile, hinting at a quiet, sophisticated sense of humour, plays about the full sensual lips. In spite of the ritualistic stiffness of the figures, reminiscent of Egyptian statues, they are, in the words of Lord Clark, 'alert and confident members of a conquering race'. However, the finest *kouroi* (not from the Acropolis) are in the National Museum and it is the reed-like maidens, the *korai*, presented as votive offerings to the goddess, that exercise the greatest fascination in the Acropolis Museum. In their main attributes they differ little from the *kouroi*, except that they are fully and stylishly dressed, and the arrangement of the hair is extremely elaborate. The *korai* represent fashionable young women of Athenian society in the aristocratic age of the Peisistratids. They are clad in a skin-tight tunic, the *chiton*, and a mantle, the *himation*, which is frequently jewelled and which falls in symmetrically-pleated folds in front of the breast. In spite of variations in size (most *korai* are about three-quarters life size), hair style and details of drapery, one is struck by the prevailing conformity.

At the entrance to the museum a large marble effigy of Athena's owl (No. 1347) establishes the goddess' symbolic authority. To the left, a charming fourth-century BC bas relief (No. 1338) depicts eight nude male figures preparing to perform a Pyrrhic dance. Room I contains part of a seventh-century BC pediment (the earliest one extant in Greece) from a small treasury, subsequently destroyed. Executed in painted tufa (traces of red, green and black), it represents the struggle of Herakles with the Hydra, whose innumerable coils are fashioned like octopus tentacles. In Room II fragments of a large, primitive pediment, possibly from the original temple of Athena (sixth-century BC), depict Herakles slaying Triton (No. 36), while a friend of Triton's, a monster with three winged bodies (No. 35), looks on. The composition - what remains of it - is full of vitality, with expressions of grotesque whimsicality on the three faces of the monster. The **Moscophoros** or Calf-Bearer (No. 624), representing a man bearing a sacrificial calf to the goddess, is a far more evolved work of art. Of four exquisitely-carved little Archaic horses (No. 575), the best-preserved are the two central ones, who turn their heads towards each other, as though engaged - somewhat shyly - in conversation.

Fragments from the early temple of Athena destroyed by the Persians are among the chief exhibits in Room III, but the greatest enchantments are reserved for Room IV. First comes the **Rider** (No. 590), which formed part of a small equestrian composition, believed to be the work of Phaidimos, greatest of Archaic sculptors. The head is a cast from the original in the Louvre, but nonetheless its charm and liveliness, with the almond-shaped eyes and firm, expressive lips set in the familiar teasing smile, make it one of the most attractive in the museum. Particularly decorative are the elaborate, bead-like curls across the forehead and the long locks, strung like corals, hanging behind the large ears. But it is the monolithic upward thrust of the torso from the wasp waist that is most impressive; a perfect achievement of grace and naturalness, in spite of the absence of movement. In the same room are the *korai*, ranged in a circle on pedestals: formal, architectonic in conception, often haughty, always amused; a world of aristocratic ease, poise and serenity, destined to perish forever in the holocaust of the Persian Wars. No. 679, the **Peplos Koré** (so called because she is wearing a heavy woollen *peplos* over her *chiton*), her bosom framed between parallel plaits of hair, is a masterpiece of sixth-century BC Attic sculpture, also probably the work of Phaidimos. The body, true, is block-like (the lower part flat at the front and round at the back), but the head is both authoritative, refined and beautifully modelled, the expression cynical, yet full of a kind of detached felicity.

Room V is dominated by a larger than life-size *koré* (No. 681), as formidable as her sisters in Room IV are diminutive. There are also fragments of a pediment from an older temple (No. 631), depicting gods and goddesses victorious over fallen giants in battle (*gigantomachia*). Passing into Room VI one is suddenly conscious of a change, a break with the past. We are in the fifth century. The mocking smile has vanished and emotion is reflected in pensive expressions and relaxed attitudes. The change of mood is most striking in the **Kritios Boy** (No. 698), a perfect reproduction of the human body, its weight evenly and naturally distributed. An effortless poise has replaced the taut formality of the strictly frontal position; but in the sweeping-away of rigid class distinctions which followed the fall of the Peisistratids, the Kritios Boy seems to have lost his sense of humour. A small slab in low relief (No. 695) represents a **Mourning Athena**. Emotion has broken through, and the limbs have grown supple in the process. Again there is the new distribution of weight, the goddess' body being slightly tilted forward, leaning on her spear; only the toes and the ball of the left foot touch the ground.

In Room VII there is a well-preserved *metope* (No. 705) from the Parthenon, portraying the struggle between a centaur and a Lapith woman (remarkable for the modelling of her body in the round), and two fine heads of horses (Nos. 1081 and 882) from the Chariots of Poseidon and Athena which formed part of the sculptural decoration of the west pediment of the Parthenon. Room VIII is dominated by **fragments from the Parthenon frieze**, stunning examples (notice how shallow the relief is) of crowds in motion, full of dash, energy and liveliness. No. 973 (relief from the balustrade of the Temple of Niké Apteros) depicts a maiden removing her sandal; although her *chiton* is so thin that the contours of her body stand out firm and rounded, deep shadows lurk mysteriously in the folds of the loosely-flowing drapery. Finally, in Room IX there is a fourth-century BC head of Alexander the Great (No. 1331), sensuous, full-lipped, conventionally handsome; also a fragment of a relief depicting a severe, authoritative Niké crowning Herakles, while Athena looks on. Also in Room IX, and more important, are the Caryatids from the Erechtheion, revealing the disastrous effects of atmospheric pollution, now protected from further decay in a chemically neutral environment.

From the museum one follows the line of the north-east rampart, past a belvedere overhanging a steep incline once cluttered with mean little medieval houses grouped round the twelfth-century church of *Ayios Nikolaos Rangaves*. Northward, below the walls of

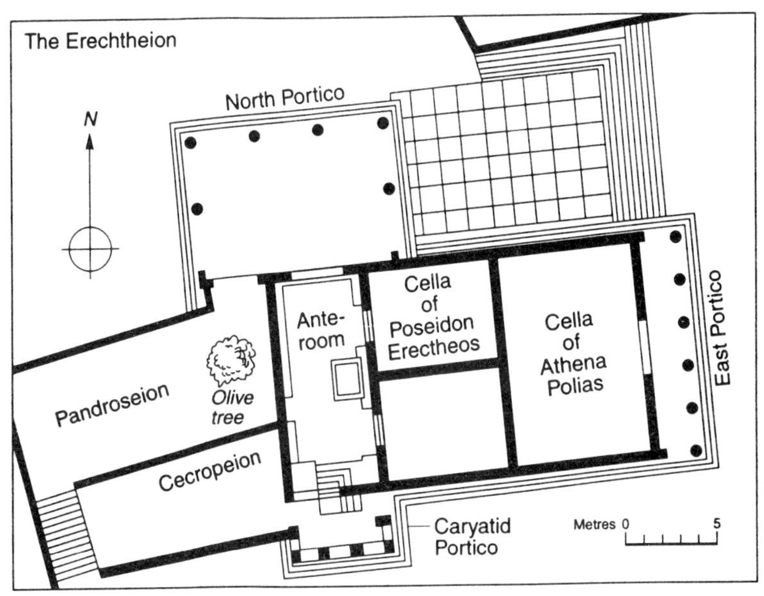
The Erechtheion
N
North Portico
Cella
of
Poseidon
Erectheos
Ante-
room
Cella
of
Athena
Polias
East Portico
Pandroseion
Olive
tree
Cecropeion
Caryatid
Portico
Metres 0
5

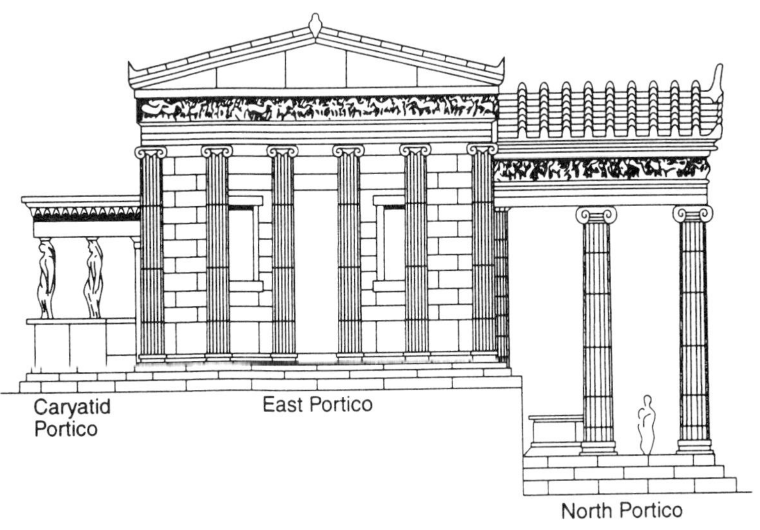
Caryatid
Portico
East Portico
North Portico

Themistocles, lies central Athens. Beside one stands the **Erechtheion**: for some, the supreme monument of the Acropolis, painstakingly restored after years of labour.

The temple, completed during the last years of the Peloponnesian War, occupied the site of the holiest place on the Acropolis. Its origins go back to the beginnings of the Attic religion. This is the spot where Athena, in her contest with Poseidon for the possession of the city, made the original olive tree spring up.

The Erechtheion is situated on lower ground than the Parthenon and its complexity is in sharp contrast to the monolithic grandeur of the larger temple. Built on different levels, on the foundations of the old temple destroyed by the Persians, it has no side colonnades but three porticoes different in size, style and execution. From every angle the spectator obtains a different view: startling, novel, sometimes confusing. The side opposite the Parthenon consists of a blank marble wall, broken at the west end by the **Caryatid Portico**; it is the least attractive side. The temple served several purposes, all of profound religious significance, and the architect, probably Mnesikles, had to cope with a sloping site as well as the inclusion of three separate shrines in one building - those of Athena Polias, Poseidon and Erechtheus - not to mention the Pandroseion, which contained the ancient olive tree planted by the goddess, and altars of other semi-deities. Architecturally, the whole edifice was intended as a counterweight - more modest in dimensions and different in style - to the Parthenon. The heavy drapery of the Caryatids may have been meant to harmonize with the fluting of the columns of the Parthenon, but these six hefty maidens, in spite of their brave yet self-conscious simper, seem to be crushed by the weight of the ornamental roof they support on their cushioned heads. Replicas have replaced the originals, one of which was bought by Lord Elgin and is now carefully preserved in the British Museum. Her unfortunate sisters were reduced to leprous anonymity by acid rain and have been moved to the Acropolis Museum for preservation, as mentioned above. The spacing of the figures is such that the porch acquires the columnar aspect of a lofty tribune. But nothing really compensates for the expanse of blank wall from which the portico projects with such aimlessness, dwarfed by the proximity of the Parthenon.

The **East Portico** consists of six narrow fluted Ionic columns of great elegance (one is in the British Museum), surmounted by elaborate capitals. Approaching the entrance, there are side views of the Caryatid and North Porticoes which break up the symmetry, but not the harmony, of the whole. It is not, however, until one has descended a flight of steps and reached the **North Portico**, through which the chamber of Erechtheus (a mythical figure, possibly another aspect of Poseidon) was probably reached, that one receives the full impact of this unique and anomalous building perched above the sprawling city, with the long line of Mount Parnitha forming a bluish-grey barrier in the north. The portico, although built on a lower level than the other two porches, gives a greater impression of thrust and delicacy and, both in its proportions and adornment, may be considered one of the most perfect examples of classical architecture. The six Ionic columns have a slight *entasis* and their bases are embellished with plaited decoration. The beautifully-carved capitals, also extremely ornate, are no less elegant. The great doorway is narrower at the top and has a lavishly-ornamented frame. An opening in the floor of the portico reveals a small vault with three holes in the rock, supposedly caused by the thunderbolt of Zeus.

One now passes out through the Propylaia before walking to the right, down the paved way into the ancient part of the town round the Acropolis. In front rises the grey, flat-topped rock of the **Areopagos**. Here sat the oldest court of justice in the world, first summoned by the gods to judge Orestes for the crime of matricide. Here, too, Demosthenes was tried for bribery and St Paul addressed the people of Athens on the 'Unknown God'. They gave the apostle a polite but lukewarm reception. Only Dionysios the Areopagite, an erudite councillor and future patron saint of Athens, took up the Christian cause with sufficient fervour to suffer martyrdom.

Further west, across a busy road and beyond a stretch of ground covered with Aleppo pines, cedars and cypresses, rises the rocky eminence of the **Pnyx**. On a semi-circular terrace of the north-eastern slope, a platform, hewn from the rock and supported by a wall of polygonal blocks originally about six metres high, has been identified as the site of the celebrated *Bema*. This was the tribune from which, in the shadow of the temples of the Acropolis, generations of orators addressed the assembly of the people of Athens. To the south of the Pnyx is the wooded hill of the Mouseion with the monument to Philopappos (second century AD) on top.

Nightly performances of *son et lumière* (Greek, English and French versions), with splendid floodlighting effects on the Acropolis, take place near the Pnyx throughout the summer. The adjoining **Hill of the Nymphs** is crowned by the old observatory, designed, like several other Athenian buildings of the mid-nineteenth century, by one of the two Hansen brothers - Danish architects brought to Greece by the King. The observatory was commissioned by the Austrian-Greek benefactor, Baron Sina, whose son paid for the University to be built. The library in the neo-classical main building is to be the nucleus of a scientific library and museum of old astronomical instruments.

The paved way skirts the north-west bastion of the Acropolis and plunges into the maze of Plaka - 'old Athens' - lively and picturesque, even though full of tourists and touts. But it is less confusing to explore Plaka, the adjacent area of the Agora and the other monuments of the 'City of Theseus' by taking a completely different route starting from Syndagma Square.

2

Athens: 'The City of Theseus'

BELOW THE NORTHERN SLOPE of the Acropolis lies a district of small shops, offices, old houses and churches, dotted with enclaves of classical ruins. To reach this district from Syndagma Square one descends Mitropoleos Street. On the left is the tiny post-Byzantine chapel dedicated to *Ayia Dynami* (the Holy Strength), intact but cowering beneath a tall Ministry building. Straddling the crowded pavement, the chapel has an air of mild protest against the impersonality of the modern building towering above it; whiffs of burning incense, drifting through its miniature portals, mingle with the smell of petrol fumes, and occasionally the chant of an officiating priest rises above the strident voices of pedestrians. The narrow canyon of Mitropoleos Street opens into a large square of the same name, where the official cathedral, constructed with materials plundered from seventy Byzantine chapels, raises its ugly, nineteenth-century façade. It suffered significant structural damage in the 1999 earthquake. Beside it, somewhat dwarfed, rests the **Little Cathedral**, known as *Ayios Elefiherios* or *Panayia Gorgoepeikoös* (the Virgin who grants requests quickly), a gem of Byzantine church architecture of the twelfth century, whose modest proportions (seven and a half by twelve metres) indicate the humble status held by Athens in the Byzantine world, at a time when the Empire's fortunes were at their peak. The drum below the small dome is slender and elegant and the exterior walls, which have a glowing, ivory-smooth patina, are studded with marble plaques. On the west front a quaint but charming fourth-century BC frieze, pilfered from some ancient monument, tells the story of the twelve months of the year. The decoration is a dotty historical jumble (something that one encounters again and again in Greece), with its ancient *stelae*, Corinthian capitals and Byzantine crosses, to which the coats of arms of the Villehardouin and the de la Roche families have been added - a reminder of that long-forgotten period of Frankish rule, when Athens was governed by the Crusaders and their Latin descendants.

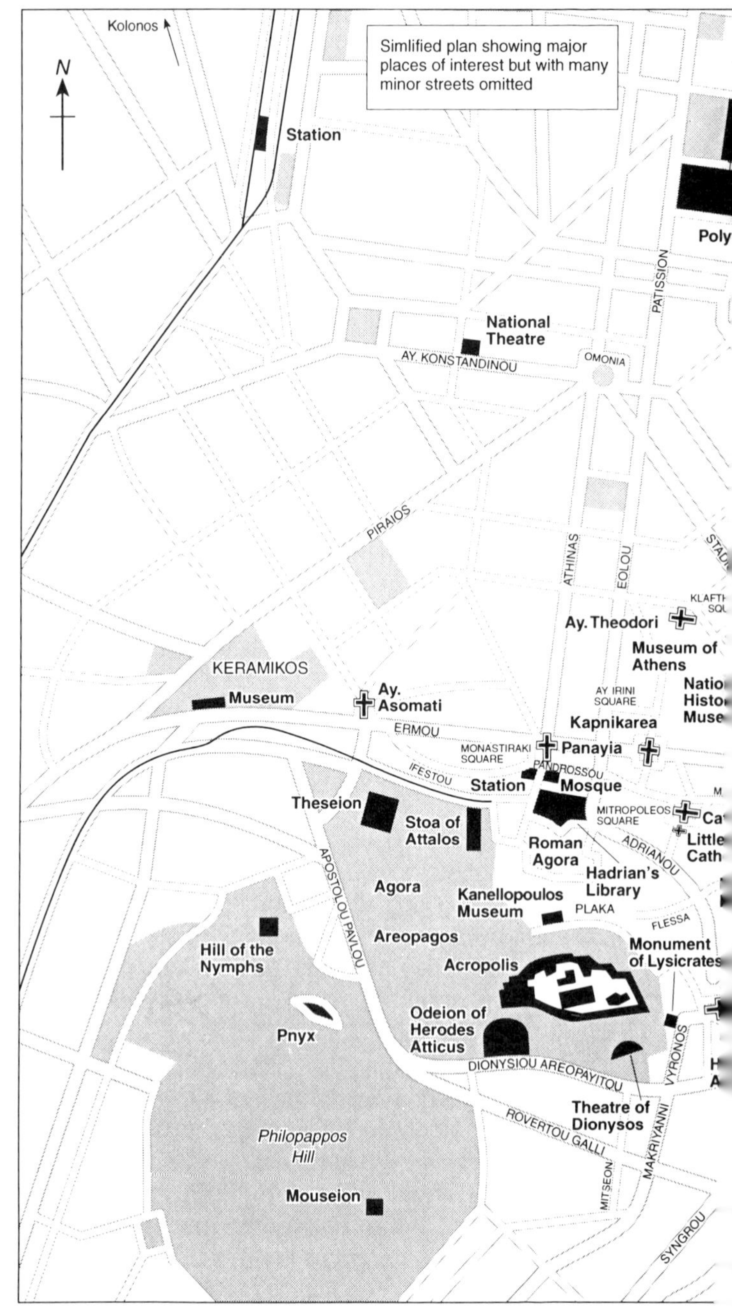
Kolonos
N
Simlified plan showing major places of interest but with many minor streets omitted
Station
PATISSION
National Theatre
AY. KONSTANDINOU
OMONIA
PIRAIOS
ATHINAS
EOLOU
Ay. Theodori
Museum of Athens
KERAMIKOS
Museum
Ay. Asomati
AY IRINI SQUARE
Kapnikarea
ERMOU
MONASTIRAKI SQUARE
Panayia
PANDROSSOU
IFESTOU
Station
Mosque
Theseion
Stoa of Attalos
MITROPOLEOS SQUARE
Roman Agora
ADRIANOU
APOSTOLOU PAVLOU
Hadrian's Library
Agora
Kanellopoulos Museum
PLAKA
FLESSA
Hill of the Nymphs
Areopagos
Monument of Lysicrates
Acropolis
Pnyx
Odeion of Herodes Atticus
VYRONOS
DIONYSIOU AREOPAYITOU
Theatre of Dionysos
ROVERTOU GALLI
MAKRIYANNI
Philopappos Hill
Mouseion
MITSEON
SYNGROU

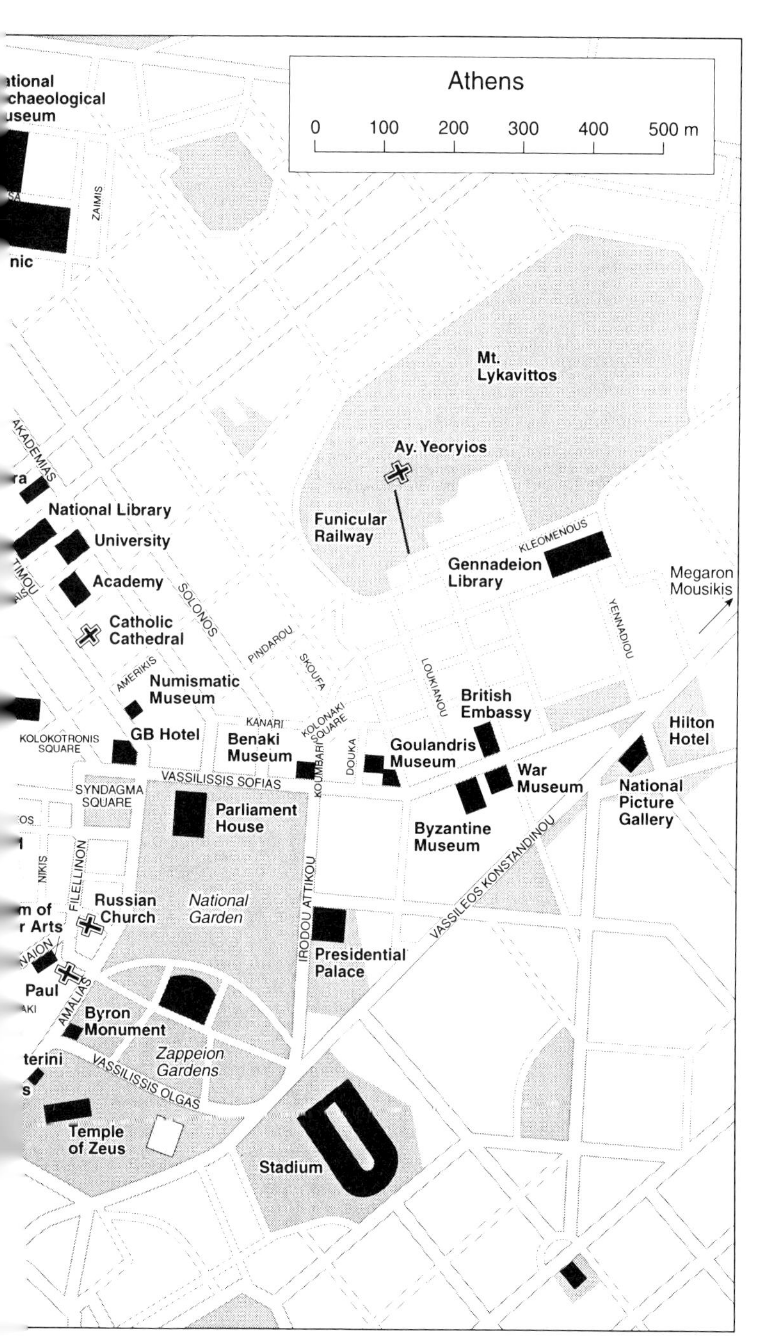

Athens
0
100
200
300
400
500 m
Mt. Lykavittos
Ay. Yeoryios
Funicular Railway
Gennadeion Library
KLEOMENOUS
Megaron Mousikis
YENNADIOU
LOUKIANOU
PINDAROU
SKOUFA
SOLONOS
AKADEMIAS
National Library
University
Academy
Catholic Cathedral
AMERIKIS
Numismatic Museum
KANARI
KOLONAKI SQUARE
KOUMBARI
DOUKA
British Embassy
Hilton Hotel
KOLOKOTRONIS SQUARE
GB Hotel
Benaki Museum
Goulandris Museum
War Museum
National Picture Gallery
VASSILISSIS SOFIAS
SYNDAGMA SQUARE
Parliament House
Byzantine Museum
VASSILEOS KONSTANDINOU
NIKIS
FILELLINON
Russian Church
National Garden
IRODOU ATTIKOU
Presidential Palace
AMALIAS
Paul
Byron Monument
Zappeion Gardens
VASSILISSIS OLGAS
Temple of Zeus
Stadium
ZAIMIS

Mitropoleos Square is a good place to watch the *Epitafios* (Good Friday Procession), when the bier of Christ, heaped with flowers, is borne through the street at night. The procession is led by the Archbishop of Athens and All Greece. He is followed by church dignitaries in tall cylindrical hats, flanked by acolytes in red and purple shifts. The acolytes totter under the weight of enormous banners. The procession is followed by a slowly-moving crowd of quiet worshippers, hands cupped round lighted candles. Everywhere there is the scent of flowers and incense. The *Epitafios* has one point in common with the Panathenaic procession that was depicted on the great frieze of the Parthenon: the people are part of the procession, not just spectators. The Cathedral procession meets processions from other churches in Syndagma Square, where the remainder of the service takes place.

At the southern end of the square, P. Benizelou Street leads into Adrianou Street, the 'aristocratic' quarter of Athens in the eighteenth and early-nineteenth centuries; now a maze of shops, including many of the better tourist and handicraft stores.

This is the beginning of **Plaka**, whose steep narrow streets and alleys criss-cross the northern slope of the Acropolis. Parts of the quarter are for pedestrians only; blaring music is not permitted and the atmosphere is remarkably peaceful and pleasant in spite of all the tourist shops, cafés, bars and tavernas - and the teeming tourists.

There are dozens of tavernas, many of them attractively sited in tiny squares or on flights of steps; whatever the food may be like, they are usually very agreeable to sit in. The food will not be a gastronomic experience, but it will usually be perfectly acceptable. Naturally most of the tavernas in Plaka cater mainly for tourists, serving the sort of Greek food that they prefer. One starts with several *mezedes* (appetizers), such as *taramasalata* (purée of dried fish roe), *melitsanasalata* (smoky-tasting purée of aubergines), *tsatsiki* (cucumber and garlic or onion in yoghourt), octopus in a vinegar sauce, perhaps a *horiatiki salata* (salad with olives and feta cheese). The main courses offered will mostly be to order - veal, pork or lamb chops, *souvlakia* (pieces of meat grilled on a skewer), liver, hamburgers, possibly fried or grilled fish, which is expensive if fresh. The larger tavernas will have a selection of ready-cooked dishes such as *moussakas*, stuffed peppers or tomatoes, pork or veal cooked with lemon, and roasts. There will not be much in the way of a sweet.

Most tavernas serve a house-wine by the carafe, usually non-

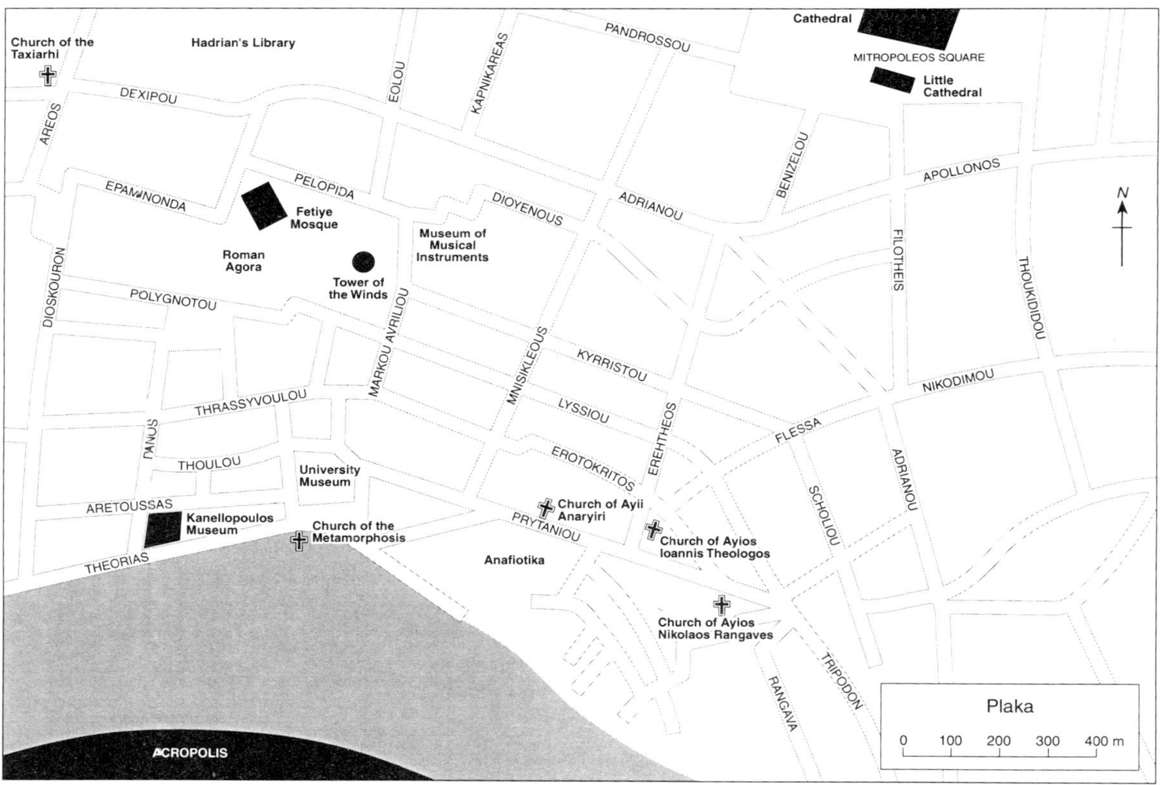
Plaka
0 100 200 300 400 m
N
Church of the Taxiarhi
Hadrian's Library
Cathedral
MITROPOLEOS SQUARE
Little Cathedral
PANDROSSOU
DEXIPOU
EOLOU
KAPNIKAREAS
AREOS
BENIZELOU
APOLLONOS
EPAMINONDA
PELOPIDA
Fetiye Mosque
DIOYENOUS
ADRIANOU
Museum of Musical Instruments
Roman Agora
Tower of the Winds
FILOTHEIS
THOUKIDIDOU
DIOSKOURON
POLYGNOTOU
MARKOU AVRILIOU
MNISIKLEOUS
KYRRISTOU
NIKODIMOU
THRASSYVOULOU
LYSSIOU
EREHTHEOS
FLESSA
THOULOU
EROTOKRITOS
University Museum
SCHOLIOU
ADRIANOU
ARETOUSSAS
Church of Ayii Anaryiri
Kanellopoulos Museum
PRYTANIOU
Church of Ayios Ioannis Theologos
Church of the Metamorphosis
Anafiotika
THEORIAS
Church of Ayios Nikolaos Rangaves
TRIPODON
RANGAVA
ACROPOLIS

resinated (*retsina*, with its flavour of turpentine, is something of an acquired taste) and will have a range of the less expensive bottled wines such as Ayiambelos, Apelia, Kourtaki retsina, Tsandali white and Naoussa Rotunda red and white.

Psistaries (Grills) offer chicken grilled on the spit, charcoal-cooked steaks and chops, and sometimes kokoretsi, a delicious mass of liver and other offal packed together and grilled.

In Plaka nearly all the tavernas are open by midday, although those away from the centre of the city will usually open later in the day. In the quieter back streets of Plaka there are tavernas patronised by the locals, where the food may be similar but the atmosphere is different, especially during Carnival when everyone goes out not just to eat and drink but to have *kefi* - to shout and sing and laugh uproariously, making as much noise as possible. Quite rapidly it can develop into a party - one lively group might send a brimming carafe over to another, especially if they are foreigners in a mainly Greek ambiance. A few of the tavernas have two or three guitarists, and there are some rather more expensive places which put on a traditional floor-show, geared largely to 'Athens by Night' groups.

Going up Adrianou Street one reaches the neo-classical façade of the old Demotic School on the corner of Flessa Street. Nearby at 8 Kyristou Street is the restored seventeenth-century Hammam Abid Effendi, now housing the small Museum of Personal Hygiene. Flessa Street then rises steeply and curves to the left. Erotokritos Street is on your right, going up between small houses, past the Byzantine chapel of *Ayios Ioannis Theologos* (eleventh and twelfth century). The chapel stands in a shady open space which, at night, is occupied by the tables of two tavernas; however in the daytime it is a peaceful place. Further along Erotokritos Street, instead of going down the steps, turn up to the left to a charming little square filled with trees and shrubs. In the top left-hand corner is a gate into the garden courtyard of a church which is a dependency of the Holy Sepulchre in Jerusalem: a tranquil spot where I sometimes spend a quiet half-hour. The church is known as *Ayii Anaryiri*, St Kosmas and St Damian, the Arabian twins, patron saints of medicine and surgery, martyred by Diocletian. The twins are called the *Anaryiri*, 'the silverless ones', because they refused to accept fees for their cures. The single-aisled church was built at the beginning of the Turkish occupation, and has a later porch with four marble columns.

Beyond and below is Mnisikleous Street and the popular taverna '*O Yeros tou Moria*' (The Old Man from the Morea). The steps between its indoor and outdoor tables lead up to Prytaniou Street, where, at the far end, is the church of *Ayios Nikolaos Rangaves*, twelfth century, but so much restored as to retain little of its original antiquity. At the top of Mnisikleous Street, up some rough steps, are more tavernas, commanding a superb view, with the pine-fringed and floodlit summit of Lykavittos crowning successive tiers of apartments.

Towards the western end of Thrassyvoulou Street, at a characterless church, one ascends the stairway on the left to reach the recently-restored Old University, the modest mid-nineteenth-century seat of higher studies, now the Museum of the University of Athens. Behind and above (taking the steps to the right) is the Church of the Metamorphosis, another charming chapel of the fourteenth century, situated below the pines and cypresses around the 'Long Rocks' of the Acropolis. The tiny altar is made from the capital of an ancient column. To the left of this church a paved path goes up between pine trees to a fine view-point, with the sheer rock of the Acropolis behind and the tiny houses of Anafiotika, like an island village, at your feet. To the right from the church, through intrusive tourist shops, is the Kanellopoulos Museum at the corner of Panos Street - a remarkable private collection of antique and Byzantine items. Outstanding are the Tanagra figurines dating from 330 to 200 BC, and icons from the twelfth to the fourteenth century AD. From here the pedestrian road, now wider, leads westwards round the Acropolis to the rock of the Areopagos.

From the Museum, Panos Street descends towards the large excavated enclosure of the Roman Agora. It is best to get to it by turning right into Thrassyvoulou Street, then going down Markou Avriliou Street past the pink, lemon and ochre-washed houses which were once the balustraded mansions of the capital's embryo bourgeoisie. A railing runs all round the complex of ancient ruins - the entrance is at the north-east corner. At night, when moonlit, it is one of the most romantic places in Athens.

Near the entrance, among trees and shrubs at the eastern end of the excavated area, stands the **Tower of the Winds**, known as *Oi Aerides* (The windy Ones), or *Horologion* of Andronikos Kyrrhestes. The octagonal tower is an architectural fantasy, the creation of a philhellenic Syrian of the first century AD. In 1676 Dr Spon of Lyons, one of the earliest Western scholars to visit Greece, identified it as a hydraulic clock. A bas-relief, portraying the features of the different winds, runs round the eight sides. The roof, an octagonal pyramid, was surmounted by a weather-vane in the form of a Triton. A small round tower against the east front served as a reservoir for the clock, which was connected by an aqueduct to the spring of Klepsydra on the Acropolis.

In the rectangle of the **Roman Agora** are the ruins of an Ionic peristyle with a double gallery surrounding an interior marble-paved courtyard. Traces of a building with a loggia at the south-east corner have been identified as the *Agronomeion*, headquarters of the market police. At the west end (Dioskouron Street) stands the gateway of Athena Archegetes (first century AD), with four heavy Doric columns surmounted by an intact, unadorned pediment. Within the excavation area there is also a square brick building with multiple domes and a colonnaded porch, once the Fetiye Mosque, built in commemoration of the visit to Athens of Sultan Mehmet, the conqueror of Constantinople, after the fall of Frankish and Venetian Greece; later it became a clearing house for archaeological finds.

Near the north-east corner of the Roman Agora is the Museum of Musical Instruments. Next to it Dioyenou Street, more of a passage, leads to a good, unpretentious taverna, the Platanos, situated in a shady, secluded little square.

From the Roman Agora and beyond the Church of the *Taxiarhi* (Archangels) one enters Areos Street; on the right rises the surviving (but fire-blackened) northern half of the west front colonnade of **Hadrian's Library**. All that remains upright of the projecting central porch, a single fluted Corinthian column, stands isolated from the smooth shafts of the colonnade, the southern half of which has completely disappeared. A considerable amount of clearing has been done recently in this area. The massive but plain east façade, also charred by fire, is in Eolou Street, looking on to a pleasant square with cafés and restaurants. On this side five heavy buttresses survive to support a projecting plain cornice. Built by Hadrian in the second century AD, the library possessed a courtyard surrounded by a hundred columns, a pool and a garden. The library was in turn sacked, burned, converted into a Byzantine church and subsequently into a bazaar, becoming the centre of Athenian life during the Turkish occupation.

The most striking feature of the adjoining **Monastiraki Square**, hub of downtown Athens, is a Turkish mosque, the former *Pazar Djami* (Market Mosque), which consists of a square block faced by a loggia and supporting an octagon. It has served as a prison and is now an annexe of the Museum of Popular Arts, containing an

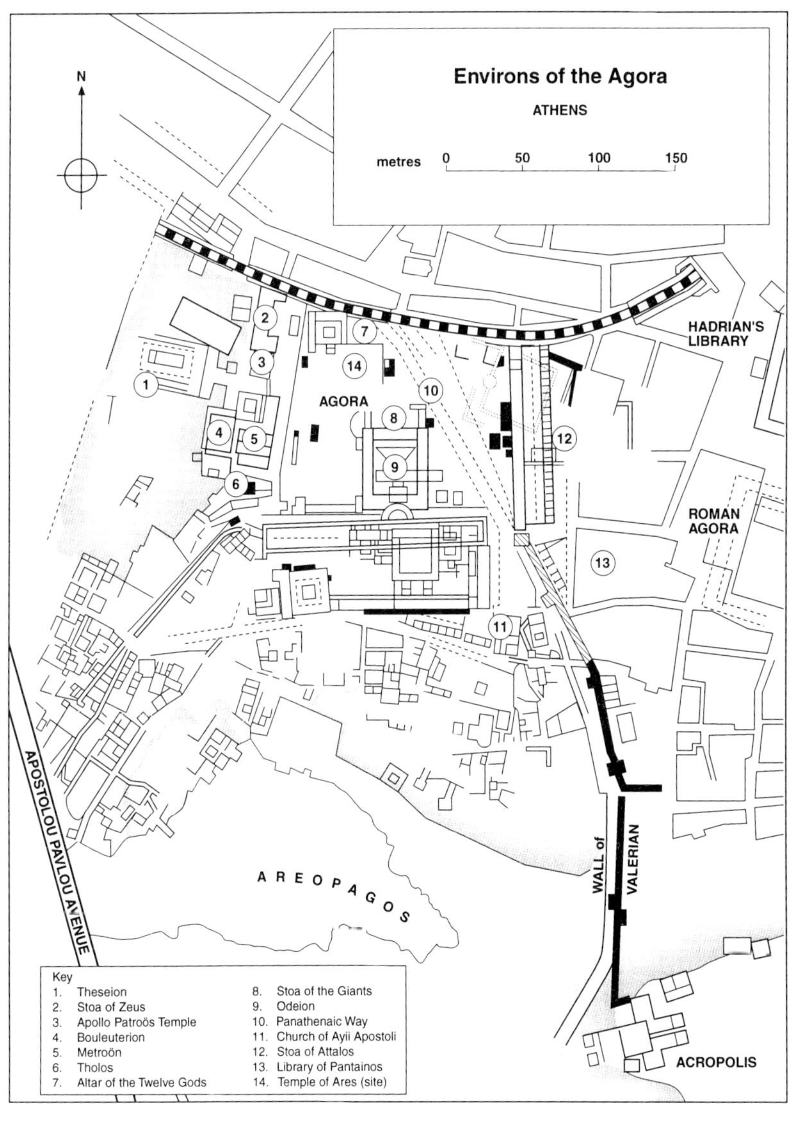

Environs of the Agora
ATHENS
metres 0 50 100 150
N
HADRIAN'S LIBRARY
AGORA
ROMAN AGORA
AREOPAGOS
WALL of VALERIAN
APOSTOLOU PAVLOU AVENUE
ACROPOLIS
Key
1. Theseion
2. Stoa of Zeus
3. Apollo Patroös Temple
4. Bouleuterion
5. Metroön
6. Tholos
7. Altar of the Twelve Gods
8. Stoa of the Giants
9. Odeion
10. Panathenaic Way
11. Church of Ayii Apostoli
12. Stoa of Attalos
13. Library of Pantainos
14. Temple of Ares (site)

important collection of ceramics. In the middle of the square rises the unusually tall drum of the modernized tenth-century Church of the *Panayia* (The Virgin). In the corner next to the mosque is the entrance to Pandrossou Street, commonly referred to in English as 'Shoe Lane'. This alley still has some antique shops and is faintly redolent of a Turkish bazaar. Hellenistic coins, Attic figurines, rugs, icons and embroideries are on sale; there is a lot of Victoriana (opaline vases, egg-cups, etc.) and filigree silverware from Ioannina in the north. Prices are high, and bargaining is the norm. However most of the shops are now given over to cheap jewellery or souvenirs for tourists.

On the right of Monastiraki railway station, Ifestou Street, a humble counterpart of Pandrossou, has a few metalworkers and there are shops full of brass and leather objects among the numerous cheap clothing and shoe shops. In an open space some way down the street is the flea market, with a fine selection of old furniture and junk. On Sunday mornings it is particularly lively, crowded and extensive, offering not only second-hand clothes and an amorphous assortment of rusty metal appliances but also a wide range of new products at cut prices.

From Monastiraki Square one joins Ermou Street at its more squalid lower end and proceeds west. Beyond the little Byzantine Church of *Ayii Asomati* (The Saintly Incorporeal Ones), its exterior brickwork decoration stylishly restored, is the entrance to a large sunken field of ancient ruins in the form of an irregular rhomboid, dominated by a large coffee-coloured modern church. The main part of this area is the **Keramikos**, a necropolis of funerary altars. (On Sundays the entrance is near the church in Piraeus Street.) The existence of more tombs and monuments, still being excavated, ruled out the construction of a branch of the extended Metro system through this area.

Lying just outside the city walls, the cemetery of the Keramikos, final resting place of countless public figures, was destroyed in the first century BC when Sulla breached the defences of beleaguered Athens. Nevertheless, the superimposition of more sepulchres raised the level of the ground and the excavation of graves continues, to this day, to yield funerary offerings. The place is now a jumble of shattered *stelae* (carved marble grave-stones) on different levels, with fosses or ditches, corresponding to the ancient pathways, cleaving through the mounds and knolls, which look like abandoned earthworks.

The surviving *stelae* - the finest are now in the National Archaeological Museum - line the right bank of the Street of the Tombs, which begins down to the left at the Piraeus Street end, whence it is best to start a tour (west to east) of the site. First, there is a relief depicting a **Roman funeral banquet** attended by the dreaded Charon, conveyor of souls to the Underworld, followed by the representation of a huge Molossian dog, its paunch seamed with protruding veins; next comes the **Monument of Dionysios** of Kokytos, crowned by a lively, well-preserved bull about to charge, and then the Monument of Dexileos - actually a cast of the original *stele*, which is now in the adjoining museum. A large, well-preserved, though artistically inferior, *stele* depicting a girl seated beside her standing mother, rises above the bank of a lateral path. Class distinctions are preserved, and the graves of slaves are marked by truncated columns. Littering the banks of the fosse are *loutrophoroi*, slender pitchers with two handles, reserved for bachelors' graves. Slender marble *lecythoi*, which resemble the *loutrophoroi* except that they have only one handle, are scattered among the shrubs. A simple and beautiful relief of a maiden bearing a vase crowns the site of the shrine of Hecate above the Street of the Tombs, toward the south-western part of the necropolis.

At the east end of the Street of the Tombs are vestiges of the city walls raised by Themistocles and restored by Konon. Next, on the left, are the ruins of the Pompeion, where all the props used in the Panathenaic procession were stored. Six small banqueting halls project from a court surrounded by a colonnade (the column bases are preserved), once a favourite haunt of that somewhat bogus philosopher, Diogenes. To the north are the stylobates and fragments of walls of the Dipylon Gate, the main commercial entrance into Athens. The Gate was connected with the Agora by a *dromos* (public way), lined with statues of poets, philosophers and statesmen. The numerous column bases, water conduits and chariot wheel-ruts in the paved ways give one an idea of the dimensions and the importance of this congested and 'monumental' entrance way.

The small **Keramikos Museum** stands by the entrance to the necropolis, in Ermou Street. In Room I are *stelae*; among the finest is the fifth-century BC **Monument of Dexileos**, depicting a warrior mounted on a frisky horse in the act of overwhelming his foe; in another, a young man - the departed soul - is represented draped in a flowing *chlamys*; a grandmother holds her dead grandchild on her lap, the folds of her *peplos* billowing over her head and following the contours of both her body and the baby's. In contrast, an earlier period is represented by a perky Archaic sphinx, its head turned at right angles to its body.

In Room II we go further back: to the funerary offerings of the late Mycenaean, Protogeometric and Geometric periods, which include a ninth-century BC bronze bowl of Phoenician workmanship, a figurine of a beast of burden carrying a load of four jars, a round terracotta work-basket with a design of swastikas surmounted by four geometric horses, and a water-jug in the form of a ship's hull. In Room III, devoted to black-figured and red-figured vases from the Archaic to the Hellenistic periods, there is a fine sixth-century BC *amphora*, found in a child's grave. It is decorated with three black figures advancing across the painted band in a Dionysiac dance processional. Room IV is the repository of fragments of the *amphorae* which received awards for their outstanding workmanship at the conclusion of the Panathenaic procession.

The **Islamic collection from the Benaki Museum** can now be found in a building near the Keramikos (corner of Ayion Asomaton and Dipylou). Among a number of objects of Turkish provenance of the sixteenth and seventeenth centuries, the show-piece is a restored **seventeenth-century reception room** from Cairo, with a mosaic floor, a fountain and a cascade from which water trickles into a small basin. The tiles are Persian, the inscriptions Cufic, the atmosphere cool and redolent of a grand Moslem house. The beautiful sixteenth-century velvet fabrics from Brusa are decorated with floral designs of brightly coloured tulips and carnations. The collection also includes sumptuous carpets from Isfahan and Samarkand.

North-west of the Keramikos, a series of dreary streets leads between garages, workshops and apartments to the Kolonos district. This is the site of Plato's Academy, the southern corner of which is marked by the Church of *Ayios Tryfon*. A very large area has recently been cleared of houses and added to the existing small park. A number of small areas of ruins, mostly incomprehensible, are in deep depressions, including some in two separate sections of park across streets. Some are the remains of a prehistoric settlement (protectively roofed): sections of walls and the foundations of an elliptical building, a temple and habitations; also a necropolis which has yielded vases and tools in obsidian; proof, if it were needed, that the Attic plain was inhabited in the Heroic Age. The enlarged park with its trees, shrubs and scattered antiquities is an interesting and very pleasant place to spend an hour or so.

The area is dominated by a flat rocky mound: the site of the ancient district of **Kolonos**, where Sophocles was born and which he immortalized in his *Oedipus at Kolonos*. A marble slab and *loutrophoros* on the summit mark the graves of two philhellenic German archaeologists. There is a small open-air theatre, but no memorial to the greatest dramatist in antiquity. Sophocles was a very old man when he wrote *Oedipus at Kolonos*. It was his last play. A deeply religious work, it is full of nostalgia for his beloved birthplace. The story - probably apocryphal - is that he died at the age of ninety, choked by a grape pip, before he could see it performed.

On the way back up Ermou Street from the Keramikos, turn right at Monastiraki Square, after crossing the railway, to enter the ancient Greek **Agora**. The ancient market place, once the social, commercial and administrative hub of Athens where business was transacted, legislation passed and gossip exchanged, lies in a hollow, littered with ruined fortifications, eroded plinths and truncated columns: a legacy of desolation left by the Heruli, a northern tribe associated with the earliest Gothic invasions.

The pathway follows the route of the Panathenaic procession. To the right, on plinths ornamented with olive branches, rise three giant statues of Tritons with elaborate fish-tails. This Stoa of the Giants - there were originally six - faces the Odeion of the second century AD (the orchestra and proscenium are easily identified). The route followed by the procession then reached the vast **Stoa of Attalos**, now entirely rebuilt of Pentelic marble, Piraeus limestone and local clay tiles: the work of the American School of Classical Studies. The original *stoa* was commissioned in the second century BC by Attalos, a philhellenic king of Pergamum. Although destroyed in the Herulian sack, much of the original masonry and materials remained *in situ* and were used in the reconstruction, completed in 1956. The *stoa* consists of superimposed colonnades of 134 columns, the lower Doric, the upper Ionic (Pergamum style). The marbles have not yet acquired the patina of age, but it is a prodigious achievement and the cool, spacious colonnades are an authentic replica of a market hall at the end of the Hellenistic era. The sculptures discovered in the course of successive excavations are exhibited in chambers, corresponding to the ancient shops, adjoining the colonnade. They include a colossal headless Apollo of the fourth century BC (unnumbered; north end of colonnade, ground floor), a Hellenistic Aphrodite with a headless Eros perched on her shoulder (No. S473), a small but athletic Winged Victory (unnumbered; north end of colonnade, ground floor), a bronze shield (No. B262) captured by the Athenians from the Spartans during the Peloponnesian War, a statue base of the *Iliad* (No I1628) with an inscription which begins 'I am the Iliad, which lived before and after Homer...', a mechanical device called the Kleroterion (N. I3967) for the assignment of public duties by lot; as well as vases, inscriptions, figurines and shards of different periods.

Proceeding clockwise from the *stoa*, one passes the foundations of several public buildings: the Library of Pantainos (the restored eleventh-century Church of *Ayii Apostoli*, slightly to the south of the Library, contains indifferent wall paintings); the Tholos, a circular fifth-century BC edifice, where dwelt fifty magistrates who constituted a permanent commission to the Senate; the fifth-century BC *Bouleuterion* (Senate); and the *Metroön*. At this point a path ascends to the **Theseion**, which dominates the Agora from a terrace laid out with flowerbeds. Myrtle and pomegranates grow in large clay pots: replicas of ancient vessels found in hollows cut out of the neighbouring rock, they were once watered by artificial streams whose source was on the Pnyx.

The temple, of the Doric order, the first in Greece to be built entirely of marble, is dated to the mid-fifth century BC (just prior to the Parthenon) and was one of the earliest attempts to restore the monuments destroyed during the Persian invasion. It is not, of course, a temple of Theseus at all. The origin of the misnomer lies in the fact that the *metopes* depict the exploits of the Attic hero. It was, in all likelihood, a temple of Hephaistos, god of forges, and the whole vicinity was inhabited by blacksmiths. Bronze statues of Hephaistos and Athena Hephaistia, patron deities of industrial workers, adorned the *cella*. It has thirty-eight columns (six instead of the usual eight on either front), with a pronounced convexity in the shaft. Of the remaining eighteen *metopes*, ten (east front) represent the exploits of Herakles and eight (north and south) those of Theseus. The *pronaos* frieze, which is very mutilated, depicts a battle (unidentified) watched by six Olympian deities. The vaulted roof of the interior dates from the fifth century AD, when the temple, like so many others, was converted into a Byzantine shrine. Although it is the best-preserved classical temple in Greece, the Theseion is not the most inspiring. The plain Doric style, so supremely effective in Iktinos' monumental plan of the Parthenon, loses much of its vitality in the smaller edifice. Its position, between the much higher

Acropolis and the western hills, may also account for its lack of authority. Nevertheless, when seen from the upper gallery of the Stoa of Attalos, framed within surrounding shrubberies, it appears startlingly alive in its exterior completeness.

The clockwise route leads down to the Agora again. On the left lie the foundations of a small temple of Apollo Patroös (fourth-century BC), followed by bases of columns and fragments of pediments marking the site of the Stoa of Zeus, in whose shade Socrates lectured to students. On the right is the site of the Altar of the Twelve Gods, the starting point for the measurement of all distances from Athens, and, beyond it, the main entrance to the Agora.

On the way back to Syndagma Square, turn left at the corner of Ermou Street into Eolou Street, a very pleasant pedestrian shopping area. A pretty garden-plant market extends across the little square of Ayia Irini, beside a church of the same name. Pots of gardenias, oleanders and hibiscus, their scarlet trumpets turned towards the sun, are ranged beside orange trees in wooden tubs and boxes filled with basil; clematis and bougainvillea trail from trellised bamboo sticks.

Halfway up Ermou Street there is a charming view of the little eleventh-century **Church of the Kapnikarea**. One of the best-preserved Byzantine churches in the capital, the Kapnikarea is a typical example of the cross-in-square plan, which was established throughout the Greek mainland in the twelfth century. It is built of stone, embellished with brick courses. The little cupola above the additional chapel on the north side is an example of the tendency to increase the number of domes. The outer porch with its two small columns has a very coquettish air, and it leads, in turn, to the beautifully-decorated door with its marble jambs and lintels. The frescoes in the interior are modern, but good.

Between the Kapnikarea and Syndagma Square the pedestrian precinct including Ermou Street becomes a crowded shopping quarter. On Syndagma Square the pavement cafés and restaurants get all the morning sun. On summer nights they are the haunt of young Athenians and tourists.

3

Athens: 'The City of Hadrian'

IN SUMMER, the city can, with the help of a strong north wind, resume its former impression of dazzling whiteness. However, the enormous spread of undistinguished blocks of apartments now covering the plain from the sea to the foothills of the surrounding mountains, is more often blanketed by the notorious *nefos* - the cloud - an obnoxious mixture of chemical fumes which has made Athens into Europe's most polluted capital. The apartment blocks, built following the demolition - restricted too late - of whole areas dating from the nineteenth and early twentieth centuries, present an endless dreary, modern sameness. The one relieving feature, the lavish use of Pentelic marble, has been abandoned since the 1981 earthquake, for fear that the slabs might be dislodged. Here and there skyscrapers tower above the relentless sea of concrete.

Several worthwhile visits can be made however, both in the ancient Roman city, an area of public gardens and residential streets lined with false-pepper trees, and in the modern city which surrounds it. One should begin at the entrance to the National Gardens and follow Amalias Avenue as far as the statue of Byron in the arms of Hellas, represented by a female figure. Just beyond this point, **Hadrian's Arch** marks the boundary between the two ancient cities - Greek and Roman. Two inscriptions on the frieze give the directions: to the west, 'This is Athens, in times past the City of Theseus'; to the east 'But this is Hadrian's and no longer the City of Theseus'.

The gateway, its Roman arch surmounted by a Greek portico, probably intended to symbolise the marriage of the Greek and Roman worlds, was not one of the happiest architectural achievements of the Emperor's reign. Hadrian was himself something of an amateur architect: a fact which may account for its lack of professionalism. It might have looked more impressive originally when its central arch was framed between the two Corinthian columns whose bases are still visible, but it could never have borne comparison with any of the great triumphal arches of Rome. The marble arch rests on two short, square Corinthian piers and there are similar but much taller piers forming the outer sides. The Greek portico on the upper level has three bays, the middle one, with fluted Corinthian columns, crowned by a pediment. The effect is one of awkwardness, of something which has not quite come off. Nevertheless, it remains a landmark, marooned in traffic-choked central Athens.

The Arch precedes the terrace of the Olympeion, the **Temple of Olympian Zeus**, supported on three sides by strong buttresses, of which there were originally a hundred. The entrance is along Vassilissis Olgas, in the north-east corner of the precinct. The history of the temple, one of the most impressive ruins in Athens, is a chequered one. It was begun by the Peisistratids in the sixth century BC on the site of an older Archaic temple. Work was interrupted by the fall of the Peisistratids and the Persian wars, but was resumed in the second century BC by a Seleucid king of Syria who would employ none but the best Roman architects. It was finally completed in 132 AD by Hadrian, who placed a majestic effigy of himself and a jewelled snake beside the gold and ivory statue of Zeus in the *cella*. During the Middle Ages the temple served as a quarry.

Near the entrance is the partially restored Propylaia of the temple and close by lie some gigantic column bases of the earlier edifice; further on to the right are vestiges of an ancient road and the ubiquitous walls of Themistocles. The foundations of a Roman thermal establishment, with column bases at the west end, partly cover one of two fourth-century BC houses; nearby the outline of a fifth-century church can be clearly seen.

The temple itself is approached from the Propylaia. With two rows of twenty columns at the sides and three rows of eight at each front, it was one of the largest in the Graeco-Roman world. The Roman architects' attempt to extend the columns to the greatest possible height, without giving them an air of exaggerated attenuation is completely successful. No Greek architect of the classical age would have dreamed of going so far. Of the 124 columns only 15 remain - tall and fluted, their magnificent Corinthian capitals adorned with elaborate acanthus leaf mouldings. Impressive at all times, they seldom look more magical than when floodlit at night, emerging from the penumbra of the surrounding gardens.

To the left of the entrance to the temple enclosure a lane with acacias, oleanders and pepper trees leads to another field of ruins in a somewhat unkempt park below the massive retaining wall of the temple terrace. It is a scene of considerable confusion, but archaeologists have identified the foundations of temples of the Archaic period and of the fifth and second centuries BC. To the right of the small church opposite is a low cliff-face: site of the Kallirhoe Spring (the beautifully flowing), the only source of good drinking water in ancient Athens.

Beyond the Temple of Olympian Zeus, Vassilissis Olgas Avenue runs between the Zappeion Gardens on one side and the Tennis Club and Sports Centres on the other. A wide formal garden between the shrubberies of the Zappeion Gardens reveals the neo-classical porch of a large horseshoe-shaped building, Athens' main congress centre. Vassilissis Olgas Avenue ends in a curved junction. Turning to the left one almost immediately reaches the **Stadium**, built in a wide fold of the pine-clad hill of Ardettos in the fourth century BC, and capable of accommodating more than sixty thousand spectators. Five centuries later its forty-four tiers were faced with marble at the expense of Herodes Atticus, a rich philanthropist. An idea of its size is obtained from the fact that as many as a thousand wild beasts at a time took part in the gladiatorial shows and Roman circuses over which Hadrian presided. In the Middle Ages the stadium was reduced to a quarry. Later travellers described it as overgrown with corn, the crumbling *diazômas* as grazing grounds for goats. In 1895 a modern Herodes Atticus, George Averoff, a wealthy cotton merchant, financed the reconstruction and refacing of the tiers with Pentelic marble, and the first revived Olympic games were held there the following year.

From the highest tier of the Stadium there is a good view of Hadrian's Athens and its twentieth-century expansion. Irodou Attikou Street, a cool shaded way, mounts gradually from the Stadium to the Presidential Palace, guarded by Evzone sentries in their distinctive white-skirted uniforms. Further up, opposite the junction with Vassilissis Sofias Avenue (corner of Koumbari Street) is the **Benaki Museum**, housed in the spacious, high-ceilinged Benaki mansion. Two generations of a family of cotton magnates from Alexandria dedicated themselves to the assembly of this impressive collection of antiqities, icons, jewellery, embroideries and relics of the War of Independence. The collection has been, and continues to be, enormously enriched by donations and bequests, including whole collections. This has necessitated both the building of a large extension at the back of the house and the removal of the Islamic and Oriental ceramic departments to other premises. Wandering through the many rooms one is constantly reminded, as one turns from bejewelled weapons to gorgeous chasubles, from religious paintings to ornate interiors, of the proximity of Italy in the west, of Islam in the east. At the same time the Museum acts as a curtain-raiser to the great religious art of Thessaloniki, Mystra and Mount Athos, where late Byzantine art flourished during the fourteenth and fifteenth centuries.

The collection of Islamic and other Arabian and Turkish objects is being rehoused in a building near the Keramikos (corner of Ayion Asomaton and Dipylou see page 30), some delay having resulted from the discovery of a section of the ancient walls on the property.

The Oriental Ceramics collection is now at the Ghika house in Kriezotou Street (another dependency of the Museum - see page 41).

The collection of antiquities on the ground floor includes a very fine example of Cycladic art (2800-1300 BC) - a small female idol with crossed arms. There are also gold cups and a silver dish of the third millennium BC, and several very good examples of Minoan and Mycenaean painted pottery.

In the later Greek and Roman rooms, where the number of items on display is a little overwhelming, there are some good sculptured heads and a small collection of strange Graeco-Roman bone carvings - crude but fascinating depictions of Dionysos, Aphrodite and various marine deities and sea monsters gambolling in the waves, thought to have been used as ornamental adjuncts to furniture.

The fascinating jewellery collection includes a number of rare Byzantine items and some elaborate Greek provincial articles such as the gold ship pendants from Patmos. Rather striking are the very convincing late-Roman funerary portraits from Fayoum, Egypt.

The outstanding Byzantine and post-Byzantine section, perhaps the richest in the Museum, includes ecclesiastical objects from various parts of Asia Minor, such as the gorgeously embroidered banner (No. 31) from the Pontos (Black Sea). From Greece itself notable exhibits are: an elaborate iconostasis in gilt carved wood; a large sixteenth-century icon of the Transfiguration (No. 123) by Damaskinos, the most important iconographer of the sixteenth century Cretan school; a **St Anne and the Virgin** in a scarlet mantle (No. 126), painted by Emmanouil Tzanes, another important Cretan painter of the same period; the **Hospitality of Abraham** (No. 64), a fourteenth-century symbolical representation of the Holy Trinity (the relaxed attitude of the figures is unusual in a Byzantine icon, and the subtle shading of reds and blues is rendered with great sophistication). Two sixteenth-century icons of the Nativity (Nos 516 and 518) and the 'Miracles of the Holy Girdle' (No. 1150) lead on to two early El Grecos: the first of these (No. 1542), a much-mutilated icon of St Luke painting the Virgin, is of purely historical interest, for it was painted in the style of the Cretan School of iconography, before the young painter left his native Crete for Venice. The other (No. 1543) is an **Adoration of the Magi**, another early work belonging to the period of the artist's apprenticeship in the studio of the aged Titian, whose guiding hand is discernible in the architectural background, the approach to foreshortening and the balanced grouping of the figures.

Greek arts and crafts of the Turkish period include a comprehensive collection of **embroideries** (mostly seventeenth- and eighteenth-century) from Epirus and the islands of Greece. The most elaborately-worked were usually reserved for household objects, such as pillow-cases, bedspreads and valances. A notable exhibit is the large seventeenth-century bed, its curtains and pillows embroidered with threads of light green, brick red and Prussian blue. There is also a magnificent collection of national costumes. The different arts employed in the decoration of interiors, especially woodcarving, are handsomely shown in the splendid reception room interior from Kozani, and beautiful room from a house in Siatista with its carved and painted panelling. Relics of the War of Independence are on show: one of the most interesting items is **Byron's portable writing-desk** (No. 955); large canvases of battle scenes by nineteenth-century Greek artists recall the swashbuckling manner of Delacroix's imitators; quite different in character is the unusual painting of the '**Battle of Karpenissi**' (No. 646); the painter was an uneducated peasant and his aerial view of the set-piece battle is crude and childish, but the detail is full of charm and fantasy.

The much expanded Museum of today no longer makes the pleasant impression of a personal and somewhat heterogeneous private collection in a private house, and may even be found a little tiring. However there is a delightful café on the second floor, with a lovely view, where one can regather one's energy.

Koumbari Street leads into Kolonaki Square (officially Filikis Eterias) on the slope of Lykavittos. The small garden, with orange trees round a fountain, is the haunt of the elderly in the mornings; the centre of a smart residential quarter, also containing many sophisticated piano bars, restaurants and discos, the square retains an atmosphere of old-fashioned intimacy, trying to come to terms with impersonal modernity (there is an efficient, new car park under the square). The sides are lined with expensive cafés where Athenians, young and old, sit for hours in the spring and autumn sunshine, interlarding their conversation with Anglo-American slang. From Kolonaki Square you return to Vassilissis Sofias Avenue via Neofytou Douka Street, where the Goulandris Museum of Cycladic and Ancient Greek Art is well worth visiting to see the beautiful and extraordinarily modern-looking Cycladic Bronze Age figurines.

Vassilissis Sofias is lined with embassies and expensive apartment blocks, which have replaced the nineteenth-century neo-classical houses of the old Athenian families. To the left, just beyond the isolated block of the Officers' Club, is the **Byzantine Museum**. Preceded by a rectangular court with a marble fountain flanked by two cypress trees, the main building is a rectangular block with a double loggia, designed in 1840 (as the residence of the Duchesse de Plaisance). The Byzantine Museum might well be visited (or revisited) *after* the traveller has been initiated into the iconographic complexities of this very long-lived art at the important sites of Dafni, Ossios Loukas and Mystra, for then the unfamiliar objects - many of a liturgical character - displayed in the museum fall into place more easily and their significance is more quickly grasped.

In 2002 the new building on the adjoining site will open, allowing many more items from the collection to be displayed. The present arrangement is described below. One recent change is that a number of icons and other objects, brought from Thessaloniki seventy years ago, have now been returned and will in due course be on show in the new Museum of Byzantine Culture. These include the beautiful and celebrated *epitafios* of Thessaloniki.

After the entrance hall, with sculptures and architectural fragments, the first room on the right is in the form of a small fifth-century basilican church, with nave, aisles and tiered seats in the apse. The marble screen closing off the sanctuary and the stone pulpit are of the period. It also contains early Byzantine sculpture: Christ shown as a boy bearing a lamb (No. 92), reminiscent of the 'Moscophoros' in the Acropolis Museum; Orpheus, (No. 93) his head crowned by an eagle, playing on a lyre to the animals, which form an open-work frame round the figure; a crude but charming nativity (No. 95) without the Virgin, but with animals and two Giottoesque stylised trees on either side. The lower section of the Flight into Egypt is on the upper part of the panel. More sculptures crowd the next room: tablets with crosses and other symbols, effigies of the Virgin and a big, winged John the Baptist - all of a much later date. After that comes a room constructed, not altogether convincingly, as a small Byzantine cross-in-square domed church, with marble revetments and a notably fine marble screen. The last ground-floor room represents a plain square single-chamber eighth-century church. It has an *iconostasis* with elaborate woodcarving, good icons and twelve panels along the top representing scenes from the life of Christ. The furnishings include a wonderfully elaborate bishop's throne, a large circular chandelier with small icons hanging from it, and a small *epitafios* (the bier for the Good Friday procession) with a canopy in the form of a Byzantine church, painted with floral designs and scenes from the life of the Virgin. On the walls are fragments of frescoes.

The first room (right) on the upper floor contains a small selection of the Museum's **icons**, among them two large fine Crucifixions: one of these (No. 169), is a beautiful fourteenth-century example with the elongated, columnar figures of an anguished Virgin and St John, wearing brown and dark blue, silhouetted against a background of the houses of Jerusalem, depicted in a narrow band along the lowest section of the panel. An icon of the Virgin and Child is framed within a sequence of the twelve feasts of the Orthodox calendar - the Dodekaorton (No. 177). The two-sided thirteenth-century carved wooden icon of St George, with small scenes of his life, is very unusual in that the Saint himself is carved in quite high relief, and painted.

The most important item is a small fourteenth-century mosaic Virgin and Child, known as the **Panayia tis Episkepsi** (The Virgin of the Visit), and also as the Panayia Glykofiloussa (The Sweetly Kissing Virgin), an outstanding relic brought to Greece by refugees from Asia Minor in 1922, which looks like the archetype of all Duccio's Madonnas.

On the walls of the second room hang carved crosses and sections of thirteenth-century frescoes; some with the tall, severe saints so often seen round the lower walls of churches and chapels. There is also the reconstructed apse of a chapel, with highly effective, though damaged, frescoes. In this room there are also a number of small religious items and pieces of jewellery.

The third room has ritual objects such as censers, chalices, sprinklers and bowls, elaborately carved reliquaries and crosses, some interesting Byzantine ceramics and, on the walls, several fine silver icon covers. There are also examples of elaborate church embroidery, which is more fully represented in the rich vestments, mitres and altar cloths of the fourth room.

Opening onto the courtyard to your right as you leave the main building is a spacious new gallery designed for exhibitions relating to Byzantine art and architecture.

Adjoining the Byzantine Museum is the War Museum; aircraft, weapons, uniforms, flags and martial miscellany. Opposite, on Loukianou Street, is the British Ambassador's Residence. This was once the home of Eleftherios Venizelos, Greece's best-known twentieth-century statesman, liberator of Crete and architect of the victorious Balkan wars. Further along Vassilissis Sofias is the Hilton Hotel - a crescent-shaped palace of marble that might have aroused the envy of Hadrian. Opposite the Hilton is the **National Picture Gallery** (*Ethniki Pinakothiki*), filled with nineteenth-century Greek paintings, some Flemish works and four El Grecos. One of these - 'The Angels' Concert' - is of considerable distinction; an unfinished work, it depicts a complex group of swirling figures mantled in draperies that follow the contours of their contorted attitudes.

At this point Ioannou Yennadiou Street leads up the slope of Lykavittos to the fine neo-classical building of the Gennadeion Library, whose collection includes books on Greece, Byronic relics and Edward Lear watercolours. Further along Vassilissis Sofias is the handsome new concert hall - the Megaron Mousikis.

The streets leading from Vassilissis Sofias up into Kolonaki ascend the lower slopes of **Mount Lykavittos**. At the top of Loukianou Street a path zigzags up to the summit of the pinnacled crag. The funicular railway starts from the corner of Aristippou and Kleomenous Streets. At Easter a Resurrection service is held in the whitewashed chapel of Ayios Yeoryios on the top and soon after midnight a long candlelight procession winds down the hill like a trail of glow-worms. Immediately below the chapel there is an expensive restaurant. On the rare days of clear visibility the view embraces the whole of the plain and the Saronic Gulf, with the distant hump of Acrocorinth in the west.

From Kolonaki, the streets which run westward, down to the centre of the city, are lined with elegant boutiques. In Kriezotou

Street, opposite the back of the Grande Bretagne Hotel, the house (now a dependency of the Benaki Museum) of the distinguished painter Ghika, houses a number of his paintings and the Museum's collection of Oriental Ceramics. Two parallel one-way streets between Syndagma Square and Omonia Square - Stadiou Street and E. Venizelou Avenue (more commonly known by its original name of Panepistimiou - University - Street) form the main axis of central Athens. Stadiou Street passes Kolokotronis Square, with its equestrian statue of the eponymous hero of the War of Independence, and a more modest marble statue of Trikoupis, a nineteenth-century statesman, standing in front of the Old Parliament building, which now houses the National Historical Museum. The Museum of the City of Athens, situated in a simple house built in 1833, King Othon's first residence in his new capital, is on the Paparigopoulou Street side of Klafthmonos Square. At the lower end of the square is the eleventh-century Byzantine **Church of Ayii Theodori**, built of stone with brick courses and an exterior Cufic frieze. Cross-in square in plan, with a tall drum (a feature of the small Byzantine churches in Athens), its proportions are exquisite.

From Klafthmonos Square, Korais Street - now a pedestrian precinct with an unobtrusive new Metro station - leads up into Panepistimiou Street. Immediately opposite rises an imposing group of neo-classical buildings. From left to right: the **National Library**, fronted with a Doric portico; the **University**, with a frescoed loggia and, in front, two statues: of Korais, champion of linguistic reform, and of Gladstone, whose government ceded the Ionian islands to Greece in 1864; and finally, the **Academy**, with a portico and pediment, and statues of Plato and Socrates seated on either side of the entrance. All three edifices were built of Pentelic marble on plans drawn up by the two nineteenth-century Danish architects, the brothers Hansen. The Academy is dominated by two tall, fluted columns crowned with statues of Apollo playing his lyre and Athena armed with lance and shield. The traffic jams, the creeping line of blue buses and yellow trolley-buses, the impatient pedestrians fulminating against the red lights - all the stridency of a modern Mediterranean street - seem to enhance the incongruity of this splendid display of neo-classical panache, emphasised by Lykavittos behind, its fantastic peak rising out of a sea of apartment blocks.

Between the University and Syndagma Square there are several landmarks on Panepistimiou Street: the Bank of Greece; the Catholic cathedral of St Denis the Areopagite; the neo-classical mansion, now the Numismatic Museum, in which Heinrich Schliemann, excavator of the sites of Troy and Mycenae, lived with his Greek wife; and a large café/restaurant, Zonar. Parallel to Panepistimiou Street runs Akademias Street, with more shops and offices and a little modern opera house, the *Lyriki Skini*, where in 1942 an as-yet unknown and plump young girl called Maria Callas, with a hauntingly deep-throated voice, first sang *Tosca.*

In the opposite direction from the University, Panepistimiou Street descends towards Omonia Square, the centre of a network of crowded commercial streets, and also a station on the Metro, linking Piraeus with central Athens and the suburbs. The handsome, colonnaded façade of the National Theatre, whose annual season (November-April) may begin with a play by Shakespeare, is a short way down Ayiou Konstandinou Street.

At the end of Panepistimiou Street, just before Omonia Square, Patission Street (28 Oktovriou), a long straight avenue, penetrates into another world: the residential area of Patissia, an uninteresting suburb dating from the inter-war years, once the mecca of the new bourgeoisie. The first large public building on the right is the marble Polytechnic School. Beyond it, a small public garden with some tired-looking palm trees forms a frontage to the **National Archaeological Museum**. Here are some, if not most, of the greatest ancient Greek sculptures in the world: Archaic, Classical and Hellenistic, both monumental and diminutive. There is a collection of painted vases ranging from huge *amphorae* to delicate *lecythoi*, so vast and varied in execution and detail that the imagination boggles at the ingenuity of the ancient potter's skill. Smaller objects, daggers, jewels, figurines, death-masks, shields, ornamental boxes, inscriptions, even toys, enable one to obtain a picture - hazy and confused perhaps, but still whole and in the round - of man's tastes and occupations, of his changing attitudes to religion, sex, death, recreation and athletics, from Mycenaean to Roman times. The existing arrangement of the exhibits is not ideal; some changes are being made to make use of the rooms vacated by the coin collection (which has been moved to the new Numismatic Museum), but they will be minor. There is, as yet, no complete catalogue but there is a useful illustrated guide.

Immediately facing the entrance is the Mycenaean room, filled with gold objects excavated from the royal shaft tombs at Mycenae and other prehistoric sites. The quantity of gold objects is breath-taking; equally astonishing is the degree of sophistication achieved by the jewellers, potters and goldsmiths of this prehistoric age.

A case facing the entrance to the Mycenaean room holds the gold death-mask of an Achaean king of the fifteenth century BC, as well as other gold masks. Exhibit No.384 is a drinking cup in the form of a bull's head, with horns and muzzle of gold and, on his brow, a golden sun, composed of strap-shaped petals. The bull-taming scenes on the famous 'Vafio gold cups' (Nos. 1758, 1759) illustrate the perfection achieved by representational art in the Mycenaean age. In the large Warrior Vase (c. 1200 BC) against the right-hand wall, heavily-armed *hoplites* march in single file, while a woman standing at the end of the processional bids them farewell. All the robustness and militaristic vigour of the Mycenaean world, as opposed to the more effete charms of palace life in Minoan Crete, seem to be represented here. Other cases in the middle and on either side contain precious objects dating from 1500 to 1200 BC. On the walls are sections of fresco from Mycenae and Tiryns showing very clearly the relationship with Minoan art.

Room 6 to the right contains objects from the earlier Cycladic culture, including many idols of all sizes. No. 3908, a crude but charming statuette, represents a male figure seated on a throne playing an unidentified musical instrument, possibly a harp. In conception and execution, it might be an object from an exhibition of twentieth-century sculpture. Its date is c. 2400-2200 BC.

It is better to return now to the entrance hall and proceed clockwise through a series of six halls devoted to Archaic sculpture. An air of essential masculinity prevails. The powerfully-built *kouroi* (young men, often athletes, later soldiers), monoliths, sometimes huge, hewn out of the crystalline rock, represent a monumental image of man. The most striking of the earlier *kouroi* is No. 2720 in Room 8, the '**Colossos of Sounion**' (late seventh century BC); the cast of his features, set and wooden, is distinctly Egyptian, but no Rameses possessed the muscular tension or freedom of pose enjoyed by this Greek youth. The Tzia kouros, No. 3686 in Room 11, of a later date, is more evolved: the formal stylization is there, but the excessive stiffness is less evident; the hair is more elaborately arranged and there is a vestige of a smile on the lips, which have grown more full and sensual. But it is No. 3851 in Room 13, the '**Anavyssos Kouros**' (Kroisos, c. 520 BC) that dominates the scene: a strong-limbed youth, marvellously self-assured, a perfect embodiment of human - though not divine - dignity. Traces of red paint are visible on the coral-shaped locks that fall down his shoulders from the head-band, and the whole surface of Parian marble has a roseate glow. His smile is more radiant than that of any other *kouros*. The modelling is opulent, the tension less extreme.

In the next two halls (14 and 15) we pass into the fifth century. The iron self-control and taut muscular strain have gone, also the Archaic smile. Realism has been substituted for symbolism. In the Eleusinian votive relief (Room 15, No. 126), Demeter presents an ear of corn to her protégé, the youthful Triptolemos, who is commanded to instruct man in the cultivation of the earth, while Koré crowns him. The 'young athlete crowning himself' (No. 3344 in the same room) is a work of Attic perfection. In spite of the low relief, the flesh has the resilient quality of youth; the boy's thoughtful expression reflects the solemnity with which victory on the running-track fills him.

The bronze **Poseidon** (No. 15161) dominating Room 15, a work of the mid fifth century, raised from the sea-bed off Cape Artemision, represents the god as larger than life-size, his left arm outstretched, his right hand holding a (missing) trident about to be hurled. Nothing better expresses the Greek concept of a god as a physically perfect man than this springy, superbly healthy Poseidon.

The next six rooms (the first three separated from the others by a central hall) contain the *stelae* (marble grave-stones some carved in relief so high that the figures appear to be sculpted in the round) which lined the alleys of the Keramikos and other ancient necropolises. The scenes represented are intimate family affairs: the departing soul, with a remote, other-worldly expression, is often depicted in the act of shaking hands with its next-of-kin. Every visitor has, or will have, his own favourites. Among the ones I never like to miss are No. 715 (Room 16), an athlete, the so-called 'Salamis youth', with his right arm raised to release a bird, his young servant leaning mournfully against a marble plinth with a cat on it. In this and succeeding rooms there are enormous sculptured marble *lecythoi* of great beauty. In Room 18 there is No. 3790, a servant girl holding up a baby in order that the departing mother may cast a last look at it. Every one of the *stelae* is a variation on the same disturbing theme of man's preoccupation with death, expressed in terms of the artist's feeling for perfection of form. In none is the perfection so apparent as in No. 3472 (Room 18), in which a pensive husband, clad in a beautifully-draped *chlamys*, bids farewell to his seated wife, Theano. In No. 869 (Room 23), the

'Ilissos *stele*', the deceased, a young hunter, superbly sculpted (possibly by Skopas), whose dog and little servant crouch at his feet, is bidden farewell by his hooded old father.

In the central hall the famous '**Jockey Boy**' (Room 21, No. 15177), a second century BC bronze, rides a disproportionately large horse, not wholly successfully restored. In rooms 36 and 37 on the left are terracotta and bronze figurines. No. 16546, Zeus about to hurl a thunderbolt, is almost a replica in miniature of the Poseidon of Artemision, but perkier, more stocky. In Rooms 40 and 41, in this corner of the Museum, there is a selection from the interesting Egyptian collection - one of the more unusual items is the carved wooden figure of a woman kneeling and kneading dough. Though theoretically a temporary exhibition, it is likely to be in place for a good many years.

Back in the central hall and through Rooms 22, 23 and 24, one enters a succession of halls filled with fourth-century BC and Hellenistic sculptures. The '**Ephebe of Antikythera**' (Room 28, No. 13396) is a hefty young man with somewhat effeminate features, holding some round object, now missing, in his right hand; it is striking, but there is a slickness, even an impersonality, about him, as in many fourth-century BC bronzes, which conjures up a vision of a highly efficient sculptor's workshop, adept at mass production. The young man is entirely physical, but unlike the sixth-century *kouroi* or the fifth-century riders of the Parthenon frieze, he has no interior life.

Less spectacular, but more compelling, are two bronze heads in Room 30: one of a 'bearded philosopher' (No. 13400), with a face of remarkable intellectual power and piercing inlaid eyes; the other, No. 14612, a young man of the first century BC, known as the 'Man from Delos' - a meditative creature with a weak, undecided mouth and anguishing doubts. Then turn back to the **Tegean Head** (No. 3602) in Room 28, believed to be by Skopas, representing Hygeia, goddess of health. In the complete harmony of its form, this oval face, crowned by soft wavy hair, is the personification of serenity, a wholly-evolved expression of idealized feminine beauty in Parian marble. Among the late Hellenistic works is the very complete Aphrodite with Pan and Eros of about 100 BC, which satisfies many people's idea of what classical art should look like. The relatively few Roman exhibits include a remarkable bronze figure of Augustus Caesar mounted (only a fragment of the horse survives) found in the sea in 1979. It is a lifelike portrait, not at all flattering or idealised.

The Museum's enormous collection of **painted vases** suffered considerable damage in the 1999 earthquake. The evolution of Greek painting from the earliest times can be traced in these products of the potter's workshop. The exhibits are displayed chronologically, but the absence of a catalogue is a handicap. First there are the vases of the Geometric period (twelfth to seventh century BC); then the Archaic period (seventh to mid-sixth centuries), characterized by Orientalizing features such as lotus flowers, palmettes, sphinxes and other animals. These are followed by Attic vases of the sixth century. The bands have now disappeared and the decoration consists of mythological scenes, the figures painted in black; luminous figures in red appear during the fifth and fourth centuries, acquiring corporeality as they move from left to right in attitudes associated with Dionysiac processionals. By the fifth century the drawing has become exquisitely fine and pure: especially in the **white-ground lecythoi**, slender funerary vessels with black bases and necks. The figures are painted in very light shades with an extraordinary economy and sureness of touch. Originally placed on *stelae*, the *lecythoi* are among the outstanding contributions made by the fifth-century BC Attic vase painters, with their melancholy depictions of sepulchral scenes in which the figures of the deceased seem to have lost all solid substance as they sit or stand wearily in a kind of occult silence, or are ferried across one of the rivers of the Underworld.

Finally, the Epigraphical Department, situated on the ground floor of the south side (entrance in Tossitsa Street), has a large collection of historical inscriptions, including Themistocles' decree of 480 BC ordering the evacuation of Athens and proclaiming naval mobilization before the battle of Salamis.

4

Attica

ATTICA IS IN THE FORM of a triangular peninsula, washed on two sides by the Aegean Sea. Its main features are its rockiness and, when the north wind blows the atmospheric pollution away, the purity of its light. The soil is poor, but with lavish watering of the gardens around the new houses, weekend cottages and modern factories, Attica has never been greener. The cities of Athens and Piraeus sprawl all over the northern part of the central plain.

The coastline is broken by barren promontories and sandy beaches fringed with Aleppo pines. Ruined sanctuaries and whitewashed chapels shelter in the folds of rocky valleys. Sheets of pale grey asphodel, the immortal flower of Elysium, spread across the hillsides and dusty paths are lined with agave and wild fig trees, from whose pliable wood theatre seats, garlands and other ornaments were made in antiquity. The streams are mere trickles, dry in summer. Goats, for centuries the peasants' main source of wealth, browse among parched shrubs. Everywhere there is the pungent scent of thyme and wild marjoram. In spring the boulders are speckled with round, apple-green tufts of spurge, and the hard ground is covered by clusters of grape hyacinths and little mirror orchids with yellow-bordered blue petals. In autumn there are deep pink cyclamen and golden crocus-like Sternbergia, whose favourite habitat seems to be around country graveyards. The landscape may not be the most beautiful in Greece, but it is seldom without interest.

Attica can easily be explored in a series of expeditions from Athens: these are described, in an anti-clockwise progression, starting from the coast to the south-west. First, at a distance of five miles from Athens, comes **Piraeus**, which is connected to the city by a flat area covered with factories, warehouses and suburbs. It has three harbours which, in ancient times, possessed nearly four hundred ship-houses (sheds with sloping ramps situated on the water's edge). One of the greatest ports of the Eastern Mediterranean and the main industrial centre of Greece, its large residential area lacks distinction.

In antiquity the open roadstead of Faliro, a mile and a half away, served as an anchorage. However, in the early fifth century BC, Themistocles realized the use to which the Piraeus headland and its three sheltered ports could be put. Sea-minded and far-sighted, he built the harbour, encircling it with walls more formidable than those of the Acropolis, and created a fleet. The harbour was completed by Kimon, and Pericles built the Long Walls connecting the capital with its port.

At the end of the Peloponnesian War in 404 BC, when Athens submitted to the superior power of totalitarian Sparta, the victorious Lysander ordered the destruction of Piraeus, as well as the demolition of the Long Walls. The defences were restored but Piraeus never regained its importance, and from Roman times on was almost abandoned. During the Middle Ages, Piraeus was no more than a fishing village, known as Porto Leone.

At the head of the port basin, a short walk from the Metro station, are the quays from which the island ferries depart. Cruise ships dock in front of the customs house on the eastern side of the harbour.

From the main harbour it is about ten minutes' walk to the more attractive **Zea**, a crescent-shaped expanse of water, lined with modern blocks of flats. Shortly before the harbour, in Harilaou Trikoupi Street, are the ruins of a little Hellenistic theatre. Beside the theatre the Piraeus Archaeological Museum displays a well-arranged collection of antique finds, including the very fine bronzes of Apollo and Athena found a few years ago. The harbour, once the battle station of four hundred triremes, now shelters a much larger number of yachts and small craft behind the greatly extended breakwater. This is also the starting point for the hydrofoils to the Argo-Saronic islands and elsewhere. A little beyond the departure point for these is the Naval Museum, and further south beyond the Naval Hospital parts of the sea-front road are buttressed by fragments of ancient walls restored in the fourth century BC by Konon, the distinguished Athenian admiral. Kanaris Square, in the centre of the main waterfront, is the site of Skeuotheke, a great arsenal which, says Pliny, contained arms for one thousand ships.

A corniche, parts of whose sides are pock-marked with grottoes and niches for votive offerings, leads eastwards to the third and smallest harbour facing the sweep of the Bay of Faliro. **Mikrolimano** (The Small Harbour), the ancient Munychia, is composed of tiers of apartment blocks clinging to two sides of a natural amphitheatre,

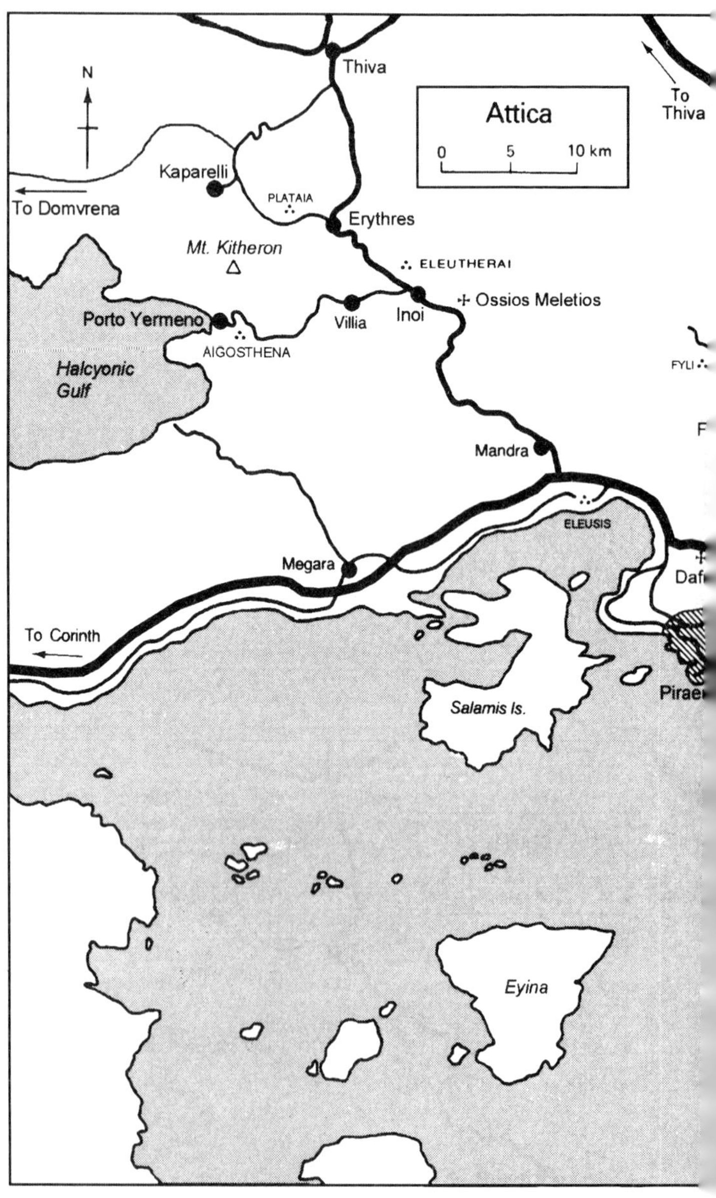
Attica
0
5
10 km
N
Thiva
To Thiva
Kaparelli
To Domvrena
PLATAIA
Erythres
Mt. Kitheron
ELEUTHERAI
Ossios Meletios
Porto Yermeno
Villia
Inoi
AIGOSTHENA
Halcyonic Gulf
FYLI
Mandra
ELEUSIS
Megara
To Corinth
Salamis Is.
Eyina

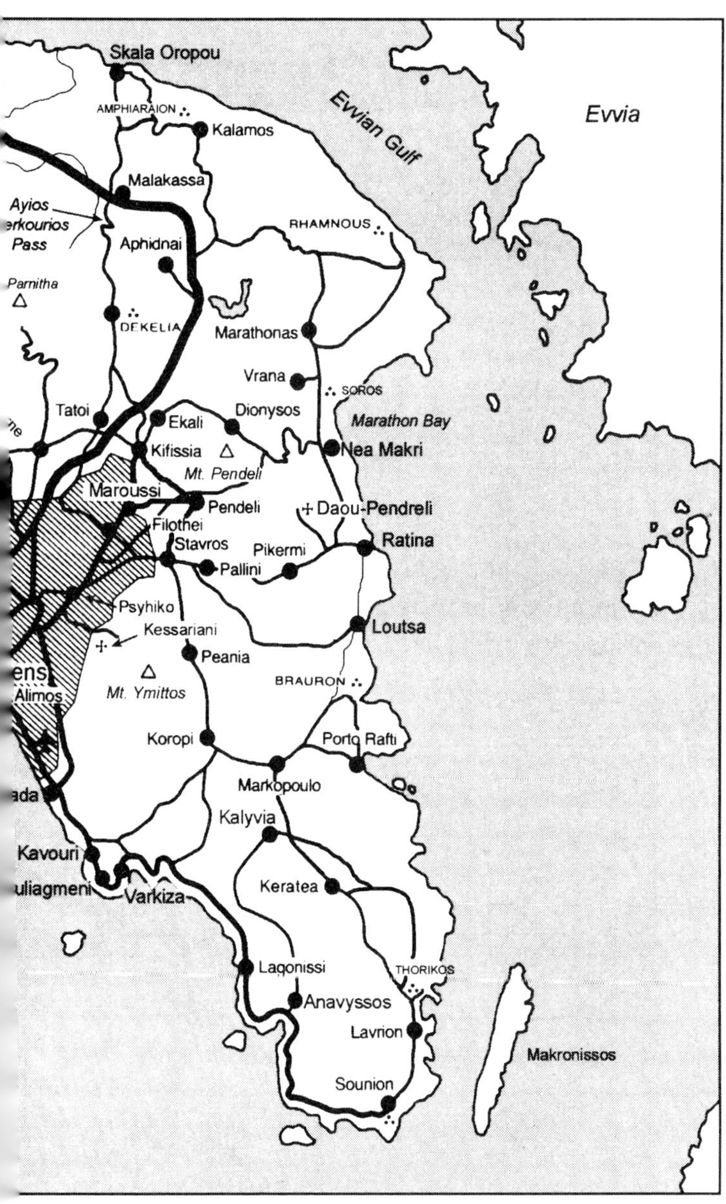

Skala Oropou
AMPHIARAION
Kalamos
Evvian Gulf
Evvia
Malakassa
Ayios
Pass
RHAMNOUS
Aphidnai
Parnitha
DEKELIA
Marathonas
Vrana
SOROS
Tatoi
Ekali
Dionysos
Marathon Bay
Kifissia
Nea Makri
Mt. Pendeli
Maroussi
Pendeli
Daou-Pendreli
Filothei
Stavros
Pikermi
Ratina
Pallini
Psyhiko
Kessariani
Loutsa
Peania
Alimos
Mt. Ymittos
BRAURON
Koropi
Porto Rafti
Markopoulo
Kalyvia
Kavouri
Varkiza
Keratea
Lagonissi
THORIKOS
Anavyssos
Lavrion
Makronissos
Sounion

with the Yacht Club on the headland forming the third. The waterfront is lined with open-air fish restaurants (indoors in winter), and yachts, caiques, *trehandiria* (fast-sailing fishing-smacks), motor launches and dinghies crowd the oily waters of the miniature harbour.

On the top of **Profitis Ilias**, the hill above the harbour, is a modern open-air theatre with fine views of the three harbours, and of Salamis and the Saronic Gulf. Traces of neo-classical architectural fantasy survive among the modern apartment blocks: peeling rosette-bordered casements and flaking spiral balustrades - sometimes a ruined Caryatid porch.

The corniche winds down to the bay of Faliro where ambitious land reclamation has so far provided space for the attractive *Peace and Friendship Stadium*, an open-air theatre, parks and a fast, new road. The Race Course is at the seaward end of Syngrou Avenue which leads back to the centre of Athens. Beyond the Race Course the coastal road passes a marina for small cruise ships and yachts, and then the cemetery for British Commonwealth soldiers killed in the Greek campaigns of the Second World War and the 1944 revolution. In December of that year British troops, greeted a month before as liberators with ringing speeches and garlands of flowers, were reluctantly drawn into a murderous five-week battle with Greek Communist-led forces.

After Alimos - the ancient Halimos, birthplace of Thucydides - and the airport, there are the beaches which are uncomfortably crowded at the height of summer. At Glyfada there are numerous hotels, another yacht harbour, nightclubs, good (and expensive) fish tavernas; at Kavouri, green with pines, the Cape Zoster of antiquity, smart villas. The two pellucid bays at **Vouliagmeni**, although lined with cabins and hotels, are the most attractive and least polluted. The small harbour is reserved for the more luxurious yachts. Nearby is the Astir Palace hotel and conference complex, one of Greece's most expensive establishments. The freshwater lake below the main road is backed by a forbidding slate-grey cliff. On the isthmus between the two bays the foundations of a sixth century BC temple of Apollo are surrounded by flowering shrubs. Varkiza comes next: a strand of fine white sand and a large number of apartment blocks, with a hinterland of rolling vine country, followed by a fiord-like inlet approached through a tunnel of rock; then more and more seaside villas and Lagonissi, with its beaches, Xenia Hotel and expensive bungalows; more resorts, then Anavyssos, once the haunt of smugglers and much of it formerly a salt marsh, where the great stocky-limbed *kouros* in the National Museum was discovered in 1936.

After Anavyssos and other untidy clusters of apartments and hotels comes **Sounion**, the southernmost promontory of Attica, with its hotels and villas, and its temple. The hills behind the steep, pine-clad coastline are bare except for bushes of sage and juniper, with a new purity of contour that suggests the proximity of the Cyclades - Kea and Kithnos are clearly visible.

An isolated, rocky headland, surrounded by vestiges of an ancient semi-circular wall, is crowned by the fifth century BC **Temple of Poseidon**, built on a massive substructure necessitated by the conical rise of the ground. The work of the architect of the Theseion, its columns - fourteen of the original thirty-eight still standing - are Doric but more slender than usual. They lack *entasis* and consequently look somewhat fragile, almost like stilts. The flutings, too, are fewer in number than usual and this also probably detracts from the stolidity associated with the Doric order. The dimensions are almost identical to those of the Theseion, except that here the architect has increased the height of the columns. As nothing remains above the architrave of the south colonnade it is difficult to judge what impression the building may have made with its *metopes*, cornice and pediments in place. In view of the spectacular nature of the position, the increased height should have added something to the upward thrust so singularly lacking in the Theseion. The marble out of which the temple was built came from a local quarry: very white and without the mellow patina that the crystalline Pentelic limestone acquires. Column-bases are disfigured with the scratching of innumerable signatures, including Byron's. The sun-dappled sea is dotted with islands; on a clear day Milos, whence came the Venus in the Louvre, is visible.

The inland road back to Athens passes through Lavrion, the ancient Laurion, where zinc and manganese were, until recently, mined in place of the silver that contributed so much to the wealth of ancient Athens; by the second century AD the deposits had been exhausted. About a kilometre along the coastal road after the former mining town, with its slag-heaps and the melancholy silhouettes of abandoned chimneys, the road to the big power station on the right passes the extremely ancient site of **Thorikos**, a Cretan naval station during the Minoan age. Later it was fortified by the Athenians and served as an important military outpost guarding the maritime approaches to the silver mines. On the slope of a hill, overlooking the slag heaps and fields, are the remains of a fourth-century BC **theatre**, unique in shape and construction: following the declivity of the hillside, the cavea is elliptical instead of semi-circular; a typical example of Greek ingenuity in adapting architectural conventions to the requirements of nature. Originally it must have been little more than a place of entertainment for garrison troops.

Beyond the branch road to Thorikos, the new road curves to the right, while the old road climbs a steep pass and descends slowly into the plains of **the Mesoyia**, passing through Keratea. This is the loveliest part of Attica, an undulating vine country streaked with olive groves and dotted with sugar-loaf hills, now in danger of being spoilt by suburban and industrial development. Far to the north-east the mountains of Evvia, a chain of peaks snow-capped in winter and infinite in their variety of forms, suggests the approach of another world. Byzantine shrines are scattered about the countryside. The most interesting are the eleventh-century Church of the *Taxiarhi* (The Archangels) at Kalyvia, believed to have been built on the foundations of an Early Christian basilica, and two churches at Markopoulo: the domeless *Ayios Yeoryios* in an olive grove and *Ayios Petros*, where fragments of Greek, Roman and Early Christian art have been discovered. All are within a short distance of the main road but, as the churches are usually locked, the keys may have to be obtained from the nearest village.

The red soil of the Mesoyia is the richest in Attica, the villages the most prosperous. Many inhabitants are of Albanian origin, and some still speak a native dialect; descendants of seventeenth-century immigrants, imported to cultivate a countryside rapidly becoming depopulated under Ottoman maladministration, they continue to dwell in their original settlements, mostly in Attica and the Peloponnese.

The east coast has a succession of sandy beaches. One of the most attractive is Porto Rafti, an almost circular bay, its seaward entrance little more than a mile wide and guarded by a small island topped by a Roman statue. A fork to the north from the Porto Rafti road leads, past a Frankish tower of the thirteenth century, into a shallow valley, where an orchard of fig trees winds towards marshland and the sea.

The marsh, bordered by low hills, is the site of the **Sanctuary of Brauron** (Vravrona). Only the foundations of the Doric Temple of Artemis remain, but excavations on the site have also revealed a large fifth-century BC *stoa* (parts of the colonnade have been restored) with a marble stylobate. A series of fifth century BC reliefs of exquisite perfection, portraying sacrificial rites in honour of the goddess, is displayed in the large, new museum; seldom have the billowing folds of women's garments been reproduced with such virtuosity. North-west of the sanctuary, on a hillside covered, in early spring, with sheets of pink and white anemones, are the ruins of an Early Christian basilica and a round building believed to have been a baptistry.

From Vravrona one can drive northwards along the coast to Loutsa, a small resort, and to Rafina, or one can go back to the main road at Markopoulo. After bypassing the village of Koropi, one reaches **Peania**, most northerly of Mesoyian villages, where there is a modern church in the main square decorated with frescoes by Kondoglou, a twentieth-century painter who has turned to Byzantium of the Paleologos epoch for his models. Every inch of space is covered with frescoes of saints, prophets, warrior angels, Fathers of the Church and all the familiar scenes from the lives of Christ and the Virgin. The great composition of the *Dodekaorton* (the Twelve Feasts) with which the traveller will soon become familiar, are as stylized as anything in the great Byzantine churches. The skill in imitation is so remarkable that one is inclined to ignore the technical virtuosity. In terms of pure pastiche, the Peania church is a *tour de force*.

The Vorres Museum, an interesting ethnic collection made by a Greek-Canadian, is housed in three restored village houses and a stable with beautiful courtyards and gardens; the striking modern wing now accommodates a large and important collection of contemporary Greek art. A road zig-zags halfway up Mount Ymittos to the Koutouki Cave, which is worth visiting; it is well lit, with multicoloured stalactites and stalagmites in several caverns. This side of Ymittos is steep, bare and desiccated, gashed with rocky ravines, and has none of the rounded smoothness of the western flanks, which often make this extraordinary mountain look like a huge grey elephant sprawling across the plain. East of here, near Spata, is the fine new airport, with a fast road connecting it to central Athens. At the Stavros flyover, north of Peania, the road to the left leads westwards back to Athens, skirting the north-eastern spur of Ymittos, which is crowned by the little Byzantine church of *Ayios Ioannis O Kynigos*, St John the Hunter, rather stylishly restored. A whole circuit of south-east Attica has been completed: a long drive.

The eastbound road from Stavros cuts across the northern Mesoyia to the Evvian Gulf and the field of Marathon. At Pallini a branch road leads to the pine-fringed beach of Loutsa. Beyond Pikermi, where there are good tavernas, the road crosses the gully where a party of distinguished English and Italian travellers, riding back from a visit to the battlefield of Marathon in 1870, were kidnapped by brigands, and subsequently murdered at Dilessi.

Shortly after Pikermi a minor road to the left climbs in a northerly direction through villas and pines until, at the top, a road to the right takes one to the **Monastery of Daou-Pendeli**, concealed in a lonely pine forest. Osbert Lancaster called the church (twelfth-century, restored in the seventeenth), 'a dotty triumph of provincial art'. It is indeed a curiosity, with numerous arches and six domes, the tallest surmounting the narthex which is on a different level from the main hexagonal body of the church. Armenian and Georgian influences, seldom encountered on the Greek mainland, have been at work here.

The main road turns north, directly to Marathon, but it is more interesting to follow the road to the east which dips down towards the sea at Rafina, a holiday resort with a busy port lined with fish restaurants, whence ferries sail for Southern Evvia, Andros and several of the northern Cyclades. From Rafina a road to the north follows the shore of the wide **Bay of Marathon**, as far as Nea Makri, where it rejoins the main road. Waves in the scimitar-shaped bay are often flecked with white horses raised by the Etesian wind; opposite rise the mountains of Evvia, denuded of vegetation, without a village in sight. Pine-covered hills roll back from the narrow coastal belt, now somewhat crowded with small houses, apartments, hotels and camping sites. Across these hills the runner, according to the apocryphal story, raced to Athens to announce the outcome of the battle, only to die of exhaustion on reaching the stadium.

Marathon (490 BC) was the first of the three great battles which the Athenians waged with such extraordinary success against the immensely superior power mobilized by Darius for what historians believe may have been an attempt at a great Asiatic invasion of Europe. The effect of the victory, though neither as important nor as decisive as Salamis (for the Persians came again, ten years later, in redoubled strength), was immense in terms of morale.

The site is now a reclaimed marshland. At the point where the foothills advance closest to the shore, a signposted road to the right leads through village gardens to the **Soros**, a mound raised over a floor on which archaeologists have found traces of charcoal and human bones: the bones of the Greek dead. Pieces of flint have been identified as arrowhead fragments, used by the Persian archers (the finds are in the Marathon Museum at Vrana, the entrance ticket for which includes the Soros). Although Herodotos says the battle was fought close to a swamp, the Soros is surrounded now by market gardens, lemon groves and the bright flowers of village houses. On one side rise the woodland spurs of Mount Pendeli, on the other flow the blue waters of the Evvian Gulf.

A kilometre beyond the turn-off to the Soros another side road runs west through the village of **Vrana**, ending at the Marathon Museum. Within the Museum enclosure is a second tumulus, overgrown with asphodel in spring, known as the Tomb of the Plataians, the only Greeks who came to the aid of the hard-pressed Athenians. In the Plataian memorial eight graves, each with a skeleton - one of an officer who is actually named - have been uncovered.

The Museum itself contains exhibits relating to the Battle, finds from the nearby estate of Herodes Atticus, banker and friend of the Emperor Hadrian, a number of prehistoric vessels and other objects found at sites in the neighbourhood. The large construction adjoining the museum covers two grave circles which contain skeletons of the undersized men who inhabited Attica in the Middle Helladic period; there is also a skeleton of a horse, equally undersized. At various points on the Marathonian plain, vestiges of prehistoric foundations and masonry suggest the extreme antiquity of this part of Attica.

Before reaching the village of Marathonas, a road to the right, signposted Kato Souli, also leads to the lovely crescent-shaped beach of Schinia, from where one can reach the Promontory of Kynosouras (the Dog's Tail, so-called after its shape) where there are vestiges of classical walls. Past Kato Souli the road turns to the north and reaches the site of the ancient township of **Rhamnous**. The sacred enclosure is at the end of a small plain on an artificial platform, supported on two sides by a retaining wall composed of blocks of white marble. The foundations of the larger of two edifices have been identified as those of a temple of Nemesis, Goddess of Retribution. Of the Doric order, probably the work of the architect of the Theseion, it contained a colossal statue in Parian marble of the goddess. The London Society of Dilettanti shipped parts of the head to the British Museum in the early nineteenth century, while the innumerable fragments of the body have recently been put together into the only surviving cult statue of the Golden Age: the work of Agorakritos, Phidias' pupil. The temple was never completely finished, for the three steps of the stylobate have not been smoothed and a number of drums of columns lying about the site have not been fluted. The small temple, almost contiguous to the larger, was a sixth-century BC shrine of Themis, Goddess of Justice, destroyed by the Persians. There is a small museum, but it is rarely open.

From the sacred enclosure a steep path, lined by tombs, descends to the shore which is dominated by a knoll on which there are remnants of the ancient acropolis, but this area is used by the Navy and cannot usually be visited. A massive fourth-century BC stone wall, almost gold in colour, emerges from the evergreens: the remains of the ancient Temple of Rhamnous. Within the acropolis, thick with brushwood and tangled vines, there are vestiges of watch-towers, barrack-rooms, cisterns and the cavea of a theatre. Clearly an Athenian garrison was stationed at Rhamnous - presumably to guard the entrance to the Evvian Gulf from Spartan incursions. The raised sacred enclosure, the lonely glen leading down to the sea, and the crumbling fortifications on the deserted shore have an austere quality which few can fail to associate with the Goddess of Retribution.

Leaving Rhamnous a road to the right leads to the village of Grammatikon, the Marathonas-Kapandriti road and the Amphiaraion, through surprisingly wild, untouched country. Alternatively, from Grammatikon you can return via Marathonas and turn off to the right at Nea Makri onto a road which climbs up into the pinewoods on the northern slopes of Pendeli, scarred by the modern marble quarries, with the Marathon dam far below you to the right. The road descends to Dionysos and northern Attica, then goes through the pines and villas of Ekali to Kifissia and down to Athens.

If, starting from Athens, you take the road to Kifissia, you will pass the residential suburb of Psyhiko, much favoured by foreign residents, and then Filothei, equally suburban, less fashionable and named after St Filothei, a well-born nun of the sixteenth century. She owned vast lands and founded a convent, a hospital and a workshop for weaving (from the profits of which she bought Greek girls out of Turkish harems). From Filothei a road westwards (the turn-off is to the right) goes to the nondescript suburb of Nea Ionia. A left turn, signposted, brings you to the twelfth-century **Omorfi Ekklissia** (The Beautiful Church) which has a pretty octagonal drum. Much of the original structure has been spoilt by later, inelegant additions. The interior is decorated with frescoes (possibly fifteenth- or sixteenth-century) which are pleasant rather than remarkable. The windows are attractively adorned with Rhodian plates.

Back on the main road the huge new Olympic Stadium is on your left. Some kilometres further on, at Maroussi, one turns right through outer suburbs towards **Mount Pendeli** (Pentelikon), a bluish pyramid, scarred with the ravages of two and a half thousand years of marble quarrying. It is one of the loveliest of Attic landmarks, although topped now with an all-too-conspicuous radar station. Towards the end of the built-up area, on the left above the main road, is the Pendeli Monastery (not to be confused with Daou-Pendeli which is much further east) surrounded by plane trees. Streams trickle down the sides of the mountain and in summer the high ground above the suburbs is popular for camping.

The slopes above the monastery are seamed with disused, ancient quarries, a lunar landscape of white rubble with mountain goats browsing among the tufts of heather and thyme which fail to conceal the centuries-old cicatrices. But one cannot approach Pendeli without a feeling of veneration. The very stuff of the mountain has furnished the raw material for some of the greatest works of sculpture and architecture in the world. 'Of Pentelic marble' - the label is familiar enough from museum catalogues. Distinguished by its opaque quality, Pentelic marble, in contrast to the snowy whiteness of Parian, contains traces of iron oxide which, when exposed to the weather, causes it to acquire a warm, honey-coloured patina.

Ascending from the monastery to the quarries, one comes to two thirteenth-century Byzantine chapels at the entrance to a cave, once the refuge of eremitical monks who chose to worship in this remote, wind-blown place high above the Attic plain. In the south chapel a fragmentary fresco of the Virgin and Child spreads across the little apse. The Annunciation is visible on the east wall. The painted decoration also includes a representation of Michael Honiates, an unusually enlightened Bishop of Athens of the late twelfth century. The decoration of crosses, eagles and inscriptions carved on the rock suggests that the chapel is of a much earlier date than the frescoes: in fact, of the pre-Iconoclastic period. The style of the best-preserved frescoes in the north chapel, which was used for burials, is of a cruder, more provincial character.

From Pendeli one can take a road over the mountain to the Nea

Makri-Dionysos road or one can go north-west to Kifissia to rejoin the road from Athens, without going back to Maroussi.

Kifissia, where some old Athenian families still spend the summer in villas set amid shady gardens, also has numerous hotels and new blocks of flats. At No.1 Metaxas Street, just off the main square, there is a famous confectioner's shop where an astonishing variety of exotic home-made jams can be bought.

From Kifissia one can join the National Road to the north, but by going straight on and crossing over it you come to the thickly wooded area of Varibobi and Tatoi on the foothills of Mount Parnitha. The taverna of Leonidas, just after a left turn, is one of the coolest spots in Attica, crowded on August nights with Athenians escaping from the stifling air and burning pavements of the city. The Greek Royal Family had a large summer villa here and, amid the pines, there is a royal graveyard. Beyond the royal estate, on the spine of the mountain, there are vestiges of the famous Spartan stronghold of Dekelia (twenty minutes' hard climb from a taverna surrounded by plane trees).

The road continues to the north and, after the pass of Ayios Merkourios, descends in loops to Malakassa, where it joins the National Road.

North of Kifissia the National Road passes below a wooded spur of Parnitha, with terraced vineyards and olive trees on the slopes of the rolling hills. The cornfields and vegetable plots in the cup-shaped valleys are partly hidden by the numerous factories beside the road. To the right there is a glimpse of the Marathon Dam and the reservoir which supplies much of the capital's water. The dam of Pentelic marble, completed by American engineers in 1926, prevents the streams that flow down the mountainside in winter from escaping through the numerous gullies into the Marathonian plain.

To the west of the National Road is the ancient village stronghold of **Aphidnai**. Beyond the village the pine-woods become thicker, more luxuriant. There are entrancing views of the Evvian Gulf which begins to contract as it nears the Evripos. Branching off the main road through Kapandriti and Kalamos one reaches the Sanctuary of Amphiaraos, the Argive seer. **The Amphiaraion** is situated in a secluded valley shaded by pine and plane trees. The wind rustling the pine branches is laden with the scent of resin; the only sound is that of a stream, its banks overgrown with maidenhair fern, trickling down to the sea.

The ruins are easily identified: as you go down the path, below you on the right are the foundations of a fourth-century BC Doric temple, with the base of the cult statue in the middle of the *cella.* Next to this is the opening of a spring, sacred to Amphiaraos, from which he reappeared from the Underworld, and into which pilgrims threw coins as a thanksgiving. Next is the substructure of a large altar, and then on the left, numerous bases of statues line the terrace. Beyond them there is a marble bench, where consultants sat whilst waiting to be allocated sleeping quarters. The bench is at the side of a long and impressive fourth-century BC *stoa*, which had a façade of forty-one Doric columns and was separated into two galleries by a row of seventeen Ionic columns. Here the consultants slept and were visited with oracular dreams. In a pine-clad hollow behind the *stoa* is the most charming ruin of all: a miniature **theatre**, famous for its acoustics. The *proskenion*, judiciously restored, has eight Doric half-columns of grey marble. Five seats for high priests, admirably preserved, are ranged in a semi-circle round the orchestra.

The road to the Amphiaraion goes on to meet the road from Malakassa (on the National road) to Skala Oropou on the Evvian Gulf. From Skala Oropou a ferry crosses to the opposite shore and the site of Eretria. Throughout one's travels in Attica the outline of Evvia, extending from opposite Rafina in the south to the Pagasitic Gulf in the north, has become increasingly familiar. There is a comfortable feeling of omnipresence about Evvia. Its peaks are nearly always visible behind the mainland ranges, and the blue streak of the channel is encountered again and again along the coasts of Attica, Boeotia and Phthiotis.

Just under Mount Parnitha, north of Athens, is the village of **Aharne** (now Menidi) where ivy, the symbol of the god Dionysos, is reputed to have grown for the first time. The village, once inhabited by descendants of seventeenth-century Albanian settlers, has now been engulfed by Greater Athens, spreading ever higher into the constraining ring of mountains. There is a road to Menidi and Parnitha from the National Road, or one can go from central Athens via Liossion Street in Kato Patissia. Beyond Menidi, which was the epicentre of the 1999 earthquake, the road ascends Parnitha, the highest though least beautiful of the mountains which enclose the bowl of Athens on three sides. A short way up is the lower station of the cableway to the top, and rather higher, about two-thirds of the way up, the firs begin. Just below the summit, where there are ski-runs, is a cluster of buildings - roadhouses, sanatoria, chalets - among the dark conifers. It is all rather Swiss. There is a luxury hotel, with a casino, swimming pool and a spectacular view of central Attica.

Liossion Street, mentioned above, also takes one via Ano Liossia (fork left about two kilometres after passing under the National Road) to the village of **Fyli (Hasia)** , which has numerous tavernas, and further into the mountains to the well-tended Convent of the **Panayia ton Kliston** (The Virgin of the Closed Defiles), probably of late Byzantine origin and perched above a ravine pock-marked with hermits' caves. The road climbs the lonely defile with its contorted rock formations, escarpments and deep crevices; behind, against the backcloth of Ymittos, there are views of Athens and the plain. The pass of Fyli (over six hundred metres) is dominated by an impressive free-standing eminence crowned by massive fourth-century BC fortifications, with the remains of ramparts and towers commanding the point of intersection of several gorges. In winter there are treacherous snowdrifts and many mountaineers and shepherds have lost their lives in the unexpected chasms. The fortifications, which replaced an earlier fortress on a neighbouring peak, guarded the shortest route into Attica from Boeotia. The drop from the fortress is precipitous. The quadrangular masonry of the walls, nearly ten feet thick, is well preserved, particularly on the east side. An interesting feature of the two entrances is that they were built in such a way as to expose the attackers' right shoulders, unprotected by shields, to the defenders within. Unfortunately the 1999 earthquake brought down a large section of the fortifications. The road continues, untarred, into Boeotia.

Before leaving Athens it would be a mistake, I think, not to take one last look at **Ymittos**, smooth and elephantine, most homely and familiar of Attic mountains. The road from the centre of Athens cuts across the populous suburb of Kessariani and enters a verdant little valley in a fold of the mountain: an oasis of cypress, olive and plane trees. At the head of the valley, under a large plane tree, a spring gushes forth: a fertility spring, according to superstition. Above the spring is the **Monastery of Kessariani**, with its church, dedicated to the Presentation of the Virgin, built in alternating courses of brick and stone. An eleventh-century foundation, for many years inhabited by monks who kept bees, it has undergone considerable restoration. The wall paintings in the narthex, apse and pendentives are of the post-Byzantine period. Around the well-kept court are the monastic bakeries, a mill and a bath-house, which was also used as an olive-press. Kessariani is not important in the history of Byzantine church architecture, but its elegant little drum and cupola, its warm red-brick roofs, even its somewhat incongruous seventeenth-century campanile, all shaded by pine trees, form a charming spectacle of rusticity on the fringe of the suburban belt.

Above Kessariani the steep mountain-side is covered with stunted shrubs: cistus, juniper and terebinth; and aromatic sage, thyme and lavender, which, together with the grape hyacinth and the purple crocus of spring, feed the famous Ymittos bees. The Greeks believed that the first bees in the world came from here; now 'Ymittos' honey is produced throughout Attica. Beyond the monastery the road climbs past the pretty little Byzantine church of Asteri to a car-park below the summit (a prohibited area) which commands an immense panoramic view of the whole of Attica and the islands of the Saronic Gulf.

The road to the west, to Corinth and the Peloponnese, crosses a ridge of hills from which there is an incomparable view, best seen at sunset, of the city spreading round its rocky hills under the 'violet crown' of Ymittos. The road now joins the Sacred Way to Eleusis, once bordered with the tombs of illustrious citizens. Today there are petrol stations and suburban houses. On the left the red-tiled dome of the church at **Dafni** and the tops of cypress trees appear above the high walls within which the Crusaders established a Cistercian community in the thirteenth century. Dedicated to the Dormition of the Virgin, Dafni is one of the most important Byzantine monuments in the country. The church is of the eleventh century, a golden age of Byzantine art - the age of the Komnenos dynasty, which held the stage for a century.

The basic plan of the interior is typical of eleventh-century church architecture: a Greek Cross with a wide, squat dome and drum, supported by four squinches, with apsed sanctuary and a narthex. But it is a variant on the classic plan: apart from having a double narthex, the sanctuary is small, allowing for the creation of a chapel on either side, as well as the long and narrow spaces at the corners (usually square) created by the cross-in-square plan. The other three high-arched spaces off the central square are also narrower than normal, and therefore on the west side there are chambers on either side of the principal entrance into the *naos*. At

Monemvassia, *Ayia Sofia* has the same plan. The mosaics have suffered from neglect and desecration (further damage was done by the 1999 earthquake), some have been restored, but enough survives to illustrate the perfection achieved by Byzantine mosaicists of this period.

On entering the church, one's first impression is of a large expanse of walls, colour-washed in brown ochre, which sets off the remaining mosaics to good effect. There seems to be little of the Byzantine 'gorgeousness' that the Benaki and Byzantine Museums promised. But each of the extant compositions merits careful

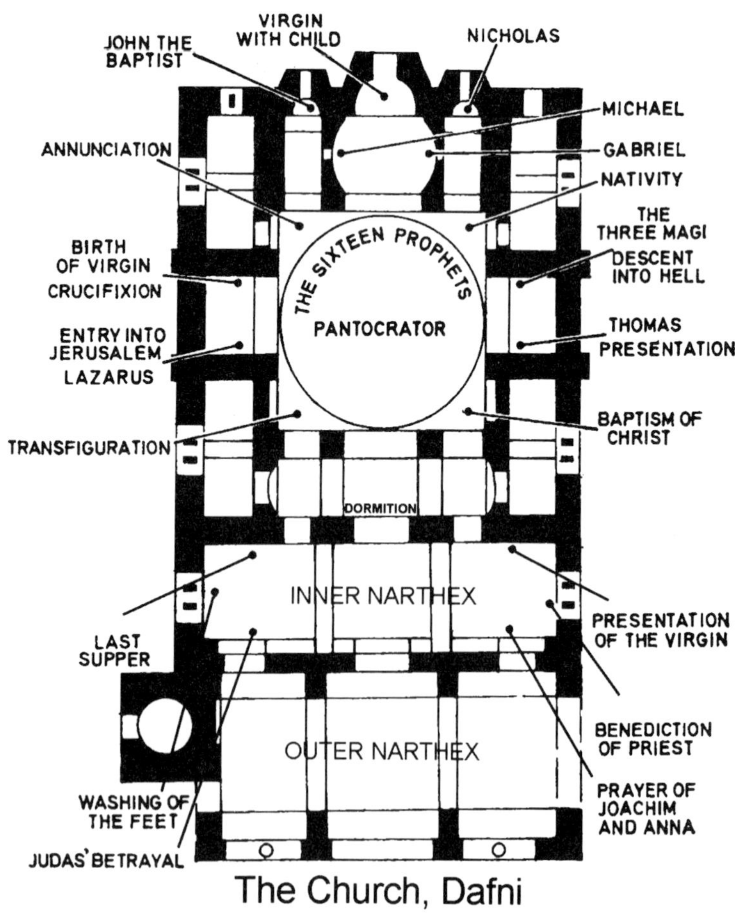

The Church, Dafni

examination; each is a work of art. The iconographic disposition is not haphazard, but strictly liturgical and symbolical, for the church is a visual image of Heaven, and the iconographer the servant of the theologian. It therefore helps to have an idea of the iconographic arrangement (mosaics or frescoes) of a typical Byzantine church interior in one's mind. The dome is Heaven, where Christ reigns in glory. He is surrounded by guardian Archangels, fully armed. Below them are the apostles or prophets who announced His coming. In the central apse, behind the *iconostasis*, the Virgin holds the Child. She, too, is flanked by Archangels. We now descend from Heaven to Earth. The walls are covered with portraits of saints, monks, ascetics and Fathers of the Church. Above them, on high panels, and in the squinches, unfold the great scenes from the lives of Christ and the Virgin, the *Dodekaorton* (The Twelve Feasts). Particular prominence is given to the Crucifixion and the Descent into Hell, which reveal the mystery of the Resurrection. Other scenes from the Gospels are often added, generally in the narthex.

At Dafni (as elsewhere) one should start in the inner narthex (the outer one is bare), where narrative tendencies are observed in the Betrayal, the Washing of the Feet and the Presentation, and then pass into the *naos*, the main body of the church, where the new 'humanism' is particularly evident in the **Transfiguration** in a squinch below the dome. The figure of Christ may be static, but it possesses an other-worldly majesty. The **Crucifixion** and the **Descent into Hell**, compositions of great poise and balance, are placed in the left- and right-hand arms of the Cross. The Virgin in the Crucifixion is the personification of grief and bereavement, her mouth slightly turned down at the sides, her almond-shaped eyes contracted as though to hide a film of tears. She is one of the most moving figures in the whole of Byzantine mosaic decoration. The drapery of the angel with enormous wings in the **Annunciation** flows with an almost classical limpidity. Note the fine, splendidly-robed figure of the **Archangel Michael** in the sanctuary. A general lightness of tone, an almost pastel quality, prevails in these jigsaw puzzles of thousands of tesserae, pink, blue and green, on gold backgrounds. But it is the formidable **Pantocrator** in the dome, one of the greatest portraits in Byzantine, or indeed any, art, that dominates the whole church - a terrifying Messianic vision. Depicted in bust, Christ raises one hand in blessing, the long bony fingers of the other clasping a jewel-studded Book of Gospels. The face, with the superbly arched eyebrows and the mouth of a man who is, beyond all things, decisive if not forgiving, is austere, Eastern, implacable. It is a Christ of Nemesis. In the Dafni Pantocrator the whole of Byzantine civilization comes into focus. He is worlds removed from the humanity of the Christ of Italian and Western art.

Near the monastery, in the pine-woods, there is a tourist pavilion where a wine festival used to be held every summer. Unfortunately this famous and lively festival has been abandoned, although more modest wine festivals are now held in many parts of Greece during August and September.

Beyond Dafni the road descends towards the landlocked bay of Elefsina. On the right are the foundations of a temple of Aphrodite and a piece of rock hollowed out into niches for votive offerings. Fragments of white marble chiselled into the form of doves, the goddess's sacred birds, were found at the foot of the rocky hillside. The crescent-shaped bay, often filled from shore to shore with laid-up, rusting ships, is sealed off from the open sea by the pine-clad island of Salamis. The battle of Salamis, the culmination of the second Persian invasion (480 BC), was fought in the narrow strait between the eastern tip of the island and the mainland, where Mount Egaleos tapers off into the sea.

We continue on the **Sacred Way**, travelled by Athenian pilgrims bound for the celebration of the Eleusinian Mysteries; once lined with statues, shrines and votive monuments, it is now a busy highway running across the Thriasian plain, bordered by factories and refineries. To the right, a few yards from the sea, is a narrow salt-water lake: the ancient Rheiti, fringed with reeds, the haunt of wild fowl since time immemorial and incongruous in this agglomeration of industrial installations. Just before Elefsina (Eleusis, birthplace of Aeschylus) a road to the right leads into the uninteresting small town and to the ruins of the **Sanctuary of Eleusis**: least inspiring of ancient Greek sites, yet second only to Delphi in religious significance. The ground is flat and featureless; Parnitha in the background does not present its most impressive aspect and smoke trails from factory chimneys in the vicinity.

Below the rocky ledge, close to the sea, extend the ruins of the principal seat of worship of Demeter and Koré, in whose honour the Eleusinia, most sacred of Greek mysteries, was celebrated every September, attended by thousands of pilgrims from all over Greece. The holy edifices, whose jumbled foundations we now see, were built and rebuilt and yet again refashioned by the Peisistratids, by Kimon and Pericles (after the Persians had destroyed the sanctuary), by Lykurgos in the fourth century BC and by the Antonine emperors in the second century AD. Literally nothing remains standing, for Alaric and his Goths seem to have gone about their usual work of destruction with unprecedented thoroughness. Moreover, the successive reconstructions and restorations on different levels over a period of eight hundred years make it very difficult to identify the foundations of particular buildings.

The sanctuary, hemmed in by a nightmare complex of industrialization, lies between the low ridge of an acropolis and the sea. Left of the Great Propylaia, an Antonine reconstruction, is the opening of a well, once the fountain around which the Eleusinian women performed ritual dances. Next comes the Lesser Propylaia, also a Roman construction, which had astonishingly opulent decoration. On the cliffs to the right two caves are preceded by a little, walled-in terrace. This is part of the Sanctuary of Hades which represented the threshold of the Underworld from which Koré emerged every spring to bring light and fertility into the world again. The outline of the god's temple is discernible in front of the larger cave.

Returning to the Sacred Way, one reaches the platform of the Telesterion, where the Mysteries were performed. Bases of columns

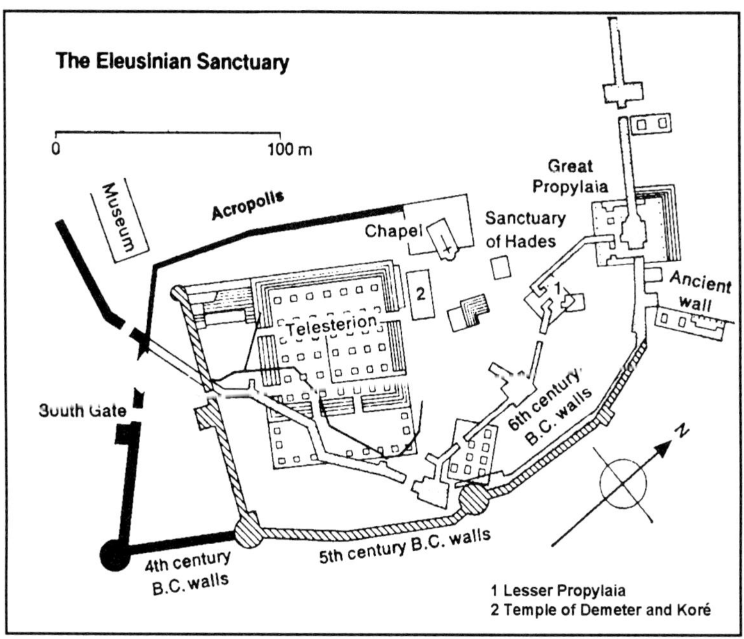

are easily identified. The fifth century BC interior consisted of six rows of seven columns, believed to have been Ionic, surrounded by tiers (those on the west side are well preserved) on which as many as three thousand people could stand. It had an upper storey with a wooden roof, where the *hiera*, the holy objects connected with the ceremony of initiation, were kept. The ruins of this extraordinary building are now no more than a mass of shattered blocks of masonry from successive restorations. Were the site less constricted by urban development and had the landscape one bit of the grandeur of Delphi or the serenity of Olympia, it might be easier to visualize the almost barbaric spectacle and to speculate on the religious exaltation experienced by the initiates, or *mystae*, as they proceeded in torchlight procession to the Hall of the Mysteries.

North of Elefsina the old road to Thiva (Thebes) winds across a rugged countryside. In March the *Anemone blanda*, with its sky-blue strap-shaped petals, grows profusely in the scrubland of the valleys below Mount Kitheron, an austere, even grim-looking mountain. Its contours are not elegant, but the steep slate-grey slopes, sprinkled with silver firs, and the lonely brushwood country at their foot, were reputed to be the haunt of Pan, god of shepherds. Here lions, bears and wild boar had their lairs, and stags roamed the forests. As one descends into a deep, sunken valley, the remains of a stone tower rise immediately on the right. It was probably part of a system of ancient watch-towers along the frontier between Attica and Boeotia. At the village of Inoi, a side road ascends to the **Monastery of Ossios Meletios**, a Byzantine foundation, considerably restored, situated on a mountain ledge among plane and poplar trees.

Beyond Inoi the entrance to a narrow pass is screened by a steep eminence with extensive fourth-century BC ramparts: the fortress of **Eleutherai**, which guarded Attica and the Megaris from invasion from the north. It failed to do so in 1941, when British Commonwealth forces retreated through the defile after a vain attempt to hold up the German panzers. Access - when driving from the east - is difficult: the track turns off very steeply from the main road. The fortifications are well preserved, particularly the north wall (eight feet thick and built in regular courses), and dotted with square towers provided with two gates in the lower storey and loopholes in the upper. The best view of the enceinte is the backward one, from the north, as one climbs the defile which ends in a bleak plateau, whence the road descends in hairpin bends into the Boeotian plain.

From Inoi a road to the left passes through the mountain village of Villia and descends in a series of wide loops between pine forests to the little harbour of Porto Yermeno on an inlet of the Halcyonic Gulf. There are enchanting views of the calm expanse of water, with the Boeotian mountains forming a screen to the north, marred only by an ugly spread of modern buildings along the shore. At the end of the descent, the remains of the fortified **Acropolis of Aigosthena** are scattered among the pine-woods. To the left of the road rise admirably-preserved fourth-century BC ramparts and the ruins of fifteen square towers, larger than those at Eleutherai, complete with gates, posterns and windows. The most impressive section, with four large, square towers crowning the east walls, is on the landward side, although the fortress must originally have been built as a defensive post against invaders from the sea. Many of the towers, especially those erected towards the end of the fifth century BC, were designed to carry wooden catapults, from which stones were hurled and arrows shot at attacking forces.

Two abandoned late Byzantine chapels add an incongruous note to the military site. On the lower ground are the foundations of an early Christian basilica. Along the placid, pebbly shore there are some modest tavernas. In summer the fields and olive groves, littered with blocks of ancient masonry, are crowded with campers, and the beach infested with horseflies. The sun shimmers on the pellucid sea and a haze screens the spurs of Elikon that ascend abruptly from a barren, deserted coastline.

5

Boeotia

MOST VISITORS TO ATHENS want to go to Delphi, and many, short of time, accomplish this as rapidly as possible, but the more leisurely approach, through Boeotia and the Parnassos Country, is very rewarding. The landscape, particularly the mountains, is superb; there are ancient sites - if fragmentary - Byzantine churches and a succession of famous battlefields.

A round trip is not practicable in Boeotia, which is virtually a large hollow enclosed between coastal ranges. Most travellers not rushing to Delphi and back, cross it in a day, with detours to the more important sites - especially Orchomenos. Two or three days in the area would allow time for visits to all the places of interest. Thiva is obviously the best base, but there is only a limited choice of accommodation, and the same goes for Livadia. Alternatively it could all be done quite easily from Halkis, a pleasant seaside town and port on the island of Evvia, less than an hour from Thiva, or even from Delphi.

Beyond the watershed between Attica and Boeotia the landscape becomes more continental, less Mediterranean. The vegetation is no longer confined to olive, cypress and oleander. Cotton, maize and other cereals take over. Flat agricultural plains succeed one another, flanked by barren foothills - austerely grey on a cloudy day, a fierce ochre at the height of summer - with hazy, fir-covered mountains in the distance and Parnassos towering above them all. The marshes, now drained and forming large tracts of wheat fields, once abounded in wild fowl. Lying on the main invasion route from the north, Boeotia has witnessed the passage of many conquerors - Dorian, Persian, Macedonian, Roman, Frankish, Norman, Spanish, Turkish and German - but today's inhabitants are mainly devoted to agriculture.

From Athens, both road and rail follow a roughly parallel course towards the north-east. After making a wide loop round a wooded spur of Mount Parnitha, they descend into the first and least interesting of the Boeotian plains and run north-westward across it. This plain is watered by the Asopos, the only local stream to flow straight into the sea without first forcing a way through an underground channel. There are tantalizing glimpses of the vivid blue streak of the Evvian Gulf at Halkis, now approaching its narrowest point. Between the road and the sea lies the field of Delion, where the Athenians, after committing the sacrilege of converting a Boeotian temple of Apollo into a fort, suffered their first major defeat of the Peloponnesian War in 424 BC.

Avlida, on the Gulf, is the ancient Aulis, off which Agamemnon's fleet was becalmed and where Iphigenia was sacrificed. The ruins of the Temple of Artemis are too negligible to justify a visit, likewise Tanagra, a little further on, once famous for its painted terracotta figurines, now has little to offer but a military airport. Soon after the toll-point the road forks, one branch leading off to Evvia; the main highway continues westward and, about nine kilometres further on, another road branches off to **Thiva, the ancient Thebes**, city of Oedipus. 'No city in Greece' we read in the *Dictionary of Greek and Roman Geography*, 'possessed such continued celebrity'. The celebrity is not always to its credit.

Theban mythology is among the richest in Greece, and Theban history, if less distinguished, is full of incident; recalling its famous past therefore, travellers are drawn to the City of the Seven Gates. They find themselves, however, in a pleasant provincial town spreading across a chain of low hills overlooking the Cadmeian plain, with scattered vestiges of ancient ruins, a fine museum and a good, lightly resinated rosé wine. It is as difficult to avoid Thiva geographically as it is to ignore the fascination of its history and renown; indeed, most of the main streets are evocatively named after the great figures of Theban mythology and history.

The centre of the town, bounded, in antiquity as now, by the streams of Dirke and Ismene, is on the highest hill, site of the ancient acropolis, the Cadmeia. Cadmos came from Phoenicia. He founded Thebes, colonized Boeotia and introduced writing into Greece (using the Phoenician alphabet which was the forerunner of modern Greek script). The record of Thebes during the Persian Wars, when its army joined with that of Mardonius in fighting the united Greeks, was beyond contempt. The slow-witted Thebans, obsessively jealous of the more lively Athenians, proved to be even more vindictive than the Spartans and after the Peloponnesian War, in which they sided with Sparta, they tried to persuade Lysander to

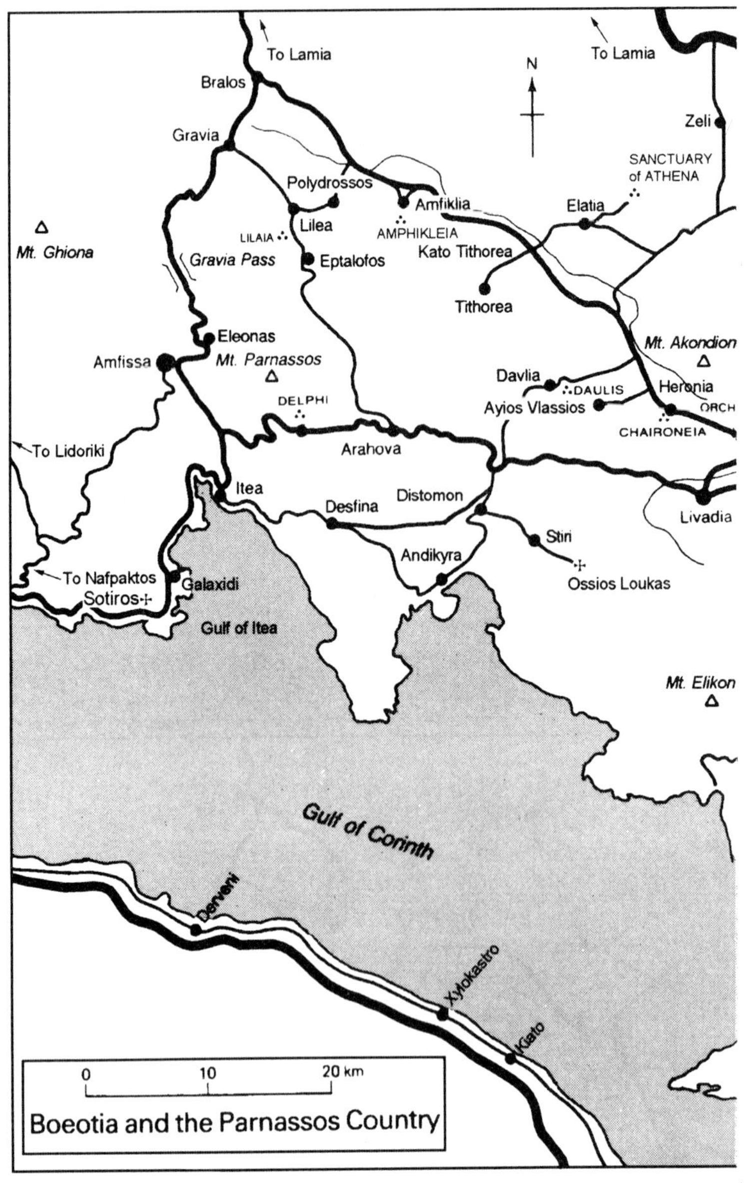
To Lamia
To Lamia
N
Bralos
Gravia
Zeli
SANCTUARY of ATHENA
Polydrossos
Amfiklia
Elatia
Lilea
LILAIA
AMPHIKLEIA
Mt. Ghiona
Gravia Pass
Eptalofos
Kato Tithorea
Tithorea
Eleonas
Mt. Akondion
Amfissa
Mt. Parnassos
Davlia
DAULIS
Heronia
DELPHI
Ayios Vlassios
ORCH
CHAIRONEIA
To Lidoriki
Arahova
Itea
Distomon
Desfina
Livadia
Stiri
Andikyra
To Nafpaktos
Galaxidi
Ossios Loukas
Sotiros
Gulf of Itea
Mt. Elikon
Gulf of Corinth
Derveni
Xylokastro
Kiato
0
10
20 km
Boeotia and the Parnassos Country

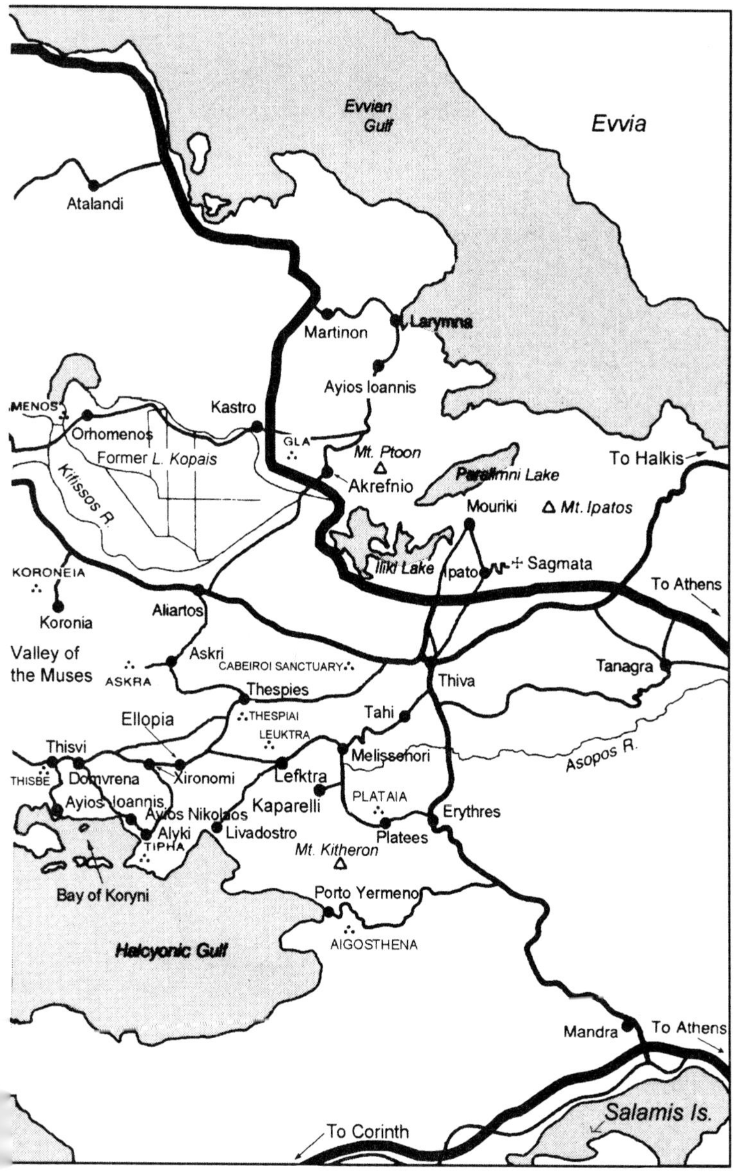
Evvian Gulf
Evvia
Atalandi
Martinon
Larymna
Ayios Ioannis
MENOS
Kastro
Orhomenos
GLA
Former L. Kopais
Kifissos R.
Mt. Ptoon
Akrefnio
Paralimni Lake
To Halkis
Mouriki
Mt. Ipatos
Iliki Lake
Ipato
Sagmata
KORONEIA
Koronia
Aliartos
To Athens
Valley of the Muses
ASKRA
Askri
CABEIROI SANCTUARY
Thiva
Tanagra
Thespies
THESPIAI
Ellopia
Tahi
LEUKTRA
Thisvi
THISBE
Domvrena
Xironomi
Lefktra
Melissohori
Asopos R.
Ayios Ioannis
Ayios Nikolaos
Kaparelli
PLATAIA
Erythres
Alyki
TIPHA
Livadostro
Platees
Mt. Kitheron
Bay of Koryni
Porto Yermeno
AIGOSTHENA
Halcyonic Gulf
Mandra
To Athens
Salamis Is.
To Corinth

raze Athens to the ground and sell the population into slavery. The Spartan leader, to his credit, refused.

In the second half of the fourth century BC, under the statesmanlike leadership of Epaminondas, oligarchical Thebes appears in a more sympathetic light. However, after his death a decline set in and later, after the Macedonian conquest, a revolt instigated by the Athenian Demosthenes called down upon Thebes the fury of Alexander the Great. The future world-conqueror ordered his scarlet-coated soldiers not only to flatten the city, but also to slay 6,000 Thebans and take 30,000 prisoners.

After this, the city sank into oblivion until the Middle Ages, when Benjamin of Tudela found it large and prosperous, and full of Jewish silk-workers whose lavish creations adorned Byzantine emperors and their consorts. The silk trade even survived a twelfth-century invasion by the Normans, who carried off many Theban workers to Palermo. The trade is dead now, but mulberry trees still grow around the town.

With the arrival of the Frankish barons, Thebes (or Estives as it was then called) became the seat of the de la Roche family, who styled themselves 'Dukes of Athens and Thebes'. The plight of thirteenth-century Athens must indeed have been tragic for the family to have chosen this dreary, humid place for their official residence instead of the Attic 'City of Light'. Theban monuments, which have never been described as beautiful, were built of dark grey Boeotian marble, giving the city a forbidding aspect, and few remnants have survived; of the ancient walls too there are only some rudimentary fragments. Alexander's sack was very thorough.

The archaeological enthusiast should start at the south-eastern end of Amfion Street (where it meets Polyneikou Street), opposite a cypress-clad hill. Here a few courses of massive, primitively-wrought limestone blocks form two round bases on either side of the street: foundations of the two flanking towers of the prehistoric Electran Gate. Crossing the centre of the town in a roughly northerly direction, one sees the foundations of what are believed to be a section of the palace archive building and a palace bathroom (corner of Epaminondas and Metaxa Streets). Turning right into Antigoni Street, one encounters some impressive ancient masonry on superimposed levels. The rubble of a palace of the Mycenaean period, in which Laios, Oedipus and Kreon probably held court, can be seen nearby, on the left, in Pindarou Street. Tablets found here are inscribed with Linear B dated to the thirteenth century BC.

At this point it is best to continue in a northerly direction along Pindarou Street to the site of one of the seven gates, from which the ancient road led to the north. The site of the Homoloid Gate is now occupied by the **Museum**, whose courtyard once formed part of the enceinte of the Frankish castle which overlooked the plain. The courtyard and garden are now filled with mosaics, tombstones, Byzantine reliefs and damaged statues. The only surviving section of the thirteenth-century fortress is the fine, squat tower, called Santameri (a corruption of St Omer) which stands on the right of the courtyard. The castle was built by St Omer, an arrogant Flemish baron who spent a large part of his wife's generous dowry in raising fortifications throughout his scattered domains in the Peloponnese and on mainland Greece.

Even the most hurried traveller in Boeotia, though unlikely to be impressed by the prehistoric rubble of ancient Thebes, should not, in my opinion, fail to visit this museum, which is small, well-arranged and now has an excellent catalogue available in English. From the entrance hall (not taking the rooms in numbered order) you pass into the Tanagra room in which are displayed the *larnakes* - cinerary urns or coffins of baked clay - dated to c. 1400-1200 BC, excavated at nearby Tanagra. Unique in Greece, these singular and beautiful urns, rectangular in shape and of varying sizes, stand on four squat legs. They contained, as some still do, the bones of distinguished Tanagran citizens who died over three thousand years ago. Stylized processionals of priests and animals with human faces are painted in black and orange - sometimes red - on the exterior surfaces. In two showcases there are prehistoric funerary gifts in the form of miniature pieces of furniture of exquisite workmanship. Once more we have an example of the veneration in which death was held by the Greeks of all periods. These enchanting little terracottas do not, admittedly, possess the lavish quality of the Mycenaean grave gifts, wrought in gold and precious stones. However, the motive, the underlying idea, remains the same: the dead are immortalized in the minds of the living by the quality of the works of art beside which they rest in eternity.

The first hall on the right contains unusual **stelae of black stone**, carved with the finest of incisions, depicting Boeotian warriors in combat at the battle of Delion, which are best seen from an oblique angle. The next hall has a display of prehistoric pottery, fourteenth-century BC cylinder seals of lapis lazuli (whose Anatolian origin suggests the existence of trade relations between Thebes and

Phoenicia), and ceramics of the highest quality from the Geometric, Archaic and Classical periods. Among the exhibits of the sixth and fifth centuries BC is a fine male torso (No. 7) displayed in the last hall. Though unfortunately headless and almost limbless, the statue is in the best fifth-century BC sculptural tradition. Among the recent finds is a fine, possibly sixth-century, funeral *stele* from Akrefnio with a relief of a youth with a cockerel. The showpiece of the museum is the sixth-century BC **Ptoion Kouros** which came from the Sanctuary of Apollo on Mount Ptoön. The youth's smile is no less enigmatic, his posture no less heroic than those of the Attic *kouroi*; only the stylized, coral-shaped locks which fall down the back of the neck are much less finely modelled.

The normal axis of travel in Boeotia is east-west or vice-versa, with detours into the foothills of the mountain ranges flanking the plains. The first such side-trip is a long one to the south and west, starting down the old Thiva-Athens road, through undulating fields, home of the *Tulipa boeotica*, a lovely bell-shaped red flower with a black centre in the form of a star. The village of Tahi (a little way off the road), where excavations were carried out many years ago, may well be the site of Potniai, a shrine sacred to Dionysos.

At the village of Erythres, on the lower slopes of Mount Kitheron, a right turn to the west leads to the ancient township and battlefield of **Plataia** where the third and decisive engagement of the Persian Wars was fought. Boeotia has always been the scene of violent armed clashes and none does more credit to Greek bravery than this battle. Plataia, in particular, had a noble record of fidelity to the Athenian alliance, which dated from the sixth century BC. During the Persian Wars it had been the only state to send a contingent to assist the hard-pressed Athenians at Marathon.

In 479 BC, after the Persian commander, Mardonius, had sacked Athens following the battle of Thermopylae, the allied Greek contingents assembled on the slopes of Kitheron. The Greeks, under the command of Pausanias, the Spartan general, numbered a hundred and ten thousand. Mardonius, one of the principal architects of the grand design for the Asian invasion of Europe, was torn between a premonitory hunch to get out of Greece before the pincers closed round his cumbersome army of three hundred thousand men and a desire to avenge Xerxes' humiliation at the battle of Salamis. He resolved to make a decisive stand on the river Asopos, where his rear would be defended by friendly Thebes. The omens warned both armies to remain on the defensive: the one that crossed the Asopos first was doomed. So for ten days the opponents glared at each other over the stream. In the end Mardonius, taken in by a series of Spartan and Athenian feints, believed the Greeks were preparing for flight. Ignoring the omens, he led a yelling, ill-equipped rabble across the stream, where it was opposed by the highly professional, heavily armed Spartan units. The Greeks took a crippling toll of the barbarian levies and, when Mardonius was killed by a Spartan, panic seized the Persians, who fled in disorder to their stockade. In the great pursuit that followed, the Greeks poured down the gullies and plundered Mardonius' sumptuous tent. The booty of silver tables, gold-inlaid couches, richly woven carpets and wagons full of goblets, not to mention droves of camels, pack-animals and Persian women, was divided equally among the allies. The sight of so much booty moved Pausanias to ask why such a wealthy people should have wanted to rob the Greeks of their only possession - their poverty. Xerxes made no further attempt to invade Greece after the Battle of Plataia.

Fifty years later, during the Peloponnesian War, the Plataians never wavered and withstood a famous siege for two years. When the depleted garrison was forced to surrender, the Thebans did not leave a single Plataian alive and they destroyed all the buildings. Plataia thus paid heavily for her loyalty to Athens. Philip of Macedon restored the city and Alexander the Great built the ramparts, which are now very ruined except on the west side; but one can walk for quite long stretches along a line of low walls overlooking the level meadows where so many Persian men, hopes and ambitions perished. These walls, about two and a half miles in circumference, can be traced round the cornfields which slope down towards the stream of the Asopos. There are no other vestiges of the ancient township except the foundations of a temple, possibly of Hera, on a terrace near the north-west wall. There is no sign of the sanctuary of Demeter around which there was fierce fighting, but on whose holy ground no Persian corpse was found. Herodotos suggests that the goddess, remembering the barbarians' desecration of her most sacred shrine at Eleusis, prevented them from setting foot in her Boeotian temple.

Shortly after the site of Plataia take the road for Melissohori and then turn left to Lefktra, a cluster of several villages now united, on a long, low hill overlooking the battlefield of **Leuktra**. This battle represented a historical milestone of a very different character. Of the victory of Thebes, led by Epaminondas, over Sparta in 371 BC at

Leuktra, Pausanias says it was 'the most famous ever won by Greeks over Greeks'. It is the familiar story of Greek tearing Greek to pieces. The site, signposted 'Tropaion' to the right as you go up to Lefktra, is marked by a monument which consists of a large circular plinth, much restored, with marble shields around the top. The battle was fought north of this - the tumulus we see nearby was probably the Spartan sepulchre. There is little else. I asked a farmer if there were any *arhaia* (ancient things) nearby. He led me across a field, scrabbled among the corn and pointed to a stone slab, which might have formed part of a *stele*, inscribed with the name *MYPON*. The inscription could not have referred to the sculptor, who, although a native of neighbouring Eleutherai, died about a hundred years before the battle. The slab, the man said, was recently ploughed up by a tractor.

From Lefktra a good road leads, through rugged scenery, to the sea at Livadostro, where, on the right, are sections of the wall of Kreusis - the Spartan invaders used this as their port.

Back at Lefktra, take the road past the Monument, which brings you out on the Thespies-Ellopia road. For Thespies turn right but, if you want to visit Alyki and the southern coast of Boeotia and ancient Thisbe, turn left - the road runs south then west through a narrow plain, between the foothills of Elikon and Kitheron. It is pastoral country and in late spring the road is bordered by banks of pale bluish-mauve *Iris xiphium* (Spanish Iris). To the south, on a clear day, one can see the peaks of the Peloponnesian mountains: a spectacular backcloth to the foreground of barren but spectacular coastal mountains. At the village of Xironomi turn left for Alyki. An excellent road climbs the hills - there is an ancient watchtower on the right - then comes out over the beautiful eastern part of the Bay of Domvrena (or Koryni) and descends to the sprawling, tawdry holiday resort or Alyki. At the far end of the long beach a rocky crag drops steeply into the sea - on it are remains of the substantial fifth-century BC walls of ancient **Tipha** (also known as Siphai), towers with polygonal masonry, and doorways with pediments, while more masonry is visible in the sea below.

Whether a squall is blowing or whether the sea is blue and pellucid, the bay of Domvrena remains, in its remoteness and intricate configuration, one of the most impressive land and seascapes on the southern mainland.

From Alyki a road follows the coast to the smaller settlement of Ayios Nikolaos, then turns inland to reach the wide valley-bowl of

Domvrena and Thisvi, large contiguous villages lying below massive rocky outcrops of Mount Elikon. The villages are now busy and prosperous; a few years ago they were undefiled and sleepy with only one taverna, serving some of the best country bread in Greece.

Next to Thisvi, on its southern side, is a long, low, flat hill littered with the stones of ancient **Thisbe** (turn left at the Primary School, and on the open plateau turn right for the most substantial ruins). There are extensive walls and squat, square towers dated to the period of Alexander the Great, when the place must have served as a military outpost against invaders from the Corinthian Gulf. The circuit, which follows the edge of the plateau on different levels, is about a mile in circumference. The masonry is regular and polygonal and the joining of the blocks reveals fine workmanship. Foundations of walls shelve down in terraces to a fertile, bowl-like valley, where flights of pigeons wheel overhead in the sky. At the foot of the plateau the rock is honeycombed with caves, thought to have served as ancient sepulchres.

Southward the road cuts across the hollow basin, following the course of an ancient causeway, built in order to prevent the whole plain being flooded when the autumn rains set in. It must have been a curious sight: one half a lake or at least a marsh; the other cultivated land. A bleak mountain stretch follows. One descends in hairpin bends to the rugged bay of Domvrena, broken by numerous coves and minute fiords. The road ends at the inlet of Ayios Ioannis. Even on this remote shore, holiday shacks and shoddy blocks of flats have sprung up. Bare headlands stretch eastward. The great bay, with its islets and numerous anchorages, has always been noted for violent squalls, as the winds funnel down the stony valleys from the mountain-tops of Elikon and Kitheron.

Returning eastwards from Domvrena turn left after six kilometres for modern Thespies (bypassing Xironomi and Ellopia). Ancient **Thespiai** shares with Plataia the distinction of being one of the two Boeotian cities that remained unrelentingly hostile to Thebes.

Modern Thespies, like its pretty twin village Leondari, from which it is separated by a shallow ravine, spreads across a shelf overlooking the plain to the south, where the barely identifiable ruins of the ancient site (notably the foundations of a Temple of the Muses) are scattered. The finds from the hitherto perfunctory excavations (apart from those in the Museum at Thiva) are in the Museum which, however, is rarely open and is more of a storehouse for antiquities.

The god worshipped here was Eros, a primeval deity, symbolizing sexual vigour, armed with flaming torches which he aimed at gods and mortals alike. It is not until Hellenistic times that Eros is sentimentalized by poets and artists, becomes the son of Aphrodite and finally the plump little Cupid rendered so popular by Roman artists. The original Greek Eros was a more virile deity. A festival in his honour, known as the *Erotidia*, was held every four years, and the cult statue consisted of an erect monolith on which every bride offered a tress of her hair, representing her youth, and a girdle symbolizing her virginity.

Near here flowed the reed-fringed stream into which the youth Narcissus gazed for so long and so intently that he fell in love with his own image. Pausanias finds the story 'absolutely stupid'; Sir George Wheler, travelling in Thespian territory in the seventeenth century was nevertheless pleased to find the narcissus growing everywhere in profusion.

From Thespies a road to the west leads to the village of Askri, from which an untarred, but good, road climbs into the rocky, cone-shaped foothills of Mount Elikon, Home of the Muses. You pass an eminence: possibly the natural stronghold to which the Thebans fled when their country was overrun by northern tribes at about the time of the Trojan War. On it stand the ruins of a medieval watch-tower (Paleo-Pyrgos) like a skeleton in stone, commanding a view of a desolate pyramidal peak crowned by a ruined Hellenic tower (Pyrgaki): all that remains of **Askra**, birthplace of Hesiod, founder of the first school of poetry on the Greek mainland. Today it seems a remote and grandiose place, from which there is a wide prospect of the Valley of the Muses. The road continues right up the valley, and near where it reaches and crosses the stream is the little that survives; one has to hunt around the stony ground for traces of an altar and the unexcavated cavea of a third-century BC theatre. The valley is pleasant enough, with vines, almond and olive trees, and poplars along the streams, but of the supposed idyllic beauty of the haunt of the Muses little remains but its evocative associations.

Back at Askri one can go on to Aliartos, or return to Thiva, in which case it is possible to visit the so-called **Sanctuary of the Cabeiroi** (reputedly the sons of Hephaistos), five kilometres from Thiva on the Livadia road. The turn-off to the south, difficult to spot, is a little way west of the major turn-off to Thespies and Domvrena. The increasingly dreadful track leads to a bridge where you should turn left, it is better to leave the car here and walk - it is less than one kilometre.

The Sanctuary lies in a fold of rolling green hills, criss-crossed with hedgerow-bordered paths. The Cabeiria were mysteries or fertility rites, possibly orgies, celebrated chiefly in Samothrace and Lemnos, but also in Boeotia. The ruins are fairly extensive but infinitely perplexing, covering a considerable chronological span. The eastern end of a temple forms the *skene* of a theatre (parts of which are well preserved), remarkable for the shallow arc of the semi-circle, which focuses on an altar: the scene, no doubt, of some orgiastic rite. On the outskirts of the sanctuary an open square is formed by what were once three chambers. Masonry as late as that of the Roman period is evident. The confusion arising from the superimposition of successive levels of foundations, all of different periods, does not detract from the pastoral quality of the scene, with wild flowers growing in the shade of luxuriant shrubs and sheep browsing on the hillsides which enclose the curiously sunken site.

Heading west from Thiva the main Livadia road leaves the melancholy plain. The ground rises, then dips down into the basin of the former Lake Kopais: now a shimmering expanse of cotton and maize fields surrounded by cliffs and mountains which, in antiquity, rose sheer from the shallow water's edge. Once the haunt of cranes, now of migratory storks, the lake or swamp was reclaimed by French and British engineers at the end of the nineteenth century. Strabo's assertion that the whole basin had been drained by the inhabitants of ancient Orchomenos is borne out by the discovery of a primitive but intricate system of dykes encircling the entire Kopaic 'lake', whereby the various streams were diverted by a network of canals into *katavothres* which disgorged their waters into the sea. Archaeologists have located long, low mounds, the remains of the ancient dykes, stretching across considerable tracts of the plain, either in unbroken lines or with gaps at intervals. Here, as indeed throughout most of Boeotia, one is constantly aware of geology: of water in subterranean channels coursing through limestone ranges; of curious hump-shaped mounds of slate-grey rock emerging out of a mirage of sun-drenched arable land; of lakes on different levels which descend like stepping stones towards the Evvian Gulf.

On the southern edge of the basin, beyond Mount Sfinghion - a grim pyramidal rock - lies Homer's 'grassy Haliartos', still surrounded by 'well-watered meadows'.

From modern **Aliartos** the traveller may be going directly to

Livadia, or may want to visit the various places of interest on the other side of Lake Kopais. The direct route skirts the base of Mount Elikon, whose constantly-changing outlines dominate much of the Boeotian landscape. Neither as grand as Taiyetos nor as beautiful as Parnassos - and not nearly as high as either - it is nevertheless well-wooded and rugged, but never forbidding.

If one opts for this route, it would be a mistake, I think, not to visit the site of yet another ancient battlefield and thus penetrate a more pastoral area of the Elikon country. West of Aliartos there is a wide arc of flat, cultivated land. A side road runs south through cornfields and olive groves between hedgerows of broom and wild pear. To the right a ruined Catalan tower crowns an isolated hill, site of ancient **Koroneia**, where the Panboeotia, a great religious festival 'common to all the Bocotians', was held at the temple of Athena Itonika. The temple stood in the plain in front of the hill.

It was on the level ground around the ancient town that the Boeotians, under the leadership of the impetuous Tolmides, inflicted a major defeat on the Athenians in 447 BC. The victory had such a tonic effect on the morale of the Boeotians that they were able to throw the Athenians out of the whole of their country. Now the ruins of Koroneia are virtually obliterated; the theatre, temple foundations and walls - all of considerably later periods than the fifth century BC - lie below and around the Catalan tower.

Leaving the acropolis hill to the left, the road climbs the mountainside, which forms the eastern arm of a great bite into the Elikon range, making a perfectly-shaped crescent around the olive groves and cotton fields. The road ends at the modern village of Koronia, perched high above the fruitful plain. Hollyhocks grow in profusion in back gardens and the scarlet of geraniums is splashed across the whitewashed walls of village houses.

An excursion around Lake Kopais, rather rambling but of greater interest, takes in sites near the main Athens-Thessaloniki road and finally reaches Livadia via Orchomenos. From Aliartos the road cuts across the cotton fields to the north-east and passes under the main Athens-Thessaloniki highway below a line of hills, whose rocky sides rise abruptly from the reclaimed swamp. Obviously one can also start directly from Athens.

A small canyon cuts through the cliff, opening out into a rugged little valley entirely enclosed by beige-coloured hills. At the village of Akrefnio, where the Thebans took refuge after their city was sacked by Alexander the Great, the road turns sharp left and a minor road climbs straight on towards Mount Ptoön, which has a triple peak and was named after a son of Apollo. To reach the **Sanctuary of Apollo Ptoion** take the first left fork on this minor road (signposted to a monastery) and then a right fork towards the Chapel of Ayia Paraskevi. It is not easy to find the ruins of the Sanctuary, an oracular seat, which are on three terraces: they are above the cluster of holm-oaks that shelter the colour-washed chapel near the road, and towards the ravine to the left (north-east). On the first terrace are the base of a *tholos* building and a rectangular cistern where consultants purified themselves before ascending to the second terrace, across which lie traces of *stoas* buttressed by a few courses of retaining wall, and finally to the third, marked by foundations of a Doric temple of Apollo. Above the temple, a spring called *Perdiko Vryssi* (The Partridge Spring) has been identified as the site of the oracle. The waters of the spring, which gush out of the rock, connect with the cistern below. Climbing from one terrace to another, one sinks ankle-deep into soft moss through which water trickles. It is as though the whole mountain had a substratum of underground rivulets. From a ledge slightly south-east of the ruins there is a fine view of the winding inlets of Lake Iliki below.

The lake itself, part of the water supply of Athens, is skirted by the Athens-Thessaloniki highway. Obviously once a crater, its configuration is of fascinating complexity - a series of figures of eight of different dimensions. Barren, rocky banks rise from turquoise water. At times the conical summits and contorted volcanic shapes overlooking the winding shore give the impression of a lunar landscape; at others of Japanese prints. A *katavothra* connects Iliki with the smaller lake of Paralimni, in an even deeper depression, which can be approached by a branch road from the highway (about fifteen kilometres back towards Athens). The road passes through the village of Mouriki and descends into a narrow, shut-in basin: unexpected and desolate, although much of the lake has been drained and the land is now cultivated..

On the way back from Paralimni one can turn off to the village of Ipato. From here a rough dirt road climbs the steep side of Mount Ipatos in a series of terrifying hairpin bends. On the higher slopes the track winds through tall *Arbutus andrachne* trees, amongst whose leathery, grey-green leaves grow clusters of creamy-white flowers and whose wood was used in antiquity for making looms. The summit, a wind-blown plateau, carpeted in spring with grape hyacinth and yellow iris, is crowned by the buildings of the **Monastery of Sagmata**, now housing only half a dozen monks. Ruined chapels below the summit suggest the monastery's one-time importance; the inhabitants of the plain, fleeing from the endless succession of invading armies, probably flocked to these chapels.

The Church of the Transfiguration, built on the site of the hermitage of a holy man, is a twelfth-century foundation of the 'golden age' of Byzantine architecture, now in some need of restoration. Rising from an irregular courtyard bordered by cells (largely of the post-Byzantine period) and monastic outhouses, the church has an exo-narthex and a narthex added in the fifteenth or sixteenth century. The plan is cruciform and tri-apsidal, with a dome (which collapsed in 1914 and was replaced by an unimpressive wooden one) supported by four slender columns of blue-veined white marble. The original marble screen of the sanctuary has been replaced by a marble *iconostasis*, but some of the original sculptural embellishment is incorporated in the wall above the south door of the narthex. The **mosaic floor** (it covers 100 square metres) in the *naos* is a fine example of the floor mosaicist's art of the twelfth century, lavishly decorated with eight circular designs within a circle and a geometric border.

Rejoining the highway and proceeding to the north-west you see, on the right, just before the village of Kastro, the long, low hill called the **Isle of Gla**, one of the strangest prehistoric sites in Greece. To reach the site take the road to the right at the major interchange, then the first untarred road to the right going in the direction of the hill. The 'isle' - it obviously was one once, washed by the shallow waters of Lake Kopais - is a natural curiosity: a low, triangular eminence with a ramp on the north side, flanked by two defensive buttresses and Cyclopean walls, two miles in circumference, which follow the contours of the cliff. Dominating the north-east basin below Mount Ptoön, it may have been a principality of the Minyans (a pre-Hellenic people who descended from Thessaly to Boeotia), forming part of a system of fortification guarding the shores of the lake. The cliffs, never higher than two hundred feet, are pitted with caves and *katavothres.* The ramp leads to a gate, on the inner side of which there was a small courtyard. Below the north-east redoubt is another double gate. Moving north-west you reach the central redoubt; to the north of this, on the highest point of the eminence, are the foundations of a palace with two L-shaped wings, built of sun-dried bricks (the base is of stone). The whole site is usually very overgrown and difficult to get around: a rough road goes right round the hill and the easiest entrance is near the north-west corner. All round, the countryside is dotted with rocky humps, like huge grey animals squatting in the cornfields of the drained marshland. It is a lonely setting, with hardly a house, a tree or even a browsing goat. Only the bees, the sage and the fennel.

East of Gla lies the ugly mining village of Ayios Ioannis. At the base of the hillside, immediately below a chapel of the same name, there is an enormous arc-shaped cave with a double entrance, which marks the site of the Great Katavothra where the Mavropotamos (the Black River), one of the main Boeotian streams, drains underground and, after flowing through the limestone barrier, pours into the Evvian Gulf.

The road continues across bleak mountain country; as it descends towards the coast, past the restored Byzantine Church of *Ayios Nikolaos*, wisps of foul-smelling smoke drift up from a straggling miners' village at the head of a deep, narrow inlet ringed round with nickel-mining installations. Site of ancient **Larymna**, whose name has been inherited by the modern village, it is believed to have been the chief port of the Minyans. In Hellenistic times Larymna, main trading centre of Boeotia and a harbour of some strategic value, was defended on the landward side by a semi-circular enceinte of strong walls strengthened with towers, substantial remains of which are identifiable; the masonry is both rectangular and polygonal, the hewn stones being of a white and sometimes an unusual tawny colour. In the choking, polluted atmosphere one may search along the shore for fragments of fourth-century BC port installations, some of which are still visible, though submerged, and gaze through watering eyes at the grandiose scree-rent cliffs of Evvia rising sheer across the water. You can return to Kastro via Martinon and the National Road.

To the west of Kastro, the Kopais road runs beside canals to the town of Orhomenos. The stream of the Mavropotamos, issues from a *katavothra* on the lower north side of Mount Akondion (the Javelin), part of a barren and forbidding chain of hills which guard the approaches to this region of fens, through which streams course sluggishly between banks of waving canes. The road goes into the town and the main street to the right leads to what is left of one of the oldest prehistoric sites in Greece, **Orchomenos**, capital of the Minyans. In the Mycenaean period it was the centre of a rich and powerful state but, like Mycenae itself, it was little more than a memory in classical times.

At the end of the main street, immediately behind the Theatre, is the most impressive surviving edifice of Minyan culture, the **Treasury of Minyas**, claimed by Pausanias to be the first treasury ever built, and 'a wonder second to none either in Greece or elsewhere'. It is actually a beehive tomb, excavated by Schliemann. It is approached by a *dromos* cut through the hillside, leading to a tapering doorway with a formidable lintel of blue schist. The diameter of the vaulted rotunda, now roofless, is almost fourteen metres. Holes for bronze rosettes are discernible on the walls, of which eight courses survive. The fact that the circular chamber is open to the sky enables the spectator to get a good impression of the concavity of the structure. On the other hand, there is a total absence of that atmosphere of centuries-old mustiness which contributes so greatly to the macabre quality of the Treasury of Atreus at Mycenae. A corridor connects the rotunda with a small square funerary chamber, with palmettes and rosettes carved in low relief on the ceiling, where the original Minyans were supposed to have been buried.

The **Theatre** is of the Hellenistic period, with well-preserved tiers and a ruined *proskenion*. Across the road, the site of the Temple of the Charities is occupied by the Byzantine **Church of the Koimesis** (Dormition of the Virgin), possibly the first church in Greece to have used the Greek-cross-in-square plan. An inscription dates it to 874. It is constructed from large stone blocks of unequal size; many, clearly of ancient origin, must have come from the Temple (such as the drums of columns built into the interior west wall). The general effect, though one of spaciousness and sturdiness, is heavy and awkward. The architect incorporated the Greek-cross plan in the central part of an essentially basilican plan but the narrow passage-like side aisles are separated from the nave by solid walls instead of columns or piers. The triple windows at the west end, each with two colonnettes, are also a basilican feature. More attractive are the courses of carved reliefs - a form of church decoration soon to disappear from Byzantine art - separating the three zones of the interior. In the pleasant park around the church are the remains of the original monastery: truncated pillars, fragments of the cornice and the closure panel of the original marble screen. Near the road the foundations of the Minyan palace have been excavated.

From here a bad road goes up between village houses to just below the citadel, passing traces of buildings of the Neolithic, third millennium BC and pre-Archaic periods. The upper terraces were reconstructed by Philip and Alexander. A steep and stony path leads up to the citadel. On the final jagged outgrowth of rock are the remains of a square tower. The ramparts, best preserved on the south side, are of the fourth century BC. Although by this time the greatness and wealth of Orchomenos were no more than a memory, Mount Akondion still possessed strategic value, dominating the bottleneck between the plains. The site is now surrounded by maize and cotton fields, criss-crossed by canals.

The end of Orchomenos came in 364 BC, as a result of the endemic feud with Thebes. Three hundred Orchomenian horsemen, aided by Theban traitors, prepared an attack on Thebes. The plot was betrayed and Orchomenos was totally destroyed, its male population slaughtered and the women and children sold into slavery. This particularly barbarous attack aroused the revulsion of neighbouring states and confirmed the reputation for cruelty earned by the Thebans.

Across the plain from Orhomenos is **Livadia**, chief town of Boeotia, spreading fanwise across the foothills of Elikon on either side of a narrow gorge. In the exceedingly unattractive, but animated, central area of shoddy apartment blocks, there is a clock tower, presented by Lord Elgin. The rocky eminence above the town is crowned by a medieval castle, and streams cascade down the hill. Higher up rises a screen of pine-covered heights. Westward towers Parnassos, misty blue in colour, its summit snow-capped from November to May, and often wreathed in cloud. In the symmetry and harmony of its forms and in its dramatic upward surge from the plain, no other Greek mountain, except Taiyetos in the Peloponnese, is more impressive.

At the foot of the castle hill, the Erkina issues from a sunless canyon. Plane trees form arbours over the ice-cold stream, which is spanned by a little arched Turkish bridge. The springs on the east bank flow into two pools: *Lethe* (Oblivion) and *Mnemosyne* (Remembrance). On the west bank, niches for votive offerings have been carved out of the cliff-side, for this was the site of the Oracle of Trophonios. The largest of these niches forms a kind of stone chamber with rock-hewn seats, the favourite refuge of Turkish governors who came here to smoke their *narghiles* and doze through long, soporific summer afternoons. Everywhere there is water: oozing, trickling, gurgling. Below the rocky precipices, among the shady planes, there are open-air cafés and tavernas, and a modern swimming pool where divers plunge into water drained from the pool of Lethe.

Near to the pools was the oracular chamber, in an underground chasm below a sacred grove. Above was the temple, with a statue of Trophonios, a Minyan semi-deity, by Praxiteles. Leake, most reliable of nineteenth-century topographers, suggests that the grove was on the eastern bank of the Erkina gorge, but not as far as the upland plateau associated with the hunting-grounds of Persephone, to which the gorge ultimately leads.

The protocol of consultation is fascinating. For several days a man who came to consult the oracle was not allowed to have a hot bath. After being rubbed with oil by thirteen-year-old boys, he would be handed over to priests who made him drink from the waters of Lethe so as to forget everything he had ever known. Afterwards he would drink from Mnemosyne in order to remember what he heard in the oracular pit. Dressed in a linen tunic girdled with ribbons, he was conducted to the fissure which was in the shape of a bread-oven. The method of entry and egress is described by Pausanias, who had consulted the oracle when he visited Greece in the second century BC. 'The descender lies with his back on the ground, holding barley-cakes kneaded with honey, thrusts his feet into the hole and himself follows, trying hard to get his knees into the hole. After his knees the rest of his body is at once swiftly drawn in... The return upwards is by the same mouth, the feet darting out first.' After this priests took charge again, placed him in the chair of Memory, which stood near the shrine, and questioned him as to what he had seen and heard. 'Paralysed with terror and unconscious both to himself and his relatives,' he was then handed over to his friends. Pausanias adds that he soon regained his faculties, as well as 'the power to laugh'.

The **Castle**, the earliest Catalan monument in Greece, is a short, steep walk up the hill from the Springs. The ruined towers, walls and archways of the keep are reminders of a strange period of Spanish rule in Greece. In the winter of 1311 a band of Catalan soldiers of fortune, originally hired by the Frankish Duke of Athens to fight the Greeks and who were owed extensive arrears of pay by him, descended into Boeotia, accompanied by an immense train of women, children and baggage, resolved to settle accounts with their debtors by force of arms.

The Catalans, though outnumbered, had laid their plans with cunning and foresight. Flooding the fields between Orchomenos and Livadia by digging canals into which the waters of the Kifissos flowed, they were thus protected by a quagmire covered with a carpet of scum that looked like grass. The Duke of Athens, waving his banner of a golden lion on an azure field sown with stars, personally led the attack, followed by his golden-spurred knights in coats of mail. Plunging their horses into the morass, they were unable to move forward or back, and men and beasts became sitting targets for the bolts and arrows of the Spaniards who bore down on them yelling 'Aragon!' The massacre of the French was appalling. The battle was decisive. Frankish power in central Greece was broken in a few hours. Henceforth Attica and Boeotia became the domain of Spanish (and later Florentine) overlords.

6

The Parnassos Country

MOUNT PARNASSOS dominates not only the country of the Boeotians, but also that of the Phocians and Lokrians: an amorphous geological complex of spurs and foothills, narrow plains, sombre defiles and cup-shaped valleys. In the centre of it all is Delphi, which can be approached from several directions. I propose to describe two of these approaches starting from Livadia: (i) The much longer route, up the Lamia road in a north-westerly arc running through Amfiklia and the Gravia Pass to Amfissa and Galaxidi on the Gulf of Corinth, then back to Itea and up to Delphi (one longish day). (ii) The direct route with a southward detour to Andikyra and the Monastery of Ossios Loukas (easily accomplished in one day).

Travellers to Delphi from Athens who do not wish to stop at Livadia, usually visit Ossios Loukas, one of the most important Byzantine monuments in the country, on the way. This journey can comfortably be completed in a day, allowing for this visit and also for leisurely stops and minor side-trips.

The first route passes to the west of the Kifissos battleground and one soon comes to **Chaironeia**, where Plutarch was born and died (AD 46-120) and wrote most of his works. Lying in the narrow plain between Mount Akondion and Mount Thourion, astride the main invasion route from the north, it was a position of great strategic importance. In ancient times it was a flowery place, the Grasse of the Hellenic world, famous for the manufacture of therapeutic unguents distilled from lilies, roses and narcissus.

Some of the antiquities in and around the modern village (Heronia) are visible from the main road: sections of city wall and, most notably, the marble Lion of Chaironeia, which stands in a cypress grove next to the road. Its artistic merit, if any, is overshadowed by its historical associations, for it is believed to surmount the collective grave of the Theban Sacred Band, wiped out in a murderous combat with the young Alexander's phalanx at the battle of Chaironeia in 338 BC. In the War of Independence, Odysseus Androutsos, most predatory of revolutionary leaders, hacked the Lion to pieces in the hope of finding it full of treasure. Subsequent excavation of the tumulus on which it lay revealed over two hundred skeletons - presumably of the Sacred Band. The Lion, put together again at the beginning of the present century, now rests on its haunches, open-mouthed, staring fatuously from its marble plinth, against the imposing background of Parnassos. In the adjacent museum are displayed prehistoric armour, weapons and terracottas from the tumulus of the Macedonians who fell in the battle.

Chaironeia was a decisive battle. By the summer of 338 BC Philip of Macedon was ready to force the gateway into Boeotia and subjugate all continental Greece. On a blazing August day, the Macedonian army, well trained, admirably equipped and expertly commanded, faced an army of disunited Greeks, held together only by the exhortations of Demosthenes.

After the engagement Philip is accused of indulging in unseemly mirth, of getting drunk on the field of battle and of jesting in the most ribald manner as he inspected the corpses of his foes piled up in the blood-soaked streams. However he is said to have wept at the sight of the Theban dead, privileged members of the Sacred Band. They had borne the brunt of Alexander's onslaught and fought with courage and self-sacrifice. They died to a man, all with chest wounds. In time the battle acquired a kind of romantic aura, its outcome being identified by succeeding generations as the end of the democratic Greek city state. Today road and rail run parallel across the stretch of level ground between the Kifissos and the battlefield.

In 87 BC another decisive battle, equally disastrous to Greek pride, was fought on the field of Chaironeia. The Hellenistic world of Alexander the Great's successors was crumbling before the irresistible tide of Roman conquest. An army of Mithridates, King of Pontos, around whom Hellenism had rallied, put up a last stand in the Chaironeian bottleneck. The forces of Mithridates were so totally annihilated that Sulla himself claimed Boeotia to be impassable for the piles of corpses.

The ancient **Theatre** of Chaironeia is to the left, above the village. The *cavea*, small and unadorned, is cut into the rock face at the base of a steep hill, with no supporting masonry at all, and the *skene* has gone. Behind it, fragments of the ruined towers and walls which enclosed the ancient city, ascend the hill.

West of Chaironeia the foothills of Parnassos alternately advance and recede into the plain, forming a fascinating sequence of different perspectives. The first turning to the left leads to the village of Ayios Vlassios and the acropolis of **Panopeos**, native city of Epeios, who built the Trojan Horse with the aid of Athena. On the hill high above the village (take the track to the left and a short, steep walk) are the remains of two well-preserved gateways and six towers of the fourth century BC.

Another spur is crowned by **Daulis** (the next turning to the south-west from the main road) which is worth visiting, if you have the time and the energy: it has a striking position on a large hill to the south of the village of Davlia. It is quite a climb up a cultivated slope, dotted with water mills, to the acropolis. There are the remains of a gateway over three metres wide between two towers - the one on the right is medieval. The square towers of the ramparts, covered in holly-oak, overhang a torrent-bed strewn with huge boulders. To the south-west a road leads across desolate, contorted hills to the Delphi road at the ancient junction known as the Cleft Way. The whitewashed Convent of Jerusalem, surrounded by cypresses, is off this road to the right, perched on a ledge of Parnassos just below the belt of firs. The course of history has flowed past in the plain below, the never-ending armies from the north hardly ever pausing to desecrate this elegiac, fennel-covered place. Only Philip of Macedon halted long enough to destroy the town, where the men, though few in number, were renowned for their height and strength. Daulis was rebuilt; we know, because Livy refers to the town's impregnable position on its 'lofty hills'.

At Kato Tithorea, 14 kilometres up the main road, another branch road to the left leads to **Tithorea** perched above the Kifissos valley. More spectacular than Daulis, Tithorea is protected to the south by sheer cliffs which terminate in a huge ledge on the flank of Parnassos. To the east the precipice plummets into a desolate ravine. The town's ancient fortifications were therefore strongest to the north and west, where the approaches were undefended by nature. Massive sections of formidable fourth- and third-century BC walls of regular ashlar masonry, with moss and ivy-covered towers, stand impressively among the village houses, forming an arc around the more exposed slopes.

Huddled at the base of the cliff, the modern village is picturesque but slightly sinister, its narrow streets interspersed with outcrops of ancient masonry. The eastern end overhangs the ravine through which flows the *Kakorevma* (The Evil Torrent). This ravine winds inland, into the heart of Parnassos. On the right, just beyond the last houses, is a cave where the Tithoreans took refuge during Xerxes' invasion.

Opposite the Tithorea turn-off, a road to the north-east crosses the Kifissos and leads to modern **Elatia**, and the site of ancient Elatia, once the most important place in Phocis after Delphi. Its capture by Philip in 339 BC, followed by the victory of Chaironeia, laid all central Greece at the mercy of the Macedonian king. The remains, just outside the village, are vestigial, but in the same area are the more impressive standing walls of the **Sanctuary of Athena Kranaia**. A good untarred road goes eastward for about eight kilometres from the Elatia site to the Sanctuary. It is advisable to contact the *fylakas* in Elatia village before making the journey.

The main Livadia-Lamia road continues to skirt the base of Parnassos. One glimpses the entrance to another great gorge and then the road by-passes the undistinguished small town of Amfiklia, the site of ancient **Amphikleia**, where orgies, which Pausanias found 'well worth seeing', were held in honour of Dionysos. A road goes uphill to the west of the town to the cemetery, where there are remains of Hellenic masonry which must have formed part of the retaining wall of the ancient acropolis. A medieval tower stands in the middle of the cemetery, commanding a view of corn and cotton fields, with formidable mountains closing in on all sides as the plain contracts into a narrow enclave.

Five kilometres after Amfiklia we finally leave the Lamia road and turn left for Eptalofos and Amfissa. Leaving the shady village of Polydrossos behind, the road runs below the precipitous slopes of Parnassos, slashed by more gorges. Three kilometres after Polydrossos and about a kilometre before **Lilea**, a large medieval tower appears on the bleak ridge of a steep hill. Nearby are the remains of ancient Lilaia which was razed to the ground by Philip of Macedon during the Third Sacred War. It now marks the beginning of a scenic detour up a mountain road to the beautiful village of **Eptalofos** - 'Seven Hills'. Amid streams and thickets of poplars and against a background of rugged cliffs remarkable for the perfection and symmetry of their form, the village is scattered across seven hills on different levels.

After passing over the ridge, one enters extensive fir forests, passes Greece's main ski centres and winds down to Arahova on the main Delphi road. In summer, driving or walking along one of the numerous tracks that wind through the cool, dark forests, one catches occasional glimpses of the scorching Phocian lowlands thousands of feet below.

Back at Lilea, one can make a another minor detour to a British military cemetery. Rows of well-tended graves contain the bones of British and Russian soldiers killed in the Macedonian campaigns of the First World War. The cemetery seems to be set in an immense crater, the shadeless level ground surrounded by the razor-sharp crests of the mountain rim. To the south a slender nodular peak guards the entrance to the **Gravia Pass**, which we now enter via the village of Gravia in order to continue the circuitous route to Delphi. The road from here, originally built by the Anglo-French army in 1917 to shorten their lines of communication with the Macedonian front, runs between the torrent-rent buttresses of Parnassos and Ghiona. Forests of ilex and fir sprcad across the higher slopes. Beyond the watershed there are glimpses of a vast sea of olive groves curling round the bases of rocky foothills and flat-topped mountain ledges. One passes through Eleonas: no village could be more idyllically-sited amid its jungle of olive trees, water cascading from one vine-covered terrace to another.

The descent ends at **Amfissa**. Built round a tapering crag planted with cypresses and littered with the ruins of a medieval castle, the town lies in the shadow of a crescent of jagged heights formed by Parnassos and Ghiona. By the nature of its commanding position at the head of the Crissaean plain, ancient Amphissa was the chief city of Ozolian Lokris.

The castle was built in the thirteenth century by the d'Autremencourts of Picardy on the site of a classical fortress, whose impregnability was mentioned by Livy and of which there remain vestiges of quadrangular and polygonal walls. Originally called Salona, it was later renamed La Sol by Catalan conquerors who made it their most important fief in the country. The castle had three enceintes, whose ruined ramparts are now fringed with tall umbrella pines. The climb is steep, the medieval ruins scanty. A fine monolithic lintel, probably of ancient origin, surmounts the entrance gate. A circular tower crowns the keep. There are also remnants of two churches - Byzantine and Frankish (or Catalan) and, at the foot of the hill to the south, a charming Turkish fountain.

The castle, which once guarded the southern exit of the Gravia Pass, formed one of the bulwarks of central Greece. In 1821, when the War of Independence broke out, Amfissa was the first citadel on the mainland to be liberated by the Greeks. Turkish troops and inhabitants, rounded up on the castle slope, were massacred to a man on the orders of the Greek chieftain Panourias. No more than a brigand turned patriot, this unsavoury man devoted his period of rule in Amfissa to the sole cause of personal gain, and the long-suffering Amfissans, having exchanged a 'foreign tyrant' for a 'national hero', were compelled to maintain his retinue of robbers. The case of Panourias is an object-lesson.

From the upper part of central Amfissa a track winds up an escarpment to a ledge on the mountainside overlooking the northern end of the plain. Here, where the olive groves contract between rocky foothills, stands the twelfth-century Byzantine **Church of Ayios Sotiras** (the building is usually locked - it is best to ask at the office of the Tourist Police). The church is a classic example of twelfth-century architecture. The exterior apse, in front of which a plane tree provides shade, is interesting in that the central window, divided by a colonnette, is placed within an arched frame, whereas the side windows are contained within square surrounds. The contrapuntal effect thus created is both harmonious and pleasing. Three parallel brick inlays decorate the window surrounds and there is considerable evidence of the tile decoration much favoured by twelfth-century architects who sought to ornament church exteriors with geometric designs. In the interior, the two columns supporting the dome are crowned by elaborately carved capitals. Some fine sculptured fragments from the original marble screen are ranged along the north wall of the *naos*.

South of Amfissa the road crosses the **Sacred Plain**, which is surrounded on all sides by lofty mountains. Peaks, ridges and slopes seem to have developed organically out of the primeval convulsion. The density of the olive trees is legendary, the gnarled trunks being among the most ancient in Greece.

This road leads to **Itea**, the port of Delphi, which lies at the head of a muddy gulf where cruise ships anchor. The place has an unfinished air, and its featureless modern buildings, so close to the sacred landscape, strike one as a profanity. However there are adequate hotels at Itea which are useful when there is no accommodation at Delphi.

The spectacular coastal road to Nafpaktos starts disappointingly along the barren shore of the gulf, the first stretch rendered hideous by extensive mining installations. Further on there are numerous fish and sea-food 'farms', the country improves and the road comes to the **Galaxidi** turn-off. This attractive little port is built on a headland flanked on one side by a bay and on the other by a pine-fringed creek, both of which provide excellent anchorages for yachts. There is a fine view across the inland sea towards Delphi and the escarpments of Parnassos. The houses, originally lived in by caique-builders, are picturesque but without architectural distinction or historical associations. Skeletons of broad-beamed caiques litter the waterfront. The bathing is not good, for the rocks are spiky, the sea soupy, and at the height of summer there are swarms of flies.

Galaxidi, however, has a thirteenth-century Byzantine church. Above the town the road ascends into the olive belt, circling a bluff overlooking the Gulf of Corinth, beyond which rise the Peloponnesian ranges, slashed by great gorges. A few kilometres west of the town, well off the main road and nestling in a cypress grove surrounded by olive trees, is the small, restored **Church of the Sotiros** (Redeemer). The church is usually locked but the keys can be obtained by asking at the police station. Towards the east end of the single-chamber church a transverse barrel vault gives the impression that it has transepts. The wall paintings are too poorly preserved to merit attention. Reliefs in the exterior apse, probably from the screen of an earlier church, are decorated with stylized pine cones and cypress branches in the angles of the crosses.

It is pleasant to take a boat from Galaxidi to Itea - a short but memorable journey. The oily waters of the gulf, dotted with barren islets like petrified porpoises, are ruffled only by the caique's wash. A silver haze hangs over the Sacred Plain, within an amphitheatre of tremendous mountains.

To reach Delphi one must go back a short way from Itea along the Amfissa road and then turn right. However it is also possible to use minor roads to reach Ossios Loukas. From Itea the road climbs to the east up one of the final seaward bulwarks of Parnassos. Providing an admirable view of the complexities of coastline, plain and mountain, it leads to a concave upland plateau on which lies the large village of Desfina. Thereafter one road descends through shadeless valleys to the deep, hidden bay of Andikyra and thence to Ossios Loukas, while another goes there more directly via Distomon.

The second suggested route for Delphi takes in Ossios Loukas. From Livadia the road winds round a series of rolling, eroded hills forming the saddle between Elikon and Parnassos. I know of no other point from which Mount Parnassos is seen to greater advantage: a well-ordered mass of soaring limestone, its buttresses and escarpments, square, regular or curvilinear, rent by deep ravines running in parallel vertical courses. It is lonely country. There is only a Vlach hamlet, some sheep-folds and a *khani*, or resting place, shaded by great plane trees. Goats scrabble among prickly shrubs on the precipitous slopes - a landscape, one feels, especially designed to guard the approaches to Delphi. On every side mountains soar above the **Cleft Way**, the ancient junction of the three roads from Delphi, Daulis and Thebes which was the scene of Oedipus' murder of his father, Laios.

Soon there is a turn-off to the left leading to Distomon. Before reaching the village a road goes westward to Itea, bypassing Delphi. From Distomon, a centre of guerilla activity in the last war, a road to the south descends abruptly to the bay of **Andikyra**, on the Gulf of Corinth. The rocky, barren coastline is dotted with mining installations. A corniche runs eastward, and the shell of a little Byzantine church lies at the mouth of a stony valley. Fragmentary remains of the walls of ancient Antikyra are scattered across a bluff.

Another road from Distomon, going east, passes through Stiri (famous for the rich quality of its sheep's milk yoghurt) and runs along a ridge of windswept hills to the **Monastery of Ossios Loukas**. The church and its dependencies overlook a bowl-like valley, with cultivated strips laid out in chequer-board fashion, enclosed on all sides by the steep, slate-grey spurs of Elikon.

The original chapel, dedicated to St Barbara, was built by the disciples of a holy man from neighbouring Stiri. He was called Luke ('Ossios' being the Orthodox equivalent of 'blessed') and his fame soon spread beyond his native mountains. He died in the middle of the tenth century. The modest shrine became a place of pilgrimage, and a monastery was founded. It was the beginning of the Byzantine Golden Age and throughout the Empire there was a surge of creative activity. In Constantinople, Theofano, wife of three successive emperors, heard of the shrine and arranged for its enrichment: her son, the Emperor Basil II the Bulgar Slayer, is believed to have given impetus to the enterprise during his triumphant tour of Greece at the beginning of the eleventh century. Ossios Loukas remains a typical example of the Byzantine tradition of imperial patronage of remote monastic establishments.

The main church (eleventh-century), the plan of which was followed at Dafni, is a tall cross-in-square edifice, with lavish exterior brickwork decoration, surrounded by monastic cells and a refectory. The windows, which possess sculptural embellishments,

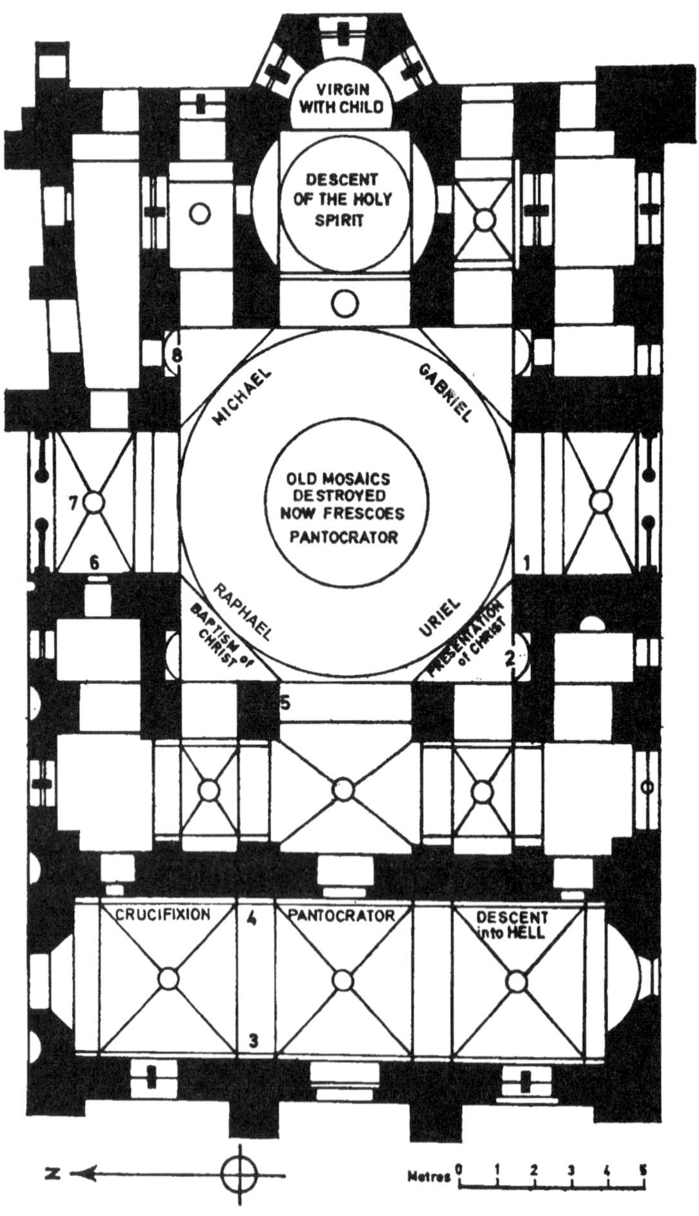

Ossios Loukas

are divided into three sections by columns of different coloured marbles. The interior is one of the finest examples extant of the Byzantine desire to create a harmonious unity of colour and form out of bricks and stone, carving, glass mosaic, marble panels, inlays and tiling. Bands of white carved marble divide the sumptuous multi-coloured revetments into two levels; the floor is of jasper and porphyry, the marble screen elaborately carved, and every inch of wall space in the narthex, the dome, the apses and the lateral arms glows with mosaics set against a golden background. There are also some less important frescoes of a later date.

The narthex comes first. The subtle and basic unity which underlies the arrangement of the figures of the apostles on the arches is achieved through their attitudes: they all ultimately point to the Pantocrator, whose image once filled the space above the door leading into the *naos*. Two of the most striking portraits are those of **St Peter** (east wall) and **St Andrew** (west wall), both with lively expressions and disproportionately large heads. Among the scenes from the life of Christ, the most impressive are the **Crucifixion** (left) and the **Descent into Hell** (right) in shallow lunettes. The bulky figure on the Cross, with its heavy tubular legs, is, in spite of its monolithic, columnar quality, contorted with physical pain.

In the main body of the church and in the side chapels, the iconographic arrangement adheres strictly to the established programme. In the first zone (vaults and chapels), saints intermingle with ascetics, prophets, bishops and provincial holy men in a gallery of portraits which, at first, tend to overshadow the narrative scenes on the upper register. There are few concessions to grace, none to sentimentality. Among the portraits, those of St Dimitrios (south transept), St Basil (lunette in north-east transept), St Merkurios, the soldier-saint, with sheathed sword (north-west arch, left on entering) and a lively St Nicholas (lunette in south-west corner) are worth noting. In the north transept there is a bust of the **Blessed Luke** himself, severe and monkish, his hands raised in worship. In numerous arches and vaults, the Archangels and military saints act as guards of honour. The busts within medallions, unlike those of the apostles in the narthex, are portrayed frontally.

High above the world of holy men extends the sphere of divine beings, at the summit of which, Christ Pantocrator (in this instance, missing) dominates the Universe. In the apse, the Virgin and Child are represented seated on a cushioned throne decorated with elaborate inlay, against a concave golden background which creates an effect of immense spaciousness. In the dome of the sanctuary, the twelve apostles are seated round the symbol of the Trinity. Below the central cupola are the spandrels in which scenes from the *Dodekaorton* are depicted: a beautiful **Nativity**, in which the figure of Joseph, with enormous black eyes, and the animals leaning over the crib, lend an extraordinarily homely quality to the scene; and a **Baptism**, in which Christ stands shoulder-high in the waters of the Jordan as two angels advance towards him bearing elaborately-decorated towels.

As there was little differentiation in colour tones, the austere, eleventh-century mosaicist at Ossios Loukas tended to over-emphasize the modelling of his figures. The mosaics at Dafni are certainly more evolved and sophisticated in technique and execution, but Ossios Loukas, in its completeness, in the power and intensity of the figures crowding its walls, in its elaborate decorative detail and majestic proportions, remains a more imposing and convincing example of the eleventh-century Byzantine church.

Below the church is the crypt of St Barbara, containing the tomb of the Blessed Luke, painted with crude frescoes of the local school of Cappadocia. Adjoining the main church is the Chapel of the Virgin, chronologically slightly earlier than the main church, and entered through a tenth-century exo-narthex with a triple portico crowned by a loggia. The dome above the cross-in-square *naos* is supported by four granite columns. The lavish Opus Alexandrinum pavement has a curious slant.

The almond orchards and patchwork fields in the cup-shaped valley are owned by the once-flourishing community of monks, now reduced to a handful of aging men living in cells in a far corner of the monastery. The restored refectory is now a museum and there is also a tourist shop on the tree-shaded, rectangular terrace. The foothills of Elikon beyond form a dark screen round the empty valley and in spring the air is heavy with the scents of broom, honeysuckle and lemon blossom.

Illustrations: *Acropolis; Athens*
Caryatid Portico, Erechtheion; Athens
Thespidos Street, Plaka; Athens
Temple of Poseidon; Cape Sounion
Christ Pantocrator, Kessariani Monastery; Attica
Tholos, Sanctuary of Athena; Delphi
Rousanou Monastery; Meteora

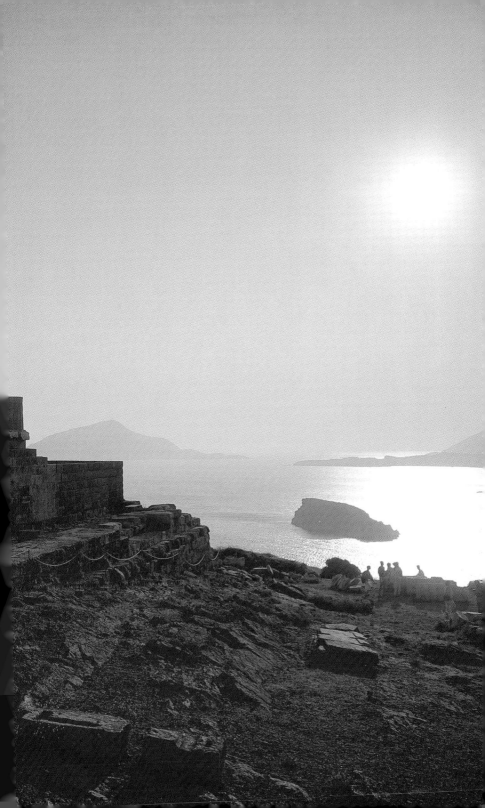

Ὁ ΠΑΝΤΟ
ΚΡΑΤΩΡ

7

Delphi

ISOLATED BY a ring of mountains, Delphi has always been subject to violent climatic and geological pressures. Earthquakes and landslides are common. Clouds dissolve and re-form, casting their shadows across the olive groves. Torrential showers blot out the landscape and thunder echoes in the hollows of the valley. In summer the heat is trapped within the refractory limestone and the cliffs, pitted with primeval fissures, reflect a peculiar radiance which seems to derive its glow from the interior of the rock.

Two ways of approaching the sanctuary have been described in Chapter Six, but the direct route from Athens through Livadia is the one most travellers take. After the turn-off to Distomon the road climbs between jagged peaks. Fir trees spread across the higher slopes. Every outline acquires a razor-edge sharpness, the atmosphere a refined quality, the blue of the sky a new intensity and one senses one is approaching a place of immense significance in the affairs of men. At the top of the pass the curtain is raised with a tremendous flourish. The gorge lies below, the mountains crowding round to complete the famous umbilical effect. In the distance a buttress of cliffs, concealing the sanctuary, juts out to meet another wall of rock; beyond it is a tantalizing glimpse of the olive groves of the Sacred Plain.

In the immediate foreground a double-peaked bastion of Mount Parnassos, nearly a thousand metres high, is covered with the grey stone houses of **Arahova.** The clocktower, donated by Lord Elgin, is perched on the summit of a crag overhanging cultivated strips which descend in terraces to the bottom of the gorge.

The modern hotels, in sharp contrast to the rustic atmosphere of this mountain eyrie, command a fine prospect of the gorge. Tourist shops display local handicrafts: woollen bags, carpets, blankets. The colours are crude and gaudy, but some of the bedspreads and tablecloths embroidered with old regional designs, and fleecy rugs called *flokates*, are attractive. The red wine of Arahova is good, if rather heady. The local cheese, made from goat's milk, its wax rind moulded in the design of a wickerwork basket, is more of a curiosity than a delicacy. Arahova is the starting-point for the ascent of Parnassos (a local guide being indispensable), for the visit to the Corycian Cave by car and for the drive across Parnassos to Gravia, via the ski centres and Eptalofos.

Beyond Arahova the road descends, through terraces planted with almond trees, into the vine belt. The duct bringing water from the Mornos river to Athens makes an ugly concrete gash in the valley below. In the narrow gorge, the ruins of an ancient necropolis herald the approach to Delphi. The road loops round a huge projecting bluff and enters the inner amphitheatre of rock. Hawks and vultures hover over the wall of cliff which rises sheer from the highest ledge of the sanctuary. In the valley below, olive trees of immense antiquity mantle the precipitous banks of the Pleistos. The ruins of the sanctuary - broken columns, polygonal walls, grey stone tiers, red-brick Roman rubble - are spread out across the steep hillside though, sadly, the most prominent architectural feature is the modern building housing the museum, with its plate-glass windows and its shrubs and flowerbeds.

Hotels and tourist shops line the few streets of the village of **Delphi**, which clings to another great projection of rock. The original hamlet, built over the sanctuary, was removed stone by stone to its present position when the excavations began at the end of the last century. Most of the hotels have magnificent views. One lunches and dines on terraces, shaded with awnings, overlooking the gorge. Well-known Athens shops have branches here and there are also, of course, tourist shops, which are better and more expensive than at Arahova.

The antiquities are confined to two areas: the Sanctuary of Apollo above the main road, and the Marmaria in an olive grove below the Castalian Spring. These (and the museum) can be rushed through in one day, but an overnight stay is strongly recommended when, at least for some hours, the place will not be overrun by day-trippers.

It is only five minutes' walk to the **Sanctuary of Apollo**. The earliest references to it are purely mythical. They tell of roving shepherds pouring forth garbled prophecies in the name of Apollo when seized by uncontrollable frenzy due to the potent vapours issuing from a fissure in the rock. In time a temple to the god was raised above the fissure. Symbol of youth, light and beauty, Apollo was the most consistently Greek of the Olympian deities. Although

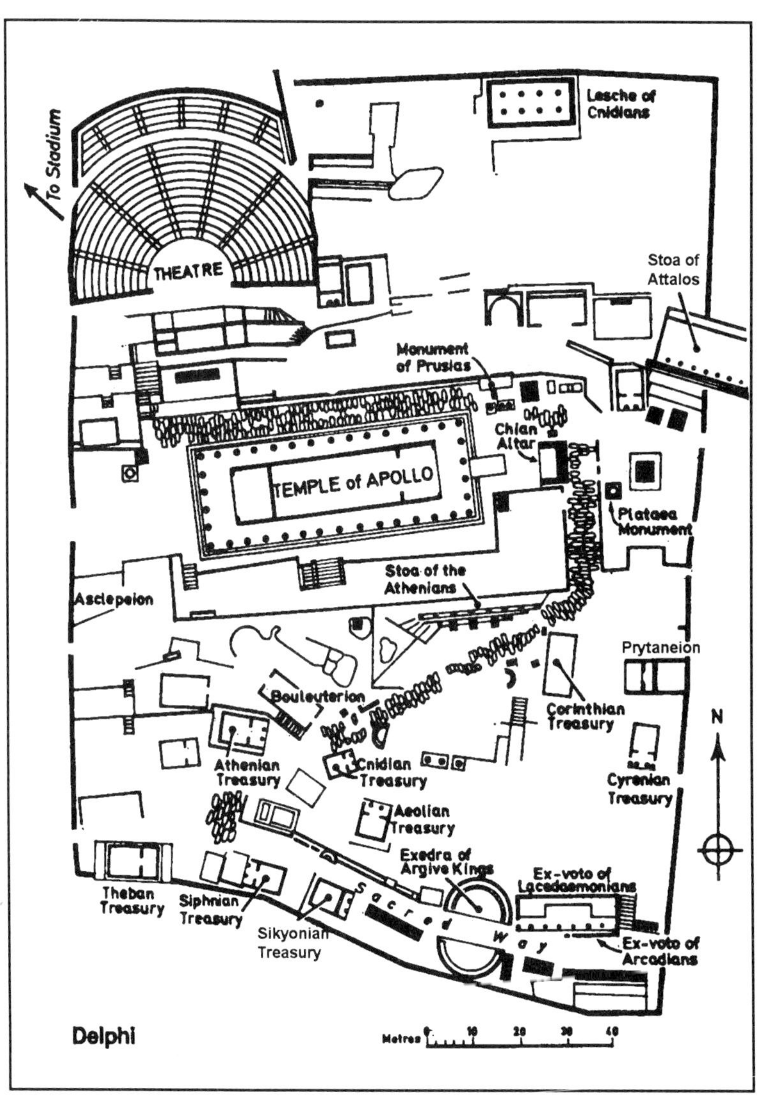
To Stadium
THEATRE
Lesche of Cnidians
Stoa of Attalos
Monument of Prusias
Chian Altar
TEMPLE of APOLLO
Plataea Monument
Stoa of the Athenians
Asclepeion
Prytaneion
Bouleuterion
Corinthian Treasury
Athenian Treasury
Cnidian Treasury
Cyrenian Treasury
Aeolian Treasury
N
Exedra of Argive Kings
Ex-voto of Lacedaemonians
Theban Treasury
Siphnian Treasury
Sikyonian Treasury
Sacred Way
Ex-voto of Arcadians
Delphi
Metres 0 10 20 30 40

vain, narcissistic and a philanderer, he had many attractive qualities: a love of music and poetry, an interest in medicine and astronomy; and traditionally he was the guardian of flocks and herds.

The Apollonian cult developed rapidly and a priestess - the Pythia - was installed in the temple, where she chanted the ambiguous riddles that exercised such a powerful influence over men's actions for ten centuries. As a panhellenic sanctuary, Delphi possessed a far more profound religious influence than Olympia, and four Sacred Wars were fought for its preservation. From the beginning, the sanctuary's purpose was purely oracular, existing solely for communicating the counsels of the gods to mortals. Strabo believes 'the position of the place added something. For it is almost in the centre of Greece ... and people called it the navel of the earth.'

The oracle was administered by five elected priests who claimed descent from Deukalion. They had complete control of administration, were responsible for the Pythia's political brief and were represented in Athens and elsewhere by agents. The fame of the prophecies was established as early as the eighth century BC; by the sixth, votive gifts were pouring in from every part of the civilized world. Croesus alone presented the shrine with a gold statue of a lion, a gold mixing-bowl that weighed a quarter of a ton and a silver wine vessel that held five thousand gallons. As an instrument of policy, the oracle's influence was by no means negligible. In the Persian Wars it tended to be defeatist, in the Peloponnesian Wars it showed a pro-Spartan bias. It was consulted among others by Oedipus, Agamemnon, Kleomenes, Philip of Macedon and Alexander the Great. To the latter the priestess cried: 'My son, none can resist thee!'

The oracles were generally extremely equivocal. Can one blame Croesus, when told he would destroy a mighty empire if he crossed the Halus, for failing to realize that the empire in question was his own? Little is known of the relations between priests and politicians, but there can be little doubt that string-pulling went on behind the scenes. Most of the problems about which people sought the god's advice related to the cultivation of crops or the sale of slaves or to journeys, to loans or love affairs or intended marriages. They had to pay a fee and sacrifice a goat, a sheep or an ox.

At an early stage Delphi was admitted into the Amphictyonic League, one of whose main responsibilities then became the safeguarding of the sanctuary's interests and treasure. However the inhabitants of neighbouring Krissa grew increasingly envious and rapacious; they exacted heavy tolls from consultants approaching the oracle, and their assaults on female consultants scandalized the Delphians. The first Sacred War (c. 590 BC) broke out and Krissa was razed to the ground. In the second Sacred War Athens and Sparta fought over the ownership of the sanctuary. In the fourth century, the Phocians, out for loot, seized the sanctuary, thus provoking the third Sacred War. In the last Sacred War the aggressors were the Lokrians of nearby Amphissa, who wanted to cultivate the plain, until then undefiled by spade or ploughshare, which the League considered sacred to Apollo. In the end Philip of Macedon had to be called in to put an end to Lokrian profanity.

In the third century BC bands of Gauls descended on the sanctuary. The invaders had the elements ranged against them: not only frost and snow, but also earthquakes, followed by landslides. Scrambling down the precipices of Parnassos, the Greeks attacked them in the rear. Panic broke out and, in their frenzy, the Gauls slaughtered each other by the hundred. It was thus left to Sulla, two centuries later, to plunder the shrine with his usual appalling thoroughness. After him the insatiable Nero carried off five hundred bronze statues to Rome. The philhellenic Hadrian and the Antonines did what they could to restore Delphi to its former splendour, but it was too late. The god's utterances no longer carried conviction. Acceptance of bribes by priests was rife and consultants became sceptical. In the fourth century Constantine the Great removed many works of art to Constantinople. The sanctuary was closed down by the Emperor Theodosios the Great in his famous edict of 393.

In time a hamlet grew up on the ancient deposits. In the seventeenth century Wheler observed traces of marble tiers on the terrace of the stadium and identified niches for statues beside the Castalian Spring. Between 1892 and 1903 the French School of Archaeology at Athens excavated both the Sanctuary of Apollo and the Marmaria.

The sanctuary is screened by a semi-circle of cliffs, the rose-coloured Phaedriades, mottled with tufts of evergreens. Stunted pedestals and foundations of treasuries spread across a hillside covered with vetch, mullein and cistus. The bronze and marble statues have long since vanished: looted by the Roman and Byzantine emperors or hacked to pieces by Goths and Visigoths. To the east the Castalian stream issues out of a rocky cleft and flows into the hollow valley, enclosed within the ring of mountains that no human hand could have fashioned with a more perfect sense of symmetry. Across the gorge, zigzag mule tracks climb the arid wall of Mount Kirfis like crude graffiti scratched by the hand of a giant. Hundreds of feet below, the Pleistos trickles sinuously between olive groves towards the Sacred Plain.

The **Sacred Way**, a steep, narrow ramp in the form of a double hairpin, begins at the lowest (east) end of the enclosure, beside the brickwork remains of a small, square Roman agora, identified by two unfluted Ionic columns. The paved ramp climbs between the foundations of buildings which once jostled against each other on the steep incline. It is all very congested and confusing and the fact that the sanctuary was built on a succession of narrow ledges further complicates the layout. In summer the sun is scorching and cicadas drone relentlessly among parched shrubs.

On the right lie the foundations of the rectangular **ex-voto of the Lacedaimonians**, with traces of a parapet, once adorned with statues of Spartan admirals. On the west side an imposing exedra, embellished with statues of Argive kings (the bases have been restored), was raised to commemorate the foundation of independent Messene. Next come the treasuries which contained the archives and national treasures of the various states. On the left are the foundations of the **Treasury of Sikyon**, followed by the sub-structure of the **Treasury of Siphnos**. The visible remains are negligible, but there is a partial restoration in the museum. Other treasuries are scattered about the hillside. To the unprofessional eye they are no more than a mass of rubble, wholly incomprehensible.

At the apex of the first loop, the restored **Treasury of the Athenians** stands on a prominent ledge, one of the landmarks of the sanctuary. Only ten by six metres, it was the first Doric edifice to be built entirely of marble. The walls grow thinner towards the top, conveying the illusion of height, and any suggestion of squatness caused by the low roof was probably relieved by an acroterion of an Amazon on horseback surmounting the gable. But it is not one of the masterpieces of classical architecture.

The Sacred Way now slants obliquely up the hill between foundations of votive edifices. On the left are the remains of the **Bouleuterion**, or Senate House, where the Committee of Five transacted business and formulated policy. Beyond it is the rock, reinforced by modern masonry, from which the Sybil Herophile, who alternately called herself wife, daughter and sister of Apollo, chanted the first oracles. A natural fissure in the ground nearby is said to have been the entrance to the lair where the serpent Python dwelt. Three steps lead up to the **Stoa of the Athenians**, in which the spoils captured from the Spartans in the Peloponnesian Wars were displayed. Three of the original eight miniature Ionic columns which once supported a wooden roof are now ranged against the massive stones of a great polygonal wall. The interlocking and irregular stones have a smooth, honey-coloured surface and were designed to reinforce the god's temple in the event of earthquakes. Opposite is the *halos*, or threshing floor, the open space upon which Apollo's victory over Python was celebrated every seven years.

At the apex of the second loop a sharp ascending turn to the left leads to the round pedestal for the votive offering, set up by all the states who fought at Plataia in 479 BC. Facing it is the **Altar of the Chians**, also commemorating the Greek victory over the Persians, composed of rectangular slabs of grey-blue marble; a conspicuous but uninspiring monument, twice restored during the present century at the expense of wealthy shipowners of Hios. Beyond it is a rectangular plinth with a garlanded frieze, once crowned by an equestrian statue of Proussias II, a vicious Bithynian king of the second century BC, much given to vulgar ostentation.

Sheer cliffs rise above the high-lying terrace. A modern ramp climbs to the eastern entrance of the stylobate of the **Temple of Apollo**, which commands a prospect not only of the whole precinct but also of the stupendous circular panorama. The perspective is enhanced by the restoration of three massive Doric limestone columns which reflect the changing light - grey, brown or gold according to the time of day - their huge weathered drums conveying an impression of the scale of the building, which was almost as large as the Parthenon.

Of the historical origins little is known, except that the Archaic temple was gutted by fire. In the late sixth century BC it was replaced by a splendid edifice raised by the Alkmaionids: a massive peripteral temple of the Doric order on a three-tiered stylobate of bluish marble, its front adorned with marble columns, several drums of which still survive. A panhellenic subscription was raised to obtain the necessary funds. This building was largely destroyed by an earthquake and the existing foundations and stylobate belong to the fourth-century re-construction. It was the sixth-century temple built under Amphictyonic protection that acquired the greatest fame.

Among the most famous of the sculptures in the temple was the golden effigy of Apollo, which was set behind an altar of eternal fire kept alive by piles of fir-wood. Little now remains of the sculptures

- only some truncated limbs from the pediment, now in the museum. The seat of the oracle was in the *adyton*, a chamber penetrated only by priests. The fissure from which the vapours emanated has not been identified. The priestess was always a young virgin, until, on one occasion, she was raped by an impious lecher. After that, only older and less attractive women were employed. She sat on a golden tripod above the narrow fissure, munching laurel leaves, and in a state of frenzied exaltation would recite the equivocal conundrums which, with the aid of qualified advisers, the bewildered consultants had to interpret. Sometimes the effect of the vapours on the priestess was so great that she would leap dementedly from her tripod, suffer from convulsions and die within a few days.

Above the temple a Roman stairway mounts to the **Theatre**, originally fourth-century BC and of white marble, but restored in grey limestone by the Romans. The *cavea*, divided by a paved *diazôma*, has only thirty-three tiers, but they are well preserved; so is the *orchestra*, which is composed of irregular slabs and is surrounded by the usual water-conduit. There is no more perfect example of a Greek theatre in harmonious relation to its setting: the sweeping forms of the stone tiers repeated in the rocky semi-circle of the Phaedriades. In the late afternoon the glow of these cliffs is reflected on the slopes of the encircling mountains which turn pink, mauve and finally a deep cobalt blue. The valley fills with obscure shadows. For all its grandeur, it is an intensely serene landscape.

To the right of the theatre is the dried-up stream of the Kassiotis, which used to water the sacred groves of laurel and myrtle and flowed through a secret channel into the *adyton* of the temple, where the Pythia drank from its waters before prophesying. Beyond this stream a path leads to the site of the **Lesche of the Cnidians**. Its walls were of unfired brick, and the interior was in the form of a rectangular atrium. Four stone sockets (*socles*) for the columns which supported the wooden roof are all that remain of this famous rest-house where pilgrims sought shade and shelter.

From the theatre, another path climbs to the left between bushes of arbutus and blackberry to the **Stadium**, the highest point of the ancient city. The best-preserved of Greek stadia, it once seated seventeen thousand spectators. Built in the fifth century BC, it probably did not possess stone accommodation until the fourth, and most of the existing tiers are of the Antonine period. Of the Roman triumphal arch four pillars remain. On the north bank, against the cliff, there are twelve well-preserved tiers divided into as many sections by stairways; on the west and south, where there is a sharp declivity buttressed by a polygonal wall supporting the mountain shelf, only six. A slight concavity in the centre was intended to prevent the spectator's view being obstructed by his neighbours.

Like the Olympic Games, the Pythian festival, also a panhellenic celebration, was held every four years. The athletic programme was the same as at Olympia, with the addition of a long race for boys and, last and most spectacular of all, a race in bronze armour. Victors were crowned with wreaths of laurel. There was no other reward except the adulation so dear to the Greek heart. The honour of a victory at the Pythian Games was second only to that of an Olympic award. Singing and music played on the flute and lyre formed an important part of the festivities.

From the stadium there is a short cut to the village. It is more rewarding, however, to zigzag down through the sanctuary, regain the main road and, walking east, reach the **Castalian Spring**. Even though coaches now park here, this remains an evocative spot. Large plane trees shade the stream, which issues from a ravine that cleaves the Phaedriades in two. Above the spring, whose water is ice-cold and extraordinarily clear, is the niche of an old shrine. Consultants and athletes purified themselves by washing their hair in Castalia's lustral water before proceeding to the temple and the stadium. A path leads a short way into the gloomy ravine between the Phaedriades, strewn with huge boulders and pitted with unsuspected crevices. Rocks occasionally crash down from above.

Beyond the café and below the road a path winds down past the ruins of the fourth-century BC **Gymnasium,** where there has recently been more excavation. This was the practice-ground for the athletes entered for the Pythian games, with a covered race-track running parallel to an open-air one. Among the weeds and thistles lies a stone slab with a groove and socket, believed to have been equipped with a *husplex*, a mechanical device that made a loud noise as it fell, thus giving the signal for the start.

Beyond the gymnasium the path continues down the hill, under shady olive branches, to the **Marmaria**, the Sanctuary of Athena Pronaia - less spectacular than Apollo's, but no less beautiful. Carpeted in spring with grape hyacinths and bee orchids, it extends across a rectangular shelf below the eastern projection of the Phaedriades. First comes the stylobate of an austere fourth-century BC **Temple of Athena**, guardian of the precinct. Foundations of other temples and buildings, slabs of bluish limestone and fragments of broken drums litter the terraced olive grove. The pride of the sanctuary is the **Tholos**, a circular fourth-century BC edifice on a three-stepped platform. A work of extreme elegance which was originally crowned by a conical roof, it had an outer ring of twenty Doric columns surrounding an inner ring of ten Corinthian columns. The gutter of the entablature had a rich ornamentation, including lion-head spouts, one of which is preserved above a restored *metope*. Three stout, yet graceful, Doric columns, surmounted by a lintel and fragments of *metopes*, rise from the stylobate. What purpose the temple served is not known. The setting, with the valley contracting to its narrowest point, is peaceful and bucolic. Chameleons slither along ruts and cracks in the masonry; bees swarm in the sweet-smelling bay trees. There is none of the overcrowding that creates such a jigsaw-puzzle effect in the Sanctuary of Apollo.

Beyond the Tholos are the substructures of two **treasuries**: the first, that of Massalia, is thought to have been an elegant little building in the Ionic style, contemporary with the treasury of Siphnos. Next comes the debris of the early fifth century BC **Temple of Athena Pronaia**, built of tufa on the site of a much earlier edifice. Three thick Doric columns still survive at the north-west corner and two enormous boulders, lying across the stylobate, provide evidence of repeated landslides. Beyond the Marmaria lies the necropolis of the ancient city.

Several paths descend through terraces of olive groves to the bed of the Pleistos. Vestiges of the polygonal masonry of supporting walls are visible. In autumn donkeys carrying huge panniers filled with olives clamber up the stony tracks. There are few dwellings: only an occasional chapel, ruined or abandoned. At the bottom of the gorge the feeling of isolation is complete. The stream of the Pappadia trickles down from the Castalian Spring, and there is a grotto, surrounded by contorted boulders, said to be the ancient **Sybaris**, where the Lamia, a sphinx-like monster which ravaged the countryside, dwelt in a subterranean lair. The walk takes about two hours.

A longer walk or ride (about six hours there and back) is to a more famous grotto, the **Corycian Cave**. The path climbs the southern wall of the Phaedriades behind the modern village to a highland plateau of stones and stunted pines, dominated by the summit of Parnassos, where it meets a rough road. The cave is at the north-west end of the plateau above the fir belt (a guide is not essential but it is a good idea to get more detailed information in the village). I confess I cannot share the enthusiasm of Pausanias, who found it, of all the caves he had seen, the finest. Euripides extols its 'mountain-chambers', of which there are said to be forty, their damp walls shining with pink and green reflections. The light of a torch reveals stalactites and stalagmites. The cave was named after the nymph Corycia, beloved of Apollo, and was sacred to the nymphs and to Pan. The start of the final ascent to the cave (twenty minutes' hard climbing) can also be reached by car along a rough road from Kalyvia, on the road from Arahova to Eptalofos.

The **Museum** at Delphi is situated halfway between the Sanctuary of Apollo and the village, its recently renovated marble façade now fitting more easily into this most classical of landscapes. Before entering, it is worth looking at two fourth-century AD **floor mosaics** at the right of the entrance. The decoration is chiefly composed of birds, though the larger one has a wider zoological range and the mosaicist has reproduced a number of stylized animals.

The interior of the Museum is spacious and well lit. For those not in a hurry it is worth obtaining the guidebook before starting. At the top of the staircase stands an ovoid stone object: a copy of the original sacred stone, the *omphalos* or so-called navel of the earth, which was placed in the *adyton* of the Temple of Apollo, its interlocking marble fillets symbolizing the continuity of life. From here on the arrangement is more or less chronological.

Room 3 is full of interest. The **Naxian Sphinx**, a heraldic work of the sixth century BC, towers above the other exhibits on a marble plinth crowned by an Ionic capital. Seated on her hindquarters with her scythe-shaped wings and a bosom ornamented with feathers, she gazes imperiously into space.

Fascinating fragments of the **frieze of the Treasury of Siphnos** are ranged along the walls. Dated to the sixth century BC, the figures are without the least trace of crudity. The sculptures, though battered, quickly come to life. In the battle of the gods against the giants (north side) a tornado of agitation galvanizes the figures into action: Apollo and an exultant Artemis aim their arrows; a stocky-limbed Ares, smirking with self-confidence, takes on a couple of giants over the prostrate body of a third. The east side depicts seated gods debating the issue of the Trojan War. The detail of the frieze is fascinating. Both the pliability of the stylized drapery and the difference in texture between the naked flesh and the long ringlets of the head-dresses point to the chisel of a master sculptor. Particularly beautiful are the manes and tails of the horses in the south frieze. The reliefs originally ran around the entire building, framed between decorative fillets. In its entirety, with the crowd of agitated figures and prancing horses, the frieze must have been a masterpiece.

Room 4 is dominated by two crude and impressive early sixth-century BC figures of **Kleobis and Biton**, the Argive boys who, in the absence of oxen, harnessed themselves to a chariot and bore their mother across the plain to the Temple of Hera, where she was chief priestess. For their pains, the goddess rewarded the youths with eternal sleep. Kleobis (right), who is better preserved than his brother, possesses all the 'inner mobility' associated with later, more polished Archaic *kouroi*. Tough, stocky, with short muscular arms, he is endowed with remarkable tension, ready to spring forward and harness himself to his mother's chariot.

Rooms 6 contains fragments of *metopes* from the Athenian treasury. In Rooms 7 and 8 there are figures (with uncompleted backs) from the Temple of Apollo, and in Rooms 9 and 10 *metopes* and fragments of the coffered ceiling from the Tholos. Here also are two bronze *kalpis* (elegantly-shaped ewers with three handles) and a fine *stele* of an athlete extending his arms to the right, while a bereaved child, no doubt his servant, gazes up from the right-hand corner.

In Room 11 the **Column of the Dancing Girls**, an unusual monument of the Hellenistic period, soars towards the ceiling. The shaft, about ten metres high, was so carved as to resemble a gigantic acanthus stalk, the foot of each drum being surrounded by luxuriant foliage. The three girls were grouped round the highest tier of leaves, performing a hieratic dance. In spite of the fundamental awkwardness of the composition, the girls' drapery is loose and flowing and they possess much of the life and grace lacked by the more solemn Caryatids of the Erechtheion. In the same room is the nude athlete, the **Thessalian Agias**, winner of fourteen awards at panhellenic festivals, a good marble copy of a late fourth-century BC bronze work by Lysippos; there is also a particularly attractive Roman work, a statue of the young **Antinous**.

The bronze **Charioteer** stands alone in Room 12, against a pale grey background (but he will be moved in a planned rearrangement of the Museum). He could not be more effectively exhibited. The life-sized figure, made up of seven separately-cast parts, belonged to a *quadriga* which was placed on the terrace of the temple, the gift of a Sicilian tyrant in the first half of the fifth century BC. Only the shaft and the yoke of the chariot survive. The heavy tubular drapery of the tunic, perfect in its symmetry and rhythm, creates a columnar effect that distinguishes this work from all other Greek statues. Viewed from all sides the figure is stately, though somewhat disproportionate, for the sculptor was endeavouring to correct the distortion which is inevitable when life-sized figures are viewed from below.

From Room 12 one has a staggering view of the Phaedriades through large plate-glass windows. Russet-coloured, they tower up on either side of the ravine that slashes them into two separate but complementary masses. On the periphery, the olive groves, watered by rivulets of the Castalian Spring, shelve down into the valley and purple shadows drift across the outer ring of mountains. The spirit of harmony that existed between the creative genius of the Greeks and the physical world in which they dwelt is not now beyond the bounds of comprehension. What is more difficult to understand is how that colossal hoax, the Delphic oracle, could have taken in so many people for so long.

8

Eastern Roumeli

NORTH-WEST OF DELPHI is the confused mountain region of Northern Greece known as Eastern Roumeli, inhabited by a sturdy people, proud of their warrior traditions and reputation for probity.

Descending from Delphi to Amfissa and taking the road north over the Gravia Pass we go straight on to Bralos, at the western apex of the Phocian Plain, and to the old main road from Athens and Thiva to the north. From Bralos village, just off the main road to the left, a road to the north-west leads into a massif of great splendour. At all points of the compass rise the peaks and escarpments of the three mountains, Iti, Ghiona and Parnassos. Winding up into the complex of ranges, the road passes through the alpine villages of Iti and Pavliani, ablaze with hollyhocks in summer, often snowbound in winter. Then the chestnut forests begin: dark tracts, the open patches covered with bracken. The altitude increases and one enters the conifer belt. About two kilometres after Pavliani a track to the right is signposted for the Funeral Pyre of Herakles. It is an extremely bad, stony road and after heavy winter rain and snow is liable to be unsuitable for ordinary cars. The road mounts the fir-covered slopes and after about five kilometres reaches a barren upland. Another signpost marks the site of the **Funeral Pyre of Herakles**, where an ancient shrine, among the loneliest in the country, was raised to commemorate the hero's metamorphosis into a fully-fledged deity.

According to tradition, Herakles, the symbol of incomparable masculine strength, ended his mortal career on this lonely two thousand metre high mountain-top. Sophocles wrote of his ascent, amid peals of thunder and flashes of lightning, to the marble halls of Olympos, where his father granted him immortality and a charming wife.

The site, which includes the outlines of a *megaron* and *stoa*, is littered with limestone slabs, fluted drums and fragments of *triglyphs*. Unexcavated, these stones have weathered time and the elements for over two millennia. In this rarefied atmosphere, the contours of the central mainland massif assume the aspect of a map. Geography is omnipresent, the emphasis on symmetry pronounced. The north-south spine of the Pindos, dividing the country in two, meets the west-east chain of Panetoliko, Iti and Kalidromo. Parallel to it, the Ghiona-Parnassos-Elikon range shuts off all Central Greece from the south. It is like an upside-down Cross of Lorraine, with the valleys and cultivated plains filling in the interstices between the lateral arms.

Back on the main road beyond Bralos, one climbs a lower ridge of Iti and descends through very fine scenery into the wide, but shut-in **Valley of the Sperhios**. Westward, hundreds of feet below, streams trickle down gorges, and *katavothres* force their way underground to pour their efflux of silt and sludge into the Sperhios and thence into the Malian Gulf. Not far from the road, the Athens-Thessaloniki railway line - a remarkable piece of French nineteenth-century engineering - winds through silent, wooded country. The line passes through seventeen tunnels and, clinging to successive ledges, descends the rocky Trachinian precipices to the lowlands below. A long viaduct spans the Gorgopotamos torrent, scene of a much publicized exploit in 1942, when Greek guerillas, aided by British parachutists, blew up the bridge, cutting one of the main German supply routes to the Libyan front.

Soon after the start of the descent there is a fork - to the left the old road to Lamia, now in bad condition, goes down to the valley and runs across a flat cereal and cotton-growing strip, watered by the streams of the Sperhios. Frogs croak on muddy banks. On moonless nights myriads of fireflies flit among the reeds bordering the streams. Achilles, who was born hereabouts, trained, from the age of six, to dispose of bears and lions in single combat and consequently developed such physical strength that, when passionately embracing the objects of his affections, he often broke their ribs.

The main road continues the descent via the right-hand fork and, in the valley, joins the National Road from Athens which bypasses Lamia after passing over the **Alamanas Bridge.** This bridge spans a tributary of the Sperhios and was the scene of a much-romanticized episode in the opening round of the War of Independence. A large Turkish force, moving out of Lamia, was met at the bridge - across which the main Athens-Thessaloniki traffic now streams - by a small band of determined Greeks under Athanassios Diakos, a deacon who had abandoned a religious vocation for a military career in the ranks

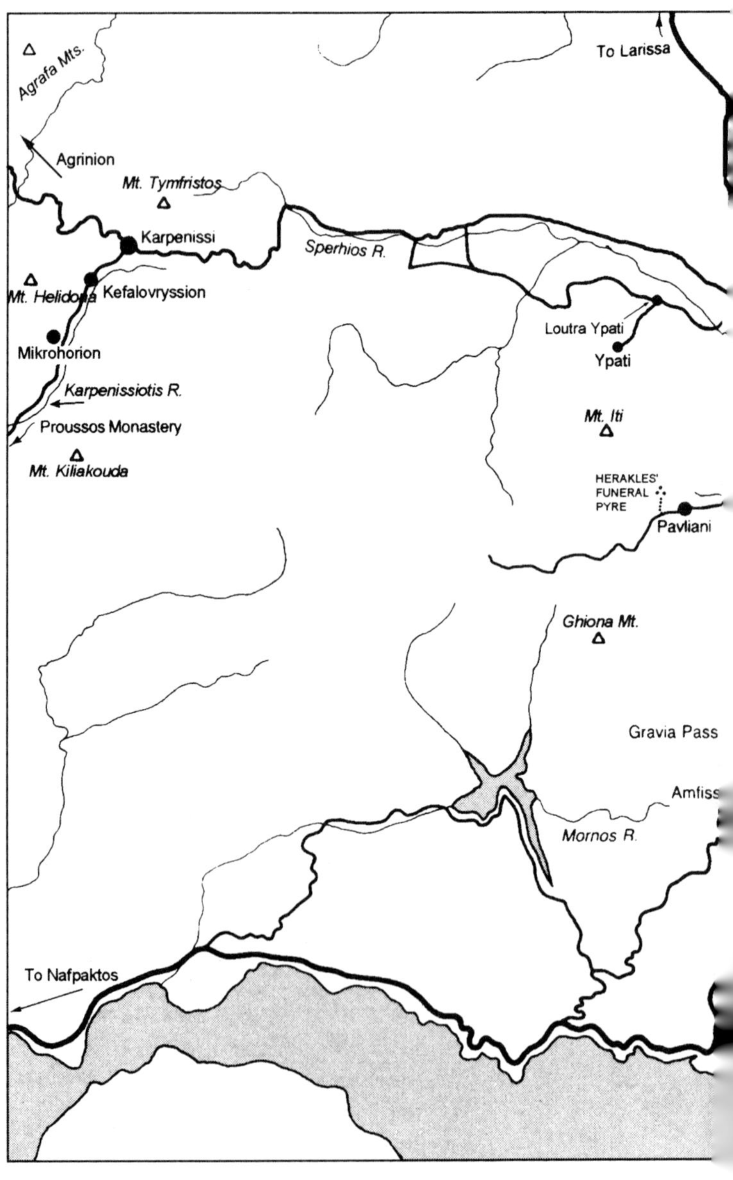
Agrafa Mts.
To Larissa
Agrinion
Mt. Tymfristos
Karpenissi
Sperhios R.
Mt. Helidona
Kefalovryssion
Loutra Ypati
Ypati
Mikrohorion
Karpenissiotis R.
Proussos Monastery
Mt. Iti
Mt. Kiliakouda
HERAKLES' FUNERAL PYRE
Pavliani
Ghiona Mt.
Gravia Pass
Mornos R.
To Nafpaktos

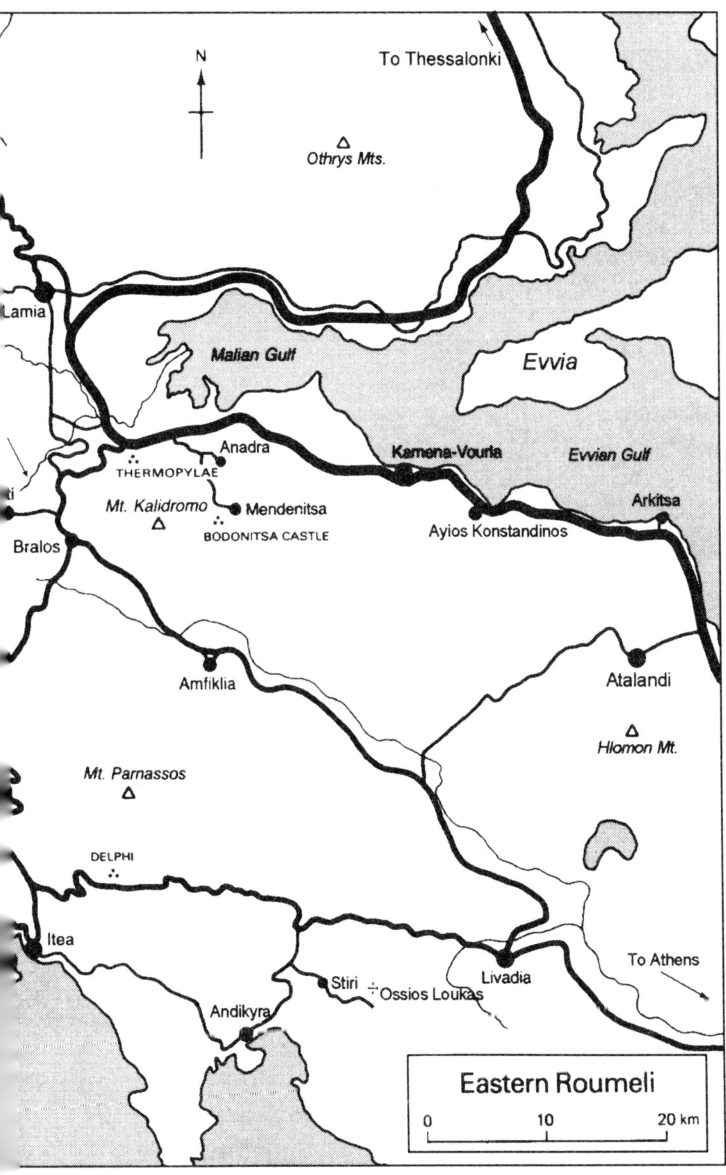
N
To Thessalonki
Othrys Mts.
Lamia
Malian Gulf
Evvia
Anadra
Kamena-Vourla
Evvian Gulf
THERMOPYLAE
Mt. Kalidromo
Mendenitsa
BODONITSA CASTLE
Ayios Konstandinos
Arkitsa
Bralos
Amfiklia
Atalandi
Hlomon Mt.
Mt. Parnassos
DELPHI
Itea
Livadia
To Athens
Stiri
Ossios Loukas
Andikyra
Eastern Roumeli
0
10
20 km

of the local militia. Diakos was youthful and lion-hearted and the members of his militia, although officially in the service of the Sultan, worked for the cause of independence with a courage and sense of responsibility rarely encountered among the Greek patriots. But an overwhelming superiority in numbers enabled the Turks to cross the stream. Diakos was captured and roasted alive. His death remains enshrined in storybook and folksong. There is a statue of the hero at the bridge and another in Lamia adorns the square, named after him, where he was roasted.

Lamia sprawls across the foothills of the Othrys range. Although a pivotal point in the lines of communication running north to south, east to west, it offers nothing in the way of sightseeing except, on a hill spiked with cypress trees above the town, a partly-restored Catalan castle with Turkish battlements, built on classical and Roman foundations. It is pleasant to sit at a café in the shade of a plane tree beside the fountain in Laou Square, drinking coffee and eating *kourabiédes*, buttery shortbread dusted with powdered sugar (a Lamian speciality, popular throughout the country).

The town has long been a military centre. When the War of Independence broke out in 1821, the Turks assembled twenty thousand men in and around the town; the cobbled streets were crowded with horses, pack-animals and ammunition dumps, while greedy-eyed Albanian soldiers ravaged the neighbouring farms.

At Lamia, the traveller coming from Bralos has the choice of four directions: north to Larissa (see Chapter Nine), east to Volos and Pelion (Chapter Ten), west to Karpenissi, and south-east to Thermopylae and Bodonitsa. I take the shorter, south-east route first which entails going down the National Road towards Athens.

As the valley opens out towards the once-marshy shore of the Malian Gulf, the mountain wall rises abruptly from the plain. The National Road passes the turn-off for Delphi and the small spa exploiting the natural hot springs of Thermopylae, meaning 'Hot Gates'. The name goes far back into antiquity, relating to the narrowness of the way between the mountains and the sea and, of course, to the springs. Beside the road on the left a modern bronze statue of Leonidas marks the site of the **Battle of Thermopylae**. No other major ancient site is more disappointing. In the fifth century BC the swamp came so close to Mount Kalidromo that it left only the narrowest passage for men and chariots, but the deposits thrown up by the hot springs have created new alluvial soil, the bog has been replaced by cultivated fields. There is no sign of the pass where five thousand Greeks made their heroic stand in August 480 BC against Xerxes' army of 'five million men' (according to the doubtless vastly-exaggerated estimate of Herodotos).

A tumulus opposite the statue of Leonidas is supposed to cover the bones of the Spartan dead. Standing on this mound, one can try to work out the different moves in the battle. But it is all very baffling. Where was the Great King encamped while he waited, bewildered and enraged at the temerity of this handful of Greeks? In the plain? But it was then an unbridgeable morass; and where was he stationed when, after launching the attack, he watched the battle? Throughout two whole days Xerxes beheld his best troops annihilated by the skilled archers of the little Greek force. Disheartened by such tenacity, he accepted the offer of a Malian traitor to lead part of the Persian army up a secret track into the heart of the mountain, whence it could wheel round and attack the Greeks in the rear. At dawn, the Persians rushed down the mountain path onto the main body of the Greeks, whose soothsayer had already foretold their doom. Leonidas, the Spartan king who claimed descent from Herakles, dismissed most of his allies, insisting that the honour of making the last-ditch stand should belong to Spartans alone (the suggestion that his allies, aware of the hopelessness of their situation, actually abandoned Leonidas cannot be ruled out). 'In the morning' says Herodotos 'Xerxes poured a libation to the rising sun and attacked the three hundred': all were warriors of mature age, personally picked by Leonidas. Caught in the pincers, the Spartans performed prodigies of valour. After Leonidas was killed, they retreated into the narrowest part of the pass, where they fought with daggers, bare hands and even their mouths, until each one fell. After it was all over, Xerxes ordered the head of Leonidas to be cut off and fixed on a stake. Later, a column was raised where the Spartans fell - there is, alas, no vestige of it left.

For centuries Thermopylae remained the only pass through which an invading army could enter Southern Greece. In April 1941, with the RAF driven from the skies, officers and men of the Australian and New Zealand brigades of the British Expeditionary Force, encamped below the ridges of Kalidromo, watched German armoured forces assemble unmolested in the plain. In the eventual attack the German tanks, like the Persians, suffered heavy casualties. The British guns might have held the pass, but a repetition of the fatal encircling movement - this time on an infinitely wider scale -

caused the Expeditionary Force to abandon the position. It is curious how each time the defenders of Thermopylae have lost the battle.

Shortly after Thermopylae a side road climbs five kilometres south-east between hedgerows of arbutus and agnus castus to the village of Anadra. Eastward, where Kalidromo tapers off into a series of jagged peaks towards the Evvian Gulf, there is a sudden view of the **Castle of Bodonitsa** crowning a tawny hill, around which the hamlet of Mendenitsa nestles among walnut trees and vegetable plots. Bodonitsa, site of ancient Tarphai, was one of the Crusaders' main bulwarks guarding Central Greece from invasion from the north. Any hostile force, attempting to round the Kalidromo range could not fail to be spotted by sentinels stationed on the battlements.

Most impressive is the north-west polygonal wall rising sheer from a sloping ledge. It is five minutes' climb from the modern war memorial to the keep, entered through a postern crowned by a massive lintel. Above it rises a squat tower. Ancient slabs, believed to have come from a temple of Hera, who was worshipped here, are embedded in the masonry among huge thistles with purple flowers. Ruined ramparts overlook cornfields shelving down to the coast. Bodonitsa was an Italian, never a French, fief, and the fame and prestige of its Marquis was comparable to the strength of his castle and elegance of his court. It is not among the largest of medieval castles in Greece but, in the grandeur and beauty of its position, it is comparable to any. In 1414 the last Italian Marquis, inspired perhaps by the proximity of Thermopylae, defended it against the Turks with a bravery and tenacity that would have done credit to Leonidas. With the fall of Bodonitsa, the whole of Central Greece passed into Ottoman hands. The Turkish conquerors destroyed the walls and sold the inhabitants, Italian and Greek, into slavery.

The enclosure is pitted with hollows: once vaulted chambers, now overgrown with wild fig trees which exude the sun-baked bitter-sweet fragrance of the milky sap secreted in their stalks. A Gothic arch, probably part of a chapel, surmounts one side of the pits beside the north rampart. The wall-walk is too ruined to serve as a promenade, but the village boys, who like to act as guides, scramble to the summit of the squat tower, where, silhouetted against a background of fir-covered peaks, they pass the time aiming stones at elusive grass snakes rustling among the thistles.

After Thermopylae the western extremity of Evvia appears across the water. The entire maritime strip was once dotted with ancient townships: for the most part unexcavated, unidentified or razed to the ground by earthquakes.

The hotels, restaurants and tavernas of **Kamena-Vourla**, a popular spa and holiday resort, are confined between the seashore and the foot of abrupt slopes sliced by wooded gullies filled with evergreens and coursed by rivulets bordered with maidenhair. After this the highway runs along near the sea, sometimes winding around shingly coves. Hotels, blocks of holiday apartments and villas line parts of the coast - it is only two hours' drive from Athens - but most of the beaches are narrow, sometimes littered with sea-weed, and the water on this side of the Evvian Gulf lacks the sparkling quality of the Aegean. **Ayios Konstandinos** is a fishing village turned summer resort, and a port for hydrofoils to the Sporades; likewise **Arkitsa**, from which a ferry plies to Edipsos, a spa on Evvia. The highway then enters a little, triangular plain of well-watered orchards, at the apex of which is the town of **Atalandi** whence a road climbs over a shoulder of Mount Hlomon to join the old Athens-Thessaloniki road in the Boeotian plain. The islet in the bay of Atalandi was fortified by the Athenians during the Peloponnesian War as a deterrent to privateers who harassed Athenian trade. After skirting the shallow bay, broken up by little spits of land, the highway climbs a saddle of Mount Hlomon and descends into the Boeotian plain at Kastro.

West of Lamia the spa of **Loutra Ypati** shelters under the wall of Mount Iti. Over it all - cafés, restaurants and hotel lounges crowded with patients suffering from skin diseases - hangs the smell of the curative sulphur. More attractive is the village of **Ypati** on a high ledge above the spa. Here Apuleius lays the scene of *The Golden Ass*, in which the lusty Lucius, after rubbing himself with an ointment prepared by the witch Pamphile, is transformed into a dumb and docile donkey.

Although there is a good road, it is possible to climb from the village square to the site of the Catalan castle, up a steep path shaded by plane trees and thick brambles which form an arbour over a trickle of water from a mountain stream. Winding round a rocky eminence, one perceives a lone crag crowned by a circular tower and fragments of ramparts. The Catalans could not have chosen a more inaccessible site on which to perch a castle, from which they could detect hostile armies threading their way through the western and northern defiles of the mountain arena. But ruined watchtowers are not the sole legacy of the Catalan conquerors. The impact made by this strange Spanish interlude on the local inhabitants was considerable and lasting. Regarded as one of the perennial scourges the Greeks had learnt to accept as a law of nature, the rough soldiers of fortune of the Catalan Grand Company stayed on, picking wives for themselves from among the Frankish aristocracy they had defeated at the battle of Kifissos and soon earning themselves a terrible reputation for cruelty.

The Karpenissi road west of Lamia follows the course of the Sperhios, north of Mount Iti, until the cereal and cotton fields peter out below the foothills of Mount Tymfristos (2315 metres), the southernmost peak of the Pindos. Its elegant tapering peak is a landmark throughout much of Central Greece. The road ascends between silver firs, affording backward views of the ribbon-like valley, skirts a village named after the mountain, and enters a shut-in alpine valley through which flows the torrent of the Karpenissiotis. At the end of it is **Karpenissi**, a summer resort with some hotels and restaurants. Largely rebuilt after its destruction by both Germans and Communist rebels during and after the Second World War, Karpenissi has nothing to offer in the way of sightseeing. But the air is crystalline. It is also one of the two starting points (the other is Agrinion in Western Roumeli, a much more difficult road across the mountains) for a visit to a famous place of pilgrimage: the Monastery of Proussos. The road is easy and picturesque, through narrow defiles and round overhanging precipices.

A short descent from Karpenissi ends in a well-watered valley of maize-fields, cherry and apple orchards. Here **Kefalovryssion** marks the site of a notable engagement during the War of Independence. A Turkish force of four thousand men was surprised one summer night in 1823 by Markos Botsaris, one of the ablest champions of Greek independence, and three hundred and fifty Souliots, a warrior tribe of Albanian descent. The Turks were taken unawares and the Souliots prevailed. Botsaris, however, was shot, although the gloom cast over the Souliots by the death of their leader did not prevent them from indulging in an orgy of plunder. The Turkish commander's tent had been pitched in a low-walled enclosure protecting beehives, which still spread across the hillside today.

The road passes near the tree-shaded village of **Mikrohorion** - site of the Souliot encampment - destroyed by a gigantic landslide in 1963 and re-built at the foot of Mount Helidona; another peak, that of Mount Kaliakouda towers immediately south of Gavros. One crosses the Karpenissiotis, bordered by ilex and plane, and enters a gorge rent with screes whose higher levels of rock reflect a bright purple light when just touched by the sun's rays. The gorge narrows to a point where it is no more than forty metres wide, with the road imprisoned between walls of granite, alternately brick-red, brown and purple. The chapel of *Ayios Sostis* (St Saviour) clings to a ledge of cliff above.

Beside the torrent of ice-cold water there is a café, from which, in the gloomy shade, one can look up at the face of the cliff and see a hatchet-shaped aperture in the rock. Through this passage the venerable wonder-working icon of Proussos is said to have flown in its quest for a final resting place. The stratification of the winding gorge becomes more curious, the rock seamed with vertical zig-zags and squiggles like notes of music. Climbing above the bed of another ice-green torrent, the Krikelliotis, one sees the distant peak of Panetoliko, the ubiquitous 'Arab's Head', which dominates the Etolian massif. As the road ascends, one looks down on ranks of nodular outcrops of rock, overgrown with tufts of ilex, rising like ninepins out of the gorge. As the gorge opens out between fir-clad heights, one catches a glimpse of the houses of Proussos scattered across a cultivated slope above an irregular bowl, out of which more rocky cones, sometimes with spherical or bulbous summits, rise in terrible disarray. Winding among these awesome precipitous bluffs, the road descends towards the bowl, making for a needle of rock crowned by a clock tower.

In the shade of plane trees, beside a chapel, lie the ruins of a Greek 'secret school', founded during the Turkish occupation by Kosmas the Etolian, who tried to instruct his uncouth fellow-mountaineers in the virtues of their Hellenic heritage. Nearby is the church of the **Monastery of Proussos**, thought to be the site of a sanctuary of Athena and later a Christian shrine which became the refuge of an anchorite. The monastery is an unattractive modern building raised on the charred foundations of several earlier monastic establishments. The church, an ordinary domed and cruciform little edifice, is strikingly situated in a deep concavity of vertical rock; it has thus been protected for centuries from the boulders that hurtle down in the course of landslides. The painted decoration of the interior is undistinguished.

In the courtyard, pilgrims holding long tapers drag themselves penitentially on hands and knees to a side chapel which contains the **icon of the Virgin Proussiotissa**, famous for its healing powers.

Patiently the worshippers queue in single file to enter the dimly-lit interior and kiss the holy image. Only the brown faces of the Byzantine Virgin and Child are visible, the rest of the ancient icon being elaborately silver-plated. The icon is apocryphally attributed to the hand of St Luke and is, to this day, in spite of its inaccessibility, venerated by streams of pilgrims especially during a whole week in August. The library and museum of the monastery contain little of interest: post-Byzantine Books of Gospels, filigree work, reliquaries and crosses.

Returning to Karpenissi, a good road to Agrinion in the west winds through the highlands of the Southern Pindos, overhanging rugged gorges which run parallel in a north-south axis. To the north rise the Agrafa mountains. For pure form and structure there is little in Greece to compare with them. Hereabouts a British military mission had its nomadic headquarters during the Second World War, supplying Greek resistance forces with arms and gold pounds; its efforts to prevent the rival Right- and Left-wing factions from fighting each other instead of the enemy were not always crowned with success. The road descends in loops through wooded country to two tremendous bridges spanning the narrowest branches of the huge artificial Kremasto Lake, formed by the damming up of the Avrafiotis, Aheloos and Tavropos rivers. At the bottom lies a submerged Byzantine church of the ninth century. On two sides of the lake, north and east, mountains rise sheer, ranged one behind the other like screens, escarpment upon escarpment, wooded on the higher levels, with the Aheloos flowing swiftly between scrub-covered hills towards the Akarnanian plains.

9

Thessaly: The Plain

THE OLD MAIN ROAD to the north from Lamia via Farsala to Larissa, and the railway, both climb the Othrys mountains, once associated with the legend of the flood of Deukalion, the Noah figure of Greek mythology. When Zeus, incensed by the degeneracy of mankind, caused a flood to wipe out the human race, Deukalion, the Phthian king, hastily built a ship in which he placed his wife and abundant provisions. When the swollen waters retreated, the vessel is said to have landed on one of the summits of Mount Othrys. The puce-coloured slopes, also associated with the seat of Hellen, son of Deukalion and founder of the Hellenic race, are featureless and unwooded, but there are fine backward views of the receding panorama of Mount Iti. The monotony of the descent into the lowlands is relieved by the ruined walls of a medieval castle on a rocky eminence above **Domokos**, which commands an immense prospect of the flat, chequer-board plain of central Thessaly.

This plain of Thessaly, the most spacious in Greece - Herodotos, supported by modern geologists, says it was originally a lake - is sealed in by mountains: in the west by the serrated spine of the Pindos, in the north by the desolate Kamvounians and Olympos, in the north-east by Pelion and Ossa, with Othrys bolting the door in the south. When Xerxes entered the plain and the guides pointed out how thoroughly shut in by mountains it was, the Great King decided that, should the Thessalians not submit to him, he would block the only exit, the Vale of Tempe to the north-east, causing the country to flood. The climate is one of extremes, and in summer a metal-coloured haze hangs tantalizingly over the legendary mountains. So heavily blanketed in cloud is Olympos that even its foothills are seldom visible from the plain. The horses of Thessaly, which still graze in the cornlands, were famous throughout Greece, and the Thessalian cavalry was an important factor in every war. Philip of Macedon found the country hard to conquer; when he did, it was useful to him for grain, horses and manpower.

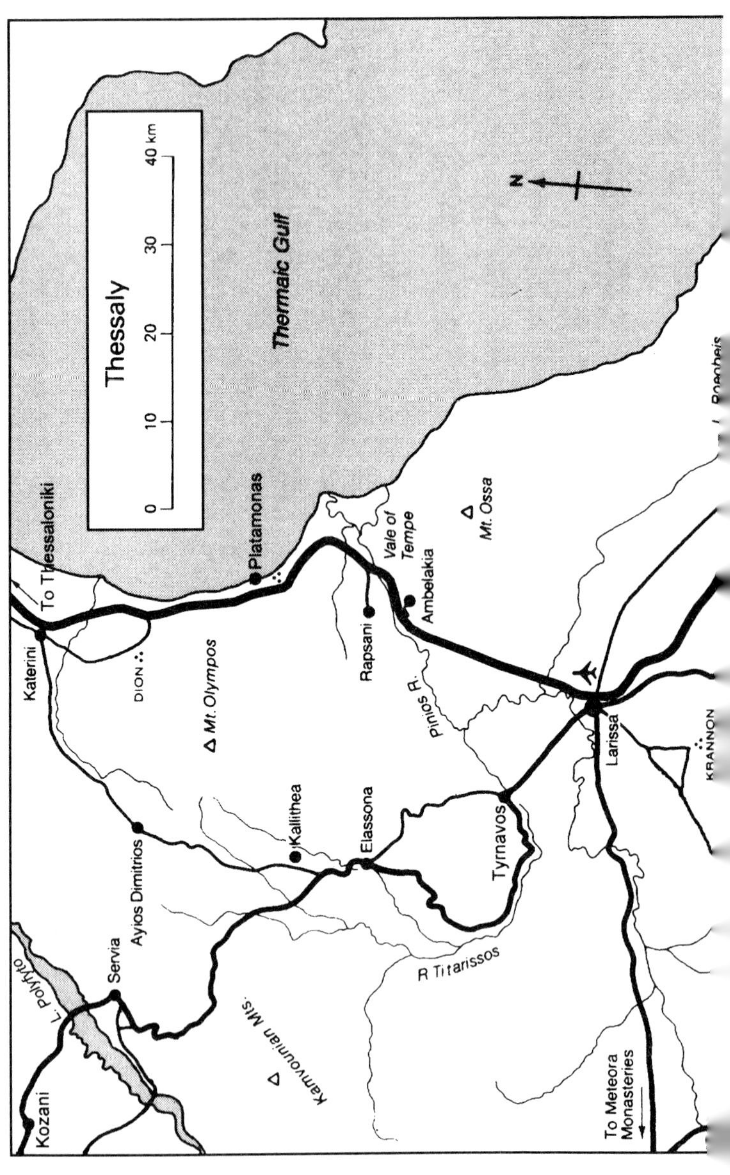
Thessaly
0
10
20
30
40 km
Thermaic Gulf
N
To Thessaloniki
Platamonas
Katerini
DION
Mt. Olympos
Rapsani
Vale of Tempe
Ambelakia
Mt. Ossa
Pinios R.
Larissa
KRANNON
Kallithea
Elassona
Tyrnavos
Ayios Dimitrios
Servia
L. Polyfyto
R Titarissos
Kamvounian Mts.
Kozani
To Meteora Monasteries

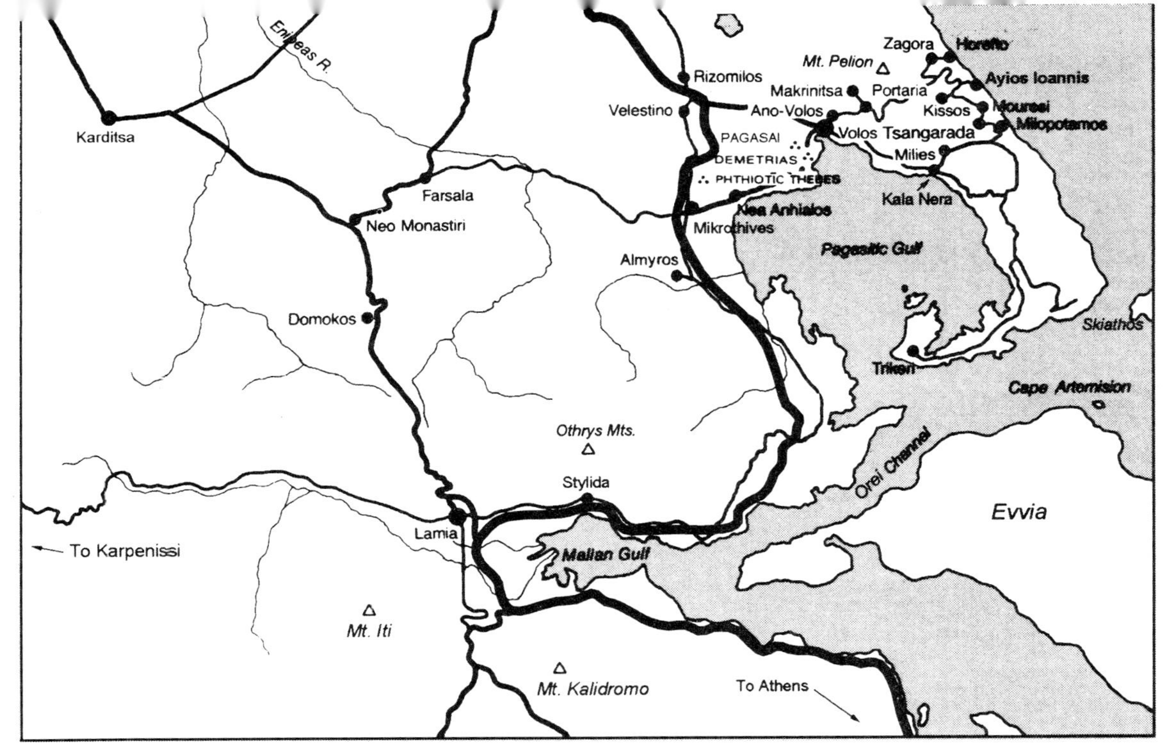
Zagora
Horefto
Mt. Pelion
Rizomilos
Ayios Ioannis
Makrinitsa
Portaria
Velestino
Ano-Volos
Kissos
Mouresi
Milopotamos
Karditsa
Enipeas R.
PAGASAI
Volos
Tsangarada
DEMETRIAS
Milies
PHTHIOTIC THEBES
Farsala
Kala Nera
Nea Anhialos
Neo Monastiri
Mikrothives
Pagasitic Gulf
Almyros
Domokos
Skiathos
Trikeri
Cape Artemision
Othrys Mts.
Orei Channel
Stylida
Evvia
Lamia
To Karpenissi
Malian Gulf
Mt. Iti
Mt. Kalidromo
To Athens

Why Strabo should call this fertile but featureless landscape, dotted with little oases of stunted trees, 'a country most blessed', remains a mystery. Deep cart-tracks furrow the corn-fields around dust-caked - in winter mud-encrusted - villages, and in spring storks perch with an air of impervious elegance on the domes of red-brick churches. Huge sows wallow beside filthy troughs, like the swine sacrificed to Aphrodite who was worshipped in the ancient cities of the plain. But most of the Thessalian lowlands defy description. How right Sterne was when he said there is 'nothing more terrible to travel-writers than a large rich plain if it is without great rivers or bridges, and presents nothing but one unvaried picture of plenty'.

At the village of **Neo Monastiri** the road divides (the well-preserved walls of ancient Proerna, a minor Thessalian township, are spread across the hillside to the right). The road to the left leads to Trikkala, the Meteora and Ioannina, while the Larissa road passes through **Farsala** the ancient Pharsalus, scene of Octavius Caesar's masterly set-piece battle. This was the first of the three engagements fought on Greek soil or in Greek waters - Pharsalus, Philippi, Actium - that decided the fate of the Roman world. Low rocky hills overlook the fields through which the stream of the Enipeas flows, and where the 'flower and strength of Rome', says Plutarch, 'met in collision with itself'. The level ground was admirably suited to the advance of Caesar's brilliantly-led battle-trained legions against the amorphous force assembled by Pompey, whose morale had already been shaken by a series of alarms and omens. 'In a few hours' Plutarch continues, 'the plains of Pharsalus were covered with men, horses and armour' and the great Pompey was fleeing towards the sea, his army routed, his tents and pavilions abandoned to Caesar's cohorts. Today Farsala is known only for the terrible earthquake of 1954 and also for *halva*, the popular sweet made commercially with sesame seeds (at Easter a different type of *halva* - more of a cake - is made at home using semolina).

Beyond the stream of the Enipeas the road crosses an east-west chain of barren hills and then continues over the plain. Occasionally there are settlements of transhumant sheep herders, Sarakatsani or Vlachs, descendants of the medieval Wallachians; dwelling in the alpine villages of the Pindos, in winter they descend into the lowlands with their sheep, women and prickly sense of personal pride. In the Middle Ages Thessaly was overrun by these nomads. After them came the Serbs, pouring over the Macedonian border.

But by the end of the fourteenth century the rivalries of Serbs, Greeks and Wallachians were swept away in the Ottoman conquest. The Turks repopulated Thessaly with peasants from Asia Minor, and leisure-loving pashas carved large estates out of the lands abandoned by the frightened Greeks. Consequently Thessaly was one of the few provinces in the country in which villages grew up with mixed Greek and Turkish populations. This triple influx - Wallachian, Serb and Turkish - left a Balkan stamp on the province.

Larissa, the provincial capital, through which the vanquished Pompey fled to the sea, lies in the north-eastern part of the plain. A garrison town and an important centre of communications, with plenty of hotels, it is a useful halt for the traveller, though there has been much un-attractive development and heavy traffic makes parking in the city centre a nightmare. More than one military plot has been hatched in the local barracks and officers' messes, and the success of any attempt at a military take-over of the country is said to depend largely on the role played by the army corps stationed here.

In antiquity the city was ruled by the Aleudai, the leading family in Thessaly, and we know that Gorgias, the glamorous Sicilian Sophist, was greatly honoured as a teacher of rhetoric at their court; they liked to be surrounded by scholars, being somewhat boorish themselves. Pindar too was a much-venerated guest, and Hippocrates died here at the age of over a hundred - a fitting life-span for the 'father of medicine'. The low acropolis hill, which overlooks a loop of the Pinios, the chief river of Thessaly, is now crowned by a modern cathedral, reached by a winding stairway with bizarre stone dressing. Near the cathedral a fluted column, an Ionic capital and some broken marble plaques mark the site of a temple of Aphrodite. East of the cathedral rises a squat block of masonry, formerly a Byzantine fort, with blind arches and a substructure which preserves features of the architectural style of the original market town to which all the produce of Thessaly was once carried by beasts of burden. Across the river is the large and very pleasant Alkazar Park.

The Archaeological Museum contains the fossilized remains of prehistoric monsters dated to the Inter-Glacial and Last Ice Ages, discovered in the sandbanks of the Pinios; also Neolithic tools and weapons from neighbouring sites - especially Sesklo, roughly carved fourth-century BC *stelae* excavated on the acropolis and reliefs with figures of mounted horsemen riding towards a symbolic tree.

Taking the Karditsa road to the south-west one comes, after

fifteen kilometres, to a turn-off on the left leading to the little village of **Krannon** and the site of the ancient city of that name. This was the seat of the Skopadai, a Thessalian royal family proverbial for their wealth and power. The site is not a tourist attraction and one is unlikely to get any local help in finding the ruins; those wishing to visit the tombs should contact the Classical Eforia in Larissa. The acropolis once spread across a low, treeless eminence, over a kilometre in circumference. Now littered with shards, it commands an immense prospect of corn and maize fields. In summer the site is best visited in the late afternoon, when the rolling fields of stubble turn pale yellow and the outlines of mountains - Pindos, Olympos, Ossa, ranged in a horseshoe round the northern end of the plain - emerge out of the heat haze.

The extant remains of Skopadic power include three extremely well-preserved fifth-century BC tombs: two of them are mausoleums with conical, beehive roofs - a small-scale survival, a thousand years later, of the early Mycenaean royal sepulchre. The first tomb I visited was circular, the second (further south) square with a square doorway supported by three half-engaged pieces of masonry resembling colonnettes, the third (still further south) possibly the resting place of the Skopadic king, had traces of painting on the wall. The masonry of the three tombs is in the best fifth-century BC tradition. Numerous mounds of earth scattered about the acropolis are thought to be more tombs awaiting the attention of archaeologists. There is a spaciousness about the scene, virtually untouched as yet by human habitation, with swallows' nests in the tholos tombs. This evocative site is being further explored - recent excavations have concentrated on the remains of the town, on and around the acropolis.

All this part of Thessaly was strongly contested by the armies of the Roman Republic in their wars with the Macedonian Empire and, after the final Macedonian defeat, it became a flourishing Roman province. Evidence for this can be seen to the east of the tholos tombs where, walking across humps and undulations, past the post-Byzantine Church of Zoodohos Piyi (The Source of Life), one comes to a large, well-preserved Roman kiln for firing pots.

From Larissa the westbound road leads to the Meteora monasteries (see Chapter eleven) and there is a choice of two routes northwards into Macedonia: the National Road goes through the Vale of Tempe (Chapter twelve) and the old main road described here crosses the western foothills of Olympos.

North-west of Larissa, the first place of any importance is **Tyrnavos**, a hot, dusty little town below a spur of Olympos. Allegedly the best *ouzo* in Greece is made here, and the cafés in the large public square are well stocked with it. On the first day of Lent an annual procession, originating in some primitive Orphic rite, winds through the streets. The participants, men only, carry large earthenware objects shaped like phalluses. They call themselves 'phallus-bearers' and take the proceedings very seriously, turning a deaf ear to the ribald remarks of the youthful spectators. The ceremony ends with a lively celebration just outside the town.

After Tyrnavos the road to the north penetrates deep into the Kamvounian range, past the ruins of a second-century BC watch-tower perched on a conical hill at the entrance to a spacious valley. Through the valley streaks the upper Titarissios, a fast-flowing tributary of the Pinios, which curls round beige-coloured hills between thickets of poplar. A gradual ascent ends in a little plain, with **Elassona**, a market town, spreading on either side of a stream spanned by an old Byzantine bridge and surrounded by hills of white clay soil.

The ancient citadel stood on a hill above a ravine, now crowned by a somewhat over-restored Byzantine **Church of the Olympiotissa** (The Olympian Virgin). Commissioned by that indefatigable church-builder, the Emperor Andronikos Paleologos II (1282-1328), the Olympiotissa is architecturally similar to many churches in Thessaloniki. The juxtaposition of a low narthex and tall *naos* is striking. Elegance is not lacking in the architect's conception. But the harmony of volumes and interrelation of planes of the earlier cross-in-square churches are markedly absent. The heightened drum, which we see again and again in Macedonia, at first excites, then palls. In the end, one realizes that it vitiates the sturdy structural unity for which earlier Byzantine church-builders were justly famous. The interior frescoes of the late Byzantine period are poor in artistic quality, narrative in style, conventional in execution. More striking are a fine marble column in the entrance door between the narthex and the nave and the carved wooden two-leafed door (west) dated c.1300. Islamic influences are evident in the ivory inlay of the panels, each of which is carved with different designs of enmeshed circles, crosses and triangles.

Beyond Elassona the country becomes less domesticated. One draws nearer to **Mount Olympos**, the huge massif buttressed by chalky foothills. There are formidable views of deep crevices, filled with snow all the year round; of Mytikas, the 'Needle', the highest peak in Greece (2917 metres), and of the dolomite of Stefani, the Throne of Zeus (2909 metres) soaring skywards. It was presumably because of this physical dominance over all other structurally more beautiful mountains that the ancient Greeks chose its summit, which represented heaven itself, as the residence of the gods.

After traversing a bleak wind-swept saddle, the road descends towards Servia in Western Macedonia and crosses the artificial Lake Polyfyto to Kozani.

An alternative route into Macedonia over the Olympos country begins at a fork nine kilometres beyond Elassona. The north-east-bound road climbs to a region of bare uplands at a very considerable altitude. Even in summer the cold can be penetrating. Crossing the watershed, the road, completing a full semi-circle of Olympos, winds through forests of beech and oak. To the south the 'Needle', now seen from a new angle, projects above a mass of naked rock; chasms fall vertically to wooded foothills. The village of Ayios Dimitrios affords a welcome sign of domesticity. The east Macedonian coastal strip comes into view and the road, after rounding bluffs and scarps, ends at the town of Katerini in the plain, where it joins the National Road.

10

Thessaly: The Pelion Villages

FROM LAMIA TO VOLOS, starting point for a visit to the villages of Mount Pelion, is an easy drive, mostly along the National Road. The road passes Stylida on the coast and one sees, to the south, the Kalidromo mountains rising dramatically above the shallow waters of the gulf: one of those deep inroads into the land so characteristic of the Aegean and Ionian seas.

Skirting the southern foothills of the Othrys range, one has some tantalising glimpses of the Orei Channel and Evvia, with great cliffs alternately advancing and receding across the water. The road then enters the rather uninteresting southern part of the Thessalian plain; after passing near Almyros the road for Volos turns off to the right. About two kilometres beyond the first village, Mikrothives, is a signpost to the site of **Phthiotic Thebes** (not to be confused with the more illustrious Boeotian Thebes); in the Hellenistic era it endured a frightful siege by Philip V, a martial king of Macedonia and an unbridled alcoholic, who ostentatiously renamed it Philippopolis. A large area of impressive ruins, with the remains of towers and ancient fortifications, extends to the left of the road.

Three kilometres further on is the small, seaside resort of Nea Anhialos, with the acropolis of ancient **Pyrasos** on the hill above the town. In antiquity Pyrasos was the port of Phthiotic Thebes but, today, there is virtually nothing to be seen on the acropolis although archaeologists have found neolithic and later remains. Much more interesting are the ruins of the town founded when the ancient inland city of Phthiotic Thebes was abandoned. These ruins are mostly of the Early-Christian period and are scattered among several separate sites, near to the main road, within Nea Anhialos. The area, not yet exhaustively excavated or even completely expropriated, is somewhat confusing, with the main road and side streets running through it. It is best to make for **Basilica A**, which is easy to identify (and is the only area normally open to the public), for it is shaded by pine and cypress trees and lies directly to the north of the main road. The ground is strewn with colonnettes, capitals, fragments of cornices decorated with acanthus leaf designs, plaques carved with rosettes, swastikas and roses. In the north aisle a Corinthian-type capital crowns an unfluted column standing amid the remains of a pebble mosaic floor with designs of lozenges, diamonds and circles. In the apse behind the sanctuary of the baptistry, where the fourth-century bishop officiated, are two large reversed capitals with finely-carved acanthus leaf decorations. Beyond it there are traces of an ancient road and behind the museum, on what could have been the paved floor of a house, the most beautifully carved capital of all: the relief is shallow, the design a variant of the acanthus leaf, so delicately executed as to give the impression of filigree work. To the east is Basilica B, a mass of rubble. The vista of destruction is appalling: the work of invading Slav hordes which set fire to the city in the seventh century.

Basilica C (sixth century), the largest of the three (easily visible but not yet open to visitors), is on the main road west of Basilica A with houses on two sides. The architectural layout, deeply influenced by the tendency towards inflated aggrandizement common in Late Antiquity - particularly in the East - is fairly clear even to the unprofessional eye: atrium, narthex, nave and sanctuary. Only bases of the nave columns are preserved, but some unfluted ones stand in what may been have a subsidiary southern chamber and a colonnade. There are several well-preserved floor mosaics, protected by plastic roofing, in the south-west corner. The stylistic history of the decoration of floor mosaics is a long one. The allegorical and mythological set-pieces of the Hellenistic era tended, in Roman times, to be replaced by landscapes and scenes from nature. Symbolism and idealism are replaced by more representational realism. By the Early-Christian period the decoration has become more formal, more stylized; a rebirth of the Greek feeling for geometry is apparent and it is as though one were witnessing the nascence of the static art of Byzantium. Here in Basilica C there are beautiful designs of ducks with green bellies, cornucopias overflowing with fruit, a deer, a lobster, all framed within medallions. Some melon-shaped capitals with lace-like carving are scattered about the site.

Continuing on the Volos road, just before the town itself you come to the sites of Pagasai and Demetrias. The **Acropolis of Pagasai**, a more ancient and venerated site than upstart Demetrias, has very little to offer in the way of visible ruins: only some fragmentary remains of ancient walls just to the left of the road and on the low hill which is crowned with a whitewashed chapel. To the north, the spurs of Pelion rise abruptly from the inland sea which took its name, the Pagasitic Gulf, from this prehistoric site. In mythology, the beach below, now lined with tavernas, was the site of the building of the *Argo*, on which Jason and the Argonauts embarked.

Nearby **Demetrias** enjoyed a measure of fame from the third century BC as a flashy and ostentatious city founded by Demetrios Poliorketes, one of the most brilliant commanders of the Hellenistic world, whose military career was spent in far-flung campaigns against the Diadochi (successors of Alexander the Great). His private life was scandalous: in Athens he indulged in outrageous debaucheries, even defiling the sacred precincts of the Parthenon. (On contemporary coins Demetrios is represented with horns, in emulation of Dionysos, his favourite deity.) The centre of Demetrias was on the small peninsula to the south of Volos harbour, but the ruins are confusing because other parts of the city were built over Pagasai which had flourished two hundred years before. There is an ancient theatre scooped out of a conch-like fold in the hill; the lower tiers are still faced with stone seats and the *orchestra*, more than a half-circle, is unusually large, probably designed to suit the tastes of its flamboyant founder. Towers rise from the enceinte of ruined walls that extend across the hillside, and there are other remains on the tree-covered promontory to the right. There is an excellent model of the two sites at the Volos Museum.

Volos lies at the head of the Pagasitic Gulf, at the foot of Mount Pelion. In antiquity this fertile mountain bastion of eastern Thessaly was known as Magnesia. It was always richer in legend than history. Destroyed by an earthquake in 1955, Volos today still has a somewhat improvised air in spite of its prosperous bourgeois provincialism. However it has a very fine waterfront promenade, lined with elegant cafés and a variety of restaurants.

The site of ancient **Iolchos**, home of Jason, has been excavated at the west end of the town. Turning right off the main road to Larissa, just after the railway, into Papakyriazi Street, and then left, one reaches the hillock of Ayios Theodoros, overlooking a brick factory. The acropolis obviously commands the entrance to the head of the Gulf. Only the remains of a medieval wall and some foundations now replace the 'well-made streets' where Jason dwelt, in a house filled with 'many servants, men and women, and costly ornaments', as described by Apollonios of Rhodes. It is not an evocative site. Strabo says that 'Iolchos has indeed been rased to the ground from earliest times'. The only identifiable feature is the dry river-bed of the Anavros, which Jason happened to be fording on a rainy day when he saw an old lady in distress amid the swollen waters. He promptly carried her on his back across the stream, whereupon she revealed herself to be Hera and promised him her patronage.

The **Volos Archaeological Museum** (Athanassaki Street), which should not be missed, possesses a fine collection of painted *stelae* from Demetrias. Among the most striking are those of an austere headless warrior (No. 235), of Choirele (No.55) and of three elegant figures (No. 355). The unpainted *stelae* include two fascinating examples of the late Roman period: one male and two female figures surmounted by bunches of grapes and the snake of Asclepios (No. 388), and a child flanked by two female figures (No. 422). Crude, rough, yet forceful, these reliefs have a distinct stylistic relation to works of the so-called 'expressionist' school of Early-Christian sculpture, in which the Hellenic ideals of grace and charm are replaced by the desire to express a more profound inner emotion. There is also a lovely little torso of Aphrodite (No. 715). Among the prehistoric objects are Palaeolithic and Neolithic tools from the very important neighbouring sites of Sesklo and Dimini. Recent research indicates that this was probably the first area to be systematically farmed in Europe. Settlers came from Asia Minor bringing with them not only basic farming techniques, but an Indo-European language, the ancestor of most European languages.

Volos is the starting point for a circular tour of the **Pelion villages**, where a striking style of local architecture, showing distinct Macedonian influences, flourished during the Turkish occupation. Tall white houses - timber-framed, with projecting upper stories - and rustic churches are scattered among the chestnut forests. I usually follow an anti-clockwise route on which the 'star' villages can be visited in two days; a night can be spent at Tsangarada. There are daily buses to all the main villages.

The road to the south-east skirts the seashore. Coastal and inland hamlets spread across olive groves and gardens filled with giant dahlias, Canna lilies and roses, from whose petals a fragrant oil is distilled; in early summer pink and blue hydrangeas, large as cabbages, speckle the silvery groves. At Kala Nera, a pleasant, small resort, the road divides: one road goes on down the peninsula to the scythe-shaped headland of Trikeri, inhabited by caique-builders whose ancestors owned the broad-beamed vessels which traded with all parts of the Levant. In the distance Evvia tapers away into Cape Artemision, off which Xerxes' cumbersome armada, strung out in eight parallel lines, fought the first major engagement of the war with the more nimble Greek triremes in 480 BC.

The other road from Kala Nera goes inland and up to **Milies**. Greek literary tradition was kept alive throughout the Turkish occupation by patriot-scholars in the Pelion villages, whose inhabitants were never tamed by the conquerors; during this period Milies possessed one of the most important libraries in Greece and a school where geography and natural sciences were taught. It was at Milies that the Thessalian standard of revolt against the Turks was raised in 1821.

From Milies the road to the east winds along ridges of heather-covered hills, alternately overlooking the Pagasitic Gulf to the west and the open sea to the east, where two of the loveliest Aegean islands, Skiathos and Skopelos, lie out beyond the coast. The soil is an unusual purplish-red hue.

The road crosses the mountain ridge and, on a clear day, one gets a sudden breathtaking view of Mount Athos, a mirage-like peak thrusting skyward through a pale sea-haze. The heather is succeeded by evergreens. There are interminable windings around vertical clefts as far as **Tsangarada**, a straggling settlement of farmhouses with some small hotels in a forest of oak and chestnut trees at an altitude of 500 metres. A Xenia Hotel overlooks wooded gorges descending abruptly to the sea. On the coast below Tsangarada lies **Milopotamos**, with a beautiful beach and two tavernas that also provide accommodation. Above the beach the ferns and brambles are luxuriant and in autumn mushrooms carpet the undergrowth. In winter the rainfall is the highest on the Greek mainland; everywhere there is the sound of running water - that wonderful crystalline water, served for drinking in thick-rimmed tumblers. Greeks do not drink water only because the body needs a certain amount of liquid. They savour it, like connoisseurs, and make comparisons between the waters of different springs - a civilised approach, Homeric in origin.

The road continues westward at a considerable altitude, through Mouresi, where hollyhocks and hydrangeas blaze in shady arbours, to the turn-off for **Kissos**, its central square overlooking green hills with the sea beyond. The village is lively, less straggling than

Tsangarada. The air is cool in summer, fragrant with sun-drenched grass and ripe fruit. The focal point is the **Church of Ayia Marina**, dedicated to St Marina, a Bithynian holy lady who dwelt in a monastery disguised as a boy and was maliciously accused of fathering the daughter of the local inn-keeper's wife. The church is a low three-aisled basilica, with a belfry pierced by arches on successive levels. The walls of the interior are covered with post-Byzantine frescoes by Pagonis, a local peasant artist, responsible for the painted decoration of many Pelion churches. His work is rustic in conception and rendering; the strict, undeviating rules of Byzantine iconography are ignored and superstition rides roughshod over the dogmas of religious painting. From the capitals demons rudely stick out deformed tongues. Although the bright gilding of the *iconostasis* creates a somewhat gaudy effect, the carving is inventive in detail: a lattice of blooms, tendrils, pert little stags and stylized lions. At the right of the *iconostasis* is a strange fresco of a church perched on a tenuous rock pillar. One wonders if the iconographer had ever visited the rock monasteries of Meteora.

Just after the Kissos turn-off a branch road to the east descends to **Ayios Ioannis**, the principal resort in the area, where there are numerous medium-sized hotels, guesthouses, restaurants and cafés.

After Kissos the main road winds through chestnut forests and round an impressive gorge in the most precipitous part of **Mount Pelion**. Occasional clearings in the forest provide fretwork frames for vistas of unbroken expanses of sea. The deserted glades are carpeted with feathery fronds. Nothing stirs in the shade of the interlacing boughs.

The mountain appears in the earliest myths, from the time when the giants piled Ossa on Pelion in a bold attempt to attack the gods on Olympos. It was on Pelion that Apollo, in one of his amorous escapades - he almost rivals his father, Zeus, in concupiscence - surprised the huntress Kyrene, who was wrestling single-handed with a lion, and carried her off to Africa.

Another mythological Pelion character is the wise old centaur, Cheiron, doctor, prophet and scholar, who dwelt below the summit where medicinal plants grew in profusion, and who was the fashionable tutor of the period, entrusted with the education of such distinguished young men as Achilles and Jason. He paid great attention to physical fitness and character-training, feeding Achilles on marrow from the bones of fawns to make him run fast and lions' entrails to imbue him with courage.

The road climbs inland through forests and orchards, meeting the direct road coming from Volos before turning to the north for **Zagora**, the showpiece of the Pelion. Like Tsangarada, the village is filled with the sound of streams running between banks of maidenhair fern. Its orchards produce several varieties of apple which are much prized in the Athenian market. Like Milies, it was a centre of learning, enjoying local self-government under Turkish rule.

The older houses of Zagora present a blank wall two storeys high to potential enemies, the projecting third one being surmounted by a roof of irregular slates. Under the Turks, folk art, generally quaint, often charming, remained unaffected by the main currents of artistic fashion and two eighteenth-century three-aisled basilicas are typical. At Ayia Kyriaki, faience plates and moulded tulips (here the Turkish influence is clear) are embedded in the apsidal wall. The **Church of Ayios Yeoryios**, situated in a paved square, has the added attraction of an exo-narthex in the form of a wooden colonnade roofed with slates running round the west front and part of the north and south sides (another characteristic feature of Pelion church architecture). On the exterior, the apses are decorated with three bands of small columns which frame marble plaques engraved with geometric patterns and rosettes: there is a small trefoil above each plaque in the top row. The interior possesses an elaborate gilt *iconostasis*, also of the eighteenth century, which gives the impression of filigree work; the pulpit is one of the largest and most ornamental I have seen in a village church. On the south wall hangs an *epitafios*, a fine piece of seventeenth-century embroidery depicting the body of Christ on the bier.

A narrow road descends from the village in hairpin bends to the beach, part sand, part shingle, of **Horefto**, fringed by olive groves and orchards of apple and Kiwi Fruit. There are several hotels and restaurants. Westward the mountain rises sheer: a backcloth of shimmering woodland.

Returning from Zagora towards Volos, the road climbs through plantations of walnut trees with streams cascading down the mountain. Beyond the beech forests of the saddle, below the radar-crowned summit of Pelion and the winter ski-runs, the road begins a winding descent to the Pagasitic Gulf. **Portaria** is a summer resort with a Xenia hotel, an ugly rash of modern villas and a church with murky sixteenth-century frescoes. From here a branch road follows the contours of a precipitous ravine for two kilometres to **Makrinitsa**, which is now unfortunately over-run with tourists and day-trippers. Tall houses, with more slate roofs than elsewhere on Mount Pelion, are built on terraces so steep that the main entrances to the old timber-framed mansions, once the homes of a flourishing agricultural society, are often on the top storey. Unlike other Pelion villages, Makrinitsa is centred round a terrace, which forms a belvedere overlooking the ravine, shaded by plane trees and flanked by the chapel of *Ayios Ioannis*, whose church bell hangs from the branch of a plane tree. From a marble fountain, decorated with carved plaques, water gushes out of a brass gargoyle.

The **Church of the Panayia** is situated on a higher level, its courtyard flanked by cypress and chestnut trees. Above the marble-framed south doorway an exterior eighteenth-century fresco depicts the Virgin, holding the Child, seated on an elaborate baroque throne. The three apses are decorated with sculptured plaques, the most striking of which depicts a lion hunt, with a chariot drawn by four horses. Within the church there is a fine thirteenth-century marble relief of the Virgin *Orans*. During the Turkish occupation, secret classes in history and theology were held in two adjoining chapels; at Makrinitsa teachers and priests went about their clandestine activities, propagating Hellenic culture and the orthodox faith, within sight of the Crescent flying from the fortress of Volos.

The descent continues. The **Kondos House** in **Anakassia** (which is signposted) is in a pretty garden below Makrinitsa's great cliff. The upper storey contains sixty square metres of frescoes by the eccentric peasant painter, Theofilos, a late nineteenth-century 'primitive', who peddled his way across eastern Greece, singing while he painted, asking for no payment other than the cost of his materials. Although his frescoes are devoid of scale and perspective, Theofilos often conveys the spirit of place and period, and his decorative detail has roots in a precise, almost classical, perception of objects. His subjects generally derive from episodes during the War of Independence (there are some splendidly-bedecked military gentlemen, armed to the teeth, with frozen expressions and ferocious moustaches). Whimsical treatment and bold use of colour combine to make the stylized scenes come to life. Mythological subjects are not ignored: Hermes in a black mantle departs on one of his divine errands; Aphrodite, with great feet, holds a trident as she rises from the foam. One of the most attractive features of the frescoes is the decorative detail: a giraffe munching palm leaves, a blue peacock with emerald-green plumage.

From Volos one drives across the plain to rejoin the National

Road to Larissa and the north. However before actually joining the National Road, one can cross it, keeping on the road from Volos for a short distance to where a side road to the south leads to **Velestino**, a small town among apple orchards: the site of ancient **Pherai**. The city was ruled by a succession of bloodthirsty tyrants, who were the scourge of Central Greece in the fourth century BC, raising Thessaly to the status of a great power. The first of these was Jason (not to be confused with the mythical leader of the Argonauts) whom Xenophon describes as 'the greatest man of his times'. By nature he was violent and ostentatious. Like him, his successors were assassinated. Of these, none surpassed in cruelty his lawless and foul-mouthed nephew, Alexander, whose sole religious exercise was the worship of the spear with which he slew his uncle. His own end was plotted by his wife and her three brothers. With his assassination, the power of the Thessalian despots declined, and the country was soon subjected by Philip of Macedon.

Next to the town's miniature public garden is a shallow pond with a tiled basin, its surface mantled with sedge: the scene painted by Edward Dodwell in one of his most charming 'Views of Greece'. In the nineteenth century the pond was fringed with minarets and trees, including a palm, and there was a broken column in the foreground. Assuming that Dodwell did not invent the column, one is justified in associating the site with the fountain of Hypereia, which was situated in the heart of the ancient city. Of antiquity all that remains today are some vestiges of a temple of Herakles and of the Larissa gate on the site of an acropolis, north of the town.

One rejoins the National Road at Rizomilos and the remainder of the run to Larissa is without interest - across the flat Thessalian plain. To the north extends the former lake of Boibeis, at the foot of Mount Ossa.

11

Thessaly : The Meteora Monasteries

THE WAY FROM LARISSA to the Meteora monasteries is across a flat, typically Thessalian, stretch of country, watered by rush-bordered streams. Geese waddle around stagnant pools; occasionally avenues of poplars shade the road, which runs parallel to the Pinios. The Palaeolithic fossils and tools excavated along this stretch of the river have been dated to a period between 100,000 and 40,000 BC. The barrier of the Pindos range, bluish in colour, gashed by chasms, draws nearer.

We start by going south-west from Larissa to **Karditsa**, a market town of Turkish origin, served by a narrow-gauge railway running from Volos to Trikkala. Storks' nests crown chimneys and other high points in the town. General Plastiras, an ambitious cavalry officer with a fierce black moustache, who always rode a black charger and became one of the more controversial political personalities between the two World Wars, plotting military revolutions and brooding in exile when out of office, was born here. His name was given to a large artificial lake, one of the loveliest in Greece, created by damming up the Tavropos. The signposted road climbs westward past a twelfth-century monastery, through oak forests into magnificent mountain scenery. A circular tour of the lake is easy and strongly recommended. At Karditsa one can join the Lamia-Ioannina road which goes across the plain to Trikkala.

A sluggish tributary of the Pinios flows through **Trikkala**, a lively market town with a small, recently restored mosque, a castellated clock tower and a stone bridge spanning the poplar-lined stream. A furnace of heat in summer, it is dominated by the crumbling walls of a Byzantine fort, site of the ancient acropolis, from whose highest tower the Turkish governor used to hurl his enemies. Projecting hooks caught the bodies as they fell; there they were left, dangling in gruesome postures - a warning to all who passed below.

A road from Trikkala to the south-west passes close by Gomfi, which has some ancient remains. At the village of Pyli, lying at the base of the Pindos, one crosses a bridge that spans the torrent of the Portaikos where it issues from a cleft in the mountain wall. A little way up this natural gateway is the **Church of the Porta Panayia**. Lofty crags frame the gorge, their higher levels speckled with deciduous trees and, in the evening, the dark mysterious tunnel is filled with shifting shadows. Mulberry, plane and cypress surround the monastic walls.

The church was founded in 1283 by Ioannis Doukas, the rebellious illegitimate son of an Epirot Despot, who ruled over Neopatras, a medieval duchy with ill-defined borders in east central Greece. Doukas allied himself with the Vlach nomads, fought both the Franks and the Byzantine Emperor, married a Vlach, eventually became a monk and was buried in the church four years after its completion. Whether its foundation was a bid for salvation on his part must remain a matter of conjecture; few Byzantines, however unprincipled in worldly affairs, were without a deep mystical faith in the Orthodox Church.

The brickwork decoration of the exterior walls of the church consists of rosettes, squares, overlapping arches and rows of elongated Z-shaped forms: a kind of embellishment repeated more lavishly in a number of churches at Thessaloniki and Arta. After its foundation the church underwent major rebuilding in the fifteenth century to rectify earthquake damage; this has resulted in its present unusual configuration. A spacious narthex (probably a remodelling of the original *naos*), is crowned by a broad dome, its drum pierced by narrow elliptical windows. The frescoes, of a late period, are very damaged. The *naos*, of a later date than the original church, is in the form of a three-aisled basilica, the height of which is increased at the east end by a transverse vault instead of a dome. In spite of this curious juxtaposition of vaulted nave and domed narthex, an air of uniformity prevails. At the west end of the south wall there is a portrait of the founder, in the act of being introduced by an angel to the Virgin and Child. The Holy Door of the marble screen is flanked by two surviving mosaics of superior quality: late thirteenth-century figures, noble and austere, of the Virgin and Child (right) and Christ (left) - a deviation from the strict code of Byzantine iconography in which Christ is normally depicted on the right.

Beyond the church the defile contracts. The road from Pyli crosses the pass over which the Despots of Epirus rode from their capital at Arta to conquer the Thessalian Lowlands. A torrent is spanned by the elegant arch of a Turkish stone bridge, under a canopy of plane trees where nightingales sing. The bridge, like all those built by the Turks in remote parts of the country, is narrow, stepped and crescent-shaped, intended for the passage of a single man or beast. There is neither a parapet nor balustrade, and one needs to be immune to vertigo to cross the slender arch. There are simple hotels at Elati from which meadows stretch to the Pertouli fir forests below the Pindos range.

The road to the north-west from Trikkala towards Ioannina is also the route to the Meteora Monasteries, and the traveller who includes them in his itinerary is rewarded with one of the most extraordinary sights in Greece. After Kalambaka the road continues westward, crossing the Pindos at over seventeen hundred metres. The scenery is magnificent, all the way down to Metsovo and Ioannina, after which the road continues to Igoumenitsa on the Epirot coast.

The small town of **Kalambaka** spreads fan-wise round a huge projection of dark grey contorted rock which thrusts forward into the plain. Behind it extends the labyrinth of rock pillars crowned by the monasteries, whose eremitical origins and subsequent prosperity form part of the history of Byzantine monasticism. One monastery alone, *Ayios Stefanos*, is visible from the town, perched on the ridge of a lofty wall of rock with a smooth polished surface, slit at intervals by horizontal seams and honeycombed with caves and eyries. Over six hundred years ago a young monk named Athanassios, hearing of this wild place, crossed the mountain in search of the refuge it offered him. He had long sought a life of unremitting prayer for the salvation of men's souls, undisturbed by their physical presence. His quest was at an end; although hermits had preceded him, he was the founder of the first 'monastery in mid air'.

The screen of dolomites is omnipresent at Kalambaka; it seems to cast its reflection across the meadows and vineyards bordering the shingly bed of the Pinios like some sombre radiation from the interior of the rock itself. There are few amenities, other than hotels, petrol stations and a main square crowded with tourist coaches, but Kalambaka does possess a venerable Byzantine Church, **the Koimesis** (Dormition of the Virgin). A three-aisled basilica, it was built in the twelfth century on the foundations of an earlier place of worship. The stone canopy of the *ciborium* above the altar, carved with intricate foliate designs, has clearly been remade from more ancient materials; so has the imposing marble *ambo*, with its panels sculpted

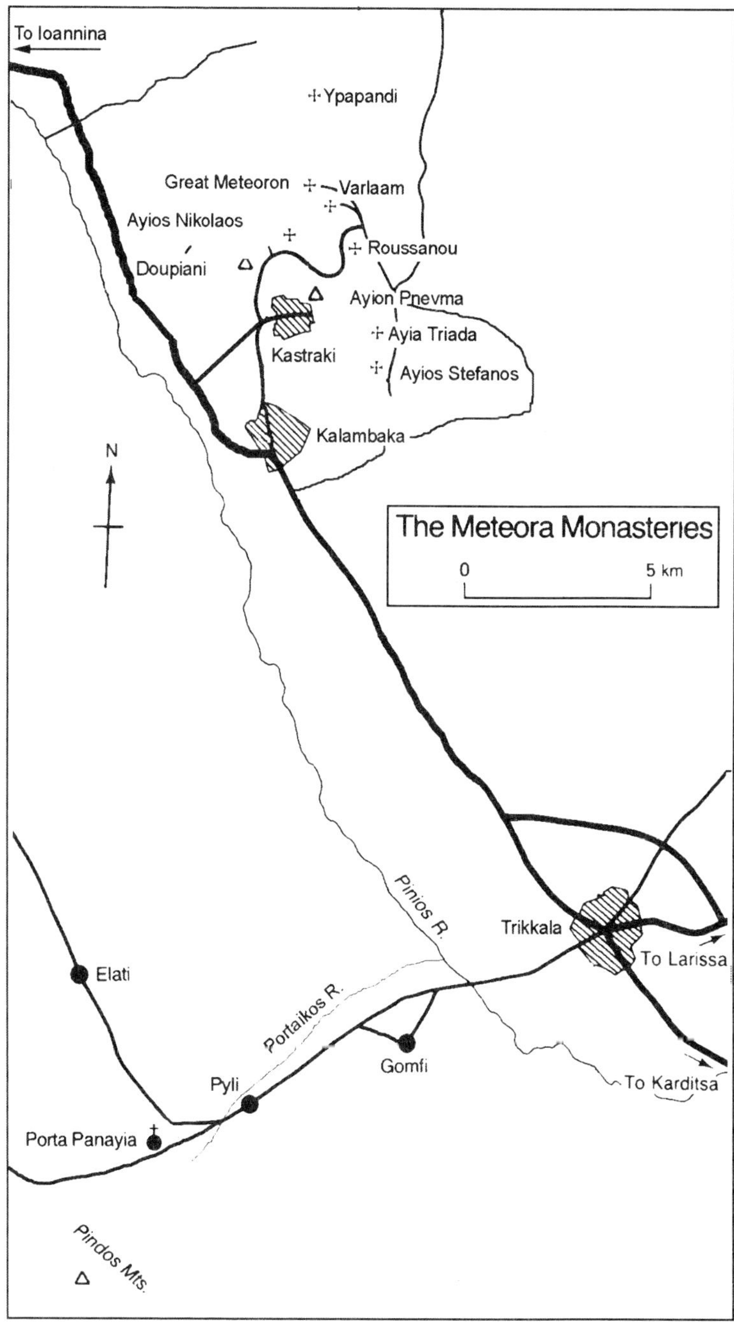

To Ioannina
Ypapandi
Great Meteoron
Varlaam
Ayios Nikolaos
Roussanou
Doupiani
Ayion Pnevma
Ayia Triada
Kastraki
Ayios Stefanos
Kalambaka
N
The Meteora Monasteries
0
5 km
Pinios R.
Trikkala
To Larissa
Elati
Portaikos R.
Gomfi
Pyli
To Karditsa
Porta Panayia
Pindos Mts.

with double crosses, its two staircases and hexagonal pulpit. The quality of the carving and opulence of the monument, which has been compared to the great *ambo* at San Clemente in Rome, suggests the prestige attached to the cathedral in the Byzantine ecclesiastical world. Among the icons there is a fine double-sided Crucifixion and Dormition. The frescoes, the work of sixteenth-century painters of the Cretan School, are blackened almost beyond recognition.

From Kalambaka the road curves round the so-called 'Black Rock' to the village of **Kastraki** sheltering among vineyards in the shade of a forest of towering pinnacles. On the lower levels the gaps between the rocks are covered with mulberries, oaks, cypresses and evergreen shrubs. Curzon, writing in the mid nineteenth-century, says '... the end of a range of rocky hills seems to have been broken off by some earthquake or washed away by the Deluge, leaving only a series of twenty or thirty tall, thin, needle-like rocks, many hundred feet in height; some like giant tusks, some shaped like pudding-loaves, and some like vast stalagmites.' A peculiar aspect of the rock formations, whose height varies between 200 and 300 metres, the way in which their surface is slit by both vertical and horizontal seams. The former have clearly been caused by the endless trickle of rain water, the latter, it is suggested, by the lapping of waves when the waters of the Thessalian lake beat against the cliffs.

Only five of the original thirteen **Meteora Monasteries** are still inhabited by small groups of monks or nuns (the numbers are actually growing) and they can all be visited in a single day. All the paraphernalia of an increasing tourist trade has not yet wholly succeeded in effacing the image of the strange life once led by the Byzantine solitaries and visionaries of Meteora nor in diminishing the grotesque splendour of the scene.

To the left of Kastraki rises the round-topped rock of **Doupiani**, studded with eyries, once scaled with ladders by the earliest hermits. Up there, far from the affairs of men, they communed with God and mortified their bodies. Deeming the flesh to be rank pollution, one monk left instructions that his mortal remains should be cast to birds of prey. Once a week the monks descended from their caves to worship communally in what is now a whitewashed chapel at the base of the cliff.

Above the village looms another huge pudding-shaped conglomerate mass, known as **Ayion Pnevma** (The Holy Ghost), crowned by two iron crosses. It is suggested that this was probably the pinnacle on which the young Athanassios first settled, but when demons were seen circling round his cave, he was persuaded to move to another rock, so lofty that even the forces of evil hesitated to scale it. Bit by bit, Athanassios climbed the formidable **Broad Rock** with the aid of ladders clamped one above another, choosing a cave - halfway up the modern zigzag stairway - as his first abode. The remains of a ladder, used by later inhabitants, still dangles from a wooden doorway overhanging the abyss. The sanctity of his life attracted so many disciples that he was finally persuaded to establish a community on the Broad Rock. A monastery thus grew up and came to be known as the Great Meteoron. No woman was allowed near it. Once, when the widow of the Serb 'Caesar' of Thessaly asked for Athanassios' blessing, he not only refused to approach her, but abused her roundly for being a woman and prophesied her imminent death; three months later she died. His successor Joasaph enlarged the church, and the monastery enjoyed a period of prosperity, which owed much to the munificence of Joasaph's sister, the engaging Maria Angelina, who married Thomas Preljubovic, the Serb tyrant, at the age of ten.

The road passes the **Monastery of Ayios Nikolaos** (to the left). The basilica, with partly restored sixteenth-century frescoes, is open although not occupied. The road continues past Roussanou on the right, then, after bearing left, ends at the **Great Meteoron**. One enters the Monastery by a steep, rock-hewn stairway. A wooden shed projects across the precipice. Here are the ropes, 124 feet long, by which men and provisions were originally hauled up. Describing his ascent, Curzon says 'the net was spread upon the floor and having sat down upon it cross-legged, the four corners were gathered over my head, and attached to a hook at the end of the rope. All being ready, the monks at the capstan took a few steps round, the effect of which was to lift me off the floor and launch me out of the door right into the sky, with an impetus which kept me swinging backwards and forwards at a fearful rate; when the oscillation had in some measure ceased, the abbot and another monk, leaning out of the door, steadied me with their hands, and I was let down slowly and gently to the ground'.

The interior of the **Church of the Metamorphosis** is spacious and unusually high. The candelabra, pulpits and iconostasis, crowned by a large Crucifixion in an ornamental cross-shaped gilt frame, heighten the atmosphere of brilliance created by the recently-restored frescoes, the work of late fifteenth-century Athonite artists. There is little subtlety of colour tone, and although the figures sometimes strike agile, even acrobatic, attitudes, they remain basically static. The large narthex, supported by four columns, is somewhat dark. The frescoes, fussy and full of stylistic mannerisms, are of a later date - the usual blood-curdling Last Judgement, and full-length portraits of Athanassios, founder of the monastery, and Joasaph, his successor, holding a model of the church: gaunt figures in long black beards.

The icons in the treasury are more interesting than the frescoes. After the fall of Constantinople, Byzantine fresco-painters seem to have been incapable of inspiration on the grand scale. No great churches were built during the post-Byzantine period; consequently demand for the painting of large wall-surfaces virtually ceased to exist. But the icon-painter, working in a less expensive medium, preserved, developed and revitalized the best elements of the old tradition. Western influences crept in and enriched narrative iconography. At the Great Meteoron there are several outstanding examples, ranging from the fourteenth to the sixteenth centuries, including an **Incredulity of Thomas**, with a perky Maria Angelina in royal robes, amongst the apostles, who are gazing at Thomas or chattering among themselves; a boyish **St Dimitrios** thrusting his javelin into the leader of a Bulgar host besieging Thessaloniki; a **Baptism**, with Christ immersed in the waters of the Jordan while St John baptises him and angels bear him towels. Equally attractive are the five Menoloyion (Calendar) icons, with lists of saints' feasts painted on gold backgrounds: typical examples of sixteenth-century painting in miniature.

The refectory, separated from the church by a courtyard with cypress trees, has a vaulted roof supported by five elegant columns. Below it were stored the enormous wine barrels drawn up by windlass. Water was supplied from cisterns hewn out of the rock.

The view from the Great Meteoron is astonishing. Twisted spectral forms, scarred and rutted, tapering into pinpoint cones, isolate the winding boulder-strewn chasm from the outside world. Occasional gaps between the rocks afford glimpses of the plain beyond and its welcome cultivated domesticity.

By the fifteenth century the number of monastic settlements had increased and, during the death agony of Byzantium, the 'monasteries in mid-air' became asylums of Hellenism and Orthodoxy, where monks could commune with God and invoke his blessing on Greek arms, undisturbed by Ottoman armies advancing across the plain below. After the Turkish conquest there was a marked deterioration in monastic morals. At one monastery a cross-eyed monk had the effrontery to introduce two women, dressed as monks, to serve as his 'companions'. For a time the Great Meteoron was ruled by a contemptible abbot in the pay of the Turks, and for his sin of treachery to the Hellenic cause (always synonymous with that of Christian Orthodoxy), he was cursed and sent into exile. When he died, his body remained uncorrupted - a sign of God's displeasure. From the seventeenth century onwards, looting, sale and fraud robbed the churches of much treasure.

All that remain of the inaccessible Monastery of *Ypsilotera* (The Highest One), which crowns an offshoot of the Broad Rock, are an image of two saints painted on the rock and traces of a wooden ladder hanging from a narrow projection just below the summit. The ruins of the little Monastery of *Ayios Ioannis Prodromos*, uninhabited for over two hundred years, are scattered across the ridge of a vertically slit hump. More spectacular is a completely detached monolith soaring skyward, capped now by nothing but a debris of wood and stone, once the Monastery of *Ayia Moni*; this and Prodromos are inaccessible.

North of the Broad Rock a path leads between misshapen tusks and perpendicular cliffs, seamed like organ pipes, to the rock of the **Ypapandi** (Presentation in the Temple). The monastery, long abandoned but partially restored, is situated in a cave halfway up the cliff, reached by a stone stairway. The tiny domeless church is decorated with frescoes of the late thirteenth to mid-fifteenth centuries. Icons adorn the elaborately-carved *iconostasis* of gilded wood.

Taking the road back a short distance, we reach the terrible abyss which separates the Broad Rock from a magnificent obelisk, on which the **Monastery of Varlaam** is perched, soaring out of a mass of bulbous rock. The retreat of a fourteenth-century anchorite who gave his name to the monastery, it later housed such valuable relics as a finger of St John and the shoulder blade of St Andrew. The church was founded by two brothers, Theofanes and Nektarios. The monks of the Great Meteoron lent them mules to carry stones to the base of the rock; but records of how the materials for the original windlass were hauled up are tantalizingly absent. The two brothers imposed a strict discipline on their disciples, partaking once a day of bread, beans and water, and praying half the night. Theofanes, avid for mortification, wore an iron chain tight round his waist, next to the skin. Shortly before he died - it was the hour of sunset and the day of the church's completion - he stretched himself on a couch, carefully arranging his limbs in the shape of a cross.

Varlaam, now reached easily across a bridge, is more animated than the other monasteries, with a number of mostly elderly monks going about their devotions and chores. The monastery buildings are in disorder, but the walls, eaves and roofs seem to grow organically out of the bluish-grey rock. They are capped by a church with two tiled domes resting on octagonal drums. A labyrinth of rotting floor-boards and worn paving-stones leads to deserted cells. One storeroom contains a barrel nearly six metres high with a diameter of two metres, which must have sorely taxed the strength of the monks at the capstan when it was originally hauled up. The disused shed where the contraption was kept, buttressed by masonry, projects like some abandoned crumbling belvedere above the ravine.

In the **Church of Ayion Pandon** (All Saints) the sixteenth-century frescoes, restored in the eighteenth century and again recently, depict the familiar scenes from the Dodekaorton. Everywhere there are swirling draperies, huddled buildings, martyrs, hermits, soldiers, the gold of haloes, the flash of swords, the reds and purples of ecclesiastical vestments. In the narthex the mourners in the **Dormition of Efraim the Syrian** are ranged round the saint's body like crude prototypes of El Greco's grandees at the funeral of Count Orgaz (painted a quarter of a century later). In the monastery museum there is a small Book of Gospels, once the property of the Emperor Constantine VII (913-959), and a fine icon of the Virgin and Child surrounded by angels and apostles in robes of pale mauve, dark green and indigo, by Tzanes, the sixteenth-century iconographer.

After Varlaam we take the road back to **Roussanou**: a small monolith crowned by three storeys of seemingly inaccessible masonry. Never one of the more flourishing monasteries, Roussanou, when visited by Curzon in 1834, was inhabited by two half-mad crones who refused to let the rope ladder down to the English traveller, preferring to jabber frenziedly at each other and shriek curses. The modern traveller is assured of a more courteous welcome from the few nuns who inhabit the quite recently re-opened convent. Scenes of martyrdom of unparalleled cruelty decorate the walls of the narthex of the church, dedicated to St Barbara.

More impressive than Roussanou is the **Monastery of Ayia Triada**, to reach which one goes back a short distance towards

Varlaam, then turns right. The balconies and arcades of Ayia Triada project above a rock shaped like a rolling-pin. A cave in the rock, halfway up the stone stairway, contains a little chapel decorated with crude paintings of ascetic saints. The exterior of the church, though spoilt by a large, ill-proportioned narthex, is ornamented with brickwork designs and the cypresses and shrubs growing around it create a pleasant rustic effect.

The road then emerges from the valley and runs along the ridge of an escarpment to the **Monastery (Convent) of Ayios Stefanos**, separated from the main rock formation by a narrow chasm spanned by a bridge. The change of scene is remarkable. Nothing towers overhead anymore. The horizon is clear. The monastic buildings are, as usual, crowned by the one rotund and two slender drums of the church which has little, architecturally, to recommend it. In relation to their commanding position on this great bastion overlooking the plain, the toy cupolas and untidy houses seem insignificant. The church still possesses treasures: a silver reliquary containing the head of St Haralambos, whose healing powers are said to have staved off many pestilences, and an *iconostasis* and bishop's throne of lavishly-carved woodwork with designs of flowers, cranes pecking at vipers and little creatures swinging censers, all meticulously executed in the fussy high relief typical of Epirot carving of the late eighteenth century. A small chapel, hewn out of the rock, with an apse suspended on the brink, is reached through an abandoned refectory. Near the doorway is a portrait of a white-bearded monk holding a scroll: the fifteenth century founder of the monastery, a certain Antonios, of the imperial family of Kantakouzenos. Today the chief glory of *Ayios Stefanos* is the view from the terrace across the narrowing valley to the dark masses of the Pindos mountains. Hundreds of feet below, at the base of the cliff, are the box-like houses of Kalambaka. Southward the plain extends in a soporific haze. There is only one way back to Kalambaka - the way you came.

In his account of the Meteora monasteries, Curzon says that Greek monks seem to be obsessed by 'everything hideous and horrible'. His choice of adjectives is open to question, but one does see what he means. At Meteora, the violence of the geographical upheaval seems to be reflected in those 'hideous' mortifications of the flesh which Byzantine ascetics considered to be the necessary stepping-stones to salvation. It is also interesting to note that there is not a single reference to the rock formations of Meteora in classical literature. The ancient Greeks were not impressed by wonders of nature - not unless they could relate them to some visible or symbolic association with a human entity or agency.

12

The Approach to Macedonia

NO TRAVELLER in Northern Greece can - or should - avoid Macedonia, the largest and richest province in the country. Thessaloniki, the capital, is usually approached from Larissa along the northbound National Road; including stops, and two worthwhile deviations to Ambelakia and Dion, the distance is easily covered in less than a day.

The Pinios, now joined by the muddy Titarissios, meanders in S-shaped loops across the north-eastern apex of the plain, which is studded with brown, cone-shaped hills. To the east rises Mount Ossa, whose quarries once supplied verd-antique and serpentine to the workshops of Roman architects and sculptors. Twenty-seven kilometres north of Larissa, shortly before the Vale of Tempe, a road to the right climbs to the village of **Ambelakia**. On the last turn but one before entering the village there is a fine backward view of the cone-shaped hills vanishing into the haze. The immediate foreground is filled by an abrupt spur of Lower Olympos, across which extends the village of Rapsani, famous for its red wine.

In the late eighteenth century Ambelakia was the site of the first co-operative in Greece. It was founded by local weavers and dyers, who used the madder grown on Mount Ossa for dying their yarn a particularly attractive shade of red. The chemical composition of the abundant waters of Ambelakia added a glossy hue to the finished product, which was exported to the markets of Europe. With the ascendancy of the Manchester cotton industry and the discovery of aniline dyes, the importance of Ambelakia and its co-operative declined. It is now rather a ramshackle place, open to the mountain breezes; so near, and yet off, the beaten track, and where one is seldom out of earshot of running water.

From the main square it is no distance to the eighteenth-century **Schwarz House**, once the property of a Hellenized Viennese family, now a museum. The constant menace of brigandage and the fear of punitive forays by Turkish soldiers account for the heavy wrought-iron grilles protecting the few windows. The ground floor, formerly used for commercial transactions, with the accountant sitting in an enclosure shut off by a wooden balustrade, consists of a wide, vaulted room with alcoves. The walls are painted with decorative designs which create an illusion of fluted columns. The wall paintings of the living quarters on the T-shaped first floor include an array of cornucopias filled with carnations and a fanciful evocation of the Bosphorus.

The high-ceilinged top floor, also T-shaped, is virtually one vast reception room with alcoves, in which the distinguished dyers and weavers of Ambelakia were entertained in style. Numerous wooden pillars crowned by carved capitals conjure up an image of colonnades receding into a succession of subsidiary chambers. On the walls are painted imaginary landscapes, flowers and foliate patterns of twigs and drooping branches. Everywhere the Turkish genius for creating a feeling of spaciousness is reflected in this work of Greek architects schooled in Islamic lay architecture. The stained glass windows are of Viennese provenance. The entire house, with its finely wrought woodwork of turned railings and corniced pillars, is a triumphant combination of architectural and decorative styles: an amalgam of the minor arts of post-Byzantium and Islam, with a touch of middle class, early-nineteenth-century Vienna thrown in. To the uninitiated traveller, it serves as a curtain-raiser to the more impressive, if less well-preserved, eighteenth-century houses of Western Macedonia.

Back on the main road one is soon at the Tembi toll-gate. Just before the tree-fringed Pinios forces its way through the mountain barrier stands a recently restored Turkish mosque where, in spring, storks perch on the dome. Here the Ottoman Government's envoys, after passing through the **Vale of Tempe**, would pause to worship before entering the plain to impose new taxes on their Greek subjects. The narrow eight-kilometre gorge, separating Olympos from Ossa, was believed by the ancient Greeks to have been cut by Poseidon's trident. Home of the laurel, Tempe was associated with the worship of Apollo; every nine years a delegation of aristocratic youths would march through the vale in procession, accompanied by a flute-player, to gather the sacred laurel destined for the god's oracular seat in Delphi. The mountain sides are steep, almost vertical, covered with dark evergreens; a mass of gnarled plane trees border Homer's 'sylvan eddies', which have become rather muddy with the passage of time. Tempe does not compare with any of the great gorges of Greece, although its importance, linking the Balkans through Macedonia with the Thessalian enclave and thence the whole of Central and Southern Greece, was appreciated by the Romans, who built a military highway, roughly followed by the present railway and road.

At the eastern outlet the change of scene is striking. Northward extends a cultivated strip, an unbroken coastline and the blue expanse of the Thermaic Gulf, into which two large rivers pour their mud and silt. This is Macedonia. A new climate. After Tempe the air is never so crystalline again, the outlines of the mountains never so sharp and dramatic, the sea and sky never so vivid a blue. There is no lack of historical sites and associations. But it is Philip and Alexander and their successors who dominate the scene.

On a bluff to the right, rise the ruins of the Crusader castle of **Platamonas**, which the Lombards lost to the Epirot Despot, Theodore Angelos, in 1218. After a brief but violent siege, the defenders fell from the castle walls 'like birds from their nests', in the words of a contemporary ecclesiastic. The well-preserved walls of the triangular enceinte, dominated by a fine octagonal tower, are outlined against the wooded hills sloping down to the village of Pandeleimonas with its sandy beach. To the north there is a string of beach resorts, and on the main road there are several hotels suitable for breaking a journey. From now on the backward views of **Mount Olympos** are superb. For the first time one is able to associate the celebrated mountain with the home of the gods. Its contours are more awesome than beautiful. Forests of oak, chestnut and beech spread across the middle slopes. In the afternoon, shafts of sunlight fill the ravines, creating new perspectives, and great precipices fall from dizzy altitudes to the plain below. Through one towering glen there is a glimpse of the Throne of Zeus, thrusting its peak into the vault of heaven itself. But as often as not the traveller will see none of this. The gods still like to conceal their celestial abode in a blanket of cloud. Those wishing to visit Olympos should take the branch road to Litohoro, whence the ascent to the Throne of Zeus begins.

Hellenistic Macedonia, over which the figure of Alexander the Great looms so large, begins at a signpost pointing west, to the ruins of **Dion**, originally a sacred city, later a huge military camp where Philip and his son trained their troops. The remains are largely of later Roman buildings, which follow (with additions) the original Hellenistic ground plan. So far, fourteen paved roads have been uncovered in the well-planned, strongly fortified city.

When in Archaic times it was a sacred city, the earth-goddess, Demeter, held sway. Her two small early temples (c. 500 BC) were later replaced by a larger Hellenistic building. Subsequently, Zeus was dominant and the city was named after him (Dios is the genative of Zeus); at his sanctuary, inscriptions were set up referring to important affairs of state, for the information of the pilgrim crowds. Aphrodite Hypolimpidia (Below Olympia) was worshipped in a small, graceful temple where her cult-statue, now in the museum, was found. Dionysos was also honoured near the Hellenistic theatre, built, like the stadium, by King Archelaos who caused the religious festivals to be enlivened with athletic and theatrical performances. Livy and Pausanias refer to the number of statues that embellished the paved ways, including Lysippos' famous bronze group of twenty-five horsemen, commissioned by Alexander to commemorate his favourite Companions who fell in the battle of the Granicus.

In the fourth century Philip was in the habit of celebrating his victories here with games and contests. Later the camp was the scene of Alexander's sacrifices before he crossed into Asia. In the course of the accompanying athletic and musical contests he entertained a hundred of his Companions in a magnificent marquee which accommodated a hundred couches. And all the time the drilling of the troops went on, the camp echoing with the din created by the marching phalanx, each of whose members was armed with a long spear and short sword, a shield large enough to protect the whole body, a helmet, a coat of mail and greaves. No foreign army had as yet faced such a solid, impenetrable front. When going into action it was said to resemble a giant porcupine unfolding its erectile spines.

The Romans continued the tradition and maintained Dion as a military encampment from where they could easily deploy their legions across the northern plain. In the Early Christian era Dion was a bishop's see, and the chants of pious choristers echoed through the basilicas raised on the ruins of the officer's messes which had once witnessed the drunken orgies of the young Alexander and his friends. Then came Alaric's visitation and a final devastating earthquake; Dion ceased to exist.

The site, which is divided into two halves by a modern road, is well arranged for the visitor: there are paved paths, occasional shelters and bridges over some of the more interesting remains. Water is everywhere, frogs croak and the wind rustles pleasantly in the trees. From the main entrance (which is in the South-Easterly section) signposted paths lead to the Hellenistic theatre which has been partially restored for use, the ruins of the Sanctuary of Zeus, the Roman theatre and other lesser remains. The two theatres were intended for pilgrims rather than for the inhabitants, as in the other principal Greek sacred towns. The Sanctuary of Zeus is not very impressive, considering his importance, but in 1999 an Altar of Zeus was identified with tethering rings for 33 sacrificial bulls.

The path continues along the canal, past a small ancient harbour, to the elegant Sanctuary of Isis, Hellenistic tolerance having allowed the superimposition of Isis on Artemis following Ptolemaic religious propagation.

Due to a rise in the water-level after an earthquake, the Sanctuary was preserved from pillage by a thick layer of mud. Excavation has been slow and difficult but the finds have included two cult-statues, which were still standing among the Ionic columns.

It is pleasant to rest amid the shaded bracken, where the Macedonian cavalry, largely composed of upper class Thessalian young men renowned for their horsemanship, also probably rested after training. It was somewhere near here too that Philip, while celebrating his presumptuously named 'Olympian' Games, bought a prize black stallion from a Thessalian horsebreeder. But the animal, with a lock of white hair across its forehead and branded with an ox-head, plunged and reared, proving totally intractable to the cajolings of even the most experienced horsemen. Plutarch tells the story of how Philip glanced, half-smiling, half-mocking, at the eight-year-old Alexander who was staring intently at the prancing steed. Approaching it unhesitatingly and realizing that it was only frightened by its own shadow, the boy turned it directly towards the sun and, after gently stroking the sleek black flanks, with 'one nimble leap securely mounted him ... and let him go at full speed'. There was no mishap. Philip, squinting out of his one eye, cried 'Oh my son, look thee out for a kingdom equal to and worthy of thyself, for Macedonia is too little to hold thee.' The boy named the horse Bukephalos (Ox-Head), and it accompanied him throughout his campaigns. A city in the upper Indus valley was named after it and, when it died of old age, the horse was accorded a state funeral. Fidelity to his loved ones was one of Alexander's more attractive traits.

Returning from the Sanctuary of Isis towards the main entrance one comes to the extensive Sanctuary of Demeter, which includes two very small 6th Century BC temples; among the earliest buildings so far found at Dion.

A small gate leads across the modern road to the entrance to the main site, among big trees. First comes the marble city gate, looking up the wide paved main street; to the left and right there are clearly discernible remains of massive walls with square towers. After the gateway there are shops on your left, and a small climb takes you to the Roman Odeion, beyond which are the huge Public baths. Several of the mosaic floors are in place, as well as the hypocaust system of the calidarium. A unique group of statues representing the six sons and daughters of Asclepios was found in the northern part of the baths.

A little way to the north from the baths are the remains of a large early Christian basilica, including a mosaic pavement bordered by a red, black and white geometrical design. The western walls are a short way beyond. Going eastward along a cross-street past partly dug areas of houses and shops, and crossing the 'main' street, one comes to the very grand **Villa of Dionysos**, revealed in 1987, with its several courts and marvellous floor mosaic of Dionysos on a chariot pulled by leopards with a young centaur on either side. There is a wide protective roof, and it is fenced in - you need someone to open the gate. Four statues of seated philosophers, unfortunately headless, were found in the Villa.

There are many excavated areas of lesser interest, and others where digs are incomplete that are not open to the public. The site is very large but, little by little, the whole area is being cleared. Returning from the Villa to the entrance, there is, on the right, a fine supporting wall with a frieze of warriors and shields. Opposite the main entrance and outside the walls is a new excavation of what is thought to be a royal villa.

The **Museum**, which is being doubled in size in view of the steady stream of finds, is in the village, just up from the hotel (a very pleasant spot for a stopover). The family of Asclepios is here, and the four seated philosophers, as well as various statues of Aphrodite Hypolympidia, who was worshipped in association with Isis. Many of the statues have that languid softness often found in Hellenistic art.

The great number of Macedonian coins found in the mound that covered the Greek theatre is displayed here, as well as votive offerings, small bronzes (note the older man with a stick over his shoulder, and the intrepid hunter apparently strangling a lion). The most unusual exhibit is a small water-operated pipe organ (Hydraulis) dating to the 1st Century AD, the most complete example ever found.

After the turning to Dion, the National Road runs further inland and, from Katerini (to which you can also go directly from Dion), it is more interesting to take the old main road, just inland from the new one. It takes a little longer to reach Thessaloniki but it is less monotonous, rising and dipping between the hummocks of a rolling green countryside dotted with prosperous villages.

Near Kitros a turning to the east leads to the site, on the coast, of ancient **Pydna**, where the passionate Olympias, Alexander's mother, was stabbed to death by order of Kassandros during the murderous wars between her son's successors. Here too the forces of Perseus, last king of Macedonia, were routed by Aemilius Paulus in a battle begun after an eclipse of the moon predicted by a Roman officer, expert in astronomy. The natural phenomenon struck such terror into the hearts of the black-frocked Thracians, mercenaries of the Macedonian king, that they fled dementedly, wailing loudly and beating their burnished shields. In this famous engagement, the scarlet-coated Macedonian phalanx was finally routed by Aemilius Paulus' experienced generalship and a formidable charge by the Roman elephants. Livy has left an account of the way in which the Romans transported the terrified animals down the precipices of Olympos, lowering them by means of a succession of broad planks, supported by wooden posts, used like drawbridges on different levels. Once they reached the low ground the great lumbering beasts felt more at home, and the thunder of their stampede across the plain, already alive, Plutarch says, 'with the flashing of steel and the glistening of brass', was decisive. The battle of Pydna (168 BC) tipped the balance. In a matter of hours, Aemilius Paulus, the Roman patrician, was master of the moribund Macedonian kingdom, a Greek defeat that opened the way to the East for Roman arms.

After Kitros there is **Methone**, where Philip lost the sight of an eye while besieging the Athenians in their last colonial stronghold in Northern Greece (354-3 BC). He allowed the inhabitants to leave the city with no more than one garment on their backs and distributed their lands among his Macedonian henchmen. Very little has been found of either Pydna or Methone.

After the village of Methoni the old road goes inland and you should rejoin the National Road which sweeps round the head of the

Thermaic Gulf. The Aliakmon River is crossed near its mouth. Higher up, at the old bridge, the British Commonwealth Expeditionary Force made an unsuccessful attempt to stem the Nazi onrush in 1941. Real rivers, rising in the Balkan highlands, now replace the oleander-bordered streams of Thessaly. The traffic increases and the flat monotony of corn, rice, sunflower and beet fields gives way to the factories on the outskirts of Thessaloniki.

13

Thessaloniki: The Second City

IN ROMAN TIMES travellers passed through the Golden Gate into what is now **Platia Vardari (Dimokratias)**. From here **Egnatia Street** crosses the city centre in a south-easterly direction, roughly following the ancient Via Egnatia, which began on the Adriatic and ended on the Hellespont and was marked throughout with milestones commemorating the names of deified emperors. Triumphal arches spanned the highway; under them marched the legions, bearers of Roman law and order in exchange for oriental riches. Here in Turkish times Edward Lear watched peasants bringing goods for sale 'in carts drawn by white-eyed buffali'. Trucks loaded with fruit and vegetables have replaced the wild oxen of the Macedonian plains, and instead of a mob of 'blackamoors and Jewesses', office and factory workers now thread their way through the congested traffic. In fact traffic is so bad that visitors with cars are recommended to stay outside the city.

For over thirteen centuries Thessaloniki has held the rank of second city of the Greek world: second after Constantinople in the Byzantine period and after Athens in modern times. Founded by Kassandros in 315 BC on the site of ancient Therma, where Xerxes stayed in the summer of 480 BC while his fleet cruised in the gulf, it later served as a refuge for the exiled Cicero; St Paul too had an affection for the inhabitants. For a time it was to Thessaloniki, strategically situated at the outlet of the Balkan trade routes, that Constantine the Great contemplated transferring the capital of the Empire; when his choice fell on Byzantium, the chagrin of the inhabitants was equal only to their indignation that such a prize should go to an upstart colony on the Bosphorus. By the end of the fourth century however, with the triumph of Christianity assured, the city's course was fixed: scene of countless sieges and hair-splitting theological disputes, it was destined, under the protection of its patron saint, Dimitrios, to play an eventful and often heroic role in Byzantine affairs.

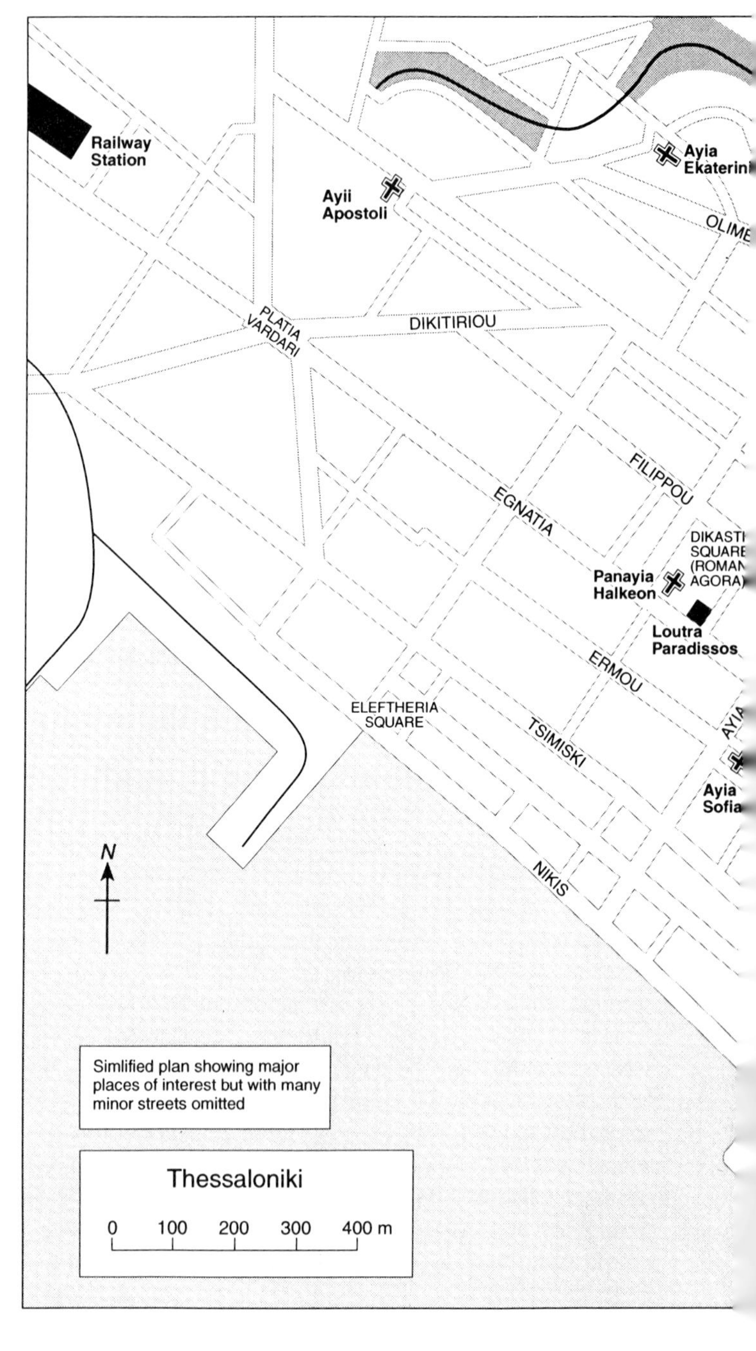

Railway Station
Ayii Apostoli
Ayia Ekaterini
OLIMB
PLATIA VARDARI
DIKITIRIOU
FILIPPOU
EGNATIA
DIKASTI SQUARE (ROMAN AGORA)
Panayia Halkeon
Loutra Paradissos
ERMOU
ELEFTHERIA SQUARE
TSIMISKI
AYIA
Ayia Sofia
NIKIS
N
Simlified plan showing major places of interest but with many minor streets omitted
Thessaloniki
0 100 200 300 400 m

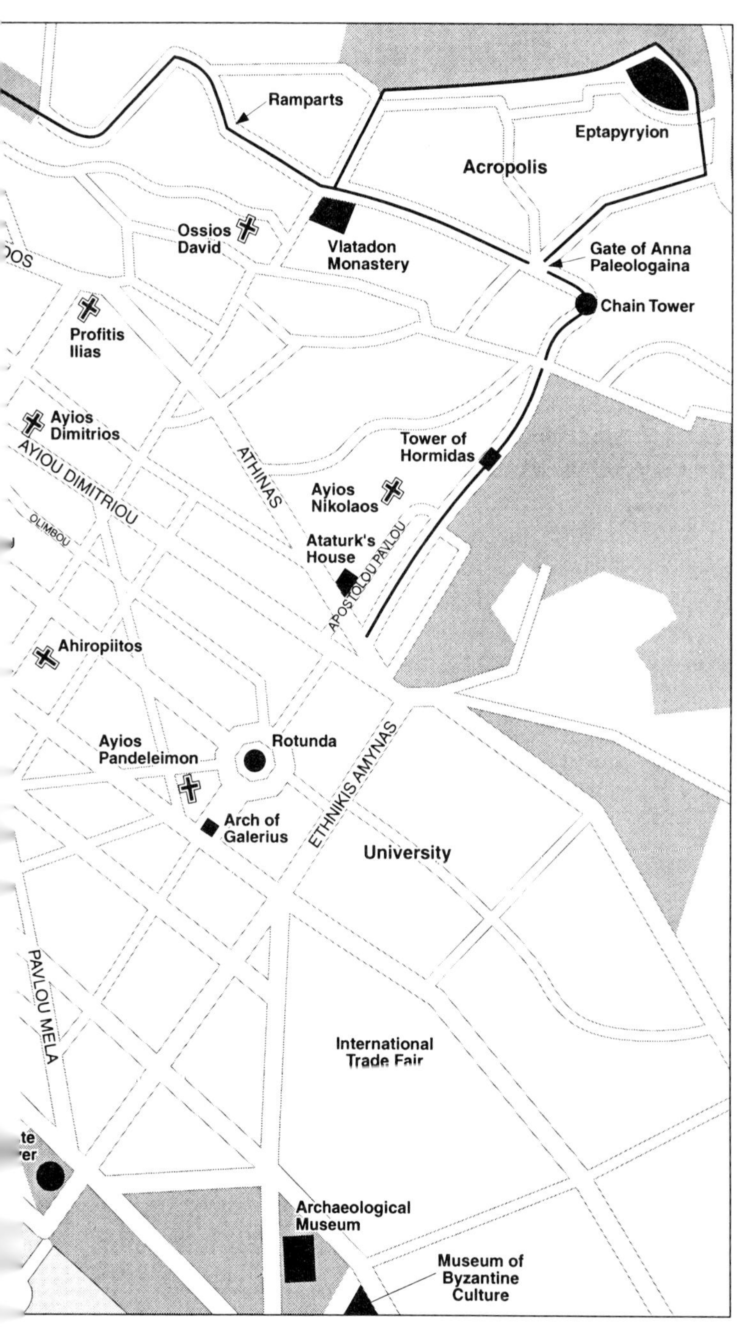

Ramparts
Eptapyryion
Acropolis
Ossios
David
Vlatadon
Monastery
Gate of Anna
Paleologaina
Chain Tower
Profitis
Ilias
Ayios
Dimitrios
AYIOU DIMITRIOU
ATHINAS
Tower of
Hormidas
Ayios
Nikolaos
OLIMBOU
Ataturk's
House
APOSTOLOU PAVLOU
Ahiropiitos
Ayios
Pandeleimon
Rotunda
ETHNIKIS AMYNAS
Arch of
Galerius
University
PAVLOU MELA
International
Trade Fair
Archaeological
Museum
Museum of
Byzantine
Culture

The modern city, not liberated from the Turks until the conclusion of the First Balkan War in 1913, is strung out along a grid of parallel and intersecting streets between the hills and the sea. Uniquely well-preserved basilicas and domed Byzantine churches, among the most important in the country, provide an air of mellowness to an otherwise wholly urban prospect. Parallel to Egnatia Street runs **Tsimiski Street**, the main shopping quarter, its pavements bordered with horse-chestnut trees. The food is better than elsewhere in the country, and the confectioners are crowded with Thessalonikian ladies devouring cream cakes and oriental pastries. There are hotels for every purse, but because of the International Trade Fair and the Greek Film Festival, it is essential to reserve accommodation between late August and mid-November. The climate is one of extremes. In winter icy winds funnel through the Balkan valleys and fog is not unknown. In summer a pall of torrid humidity hangs over the tall new blocks stretching round the bay towards the eastern suburbs.

For many travellers Thessaloniki is, above all, a Byzantine pilgrimage. The traveller in a hurry can look briefly at the mosaics of *Ayios Dimitrios* and visit *Ayia Sofia* (as well, of course, as the Museum), but the Byzantine enthusiast should allow three days and visit the twelve most important churches. The evolution of styles, architectural and decorative, covers the whole span of Byzantine history and the proposed itinerary, a little round-about, is roughly chronological. Roman ruins and Byzantine monuments are all enclosed within a horseshoe-shaped enceinte of Byzantine ramparts with Turkish additions.

It is best to begin at the end of the waterfront, at the cafés among the shrubberies below the **White Tower**, the only surviving fort of the maritime defences. Within the circular walls of the tower a body of mutinous Janissaries, swollen from a praetorian guard into a power-hungry rabble, were put to the sword in 1826, when Sultan Mahmud II the Reformer carried out a wholesale liquidation of this increasingly reactionary corps. The 'Bloody Tower', as it came to be known, has now been put to rather more peaceable use, housing an interesting small museum of religious art. On the landward side of the tower there is a public garden speckled with the peony-like flowers of Syrian hibiscus, their large curled petals creating a spangled effect against the dark green bushes on moonlit nights.

To the north of the gardens lie the grounds of the International Trade Fair (held every September), whose origins go back to a medieval market held on St Dimitrios's day to promote the city's handicrafts. Facing the gardens is the **Archaeological Museum,** housed in a well-designed modern building. The wide range of exhibits, both as regards style and provenance, reflects the proximity of those parts of northern Greece which have done so much to shape the history and character of Thessaloniki.

There are the usual ancient vases, greaves, weapons, terracottas, animal figurines, bronze kraters with mouldings of sphinxes and grotesque theatrical masks; all, or mostly all, of Macedonian provenance. They make nonsense of the once-popular belief that the 'barbarous north' was incapable of producing first-class craftsmen. But the museum is, above all, a treasure house of the Hellenistic objects of intricate workmanship found in Macedonian tombs.

Wonderful as the famous finds from Veryina (now back at Veryina) are, they do not completely eclipse other great finds made earlier, such as the gold objects from the cemetery at Sindos, now an industrial suburb of Thessaloniki, and, above all, the **Derveni krater**. The bronze surface of this huge urn is covered with appliqué silver-gilt figures in a crowded bacchanalian procession: prowling animals intermingle with human forms striking ecstatic attitudes, vine tendrils terminate in ornate leaves and maidens and youths recline gracefully below the lip of the vessel. One moves round the glittering object with increasing fascination. Attributed to Lysippos, one of the great Peloponnesian sculptors and a contemporary of Alexander the Great, the Derveni krater possesses all the natural ebullience of Hellenistic art before the elegance and discipline inherited from the Classical age was tarnished by over-sumptuousness and florid ostentation.

Among the other interesting objects in the museum is the series of small **stelae of the Thracian Horseman**, funerary or votive offerings to a primitive cult figure who exercised a profound influence on the national consciousness. The horse was the emblem of the Scythians whose territory bordered that of Thrace. Consequently, the religious cults of both peoples possessed many points in common. In the early carvings, roughly modelled in shallow relief, the enigmatic Horseman is represented as a hunter holding a spear and galloping towards a tree, around which a snake is coiled. Later the heroic hunter assumes a semi-divine character and is depicted crowned with a wreath. In Roman times he wears military dress. In the Early-Christian period the memory of him helped to mould the popular image of St Dimitrios. He is still mounted, but now proceeds in stately fashion towards an altar crowned by a pine-cone in front of the serpent-entwined tree. A composite figure, probably some father-figure of the Thracian race, he is also part Asclepios, god of healing, whose emblem was the snake that possessed curative properties, part Rhesos, leader of the Thracian contingent in the Trojan War.

Nearby is the new Museum of Byzantine Culture in a very spacious, and still rather empty, new building. It will, in due course, house a fine collection of Byzantine art, including much that was taken to Athens seventy years ago to be housed in the Byzantine Museum, and has now been returned permanently to Thessaloniki. Among the items returned is the beautiful and celebrated **epitafios** of Thessaloniki: an exquisite fourteenth-century embroidery depicting the Lamentation over the body of Christ. At once a technical *tour de force* and a masterpiece of one of the minor arts, it is composed of three panels, with the outstretched body dominating the middle one. The figures are woven with gold and silver threads and stencilled with blues and greens against a gold background; the stitches are so varied that they create an impression of constantly changing colours.

At present, and for some time to come, there is only a fairly small, but extremely interesting Paleo-Christian exhibition. Among the striking objects on display are a sixth-century wall-painting of St Kosmas and St Damian from the Agora, some fine painted tomb chambers and two small statues, late Roman in style, of a youthful Christ with a lamb over His shoulders - 'The Good Shepherd'.

From the museums it is five minutes' walk to the junction of Ethnikis Amynas and Egnatia Streets, with the Aristotelian University on the right. All this area, which once formed part of a vast imperial compound of palace, circus and mausoleum, is now a commercial and residential quarter, dominated by the **Arch of Galerius**, the Dacian shepherd who became a Roman Emperor - and not a very attractive one. The south-east half of what was once a double gateway has gone, as also has the south-west pier of the other half, but the middle piers survive, carved with stone reliefs of puny figures devoid of grace or individuality. An unimpressive replica of the great triumphal arches of Rome, it was probably considered good enough for a provincial capital. The sculptures tell the story of the success of Roman arms against the Parthians in the early fourth century.

To the south-east of the arch extended the circus, scene of a horrible massacre in the year 390. The most popular charioteer of the day courted the favours of a boy slave of Botheric, the hated Gothic commander of the local garrison. Shocked by the laxity of Mediterranean morals, Botheric imprisoned the charioteer, whose outraged followers promptly murdered the commander and his officers, their bodies being dragged through the streets amid scenes of great acclamation. The prudish but choleric Emperor Theodosios the Great, who relied on his Gothic commanders for discipline in the army, ordered a swift and savage retaliation. The people of Thessaloniki were summoned to the circus to applaud the released charioteer. The exits were barred and Theodosios' troops fell on the unsuspecting crowd with drawn swords. According to Gibbon, the carnage lasted for three hours; at a conservative estimate seven thousand Thessalonikians had been slaughtered.

The area between the Arch and the seafront contains many other reminders of Galerius, most notably his once sumptuous palace between Gounari Street and Platia Navarino. Recently more of it has been exposed to the west, including an octagonal hall, possibly the throne room. Along the north side is a very long court with floor mosaics which have been partly restored. A great deal has been done to tidy up and preserve the ruins - some say too much.

A little to the north of the Arch of Galerius is the prominent circular building raised as a mausoleum for this 'notorious and faithful servant of the demons', as a medieval monk described the bull-necked, pale-faced Caesar, arch-persecutor of the Christians. Destiny however played a trick on Galerius: in the late fourth century his mausoleum was converted into a Christian place of worship, later dedicated to St George, most popular of Eastern warrior-martyrs. During the Turkish occupation the church was converted into a mosque and a minaret raised beside it. The building, known as the **Rotunda of Ayios Yeoryios,** is again a church, and functions as such twelve times a year. It is normally open to the public, but the mosaics will not be properly visible until the extensive restoration work is completed. The vast echoing interior, with sculptural fragments in the bays and the celestial fantasies of masterly mosaicists below the dome, has been used as a museum of Early Christian art and has provided a unique setting for occasional concerts of Byzantine and classical music.

Architecturally the Rotunda owes much to the circular buildings which Galerius probably saw when campaigning in the East. The basic plan is simple and grand: a towering cylinder with eight bays supporting a wide dome. Its Eastern character remains unaffected by the transformation of the arched recess opposite the entrance into an apsidal altar-space. Fragments of sculpture, Roman, Early-Christian and Byzantine, ranged along the walls of the other bays, include a fine tenth-century **plaque of a Virgin Orans** (the Virgin with arms outstretched in an attitude of prayer). The symmetrical yet gentle pliability of the folds of the mantle recall the drapery of classical Greek sculpture. Equally impressive is another tenth-century **plaque representing the Ossios David**, a holy man in the act of prayer.

Mosaics surviving from the original Christian decoration include Alexandrian motifs of birds and fruit within the octagonal medallions which decorate the soffits of several bays. However it is the huge **mosaic panels**, originally made up of some thirty-six million *tesserae*, in the circular band around the shallow dome, that provide the mystical quality peculiar to this extraordinary building. Only seven panels survive. In each, two martyr saints, ritualistic figures with arms outstretched in the *orans* gesture, stand against crowded architectural backgrounds of immense fantasy. Examination of detail is unfortunately ruled out by the height of the dome, but photographs reveal the refined modelling of the martyrs' heads, the vivacity of their expressions and the classical folds of their *chitons*. These fantasies, which were to exercise a powerful influence on later book illumination, are full of Eastern motifs: knotted columns crowned with Corinthian capitals, arches, friezes and cupolas. In each panel, pavilions frame the centre-piece, generally an apse or *exedra*. The mood is elegiac: peacocks strut across parapets and swans float above the ornamental cornices; candelabra hang from bejewelled canopies and turquoise curtains are drawn back to disclose pendant lamps or lighted candlesticks. There is little hint of Byzantine austerity. All the ecstasy of Eastern Christendom is symbolized in this opulent image of the Church Eternal.

To the west of the Rotunda, on a small square where the local inhabitants assemble on hot summer evenings to gossip, rises a shapely brick-domed drum crowning the twelfth-century **Church of Ayios Pandeleimon**, once a dependency of an Athonite monastery.

Regaining Egnatia Street and turning right up Ayia Sofia Street, one reaches the fifth-century **Basilica of Panayia Ahiropiitos**, squatting in a sunken square. Restored in 1910, its exterior architectural severity reflects the dignity implicit in its polysyllabic name - *Ahiropiitos* (Not made by human hands) - so-called because in it once hung a miraculous icon of the Virgin which, according to legend, no human hand had fashioned.

The interior of the church has, in spite of a certain bleakness, an imposing overall architectural unity. The windows, divided by short columns, are disposed symmetrically in two rows, thus relieving the general design of both monotony and clumsiness. Columns of greyish-white marble are crowned by magnificent **Theodosian capitals**, an elaborate version of the Corinthian - the spiky acanthus leaves turning back on themselves as though windblown - which evolved in the fifth century and was named after the Emperor Theodosios II. The fashion spread, but it was in Thessaloniki and Constantinople that this sumptuous marble embellishment achieved its most sophisticated form.

Many images were probably removed during the Iconoclast periods of the eighth and ninth centuries, when the reproduction of the human form in religious art was proscribed by the puritanical emperors of the Isaurian dynasty; consequently only a few **mosaics** - decorative work of a high order - survive in the soffits of the arches. The colours are unusually lavish, with lilies, poppies, sunflowers, nasturtiums and fruit-bearing branches sprouting from ornate vases; foliate wreaths wind round crosses and sacred books; gold backgrounds swarm with fish and plump blue pheasants.

Ayia Sofia Street mounts directly from the *Ahiropiitos* to Ayiou Dimitriou Street along which, to the left, is the holiest spot in Thessaloniki: the site of St Dimitrios' martyrdom. A spacious church with sloping roofs and rows of arched windows spreads across a narrow square. The unweathered brick indicates a modern construction, but the amplitude of the proportions suggests an ancient design. It is, in fact, a faithful reconstruction - the result of years of patient archaeological research - of the **Basilica of Ayios Dimitrios**, twice destroyed by fire, most recently in 1917. On feast days the ringing of the bells of the Basilica echoes across the roofs of the hotels and office blocks shelving down a slope once crowded with medieval mansions, hospices and public baths. The whole history of Thessaloniki is bound up with this church. It is the spiritual centre and common meeting-ground of the inhabitants in a way that no other Christian place of worship in Greece has ever been.

Of Dimitrios himself we know little except that he was an upper-class young man whose military prowess won for him the patronage of Galerius. His conversion to Christianity, however, infuriated the Caesar, who promptly imprisoned him in a bathing establishment. To make matters worse, Nestor, an athlete friend of Dimitrios, also a Christian, challenged and killed the champion gladiator, the imperial favourite of the moment. This was too much for the irascible Galerius. Nestor was summarily executed and Dimitrios speared to death in the public baths (now the crypt of the church), where he was afterwards buried by Christian friends. From this contemptible exhibition of human vindictiveness an obscure martyrdom derived its venerable character and a great cult centre acquired its popularity.

The church has been rebuilt on the fifth-century plan. Original materials, such as chancel portico arches, Theodosian capitals and column shafts of green and dark red marble, were re-used in the modern construction. However the frescoes, porphyry revetments and the mosaics which used to adorn the north aisle were lost forever in the 1917 conflagration.

It is curious that the Iconoclasts removed neither the north aisle mosaics nor the few panels elsewhere which have been preserved in their original positions. They may have feared a public outcry. Healer of the sick, protector of children, Dimitrios was also guardian of the city. He is the city. When Thessaloniki fell to the Turks in 1430 only the shrine of St Dimitrios was spared from desecration; all other churches were converted into mosques, and many of the inhabitants were put to the sword. The fall of Thessaloniki, which preceded that of Constantinople by twenty-three years, was the penultimate warning to the pusillanimous leaders of the West, who stood by, as though bemused, watching the downfall of an empire which, for all its cruelty and corruption, was still the heir of Athens and Rome and the repository of every human value they cherished. Within a century the Ottoman armies had entered Budapest and were besieging Vienna.

The layout of the reconstructed basilica is clear: narthex, nave, with each side a double aisle divided by a colonnade, short transepts and galleries over the aisles and the narthex. At the west end of the south aisle colonnade, a Theodosian capital of great fantasy surmounts an ancient pilaster. Stone images of birds nestle among bunches of grapes, and fat peacocks with rippling feathers drink out of a *cantharos*. Other fifth- and sixth-century capitals crown dark green columns with strange effigies and serrated lace-like leaves which, carved in deep relief and curled backwards, create astonishing effects of light and shade.

The surviving **mosaics**, probably of the early seventh century, are half-hidden among the aisles and piers. The technique of mosaic work was even more highly-developed in Thessaloniki than in Italy. In the grading and setting of *tesserae* (the average measurement in the St Dimitrios panels is four millimetres), in the blending of colours and the creation of shading effects, Thessaloniki was in advance of Rome. Even at times of acute military crisis the mosaic workshops hummed with activity. The panels, which are not disposed in any apparent order, were votive offerings to the saint. The holy persons are represented frontally; great attention is paid to symmetry and, in spite of their wooden attitudes, they emerge as figures of great nobility.

The two panels on the north-east pier of the nave, placed like icons in front of the sanctuary, are impressive. The first is of **St Dimitrios and the children**. The young saint has thick, wavy hair and the expression of his large black eyes is compassionate yet penetrating. The round-eyed faces of the two children, over whom the slender saint towers protectively, are so lifelike that little seems to distinguish them from the small boys playing hide-and-seek among the marble columns, to the accompaniment of their mothers' unabashed chatter in the side aisles. In the other panel, the Virgin and St Theodore, the colouring is more sober. The slim, elegant figure of the Virgin is represented in the act of intercession on behalf of mankind. St Theodore, a military gentleman, black-haired and black-bearded, hands outstretched, possesses all the weight and volume that the ethereal Virgin lacks. There seems to be no relation between the two figures, as though their juxtaposition were a matter of pure accident.

The three panels on the south-east pier are probably the best-known. The faces are clearly portraits, the style monumental; there is no attempt at symbolism. In the central panel we see **St Sergius**, a young Roman officer martyred in Syria, where the desert nomads revered him as their patron saint. There is an unmistakable similarity between the modelling of the saint's face and that of St Dimitrios in the panel with the children. Perhaps both mosaics were the work of the same artist. Both are equally moving. The flanking panel depicts **St Dimitrios between the founders**. The figure of the young martyr, just perceptibly levitated so as to suggest his saintly status, is grand and noble. The ascetic face is unusually small and somewhat pinched, and although it lacks the spiritual quality of the beautiful head towering above the children, the eyes retain the same penetrating expression. The founders, by contrast, are robust, stocky officials with slab-like beards, their feet planted firmly on the ground. The third panel represents **St Dimitrios and a deacon** who was so distressed by the church's destruction by fire that the saint took pity on him, visited him in a dream and prophesied its imminent restoration. A report of the dream reached the ears of a senior cleric, and shortly afterwards some wealthy patrons were persuaded to commission the rebuilding of the church (the seventh-century edifice). The saint's right hand is placed affectionately on the shoulder of the deacon, a stolid wooden figure, who reverently touches his protector's *chlamys*.

A stairway to the right descends through brickwork chambers to the **crypt**. Adjoining a marble-paved cloister, lighted by windows at street level, it is an apsidal chamber, connected with the sanctuary by two stairways, incorporating part of the original structure of the Roman baths where Dimitrios was murdered. This is the centre of the cult. A shrine built above the martyr's grave possessed healing powers and thousands of pilgrims flocked to it to be cured. In the fifth century Leontios, a prefect of Illyricum, was so impressed by the relief that he obtained from a paralytic condition, diagnosed as incurable by his physicians, that he commissioned the construction of a magnificent church (the original building, destroyed in the seventh century) in honour of this new Asclepios.

Proceeding down the south aisle, past remains of wall paintings of a later period, one reaches the last major mosaic, depicting **St Dimitrios and a woman and child**, on the west wall. It is fragmentary but beautiful. The saint, wearing a gold *chlamys*, stands in front of a *ciborium*. His pale face, with luminous, almond-shaped eyes, is more mature than in the other panels. On the right a mother and child, bending forward in attitudes of humility, approach through a garden in which a stylized tree grows behind a pilaster surmounted by a vase. The contrast between the Eastern-style background and the Hellenic symmetry of the draperies is characteristic of Thessalonikian ambivalence towards artistic influences during the Early-Byzantine period.

One returns to the nave, where at the end of the south aisle is the **Chapel of Ayios Efthymios**, a miniature three-aisled basilica, donated by an official in the Byzantine administration. The work of a single painter, its early fourteenth-century frescoes provide evidence of the more attractive characteristics of Late-Byzantine painting: light, fresh colours, a predilection for free brushwork and statuesque figures given to dramatic attitudes. The episode from the Communion of the Apostles in the sanctuary is an outstanding example.

From *Ayios Dimitrios*, going back down Ayia Sofia Street, past the *Ahiropiitos*, one crosses Egnatia Street into a small square with palm trees. At its east end lies the domed **Church of Ayia Sofia** of the eighth century. The exterior is plain, with an ugly ochre wash above the brick course of the façade, but unfortunately work on the mosaics and on the actual structure means that the interior is often partly obscured by scaffolding. The unusual layout seems to be an attempt to combine a square, domed central area with an aisled basilica: it is not altogether successful, though impressive. The aisle columns are crowned with massive capitals and the whole of the square *naos* is filled with a pale gold light, spreading downwards from the shallow dome (not a circle but a square with rounded corners), which is decorated with well-preserved mosaics depicting the Ascension, probably of the tenth century. Only the Christ Pantocrator, in a medallion supported by two angels, is an earlier work, possibly of the late eighth century. Much of the disproportion evident in the mosaic decoration of the church stems from the Byzantine artist's attempt to present a seated figure within a curved surface to the onlooker below. As yet he knew little about perspective correction.

Chronologically (and topographically), the next church is the **Panayia Halkeon** in Egnatia Street, called 'The Virgin of the Coppersmiths' because it served as the mosque of the Turkish coppersmiths in whose noisy quarter it lay. The din of hammers crashing on anvils has been replaced by the cries of fruit-sellers from the neighbouring market. Founded in 1028 and heavily restored in 1934, the church is small in comparison with the spacious basilicas. The transitional style, as represented by *Ayia Sofia*, is now succeeded by that of the cross-in-square church. The triangular pediments and the vaulting of the arms of the Greek Cross of the *Panayia Halkeon*, as well as the exterior brickwork decoration (a faithful reproduction of the original), are forerunners of the inventiveness of later architects. The interior of the church (it is not always easy to get in) is noteworthy for the faded remains of its original fresco decoration.

To the right of the church (east) there is a charming relic of Turkish times: a nicely-restored brickwork *hammam* with multiple shallow domes, in use as a bath-house until 1969, and still known as **Loutra Paradissos** (The Baths of Paradise). It rests on Roman foundations, which are clearly visible from the street. To the west is an octagonal former mosque with shops around it, known as the **Alcazar** from the cinema it once housed. Thessaloniki has several of these little Turkish 'islands', but it is a pity that the minarets have gone - for the most part demolished in an orgy of nationalism unleashed by the assassination of George I. The king, founder of the ill-fated Glucksberg dynasty, was shot while taking a walk in Thessaloniki one spring afternoon in 1913. The assassin was a lunatic whose only grudge against the sovereign was that he had once begged money of him and allegedly been refused.

The *Panayia Halkeon* and the *Loutra Paradissos* are both in Platia Dikastiriou and behind them is a small park. Beyond that, looked down on by undistinguished modern blocks, is the large **Roman Agora,** excavation of which is still in progress,. The most noticeable feature of the Agora is a long portico, or *stoa*, on the south side. A number of columns have been put back in place, some with their capitals. Under the portico, clearly visible, is the *Cryptoportico*, a long, wide, barrel-vaulted passage, with arcades on each side, the arches being supported on piers. A flight of steps leads down to a chamber, penetrated by opaque shafts of light from arched windows, where a stone pedestal is preserved. On it stood the auctioneer, ringing his bell, amid the crowd of Jews, to whom St Paul addressed his letters. The *Cryptoportico* is to be restored as an exhibition centre. In the north-east corner is the **Odeion**, its entrance paved with fragments of mosaic, and its *proskenion* provided with arched recesses in which musicians played in the instrumental concerts popular with the Romans. At the south-east end of the portico is what may have been an Early Christian chapel: catacomb-like, safe from the prying eyes of Galerius' spies, the wall-painting of St Kosmas and St Damian came from here. Fragments of ancient wells and an intricate system of waterworks, including stone bath-tubs, have been identified along the east-west axis of the site.

On the harbour, at the end of the waterfront, is **Eleftheria Square**. In the tenth century the arms of a mole, originally constructed by Constantine the Great, enclosed the inner port in which even the largest vessels could seek protection from Saracen pirates. However, one day in 904 sentinels observed the Arab fleet, consisting of fifty-four galleys, nosing its way around Cape Ayia Triada. As the blood-curdling yells of Arabs and Ethiopian mercenaries drew nearer, the Thessalonikians gave themselves up to loud lamentations. Fire belched forth from the enemy's long copper guns, and cages filled with half-naked negroes waving scimitars were swung over the seawall. Arrows, stones and fiery missiles rained down on the dazed defenders, who were rapidly overwhelmed. The massacre that followed was total and indiscriminate. In spite of their success, the conquerors, glutted with loot, slaughter and slaves, sailed away after two days, but the pattern of Arab aggression was set for years to come.

Taking Eleftheria Square as the starting-point for a tour of the ramparts and churches of the Late Byzantine period, one may take a bus or climb to the **Monastery of Vlatadon**. It is the last-surviving monastic establishment of the twenty that once flourished in this most Orthodox of Greek cities. Situated on a ledge below the ramparts, overlooking the city and the gulf, the fifteenth-century church, largely rebuilt in the nineteenth, is of little interest, but the garden is pretty. Behind the monastery rises the huge neo-Byzantine Institute of Patriarchical Studies, next to a line of **watch-towers**, forming part of the defensive circuit of the medieval city. The ruined ramparts descend on both sides of the steep escarpments.

The line of towers runs eastward to the area where the Sultan's troops poured into the city in 1430, killing every Christian they encountered. The fourteenth-century **Gate of Anna Paleologaina** (named after the wife of the Emperor Andronikos III) leads to the ruins of the **Eptapyryion**, which consisted of seven strong towers, linked by ramparts. The central tower, the most formidable, now restored, was built by the Turks a year after they captured the city. At the corner formed by the arms of the north and east walls rises the **Chain Tower** with a fine circular keep. From here the ramparts descend to the sea. The surviving section of the east walls includes the well-preserved Tower of Hormidas, built at the time of the Emperor Theodosios the Great by a Sassanian prince who, according to an inscription on the upper part of the bastion, 'completely fortified the city by indestructible walls'.

The descent from the Monastery of Vlatadon leads through the heart of the former **Turkish Quarter**, once an area of winding, precipitous alleys, bordered by vine-trellised yards with priests in pill-box hats panting up stepped paths. Doves cooed in walled gardens, while children with huge, black eyes stared at you from under stunted acacias, and flea-ridden donkeys loaded with panniers of fruit stumbled across the cobblestones. The smell of dust, dung and over-ripe vegetables may linger in places, mixed with that of syringa and jasmine.

At this point the clock has to be turned back - over fifteen hundred years. Tucked away in a little garden filled with pots of basil and fuchsias is the fifth-century **Chapel of Ossios David**. Originally a square building, subsequently truncated, it was once part of a large monastery. Contained within its apse is a damaged but very beautiful mosaic, primitive but profound in religious feeling, not inhibited by the more sophisticated techniques of later centuries. The crowded composition depicts the **Vision of Ezekiel**, who raises his hands in fear with an almost elfin expression on his face. Opposite him Habbakuk, more meditative, records the miracle in an open book. Above the prophets, a young and beardless Christ sits on a rainbow, with shafts of light radiating from him like spokes from the hub of a wheel. His face, more Early-Christian than Byzantine in feeling, emanates sanctity, compassion, authority. At his feet flow the four rivers of paradise, in whose waters two fish and a frightened river god, symbolizing paganism, take flight.

From *Ossios David* you descend to the **Church of Profitis Ilias**. Probably of eleventh-century origin, built on the site of a Byzantine palace overlooking the city, this bulky edifice, frequently reconstructed, is architecturally very complex. Additional north and south apses create a trefoil effect, and an elongated central apse projects clumsily from a box-like, cruciform structure which is crowned by a high polygonal drum decorated with blind arches.

To the west, near the city wall but nestling among painfully modern houses, is the more attractive **Church of Ayia Ekaterini**, in the purest architectural style of the fourteenth century. Airy little cupolas crown tall polygonal drums and a portico surrounds three sides. The exterior brickwork decoration is elaborate. The fragmentary frescoes, depicting Christ's miracles, were badly damaged when the church was converted into a mosque, but the artist's endeavour to create an illusion of architectural depth by means of successive planes, whilst modelling the rounder, somewhat fleshy, faces in a more free, more painterly manner is evident. Although lacking the sturdiness of Early-Byzantine architecture, *Ayia Ekaterini* possesses all the elements that make up the typical small church of the Paleologos period: warm-coloured brickwork decoration, multiple domes, arched windows, arcades with glass frontages and a clearly-defined Greek Cross plan.

The westerly route continues downhill past traces of the western rampart. It is best to head for Ayiou Dimitriou Street, cross it and enter a little square, where the walls, apses and domes of the early fourteenth-century **Church of Ayii Apostoli**, girdled with multiple bands of brick inlay, rise out of a sunken enclosure. On summer evenings, when the sun goes down, a priest waters the orange trees and flower-beds in the court, as women drop in for vespers.

Church of Ayii Apostoli, Thessaloniki

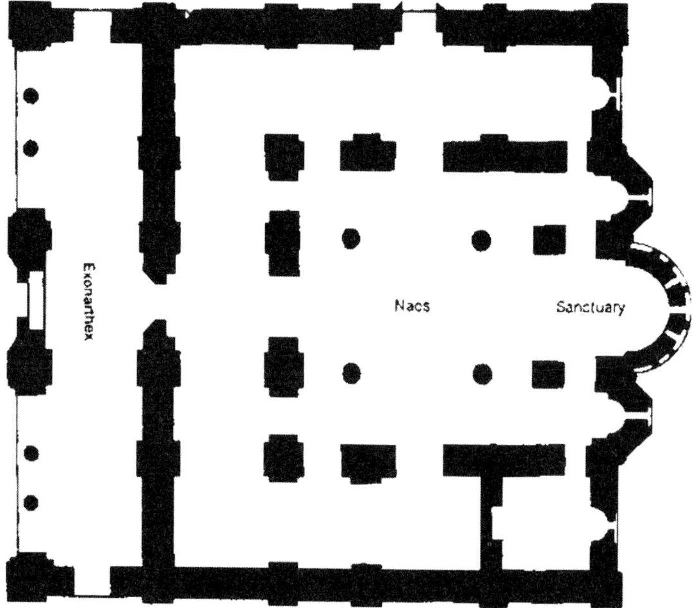

little architecturally from *Ayia Ekaterini* (except that it is larger), with a lofty central dome on a drum and four subsidiary ones at the corners of the square. The west façade has a large window on each side within an arch which is supported on two columns with Theodosian capitals; the space above is filled with brick inlay. The whole exterior is a masterpiece of the lavish and ingenious interplay of stone, mortar and brick. The fashion certainly had earlier origins, but it is not until the fourteenth century that Byzantine architects achieve an extraordinary virtuosity in the creation of unlimited geometrical permutations with bricks of different colour, size and shape, which they handle with the skill of a mosaicist. This art, a minor yet characteristically Byzantine one, is nowhere better-illustrated than at the *Ayii Apostoli* (though there are other outstanding examples at Arta and Kastoria). The zigzag cornices, rosettes, crosses and colonnettes, the string courses and step-patterns, especially those of the three apses, are integrated with the harmony and brilliance of design of a Persian carpet, and with as much feeling for poetry as for geometry. An element of frivolity, almost of skittishness, is sometimes apparent in the garlands of hieroglyphics.

This last phase of artistic creation at Thessaloniki, of which the

Ayii Apostoli is the highlight, corresponds with the development of the Hesychast movement, which set priest against priest and split their flocks into hostile factions. Bricklayers and mosaicists were adding their final touches to the *Ayii Apostoli* when the storm of the Hesychast dispute swept Thessaloniki. The word is derived from *hesychia*, the Greek for quiet, and the Hesychasts - like Hindu exponents of Yoga, with eyes staring at their own bodies and their limbs arranged in specially-prescribed postures - devoted themselves to prayer and meditation, their spiritual concentration being assisted by these physical means. The battle raged throughout the fourteenth century. At the *Ayii Apostoli*, gorgeously-robed prelates hurled anathemas at each other. The unity of the Church was threatened and families, in the best traditions of Greek party politics, were split in two. In the sphere of art, the static liturgical canons of Byzantine iconography, so tenaciously preserved for nearly ten centuries, were not unaffected. The greater stress on physical movement seen here, and strictly denied to the monumental figures of an earlier age, may owe something to the Hesychast contention that the body in itself is not evil, as well as to the fact that Byzantine artists, now visiting Italy in increasing numbers, were unlikely, on returning home, to have forgotten wholly the lessons they learnt in the West.

The *naos* of the *Ayii Apostoli* is a perfect Greek Cross, with four marble columns, crowned by Theodosian capitals, supporting the central drum; behind the sanctuary are three elliptical apses. The smell of incense is strong. The greater part of the walls is washed a dirty pink. Turkish graffiti pock-mark the damaged frescoes of the lower level.

The surviving mosaics, stylistically typical of the so-called Paleologos ‘renaissance’ in religious art, are clearly the work of first-class Constantinopolitan artists. The emphasis is on movement and tension. In the **Entry into Jerusalem** (north side of the west vault) the elders rush forward to meet the procession against a background of towers, roofs and domes. The **Descent into Hell** in the north vault (east side) is treated in a very dramatic fashion. A dour, purposeful Christ with heavy-lidded eyes, the corners of his mouth turned down, his mantle blown back by the wind, raises the aged Adam from Limbo, while Eve, her hands outstretched, awaits her turn in front of a crowd led by Abel and a prophet. The balance and symmetry of the central, interlocking figures of Christ and Adam are apparent in every line, whether of limbs or drapery.

In the **Nativity** (east side of the south vault) the crouching

Joseph and the shepherds who bear the tidings are simple rustic creatures. The faces of the mourning apostles in the **Dormition of the Virgin** above the main doorway are treated as portraits with individual expressions. The cruel bony hand of the Pantocrator in the dome hints at the familiar representation of a militant, uncompromising Christ, a saviour of souls on his own terms. Of the four Evangelists in the pendentives, the contemplative **Matthew** is the best-preserved. Occasionally, a hint of preciousness is evident in the facial expressions. In his desire to dramatize, to stress human individuality, the fourteenth-century artist no longer appears to be filled with the same deep religious fervour that inspired the great static monumental figures of the *Ayios Dimitrios* panels. Only in the frescoes, which are in a much poorer state of preservation, one observes a more monumental character, reminiscent of slightly earlier models.

There remains one last Byzantine visit; on the way, however, the sightseer must project himself for a moment into the closing years of the Ottoman Empire. From the *Ayii Apostoli*, Ayiou Dimitriou Street goes eastward; near its end, on the corner of Apostolou Pavlou Street is the Turkish Consulate, and behind it a plaque on a brightly-painted house identifies it as the **birthplace of Mustafa Kemal**. The son of a local customs official and a fair-skinned Macedonian lady of Moslem faith, the future Ataturk, 'father of the Turks', grew up here in the late nineteenth-century squalor of the decaying Levantine port, where shadows of minarets lay across potholed streets littered with dung; in dimly-lit cafés screeching, pig-tailed schoolgirls mingled with groups of soldiers bristling with sabres, daggers and pistols, their close-cropped Tartar heads crowned with furry black fezzes. At the army cadet school, Kemal galvanized the Thessaloniki branch of the 'Young Turk' movement and plotted the overthrow of the corrupt regime of Sultan Abdul Hamid II: the first step in a programme of national regeneration which was to culminate in the expulsion of Greeks from Asia Minor, the foundation of the Turkish republic and the doom of the *Megali Idea* (the Great Idea) of a revived Byzantine Empire, romantically fostered by Greek nineteenth- and twentieth-century politicians.

Not far from Ataturk's house is Platia Kallithea and the small but important **Church of Ayios Nikolaos Orfanos** (St Nicholas the Orphan), which once formed part of a fourteenth-century convent and became, in the seventeenth century, a dependency of the Vlatadon Monastery. Built with a narthex in the shape of a Greek letter π, it is chronologically the last of the surviving Byzantine churches in Thessaloniki. Good lighting and the church's diminutive proportions enable one to devote attention to the details of the paintings which the lofty, ill-lit interiors of earlier churches preclude.

The **frescoes** are not among the masterpieces of late Byzantine art. Illustrative, picturesque, even fussy, they nevertheless possess a quality of ingenuousness which is wholly disarming. Take the narthex first. Across the east wall extend two bands of small compositions depicting the miracles of St Nicholas, the Lycian bishop who was patron of sailors, merchants and pawnbrokers. The cycle is full of story-book detail. In one episode the saint, standing in a boat propelled by five rowers, gazes up at a billowing, crescent-shaped sail as he prepares to cast a phial of soothing magic oil on the troubled waters. The south wall is devoted to **scenes from the miracles of Christ**. In the Wedding at Cana, the bridal couple, crowned and wearing jewel-studded robes, are seated at an ornate table loaded with food, while the Virgin whispers in Christ's ear: 'They have no wine.' On the north wall a beautiful Christ, depicted as a beardless boy with haunting eyes, is seated on a throne surrounded by priests and choristers.

In the apse the **Virgin Orans** stands on a golden dais, flanked by two adoring angels: a figure of authority, her eyes fixed in an oblique glance to the left, her gold-fringed robe draped in symmetrical folds. The cycle of the *Dodekaorton* (the Twelve Feasts) spreads across the nave, with the Transfiguration flanked by the Entry into Jerusalem and the Crucifixion, and the Ascension up above. In the **Nativity**, subsidiary episodes full of homely detail are grouped round the conch-shaped manger: Joseph meditating; the rustic shepherds hearing the news; the bathing of the Child in an ornamental basin into which an attendant pours water from a gold ewer, while another dips her hand in to test the temperature. At the east end of the south aisle Christ holds an open Book of Gospels. The austerity of previous centuries has been tempered. His beneficent expression is identical throughout the church - an indication that a single artist employed the same model for all the portraits of Christ.

Everything is on the minutest scale; but colour, opulent as a peacock's plumage, is used unsparingly to match, blend and contrast. Lime greens vie with sealing-wax reds, sombre purples fade into amethyst shades, and the brown, maroon, puce or copper tones of gold-fringed robes glow against inky-blue backgrounds. No longer are the heavenly beings the austere symbols of a mystic revelation;

beautiful, pert, playful, contemplative - they are all somehow identifiable: the plump, lavishly-bedecked page attending the horses in the Adoration; the aquiline-faced apostles in the Washing of the Feet; the forbidding Caiaphas giving counsel to the Jews; a bored, indifferent Pilate washing his hands; the compassionate Christ who appears above the myrrh-bearers in the garden; the prophets and saints in the lower register. One sees their faces in Thessaloniki every day.

14

Western Macedonia: The Lowlands

THE LOWLANDS of the large province of Macedonia extend to the west of Thessaloniki. The Hellenistic sites, including Pella, birthplace of Alexander the Great, Lefkadia and Veryina can be visited in one long day. However to visit these sites and the three neighbouring towns of Edessa, Naoussa and Veria, which are beautifully situated on the mountain periphery overlooking the Imathian Plain, at least three days should be allowed.

Twenty kilometres west of Thessaloniki the road to Edessa crosses the National Road from Athens to the Yugoslav Macedonian border (near which, at Polykastro, there is a British military cemetery - reminder of the long, frustrating campaigns of the 'forgotten front' of the First World War). The Edessa road continues westward and, shortly after the bridge over the Axios, passes a south-westerly fork (to Veria) and enters the reclaimed marshland of Imathia. In the middle of it lies **Pella**, founded by King Archelaos (413-399 BC), where later, in the royal residence of Philip of Macedon, the conquest of Asia was conceived. To the south, Olympos looms in the haze; in the west, the Vermion range forms a barrier, thickly wooded, above endless orchards. The site was not discovered until 1957 and excavation continues. Foundations of Hellenistic houses paved with floor mosaics cover a wide area previously hidden under the fields. The discovery of the vast *Agora*, and uncovering of a large part of it, has added a new dimension. The low hill to the north has proved to be the site of a great palace (as long as excavation and clearing continue, visiting is not permitted). It is not, however, the Palace of Archelaos where Alexander was born, which has still to be identified.

In antiquity Pella was surrounded by navigable marshes extending from the acropolis to the Thermaic Gulf. It is, for most of the year, a damp, torrid place. Livy says the citadel rose 'like an island from the part of the marsh nearest to the city, being built upon

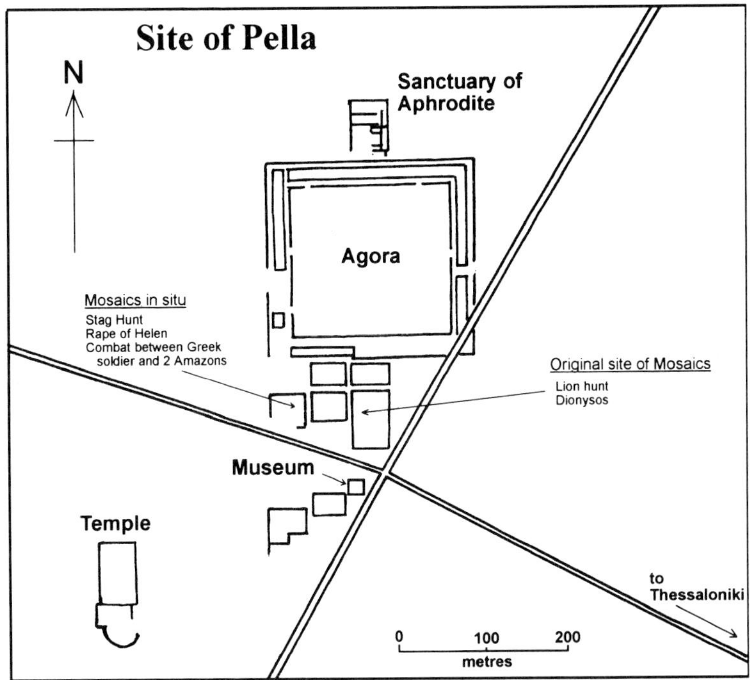

an immense embankment which defies all injury from the waters'. He also mentions 'a wet ditch' spanned by a single bridge 'so that no access whatever is afforded to an enemy...'.

Plutarch relates much of the somewhat fanciful history of Philip II's life and we are told that one day he discovered his wife Olympias lying in such a compromising position with a serpent that he presumed her to be having intercourse with a god in disguise. God or serpent, it was exactly nine months later that this extraordinary woman gave birth to Alexander. At the very hour of his birth, according to Plutarch, the temple of Diana at Ephesus was destroyed by fire and panic-stricken soothsayers ran through the city, prophesying that 'this day has brought forth something that will prove fatal and destructive to all Asia.'

The palatial houses to the north of the main road have pebble mosaic floors. To your right as you enter the site, bordered on both sides by ancient streets, lies the clearly outlined structure of the late fourth-century BC **House of the Lion Hunt** (so-called after the mosaic pavement found there, is now in the Museum), which consists of a succession of chambers with a peristyle court surrounded by fluted Ionic columns. In several rooms decorative pebble floor mosaics are *in-situ.* The ruined house lends scale and perspective to the whole site. Fragments of plaster-work, bronze door fittings and ornamental blocks suggest that it was an important official residence. In some such colonnaded court it is possible to imagine Philip, one-eyed and lecherous, surrounded by his under-age concubines, indulging in nightly debauches. On one of these occasions, relates Plutarch, he so infuriated Alexander that the young prince seized a wine-cup and hurled it at his father. There was little family unity at Pella, and soon after this incident Alexander fled with his morbidly possessive mother to the court of her brother, Alexander, King of Epirus.

West of the House of the Lion Hunt, across the foundations of a large square building, is the house with the magnificent mosaic of the **Stag Hunt**, which has been restored and replaced. A stag is about to be slain by two naked young hunters armed respectively with a sword and a double-headed axe. Anatomical details - muscles and joints - are subtly emphasized by shading effects; fingernails and toenails are outlined in black pebbles, and the hunters' wavy hair is reproduced by the juxtaposition of alternately light and dark-coloured stones. In spite of the formal framework the figures remain intensely alive, and their predatory expressions reflect the excitement of the kill. In contrast, the border - a formal flower pattern - is pastoral and tranquil in tone: crocuses, lilies and honeysuckle are drawn by an artist with a professional knowledge of botany. The floor of the next room has the **Rape of Helen**, also restored and replaced - a charioteer, horses and the flowing garments of a handmaiden are the best-preserved sections. Another room on the same court has the mosaic of a Greek and an Amazon fighting.

The immense square of the *Agora,* surrounded by a Doric colonnade, which used to shelter market stalls, workshops, fountains and meeting places, has been largely revealed. Architectural evidence suggests that the water supply and drainage would have done credit to any modern urbanisation. In the south-west corner another complex structure has been uncovered, and just north of the *Agora* is the large **Sanctuary of Aphrodite**. As both the main road and the branch road to the modern village cut across the huge site, there are numerous remains not often visited. The most important is a sanctuary to the south-west of the Museum.

In the **Museum** some of the great **floor mosaics,** composed of large pebbles of different colours, are displayed. In late-Classical and Hellenistic times the subjects of this lavish form of house decoration were generally confined to historical and mythological events. The Pella mosaics are among the earliest and grandest examples extant. The first is the **Lion Hunt**, in which two male figures, brandishing swords, attack a lion with dark mane and erect tail. The attitudes of both men and beast, with the agitated backward sweep of the hunters' cloaks, form a perfectly balanced composition; clearly outlined shading, achieved by the use of grey pebbles, marks the sinews of naked limbs and folds of drapery. The second mosaic represents **Dionysos riding a leopard**. The god is depicted as a flabby young man holding a *thyrsos*; his soft, effeminate body provides a striking contrast to the lithe and powerful animal. There are also mosaics of a griffin attacking a deer and a female Centaur approaching a cave.

Also in the Museum is an outstanding small bronze Poseidon, attributed to Lysippos, as well as a large assortment of architectural fragments, jewellery, Hellenistic paintings and a number of small terracotta figures of the first century BC, some of them very attractive. Among the sculptures are a fifth-century BC life-size dog couchant, relaxed yet alert, and a small male torso crowned by a Hellenistic head with a voluptuous expression and tiny horns, thought to be Alexander as Pan. The bronze figurines include a supple little panther devouring a stag, a masterpiece of anatomical observation.

Much excavation remains to be done at Pella before we know more about the actual physical surroundings in which Alexander spent his childhood with Aristotle, his tutor, and the savage Thracian women whom Olympia, his mother, brought from the Aimos Mountains. After Philip had been assassinated and Alexander had embarked on the conquest of Asia, Antipater became Governor of Macedonia and kept his official residence at Pella. However, when the Macedonian Empire began to split up after the death of Antipater in 319 BC, his son Kassandros, established a new capital, named after his wife Thessaloniki, Alexander's sister. Pella subsequently declined in importance, in spite of being on the Via Egnatia.

Beyond Pella the plain is dotted with pine-clad mounds; patches of swampy ground among the wheat fields recall the marshes described by Livy. After Yannitsa, once a Moslem holy place in whose neglected mosque descendants of the Ottoman conquerors of Macedonia are buried, the plain contracts, cows graze in the meadows and avenues of trees relieve the monotony: not the cypress

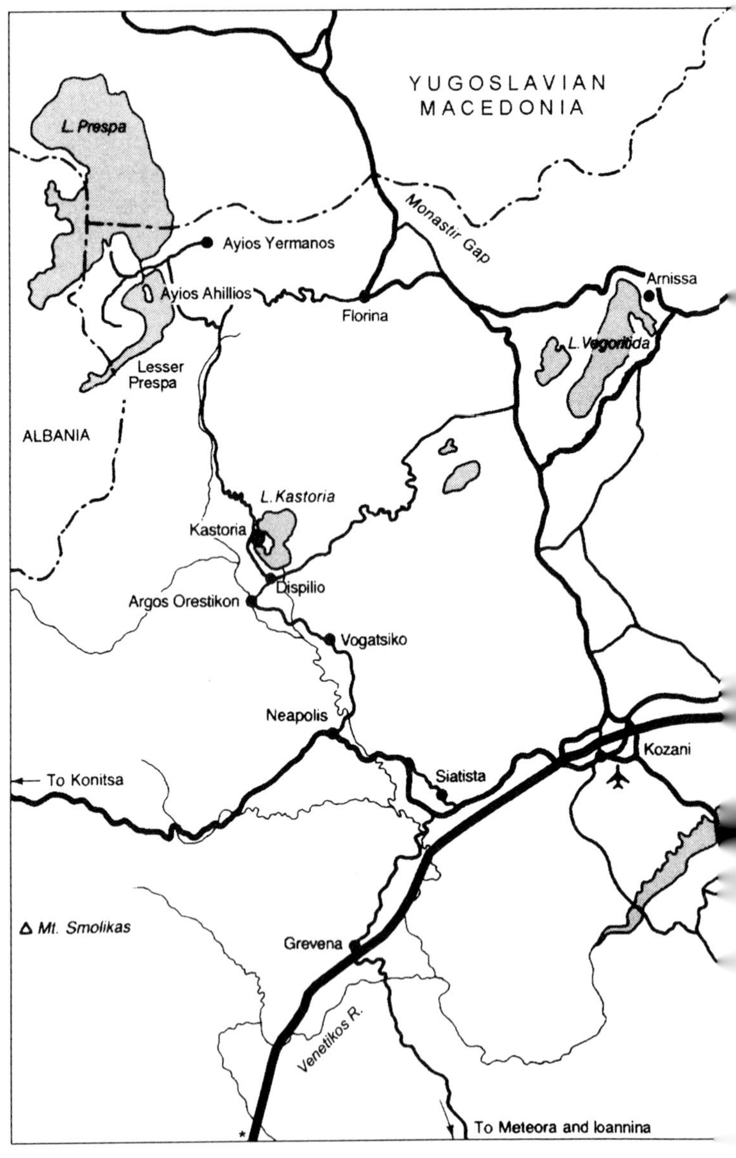
YUGOSLAVIAN
MACEDONIA
L. Prespa
Monastir Gap
Ayios Yermanos
Ayios Ahillios
Florina
Arnissa
L. Vegoritida
Lesser
Prespa
ALBANIA
L. Kastoria
Kastoria
Dispilio
Argos Orestikon
Vogatsiko
Neapolis
Kozani
To Konitsa
Siatista
Mt. Smolikas
Grevena
Venetikos R.
To Meteora and Ioannina

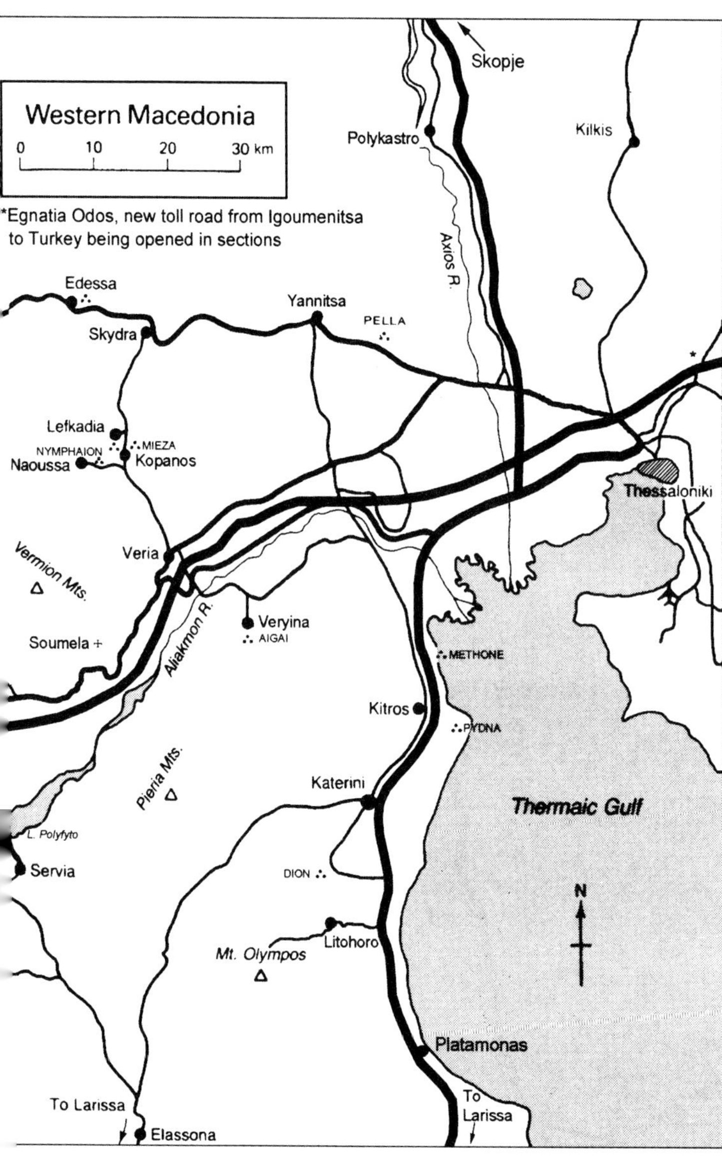

Western Macedonia
0
10
20
30 km
*Egnatia Odos, new toll road from Igoumenitsa to Turkey being opened in sections
Skopje
Polykastro
Kilkis
Axios R.
Edessa
Yannitsa
PELLA
Skydra
Lefkadia
NYMPHAION
MIEZA
Naoussa
Kopanos
Thessaloniki
Veria
Vermion Mts.
Veryina
AIGAI
Soumela
Aliakmon R.
METHONE
Kitros
PYDNA
Pieria Mts.
Katerini
Thermaic Gulf
L. Polyfyto
Servia
DION
N
Litohoro
Mt. Olympos
Platamonas
To Larissa
Elassona
To Larissa

and olive of the south, but aspens and Lombardy poplars, limes and dwarf oaks. At Skydra, a fruit-canning centre through which the River Edesseos (or Voda) flows sluggishly, there is a fork. One road mounts to Edessa, the other runs southward, parallel to the railway, as far as Veria.

As the road begins climbing up to Edessa, a road to the right, signposted for the Monastery of Ayia Triada, leads in just over a kilometre to the substantial ruins of **ancient Edessa**, near to the Monastery gates. The walls stand to a great height with a massive gateway leading to a fine paved street with the remains of numerous houses and other buildings: a site well worth the small detour. Edessa was, until Veryina's importance was revealed, believed to have been ancient Aigai.

The road continues up through orchards to the modern town of **Edessa,** strung out across the ridge of a wooded escarpment of Mount Vermion. Factory chimneys have now replaced the minarets that once thrust their pointed turrets out of shady groves: a scene which Edward Lear found 'difficult to match in beauty'. The ascent, streaked by cascading streams, ends at the hotel and tourist pavilion above the waterfalls for which Edessa is renowned.

In Edessa itself there is nothing older than an arched Roman bridge that carried the Via Egnatia. In medieval times the town, then called Vodena, was strongly fortified. During the Latin occupation, after the knights had lost what little control they had ever exercised over Macedonia, it became a battle-ground between the armies of the rival exiled aspirants to the Byzantine throne. The Byzantine Church of the *Koimesis*, beside the modern cathedral, has some ancient columns and damaged frescoes. Alleys, with some surviving old Turkish houses with projecting wooden balconies, lead up to an open space where a Turkish mosque with a well-preserved porch has a large tea-cosy dome. Remains of Byzantine capitals and inscriptions are displayed within. A minaret with a crumbling circular balcony casts an oblique shadow. Under the Turks, Edessa was a flourishing commercial and industrial centre; carpets are still produced.

Edessa, however, is mainly visited for the **waterfalls**. On the plateau behind the escarpment the Edesseos divides into two streams which flow between weeping willows before cascading into the plain. This plain stretches eastward in a haze of fruit orchards and poplar groves. A cool shadowy public garden, neatly laid out with flower beds and filled with rustic belvederes and kiosks, at which hideous souvenirs are sold, overhangs a vertical bluff. Down its sides roar the waters of the Edesseos, spray drenching the leaves of the walnut, pomegranate and wild fig trees which sprout from mossy ledges, thick with maidenhair ferns.

Returning to the fork at Skydra, one follows the road south, below the foothills of Mount Vermion where, in spring, a mist of pink peach blossom stretches for miles across the orchards. This fringe of the Imathian plain is littered with sepulchres containing the ashes of princes and generals who fought fratricidal wars for mastery of the East, whence they brought back the orientalizing influences that characterize so much of the art and architecture of the Hellenistic period.

The village of **Lefkadia** is just off the road to the right, about fourteen kilometres from Skydra; two kilometres further along, on the main road, is another village: Kopanos. The area between these two villages contains a great deal that is of archaeological interest. Excavations on both sides of the main road are revealing the remains of a very spread-out city: **ancient Mieza**. The most notable feature of the area is the series of Tombs on or near the main road.

Shortly after the turn-off to Lefkadia, a track to the right leads in one kilometre to the **Tomb of Lyson and Kallikles** (second-century BC), so-called after an extant inscription on the doorway. This is the least imposing but most curious of the four tombs. Entry is not normally permitted, but specialists can obtain a permit to enter this and the other tombs from the *Eforia* (Inspectorate of Antiquities) in Edessa, which must be taken to the *fylakas* (curator) at the Great Tomb (see below).

The tomb, which has become almost completely buried with the passage of time, has not been excavated and the entrance is through what looks like a well-head, flush with the ground. An iron stairway descends a narrow shaft into a subterranean chamber, once the sepulchre of a princely Macedonian family. The walls are painted with garlands and an altar on which writhes a snake, symbol of the underworld. Twigs and pomegranates painted on either side of the columns, just below the capitals, give the impression of being suspended on hooks. Outlines of towers and ramparts decorate the ceiling of the vault. There are *Trompe l'oeil* weapons, one of them decorated with a star within a border of laurel leaves, and pieces of armour seemingly hung from nails. Twenty-four ossuaries can be counted in niches on the walls. Of the gold objects offered to the dead none remain - the result of looting. There is little oxygen in this macabre folly of a charnel-house, and it is a relief to return to the light of day.

About a hundred metres after the turn-off to the Lyson and Kallikles tomb is the **'Kinch' Tomb** (named after the archaeologist who found it), on the left side of the road. Its exterior can be seen, but again, one cannot enter it. It is built of ashlar masonry and dates from the middle of the third century BC. The façade, covered with a thin layer of marble, is crowned by a frieze: six yellow *metopes* and a cornice with painted moulding. An antechamber, around which runs a narrow seat with traces of floral decoration, leads into a vaulted sepulchre, also once painted.

Several hundred metres further down the Veria road a side -road to the left crosses the railway line to the other two tombs. The first is the most important of the four at Lefkadia: known as the **Great Tomb,** it is the largest known Macedonian tomb and has been dated to the period of Alexander the Great. The *fylakas* responsible for the four tombs can be found here. Unfortunately, although protected by a modern concrete shelter, the fabric of the tomb has deteriorated so badly that it is closed until the very extensive renovation necessary has been completed. The façade can sometimes be seen, behind scaffolding, when the metal gates are opened. The quasi-oriental monument makes an astonishing impact - a two-storied structure, composed of large stone slabs set in regular courses, emerging, like some Babylonian temple in miniature, out of an excavated pit. On the façade of the lower storey there are panels, framed by columns, with the remains of unique life-size paintings. They are, alas, all badly faded, but they depict from left to right: (i) the deceased, holding a spear and the sheath of his sword; (ii) Hermes in his role of conductor of the dead to the Underworld; (iii-iv) Aicos and Rhadamanthus, Lords of the Elysian Fields. On the upper part of the lower storey façade, sculptured and painted *metopes* depict the battle of the Centaurs and Lapiths. Just above, there is a sculptured frieze, also painted, of skirmishes between Persians and Macedonians. The upper storey consists of six Ionic half-columns alternating with painted doors within frames. Little remains of the architrave and pediment. Beyond the façade, an antechamber leads into the vault, on the walls of which columns alternate with painted panels. As an example both of architectural complexity and of the Hellenistic attachment to the symbols of human mortality, nothing could be more arresting than this grotesque monument.

A short way beyond the Great Tomb is the **Anthimion Tomb** (also known as the tomb of the Palmettes) which is the only tomb open to the public and is shown to visitors by one of the wardens. It too, is now protected by a huge concrete structure: a wide *dromos*, built partly of ancient stone, leads down to the handsome and more traditional façade, with four Ionic columns. Its huge stone doors can be seen lying on the floor inside. Two sarcophagi remain in place, and the wall and ceiling paintings are in fair condition.

Half a kilometre beyond the turn-off for these two tombs, an untarred road to the right leads to the not very impressive theatre and to other, somewhat unrewarding, remains higher up.

Further on to the south, from the top of a rise in the village of Kopanos, a road to the right, poorly signposted, leads to the **Nymphaion**, or School of Aristotle, also known as the Baths of Alexander, a lovely spot, much favoured for picnics. Here in the foothills, between banks of campion and golden drop and patches of butterfly orchids, is the way to the **Sanctuary of the Nymphs** of ancient Mieza. At a confluence of little streams a path leads up through moss-covered boulders and clusters of giant mullein. It is an enchanting spot, discreetly arranged for visitors. Opposite rises a wall of cliff divided into barely perceptible ledges, believed to be the site of **Aristotle's Academy**, founded by Philip of Macedon within the Nymphaion. Here, in a tranquil atmosphere far from the palace intrigues of Pella and the overpowering influence of his mother, the thirteen-year-old Alexander could be instructed in the art of government and kingship. He was taught ethics, physics, politics and geography. It is said that, in later years, he never went to bed without a well-thumbed copy of the *Iliad*, annotated by Aristotle and kept in Darius' jewelled casket beside his unsheathed dagger. In practice, he paid little attention to the application of his tutor's principles on the art of government, but the seed of the love of learning, implanted at Mieza, prevailed throughout his brief, meteoric career.

Bas-reliefs of gorgons, lions' heads and floral decorations, as well as Roman coins, have been found and, in the small caves in the escarpment, there is evidence of the grotto with stalactites mentioned by Pliny. There are also the remains of a Hellenistic stairway and of structures, including an Ionic portico, at the top of the ledge from which water cascades into copses of oak, walnut and Judas trees.

This by-road (the main road is a little further south) continues to **Naoussa**, ascending the foothills where vineyards alternate with apple orchards. A terrace with a belvedere and cafés, shaded by great pines, overlooks the cultivated plain that was formed centuries ago by the silt of numerous streams pouring down from the sides of the Vermion range. Naoussa has little to offer, although the park of Ayios Nikolaos, about four kilometres to the south-west, is lovely, with turbulent waters gushing among huge, old trees. On Sundays and holidays, what seems like the entire population of the town can be found in the park. In the mountains the village of Seli is an important ski resort.

Regaining the main road, one ascends the escarpment again: this time to **Veria**, spreading across a wide natural terrace below the foothills. As in many Macedonian towns, a somewhat muted air prevails. Instead of the usual Greek dust there is running water; instead of brilliant light, an opalescent haze. Outlines are blurred and rounded. It is a painter's scene, not a sculptor's. A number of old Turkish timber-framed houses put up a brave show among the cheap modern buildings.

The **Museum**, in a park with a view over orchards, houses fragments of idols and axes of about 6200 BC from Nikomedia, the oldest Neolithic site in Greece, situated in the plain below. Of much later date there are terracotta figurines, some fine bronze urns for ashes, a Hellenistic Aphrodite and a large tablet with the second century BC Laws of Verroia. In the garden are a number of Roman sarcophagi, column bases as well as Roman and Early Christian carved gravestones.

At the upper end of the town, where Pompey spent the winter assembling his legions before the battle of Pharsalus, a ruined tower of the third century AD is conspicuous. Parts of the old Roman walls have attractive old houses built on top of them. St Paul also stayed here for three months, converting large numbers of the inhabitants. In Byzantine times the town was a bulwark guarding the western approaches to Thessaloniki, and consequently one of the first objectives in the lightning campaign waged by Theodore Angelos, Despot of Epirus in the thirteenth century, when this fiery claimant to the Byzantine throne freed all Northern Greece of Franks, Bulgars and other foreigners.

The upper town has many post-Byzantine churches and, tucked away in secluded courtyards, are timber-framed chapels where Christian devotions used to be performed in the privacy of the family circle, without drawing undue attention from hostile pashas and fanatical imams. Most important is the fourteenth-century **Church of Christou** in a sunken garden in Kotoyorgaki street, a single-aisle basilica with fourteenth-century frescoes by Kalleryis, who is described in an inscription as 'the best painter in Thessaly'. His style is elegant and fluent, probably influenced by that of icon painting, and his faces are remarkable for their liveliness of expression. In the Descent into Hell, Christ, wearing luminous yellow garments instead of the usual scarlet mantle, is more the gentle saviour of mankind than the formidable judge of the souls of the dead, so dear to earlier Byzantine iconographers.

Mitropoleos Street neatly divides the upper town: the section to the left containing most of the old houses and picturesque Turkish remains. The street itself was once part of the Roman Via Egnatia, many paved sections of which have been left in place in the middle. The maze of streets on the right-hand side contains several crumbling Turkish buildings, the partly restored Jewish quarter and the curious basilica of the Old Mitropolis which can be visited by arrangement with the Byzantine *eforia*. The original structure goes back to the fifth century - there are rather vague plans for extensive restoration. On the north side of the spacious *naos*, there is a colonnade of ninth-century columns. The last transformation was made in the fifteenth century when the frescoed walls were whitewashed, Christian symbols ripped off the desecrated sanctuary and a Moslem congregation appropriated the *naos*.

Six kilometres south of Veria, in the south-western corner of the plain, the road crosses the reed-fringed Aliakmon, flowing out of a defile between the Vermion and Pieria ranges, then turns east to the village of **Veryina**, named after a legendary queen of Veria. The village, like the ancient site, is spread across the lower slopes of the hills behind. Just beyond the village a square kilometre of the plain is dotted with more than three hundred small tumuli, many little more than a metre high. This **Cemetery of the Tumuli** was used for some eight hundred years by the tribesmen who dwelt on the wooded Pierian Mountains, the oldest graves, often in distinct groups indicating clans, dating from the Early Iron Age (1000-700 BC). These burial places attracted much greater interest with the discovery of the first Macedonian tomb here by Leon Heuzey in 1861. Six years earlier this young French archaeologist had been shown the imposing but forgotten ruins of a palace a little further to the south-east. He engaged the interest of the Emperor Napoleon III in his find and returned with a research expedition. A subterranean vaulted building, flooded during his first visit, could at last be explored. The unusual features and originality of style were duly noted and the marble doors, the first example of their kind, were removed to the

Louvre; but still the full significance of the discovery was not recognized. It was only in 1938 that the second Macedonian tomb in the area was found, on the terrace north-west of the palace, and proved to be a royal sepulchre.

A huge mound on the western edge of the Cemetery of the Tumuli - now within the village - 12 metres high with a diameter of 110 metres, unique in the Greek world, had been observed by Heuzey. Excavations by the late Professor Andronikos did not begin in earnest until 1976 but, within three years, they yielded discoveries that have completely changed our idea of Macedonia before Alexander. **The Great Tumulus** had been raised to cover four royal tombs, including the untouched resting place of Philip II. These remains, together with the excavations of the acropolis wall, a temple with votive offerings from Philip's mother Eurydice, and above all, next to the palace, the theatre answering to the description of the one in which Philip was assassinated, leave little doubt that this - and not Edessa - is ancient **Aigai**. First capital of the Macedonian kings, Aigai remained their burial place until the time of Alexander. In 336 BC it was the scene of a splendid ceremony in honour of the marriage of Philip's daughter to an Epirot prince, but the festivities ended in disaster when an assassin's knife was thrust into the kings's back as he entered the crowded theatre.

Glory returned in the last years of the fourth century BC with the construction of a new Palace, the most outstanding of all Macedonian buildings not merely because of its size, but even more because of its architecture and execution.

Veryina is now one of the most important ancient sites in Greece. The **Royal Tombs** are on the left, in the reconstructed mound towards the southern end of the village. The brilliantly successful way that the interior has been laid out, with the tombs and the display of the items found in them, alone justifies a visit to Veryina. The huge interior space seems at first very dark, and one needs several minutes to become accustomed to the subdued lighting. All four tombs are within this space and, in well-lit cases nearby, the items found in them.

The **Tomb of Philip II** (Tomb II) is now world-famous for its wall-painting and for the treasures buried with the king. Visitors descend to the façade, which is brilliantly lit, and can thus have a good view of the large hunting scene painted right across, above the entrance. Among the wonderful objects displayed nearby are the two gold caskets of splendid workmanship that contained his, and perhaps, the queen's bones, the royal diadem, gold jewellery, the king's gold-woven robes, his armour and shield. There are also the remains of two couches elaborately decorated with small figures in ivory; among these there are likenesses of Philip and Alexander. Using a variety of skills it is now possible to create an image of the whole head from a skull or even part of a skull. When this was done with the male skull from the tomb, the result was unmistakeably Philip II, with the terrible wound over his right eye.

The plain façade of the **Tomb of the Prince** nearby (Tomb III) can also be viewed from close quarters. The interior (not visited) contains brilliant wall-paintings of chariot racing of which reproductions are on show. Tomb I, the furthest, contained the remains of a woman with a baby and a young man. Unlike the others it is a simple chamber: the wall-paintings, detached and shown above it, tell the story of the Rape of Persephone. Next to Tomb I are the remains of a shrine to Heroes.

Tomb IV, like Tombs II and III, is in the form of a small temple whose roof has largely fallen in, and this gives one an idea of the interior of these tombs. It is not known who it was for. On display in the well-lit glass cases are many other items of considerable interest.

The road below the car park leading out of the village turns up towards the hills and takes one to the '**Macedonian Tomb**', the Palace and the Theatre. The Tomb, discovered in 1938, is nearly a kilometre up the road, on the left, with a keeper in attendance. The façade resembles that of a little Ionic temple, with four half-columns, a frieze of painted flowers and a pediment. Marble slabs, which formed part of the doorway, lie across the floor of the antechamber. In the barrel-vaulted burial chamber there is a ledge on which the urn containing the ashes of the deceased was placed, and also the damaged but imposing throne of a Macedonian king. The arm-rests are supported by carved sphinxes. Traces of painted griffins devouring a yellow stag against a red ground are visible on the sides and foot-stool. Though robbed like most tombs, the marble throne left no doubt that this was indeed a royal burial chamber, most likely of the third century BC. There are other tombs nearby and elsewhere on the site.

Higher up, on a large terrace looking down over the strange necropolis of burial mounds extending down to the plain, are the ruins of the **Palace.** Built in the early third century BC of buff-coloured limestone it surrounded a colonnaded court which measured

105 metres by 90 metres. These dimensions alone suggest royal pomp of the first magnitude, certainly this is the early third-century BC residence of Antigonos Gonatas. The ruins are scarcely more than shoulder-high, but the architectural layout is clear. A pedimented portico flanked to the north and south by four large rectangular chambers led into the *propylaia* - the small Ionic columns previously decorating the upper storey are now strewn about the ground - and finally into the court, once bordered by sixty massive Doric columns but now littered with pieces of cornice and architrave, drums and capitals, all eroded by time and weather.

Next to the *propylaia* was a circular chamber, believed to be the ceremonial room in which the king received ambassadors and generals. One of the rooms along the south side has a well-preserved floor mosaic which may have had erotic details, removed later by more prudish inhabitants. Excavations at the south-west corner of the palace have revealed a colonnaded open court, beyond which were porticoes and chambers forming an annexe to the tetragon of the palace proper. There are several paved chambers on the west side, but the north side has been completely destroyed. A short distance below the palace terrace are the remains of the theatre in which Philip was assassinated.

Thrusting aggressively from the ledge above the plain, the palace, in its now somewhat naked geometric state, still remains a very impressive ruin. Veryina was partly destroyed by the Romans; some sections of the palace survived, however, to serve different - probably religious - purposes during later periods.

15

Western Macedonia: The Highlands

NORTH TO SOUTH, the mountain mass is seamed with tracts of agricultural land - rice paddies, orchards, fields of corn and sugar-beet - and through it the Aliakmon flows in a great horseshoe loop. The forests, lakes, snow-capped ranges and passes are not yet the haunt of tourists. The goal of most travellers is Kastoria, one of the most important Byzantine sites in Greece. The landscape is varied, often magnificent, but never classical; at no point is the Mediterranean visible. It is a journey into the periphery of the Balkans, whose remoteness ensured the survival of folklore traditions during four centuries of Turkish occupation.

Kastoria, where it is worthwhile spending two nights, can be approached either from Veria across the Vermion range and along the course of the Aliakmon, or from Edessa whence the road runs parallel to the border with Yugoslavian Macedonia and then turns south. The former route, which I describe first, is the longer one.

West of Veria the road climbs Mount Vermion between beech forests where primroses grow. The celebrated monastery of the **Panayia of Soumela** is high above the road on the right. Refugees from the Trebizond area of Turkey brought the holy and miraculous icon of the Panayia with them; the shrine now attracts thousands every day. At the top of the pass there is a tremendous aerial view of the **Aliakmon Valley**, with the river winding between green banks against a prodigious background of the wooded Pieria ranges, which rise to over 2000 metres. The scale is immense. A long, dizzy descent in hairpin bends terminates at the unattractive town of **Kozani**, a road junction in the plain of Ptolemais, where lignite mines have brought heavy industry and prosperity to the region.

From Kozani the Kastoria road, to which we will return, continues westward through undulating countryside. The southbound road (the old main road from Thessaloniki to Athens) crosses the elongated Polyfyto lake, formed by the damming-up of the

Aliakmon, on a very long bridge. A gap suddenly appears in the mountain barrier, with a group of twisted outcrops of rock guarding the entrance to a deep defile. At their foot lies the sleepy little town of **Servia**, originally founded by Serbs settled here by the Emperor Heraklios in the seventh century to defend the strategic pass into Central Greece. Opposite the needle-shaped rocks a hill is crowned by the ruined towers of a Byzantine fortress overlooking a loop of the Aliakmon. Little else survives of the military fortifications of this former key town, where Michael II, the violent and hot-blooded Despot of Epirus, met his pious consort, Theodora, and carried her in state across the mountains to his capital at Arta. South of Servia, a number of narrow passes are succeeded by tracts of inhospitable moorland whence the road descends into Thessaly at Elassona and goes on to Larissa.

The road from Kozani to Kastoria continues westward and after 24 kilometres there is a turn-off to the right for Siatista. A little further on the road from Kozani meets the road from Kastoria to Thessaly via Grevena - a road which has little to offer but its spectacular climax. In summer, heaps of melons are piled up in gigantic pyramids in the main square of **Grevena** - I know of little else to recommend this dreary provincial town. After Grevena the road crosses the ravine of the Venetikos, its rocky banks eroded into strange forms above pools of ice-green water. This is the ancient country of Elimeiotis, across which the nineteen-year-old Alexander, just crowned king and flushed with a resounding victory over the Illyrians, force-marched his army at a pace then unknown in military history, in order to reach Southern Greece and chastise the rebellious Thebans.

Descending gradually across a barren, melancholy mountain tract, one is rewarded by a novel and superbly theatrical view of the Meteora rock-pillars barring the way into the Thessalian plain. To the west the Pindos mountains rise sheer, with dark chasms biting deep into the range. Between awesome heights, the road, by contrast, follows a lovely fertile strip traversed by a stream which feeds the Pinios. Plane trees shade a jungle of brambles and wild fig; there are mulberry groves and the long grass sizzles with the chirping of cicadas; hornets and dragon-flies whirr crazedly in the sun-drenched foliage. The road enters the plain at the base of a cluster of obelisks and pinnacles of stratified conglomerate, rent by gloomy caverns leading into the heart of the valley of the Meteora, and joins the main road from Lamia to Metsovo and Ioannina, capital of Epirus.

Just off the Kozani-Kastoria road is **Siatista**, seat of a remote feudal society that flourished in the twilight era after the fall of Constantinople. The branch road climbs into limestone mountains with fine structural forms uncommon in these parts. The multi-coloured houses of Siatista spread across a line of broken hills. Once inhabited by rich furriers, Siatista seems to have been left unmolested by the Turks. Straddling no centre of communications, it was a retreat to which wealthy merchants retired, untroubled by Turkish tax-collectors. They dwelt in lofty houses with projecting third stories supported by wooden brackets and painted with stylized flowers and foliate patterns below the cornices. The chief interest of the timber-framed houses, some recently restored, lies in their oriental-style interiors and frescoed walls, evocative of a rural, seigniorial way of life, swept away in the holocaust of the War of Independence. There is no feeling of continuity here. Unlike Edessa, Veria or Kastoria, Siatista has no roots in Macedonian history. A phenomenon of the post-Byzantine age, it was the product of its own inaccessibility.

Several of the eighteenth-century houses can be visited. First the **Nerantzopoulous House**, which is still inhabited. As in most large residences of the Turkish period, storerooms and wine-cellars are on the ground floor, sleeping quarters on the first, reception halls on the second. The exterior walls are whitewashed, pierced with windows protected by coffered shutters and wrought-iron gratings fashioned in squiggles and spirals. The nail-studded gate is secured at night by a heavy bar, intended to keep out the brigands who once roamed the encircling mountains. The interior painted wall decoration is primitive and rustic, with still-life compositions of bowls of apples and pears, slices of water melon and stylized flowers.

The **Manoussi House** is more impressive. The exterior walls of the second storey, protected from rain and sun by wide eaves, are painted with geometric designs which create an impression of faience, reminiscent of the ceramics embedded in the exterior apses of chapels in the Pelion area. Despite the ravages of damp and woodworm, many of the rooms still preserve a faded image of the work of the rustic interior decorators who plied their craft throughout Macedonia in the seventeenth and eighteenth centuries. The woodwork is admirably carved, and the variety of differently-shaped bannisters add a further touch of fantasy to the architectural embellishment. A maze of little galleries and panelled halls on different levels leads to the spacious, low-ceilinged reception chamber, reserved for formal name-day celebrations, for wedding festivities conducted with all the pomp dear to a small-town community, and also for night-long death laments chanted by black-draped crones.

The walls of the sun-parlour, its bay windows supported by columns like a miniature loggia, are adorned with mock-heroic frescoes: a stag-hunt with blackbirds perched on tree-tops or flying across a lemon-yellow sky; a kilted hunter with long black moustaches drawing his sword, preparatory to killing a lion which sticks its tongue out at him. The drawing is like that of a child and has a dream-like quality; Islamic influences are evident. The bedrooms are distinguished by a curious architectural feature: fireplaces in the form of apse-like pyramids, their bases surrounded with marble kerbs and each surmounted by a cone capped with a cross, like some Christian version of a Moslem monument. Arched windows are filled with panels of stained glass set in stucco: an importation from the Danubian states, with which the local furriers and wine merchants traded. Perched on the top floor of the house is the minute and only lavatory - Turkish style, a hole in the floor - projecting above the neglected garden. The house must have been a place of fantasy to live in, set against the background of desolate mountains, from which jackals descend at night to shriek in the stony wastes around the village.

Rejoining the main northbound road after the visit to Siatista, one continues along the upper valley of the Aliakmon. At Neapolis one leaves the excellent road to Konitsa and turns north for Kastoria. Westward runs the spine of the northern Pindos, capped by the formidable snow-capped peak of Smolikas (2650 metres). Groves of poplars spread across shallow gullies through which mountain streams feed the Aliakmon. The village of Vogatsiko, built on seven hills and surrounded by oak and beech woods, overlooks the river valley. Barns with thatched roofs suggest the increasingly northern character of the country. The road by-passes the town of Argos Orestikon, the centre of a trade in sheepskin rugs. Near Dispilio a pre-historic settlement has been recreated. Soon the road is winding along the shore of Lake Kastoria. Mist clings to the banks in the early morning, and wild fowl skim the placid waters.

The buildings of **Kastoria** rise from the twin shores of an isthmus onto a rocky headland. Among the highest of them, the Hotel Xenia commands a prospect of the ice-blue lake with its fringe of poplars; behind, a screen of wild mountains piles up towards Albania in the west and Yugoslavian Macedonia in the north, the whole dominated by the cone-shaped peak of Vitsa. Byzantine churches and chapels spread fan-wise round the hotel, which is a good starting-point for sightseeing. A full day is required to visit the main churches and the surviving, tower-like eighteenth-century houses overlooking dark courtyards. (A lot of time is usually spent hunting for the custodians of these houses.) The climate is harsh and northern. In winter the lake freezes; in spring adders glide in the undergrowth; summer does not come till June. Perch, pike and eels are fished in the lake, but it was the fur trade that brought prosperity to Kastoria: for centuries it was a recognized dumping-ground for scraps of mink and other pelts discarded by the more fastidious furriers of Europe and America - but now the trade is very much reduced.

The history of the town, the ancient Keletron, is uneventful until the Middle Ages when a succession of invaders made it an important staging-post on the way to the East. Among the first was Robert Guiscard, Norman Duke of Apulia and Calabria, who opened the eyes of western princes to the glittering prospect of the dismemberment of the Byzantine Empire. Later, during the Frankish occupation, Michael II conducted a guerilla war in the neighbouring hills against the Eastern aspirant to the Byzantine throne. Then came the Albanians, the Turks, who stayed for over five centuries, and the Jews, who developed the fur industry. In 1947-49 insurgent Communists waged a two-year struggle against the Greek army from hideouts among the surrounding villages.

The important churches are wholly Byzantine, but there is no evidence of the multiple domes that crown the Paleologos churches; here the more austere basilica form endures almost unchallenged, the angular planes of its sloping roofs conforming harmoniously with the northern setting. On summer evenings, however, the elaborate brickwork decoration of the exterior walls glows with a warm, roseate hue. Of the seventy-two churches and chapels, at least six are worth visiting. They belong to the tenth to fourteenth centuries. It is essential to start by visiting the **Byzantine Museum** where the keys to the important churches are kept. The Museum, which is on the hill near the Hotel Xenia, has a small and well-arranged collection of icons and frescoes of the thirteenth to fifteenth centuries. It may be possible to arrange for a guide to take you to the important churches, however staff may not be available and it will then be

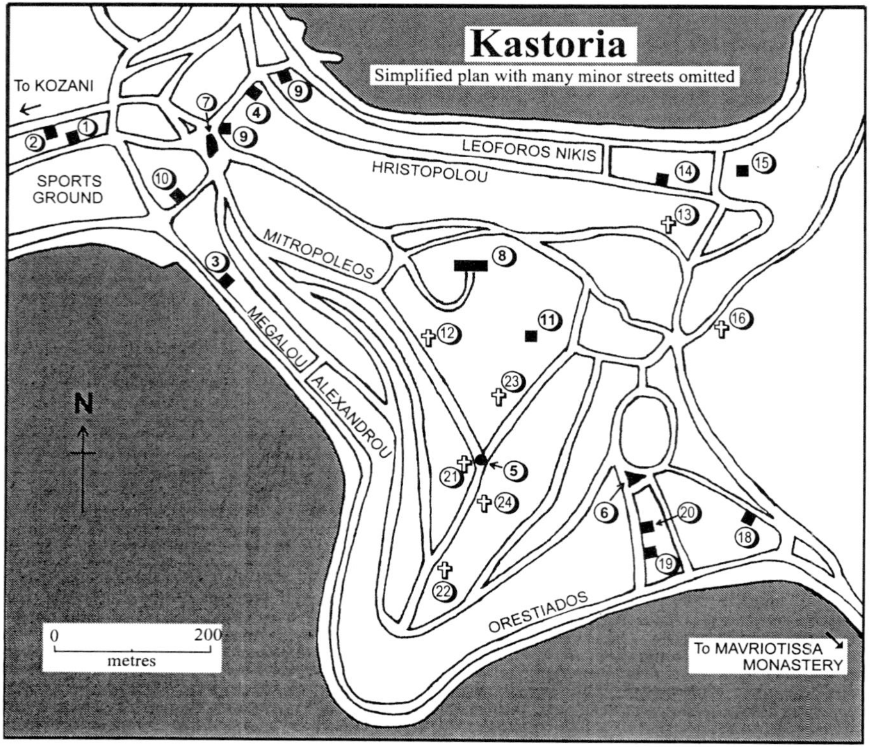

Kastoria

Simplified plan with many minor streets omitted

PLACES OF INTEREST

1. Bus Station
2. Police
3. Post Office
4. Town Hall
   Tourist Information
   Market
5. Platia Omonia
6. Platia Emmanouil
7. Platia Davaki
8. Hotel Xenia
9. Byzantine Walls
10. Medresseh
11. Byzantine Museum
12. Ayios Nikolaos
13. Ayii Anaryiri
14. Sapountzi House
15. Tsiatsapa House
16. Ayios Stefanos
18. Folklore Museum
19. Natzi House
20. Emmanouil House
21. Ayios Nikolaos Kasnitzi
22. Mitropolis
23. Panayia Koubelidiki
24. Taxiarhi

necessary to wait to join a group or go to each church in the hope of finding it open. The staff at the Museum will advise you if any of the churches are closed for restoration work and how to gain access to the less important ones.

Below Platia Davaki, next to the Town Hall (*Dimarhion*), one can see fragments of the Byzantine ramparts which used to protect the isthmus from the west. From here, Mitropoleos Street climbs up to Platia Omonia. A turn to the left takes you to the Hotel Xenia and the Museum. The order in which you visit the main churches will depend on your guide - here we will follow a roughly clockwise circuit, including other buildings on the way.

In a side-street between Mitropoleos Street and the Museum stands the little eleventh-century **Church of Ayios Nikolaos**, with some sixteenth-century frescoes, of which the most striking (left, on entering) represents a melancholy youth wearing a fez, who died at an early age; his bereaved mother laments beside him.

Going northwards and then to the right below the Xenia Hotel, a sharp descent leads eastwards to the attractive **Basilica of Ayii Anaryiri** (Saints Kosmas and Damian), one of the oldest churches in Kastoria. Destroyed, it is said, by the Bulgarian Tsar Samuel in the tenth century, the church was refounded by the Emperor Basil II when he spent the autumn of 1018 in Kastoria, celebrating his triumph over the Bulgars. The exterior walls are decorated with an intricate pattern of brick inlay. Two sun-discs frame an arched window divided by a colonnette above the apse. Symmetry and picturesqueness are nicely blended. Exterior frescoes dating from the eleventh and twelfth centuries - another provincial feature - break up the monotony of the western façade. Figures of St Peter and St Paul flank the doorway; on either side of them the two patron physicians, Kosmas and Damian, stand protectively. The interior is very dark but, if the doors are opened, the figures in the blackened frescoes assume identifiable forms. In the narthex a grim, bearded St Basil, with a nasty turned-down mouth, reflects an unusual aspect of the beneficent bishop, who devoted his life to relieving the miseries of the poor. In the later frescoes of the *naos* the faces are softer and the garments less rigid. In a haunting vision of the Pentecost, rays of light fall on the heads of the apostles grouped on either side of a double arched window.

Several tower-like houses of the seventeenth and eighteenth centuries survive on or near the northern waterfront and in the southern quarter. Built for prosperous furriers and once the grandest in Macedonia, many were left to decay beyond repair and were finally pulled down. In about half a dozen the frescoed sun-parlours, panelled halls, painted ceilings and ornamental doorways have been restored. In a lane behind the northern waterfront (Leoforos Nikis), the **Tsiatsapa House** is distinguished by latticed windows, recessed balconies and wooden brackets. Cobbled alleys lead west to the **Sapountzi House**, architecturally very formal and symmetrical, approached through a court. The first two stories are of stone, the third timber-framed, shaded by eaves that protect the walls from the drip of melting snow in spring.

A little south-east of Ayii Anaryiri is the small tenth-century **Basilica of Ayios Stefanos**, with single columns separating the nave from the diminutive aisles. Its unusual height, together with the smoke-blackened surface of the walls, produces a sombre effect. More interesting is the brickwork decoration of the exterior, a conspicuous regional feature, which has a complex interplay of cubes, crosses, lozenges, half-moons and wheel-spokes within sun-discs.

In the southern quarter, Kariadi, near the lake waterfront there are a number of fine old mansions, some restored, notably the **Nerantzi House**, now transformed into a folklore museum. The **Natzi House**, preceded by a little loggia, is one of the finest in Kastoria. A musicians' gallery, its walls painted with garlands of flowers, overlooks a reception room, where engagements and marriages were celebrated. The *saloni* (or drawing room) and halls are elaborately frescoed and the decoration has all the story-book whimsicality of Siatista. Nearby is the Emmanouil House.

Up the hill again, towards the Museum, is Platia Omonia, an irregular open space lively at night with tavernas and cafés, and crowned by the little single-chamber Basilica of *Ayios Ioannis Prodromos*. More important is the twelfth-century **Church of Ayios Nikolaos Kasnitzi**, which repeats the familiar architectural and decorative pattern of the Kastorian basilica. In the thirteenth-century frescoes the well-known figures play their accustomed liturgical roles. In the apse the Virgin *Orans* is flanked by two angels bearing kerchiefs. Their movements are free and articulate. Above the apse presides another effigy of the Virgin, this time of greater dignity, approached by the Angel Gabriel with an alert expressive face. Above the west door the Dormition of the Virgin is crowned with mourning figures in pastel-shaded garments. Above the Dormition, the Transfiguration depicts Christ as an emaciated figure with matchstick legs, his white garments fluttering in the breeze. The frescoes of *Ayios Nikolaos Kasnitzi* are not among the great masterpieces of Byzantine painting, but they possess freshness and vigour, tempered by an engaging rustic simplicity.

A short distance southwards, towards the *Mitropolis,* is the eleventh-century **Basilica of the Taxiarhi** (Archangels) which, in spite of the jigsaw puzzle of brick inlay, produces an almost barn-like effect. Frescoes spread across the façade: Archangels flank the entrance and the two pygmy-like figures of the donors, a Bulgarian prince and his half-Greek mother, cower at St Michael's feet. The fourteenth-century frescoes in the interior possess unmistakable affinities with the Southern Serbian school of Byzantine painting. There is a realism and a fluidity of movement, a suggestion of three-dimensional style foreign to the classical, more static, iconography of Constantinople.

A short way north of Platia Omonia, in front of the High School, stands the picturesque little **Church of the Panayia Koubelidiki**, which is another early foundation. The usual exterior brickwork decoration is tidier though less inventive than elsewhere, but the fifteenth-century frescoes of the exterior walls of the narthex give a coquettish air to this little architectural folly.

The south shore of the isthmus is bordered by plane trees. After skirting a sandy beach littered with hulks of half-constructed boats, the narrow road, bordered by weeping willows, becomes a favourite strolling ground, with cyclists and holiday-makers bound for the lakeside tavernas. Flat-bottomed fishing boats with blunt bows glide across the slime-covered waters of the southern bight of the lake. In the evening, loaded with perch and carp, they emerge ghost-like out of the mist, nosing their way towards wooden jetties.

Between the shore and a rocky hillside, the **Monastery of Mavriotissa** nestles in the shade of the plane trees. A landing was effected here by a Byzantine army led by Alexios I, most astute of Komnenos emperors, who laid seige to the Normans occupying Kastoria; the Emperor probably founded the monastery later. It was considerably rebuilt during the fourteenth-century Serb occupation.

The church, chapel, some cells and a belfry spread along the lakeside. It is a secluded place, once the haunt of Byzantine and Slav princes who came here to worship. The exterior side wall of the chapel of *Ayios Ioannis Theologos* is painted with crude post-Byzantine frescoes of saintly figures. But in the Last Supper (interior north wall) there is a charming arrangement, totally devoid of perspective, with glass and cutlery, plates, goblets and bowls laid out on a half-moon table.

In the main church, a single-aisle basilica with narthex, the frescoes of the late twelfth century are, in spite of clumsy execution, vigorous in conception, with detached groups of figures depicted in a state of arrested movement. Within the narthex there is a crude but animated Last Judgement, crowned with militant angels and deformed, cringing creatures representing the various categories of sinners: slanderers, moneylenders (hanging upside down) and harlots with long black ringlets. A wooden door carved with crosses and diamond-shaped lozenges leads into the *naos*. The dominating fresco is the **Dormition of the Virgin** (west wall) which is grand and tragic, the figures stilted but expressive, the mourners' faces turned towards the bier so that the focus is on the centre of the picture, where lies the formidable, almost masculine, corpse. There is a grand **Ascension**: first a frieze of apostles between stylized trees, with the Virgin *Orans* in the middle; then Christ, with a terrible Messianic expression, a protruding stomach and short legs. Neither faulty drawing nor clumsy execution deprive the composition of power or intensity of feeling.

The numerous post-Byzantine chapels scattered about the headland are destinations for walks. The walls of many, both interior and exterior, are frescoed. In the Apazari quarter (north shore), the Church of *Ayios Ioannis Prodromos* is worth visiting, if only to look at the frescoes in the women's gallery. Demons are seen torturing the malicious gossiper, the cheating miller and the female usurer; an adulteress suffers ignoble torments inflicted by a demon in the form of a snake, while the most shocking treatment of all is reserved for the harlot.

The beginning of the shorter northern route from Edessa to Kastoria follows the upper reaches of the **River Edesseos** (Voda). The configuration of the land, with its wooded ledges ascending the Vermion range, has none of the dramatic quality of the Central Greek mountain formations. Everything is tamer, somewhat lacking in definition. It possesses all the fertility of the Imathian plain but without any of its domesticity. There are no towns, few villages. The route must be the one followed by Alexander when, weary of the rumbustious brawling of family life at Pella, he retired to sulk in Illyria.

After leaving the Edesseos valley, the road crosses a small plain where rushes grow, surrounded by ilex-covered hills. Below, to the west beyond the maize fields, appear the sparsely inhabited shores of **Lake Vegoritida**, its pale blue waters making deep inroads into the arid mountain sides. At the north-east end of the lake a huddled village is all that remains of ancient **Arnissa**, better known as medieval Ostrovo, once a station on the Via Egnatia, which was fiercely disputed by the armies of rival claimants to the Byzantine throne when Frankish Greece was beginning to fall apart; in the general confusion of civil war, the shores of Vegoritida were often littered with the abandoned impedimenta of defeated armies. There are ruins of a Turkish mosque on an islet off Arnissa, once the centre of a village said to have been submerged in the lake.

The direct road to Florina from Arnissa goes through sparsely inhabited valleys and scrub-covered highlands where the armies of the Emperor Basil II and the Bulgar Tsar Samuel contended for the strategic prize of Ostrovo in the early eleventh century. It is a melancholy scene, with several abandoned stone-built villages, but the descent leads into a warmer climate, with a fertile plain running north to south between hazy mountain ranges. To the north, at the head of the broad strip of cultivation lies Pelagonia; here the Byzantine emperor in exile decisively defeated the Frankish armies in a battle which preceded the expulsion of the Crusaders' descendants from Constantinople by only two years. More recently, in the twentieth century, Balkan and German invading armies poured through the so-called 'Monastir Gap', in fact a wide plain between the mountains.

Across the plain the garrison town of **Florina**, fought over during the First World War and largely destroyed during the civil war of 1947-49, stands in a commanding position at the mouth of a mountain valley. This is the ancient land of Lynkestis, famous for its waters, which were said to possess intoxicating qualities, and whose royal house married into that of the Macedonian kings, only to find the connection used as a pretext for the annexation of the country. There is little to say about Florina; a reorganised museum and an art gallery fail to compensate for extremes of climate and a surfeit of concrete. Unsmiling, square-faced peasants bring their produce to market and bored-looking soldiers stroll along the unattractive streets. Both seem as remote from Mediterranean Greece as the Balkan landscape itself. But there is one last lap: to the Prespa lakes.

To the west of Florina the Kastoria road climbs a flank of the mountains above a fertile valley; otherwise the country seems uninhabited, muted. One senses the proximity of frontiers, of an end to all things Greek. The road goes over the Pisoderi pass at nearly 1500 metres and then, after winding between puce-coloured hills, one is suddenly peering over the rim of a great bowl surrounded by the mountains. The configuration is confusing: north to south runs the lake of **Lesser Prespa**, appendix-shaped; a Greek-Albanian lake, its surface is a cold, hard blue. Beyond an isthmus extends **Greater Prespa**, whose waters are shared by Greece, Albania and Yugoslavian Macedonia, heart-shaped in the north, tapering at the southern end into an inlet which runs parallel to Lesser Prespa, biting deep into Albanian territory. To the west rise the stark Albanian mountains, at the foot of which once wound the Via Egnatia. The descent to the lakes is through domesticated but seemingly deserted country, the red soil contrasting sharply with the naked grey mountains on whose ridges snowdrifts lie in crevices. The scale and range is immense, the desolation grandiose. I know of no more inhospitable place than this meeting-point of three countries. In this inaccessible area Alexander defeated the Lynkestrian tribes, whose subjection ensured the safety of his rear, at a time when he was concentrating the bulk of his forces in the east for the passage into Asia. Here too, in the late tenth century Tsar Samuel established his military headquarters and a court, noted for its savagery, from which he waged a long, defiant and ultimately hopeless struggle for possession of Northern Greece.

Along a level stretch of shore, washed by Lesser Prespa, extends a **bird sanctuary**, to which birds from all over south-eastern Europe migrate; about 200 species have been recorded and it is one of the few sites in Europe where pelicans are known to nest. A hide has been built for the benefit of birdwatchers. On the islet, somewhat quaintly named Ayios Ahillios, to the south of the narrow isthmus between the lakes there are various Byzantine ruins, including a basilica, founded in the tenth century by Tsar Samuel, with remains of contemporary frescoes. The road continues close to the north-east shore of Lesser Prespa as far as Ayios Yermanos, which lies at the foot of beige-coloured hills, the last village this side of the border with Yugoslavian Macedonia: a bucolic place with houses scattered among poplars in which myriads of birds twitter. One hears villagers talking Serbo-Croat as well as Greek. This is the end of the road, as there is no border crossing.

Returning to the main road, and after re-crossing the line of hills above the Prespa basin, there is a fork - the road to the right goes to

Albania. The road to the south runs through shut-in, wooded country. Donkeys are tethered to tree-trunks in groves of silver plane trees and goats browse in terraced glades where the parched grass of summer replaces the narcissi of early spring. Streams unite and separate, forming shady pools where the water freezes hard in winter; the whole place is alive with bird-song. In antiquity the Orestai, a barbarian tribe, dwelt here, more happily blessed by nature than many of their neighbours, until they were subjugated by Philip II and their well-watered valleys were annexed to 'Greater' Macedonia. The road climbs through beech woods and then winds down in successive loops, each of which affords a more entrancing view of the northern shores of Lake Kastoria, the tall houses and buildings of the town strung out along the isthmus and the mallet-shaped headland projecting into the shallow waters.

For those not wishing to visit Florina and the Prespa Lakes it is possible to follow the road from Arnissa down the east side of Lake Vegoritida and then use a beautiful mountain road to reach Kastoria.

16

The Halkidiki

THE TRAVELLER IN MACEDONIA has a wide choice of places to visit in the central and western parts of the area, but there is also much that merits attention east of Thessaloniki. Most of the important sites can be visited by means of two main itineraries: (i) the highway running eastward across the rest of Macedonia and Thrace to the Turkish border (Chapters 18 and 19); (ii) a somewhat circuitous tour round the Halkidiki peninsula, starting from Thessaloniki and including several detours - which I describe here. The long, two-day drive can be broken at one of the many hotels in the area, although the large modern hotels situated on, or overlooking, the beaches are likely to be full during the summer and closed out of season. The two westerly prongs of the peninsula have been developed into what the brochures describe as a 'tourists' paradise', with all the amenities of good roads, conference centres, hotels with swimming pools and discos, villa complexes, yacht anchorages and camp sites.

South-east of Thessaloniki the Halkidiki juts out into the Aegean like a huge deformed lobster with three claws. Much of the woodland country (as opposed to the sometimes over-developed beaches), across which Xerxes' army marched in the summer of 480 BC, is still sufficiently off the beaten track to recall a virgin land. Washed by the Thermaic and Strymonic Gulfs, the peninsula has, by the nature of its strange contours and sparsely-populated forests, remained a self-contained geographical unit, with a character different from the rest of Macedonia. The original inhabitants, the Paeonians, a rustic people cut off from the two-way traffic of trade and ideas that crossed the neck of the peninsula, developed independently of the Thracians; but in the eighth and seventh centuries BC the coast was colonized by settlers from Euboea (the modern Evvia) who intermarried with the natives. For centuries the forest tracts remained wild and uninhabited, the thirty cities founded by the colonizers being strung out along the shores of the three prongs. Athens too founded colonies here. Corinth and Sparta objected and the Peloponnesian War followed. Finally Philip II of Macedon reduced the country to subjection. The poor state of preservation of the antiquities sometimes belies their historical importance. The indigenous inhabitants, formerly woodcutters and fishermen, are a dark, taciturn people; unlike most Greeks, they seem, except in the tourist centres, to be impervious to the presence of strangers, indifferent to their provenance or destination.

From Thessaloniki the road to the south runs through dreary suburbs to the nineteenth-century Villa Alatini, a landmark situated on a bluff above the sea, where Sultan Abdul Hamid II, 'The Damned', was interned after his deposition in 1909. Just before the villa, a branch road to the north climbs Mount Hortiatis to Panorama, a summer resort of red-roofed houses amid dark green conifers. There are hotels, restaurants and a panoramic view of the city, the Thermaic Gulf and Western Halkidiki; on torrid summer evenings the air is wonderfully bracing. The road continues through upland country with much unattractive development on either side and ends at the village of **Hortiatis**. Here, beside the ochre-coloured modern church, there is an unassuming little twelfth-century Church of the Metamorphosis, with four niches in the interior angles which create the illusion that the building is octagonal. It is crowned by a shallow windowless dome, probably a later addition of the Turkish period. The narthex has disappeared to make room for an adjacent house. The original frescoes are unfortunately covered with plaster, but vestiges of the fine head of a young saint within a sombre-coloured halo suggest their quality.

The southbound road from Thessaloniki continues past crowded beaches and the airport. Fifty kilometres from the city a branch road runs north to Petralona, where the cave of *Kokkines Petres* (The Red Stones), famous for its shiny stalactites, is situated at the base of a foothill of the Holomon range. One day in 1960, a party of visitors entering the cave stumbled on a fossilized skull, later identified as that of a Neanderthal woman who probably lived some seventy-five thousand years ago. Later a complete skeleton was found, possibly 700,000 years old, which would indicate that Homo Sapiens existed in Europe rather earlier than previously believed.

The main road runs across open country - a golf-course landscape with views of distant, cone-shaped hills. Soon the land contracts into a very narrow isthmus; here begins the geographical area associated with the 'Thracian tribute': the detested levy exacted

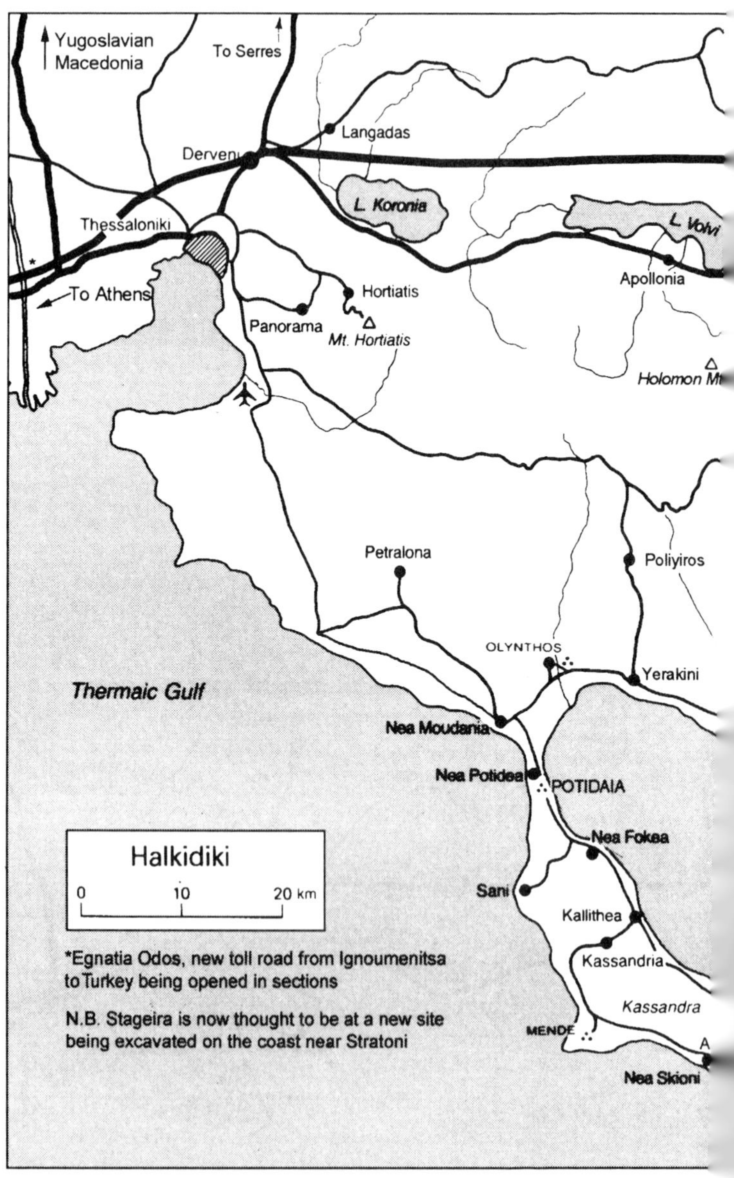
Yugoslavian Macedonia
To Serres
Langadas
Derveni
L. Koronia
L. Volvi
Thessaloniki
To Athens
Hortiatis
Apollonia
Panorama
Mt. Hortiatis
Holomon Mt
Petralona
Poliyiros
OLYNTHOS
Yerakini
Thermaic Gulf
Nea Moudania
Nea Potidea
POTIDAIA
Nea Fokea
Halkidiki
0
10
20 km
Sani
Kallithea
Kassandria
Kassandra
MENDE
Nea Skioni
*Egnatia Odos, new toll road from Ignoumenitsa to Turkey being opened in sections
N.B. Stageira is now thought to be at a new site being excavated on the coast near Stratoni

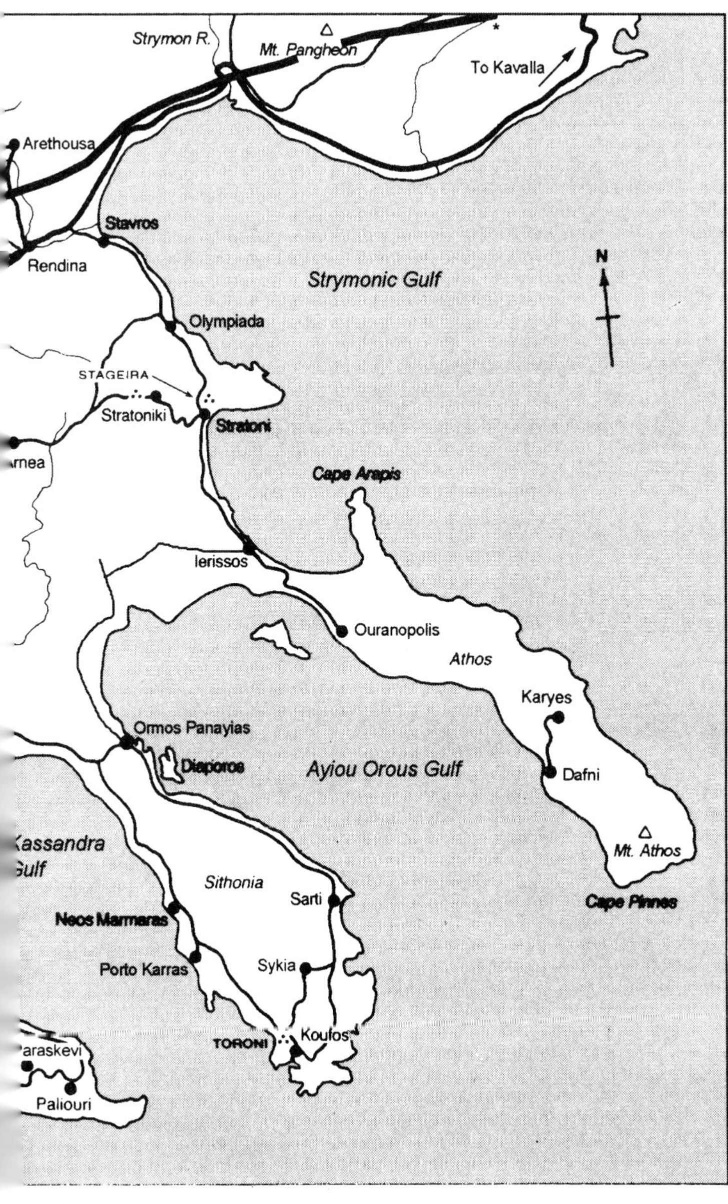
Strymon R.
Mt. Pangheon
To Kavalla
Arethousa
Stavros
Rendina
Strymonic Gulf
N
Olympiada
STAGEIRA
Stratoniki
Stratoni
Cape Arapis
Ierissos
Ouranopolis
Athos
Karyes
Ormos Panayias
Diaporos
Ayiou Orous Gulf
Dafni
Mt. Athos
Cape Pinnes
Sithonia
Sarti
Neos Marmaras
Porto Karras
Sykia
TORONI
Koufos
Paliouri

from the colonies allied to Athens under duress in the fifth century BC. At **Nea Moudania**, a nondescript town with a fishing harbour, there are tavernas and a small hotel.

To reach the Kassandra peninsula (the western 'claw' of the whole Halkidiki peninsula) take the southbound road after the town over the muddy canal that crosses the isthmus. At the hinge of the 'claw', the site of ancient **Potidaia** extends beyond this canal. Xerxes' fleet, supporting his invading army, anchored here in 480 BC and took on provisions. Half a century later, the Corinthian-inspired revolt of Potidaia against Athens was one of the incidents that triggered off the Peloponnesian War. Athenian pride, stung by the insolence of Potidaian defection, demanded instant retribution. However, neither battering ram nor other aggressive weapon could help the assault troops, led by the brilliant Phormio, to break the defenders' resistance. Blockaded by the Athenian fleet, the Potidaians were also decimated by the plague spread by reinforcements from Athens, where the epidemic was raging. It took the besiegers two years to reduce the city; the epitaph of those who fell is in the British Museum. It was here also, in the Halkidiki, geographically so remote from Athens and Sparta, that were fought some of the most decisive campaigns of a war in which the whole Hellenic world was involved. In the Hellenistic period, Kassandros, who had assumed Alexander the Great's mantle in mainland Greece, founded a new city on the site and called it Kassandreia.

At **Nea Potidea** brightly-painted caiques anchor in the creeks where the Macedonian triremes were once built - Livy talks of a hundred vessels at a time being constructed in the docks. Blocks of masonry near the sea mark the point where the line of forts guarding the entire headland once began. I have counted eight ruined towers extending across the isthmus - all medieval - in which classical masonry has been re-used, and archaeologists have identified ancient slabs among village rubble. It must have been somewhere near here, in the days of the great siege, that Socrates saved the life of the young Alcibiades, thus cementing - if the story is not apocryphal - his famous friendship with the most controversial personality of the late fifth century BC. Fishermen talk of ancient under-water stairways: visible only when the sea is calm and translucent.

From Potidea the **Kassandra** headland runs southward in a series of low, neatly-sliced cliffs. The road follows the east coast of the prong; above the beaches, reddish-brown cliffs are studded with tall pines whose wood was used in the construction of the triremes; at

Nea Fokea, a medieval tower crowns a cliff overlooking the little harbour. The countryside, until recently inhabited exclusively by sheep-farmers, has been developed into a complex of camp-sites and tourist hotels, though in the shady, still undesecrated woodland the copses are pock-marked with beehives. At Kallithea, cliffs screen a number of large hotels situated on a beach of fine sand. Beside them is an ancient ruin: the foundations of a fourth-century BC temple of Zeus Ammon, with a north-south axis (instead of the usual east-west), strewn with Doric, Ionic and Corinthian capitals. A nearby spring, which provides water for the hotels, is popularly associated with the stream diverted by Zeus to flow underground from Mount Olympos in order to irrigate his maritime sanctuary.

Southward, large hotels and villa complexes succeed each other as far as the Xenia at Paliouri, where the coastline, now more broken, offers greater variety. The road turns inland across the saddle of the prong and passes through the village of **Ayia Paraskevi**, where there are traces of the architecture of the Turkish period. Children playing in pot-holed lanes glance at one and go on with their games; in the café, men briefly look up from their backgammon boards and continue to rattle dice. But no Halkidikian, for all his lack of inquisitiveness (so rare in Greece), is likely to be unfriendly when asked for help.

At **Nea Skioni** on the west coast of the prong, below the pine-clad hills carpeted in spring with shrubs of bright-coloured cistus, is the site of ill-fated Skioni, where the Athenians took revenge on the inhabitants for welcoming Brasidas, the Spartan leader. Retribution took the form of the massacre of the entire male population of the city, which had held out against the Athenian siege for so long and so courageously in 423 BC. Some exploratory archaeological work has been done but, so far, no major excavation has been carried out.

The road passes above another fine beach and reaches a wooded bluff with a modern hotel on it, the Mendi: site of ancient Mende, once famous for its delicious wine. Here too there was fierce fighting during the Peloponnesian War, with triremes manoeuvring along the coast.

The northbound road back to Potidea and the isthmus continues across low, flat-topped promontories. After crossing the isthmus take the Sithonia road, to the right, along the head of the Gulf of Kassandra and, after about three kilometres, take the second of two successive turn-offs to the left for Olynthos. The fields are dotted with clumps of chestnut trees, the air is heavy with humidity and the drone of cicadas is deafening. At the park-like entrance to the archaeological site is the custodian's house and ticket office with a small, informative exhibition.

The ancient city of **Olynthos** covers most of a long, flattish eminence rising steeply on all sides out of the fields and pastures. Lilac-coloured, nutty-scented heliotrope spreads around the base. The walk to the top is short and is not very steep; in spring the track is ablaze with wild flowers.

By the early fourth century BC, the political prestige and economic prosperity of the Olynthian Confederacy had become a byword. Narrow nationalist motives, however, induced the neighbouring cities of Akanthos and Apollonia to solicit the intervention of Sparta, whose gimlet-eye had long been fixed on this progressive and potentially powerful state. At first the Lacedaimonian attackers made little progress and even suffered humiliating defeats. The besieged Olynthians had a grandstand view of their cavalry charging down the hill towards the Spartan *helots* massed before the walls. However a sustained blockade (382-379 BC) ended in surrender and the Olynthians had to accept subjection to Sparta. The destruction of the confederacy was a blow to Greece and the nascent democratic ideal. Some thirty years later Philip of Macedon unleashed an avalanche of conquest on Eastern Macedonia. Sparta sullenly refused to raise a finger in aid, and Athenian assistance - fourteen thousand men and fifty triremes - came too late to be of use. Shorn of all power by their Spartan 'protectors' and undermined by treachery, the Olynthians surrendered to the Macedonian phalanx. On the site of the battle Philip staged a festival, with athletic and, for the Macedonian king had his softer side, poetical contests.

Little of major importance has been uncovered although the American School of Classical Studies has carried out extensive excavations, and the whole site has now been tidied up by the Greek Archaeological service. Cisterns and substructures seem inadequate legacies of a city once so politically mature for its times, but the area does give a very good idea of domestic architecture of the period and of the sophistication of the town-plan. Vestiges of neolithic dwellings on the higher, southern part of the hill reveal that it was inhabited as far back as the third millennium BC. In the same area is an elaborate system of cisterns of much later date; at the south end of the site are the remains of one of the defensive towers.

Beyond Olynthos, the road continues eastward past the tourist beach of Yerakini. 25 kilometres further on there is a fork in the road. One way leads left, across the next isthmus to the Ayiou Orous Gulf; the other penetrates the middle 'claw' of the Halkidiki: hilly, wooded **Sithonia**, upon which the cities of the earliest colonizers were once scattered. Range upon range of hills of ever-increasing height, sliced with gullies filled with plane and olive trees, rise from the sandy coves of the west coast. An abandoned dependency of an Athonite monastery - windowless buildings with slate roofs and tall chimneys, amid poplars and cypresses - spreads across the mouth of a valley. The beaches continue, pine-fringed. Beyond the harbour of Neos Marmaras and its cone-shaped islet, the purpose-built resort of Porto Karras is the largest and most comprehensive tourist complex in Northern Greece, with hotels ranging from luxurious to relatively modest. From here the road climbs into the hills, past the huge Karras agricultural estate; its terraced vineyards, olive groves and citrus orchards affording sudden glimpses of the sea, wooded spits of land and rocky islets. From a considerable altitude one looks down on an inland bowl which conceals another ruined dependency of an Athonite monastery. The descent to the coast leads through avenues of mulberries to pine-fringed lagoons. To the south rises the hatchet-shaped bluff of Vigla. At the southern end of the crescent-shaped bay another bluff, which repeats in miniature the forms of Vigla, marks the site of the acropolis of ancient **Toroni**. There is still not much to see (although excavations are proceeding), but it is one of the most evocative places in Northern Greece. Toroni was the chief settlement of the early colonizers. During the Peloponnesian War, although allied to Athens, the city welcomed the Spartans as liberators. However when Kleon, the Athenian demagogue-general, recaptured it, the Toronians paid for their fickle behaviour: the male population was deported to Athens and the women and children sold into slavery.

Vestiges of Byzantine fortifications can be identified along the line where the ancient ramparts extended, and Hellenic masonry is embedded in the soil of the strip of land connecting the acropolis with what must have been the ancient town. The visible blocks of granite probably formed part of Hellenic structures. It is a remote and unfrequented place.

Immediately to the south, the deep inlet of Koufos is cunningly concealed by the Toroni promontory which scythes around to create a lovely landlocked bay with a sandy beach and perfect anchorage. The road now climbs into hills covered with heather and arbutus.

Vultures perch on rocky ledges; they suddenly flap their wings, then wheel, hover and swoop down to peck at a carcase. The east coast is very rugged, less wooded, more sparsely inhabited than the western shores. From above the bay of Sykia there is a spectacular view of the Athos peninsula to the north-east, with the tip, Cape Pinnes, crowned by a conical peak which is repeated, at a much greater altitude, by the dramatic summit of the Holy Mountain itself. Monasteries, hermitages and maritime arsenals are discernible along the length of this tremendous backcloth.

North of the bay and beach of Sarti, the coast becomes grander, its broken forms more intricate. Pine-clad spits project into the still waters of the Ayiou Orous Gulf. Poplar-lined lagoons girdle the low, sand-fringed islet of Diaporos. From the inlet of Ormos Panayias it is possible to drive round the head of the gulf to Ierissos, but the route proposed here turns westward, back to the point where the road penetrates the Sithonian headland.

At the head of the Gulf of Kassandra, not far from the Yerakini beach, a road climbs the Holomon range, the central massif of the Halkidiki, winding between hills of increasing height covered with arbutus, whose wood was used for making flutes, and whose large berries taste like strawberries. **Poliyiros**, a pretty little town with red-tiled roofs, spreads among poplars in the folds of hills where myriads of birds sing. Hereabouts, according to Xenophon, was the site of Apollonia, one of the cities which undermined the Olynthian Confederacy by inviting Spartan intervention. Beautiful silver coins, minted in Apollonia and showing the head of Apollo, can be seen in the Numismatic Museum in Athens. Further north take the road to the right, which climbs, dips and winds around oak-covered ridges past the highest point in the range. The landscape is unlike any other in Greece. The massif is cut by no deep valleys, conceals no high-lying plains; there are no bold dramatic contours, no vast perspectives. Foreground and background melt into each other in gentle undulating folds; a faint opacity tinges the light; wisps of smoke spiral up from woodcutters' fires. The road descends around hairpin bends through silent chestnut forests has an sombre quality. A muted feeling seems to hang over the little town of Arnea, its large square bordered by lime-washed houses, their balconies ablaze with morning glory and climbing roses. Around here once stretched a tract of virgin forest, home to lions, which, in 480 BC, attacked the caravans of camels loaded with Persian stores.

The descent continues and, on the right, at **Stayira**, the statue of an ancient Greek figure holding a scroll stands commandingly on a ledge. The effigy, which is modern, glossy and without artistic merit, represents Aristotle, and the terraced ground is the site of ancient **Stageira**, the philosopher's birthplace. The son of a local physician, he spent his childhood roaming the woods, absorbed in the study of natural history. After the peninsula had been laid waste by Philip, Aristotle persuaded his pupil, Alexander the Great, to rebuild Stageira, of which he always remained a citizen; but by the first century AD Strabo found the city totally abandoned. Substructures of Hellenic masonry can be identified around the terraced ground. There are also ruins of a tower and an edifice with built-in arches of a later period.

The road continues through the village of Stratoniki and the coastline of the Strymonic Gulf is reached at Stratoni, below a forbidding cliff where the mines, now producing magnesite, once provided silver for coins. Sandy beaches littered with grotesque outcrops of rock stretch southward as far as **Ierissos**, once Akanthos, the jealous rival of Olynthos. Beyond the town, the last prong of the trident culminates in the peak of Athos, hidden by the headland of Cape Arapis. The mole, which affords shelter to small craft from the winter gales that lash the Thracian sea, is built on Hellenic foundations. Weather permitting, boats sail daily from Ierissos to the monasteries on the east coast of the Athos peninsula. Ancient marble slabs and square granite blocks are scattered across the hill above the town, where the acropolis once stood, and vestiges of the tombs of a classical necropolis have been excavated on the sands. Here Xerxes was received with pomp during his westward march, and Brasidas, who was 'was not a bad speaker for a Lacedaimonian', according to Thucydides, once again won over the local inhabitants with his 'seductive arguments'. The modern town has little to offer, other than its fine beach and some hotels, useful to travellers bound for the monasteries. A prevailing air of melancholy is only relieved on summer nights when the seashore tavernas are visited by an itinerant bouzouki band.

The road across the mile and a half-wide isthmus roughly follows the course of **Xerxes' Canal**, dug by his engineers to allow the passage of the Persian fleet, two triremes abreast. Men of all nations were employed in shifts 'and put to the work of cutting a canal under the lash', for, according to Herodotos, the Great King 'wanted to show his power and to leave something to be remembered by'. There is evidence of wall substructures and some man-made mounds but the ditch itself is now filled with soil. The area is being systematically investigated by the British School of Archaeology, using a variety of electronic instruments to establish more exactly the form of the canal.

On the south side of the isthmus the little port of **Ouranopolis** shelters in a wide, tranquil bay skirted by sandy beaches and dotted with wooded islets. A first-class hotel, the Eagle's Palace, and the more modest Xenia, both with bar, restaurant and private beach, offer a pleasant refuge for weary travellers. A daily boat carrying a passenger-load of shaggy monks and unshaven pilgrims chugs into the port from the monasteries of the west coast of Mount Athos. The village, built in 1923 by refugees from Cappadocia on the site of a Hellenistic city and now a holiday resort, is tidier and more attractive than Ierissos. The five-storied **Tower of Prosfori**, with gun-slits and wooden balconies, dominates the surroundings from above the mole between two coves. Once a lay dependency of the Athonite Monastery of *Vatopedi*, the abandoned tower was bought in the 1920s by an Anglo-Australian couple who converted the ground floor into a workshop, where village girls learnt to weave knotted rugs decorated with traditional Byzantine patterns.

From Ouranopolis one can return to Stratoni and then continue north-west to complete the circular tour of the Halkidiki. Leaving the road to Stayira to the left, one climbs a seaward spur of Holomon and descends in hairpin bends to the shore of the Strymonic Gulf. Beaches of white sand are broken up by rocky inlets. Chestnut forests spread across the flanks of the valleys, and ice-cold streams trickle through shallow gullies to the sea. The smell of iodine and wet sand is mixed with that of pungent evergreens. To the east rises the outline of mountainous Thassos. There is probably no finer series of beaches in Greece - in spite of the uncontrolled development of villas, hotels and camp sites.

At **Olymbiada**, the ancient Kapros, port of Stageira, a wooden jetty extends into the poplar-fringed bay, where rowing boats, moored to an island mentioned by Strabo, rock in the oily swell. At night, flotillas of brightly-painted fishing caiques put out to sea, their carbide flares, which attract the fish, strung out across the dark in phosphorescent formations. To the north-east, where the Strymon flows into the sea through a wide estuary, looms Pangheon, the mountain of gold. At **Stavros**, plane trees skirt the shore and a broad walk is lined with cafés. The little port was discovered by the British army, based in the Strymon valley during the First World War, when it became a rest camp provided with swimming facilities and tennis courts in summer, woodcock-shooting in winter. In spring and summer there is the song of nightingales in the cool, dark arbours formed by the giant planes.

Soon after Stavros the road joins the main Thessaloniki-Kavalla road and we turn westward through a beautiful ravine to the village of Rendina, which has some visible but not very interesting ancient remains. Nearby was Arethousa (nothing to do with the modern village of the same name to the north), where the aged Euripides, driven out of Athens by a campaign of calumny provoked by his cynical questioning of the gods' infallibility, was torn to pieces by the dogs of the Macedonian king, set upon him by rival poets. Later, Arethousa became a staging-post on the Via Egnatia. There is little to see now, but archaeologists are busy both here and at Rendina. Beyond Rendina the main road follows the course of the Via Egnatia across a featureless plain beside the shallow waters of Lake Volvi, near the southern shore of which is the modern village of Apollonia (not to be confused with the Apollonia near Poliyiros). St. Paul and Silas passed through here when they left Philippi after the earthquake. Another lake, Koronia, is equally without scenic distinction.

At the end of this lake the road meets the Thessaloniki-Serres road near **Derveni**, where some of the treasure exhibited at the Archaeological Museum in Thessaloniki was discovered in fourth-century BC burial chambers. The Derveni to Serres road leads shortly to a turn-off to the right, crossing the plain through avenues of poplars to **Langadas**. Here a macabre religious rite is performed by a sect of Thracian firewalkers on the feast of Saints Constantine and Helena (21 May). The firewalking rite, manifestly pagan in origin, translated into thinly-veiled Christian terms, has recently received the blessing of the Church. So the slaughter of animals, the burning coals and the primitive music are now invested with all the trappings of officialdom, and the ceremony, held on waste-ground near the cemetery, draws increasingly large numbers of visitors.

The ceremony begins in the morning. A garlanded calf with candles stuck in its ears is led out, to the accompaniment of ritual dances and the thud of drums. Clarinets wail; occasionally there is a fanfare of trumpets. The moment the knife is plunged into the squealing animal a great moan escapes the crowd. Women's shrieks pierce the air. In the afternoon the bonfire is lit and the firewalkers, bearing the holy icons, caper shoeless on the red-hot coals, accompanied by banging tambourines; sometimes they shout and leap in the air. In the tavernas wine and ouzo flow. Doctors are said to have testified that the soles of the firewalkers' feet are neither blistered nor discoloured. After 21 May Langadas lapses for another year into the routine of agricultural domesticity. Only cinders remain, scattered over the waste-ground until the autumn rains turn them into squelching mud.

17

Mount Athos: A Traveller's Journal

THE THOUSAND-YEAR-OLD monastic republic of Athos, nominally independent of the Greek state although policed by its officers, extends along the eastern prong of the Halkidiki peninsula. Fortified medieval monasteries fringe the wooded coast; hermitages and eyries cling to the sides of vertical cliffs. Some settlements are abandoned; others are still inhabited by a handful of monks who celebrate daily services in frescoed churches filled with icons, golden candelabra and carved, gilded *iconostases*. Outwardly it remains the truest extant image of Byzantine monasticism. In reality it is a twilight place, nostalgic, muted, dying of apathy and dereliction, though there has been some revival over the past twenty years, to the extent that there is a shortage of accommodation for new recruits - a result of the earlier neglect of vacant buildings.

The fertility of the promontory is legendary and the landscape, with the Holy Mountain soaring to a tapering peak at the south-eastern extremity, could not be more splendid. The Virgin herself found the prospect so bewitching that she fell in love with it when she was forced to land in the Bay of Iviron, after her ship, bound for Cyprus, where she and St John were about to pay a visit to Lazarus, had been blown off-course. Enchanted by the shady forests and flowery meadows, she annexed the peninsula, declared it her private garden and forbade any member of her sex to enter it. The whole spiritual development of the community stems from the worship of the Mother of God, and her mantled form, the monks say, still haunts the groves and coppices below the woodland monasteries

The earliest hermits came in the eighth century, seeking refuge from the persecutions of Iconoclast emperors. The first recorded solitary was Peter the Anchorite in the ninth century. Beset by demons and wild beasts, he dwelt for fifty years in a cave on the marble mountain. The influx of anchorites increased and in 872 the Emperor Basil I granted them a special charter of protection. The future pattern of the republic was established by St Athanassios, a

Bithynian monk, who founded the first monastery, the Grand Lavra, and reaffirmed the Virgin's injunction that no woman or female animal should enter the holy territory (an edict that still holds good today).

Pious men, anxious to escape from the world of temptation, flocked from the Orthodox countries and founded monasteries which were financed by princes and statesmen and which, while preserving their independence, acknowledged the suzerainty of the Byzantine emperor. Artists from Constantinople, Thessaloniki and Crete were commissioned to fresco the walls of churches and instruct the monks in the art of iconography. Religious learning and scholarship flourished, with the best brains in the ecclesiastical world gravitating to the Holy Mountain, which gradually became the symbol of the Church's undisputed influence over every sphere of national consciousness. In the fifteenth century the idiorrhythmic system, which meant that each monk fed and clothed himself from his own resources, was introduced in several monasteries where the rule was milder than in the cenobitic or communal (and more austere) establishments.

During the centuries of Latin, Slav and Ottoman occupation the monasteries preserved the prestige of Byzantine religion undiminished and, when the War of Independence came in 1821, Finlay was justified in saying that Mount Athos 'held a more revered place than the memories of Marathon and Salamis' in the minds of ordinary Greeks.

In the nineteenth century wealth poured in from Tsarist sources and the number of novices from Slav countries threatened to exceed those from Greece and Asia Minor; but the Russian Revolution put an end to that. After the Second World War the flow of recruits from the other Slav countries was also cut off at source. Thus, where there were once forty thousand monks, there are now about fifteen hundred, and narrow Greek nationalism paralyses any form of twentieth-century theological stimulus.

Most of the monasteries, which are filled with treasures of religious art, provide little more than a refuge for aged monks of peasant origin and limited education. Almost all artistic activity has ceased; the fields and vineyards owned by the idiorrhythmic orders are largely abandoned; parasitic plants wind murderous shoots round the trunks of fruit and nut trees; deforestation is rife and the bracken grows so high that it is difficult to locate the shady mule-tracks that once linked one monastery with another. What remains to be seen?

Just some decaying monasteries inhabited by a few aged, illiterate monks? No. Each monastery is a castellated stronghold. The architecture, if not always good, is either striking, picturesque or spectacular. In every instance the monastic buildings gravitate round the main church, which is usually Greek-cross plan, but with notable variations and with one or two side chapels. All contain frescoes; mostly of the late Byzantine and post-Byzantine periods - some very good, others indifferent. Many of the libraries and treasuries possess priceless works of silverware, icons and illuminated manuscripts, as well as a variety of other religious works of art wrought in gold, bronze, jasper and marble, including holy relics so dear to the Orthodox faithful. There are also some mosaics.

It is helpful to bear in mind the uniform iconographical arrangement of an Athonite church, which, generally speaking, applies to every Byzantine church in the country: in the dome of heaven reigns Christ Pantocrator, surrounded by worshipping angels, while the Virgin and St John the Baptist intercede on behalf of mankind; in the central apse (there are three) the Virgin and Child sit enthroned within a golden aureole above the altar. Around this focus of divinity, in the pendentives and vaults, unfold the scenes of the Twelve Feasts and the Passion (these sometimes overflow into the narthex). On the lower register - the terrestrial one - prophets, saints and holy men are ranged in strict order of precedence. Finally, monks and lay worshippers assemble on the historiated pavements. The church thus represents the universe in miniature.

The traveller will encounter hardship and frustration, an unappetizing diet and (sometimes) dirty sheets. He may even encounter something unusual in Greece - unfriendliness. However, the loneliness and the tranquillity, the emphasis on superstition and demonology, the obsession with the past and the indifference to the future, the sheer anachronism of it all, combine to produce in one a state of almost traumatic fascination. The journey may be the most arduous in Greece; it is also probably the most exciting. The lover of landscape will find little in the whole country to match some of the prospects encountered.

A three-day tour enables the visitor to visit two of the three senior monasteries - Iviron, Vatopedi and the Grand Lavra - and cast a quick glance at the frescoes of the Protaton at Karyes en route. Yachtsmen, after going through the usual formalities at Karyes, can sail round the peninsula, visiting any monastery (or indeed all) at will.

On my last visit I worked out a practicable eight-day tour by *caique* (*see Appendix*), starting at Ouranopolis This is the minimum time required to visit the ten most important monasteries. I have described the journey in the form of a personal journal, hoping that it will give the traveller some useful hints as to what to expect from Athonite habits and monkish idiosyncrasies. Mount Athos is not the mere sum total of its monasteries and hermitages. It is a way of life; to understand it requires a little insight into the character of its strange inhabitants.

Some practical details on travel, formalities and accommodation are given in the Appendix.

21 August

We left Ouranopolis at ten o'clock by the public caique. Among the passengers were three elderly monks who had been visiting relations in what they call 'the world'. A profound, almost reverential, silence descended as we sailed into holy waters below pine-clad cliffs fringed by sandy beaches. Occasionally an abandoned hermitage appeared in a clearing in the woods. In the south-east the peak of the Holy Mountain, a pyramid of white limestone, was wreathed in wispy clouds, its tapering form repeated in a similar cone at the tip of the promontory. Strabo calls it 'breast-shaped'.

Arsenals - fortified tower-like structures, surrounded by disused port installations which serve as landing-stages for the monasteries - began to skirt the shore. The first was that of Zografou, where logs of wood were laid out in rows along the beach, awaiting export, and from which the *arsenaris* (arsenal-keeper) waved to us from a projecting balcony; then that of Dohiariou, crowned by a crenellated tower flanked by cypress trees; Xenofondos, its wooden galleries overlooking the placid bay; Ayios Pandeleimon, with its lime-green onion domes and derelict warehouses, and Xeropotamou, an inland monastery. We were soon entering the port of Dafni, a huddle of small houses at the foot of a steep hill.

After showing our passports and having lunch (an oily stew served stone-cold) in a *taverna* under a vine trellis, we took the afternoon bus to **Karyes**. The passengers included two men wearing caps with the badge of the double-headed eagle - emblem of the ecclesiastic police force. Climbing potholed hairpin bends, we passed the Monastery of Xeropotamou which spreads across a shady ledge with deep ravines on either side, and ascended through a jungle of shrubs. The smell of sun-baked myrtle was pungent. The forest now

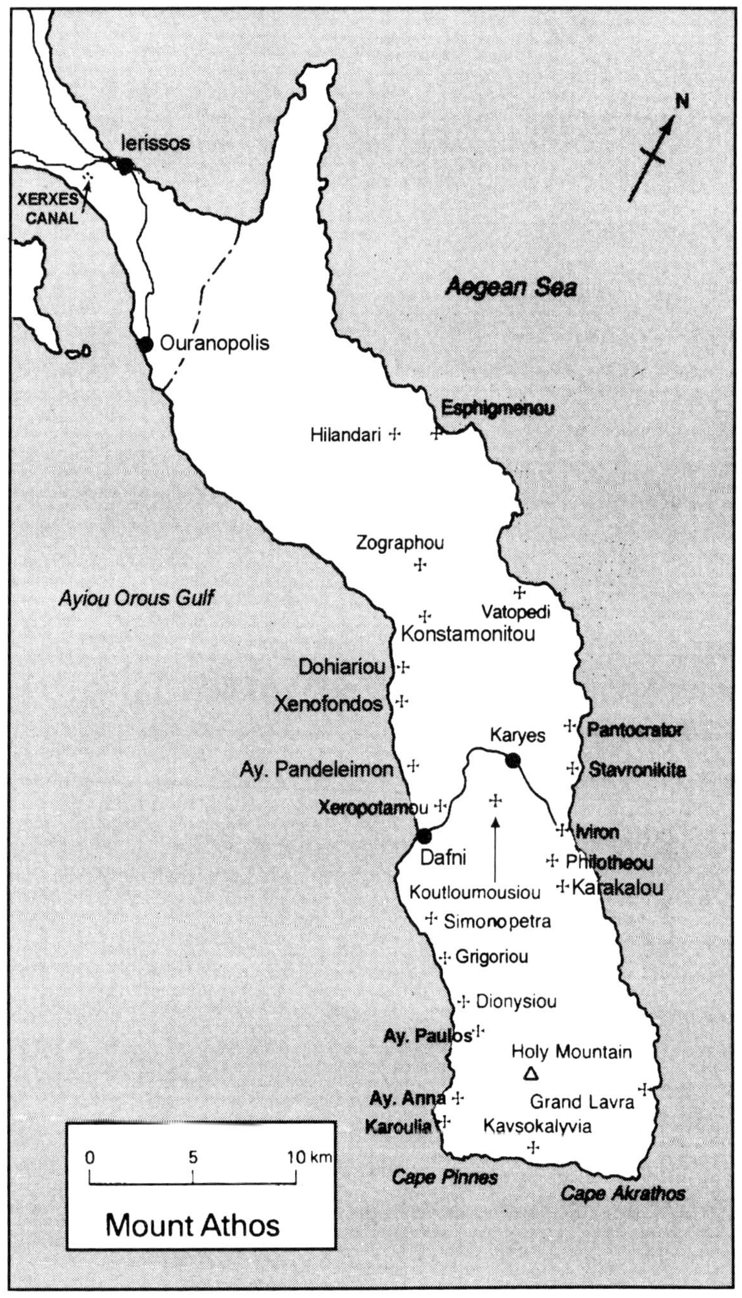
N
Ierissos
XERXES
CANAL
Aegean Sea
Ouranopolis
Esphigmenou
Hilandari
Zographou
Ayiou Orous Gulf
Vatopedi
Konstamonitou
Dohiariou
Xenofondos
Karyes
Pantocrator
Ay. Pandeleimon
Stavronikita
Xeropotamou
Iviron
Dafni
Philotheou
Koutloumousiou
Karakalou
Simonopetra
Grigoriou
Dionysiou
Ay. Paulos
Holy Mountain
Ay. Anna
Grand Lavra
Karoulia
Kavsokalyvia
0
5
10 km
Cape Pinnes
Cape Akrathos
Mount Athos

closed round on all sides, and we drove through a tunnel of trees, whose trunks, entwined in creepers speckled with purple berries, grew out of a bed of ferns so dense that no path has ever been cut through it. After crossing the watershed the road descends into a bowl-like valley, seamed with verdant gullies and scattered with nut-groves and farm-houses. 'Karyes!' called the driver with a flourish, and we observed the domes of churches and ecclesiastical colleges crowned with crosses glistening in the afternoon sun.

In Ayiou Pnevma (Holy Ghost) Street, where the bus stops, there are grocers, cobblers, the only post office on the peninsula and a shop filled with postcards, rosaries, wooden wine-jugs and eucharistic bread-stamps carved by monks in outlying *skitis*. Respect for the Holy Ghost precludes smoking, wearing a hat or short-sleeved shirt in the street. We climbed a cobbled lane between well-watered gardens to the house of the Archimandrite, to whom we had a letter of introduction. Pigeons piped in the surrounding orchards. A white-bearded *yerondas* (servant of a senior cleric) brought us coffee and *ouzo* in the courtyard filled with roses, oleanders and hydrangeas. He told us he had not been outside Karyes for forty years. The Archimandrite, who was more worldly (an iconographer and landscape-painter), conducted us to the authorities who issued us with residence permits. We looked at the Assembly House of the Holy Community, where novices hurried across the marble halls carrying cups of coffee to high-ranking prelates, while the Archimandrite fetched the key of the church which is the chief glory of Karyes.

The **Protaton** or Church of the Holy Community, joint property of all the monasteries, is a basilica of the tenth century, restored in the thirteenth and sixteenth. The belfry, with striped bands, is a later addition. The exterior is plain enough, but the walls of the *naos* are covered with early fourteenth-century frescoes of the Macedonian School. The best of them are probably by Manuel Panselinos, an enigmatic figure of Thessalonikian origin, whose work is characterized by sturdy modelling, depth of expression and a realism apparent in both portraiture and detail.

Unhampered by the architectural complexities of the Greek Cross plan, the master painter was able to achieve an unusual unity of composition across large surfaces. The painted decoration is divided into four distinct zones, with the topmost reserved for standing figures of, for the most part, Christ's ancestors. Across the third zone (from the bottom) spread the noble groupings from the life of Christ and the Virgin in a flowing, frieze-like continuity. In the **Birth of the Virgin** St Anne's exhaustion from the pangs of labour is suggested in the support she seeks from her attendants while trying to take some food. In the **Presentation of the Virgin in the Temple** a timid little Virgin appears before the hoary old priest, followed by maidens carrying lighted candles. Puckish figures, in the form of Hellenic river gods personifying the Jordan and the sea, retreat before the Lord's displeasure in the **Baptism**, while three children dance across the bridge spanning the river. Architectural backgrounds are used to stress the unity of the compositions, as in the **Incredulity of Thomas**, in which Christ stands in the central arch, the apostles in the other two. A similar symmetry of arrangement, both of figures and architectural features, is apparent in **The Last Supper**. Harmony becomes the keynote.

Representations of evangelists, prophets, military saints, bishops and martyrs extend across the two lower zones. An austere spirituality haunts the faces of the ascetic saints, each of whom is depicted with a distinct individuality rare in Byzantine iconography: particularly the white-bearded **Efthymios**, who lived to be ninety-six, his sunken eyes reflecting the disillusioned wisdom of his years; **Ossios David of Thessaloniki**, whose gnarled, knobbly features recall those of generations of Greek monks; **St John the Baptist**, tragic in the force and intensity of his expression. In the *prothesis*, within the sanctuary, there is an unusual portrait of a **youthful Christ**, full of vigour and freshness. Throughout the church the colour scheme is remarkable for its glow of different shades of pink and red (coral, flame and claret, pale and ruddy flesh tints) set off by sea blues, ambers and silvery greens. Shading is effected by black or indigo and green brush-strokes. The use of yellow against white produces a bold effect. Everywhere luminosity and chromatic harmony prevail.

In the Protaton we saw the holy icon of *Axion Esti* ('It is meet and right'), which was found in a cell near Karyes, where a tenth-century monk was visited by the Archangel Gabriel and instructed how it was 'meet and right' to glorify the Virgin. On Easter Monday the image, shaded by an umbrella, is borne in procession to the homes of the local representatives of each monastery, who sprinkle rose water and incense over it while church bells ring and spectators shout: 'Long live the Virgin!'

It was too late to visit the nineteenth-century Russian *skiti* of St Andrew, a fantasy of onion domes and coloured roofs, crosses and towers, set among groves of hazelnut trees to the north of the village. Its most important possession is a relic of St Andrew - part of his forehead. We went instead to the inn for supper. I do not remember what we had to eat (perhaps it is just as well), but we drank resinated wine. We slept in a room with six beds, after asking for clean sheets. Washing arrangements were confined to a cold water tap in the court where we dined. But the view from the rickety wooden balcony outside our room was unforgettable. The steep side of the Holy Mountain rose sheer above woods and vineyards, haunted, it is said, by seductive Nereids who have trespassed into the Virgin's garden. The whole countryside was mantled in a velvet sheen of moonlight. Occasionally the shriek of a jackal broke the spectral silence.

22 August

We got up at 6 am to catch the bus to the Bay of Iviron. The cobbled alleys of Karyes were deserted. The absence of women's and children's voices had begun to make an impact. Some travellers find that this feeling of absence grows stronger the longer they stay on the Holy Mountain, until they finally become aware of a great void at the heart of things. It is hard to get used to the idea that nobody has been born here for over a thousand years.

The road wound down to the coast, past the Monastery of Koutloumousiou, its crimson church surrounded by high walls. The gullies were a paradise of vegetation: oleanders, mulberries, olives, walnuts and hazels; ferns, ramblers, spiky shrubs and thick coverts where jackals hide. The smell of aromatic herbs drifted across the hillside. To the south a wisp of cloud formed a perfect halo round the peak of Athos. At the landing stage of Iviron the *caique* had just put in. A high sea was running, the *meltemi* - the etesian wind that funnels through the Hellespont and hits the Aegean with redoubled force - breaking the waves in sprays of foam against a primitive sea wall. We hurled ourselves and our luggage into the pitching *caique*. One of the passengers, a policeman, his complexion the colour of his uniform - pea-green - groaned and leant, gurgling, over the rail.

The coast is wild, grand and rocky, fringed with bluffs and crags from which a succession of monasteries overhang the sea: the medieval tower of Stavronikita crowning a huddle of monks' cells, 'like a Gothic castle perched on a beetling crag' said Robert Curzon, who travelled to Mount Athos in 1837; Pantocrator, astride a cliff lashed by waves so high that our caique could not enter the minute harbour; Vatopedi, largest of all the monasteries, a fortress sprawling across a sea-washed woodland; Esfigmenou, compressed, as its name - the Squeezed-together One - implies, within a narrow, green valley.

About mid-morning we reached the arsenal of **Hilandari**, the first monastery on our itinerary. The way inland is up a gentle incline. It took us almost an hour to walk - carrying our bags. On the left a fine thirteenth-century watch-tower commands the maritime approach. The country is green and open. We did not pass a single human being, not an animal. At last we saw kitchen-gardens, then the encircling walls of the great Serb monastery within a ring of hills covered with pine and chestnut trees and dark cypresses thrusting their tips through latticed olive branches. The only sound was the low piping of wood pigeons which nest in the arbours of ash and pine.

The monastery was founded in the twelfth century by Stephen Nemanja, unifier of the Serbs, who donned a monk's habit and died here. A century later, when it was the fashion for Slav princes to marry into Byzantine ruling families and found churches, hospitals and charitable institutions on Greek territory, the monastery was enlarged by Stephen, son-in-law of the Emperor Andronikos II Paleologos. Hilandari soon became a cradle of Slav culture, visited by Serbian kings and national heroes. It is now inhabited by some twenty monks, mostly anti-Communist refugees from Yugoslavia. Relations with Belgrade, however, are not severed, and Marshal Tito presented the house with a tractor.

We passed through a frescoed gateway into the court, the loveliest on Mount Athos. The layout of the monastic precincts is more or less identical throughout the peninsula: a central court, varying in size, with the church in the middle and the refectory, cells, chapels, oratories and sometimes cloisters grouped around it, the whole encircled with high walls. Fan-shaped, the court at Hilandari is a perfectly composed complex of tall brick buildings - rebuilt after a fire in 1722 - with whitewashed upper storeys supported by wooden brackets. A fourteenth-century tower, its windows set within arched frames, overlooks slate roofs of a dull pink colour and domes crowned with crosses. In the late afternoon a roseate glow is reflected from walls striped with tiles of different brick-red shades. In the centre of the court stands a seventeenth-century octagonal *phiale*, a holy water basin, roofed with a domed canopy. Beside it rise two tall, ancient cypresses, in whose foliage the monks once hid their treasure of relics, icons and manuscripts when Latin pirates attacked the monastery. Nature came to their rescue: a clammy fog rose suddenly from the valley, enveloped the pirates as they scaled the walls and completely confounded them. Losing their bearings in eddies of white mist, and panicking, they slaughtered each other. Only three survived; They were succoured by the monks and converted to the Orthodox faith. Their portraits adorn the walls of the refectory.

The guest-master led us to a cool, spacious gallery with settees ranged along the walls. We were offered *ouzo*, coffee and *loukoumi*, and shown our sleeping quarters - an enormous dormitory, all to ourselves. The primitive lavatory overlooked a sun-dazzled glade surrounded by cypress and olive trees thrumming with cicadas. We had lunch - boiled marrows, tomato and onion salad, gherkins, bread and wine - with the abbot (who was fond of his glass of wine) and a theology student from Athens University who gave Greek lessons to the Serb monks during the summer vacation. After a siesta we started sightseeing, conducted by the librarian.

The **Church of the Presentation of the Virgin** is of the twelfth century, enlarged in the fourteenth, with later additions and transformations. The exterior brick decoration, largely composed of striped bands and arched surrounds, tends to obscure the purity of the architectural ensemble, with its five domes, apses, arches and barrel-vaults. You enter through the exo-narthex, built across the west front of the church, and then come to the large square inner narthex, known as the *litis*, a feature of Athonite churches and sometimes larger than the *naos*. The *litis* opens into the Greek-cross *naos* (in some churches there is no division) with a gilded *iconostasis* pierced by three doors, and a tri-apsidal sanctuary. At Hilandari the *naos* is distinguished by a beautiful twelfth-century **pavement of Opus Alexandrinum**: slabs of verd-antique within a border of petals and concentric circles of different marbles - grey, blue, green and off-white - with cubes and rectangles superimposed. Most of the frescoes (c. 1300) have been ruined by tasteless nineteenth-century repainting. Noteworthy exceptions are the untouched portraits of Stephen Nemanja, the founder, and King Stephen Milutin, the thirteenth-century benefactor, on the south-west pilaster above the tomb of the former.

Beside the Bishop's throne hangs the miraculous icon of the Virgin Triheroussa. The face, brown with age, is surrounded with votive gifts - jewelled crosses, gold, strings of coins. Next to the icon is a bejewelled staff belonging to the Emperor Andronikos I Komnenos, who paid for his crimes by being paraded, strapped to a camel's back, through the hippodrome where he was torn to pieces by an angry mob in 1185. Above the Bishop's throne is a set of charming thirteenth-century miniatures.

In the **Library** we saw an eleventh-century edition of the homilies of St John Chrysostom and a fourteenth-century illuminated **Book of Gospels** of Serbian origin with letters of gold and silver on white parchment. This was much admired by Robert Curzon, who seems to have had no scruples about exacting precious manuscripts from ignorant monks in exchange for a few drachmae, and it is to the credit of the monks of Hilandari that they did not fall to his usual blandishments. We looked at a small **mosaic panel of the Virgin and Child** in the grand, austere manner of the twelfth century. However, our unstinted admiration was reserved for a set of superbly painted **icons of the fourteenth century** which are probably the finest on Mount Athos: four contemplative Evangelists holding bejewelled Gospels, clothed in mantles of subtly matched purple, olive green and smoky blue shades; a *Deisis* - Christ, authoritative and compassionate, between the Virgin and St John; the Archangels with Gabriel in blue and green robes. A softness of texture and limpidity of outline, suggestive of Slav influences, distinguishes these beautiful panels.

The refectory, largely disused, is less interesting. Apsidal and T-shaped, its walls are covered with seventeenth-century frescoes representing, *inter alia*, the life of St Sabbas, the pious son of Stephen Nemanja. The figures are loutish and lifeless. The Last Judgement, which always figures prominently in the apses of refectories, is more attractive, with its semi-circular architectural background of arches and towers.

Descending into the court, we saw an old monk with a flowing white beard beating the *simandron*, an oblong wooden board which is tapped with a wooden mallet to summon the community to prayer. The whole place - the weed-grown court, the flimsy wooden stairways, the maze of cells and chapels, echoed with the repetitive beats which obviously derive from a set score, the introductory *lento* passage working up to a lively *vivace* climax, only to die down and begin all over again. Soon we heard the rise and fall of a feeble voice chanting the litanies in Slavonic. As it grew dark the cypress trees flanking the *phiale* stood out like sentinels, guarding the isolation.

We dined with the friendly abbot and the theology student. By the time we went to bed - about nine o'clock - the galleries overlooking the court were empty. No light showed anywhere, except a kerosene lamp fixed in a bracket pointing the way to the lavatory. A bat was making frenzied gyrations around it.

23 August
The abbot placed Marshal Tito's tractor at our disposal to carry our bags to the arsenal. We bathed and had a picnic lunch on a sandy beach. Later the abbot, who was on a visit to the *arsenaris* and had exchanged his cylindrical hat for a floppy straw one, trailed across the sands and presented each of us with a little bunch of sea-daffodils. Except at Dionysiou we were not to meet with such friendliness again.

The *caique* left at two o'clock. The theology student, on his way to post letters at Karyes, was seated next to me. As we pitched and rolled between huge waves, he inveighed against the iniquities of British foreign policy in Cyprus and British ingratitude (it would have been American ingratitude had I been an American) to Greece, which had saved the Western world from Communism, etc. etc. Illogical, rhetorical, cliché-ridden, the discourse continued relentlessly, though, politics and heroics apart, the young man was both charming and intelligent. Typically, we parted the best of friends.

The climb from the landing-stage to the **Monastery of Vatopedi**, screened by wooded hills watered by streams, is steep but short. A squat watch-tower overlooks the arsenal and a huddle of woodcutters' huts. A crescent-shaped bay sweeps northward at the foot of hills seamed with valleys where pomegranates and Japanese medlars grow between hedgerows of blackberry bushes festooned with clematis and wild vine. On late summer evenings caravans of mules wind down the paths to the monastery gates where logs of wood (the monks' sole supply of fuel in winter) are unloaded. You enter the monastery through a porch in the shape of a canopy guarded by an icon of the Virgin. A Turkish soldier once had the temerity to shoot at her hand. The Virgin retaliated swiftly. She drove the Turk so mad that he hanged himself from a tree, whose branches subsequently withered and died.

After a long wait in the guest-house, a sulky guest-master offered us coffee (no *ouzo* or *loukoumi* here). We wandered round the **polygonal court** - larger than that of Hilandari, less well composed, but suffused with an even brighter glow from crimson stuccoed walls and brick courses with fantastic geometric designs. A warren of cells, chapels and storerooms extends across a slope within fortified walls. Here patriarchs, bishops and archimandrites once strolled and aristocratic novices mingled with the suites of princes and statesmen from every quarter of the Orthodox world. Vatopedi was always the 'smartest' of Athonite monasteries, its wealth exceeding even that of the Grand Lavra. Here stayed John Kantakouzenos, a statesman who fomented a civil war in Constantinople, usurped the throne, became one of the outstanding emperors of the late Byzantine period and finally a nomadic monk. Now there are about thirty monks, as bigoted as any on the mountain, who stare suspiciously from wooden balconies at modern pilgrims, loaded with rucksacks and thermos flasks, desecrating the place with their unseemly garments and clicking cameras. The skyline is broken by turrets, domes and belfries of different periods. The octagonal *phiale* has a circular colonnade and a frescoed *baldacchino*. A painting of the Eye of God and a chocolate-coloured puppet figure of a Saracen, who strikes the hours on a church bell, add the final touch of fantasy.

In Athonite legend, the origins of the monastery go back to the fourth century, when Arkadios, son of the Emperor Theodosios the Great, was shipwrecked off the coast. The Virgin took pity on the boy and permitted him to land in her garden, where he was found resting in a blackberry bush. So the place was called Vatopaidi - 'blackberry bush boy' (the spelling is now Vatopedi, which means 'blackberry field'). The Emperor was so grateful to the Virgin that he built a monastery on the spot and dedicated it to the Annunciation. According to the historical record, the house is a tenth-century foundation.

I had time before vespers to look at the **Church of the Annunciation** (known as the Katholikon, the term used for the main church in all monasteries), the most important on Mount Athos. The exterior, whose walls are painted bright crimson, is a jumble of domes, arches and apses. The interior of the colonnaded outer narthex is covered with eighteenth-century frescoes, whose whimsical folklore character is epitomized in the coy expression on the faces of the damned souls floundering in the river of Hell. Above the entrance into the narthex are three mosaic panels: a severe, unsmiling Deisis of the eleventh century, flanked by the Virgin and the Angel of the Annunciation (fourteenth-century). The figures are heavy and forceful, in the monumental style. The magnificent fourteenth-century **bronze doors** are decorated with designs of leaves and birds and

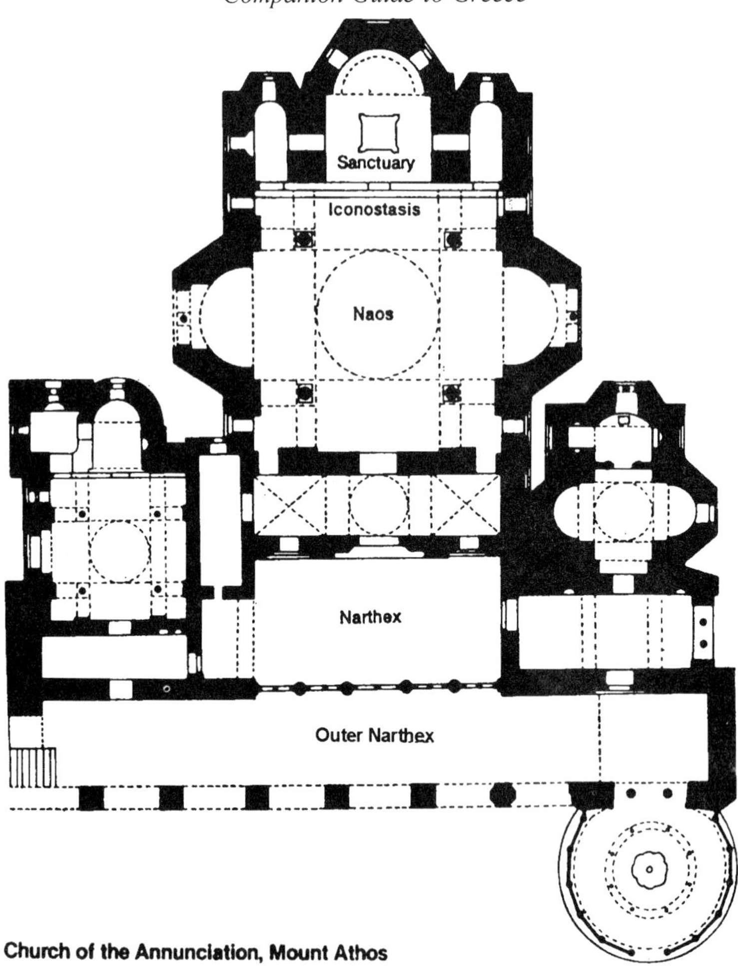

Church of the Annunciation, Mount Athos

figures of the Virgin and the Angel Gabriel. The early fourteenth-century frescoes in the narthex are distinguished by a pink glow reminiscent of the Protaton.

From the narthex I passed through sixteenth-century ivory-inlaid doors into the *naos*, which is paved with lavish polychrome marbles laid out in geometric designs. The dome is supported by granite columns with brass rings. The **frescoes**, despite restoration in the eighteenth and nineteenth centuries, are among the supreme achievements of the Macedonian School of painting in the early fourteenth century. An important new trend, later developed in other Athonite frescoes, is observed for the first time: a series of individual pictures seems to replace the strictly liturgical sequence of symbolical scenes. Overall uniformity is sacrificed to narrative. The colours are colder than usual: perhaps owing to restoration. An austere blue predominates and the familiar figures of the Dodekaorton pursue their tragic destinies in an inky haze, through which it is not always possible to distinguish the detail.

The grandest compositions are the **Entry into Jerusalem** and the **Crucifixion**, both larger than life-size. The atmosphere of expectancy prevails in the Entry. Christ in luminous dark blue robes rides on the donkey as he listens to the arguments of the Apostles, while the people of Jerusalem pour out of the ornamental city gate. The branches of the palm tree wave in the breeze. The background is a tortuous complex of domes, roofs, cornices and pediments, red against an inky, star-studded sky. In the Crucifixion the use of rigid straight lines - in the draperies of the stricken Virgin and the anatomical details of the figure of Christ - heighten the sense of anguish. Only the figure of St John is conventional and unconvincing.

Two thirteenth-century icons flank the sanctuary: a Holy Trinity, disfigured by flashy haloes in gold filigree, and a Virgin and Child distinguished by the poignancy of the Virgin's expression. Above are dark mosaics of the Virgin and the Angel of the Annunciation, protectors of the church, guarding the entry into the sanctuary. The eighteenth-century *iconostasis* is very elaborate, the work, probably, of some monkish woodcarver with a love for pastoral life: stags, hunters and boys picking grapes frolic among flowers, pine-cones and vines.

It is important to get permission to enter the sanctuary. Here are kept tenth- and fourteenth-century icons of the Virgin and Child, St George and the Archangel Michael. Some of the most venerated **relics** of the Orthodox Church are also kept here and only shown to the visitor on request (and under strict surveillance). They include parts of the True Cross, the index finger of St John the Baptist, the skull of St Gregory of Nazianzus, a ninth-century gold and silver reliquary embossed with scenes from the life of St Dimitrios, which contains a piece of blood-soaked earth from the public baths at Thessaloniki where the martyr was speared to death. However the most revered relic of all is an enamelled box studded with gems containing a fragment of the Virgin's girdle: a piece of russet-coloured ribbon woven with gold thread and subsequently sewn with seed pearls by the Empress Pulcheria, a cultivated Athenian lady of the fifth century. Dropped by the Virgin on the site of Golgotha, it changed hands several times, was carried from country to country, allaying epidemics of the plague, and was finally presented by a fourteenth-century Serb prince to Vatopedi. When Curzon visited the monastery in the 1830s, afflicted persons were allowed, he says, in return 'for a consideration', to kiss it and be cured.

We dined in the guest-house with some itinerant monks. The fare was vegetarian, without wine. There was no conversation, not even polite formalities. We went to our room overlooking the mysterious velvety hills. It was about eight o'clock. We talked for a while in whispers. Suddenly there was a loud knocking at the door and the angry voice of the guest-master was heard inveighing against our irreverence in this house of God.

24 August

We got up at six and breakfasted on biscuits and Nescafé (our own). We visited the beautiful church again and persuaded a relatively amiable monk to let us see the library and the refectory. Visitors need waste no time on the latter. It is cross-shaped with marble-topped tables and ugly frescoes of the eighteenth century. The most striking object in the library is an extremely elegant specimen of Byzantine silverware: a **jasper cup** of the mid-fourteenth century on an octagonal stem with the monogram of the donor, Manuel Kantakouzenos, Despot of Mystra, inscribed on the base. Among the six hundred manuscripts - over half on parchment - are an eleventh-century psalter with the monogram of Emperor Constantine IX Monomachos and one of the few illustrated copies of Strabo's *Geography* in existence, with a crudely drawn but extraordinarily accurate map of the course of the Nile.

We looked at the ruins of the Theological School above the monastery, then descended along lanes between ilex, arbutus and Judas trees to the crescent-shaped shingly beach, where we ate our picnic lunch. Horseflies and wasps plagued us, while striped butterflies fluttered among the blackberry bushes. We then took the southbound *caique* and sailed back to the Bay of Iviron.

The ascent from the arsenal to the **Monastery of Iviron**, which spreads across a densely-wooded ledge, is easy by Athonite standards. The monastery was founded in the tenth century by three Georgian monks. Its maritime situation invited pirate raids and the monastery suffered much from Saracen attacks. In the fifteenth century the King of Georgia financed its reconstruction. However fire and earthquake took their toll, and most of the surviving buildings around the large irregular court, including belfry and *phiale*, are of the seventeenth century and are not very distinguished: some of the chapels are painted red and one bright mauve. The south buttress wall, cracked from top to bottom by an earthquake, supports a ruined tower, one of the five that formerly crowned the walls.

Before the sun went down we looked at two of the smaller churches. First the **Chapel of the Portaitissa**, situated where the Virgin addressed the pagan inhabitants and forbade any woman or female animal ever to enter her private garden. Ivory-inlaid doors lead from a hideously frescoed narthex into a small *naos* where the miraculous gold-sheathed icon of the Portaitissa (The Virgin of the Gate) is kept. The dark brown face is discernible through an overlay of gold decoration, surrounded by votive gifts. The monks claim it to be the work of St Luke. According to a popular Athonite legend the icon, cast into the sea by its owner during the Iconoclast persecution, appeared seventy years later in the Bay of Iviron, standing upright on the waves. Above it, a column of fire rose to heaven. The monks set out in rowing-boats to rescue it, but each time they approached the image it retreated and a celestial voice was heard saying that only Gabriel, a Georgian anchorite who dwelt in a cave above the monastery, was worthy of recovering it. So Gabriel was summoned from his eyrie; after walking on the waves he grasped the image and carried it lovingly to the church. But every night the image moved of its own accord to the monastery gates, until the Virgin told the perplexed monks in a vision that she had not come to Mount Athos to be protected, but to protect them, and not until they were all gone would she leave her beloved garden. So a chapel was built near the gate and the icon has stayed there ever since.

The second chapel, that of St John the Baptist, is built, superstition has it, on the site of a pagan temple, where the idols fell down when the Virgin landed here. Disappointment awaited us in the Library, where all the illuminated manuscripts (several hundred) were packed and ready for removal to a new museum.

Our sleeping quarters overlooked a steep slope of woodland - the drone of insects and cicadas in the hot, airless valley was deafening - with just a glimpse of the Holy Sea beyond. The room was primitive, but there was no sign of the 'numberless tribes of vermin' which tenanted Curzon's chamber in the mid-nineteenth century. A tap at the end of the gallery provided us with washing facilities. For dinner (served in an annex of the kitchen) we had boiled beans and bread soaked in rancid olive oil, supplemented by our own processed cheese and *loukoumi*. There was as much wine as we wanted. We sat up late talking to the guest-master, who was an authority on Athonite legends. It was very pleasant after the regimentation of Vatopedi.

25 August

In the morning we visited the **Church of the Koimesis** (Dormition of the Virgin). The frescoes in the outer narthex and narthex are over-restored and unattractive, but a set of beautiful Iznik tiles set into the interior wall of the outer narthex serve as a curtain-raiser to the quasi-Oriental lavishness of the *naos*: a scene of exceptional opulence, with pendant silver censers, bronze candelabra from which lighted tapers flicker in front of a gilded *iconostasis*, a huge chandelier, frescoes on the upper register and icons with gold backgrounds hanging on walls and pillars. The tenth-century **pavement of Opus Alexandrinum** - marbles of orange, pink and mauve blending with ophite, porphyry and verd-antique - is contemporary with the original foundation. The great chandelier, a trophy captured by a Byzantine emperor in a campaign in the East, is carved with pygmy-like effigies including an allegory of Love, a Buddha-like deity and Persian soldiers; the immense enamelled corona which surrounds it came from Moscow in 1902 and is decorated with crosses, double-headed eagles and arched frames for icons. Behind the *iconostasis* there are chalices, crucifixes and a beautiful **silver gilt cross**, a masterpiece of Byzantine silverware. The whole church is lambent with copper, brass, gold and silver; the effect is almost barbaric in its splendour. It is not easy to forget its Georgian origins.

Frescoes cover every inch of wall space in the upper register. The finest is the **Pantocrator** in the dome (probably twelfth-century) set against a gold fan-shaped background ribbed with lines like the spokes of a wheel, the hub of which is Christ's head. His expression is haggard but serene. Below Him are the Virgin *Orans* and the Archangels (fifteenth-century).

The church is rich in icons which include an early image of the Virgin, set in a rococo frame, holding the Child and surrounded by angels (north transept) and a magnificent **Deisis** (south-west transept) overlaid with gold plate so finely embossed that the draperies recall the work of some ancient sculptor. More icons, some of which are ancient and a few beautiful, adorn the walls of the restored refectory.

After lunch I walked over a shoulder of steep woodland north of the monastery and looked down at the coastline: at the castellated pile of Stavronikita and the waves breaking on the cliff of Pantocrator. Higher up the valley, abandoned hermitages were scattered among copses of poplars, and the domes of Karyes glistened in the sun.

The *caique* for the Grand Lavra arrived at about four o'clock; the wind had dropped and the Holy Sea was smooth, with just a faint swell. As we chugged to the south-east the coast became more abrupt; forest smells drifted across the water, which turned from indigo to aquamarine and pearl grey. The peak of Athos, divested of its nebulous corona, tapered into the clear air. A waste of sea stretched east and south. Beyond the arsenal of the inland monastery of Filotheou we caught a glimpse of Karakallou and its handsome tower surrounded by cypress trees and nut groves. The coast, almost unbroken, became more wild and desolate. Suddenly we were sailing into a hidden creek, like a pirates' lair, in the shadow of a concrete tower - the arsenal of the **Grand Lavra**. We climbed for over half an hour up a steep hill pock-marked with bushes of holly-oak and arbutus, along the path that St Athanassios climbed, fighting prowling demons all the way, to found the first monastery.

In the failing light we discerned grey stone shapes ahead: a tower and rampart; then the wall-girt buildings of the monastery stretching across a ledge surrounded by vineyards and dominated by a rocky spur of the Holy Mountain. The sun had just set and we heard the creak of wood on ancient hinges as the gates were slammed behind us. We passed through a domed porch and entered what seemed to be a small medieval town: a maze of cobbled alleys, vaulted passages and small courts surrounded by low buildings with cupolas and slate roofs. Monks were chatting with lay labourers. A German student, who had left Dionysiou early in the morning and walked all day across the wildest and stoniest part of the peninsula, told us of views of 'unparalleled splendour'; his shoes were in a terrible state. We ate dinner in the guest-house - over twenty of us, all lay visitors. By nine o'clock everybody had gone to bed. From the gallery above the court, speckled with shadows of lemon trees, I could hear jackals shrieking in the vineyards. Gradually the unearthly whine drew nearer until I had the impression that entire packs of these scavenging beasts were prowling below the walls, hunting for carrion.

26 August

Early in the morning the court was full of animation. Monks were unloading baskets of marrows from the backs of braying donkeys, gardeners carrying picks and shovels, accompanied by shouting boys, set out for the fields and vineyards. Fruit trees and vine trellises, beds of straggling zinnias and pots of flaming salvias give the Lavra a rustic village-like air. There is little order in the layout of chapels, cells, arched troughs, wooden stairways and turrets, covering an area of several acres and all surrounded by grey walls. The court preserves something of the original *lavra*, a community of hermitages which existed before the monastery was built in 963. The foundation arose out of the friendship between Athanassios, a Bithynian ascetic, and a dour, puritanical General, Nikeforos Fokas. At the outset of the Cretan campaign (961) the General persuaded his pious friend to bless Byzantine arms. As soon as victory was won, he vowed, he would himself become a monk. However, after inflicting a decisive victory on the Saracens, Fokas found the prospect of usurping the throne more attractive than fulfilling his promise. So he placated Athanassios by founding the monastery which was to take precedence over all others on Mount Athos. Unlike most Athonite monasteries, the Grand Lavra has never been destroyed by fire and the main tower is part of the original tenth-century foundation.

The librarian guided us round the sights. The *phiale*, a seventeenth-century restoration of an earlier construction, shaded by two ancient cypresses, is the most beautiful on Mount Athos: a tea-cosy dome resting on arches filled with brick inlay and supported by little columns crowned with block capitals. The balustrade is composed of marble panels carved with designs of rosettes, birds, leaves and pine-cones. At Epiphany the holy water is consecrated in the huge porphyry basin before the whole community of monks. On either side of the main church is a large cross-in-square chapel, thus creating a triple façade. The Katholikon itself, the **Church of the Koimesis**, the architectural plan of which became the model for Athonite churches, is not without blemish. There is a squatness about the proportions, with weighty vaults and massive apses; the cupola is the largest on Mount Athos; the exterior walls are painted bright puce. The frescoes of the outer narthex and narthex are tasteless examples of early nineteenth-century work. Impressive metal-faced oak doors of the Middle Byzantine period, elaborately decorated in *repoussé* technique with rosettes, petals, scrolls, vine leaves and crosses studded with gems, open into the *naos*, which is less splendid than that at Iviron. The two columns at the west end are part of the original tenth-century structure. On the screen - a nineteenth-century castellated stone monstrosity - hang two splendid **icons**, gifts of the Emperor Michael IX Paleologos (1293-1320): the Virgin with doe-like eyes; and Christ, with aquiline features and a deep, penetrating expression, holding a Book of Gospels. Part of the main apse is hallowed ground and no human foot is allowed to tread on the spot where St Athanassios fell, broke his back and died, while helping to raise the dome. The Chapel of the Forty Martyrs on the left contains his tomb, encased in silver and draped in a mauve cloth decorated with crosses.

More important, though restored, are the **frescoes** of the *naos*, the work of Theofanes, a master of the Cretan School of painting, who died at the Grand Lavra in the early sixteenth century. His work seems more monkish and mystical than human and emotional; but his draughtsmanship and feeling for clarity are apparent in the grandiose Dormition of the Virgin, dominated by the noble figure of Christ holding the Virgin's soul. For an agreeable blend of colours one should turn to the Transfiguration, with its ochre rocks and mauve-tinted draperies and to the procession of saints and fathers of the church on the lower zone. Every known trick of the brush is used to make the figures identifiable and to heighten the dramatic allegory.

The walls of the disused **refectory**, the largest on Mount Athos, built in the shape of a cross, are also covered with frescoes by Theofanes and his Cretan disciples. The Last Supper spreads across the west apse, where the abbot once sat. Other scenes have to do with eating: the miracle of the loaves of bread, the supper at Emmaus, Elijah fed by the raven. More moving is the **Dormition of St Athanassios** in the north apse, a lyrical scene filled with mourning figures, a pink church symbolizing the dome that caused the saint's death. The south transept is filled with a panoramic vision of the **Last Judgement**, a confused assemblage of figures, incidents and allegories.

To the right of the refectory, a huge *simandron*, three metres long, beaten only on the most solemn of occasions, hangs from metal chains beside a bell-tower. We passed the goldfish basin, dragged up the hill in the form of a block of unhewn stone by St Athanassios, as he warded off the assaults of demons who were finally driven off by blows from his metal-tipped staff. The spot where the saintly foot was imprinted on the rim of the basin in the course of the skirmish is marked with a cross.

The librarian, anxious to hurry us on, and inclined to gabble his information, led us to the **treasury**, which houses the gifts of two Emperor-benefactors of the tenth century: the chasuble of Nikeforos Fokas, which he wore over a hair shirt; his imperial crown, studded with pearls and precious stones and surmounted by a jewelled cross, and his **Book of Gospels**, a superb piece of Byzantine gold and silver work; an early **mosaic icon of St John the Divine**, presented by John I Tsimisces, set within a frame of mosaic medallions in each of which a saint is portrayed, and an exquisitely wrought jewel-studded **gold cross**, in whose arms splinters of the True Cross are concealed.

The library contains eight hundred manuscripts on parchment. We looked at some leaves of St Paul's Letters to the Corinthians and Galatians from a sixth-century codex, a tenth-century illuminated manuscript of Dioscorides's *Manual of Botany* and a fifteenth-century edition of Homer - its first printing.

After an early lunch of bean soup and tomatoes, we descended to the arsenal to catch the two o'clock *caique*. The wind had dropped and the sea was smooth, metallic. The *caique* hugged the coast, which became increasingly abrupt and desolate beyond the arsenal of the Romanian *skiti* of Prodromou. Nothing could be more spectacular, or in a sense more forbidding, than the journey round **Cape Akrathos**: we passed the mouth of the **Cave of the Wicked Dead** high up on the cliff-side. Its fetid chambers, the exile of excommunicated monks, were said to have been littered with bloated corpses, their nails turned to horny talons and their hair growing to their ankles, for the bodies of renegade monks, contrary to the laws of nature, did not undergo decomposition.

We rounded the cape. Towering screes are fringed with gigantic boulders that hurtled down in primeval landslides, forming ramparts of contorted stone. Grottoes are made up of a succession of arched tunnels in which the water swishes and gurgles. Around here, Mardonius' fleet was smashed to pieces in a storm in 492 BC and the Persian soldiers were 'seized and devoured', says Herodotos, by the 'man-eating monsters' that infested the waters.

The Eastern mystical tradition of attaining the good life through the purest asceticism is easily comprehended in this savage setting: sailing between razor-edged reefs, we saw two seemingly inaccessible *kellia* (solitaries' eyries), perched hundreds of metres above the sea, and the formidable ravine up which Peter the

Anchorite, the first hermit, climbed single-handed. Another cave, until recently inhabited by a solitary, overhangs a dizzy ledge, forming part of the eyrie of St Neilos, from whose corpse myrrh was said to have trickled down the side of the scree and floated on the waves in patches of luminous gold so that sailors came to collect it and afterwards sold it to pious worshippers.

Two thousand metres above towers the limestone crest of Athos, crowned by a white chapel. Strabo said that people who scaled the final peak could 'see the sun rise three hours before it rises on the seaboard', and its shadow is supposed to be cast across the Aegean as far as the island of Skiathos, which means 'in the shade of Athos'.

Suddenly the desolation is relieved by a glimpse of human habitation. The *skiti* of **Kavsokalyvia**, a dependency of the Grand Lavra, winds vertically up the side of a fertile valley. Chapels with domes and slate roofs, and whitewashed cottages inhabited by monkish wood-carvers are surrounded by clusters of bay trees from whose berries laurel oil is pressed. Here dwelt St Akakios, who took flight one day in a religious transport and floated up to the summit of Athos where he met the Virgin.

We passed two rowing-boats propelled by black-robed hermits with white beards. They waved and went on fishing. As we rounded Cape Pinnes, where the screes acquire a deep pink, almost fiery hue, the *skiti* of **Karoulia** burst into view: a chain of eyries straggling up a perpendicular streak of vegetation. They are connected to each other by a cobbled track, just wide enough to allow the passage of a single mule, which has replaced an ancient system of communication whereby the hermits, on visits to each other, clung to ropes or chains passing over makeshift pulleys. Little shelves of soil are terraced one above another, planted with vegetables and a few vines, surrounded by cacti. It is like the Ladder of Heaven in the Last Judgement. A blue dome was visible and some huts where more worldly hermits carve religious souvenirs and crosses from deer-horn, which are sold in Karyes.

The next *skiti* was **Ayia Annas**. Each shelf of the vertical succession of eyries is connected with the next by primitive aqueducts made of hollowed-out trunks of pine and cypress, through which streams cascade from one vegetable plot to another. Modern icons are painted by the inhabitants of these vertiginous abodes. In the Church of Ayia Annas there is a venerable relic: St Anne's left foot.

We had now rounded the promontory and put in at Nea Skiti, an eighteenth-century dependency of the Monastery of Ayios Paulos, where the woollen socks worn by Athonite monks are knitted by hermits. The slope of the mountain is less abrupt here and there is a green foreshore, with some modern houses scattered among orchards.

We sailed into the Singitic Gulf. To starboard, high up on the mountainside, rises the fortress of the Monastery of Ayios Paulos. The coast was still steep, but wooded and more broken; one could imagine men dwelling in this country. We were chugging towards the **Monastery of Dionysiou**: four stories of whitewashed cells with projecting balconies, roofed with slate tiles and crowned with a medieval tower, soaring above an immense foundation wall that rises like a stone pier from an isolated bluff above the shore.

From the arsenal we climbed a cobbled path between plane and walnut trees overhanging the torrent-bed of the Aeropotamos (The Windy River), so-called because sudden currents of cold air whistle down it from the mountain. Terraced kitchen-gardens were bordered with oleanders and we noticed peach trees heavy with golden fruit. By the entrance gate there is a fountain of cold water and a belvedere overlooking the peaceful gulf. The rock on which the monastery is perched allows no room for outward expansion. Cells, storerooms and galleries pile up, supported on struts, one above the other; at the summit of the pinnacle is the crimson-painted church within its cramped court.

The origins of the monastery's foundation go back to an eremitical vision. In the fourteenth century a hermit called Dionysios dwelt in a neighbouring eyrie. One night he noticed flames leaping heavenward from the bluff above the sea. Every night the supernatural blaze grew brighter. Interpreting the message correctly, he begged his brother, a Trapezuntine bishop, to persuade the Emperor Alexios III of Trebizond to build a monastery on the holy spot. It was called after him - Dionysiou.

It was five o'clock and we were hustled off to dinner in the refectory. The rhythm of life would be different here. We were in a cenobitic house - one of the friendliest and most beautiful on the peninsula. The monks here are not just refugees or vagabonds from the world, anxious to secure free board and lodging in return for the gabbling of praises to the Lord, parrot-fashion, in a haze of incense; here the spirit of contemplation and communion still exists, and frugality has some relation to godliness.

The beautifully proportioned **refectory**, entirely frescoed, is T-shaped, with arches at the point where the arms join the stem. As we ate - a Lucullan feast by Athonite standards: *pilaff* with fried squid, tomatoes stuffed with rice and garlic, peaches, bread and rough red wine - a deacon mounted the brightly painted pulpit and read from the menology, while we gazed round the frescoed walls. Shafts of light, slanting through the windows, fell on gruesome scenes of martyrdom: severed heads, surrounded by golden nimbuses, rolling on marble floors, ferocious Roman legionaries brandishing blood-stained swords. The principal frescoes are of the sixteenth to seventeenth centuries: the Last Supper in the east apse above the abbatial table, and a vast **Last Judgement**, in which the Ladder of Heaven is full of animation, with figures scaling the celestial rungs, urged on by officious angels. At the top they are received by Christ standing against a star-studded sky. The cool, pleasant cloister of the refectory is frescoed with lively apocalyptic scenes: the Four Horsemen, martial and purposeful, and the Earthquake, with the roofs of buildings collapsing in a strangely geometrical fashion.

We attended vespers in the dark, frescoed church, spellbound by the voice of a young, beardless monk chanting the litanies in a soaring tenor, while hoary old men, bent double with fatigue and infirmity, muttered '*Kyrie Eleison! Kyrie Eleison!*' They then kissed the holy images and shuffled out, removing the veils they attach to their hats during the liturgy. There was little to do but retire to our bedroom on the top floor of this complex eyrie of corridors and projecting balconies. From the windows there was a drop, absolutely sheer, of hundreds of metres, to the base of the bluff fringed by a rocky shore.

28 August

In the morning an amiable librarian took us sightseeing. The **Church of Ayios Ioannis Prodromos** follows the usual Athonite plan. The sixteenth-century frescoes possess a harmony, a fluidity of design and a freshness of colour rare in the grandiose wall-paintings of the ancient and more venerable churches of Vatopedi and Iviron. Less opulence, in the way of gold and marble decoration, creates an atmosphere of greater restraint and concentration. The artist was Zorsi, a native of Crete, possibly of Venetian origin. His work is more Italianate, less monkish, than that of his compatriot Theofanes. His draperies billow and swirl and his architectural backgrounds are more integrated. From the dome the Pantocrator blesses mankind, with angels, standing on a green lawn, surrounding him. Opposite the Nativity, on the barrel vault of the south apse, St John baptizes Christ, who is immersed in the waters of the Jordan, against a star-studded sky.

In the library we saw the famous **chrysobull of Alexios III of Trebizond**, the imperial charter confirming the foundation of the monastery, which Finlay calls 'one of the most valuable monuments of the pictorial and calligraphic arts of the Greeks in the Middle Ages'. On the piece of parchment, more than three metres long and twenty centimetres wide, a majestic Christ is depicted in the act of blessing Alexios and his Empress, the scarlet of the imperial ink vying with the golds and bluish-greens of uncials entwined with tendrils. Among the manuscripts are a twelfth-century Book of Gospels, its cover decorated with a figure of Christ on the Cross between the Virgin and St John, and another of the thirteenth century with an earlier cover minutely carved in wood with scenes from the *Dodekaorton*.

After nine o'clock lunch in the refectory we chartered a *caique* to take us to the Monastery of Ayios Paulos. From the jetty we saw baskets of peaches, dangling at the ends of long ropes, being hauled up by monks to a balcony that projected above the great supporting wall. We struck a bargain with the *caique-master* and chartered his boat for the next two days. This would enable us to visit the last group of monasteries on the west coast without having to spend a night in each of them.

From the arsenal of the **Monastery of Ayios Paulos** we walked for over an hour up a stony path in a wild and rocky landscape. The monastery straddles the mouth of a savage ravine against a background of terrific precipices, its walls rising like a vast medieval stronghold out of the scrubland. To the east, a lofty crenellated wall protects the monks' cells from the icy blasts that funnel out of the ravine in winter. The approach is strewn with boulders washed down by torrents or thrown across the thyme-scented mountainside by landslides. The last lap of the painful ascent is along a cobbled path, trellised with vines. Beside the gate there is a pergola where we rested, listening to the gibberish of a lay vagrant - one of the many who roam the peninsula in search of a bed and a free meal - whose limbs shook as though he was stricken with the palsy. Fumbling in the pockets of his verminous clothes for a Book of Gospels, he then read several passages aloud, looking up occasionally to leer obscenely at us. Wandering through empty courts and galleries, we finally tracked down the guest-master who led us to a spacious guest-house overlooking the stony waste and offered us plum jam, coffee and *ouzo*.

The original establishment was founded in the tenth century by a hermit named Paul, a contemporary of St Athanassios, who heard an unearthly voice instructing him to build a house of God on the site of his cave. The monastery was largely destroyed by fire in 1902. Monkish carelessness, the lavish use of woodwork for constructional purposes and candles burning beside holy images have all contributed to the outbreak of these devastating conflagrations, in which much of the original structure of numerous Athonite houses has perished. At Ayios Paulos, only the Chapel of Ayios Yeoryios, the great east wall and the sixteenth-century tower (which is the tallest on Mount Athos) survive. The other buildings are modern and of little interest

We climbed a series of wooden stairways to the **Chapel of Ayios Yeoryios**, built into the fortified wall which forms the backcloth of the monastery against a screen of stupendous cliffs. The chapel, overlooking the domes of the Church of the Presentation of the Virgin, is small: a single-aisle church with a narthex. An inscription, possibly spurious, dates it to 1423, but the frescoes are more closely related to the Cretan School of the sixteenth century. Whatever their date, they have the distinction, rare among frescoes of Mount Athos, of being wholly unrestored. In their freshness and luminosity, in the subtlety, delicacy and transparency of their colour tints, they compare favourably with the best work of the late Byzantine period. The tone is set immediately by the saints and ascetics ranged around the walls of the narthex; each figure stands out as an individual. The frescoes of the *naos*, battered though untarnished, still glow with much of their original variety of colour. The faces are expressive and the garments lavish. The mood of the **Nativity** is serene and pastoral, with a relaxed Virgin reclining on a faded pink couch while the Child lies swaddled in the crib. In the **Raising of Lazarus**, white-bearded figures in robes of dove grey and pink, framed between yellow rocks, watch the unwinding of the shroud against a snow-white, castellated background beneath a sombre sky. Across the vault are medallions of the Virgin and Child and six prophets, each a compelling portrait.

We walked down to the arsenal in the sizzling heat. Lizards scuttled among scorched shrubs. We swam off a pebbly shore in what are said to be shark-infested waters. Centuries ago, the inmates of Dionysiou, perched on their highest balcony, watched a shark frustrated in the act of swallowing a monk bathing in the cove below; stretching his arms outwards, the holy man arranged his body into the shape of a cross so that the shark was unable to devour him. But no sea monsters disturbed the translucent waters on this occasion. The boulders and cliffs, rising sheer above, are horizontally seamed with brightly coloured stratifications: puce, brown, amber, olive green and pink.

We got back to Dionysiou to find the monks in a state of unusual animation. It was the eve of the feast of the Assumption of the Virgin and the beardless chorister whose voice had so impressed us the night before wandered round the monastery, beating the *simandron* with his little mallet. The tinkling tune echoed across the galleries girdling the crimson church, and there was a strong smell of incense.

The service lasted all night, without a break. We went into the church several times. Some of the weary, hungry monks, who had not touched meat or fish for a fortnight, slept as they leant on their staffs; others sneezed when a deacon swung a censer under their noses. There was no formality - the absence of pews in an Orthodox church tends to make clergy and congregation wholly unselfconscious. Priests came and went. Hour after hour the Divine Office went on, to the accompaniment of the plaintive eight-tone chant. In the cloisters and passages veiled, black-robed figures lingered, whispered for a moment and disappeared into church, crossing themselves.

29 August

Early in the morning we sailed in our chartered *caique* to the **Monastery of Grigoriou**. Like Dionysiou, though less beautiful and interesting, it is perched on a bluff above a creek. A ruined tower and a wilted palm tree crown the pile of buildings, whose wooden balconies of different colours overhang the sea.

We were received by the abbot, who led us to an ugly refectory where, with all the monks, we lunched on pieces of dried cod fried in the most rancid oil I have ever tasted, followed by custard, washed down with vinegary wine. We soon recovered our spirits, however, in an airy gallery with walls painted sky blue, from which there was a prodigious view of the wild, steep coastline stretching southwards. A heavy bank of cloud was settling on the peak of Athos.

The monastery was founded by Gregory, a hermit of Mount Sinai, in the thirteenth century. Fire destroyed it in the eighteenth and all the buildings are relatively modern. The exterior walls of the **Church of Ayios Nikolaos** are painted blue, with dark magenta drums supporting grey domes. The eighteenth-century frescoes of the interior are without distinction. In the *naos* there is a venerated but not very ancient icon of the Galaktotrofoussa (The Virgin Giving Suck), in which the Virgin is depicted with a peevish expression, offering her breast to the Child.

By mid-morning we were sailing north-westward below the fourteenth-century **Monastery of Simonopetra**, seven stories of strut-supported wooden galleries crowning a foundation wall twice as formidable as that of Dionysiou, soaring into the air out of the dark green woods three hundred metres above sea level, and joined to the mountainside by an imposing aqueduct with a double tier of arches. During a great fire in the sixteenth century, panic-stricken monks hurled themselves over the balconies and were dashed to pieces on the boulder-strewn vegetable plots below. The monastery is about an hour's steep climb from its arsenal on the rock shore. Simonopetra's façade may be the most theatrical on the Holy Mountain, but otherwise it has little to offer except an aerial view of the peninsula and gulf.

Beyond the arsenal of Simonopetra the scenery becomes tamer. We put in at Dafni, our original starting point, in time for a second lunch, then continued by boat, hugging the coast, the most domesticated on Mount Athos. The sky had become overcast and, by the time we reached the Arsenal of Ayios Pandeleimon, drops of rain were falling on an oily grey sea. A gentle ramp leads from a waterfront of tall, gutted warehouses and woodcutters' shacks into a fantasy: a miniature 'Russian' town.

The **Monastery of Ayios Pandeleimon**, commonly called Roussiko (The Russian One), is one of the most extraordinary sights on Mount Athos; not because of its antiquarian interest - it has none - but because of its decayed splendour: a vast nineteenth-century Russian enclave of spires, bell-towers and paved courts on different levels, with thirty churches and chapels, their red roofs crowned with onion domes and gold crosses, all in an Aegean setting of pine-woods, cypress thickets and olive groves.

The early twelfth-century foundation was dedicated to St Pandeleimon, a court physician and convert to Christianity, whose martyrdom in the reign of Diocletian was distinguished by the extraordinary resistance shown by his head to every attempt at severance by the most stalwart executioners; it finally succumbed, wreathed in a resplendent halo, to the blows of the mightiest axe in the Roman Empire. St Pandeleimon remains a popular patron of doctors and medical institutions.

After the Byzantine era the monastery fell on bad days and it was not until the early nineteenth century that the influence of Mother Russia, head of Christian Orthodoxy since the fall of Constantinople, reached the Aegean and led to a rapid influx of Russian monks. The Russian Government, always eager to secure support in Greece against their traditional common enemy, Turkey, exploited the link between the sister churches and showered wealth on the Holy Mountain and on Ayios Pandeleimon in particular. At the turn of the century it was the largest and most active monastery in the whole Athonite community, the number of Slav monks on the peninsula amounting to two thousand, as against three thousand Greeks. This was the culmination of a connection between the Byzantine and Slavonic worlds, first made a thousand years before, when St Cyril and St Methodios left Constantinople to convert the first Slavs to Christianity. However, after 1917 few novices found their way to Ayios Pandeleimon. Less than a dozen monks, flat-faced Russian peasants, have survived to drag out their last senile years in this decaying nineteenth-century stage set.

We carried our bags along tiled paths, past deserted chapels covered with lichen, until we reached a large, unkempt court. An old monk with a matted red beard, prominent cheek-bones and light-coloured, rheumy eyes was crouching on the ground. As we drew nearer we observed that he was feeding armies of ants with bread-crumbs. We addressed the monk in Greek. He replied in Russian, but seemed to understand what we wanted. Arranging his breadcrumbs in a little pile on the ground, he shuffled off, returning after a few minutes with a lay guest-master, who led us through a gloomy gallery to a shuttered drawing-room filled with peeling leather armchairs and sofas covered with antimacassars. Photographs of the Tsar, Tsarina and Tsarevich and related royalty (Edward VII, the Kaiser) hung on the walls. The ritual coffee and *ouzo* were produced.

Later, shafts of sunlight, penetrating the cloud bank, shone on gold crosses and green domes as we wandered among trellised passages, across tiled courts, up and down stairways with ornamental balustrades and past neglected flowerbeds shaded by limp palms. We saw a chapel, its columns crowned with Corinthian capitals, a fountain, and pedestals with cornucopias from which dusty ferns drooped languidly.

The exterior of the Church of Ayios Pandeleimon is pleasing, its walls painted coral pink, its domes sheeted with grey metal. The interior is a mass of gold and gilt, with an outsize chandelier and corona. The frescoes would have done credit to the illustrator of a children's book of Bible stories published in about 1910. Across the inner court, opposite the church, is a huge refectory in the shape of a basilica with barrel-vaulted aisles and an apse at the west end; 1500 monks used to dine here. A belfry on three stepped levels, topped by a lime-green spire, surmounts the edifice.

On the highest level of the monastery, crowning the whole fantastic pile, are the two enormous **Chapels of the Protection of the Virgin and Saints Alexander Nevsky, Vladimir and Olga**, which together virtually form a single large cathedral, all gilt and ormolu with gold crosses and rococo columns, capable of accommodating a congregation of two thousand. The walls are hung with hideous icons, and marble pillars with Ionic capitals support the gallery. After this we visited the official reception hall of the guest-house, filled with more gilt-framed photographs of Tsars and other royalty, of Rasputin and famous abbots. All that was lacking, one felt, was an empty ballroom, ghost-like, echoing with familiar tunes from *Swan Lake*. (Since this visit to the monastery, fire has once more ravaged several buildings described here. Restoration work is in progress.)

Meals are no longer served in the refectory so we dined by candlelight in the kitchen of the guest-house. Afterwards there was nothing to do but wander across the empty courts and watch sheet-lightening flash across the southern sky above the Holy Mountain. Stumbling along a dark gallery I heard mice scuttling about and thought I saw a gigantic spider hanging from a beam in the ceiling. No other monastery on Mount Athos has such a haunted air.

30 August

Early in the morning we walked to the **Monastery of Xenofondos**: two stories of projecting balconies crowned by domes and broken towers, supported by strong walls and overlooking a sandy beach. It is a peaceful place surrounded by green hills. A convoy of donkeys, carrying loads of wood, wound through the groves. The monastery owes much to Balkan benefactors. Founded in the eleventh century by a pious Byzantine nobleman called Xenophon, it was restored in the sixteenth century by Moldo-Wallachian princes and in the eighteenth by Romanian hospodars.

Steps lead up from an irregular sloping court to the **Church of Ayios Yeoryios**, frescoed by two sixteenth-century artists of the Cretan School, Antonios and Theofanes (not to be confused with the more important Theofanes who worked at the Grand Lavra). Though their work is somewhat cold and hard, that of Antonios is nonetheless bold and original and the large scenes in the upper zone merit attention. The tragedy of the **Crucifixion** is stressed by sharp angularities, by hooded effigies of the sun and moon illustrating the darkness that fell over the earth between the sixth and ninth hours. The **Entry into Jerusalem** has a quality of starkness, an absence of architectural and incidental detail rare in this composition. Antonios' skill as a draughtsman may be halting, but he possesses remarkable virtuosity in the manipulation of colour; in the violence of his contrasts he is often extremely original, using pitch-black skies as a background for his favourite Sienna reds, corals and clarets. Here, more than anywhere else on Mount Athos, it is possible to discern the origins of that explosion of luminosity and dramatic impressionism which was to distinguish the masterpieces of El Greco less than half a century later. In comparison, the work of Theofanes in the same church seems trivial and insipid.

As the monastery grew in size and importance in the early nineteenth century, the church became too small and a larger edifice, also dedicated to St George, was raised further up the slope. It is unfrescoed but possesses a fine collection of icons, a reliquary containing a drop of St John the Baptist's blood and two magnificent **mosaic panels** of the thirteenth century, representing St George and St Dimitrios. They are executed in the minutest *tesserae*. Both faces emerge as portraits: young men of nobility, virile, sensitive and chivalrous.

Later, descending the ramp to the beach, we saw a little stream of fresh water trickling through the pebbles on the spot where an icon of St George was found by monks centuries ago. Roughly handled by Iconoclasts, the icon is said to have oozed blood from a crack in the panel and was thrown into the sea. Months later it was tossed up on the shore of Xenofondos, whereupon the holy spring, whose waters are said to be purgative, gushed forth for the first time.

We began the last lap of our journey and were soon dropping anchor off the landing-stage of the **Monastery of Dohiariou**. From the sea the monastery can be seen to be one of the finest architectural ensembles on the peninsula, its buildings and dependencies spreading fan-wise against a background of hills speckled with pines and cypresses. Balconies overhang stout walls with elliptical blind arches, and a geometrical pattern of belfries, chimneys and slate roofs is dominated by a tower flanked by cypresses. A frescoed porch leads through a labyrinth of cool, shady passages painted with murals, into a small court. Pomegranate trees grow in the shade of walls covered with flowering creepers.

The monks say the monastery was founded by Efthymios, superintendent of stores (*dohiarios*) at the Grand Lavra and a personal friend of St Athanassios. According to the historical record, the site was purchased from the monks of Xenofondos in the eleventh century and the church dedicated to the Archangel Michael, a staunch champion of Athonite holy men against Saracen pirates. The monastery enjoyed imperial benefaction and later that of the Voivodes, the Moldo-Wallachians who restored the church after its destruction by corsairs in the sixteenth century.

In the shadow of the great tower, dated to the early sixteenth century, the wooden loggia of the charming guest-house overlooks roofs and domes on different levels. After the usual refreshment, we visited the **Church of the Archangels**, the largest and one of the most beautiful on the Holy Mountain. The exterior is of brick - a welcome change from the usual crimson stucco - and the blind arches are inlaid with dark, wedge-shaped tiles. The interior is covered with sixteenth-century *frescoes* of the Cretan School, possibly by Zorsi, who worked at Dionysiou; mid-nineteenth-century restoration has not deprived the paintings of their original liveliness. Across the north wall of the exo-narthex there is an enchanting representation of the **Dormition of St Efraim**, the Mesopotamian bath-keeper who became one of the most popular hymnographers of the fourth century. The mourners fan out around the bier, long white beards, draperies and striped vestments forming a symmetrical pattern of vertical lines. The conch-shaped centre-piece is framed within bucolic scenes of eremitical life: hermits praying, reading holy books, riding donkeys and tending fields. A stylite perched on a column casts a rope to haul up a basket of provisions. An air of muted serenity pervades the composition and the lyrical mood recalls the Dormition of St Athanassios at the Grand Lavra.

The *naos* is lofty and beautifully proportioned, the tall central drum supported by four granite columns. As in the two narthexes, every available inch of wall space is frescoed. On the gilded *iconostasis*, a typically fussy example of eighteenth-century wood-carving, biblical episodes intermingle with bucolic scenes in which hunters stalk their prey among stylized bushes. A slab of green marble on the pavement commemorates one of the Archangel's miracles: a shepherd boy of Sithonia, who had found hidden treasure, was assaulted by monks possessed by demons. They tied a marble slab to his neck, dropped him into the sea and made off with the treasure. Floundering in the waves, the boy called on the Archangel for help. St Michael promptly came to the rescue, carried him tenderly to the shore and laid his body, dripping wet, on the floor of the church at Dohiariou, where he was found by a monk beating the *simandron* just before matins.

Outside the church we admired the charming *phiale*, the interior of whose dome is frescoed with scenes of monastic vessels pursued by Saracen fleets and defenceless monks being rescued from corsairs by the Archangels; the monastery, rising directly from the water's edge, was always an easy target for maritime marauders. A cool, frescoed colonnade leads to the sombre little shrine of the *Panayia Gorgoepeikoös* (The Virgin who grants requests quickly), which possesses a wonder-working tenth-century icon of the Virgin, strung with votive offerings. A careless monk once allowed the smoke from his candle to blacken and disfigure her face. The Virgin commanded the monk to be more careful but, forgetful by nature, he repeated the offence. This time the Virgin, acting like an outraged Athena or Artemis, instantly blinded him. The stricken man pleaded for mercy, whereupon the Virgin appeared to him in a vision and declared: 'Monk, your prayer has been heard and you shall see again as you used to, for I am the Ready-Listener'.

The refectory is frescoed with apocalyptic scenes, slightly earlier in date that those in the church. The most remarkable of these is a strange representation of **God Enthroned** against a background of lighted arches: an elderly, haloed figure with a homely expression, holding the bejewelled book 'sealed with seven seals' which could only be opened by the Lamb with seven horns (Revelation, V:1). The white lamb is depicted here with green horns; it stands on its hind legs, about to receive the book from God.

We left Dohiariou and its atmosphere of tranquillity with regret. The sea was calm, the sun hot, as the *caique* chugged westward - back to the world. We bathed off a sandy beach at the foot of a pine-clad cliff crowned by the ruined buildings of a deserted *skiti*. The shore was littered with beautiful pebbles of different colours, smoothed into oval shapes by the endless friction of the waves.

In the late afternoon we saw the Tower of Prosfori rising above the port of Ouranopolis. On landing, we found the car, parked under the shadow of the tower, caked in dust. We sat at a waterfront café. A few tables away, two boys in jeans and striped shirts fiddled with a transistor radio which emitted snatches of the duet from the first act of *Traviata*. A girl in a multi-coloured cotton dress brought us iced lemonade and the sudden realization of where we now were, of where we had been, was breathtaking. A child was cuffed by another and began to howl. Its cries drowned the last echoes of wood pigeons piping in the copses of the Virgin's empty garden.

18

Eastern Macedonia

NORTH AND EAST of the Halkidiki lies Eastern Macedonia, originally Thracian country but annexed by Philip II to the Macedonian Empire after a series of lightning campaigns in the fourth century BC. Fertile, but less beautiful than the Halkidiki, it is full of military associations. Rivers flow north to south through marshy estuaries into the Aegean. The climate is one of extremes, and the winters are of unparalleled coldness by Mediterranean standards. Xenophon refers to the soldiers wearing fox-skin caps, and to wine being frozen. Oxen and cattle, now as then, are plentiful; so are the eels in the river mouths. In antiquity the natives were noted for their barbarous character; disloyal and faithless, they did not hesitate to sell their children. They spoke an uncouth non-Hellenic tongue, were idle by nature and drunken by predilection. Today, by contrast, the inhabitants are thrifty manufacturers, merchants and small farmers.

The journey from Thessaloniki to the River Nestos, on the border of the province of Thrace, and back can be accomplished in one day; but this allows for few deviations, one of which at least, to Philippi, is of outstanding interest. By spending the night at the attractive port of Kavalla, one can also visit Serres and Amphipolis and then either return to Thessaloniki or penetrate deeper into the Thracian plains.

The road from Thessaloniki to Serres, after crossing a rolling, featureless landscape, descends to the west bank of the **River Strymon**. Throughout Greek literature great emphasis is placed on the omnipotent character of the river and the winds that blow across its spacious valley, affecting the weather of the whole country. In 1916-18 the river constituted the demarcation line between the armies of the Allies and those of the Central Powers; and in 1941 German tanks streamed down the valley from the Bulgarian frontier, to reach Thessaloniki within three days. About twenty kilometres east of the Strymon, at the foot of Mount Vrondou (Thunder) lies **Serres**, the ancient Sirris, where Xerxes left large numbers of sick and wounded during the retreat after the battle of Salamis.

The modern town, seat of a bishopric, once a tobacco-growing centre but now supplying a wide range of agricultural products, is distinguished only by its pleasant rectangular square (*Platia Eleftherias*), which is bordered by poplars and weeping willows, with a basin in the centre around which peacocks strut and, on the western side, a rather fine, large Turkish building crowned by six domes, which is now the archaeological museum. At the foot of the castle hill the basilica of the **Old Mitropolis**, dedicated to the Holy Theodores, rises out of a depression, surrounded by blocks of flats and houses. It is a tall brick edifice, somewhat cumbersome in outline, probably built in the eleventh or twelfth century. Largely destroyed by the retreating Bulgarians at the end of the second Balkan War in 1913, it has now been completely restored. The little domed chapel at the north-west corner used to be connected with the medieval keep by an underground passage and was used by Stephen Dusan, the Serbian national hero, who conquered large tracts of Northern Greece in the fourteenth century. The proportions of the interior are lofty and harmonious, four of the original six grey marble columns are preserved, and high up in the bare walls is a small tall-arched tribune gallery. Fragments of an eleventh-century mosaic of the Last Supper, said to have been of outstanding quality, can be discerned in the apse. Outside there are some finely-carved bas-reliefs: a Pantocrator in low relief, elaborate crosses, griffins and horses.

A winding road leads to the summit of the pine-clad hill overlooking the city, where a single bastion stands over the remains of a Byzantine castle. As the tides of war swept back and forth across the Byzantine empire the castle was occupied in turn by invading Franks, Serbs and Turks. Southward, beyond the ugly urban agglomeration, extends the cultivated plain in a pale yellowish-green haze. To the north, chalky cliffs and shallow ravines filled with pines and evergreens mount in a series of rugged forms towards the desolate heights of Mount Vrondou, among whose snow-capped peaks the thunder is said to roll more loudly than anywhere in the world.

About halfway down the east slope of the castle hill a side-road leads through the trees to the little fourteenth-century Byzantine **Church of Ayios Nikolaos**. Recently restored, with its red-brick walls bright against the dark green of the trees, it is something of an

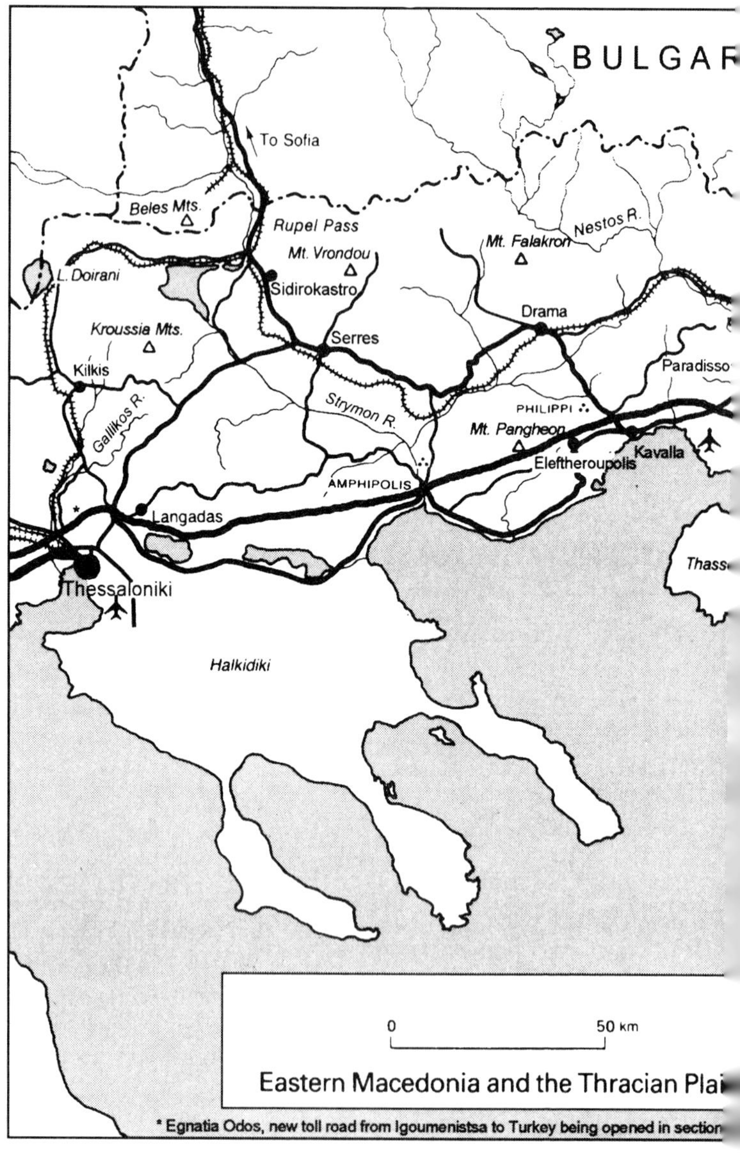

Eastern Macedonia and the Thracian Plai

* Egnatia Odos, new toll road from Igoumenistsa to Turkey being opened in section

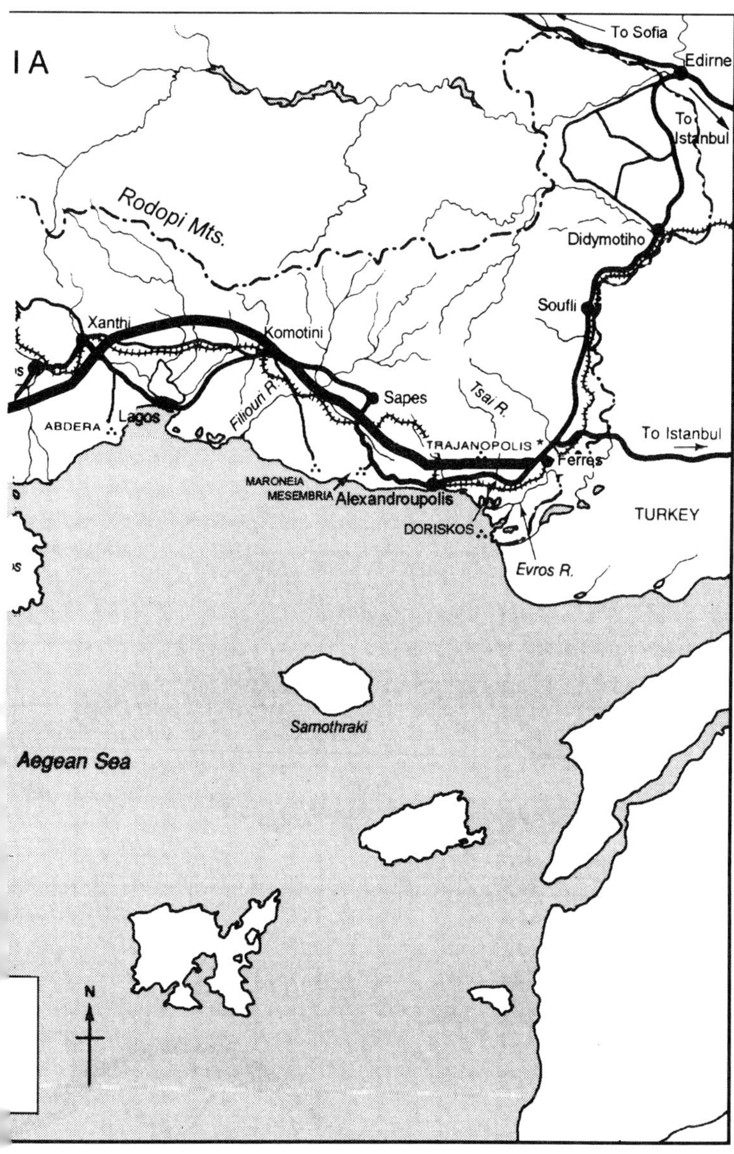
IA
To Sofia
Edirne
To Istanbul
Rodopi Mts.
Didymotiho
Soufli
Xanthi
Komotini
Filiouri R.
Sapes
Tsai R.
ABDERA
Lagos
TRAJANOPOLIS
Ferres
To Istanbul
MARONEIA
MESEMBRIA
Alexandroupolis
DORISKOS
TURKEY
Evros R.
Samothraki
Aegean Sea
N

architectural extravaganza. The *exo-narthex*, which is wider than the main body of the church, has two low domes and a belfry attached at the south-western corner. Three absurd little cupolas sit on top of the western part of the church itself, one on the east, and a well-proportioned dome and drum surmount the whole edifice. The interior is without interest; but it is a secluded place, and the air is balmy with the scent of resin.

From Serres the road runs eastward across highly-productive farming country, its monotony relieved only by the snow-capped shape of Mount Pangheon to the east. After branching south towards the coast, a sign-posted road near the mouth of the Strymon winds up to the village of **Amphipolis.** The visitor should call at the Museum for a plan of the area and advice about going round the scattered ruins of this once-important ancient city (some of the ruins are locked and have to be opened by a curator).

However much can be seen without assistance. The main site is on the flat hill-top above the village - most of the remains are of later churches (with mosaics), but the inner walls of the city can be clearly seen. In separate enclosures are the remains of houses (also with mosaics), a shrine and sections of the outer wall.

The flying ants are a pest, the brushwood thick and prickly, and the distances between the groups of foundations considerable; but one is impressed by the sprawling dimensions of the site and its commanding position between the Strymonic Gulf and the interior plains, with the river winding in two wide loops round the hill before flowing through a lagoon into the gulf. To the east rise the spurs of **Mount Pangheon**, whose gold and silver mines and forests contributed so much to the prosperity of the city. In the south the wooded Halkidiki massif ends in a distant headland crowned by the magical peak of Athos.

The history of the place, which was at the junction of nine strategic roads, is eventful. During the period of Athenian imperial expansion, a new city was founded on the site and it was colonized by Athenian settlers who lost no time in exploiting the mineral and agricultural resources of the region. Thus Amphipolis came to be regarded as one of the chief jewels of the Periclean maritime empire. During the Peloponnesian war, this commercial prize was bitterly contested by Athens and Sparta, and it finally fell to Brasidas in 422 BC at the battle of Amphipolis: a Spartan victory of the first magnitude, though Brasidas himself, the architect of the triumph, was killed. The Athenian defeat became an undignified rout and

Thucydides, in command of the Athenian triremes, failed to recapture the city. After the battle Athenian prestige was never to stand so high again; and moreover, the double event of the Athenian defeat and the death of Brasidas made such an impact on Hellenic consciousness that it increased the influence of the pacifist parties, enabling them, a year later, to negotiate the abortive Peace of Nikia. Over half a century later Amphipolis fell to Philip of Macedon.

So much history, and how little to show for it! Of archaeological excavation there has been relatively little, considering the size of the site. At intervals across the cornfields of the rolling eminence you see truncated pedestals of grey marble, white unfluted columns lying in hollows, a trench in which broken pillars stand in a row, fragmentary remains of walls, some Corinthian capitals and, far removed from any other vestige of antiquity, the legs and buttocks of a large marble horse. At the bottom of the hill, going north, a track leads left to the river, where massive sections of the walls and the wooden piles of the ancient bridge can be seen. Elsewhere signposts show the way to two Macedonian tombs to the east of the main road: one is a natural tumulus, out of which the sepulchre of a Macedonian prince has been carved. Steps descend into a barrel-vaulted chamber with an L-shaped stone couch (or tomb), sufficiently large and imposing to have been the last resting-place of a person of considerable distinction.

The **Lion of Amphipolis** is across the wide bed of the Strymon (over which Xerxes built a bridge for his prodigious army) near the old bridge, about two kilometres north of the new bridge on the Thessaloniki-Kavalla road. The Lion stands on a stepped pedestal in a straggly pine grove, a colossal animal, with magnificent mane and gaping, predatory mouth, reassembled from fourth-century BC fragments. With his eyes fixed across the estuary on the flat-topped acropolis of Amphipolis, he is a superb beast, guarding the mouth of the river. In Hellenistic times these monumental lions, symbols of virility, were generally raised as war memorials. At Amphipolis this one is thought to crown the tomb of some distinguished Macedonian prince.

East of the estuary there is a choice between the coastal road which follows the shore into Kavalla's waterfront, and the main inland road which follows the base of Mount Pangheon, whose ancient gold mines were the goal of every invader and would-be conqueror. From earliest times the mountain, with its bulbous spurs and knobbly summits, exercised a powerful hold over Greek imagination, both as a haunt of the deities and as a source of economic wealth. The gold mines figure in mythology, for the wealth of Kadmos, founder of Thebes, is supposed to have come from the precious ore of Mount Pangheon. The deposits - gold, silver and other metals - were situated on the lower slopes, which rise directly above the road. At (or near) Eleftheroupolis, now an agricultural centre, Thucydides had an estate, whose soil was seamed with veins of gold and to which he retired after the debacle at Amphipolis. It was here, according to Plutarch, that under the shade of a plane tree he began to write his history of the war. When the mines were exhausted is not established, but as late as the first century AD Strabo refers to inhabitants finding nuggets of gold throughout the country between the Strymon and the plains of Philippi.

After Eleftheroupolis the main road skirts the southern end of the plain of Philippi and zigzags down a wooded hillside, offering an enchanting view of the port of **Kavalla**, protected by a headland crowned with crenellated Byzantine walls. Colour-washed houses rise steeply up the pine-clad slopes; ferries ply between the port and the offshore island of Thassos. During the campaign of Philippi the galleys of Brutus and Cassius were anchored in the harbour, which was called Neapolis in antiquity. An emporium for the once mostly tobacco-growing plains of the hinterland, the port was a bone of contention between Greece and Bulgaria for many years. In both World Wars the Bulgarians seized and occupied it, but have left no trace of a Slav minority behind them. Today it is the second-largest town in Northern Greece and, although the central area is dominated by large, modern buildings, it is still one of the most attractive, with an animated waterfront and picturesque old Turkish quarters. Gaily-painted houses and crumbling, neo-classical nineteenth-century mansions, interspersed with modern blocks of flats, mount in terraces up a crescent-shaped screen of wooded hills.

It is worth spending a day in Kavalla, for the town itself and for the interesting and well-arranged **Museum**, which is to the west of the waterfront. In the Neapolis hall (first on the left) are fragments of seventh-, sixth- and fifth-century BC pottery, terracotta figurines and two squat fifth-century BC fluted columns with elaborate Ionic capitals from the Temple of Parthenos, the virgin goddess of Neapolis. However the Amphipolis hall (second on the left) is more rewarding: there is a delicate mid-fourth-century BC ewer with two gilded wreaths, a fourth-century BC statuette of a siren in a state of

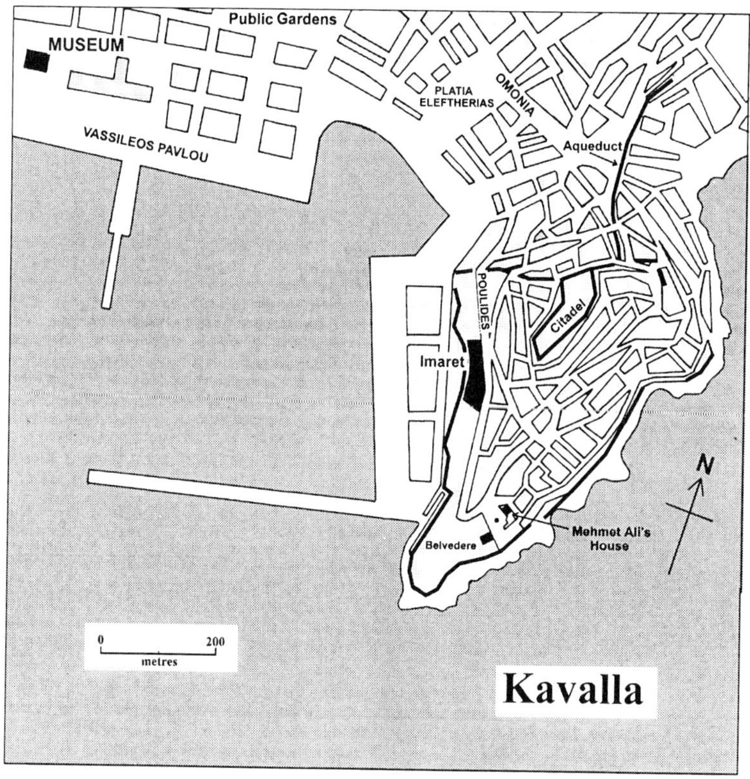

exaltation and a fourth-century BC *stele* of a funeral banquet in which a reclining male figure (the departed soul) is surrounded by his mourning wife, children and attendants. There is some beautiful jewellery on display, a fine fifth century BC tombstone of a youth in high relief, and two terracotta busts of women. But the most impressive object is the partial restoration of a double Macedonian tomb from Amphipolis, faced with fragments of original frescoes. A gold wreath and a beautifully-shaped silver hand-mirror, found in the tomb, are displayed in a special showcase. Like the exhibits in the museum at Thessaloniki, they tell the same story: the sculptor's art in Northern Greece never achieved the perfection reached in Southern Greece but, in the Hellenistic age, the Macedonian artist's observation of nature, his sense of fantasy and delight in variety seldom fails to charm.

What is left of **'Old' Kavalla** can be seen in a two-hour walk with some steep climbing. It is best to start from Platia Eleftherias and go to the right along Omonia Street to the conspicuous landmark of the sixteenth-century Turkish aqueduct, known as the *Kamares*, which straddles the isthmus joining the citadel-topped bluff to the mainland.

From the aqueduct one should return towards the harbour and then go up Poulides Street, climbing the west side of the headland, along the ridge of which run well-preserved Byzantine walls. This is the heart of the old Turkish quarter: a maze of steep alleys and sudden, unexpected declivities. The area has become rather fashionable, and many of the old Turkish-style houses have been privately restored. On the right are the low, shallow-domed buildings of Mehmet Ali's **Imaret**, an almshouse for the aged and needy. The complex, built on many levels, has been partly restored, and now houses a large and attractive café-restaurant and a taverna among other businesses. The *Imaret*, however, still reflects a forgotten aspect of a vanished Moslem world. A colonnade surmounted by eighteen metal-sheeted tea-cosy domes surrounds a sunken, irregular-shaped courtyard. Here the aged turbaned figures would wander, when they were not snoozing in the cells which contained three hundred divans. At one side of the court a convex projection like a bastion, surrounded by a water conduit where the old men performed their ablutions, supports a domed mosque with a portico overlooking the court. A second colonnaded court, square this time and full of the sound of cooing doves, has the remains of fretwork screens between square columns.

Beyond the *Imaret*, Poulides Street mounts to a belvedere overlooking the Thracian sea. A pedestal is crowned by a bronze equestrian statue of Mehmet Ali, his scimitar drawn, mounted on a splendidly-caparisoned horse impatiently pawing the ground. A prosperous Albanian farmer, born in Kavalla in 1769, Mehmet Ali was to become Pasha of Egypt and founder of the Egyptian royal dynasty which ended with Farouk. Beside the statue is his birthplace, a rambling Turkish house in an excellent state of preservation, thanks to the care and money expended on it by the Egyptian Government.

Steep cobbled lanes and alleys mount through a picturesque confusion of old houses to the formidable citadel, entered from the east side, from which there is a fine view.

Fifteen kilometres inland on the Drama road, the ruins of **Philippi** extend across a fertile plain at the foot of a pyramid-shaped hill. From no other point is Mount Pangheon - a huge isolated cone rising out of the aspen-studded fields - seen to better advantage. Originally called Krenides, the place was fortified and renamed by Philip of Macedon, who needed the gold of Mount Pangheon to wage the wars that would make him master of Greece. In 42 BC Philippi became famous as a battleground when the two largest Roman armies ever engaged in hostilities against each other manoeuvred across the plain, much of which was then a marsh. The strategic importance of the site of this decisive battle is self-evident: by guarding a section of the Via Egnatia which passed through a narrow gap, it ensured the security of Neapolis and the maintenance of maritime communications with Asia Minor.

The inevitable result of the struggle for power following Caesar's murder, was the Battle of Philippi, between the Republicans and Octavian, Caesar's heir. The battle consisted of two separate engagements, both fought west of the town between the marsh and the eastern ring of hills. Both battles were initiated by the Republican leaders - Brutus and Cassius - who seem to have repeated Pompey's mistake at Pharsalus of provoking an untimely, head-on clash, instead of trying to wear the enemy down. In the first engagement, Octavian, feeling wretchedly ill, was completely routed by Brutus' legions. The sickly future master of the world escaped capture by fleeing to the camp of his ally, Antony. Cassius, however, was worsted by Antony and, in his despair, committed suicide. Deeply distressed by the death of his friend, Brutus decided to 'try fortune in a second fight'. This time Antony's legions infiltrated the Republicans' position and Brutus was trapped and overwhelmed, whereupon he too 'retired to a hill', says Suetonius, 'and slew himself in the night'; thus perished the Roman Republic on the marshy fields of Thrace. The way now lay open for a final struggle, eleven years later at Actium, between the two victors of Philippi. After that battle Octavian, now Augustus Caesar, remembered the strategic value and agricultural wealth of the plain and sent colonists to Philippi, so that by the time of St Paul's visit it was a completely Roman city, its wide and beautiful streets crowded with strutting praetors, lictors and magistrates.

When St Paul reached Philippi the religion of the people was still that of the indigenous Thracians who worshipped the goddess Bendis, an Underworld deity, and the heroic Thracian Horseman; the

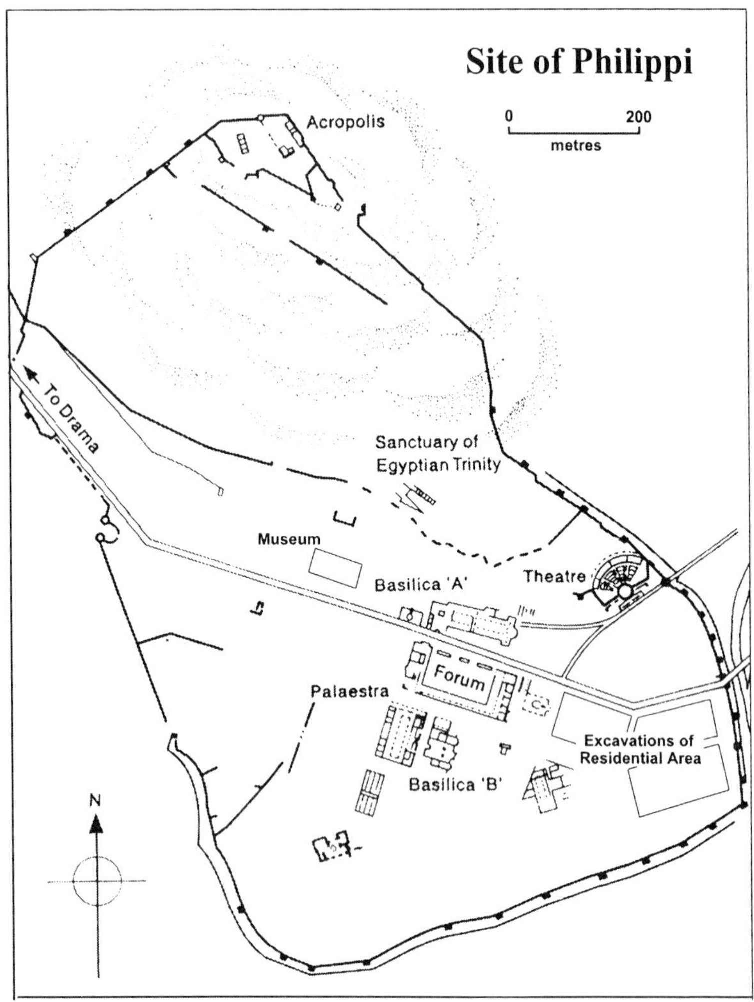

official faith of the governing class, of course, was that of Pagan Rome. Beside a stream outside the city St Paul met and baptized the soothsayer Lydia and her household. Neither the Thracian multitude nor the Roman magistrates took kindly to the Apostle's exorcism of the damsel's evil spirit; so they rent his and Silas' clothes in the market place and cast them into prison.

The main road runs through the site, but the ruins, Early-Christian rather than Roman, are extensive, impressive and easy to identify. Visiting first the area on the right, above the road, you climb a stairway to reach **Basilica A**, probably destroyed in an earthquake, leaving a confusing mass of stone. Dated to the fifth century, it is an aisled basilica with transepts and a semi-circular apse. Among the debris are several fragments of the sculptural decoration that once adorned the interior: Corinthian capitals, pieces of cornice, carved plaques and column bases. The marbles, grey and Thessalian, must have added splendour to the scene as the sun's rays, piercing the clerestory below the timber roof, fell obliquely across the colonnades separating the aisles. With the eclipse of the Roman Empire in the West, the Via Egnatia had declined in importance, and Philippi might no longer have been an important commercial centre; but the size of its churches and their surviving decoration provide evidence of the city's prominence as a place of pilgrimage, the first in Europe at which the Gospel was preached.

Nearby, a little lower, a barrel-vaulted chamber is said to have been the **prison of St Paul**. But nothing remains of the doors that the earthquake caused to open, rocking the foundation of the cell and loosening the prisoners' bonds, whereupon the panic-stricken guards were promptly converted and the Romans, both frightened by the earthquake and tired of the Apostle's nuisance value, let him and Silas go unmolested on their way to Amphipolis.

From here a path climbs to the terrace of the **Sanctuary of the Egyptian Trinity**, where more than one *cella* and the remains of stuccoed walls are discernible. The incongruity is bewildering. It is difficult to avoid a feeling of historical and geographical disorientation. Flying insects sting one and lizards slither across the path as the ascent grows steeper, until one reaches the acropolis, on the summit of the conical hill which dominates the ruined city. Identifiable fragments of the medieval enceinte are superimposed on the fourth-century BC walls, with three towers silhouetted against the skyline.

Starting from Basilica A again and going to the right, one passes first a series of curious rock-hewn chambers: tall vertical niches, possibly connected with the worship of Bendis; then a railed-in enclosure with a well-preserved chequered marble pavement and two tall columns crowned with impost capitals. Finally one reaches the **Theatre**. Originally a Hellenistic edifice, it was remodelled in the second century to suit Roman tastes: an unusually large *orchestra* was created, to allow sufficient room for gladiatorial shows and the original Greek *proskenion* was removed to make way for more showy imperial embellishments. There are about half-a-dozen Roman tiers built of limestone, the rest of the *cavea* being somewhat tastelessly restored in the late 1950's. The theatre is frequently used during the summer and is one of the two venues of the Philippi-Thassos Festival of ancient drama. From the topmost tier, alongside which ran a vaulted gallery, there is a fine view across the agricultural plain to a ridge of wooded hills separating the hinterland from the sea.

But the more impressive ruins lie south of the road, opposite Basilica A, on flat ground. First, after the wide paved road running below and parallel to the modern road, is the rectangle of the **Forum**, on a truly Roman scale, much of it dated to the reign of Marcus Aurelius. Little remains standing above waist-level, but many of the stone and marble slabs, carved with Latin inscriptions, are of great size. With a little patience and imagination one can identify the main features: the foundations of two temples at the north-east and north-west angles, and a library on the east side; to the north a stepped tribune, whence St Paul probably preached the Word; around it lie fragments of Roman statues. At the south-east end fluted columns stand on huge plinths; at the west end is a well-preserved stretch of paved road, flanked by a parapet with a row of slender, unfluted columns. The havoc and destruction of the Forum is nightmarish and the sheets of forget-me-not that carpet the ground and the clusters of asphodel that sprout from crannies in the shattered masonry in spring, only seem to emphasize the totality of the city's ruin. Recent excavations just east of the Forum have revealed the foundations of an octagonal Early-Christian church, which had an altar on one side and colonnades on the other seven. East of the Forum large, mainly residential areas have been excavated: houses with courtyards, fine paved streets and small public buildings.

Immediately south of the Forum extend the ruins of Philippi's chief glory, **Basilica B**, the warm, cream-coloured stone of its surviving piers dominating the ruins. Dated to the reign of Justinian, the plan in itself must have been exciting: a domed basilica, with an additional cupola above the sanctuary, taller and higher than the shallow one covering the nave. These were lighted by a clerestory and preceded by a vaulted narthex with three entrances. But disaster intervened before the intriguing architectural experiment (which represented a step in the transition between the Hellenistic-style basilica and the Byzantine domed church) could be completed: the great dome above the sanctuary collapsed and the architects lost heart. The would-be great church remained unfinished and was never consecrated. The weakened west end also collapsed, and all that remained of this ambitious experiment, the narthex, was converted into a much smaller church by the addition of an apse.

The narthex arch, a perfect ellipse of brick, is flanked by piers composed of rectangular slabs of re-used ancient masonry. At the north-east end rises another pier with courses of carved decoration. On the east side stand two truncated columns of tessellated marble. The sculptured decoration is of the highest order and all the Early-Christian love of zoological and botanical detail inherited from Hellenistic Asia and pagan Rome, is exploited. Most beautiful of all are the two nave capitals and imposts which crown pieces of a pillar and a base. The acanthus leaves, which appear to grow organically from roots embedded in the impost, are so beautifully and so deeply carved that, with sunlight playing on them, they appear to be real.

Leaving the basilica through the narthex arch, one enters the pagan *palaestra*. Apart from a fine acanthus-leaf capital, the debris of this ancient exercise-ground for Macedonian and Roman youth conveys little to the unprofessional eye. To the south-west there is a remarkable, if unbeautiful, monument of Roman times: seven steps descend to a doorway with a well-preserved lintel, which leads into the rectangular sunken court of the public latrine. The marble seats are ranged in rows along the sides of three walls. I counted more than twenty in a tolerable state of preservation.

East of the ancient enceinte extend the foundations of the **Basilica 'Extra Muros'**, littered with slabs, which may have been a fourth-century edifice, subsequently restored and modified. Its main interest lies in the sixteen crypts below what was once the nave; according to epitaphs discovered *in situ*, these were the sepulchres of distinguished Philippian prelates. Fragments of floor mosaic are also preserved. The Museum, a little beyond Basilica A on the north side of the main road, seems to be in a perpetual state of reorganisation, so that its interesting collection cannot to be seen.

East of Kavalla the main road into Thrace crosses open country as far as the village of Paradissos, which overlooks the **Nestos** as it flows out of a narrow gorge. To the north, the labyrinthine intricacies of the Nestos Gorge are penetrated only by the nineteenth-century railway designed, by the Turkish rulers of Macedonia, to follow a course out of range of the guns of the Greek fleet. This railway, which takes an extraordinarily roundabout route from Xanthi to Drama - obviously conceived in purely military terms -

nevertheless gives the traveller the opportunity to see a part of Greece that is not covered in the normal itinerary by car. To the north of Paradissos the defile is, at first, sombre and constricted, with the river flowing swiftly between precipitous cliffs eroded into strange forms studded with evergreens; later the gorge opens out, the aspect becomes grander, the banks are lined with poplars and the upper slopes are covered with ilex, pines and Judas trees.

After Paradissos the road from Kavalla goes on to Xanthi, from where one can return to the west on another road which joins the line of the railway fifteen kilometres north of Paradissos and follows it as far as Drama which is also connected by a good direct road with Kavalla.

Drama, the ancient Drabeskos, where the Athenian colonizers of Amphipolis, venturing too far inland, were cut off from their base and slaughtered by Thracian tribesmen, lies at the foot of Mount Falakron. The town has little to offer to the tourist. Southward extends rich agricultural country, the so-called 'golden plain'.

The road from Drama to Serres runs at first below Mount Pangheon, buttressed by its subsidiary ranges. After Serres the road (one route to Bulgaria) turns sharply to the north, towards **Sidirokastro**, picturesquely situated at the foot of rocky hills, one of which is crowned, as the town's name implies, by a 'castle which is strong as iron'. To the north rise the gloomy ranges of Bulgaria, the Beles mountains, at the base of which the road joins the upper reaches of the Strymon where it emerges from the **Rupel Pass**: a strategic entry-point for every invader, commanding the wedge-shaped Strymonic basin, key to all Eastern Macedonia.

The Rupel Pass became famous in the First World War, when the country was split between two opposing factions: the pro-German Royalist Government of King Constantine I and the pro-Entente Liberal opposition headed by Eleftherios Venizelos. To demonstrate Greece's benevolent neutrality to the Central Powers, the Government surrendered Fort Rupel, which defends the pass, to the Bulgarians. So great was the outrage of the majority of Greek public opinion that the 'Rupel' incident proved the mainspring of a chain of events which culminated in the formation of the Provisional Government under Venizelos at Thessaloniki, the exile of King Constantine under the guns of British and French battleships and the entry of Greece into the war against the Central Powers.

Leaving the road to Bulgaria here and turning west, we come in due course to Lake Doirani, where scattered hamlets spread across the border of Greece and Yugoslavian Macedonia. The road then turns sharply to the south, fringing the eastern shore of the lake and, beyond Kilkis, a garrison town at the foot of the Kroussia mountains, descends along the banks of the Gallikos river towards Thessaloniki.

19

The Thracian Plains

TO THE EAST OF THE NESTOS extends the area known politically as Western Thrace which, like most of Northern Greece, remained under Turkish rule until 1913. Flat plains of corn, tobacco and cotton, relieved only by the occasional poplar or aspen, are enclosed between the sea and the Rodopi mountains. The area is largely inhabited by ethnic Turks who, though Greek subjects, speak their own tongue, attend their own schools and worship at their own mosques. One might also see groups of dark-skinned Sarakatsanis, members of nomadic communities occasionally found in Northern and Western Greece.

It can all be seen pleasantly in two days. For the traveller driving to or from Turkey (few come to this area for its own sake) Alexandroupolis is the obvious place to stop; it has the best hotels and an airport. This is a journey into an incongruously un-Greek world. The plains, traversed by muddy streams, and the shapeless mountain ranges shrouded in haze or cloud, have little in common with the shimmering plains of Greece encircled by grandiose mountains. The light, landscape, architecture, even the people, herald a new climate. It is in fact a prolonged frontier region, with the Turkish border as the goal.

Before reaching Xanthi, on the road from Drama, there is an undecorated Macedonian tomb three kilometres from Stavropolis, off the Komnina road, a pleasant spot for a picnic.

Coming from the west, **Xanthi** is the first stop in Thrace; whether you have come from Kavalla, or by the more attractive route from Drama, through part of the Nestos valley. Vasileios Konstandinou Square, with its little *hammam* and clock-tower is the town's hub. Even the kiosks have Turkish-style pointed roofs, once crowned with crescents. Pigeons murmur in acacia trees, and rivulets flow under miniature arched Turkish bridges. North of the square there is a fruit-market and, further up, a lot of old Xanthi survives, with some quite grand Turkish houses, one of which is to be restored as an orphanage. Cypresses surround a fine minaret against a background of steep, pine-clad hills, across the higher slopes of which spread the whitewashed buildings of a monastery. Another hill to the west is crowned by the ruins of a medieval castle, which once guarded the opening of the defile against Bulgar invasions.

From Xanthi it is easy to visit ancient Abdera. Take the Lagos-Komotini road and turn right at Vafeika, towards the sea. To the north extends the chain of the Rodopi mountains: stony, inhospitable, matt-grey in colour. The rocky coastline sweeps westward in a wide crescent, the southern end of which gives the impression of being joined to the island of Thassos. Some way after Avdira village, just before the road reaches the sea, is the site of **Abdera**. Founded, according to legend, by Herakles, in honour of his favourite, the youth Abderos, who was devoured by the man-eating mares of Diomedes, King of Thrace, this ancient city was famous throughout Greece for its beautiful coinage and also, incongruously, for the dullness of its inhabitants. Xerxes was entertained here with such pomp in the summer of 480 BC that the inhabitants were crippled financially. However on his less triumphal return journey, he remembered their hospitality and had the grace to present them with 'a tiara and scimitar of gold'.

Today the scattered ruins are not impressive. The main site is on the left, just after the road down to the houses of Ayios Pandeleimon. A large area of the inner city has been uncovered and further excavations each year reveal more: streets, Hellenistic and Roman houses, baths, walls, towers and gates of various periods, as well as many underlying remains of the Classical city. Noticeable are the foundations of a large Hellenistic edifice consisting of two courts and twenty-six chambers, often filled with slimy water. Frogs keep up an interminable croaking and mosquitoes whine overhead. To the right of the road, up in the pines above the sea, on the site of the ancient acropolis are substantial sections of walls and city gates as well as the remains of several churches.

About a kilometre up the road and along a track to the left is the theatre, of which little is visible. Nearby there are remains of the outer walls: the huge circuit reached the sea about two kilometres east of the main city.

After Abdera one can drive eastward beside the sea and then, going inland via Mandra, join the main Lagos road as it makes for the coast. As one approaches Lagos there are salt-pans on one side and, on the other, a huge muddy lagoon, famous for duck-shooting and bird-watching. The fishing port of **Lagos** is remarkable for the intricacy of the channels joining the lagoon with the sea and for its Church of *Ayios Nikolaos* squatting on an island in a shallow inlet. Waterfowl fly overhead and innumerable causeways cross the lagoon, giving one a strange feeling of disorientation. The road veers inland across cattle-grazing country to Komotini, the principal town of Thrace.

The shorter but less interesting route from Xanthi to Komotini passes near the ruins of the Byzantine fortress town of Anastassioupolis, hidden in a dense wood. The new Via Egnatia, sections of which incorporate existing roads, follows this route.

A market centre for tobacco and agricultural produce, **Komotini's** population is almost half racially Turkish. The tempo of life is slower than elsewhere but, if the atmosphere is somewhat Turkish, it possesses little oriental glamour. The Bulgarian frontier lies only twenty-two kilometres to the north, but the Bulgarian-speaking Pomak minority, swarthy, taciturn Moslems, makes little impact. The Mosque of *Yeni Djami* in Ifestou Street, its wide dome crowned by a gold crescent, stands among cypresses; while the less picturesque *Eski Djami* in Hrysanthos Square is box-shaped, with yellow walls pierced by white arched window frames. The minaret, which has two balconies carved with elaborate fretwork, is striking and beautiful, but for the traveller coming from Turkey, neither mosque is really worth bothering about. Of much more interest is the *Mitropolis* which is like no other church in Greece - it resembles a rich Turk's country house of long ago, with a spacious verandah on two sides and rows of windows above. The interior, however, is more conventional. Nearby are the remains of the Byzantine fortress.

The Archaeological Museum should not be missed: a new building in a pleasant garden, with a small, but very well-arranged, collection. There are reliefs of the Thracian Horseman, a fine painted Clazomene-type sarcophagus of about 500 BC from Abdera and the striking golden bust of Septimus Severus.

From the centre of Komotini a road goes south to the village of Maronia and the ancient site of the same name near the sea. It is as well to ask in the village for directions.

Though ancient **Maroneia** had a very long history, not much is known about it except that for a long time it was prosperous and very large - the circuit of the walls was over ten kilometres. The very scattered remains, on wooded slopes leading down to the sea, give one little idea of what the city may have been like. Well before reaching the sea a rough road to the left leads to the unenlightening remains of a sanctuary, and then to the theatre, of which a considerable amount remains. It is built over the bed of a winter torrent and, at the back, the stone channel for the rushing waters is still in place. Beyond the theatre is a section of the city walls.

Back on the tarmac road, and continuing down towards the sea, one comes to the Hellenistic Mosaic house; the fine floor mosaic is covered up in winter months. A little below are substantial remains of the later Byzantine walls. Among the scattered houses of the village of Ayios Haralambos various buildings have been excavated: on the left are houses, a shrine and a Byzantine church. Just to the right of the road are the remains of a monumental gateway. The harbour mole below contains sections of the ancient mole.

It is not necessary to return to Komotini: from Maronia village, via Palia Krovili, one can join the Alexandroupolis road.

If you have come directly to this point from Komotini without visiting Maroneia, you will have seen the Roman bridge crossing the Filouri stream at Arisvi and passed by the small Turkish-speaking town of **Sapes**. The Rodopi chain, among whose uninviting mountain fastnesses the Thracian Dionysos had a sanctuary, is now far to the north. After climbing scrub-covered hills, the road descends through olive groves - a rare sight in north-eastern Greece - to a flat, unbroken coastline.

After thirteen kilometres there is a turn-off to the right for the village of Dikella and, a little further on by the sea, another interesting, recently excavated archaeological site, **Mesembria**. The city was founded in the seventh century BC by colonists from the island of Samothrace, but was never a place of great importance. The ruins, on a gentle slope immediately above the sea, are substantial, interesting, compact and very easy and pleasant to visit. To the left the remains of the inner walls run above a gulley; houses (one has a small terracotta bath in place) and a sanctuary of Demeter occupy the area above small cliffs - unfortunately the sea below keeps eating away sections of the sea walls. To the right, a little up the slope, was the sanctuary and temple of Apollo, and further up a large area of houses. Dozens of storage jars are still embedded in earth, where they were placed to keep their contents fresh.

On the west side, towers and long sections of the walls, going up from the sea to the hilltop, survive, though not to any great height. The most interesting part is the south-west corner, where there is a tightly-packed little city with its own fortifications within the larger city. One of the houses has a clay oven or kiln which may have been used for smelting.

Shortly after returning to the main road one enters the town of **Alexandroupolis**, which has little to offer but some wide streets and a claustrophobic provincial air. It is, however, a useful base for travellers bound for the Evros valley and has a small port with a ferry service to Samothraki.

One continues along the course of the Via Egnatia. Fifteen kilometres east of Alexandroupolis a hill to the north, said to be an extinct volcano, marks the site of **Trajanopolis**, an important staging-post founded by the Emperor Trajan. The scattered masonry on the northern bank of the River Tsai is Roman, incorporated into later Byzantine defence works. All this country was once peppered with Roman forts at strategic points guarding the vital highway. There is a spa, Loutra Traianopolis, nearby.

Seven kilometres beyond Trajanopolis a signpost on the right points the way to **Doriskos** (the signpost to the left is for the modern village of the same name); there are no ruins, but this was where Xerxes built a fortress and stopped to count the troops of his mammoth army. The grand total, says Herodotos, doubtless exaggerating, 'turned out to be 1,700,000'. The counting, he continues,

> 'was done by first packing ten thousand men as close together as they could stand and drawing a circle round them on the ground; they were then dismissed and a fence was constructed round the circle; finally other troops were marched into the area thus enclosed and dismissed in their turn, until the whole army had been counted.'

Beyond the turn-off to Doriskos the road continues up the Evros basin, with the hills of Turkish Thrace rising to the east. In the Middle Byzantine period the country around here enjoyed considerable prosperity, with a corresponding increase in population, for the Komnenos emperors rightly considered it a vital area, guarding the approaches to Constantinople from the West. It is worth stopping at **Ferres**, a dusty town built round a hill on which stands the twelfth-century Byzantine **Church of the Panayia Kosmosotira** (All-Holy Mary, Saviour of the World), once part of a monastery. Its proportions are sturdy and harmonious, with five domes and a spacious three-apsed east end. Deeply recessed arches form the other three sides; the western arch is supported by pairs of columns with remarkable capitals. Traces of tile decoration, both in the apse and on the small south-east dome, as well as a plaque with an effigy of an heraldic eagle on the wall below the south-east dome, indicate that the church was no mere provincial house of worship, and the badly-damaged frescoes are obviously not the work of a provincial iconographer.

Driving north from Ferres you will see, on the right, a ruined nineteenth-century aqueduct. After the highway (which follows the Via Egnatia) has turned east to Istanbul, the road to Didymotiho passes through featureless country associated only with the march of countless conquerors ever since the Persian army, composed of small, dark-skinned men wearing soft felt caps, embroidered tunics and coats of mail, and armed with spears, cane arrows and wicker shields, tramped past in 480 BC.

Soon the wide streak of the Evros appears, winding between fields and orchards and marking the frontier with Turkey. The road passes through Soufli, centre of the silk trade, on a green hill overlooking mulberry groves, often flooded by the fast-flowing river. The banks are fringed with reeds which are cut into strips to make brooms. Gold was once found among its sandbanks, says Pliny, and nearly two thousand years later a French nineteenth-century traveller saw men searching the sands for the grains of gold washed down from the river's Bulgarian sources.

At last, out of the flat, watery expanse rises the circular hill of **Didymotiho**, crowned by the ruins of its medieval castle and surrounded on almost all sides by tributaries and branches of the Evros. This is the end - ultimate objective of the traveller in north-east Greece. Beyond lies Turkey, and this is, really, a mere frontier post. Houses climb steeply up the castle hill from the rather ordinary lower town. On Platia Dimarhiou there is a large and imposing block-like mosque with a tall minaret and a pyramidal roof and in Katsandonis Street a timber-framed house with a perfectly-preserved exterior - a fine example of Turkish domestic architecture. A little above the *platia* a more western-style mansion houses the Folk Museum.

On the way up towards the castle, village houses have been built into the fortifications. Higher up, great masses of ruined masonry, crumbling bastions covered with lichen, look down on the town and across to Turkey. There are well-preserved sections of Roman, Byzantine and Turkish defensive walls and the grassy summit is littered with fragments of unidentifiable masonry. The view embraces a patchwork of fields and fruit orchards - Greek and Turkish - with the streams of the Evros meandering in loops in all directions; there is a feeling of water everywhere. On a hill to the north-east, across one of the tributaries, khaki-clad figures can be seen bustling about parade grounds, barracks and other military installations.

On the south side of the hilltop is the cathedral of St Anastassios near some fine sections of ancient wall. Next to the cathedral is the curious ruin of a Byzantine building, possibly a hostel, which opens into caves cut in the rocky cliff. Here, it is believed, Charles XII of Sweden was imprisoned by the Sultan.

The road continues north of Didymotiho to Kastanea, the Turkish border and Edirne. But if one is not going that way, there is nothing left to do but turn one's back on the east.

20

The Approach to the Peloponnese: The Isthmus and Corinthia

THE JOURNEY FROM ATHENS TO CORINTH, including detours to Perahora and Isthmia, the site of Ancient Corinth itself with its Museum, and the ascent of Acrocorinth, could be done in one rather over-full day; but it would be better to allow two days and include the excursion to Sikyon, Stymfalia and Nemea.

From Elefsina the coastal highway continues in a westerly direction, with backward views of the landlocked Bay of Salamis, crowded with laid-up ships. The road then skirts **Megara**, an undistinguished modern town spreading across a small plain.

Every spring the Megarian Games were held here. A feature of the Games was the kissing contest between youths, at whose conclusion, says Theocritos, 'whoso sweetliest presses lip upon lip, returns laden with garlands to his mother'. Modern Megarian festivities are of a more conventional nature.

Beyond Megara the old road to Corinth is more interesting than the National Road because it keeps closer to the sea. This coast is haunted by the myths of Theseus and his journey from Troezen to Athens, in the course of which he rid the countryside of several disagreeable characters. The corniche, known as the *Kakia Skala* (The Evil Stairway), is hewn out of the side of the lofty **Scironian Cliffs** and overhangs coves of crystal-clear green water. Beyond the cliffs, pine trees – a particularly vivid shade of emerald green – fringe a long beach of white shingle called Kinetta, thick with villas and camping sites. The currents are strong in this part of the Gulf, which begins to contract as the opposite shore of the Peloponnese draws nearer, and even at the height of summer the sea is relatively cold. Past the village of Ayii Theodori (the ancient Krommyon, where Theseus slew Phaia, the Grey Sow who fed on human flesh), there is a terrible blot on the landscape: the huge sprawling installations of an oil refinery.

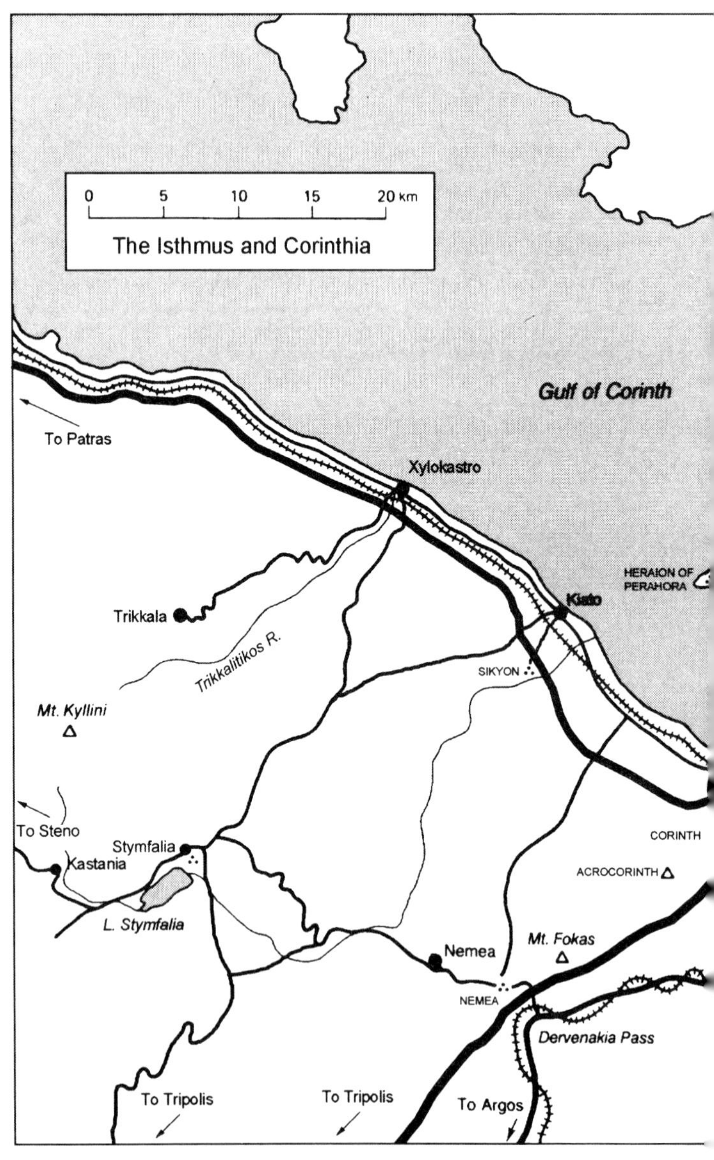
0
5
10
15
20 km
The Isthmus and Corinthia
Gulf of Corinth
To Patras
Xylokastro
HERAION OF
PERAHORA
Kiato
Trikkala
Trikkalitikos R.
SIKYON
Mt. Kyllini
To Steno
Stymfalia
Kastania
L. Stymfalia
CORINTH
ACROCORINTH
Mt. Fokas
Nemea
NEMEA
Dervenakia Pass
To Tripolis
To Tripolis
To Argos

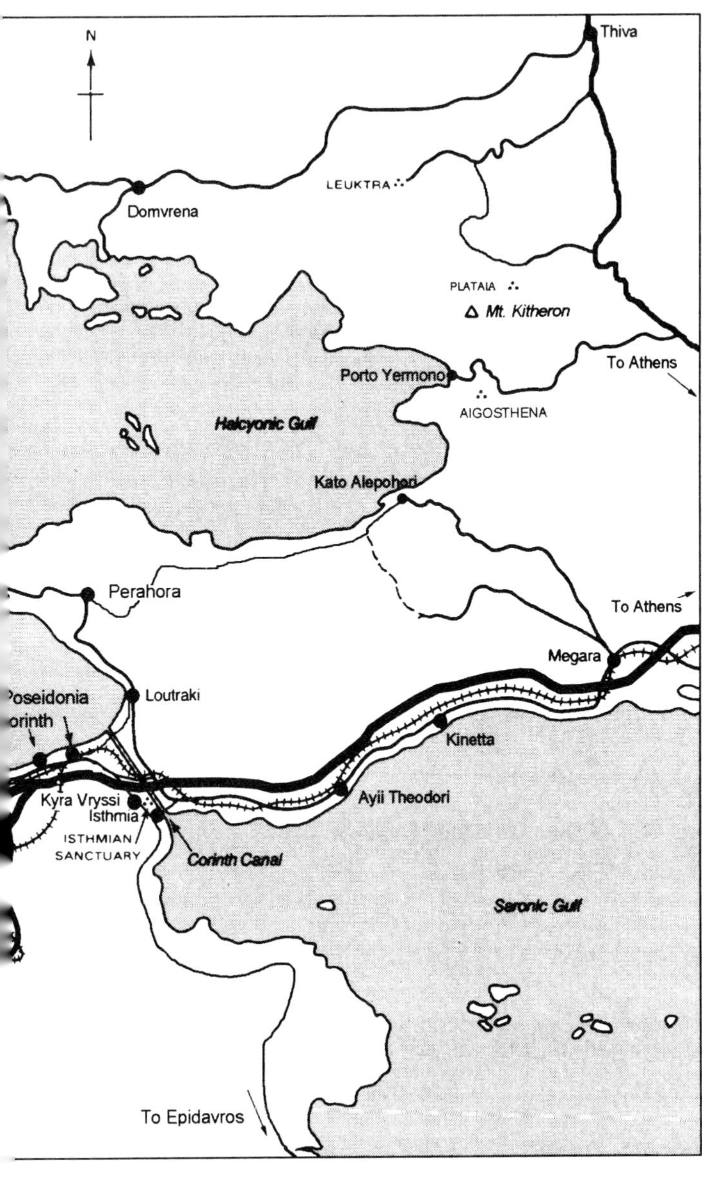
N
Thiva
LEUKTRA
Domvrena
PLATAIA
Mt. Kitheron
To Athens
Porto Yermono
AIGOSTHENA
Halcyonic Gulf
Kato Alepohori
Perahora
To Athens
Megara
Loutraki
Poseidonia
Corinth
Kinetta
Ayii Theodori
Kyra Vryssi
Isthmia
ISTHMIAN
SANCTUARY
Corinth Canal
Saronic Gulf
To Epidavros

The road crosses over the National Road and goes to the old bridge over the Canal, just before which a branch road leads northwards to Loutraki, a popular but horribly overbuilt resort and then, with fine coastal scenery, up to the big village of Perahora. To the west of the village a long promontory of bluish-grey limestone with a jagged ridge projects into the gulf. On the headland is the **Heraion of ancient Perahora**, a sanctuary of the goddess Hera, the earliest records of which date back to the Geometric period. The road down from modern Perahora passes through a huge area of burnt pine forest and by a large, tree-fringed lagoon, with many holiday houses and other buildings. After turning right there are traces of ancient masonry, often on private property, and shortly before the car-park there is, below the road to the left, an Archaic cistern with a subterranean stairway leading down to water level. Climbing down the south side of the headland from the car-park, one reaches the prominent small chapel of *Ayios Ioannis*, just above which to the left is another very large cistern, Hellenistic this time with rounded ends. Further up to the left is the substantial conduit bringing water down from the catchment area higher up, and then the foundations of the eighth-century BC **Sanctuary of Hera Limena**. Descending to the small bay you come immediately to a fifth-century BC *stoa*, then a classical altar with triglyphs, facing the confusing remains of three temples of different periods dedicated to Hera Akraia, one of them apsidal. Shortly beyond this, tucked in beneath the cliffs, are the remains of the *Agora*.

It is a remote place: a land's end with a lonely lighthouse, but now attracting many visitors, some of whom come only to bathe in the little bay, the **Sacred Harbour**, ideal for deep-water swimming. Behind are the steep brush-wood foothills of Yerania with the Halcyonic Gulf to the north. To the south, across the narrow waters of the Corinthian Gulf, the Peloponnesian mountain ranges rise above a fertile coastal belt. When the sea is calm, schools of dolphins follow in the wake of ships, bounding in and out of the wash; they are the friendliest of animals to men, always ready to carry gods and mortals on urgent errands across the ocean. (From modern Perahora there is a road over a spur of Yerania and down to the Halcyonic Gulf which, further along the coast, meets a direct road to Megara and thence back to Athens.)

The **Corinth Canal**, a dead straight ribbon of water between high banks of sand and rock, is five and a half kilometres long and little more than 30 metres wide. It was completed in the late nineteenth century by French and Greek engineers, the project having first been contemplated more than two and a half thousand years before: first by Periander, Tyrant of Corinth; later by the Roman Emperors. In 67 AD Nero went so far as to import thousands of Judaean prisoners to undertake the work, the Emperor himself hacking the first handful of earth with a golden axe. The project, however, was abandoned when he was summoned to Gaul to suppress the revolt of Julius Vindex. The canal shortens the journey from Piraeus to the Adriatic by nearly two hundred nautical miles.

From the old bridge you have a good view of the canal – from the new National Road bridge further east there is no view at all and no opportunity to stop. Shortly after the old bridge you can take the road to the left (from here you can join the National Road: west to Patras or the south-westerly branch to Tripoli) which crosses the earthquake-prone isthmus, descends through pine trees to Isthmia at the east end of the Canal, and goes on to Epidavros.

About a kilometre beyond all the tourist establishments another road to the left, also signposted for Epidavros, soon brings you into the village of Kyras Vryssi, at the end of which are the ruins of the **Isthmian Sanctuary** where the Isthmian Games were held every four years. It is a good idea to visit the **Museum** first, from which there is an excellent view over the site. Like many of the lesser museums, it contains little that is beautiful or of major importance, but much that is of great interest, particularly things connected with athletics. Other exhibits include a very attractive seventh-century BC basin supported by archaic figures, a charming small terracotta bath, with a seat, and a huge, imposing but headless Roman bust. Most important is the series of *Opus Sectile* panels – a form of mosaic done with large pieces of glazed ceramic or glass. These panels were never put in place – they were found at the nearby harbour, still packed, so they must have been imports. Some are fairly complete and easy to understand: flowers, birds and scenes of a harbour with temples.

The Games were dedicated to Poseidon, and within the enclosure, once lined with statues of famous athletes, are the prominent remains of the fifth-century BC *Temple of Poseidon*, built on rock. In the later *Stadium*, on the south side of the Sanctuary, across the road, is the starting line for races, with the starter's pit and sixteen shallow grooves for cords. These were kept in position by bronze staples and the starter, in his pit, could release the cords simultaneously to start the race with absolute fairness. There are remains of water conduits and basins and near the south-east corner of the Temple, part of the earlier Stadium has been identified. North-east of this was the Theatre, of which only the retaining wall and the foundations of the *proskenion* remain.

Isthmia had neither the religious significance of Delphi nor the panhellenic spirit of Olympia, but during the festival it was the scene of considerable animation, with touts, conjurors and fortune-tellers swarming around the stadium.

To the east and north of the Sanctuary are the remains of a fortress built by Justinian in the sixth century as an addition to the Isthmian Wall, itself built by the Spartans in 480 BC. The Wall crossed the isthmus and the Spartans would have mounted a last-ditch stand here against the Persians if the battle of Salamis had failed to turn the scales against the invaders. In some sections as many as nine courses of fifth-century BC masonry are visible. In the small valley north of the main ruins a large Roman bath establishment has been revealed and is undergoing extensive conservation. One chamber has a very fine floor mosaic of sea themes – Tritons, Nereids, dolphins – in excellent condition. The main site shelves down to a corner of the Saronic Gulf, where one can see tugs preparing to pilot ships through the canal. From Isthmia a good road with some wonderful scenery goes along the coast and eventually turns inland to Epidavros.

After the Kyras Vryssi turn-off, the road runs down into Corinth, with a road to the right leading to its port, Poseidonia. The port is at the western entrance to the Canal, where there are traces of the ancient Diolchos, the paved road across which boats were hauled from one sea to the other: a short cut used by Octavian during his pursuit of Antony and Cleopatra after the battle of Actium. Poseidonia is connected with Loutraki by a submersible bridge - there is one at each end of the canal.

Modern **Corinth** has only stood on its present site since 1858, after the destruction of Old Corinth by a devastating earthquake. Levelled by another earthquake in 1928, it is an undistinguished town. The complex topography - the isthmus, the two seas, the mainland and the miniature sub-continent of the Peloponnese - now comes into focus. Corinth is clearly the gateway to the Peloponnese; there is no other land approach. A few kilometres beyond it, the roads for Nafplion, Tripolis, Patras, Ancient Corinth and Acrocorinth, separate.

The inhabitants of Corinth tended to be mariners. They were the men who founded the colonies of Syracuse and Corcyra in the seventh century BC and who, according to Thucydides, built the first triremes. Their naval enterprise assured the city's commercial pre-eminence, its wealth being increased by the fertility of the coastal plain, which extends in a crescent-shaped sweep of vineyards, citrus orchards and olive groves from the base of the 550-metre-high citadel of Acrocorinth to the foothills of Sikyon. Wealth promoted hedonism, and the Corinthians acquired the reputation of being the most licentious people in Greece. With Aphrodite as patron goddess, the marketplace abounded with prostitutes, often women of refined accomplishments, dedicated to the art of venal love as to a religion, which in fact it was, for they were all priestesses in the temple of Aphrodite. Among the most renowned was Lais, whose bosom was so perfect that painters from all over Greece came to Corinth to reproduce its divine form. Prostitution in Corinth, like pederasty throughout Greece, was not considered a vice, but was an accepted way of life. To abjure either would, for a beautiful girl in Corinth or a handsome youth in any Greek city state, have argued considerable eccentricity.

It was under the vigorous Periander (625-585 BC) that Corinthian trade and navigation began to flourish. Government remained oligarchical, with the well-fed, pleasure-loving merchants showing little interest in the ideals of political democracy. The growth of the democratic Athenian empire aroused their jealousy and consequently Corinth associated herself with Sparta, emerging with considerable benefit from the Peloponnesian War. Eclipse came two and a half centuries later in 146 BC, when the Achaean League, of which Corinth was a member, was foolish enough to challenge the growing might of Rome; the Corinthians went so far as to pour excrement from their windows onto the heads of the Roman ambassadors. For this senseless affront they paid with massacre and the sack of their city by Mummius. Corinth literally ceased to exist. The paintings, for which the city had been famous, were carried off to Rome and it was not until 46 BC that Julius Caesar made amends by rebuilding the city. When St Paul visited it a century later it was a flourishing Roman colony; its key position at the crossroads of the Roman world had assured its rebirth. But the Corinthian sky, unlike that of other Greek city states, was never lit with the radiance that emanated from a creative, sophisticated intelligentsia; throughout history, Corinth remained in virtual intellectual obscurity.

The ruins of **Ancient Corinth**, one of the most celebrated cities of antiquity, are packed into a confined area at the foot of the massive rock of Acrocorinth and are superimposed with Roman structures. The shambles of the ancient *agora* is dominated by seven massive Doric columns of porous limestone crowned by flat capitals, which were once covered with stucco. The columns, still surviving from the golden age of Periander, formed part of the **Temple of Apollo**, one of the oldest in Greece. It was built on a raised platform and was originally enclosed within a rectangle of monolithic pillars. The southern end of the temple terrace was bordered by the north-west *stoa*, of which only the stylobate is preserved. In Greek times the *agora*, once bordered by shops and small temples, was paved with large pebbles which were replaced with marble slabs by the Romans. Across the central open space of the *agora* one can distinguish, in front of the fourth-century BC south *stoa*, the six stone courses of the large base of the **Bema**, or Roman Governor's tribune. The *stoa* itself, a once-magnificent two-storey building whose outer colonnade alone consisted of seventy-one columns (not one survives), would have been crowded with shops and tavernas, with merchants discussing market prices and local politics.

This was the scene of St Paul's arraignment by the Jewish community, who accused him, in the presence of the Roman governor, of corrupting their faith. At first few Corinthians, Greeks or Jews were impressed by the Apostle's preachings. He was a disturbing element and on one occasion his preaching in the synagogue provoked a riot, in the course of which he was beaten up by Greek hooligans. Nevertheless, he spent eighteen months here, plying his craft of tent-making and preaching the Gospel. He must have been an incongruous figure in this city of the most sophisticated carnal pleasures, picking his way among the affluent merchants and flamboyant prostitutes. In those times of political and spiritual upheaval, the pursuit of his missionary task was often put to the severest test. Yet his sojourn in Corinth was not in vain, for it inspired the two great *Letters* that proved to be among the most profoundly formative influences in the development of the Christian faith.

On the north side of the *agora* there is a ruined Roman gateway, the **Lechaion**, once surmounted by two gilded chariots in which Helios and Phaethon, the sun-god and his offspring, were to be seen riding across the heavens. The road, which connected Corinth with its western port, entered the city through this gateway. The outline

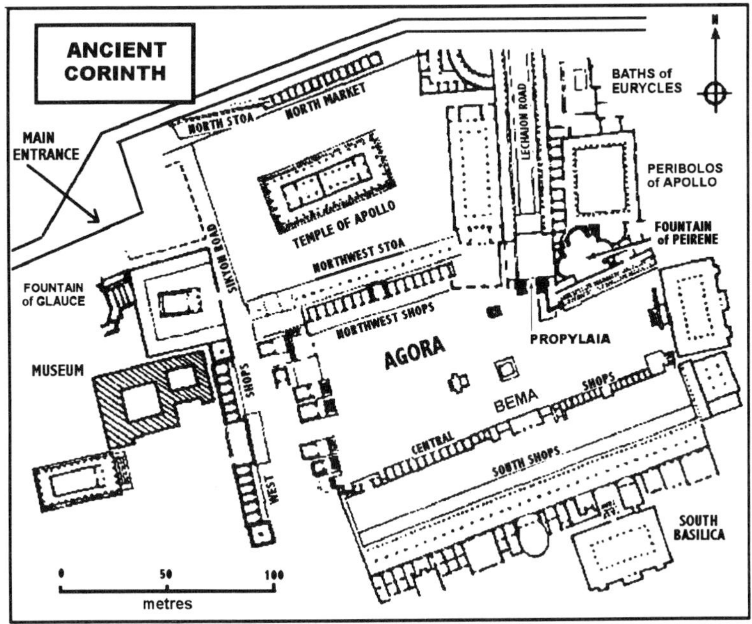

of the road, paved with limestone slabs in the first century AD, is plainly visible and the paving is well-preserved in parts. It follows an almost straight line, once flanked by shops behind colonnades (a few truncated columns survive), now cutting across fields of thistle and stubble.

To the east of the gateway lies the most attractive extant monument on the site: the **Fountain of Peirene**, a lady who was turned into a spring because of the unquenchable tears she shed for her son, accidentally killed by Artemis. Six rectangular chambers, each faced with an arch during the Roman period, contain basins connected with an underground reservoir fed by two different springs. Long before the Romans came, Pindar had admired the fountain and described Corinth as 'the city of Peirene'. Situated in the centre of the *agora*, the spring was surrounded with successive architectural adornments from the sixth century BC to Byzantine times. In the second century AD, Herodes Atticus had the entire front faced with marble. In front of the middle arch stand two columns, one crowned by a Corinthian capital. It is pleasant to sit in the shade of the arches and listen to the water trickling behind the dark chambers. Here the ancient *archons* of Corinth gathered on summer evenings to play draughts and dice. At a later period the gardens of the Turkish governor extended around the fountain.

The **Museum** is unfortunately fusty and old-fashioned, contrasting very unfavourably with some of the newer museums such as Nemea and Komotini. A few years ago it was broken into and a number of precious exhibits, a whole truckload in fact, was stolen. In October 1999, almost all the loot was found, stored together in Miami. When it returns to Corinth there is bound to be a wholesale rearrangement of the Museum. The remarks that follow refer to the arrangement in early 2000.

Of the famous Corinthian paintings, only the lively bird and animal designs on the vases remain to remind us that Corinth, despite its lack of intellectual pretensions, was a centre of painters and craftsmen. Up to the sixth century BC large quantities of ceramics were exported to Italy; Corinthian potters, unlike those of Attica, were chiefly interested in the export trade. In spite of mass-production, the quality of their products remained high until the middle of the sixth century when the Athenians captured the principal markets. The designs then became larger and coarser; there was more lavish use of reddish-purple paint, and rosettes and other floral motifs were employed to fill in an already crowded background.

The room to your right displays, along its left wall, ceramics more or less in chronological order: Prehistoric, Mycenaean, Geometric (including a very fine pitcher elaborately decorated in red and with its own three broad legs, eighth century BC), and the various stages of Corinthian pottery. The most effective are Early Corinthian, 625-600 BC, such as the jug or aryballos with warriors – though some of the pots of the next period, Middle Corinthian, are certainly very decorative, with their flowers and rosettes, animals and birds, sometimes a little too crowded. An exception is a fine two-handled pitcher with a very elegant horse.

In the same room is an incomplete painted terracotta sphinx, and a complete stone sphinx with a lovely archaic smile, both of about 550 BC. One showcase contains votive offerings to Asclepios, god of healing, representing the afflicted parts, breasts, genitals – even a hand with a cancerous growth – successfully treated by the god. Nearby is a very fine bronze mirror cover in relief, and two lovely and highly sophisticated but incomplete terracotta figures.

One of the earliest Greek pebble mosaics, c.400 BC, of griffons mauling a horse, is in the entrance hall. The long gallery to the left contains a large amount of not very distinguished sculpture, mostly Roman. Among the finer items are a very good head of Nero, a Roman copy of the head of Doryphoros by Polykleitos, a head of Dionysos with a mass of hair painted red, a beautiful grave stele of a hunter and his dog, and part of a Roman sarcophagus with 'The Seven against Thebes' in relief: really exceptional work of the second century AD. The far end of the gallery is dominated by the two huge Phrygian prisoners from 'The Captives Façade'.

In the left cloister of the courtyard are displayed reliefs from the Roman Theatre of the Battle of the Amazons, and the Labours of Herakles, fragmentary but impressive.

The Asclepeion Room can be visited on request.

The road goes up to the gateway of **Acrocorinth**, from which one climbs the great rock, dominant and aggressive but fitting harmoniously into the complex configuration of land and sea. The view from the top is tremendous. In the immediate foreground the fertile strip extends to the wooded hills of Kyllini which rise to barren, metallic-coloured peaks. The strangely-eroded mountains of the Argolid roll southwards; to east and west lie the two seas, separated by the isthmus; to the north, behind the tapering headland of Perahora, extends the placid expanse of the Halcyonic Gulf bounded by Mount Elikon and to the north-west, the hazy massif of Parnassos exercises its eternal fascination.

Although there are remains of Byzantine, Frankish and Turkish fortifications, it is the skill of the Venetian military architects that is most striking: in the watch-towers, the crenellated ramparts and the three imposing gateways connected by ramps. The route followed from the entrance is very steep. You first cross the shallow moat, once spanned by a drawbridge, and pass through the outer gate to the second line of defence. The successive levels of formidable masonry, which seem to grow organically out of the increasingly precipitous incline, permitted the defenders to annihilate all assailants with devastating fire from above. After passing through another gate, which is square outside with an arched passage within, paths lead to the two peaks. The steep path to the right leads to the lower, west peak and the ruins of a Frankish dungeon. Following the main path one first passes the shell of a ruined mosque, behind which is a postern (scattered all round here are vestiges of former chapels, minarets and barrack-rooms). Climbing up along a trough of ground overgrown with spiky shrubs and long grass, the path winds up to the east peak, once crowned by a temple of Aphrodite, where the goddess of love was worshipped in the most sumptuous manner. Within the ring of fortifications there is not a single habitation, not a single living creature, except the odd sightseer, ants, bees and lizards.

The National Road from Corinth to Patras runs a short distance in from the coast: it is faster but less interesting than the old road, which runs through flowery villages among orchards, vineyards and, unfortunately, a lot of shoddy urban development. As the season advances, pale blue hydrangeas and climbing roses are succeeded by the scarlet of hibiscus, the confetti-pink of oleander, and the striking reds of massed bougainvillea. From Kiato two roads climb into the hills: the first goes up to and through the village of Vassiliko to the Museum and the ruins of Hellenistic **Sikyon**, a beautiful minor site but rather neglected and overgrown.

The Museum (unfortunately usually closed), built into the partially reconstructed Roman baths, contains Corinthian pottery, figurines and Roman mosaics.

The ancient city, of which little is to be seen, was down below the Museum to the north, extending over the small plain which descends to the sea. It was in the seventh century BC that this salubrious little town, open to all the breezes of the Corinthian Gulf, began to acquire political prominence under the rule of Orthogoras, who founded a Sikyonian dynasty which lasted over a hundred years and whose government was praised by Aristotle for its tolerance. In 293 BC Demetrios Polyorketes, during his attempt to wrest most of Greece from the rival aspirants to the throne of Alexander the Great, built a new city on the table-land above. Defended on both sides by shallow precipices the city was concentrated around its citadel. In his usual extrovert way, he gave it the name of Demetrias; in the Greek mind, however, it always remained Sikyon - 'the town of cucumbers'. The Acropolis of the new city was still further up, on a small, higher plateau.

Sikyon's real national hero did not emerge until later in the third century BC, when the city was governed by a usurper-tyrant. Aratos, the exiled heir to the throne, stole up on a moonless night with a handful of patriots and, despite the alarm sounded by a pack of howling dogs, scaled the walls. The coup came off and it became Aratos' life-work to strengthen the Achaean League and break the stranglehold of the warring heirs of Alexander. He was buried at

Sikyon with great pomp after being poisoned by Philip V, the able, if contemptible, Macedonian king. In the first century AD the city was destroyed by a terrible earthquake, and when Wheler visited the site in the seventeenth century he found it inhabited by only 'three families of Turks and about as many Christians'.

From the coast green fields, olive groves and orchards slope up to the base of the large triangular shelf of Sikyon. Across the Gulf, Parnassos and Elikon provide a dramatic backcloth, with the hump of Acrocorinth in the east. The main archaeological site is opposite the Museum: the base of a temple can be made out, and the outline of the large Bouleuterion. A little further up you reach the **gymnasium** on a cool, windy site. It was built on two levels surrounded by colonnades: the lower, Ionic; the upper, Doric. Unfortunately only one column remains, but the fine stone fountain built into the dividing wall has been partly restored.

It is a pity that there is not a single statue left to recall the fact that Sikyon was once an important artistic centre: the site of one of the earliest schools of statuary and painting in Greece. Lysippos was born here, and Apelles - most celebrated of Greek painters - came here to acquire a final polish to his style. Pliny says that drawing in outline was invented by a native of Sikyon, which he calls 'the home of painting'. The city was also a centre of fashion, famous for the taste and skill shown by the weavers and cutters of the flowing garments worn by its inhabitants.

The road continues from the Museum to the **Theatre**, dug into the natural slope, and rather better conserved than the rest of the site, though the upper tiers remain buried, beneath a little forest of pines. The tiers were intersected by sixteen stairways – an unusually large number in relation to the width of the auditorium. Apart from its position and its solitude, there is the novelty of approaching the *cavea* through one of two once-vaulted passages. The cavity in the *proskenion* was intended for the appearance of figures from the Underworld. A rough road goes on further up the hill to the outline of the **Stadium**, in a natural elongated valley, overgrown with corn. All over the hillside, broken slabs of limestone are concealed among thistles, mullein and pungently-scented shrubs. The asphalt road continues up from the Theatre to the upper plateau and the Acropolis, of which little has been found.

The other road from Kiato also leads southward, but climbs much higher, winding through clefts and gulleys filled with thickets of cypresses, towards the windy plateau around the base of Mount Kyllini. By the time the coast is out of sight, a boundary has been crossed. We are no longer in Corinthia, but on the northern fringe of Arcadia. The narrow upland valleys converge on a ten-kilometre-long plain. Savage mountains crowd in on all sides: to the north rises the formidable mass of Kyllini, slate-grey, breathtaking in its cruel desolation; a projecting spur, Mount Stymfalos, rises sheer from the plain and at the southern end, below Mount Oliyirtos, the waters of **Lake Stymfalia** flow into a subterranean channel. The shallow lake, which shrinks considerably in summer, is full of weeds and patches of waterlilies; bordered with reeds, maize fields and a few poplar trees, its waters, fed by mountain streams, are ice-cold, even at the height of summer. Nothing could be less 'Arcadian' than this forbidding place.

The road runs along the western side of the lake passing, on the left, the shell of a Gothic church, a Crusader foundation, with three naves and windows with pointed arches. A little further on, also to the left, are the negligible remains of an ancient acropolis on a little rocky promontory jutting out into the marsh. There are vestiges of a temple of Athena Polias and, to the south-west, traces of foundations of public buildings, often submerged when the water level of the lake rises. Past the lake the road rises into the pine forest and goes through Kastania, where there is a pleasant hotel, and Steno before rejoining the Patras road.

Shortly before Stymfalia a road to the east rises to cross the saddle of a jagged mountain and, after descending into hilly vine country with streams and poplars, reaches Nemea with a direct link to the National Road to Tripolis. A lesser road, going more or less eastwards, crosses another hill and enters a narrow, vine-clad valley five kilometres long and little more than a kilometre wide, where the village of Iraklion marks the site of ancient Nemea.

Never a township, **Nemea** was a Sanctuary of Zeus where one of the four great panhellenic athletic festivals was held. The grove of cypresses that surrounded the sanctuary has disappeared, but dwarf cypresses grow in profusion on the neighbouring hills. To the north-east, flat-topped Mount Fokas looks as though its summit has been sliced off by a gigantic axe.

Ancient Greek athletics, like the games organized by Achilles round the funeral pyre of Patroklos, were often associated with ceremonies intended to speed the passage of souls to Elysium. The origin of the Nemean Games lies in a melancholy event: one day Opheltes, the child of a priest of Zeus, was laid by his mother upon a bed of wild celery in a meadow at Nemea, while she fetched water from the spring for the seven Argive leaders bound for the siege of Thebes. On her return she found the child poisoned by a snake-bite. The Seven then founded the Games to commemorate the child's death. Thereafter judges at the Nemean festival wore black in mourning for Opheltes; the victor's crown was of wild celery.

The Games, held every second year, consisted of running in armour, discus-throwing, chariot-racing, throwing the javelin, shooting with the bow, boxing and wrestling. By the sixth century BC the festival had acquired the status of a panhellenic assembly and to win the crown of wild celery was the aim of every Greek athlete.

The grove in which the Games were held was crowded with public buildings, many of which have been revealed in recent excavations and made easily accessible through a garden with lawns and rose bushes. Most prominent is the fourth-century BC Temple of Zeus, which marks the transitional period between Classical and Hellenistic Doric; the influence of Skopas, who designed the temple at Tegea, is evident. It had twelve limestone columns at the sides and six at either end. Three, of which two support a fragment of architrave, still rise from the stylobate - the columns are unusually slender and their height is thereby apparently increased. Nearby lie the drums of many other columns, some of which are being re-erected.

Across the centre of the precinct there was a series of irregular chambers, some very large, thought to have been Treasuries. Parallel and further south, are the substantial remains of the *Xenona*, or hostel, which are rather confused by what is left of the Christian church built over them – the Baptistery is easily identifiable. The very big roof just beyond shelters the fourth-century BC Bath House, with much of its installation in place – well-presented and quite fascinating.

On the other side of what is left of the river, the Heroön has been identified, but cannot be visited. The **Stadium**, the centre of all the activities, is actually a little distance away, to the south-east – various parts of it have survived, including the starting-line.

The excellent small **Museum** includes very informative plans, models and photographs, as well as the usual interesting archaeological miscellany.

Five kilometres beyond the Sanctuary the road, after passing over the National Road to Tripolis, joins the main road from Corinth to Argos at the Pass of Dervenakia. In the undulating plain to the east of the pass, surrounded by deeply eroded foothills, one of the decisive battles of the War of Independence was fought, when the northbound army of Dramali Pasha was ambushed by the Greeks. The church of *Ayios Sotiras*, visible from the road and surrounded by cypresses on the side of a steep hill, commemorates the victory. A large Turkish army was wiped out by 2000 Greek insurgents, aided by contingents of armed peasants from neighbouring villages. The Greeks captured an immense quantity of booty and horses' skeletons littered the highway for years. After the pass the road follows down the course of a dried-up torrent whose stony banks are bordered with oleanders and emerges into the Plain of Argos.

21

The Argolid: The Plain

THE ARGIVE PLAIN, roughly triangular in shape, opens out to the south after one has come through the Pass of Dervenakia between the twin summits of Mount Tretos. Taking the mountain as the northern apex, the triangle stretches down to the east, towards the citadel of Nafplion squatting above its pellucid bay and, in the west, to the fortified conical crag of the Larissa which dominates the town of Argos. Fringed by the Gulf of Argolis, the plain has a warmth and a radiance that herald a new climate. Today, flocks of sheep have replaced the mares of Diomedes which, according to Homer, were once pastured here. Fruit and vegetables grow in abundance and each evening convoys of trucks roll northward with produce for the Athenian markets.

A well-marked turning to the left (east) leads from Fihti through the modern village of Mykines, up some low hills and between banks of luxuriant oleanders, towards the ancient site of Mycenae, which overlooks the shimmering plain. There is no shade, but breezes sometimes blow across the two peaks above the citadel and there is a pungent smell of herbs. As the valley begins to narrow, large slabs of Cyclopean masonry can be seen on the slopes. With one's back to the plain, the scene acquires a rugged, denuded aspect. The citadel of **Mycenae**, once a stronghold of immense strategic importance girdled by formidable walls, crowns a rocky eminence above the confluence of two boulder-strewn ravines and commands the upper part of the Argive plain. In antiquity all the roads from the Gulf of Corinth united here and passed under the great natural bastion.

That Mycenae was influenced by the Minoan civilization has become clear since Heinrich Schliemann, the indigo merchant-turned-archaeologist, excavated the cities of Mycenae and Troy, and Sir Arthur Evans, brought up in an environment of more conventional scholarship, revealed the sophisticated splendours of the Palace of Minos. In the later stages of the Minoan civilisation the use of

Mycenaean Greek, as shown by Linear B tablets, reveals that Knossos had come under Mycenaean control. After the destruction of Knossos and the eclipse of Minoan supremacy, leadership of the whole Aegean basin passed into the hands of the Mycenaeans (c. 1400 BC). As sailors and colonists they surpassed the Minoans, whose trade they absorbed and developed, introducing their civilization into islands as far away as Cyprus. At this time a period of great architectural, even artistic, activity seems to have set in: grim, barbaric edifices of sun-dried bricks were raised on bases of clay-set rubble; lime plaster, sometimes decorated with frescoed designs or descriptive scenes, covered the floors and walls; the doors were wooden, the windows small, the roofs flat; baths consisted of pottery tubs. The poorer classes dwelt in huts with floors of beaten earth, but it is no exaggeration to say that Mycenaean palaces, and some of the *tholos* tombs of their kings, are the only buildings in Europe before the Hellenic period in which artistic as well as functional ends were aimed at by the architects.

The view of the citadel is magnificently forbidding: a heap of prehistoric masonry that ascends abruptly out of the gorge, surrounded by huge polygonal walls consisting of limestone slabs skilfully fitted together and of an average weight of six tons. The wall reflects the fierce sunlight beating down on the scorched, treeless terrain. This was once the nerve-centre of a maritime empire that dominated the Aegean - other fortified cities were scattered about the Argive Plain, as well as elsewhere further north, but they all had a common culture centred on Mycenae. Precious objects of the minor arts were produced here that have still to be surpassed for excellence of workmanship and elegance of design; no prehistoric tombs have yielded such varied and sumptuous treasure as those of Mycenae.

Under Agamemnon the Mycenaean kingdom, which included Corinth and Sikyon, led the grand alliance of Greek states in the successful war against its commercial rival, Troy. In the late twelfth century BC the infiltration of Dorians from what is now Northern Greece and a combination of natural and other causes destroyed the kingdom and the great palaces of Mycenae, Argos, Tiryns and Pylos went up in flames. After that the Dark Ages descended on Greece; Mycenae did revive for a short period in Hellenistic times, but not as a great power.

The road ends at a large car-park from where there is a short walk up to the **Lion Gate**, which is surmounted by the earliest piece

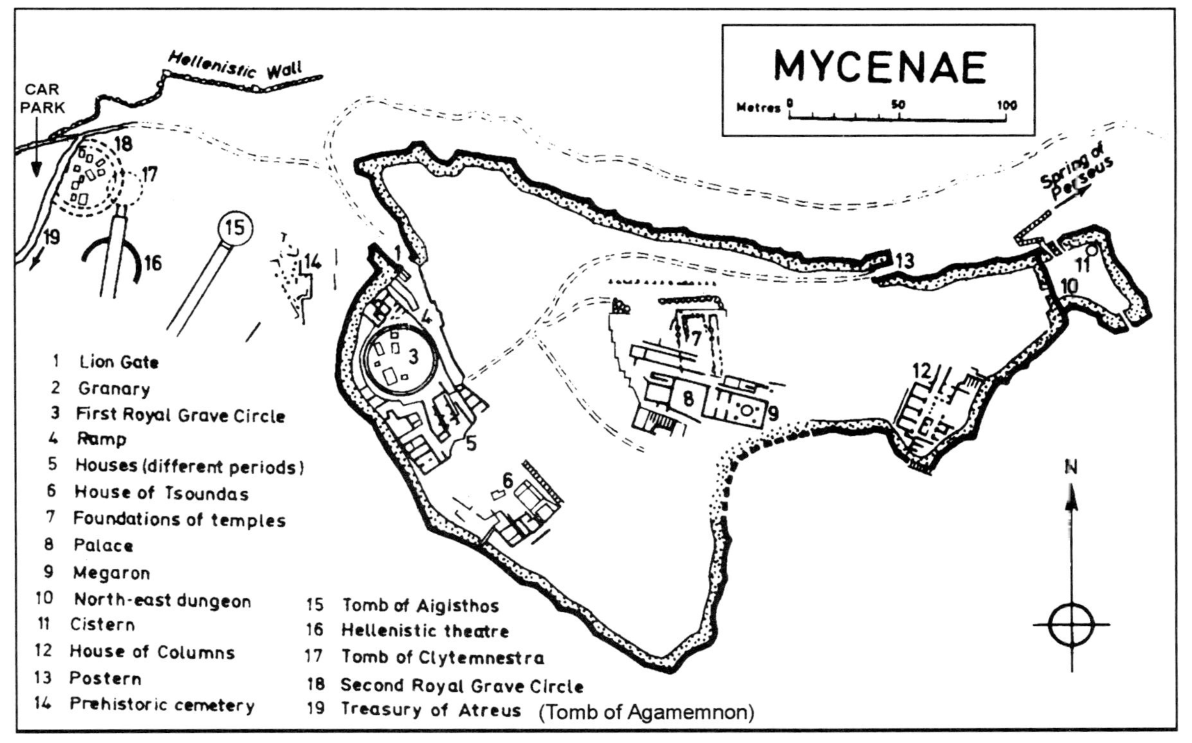

MYCENAE
Metres 0 50 100
Hellenistic Wall
CAR PARK
Spring of Perseus
N
1 Lion Gate
2 Granary
3 First Royal Grave Circle
4 Ramp
5 Houses (different periods)
6 House of Tsoundas
7 Foundations of temples
8 Palace
9 Megaron
10 North-east dungeon
11 Cistern
12 House of Columns
13 Postern
14 Prehistoric cemetery
15 Tomb of Aigisthos
16 Hellenistic theatre
17 Tomb of Clytemnestra
18 Second Royal Grave Circle
19 Treasury of Atreus (Tomb of Agamemnon)

of monumental statuary in Europe: two lionesses sculpted in relief in the triangle above the monolithic lintel. The two heraldic beasts (whose heads are missing) are clumsily modelled, their hind legs more like those of an elephant; the detail too is primitive, but there is a grandeur, even a dawning elegance, in the angles of their bodies and shoulders, designed to enable the lions' features to face those approaching the gate. References in the *Agamemnon* of Aeschylus and the *Electra* of Sophocles suggest that the scenes of both tragedies were set in the vicinity of the Lion Gate.

Within the Lion Gate, through which men, horses and chariots passed, there was a sentry box - the narrow niche, on the left as one enters, is still visible. Passing through the gate, to the right the **Royal Grave Circle** is marked by a double row of erect stone slabs. The chief interest of this circular graveyard (twenty-six metres in diameter) lies not only in its age (c.1600-1500 BC) but in the treasure of gold and precious objects that Schliemann discovered here in the summer of 1876 and which is now housed in the National Archaeological Museum in Athens. Schliemann found six tombs containing sixteen skeletons, judged to be royal personages because of the richness of the treasure interred with them. Gold masks, like the so-called 'Agamemnon death-mask' covered the faces of the men; gold fillets decorated those of the women. Tombstones, some carved, others plain (two of the latter are *in situ*), marked the graves. When the great citadel wall was built, the Cyclopean blocks were made to curve round the bulge created by the grave circle so as to include it within the royal perimeter. The vast hoard of gold lay under the soil of the hillside for three thousand years, unsuspected by passing brigands, plunderers and conquerors.

South-east of the grave circle, huddled together against the polygonal wall, are the foundations of small houses, believed to have been inhabited by middle-class Mycenaeans: the House of the Ramp, the House of the Warrior Vase, the South House; also a minor palace, the House of Tsoundas (named after the archaeologist who discovered it), in the north-east corner of which there was a small court, with a flight of thirteen steps leading down to a corridor and what are presumed to have been storerooms. All that is known of the furnishings of these houses - as, indeed, of all Mycenaean houses - is that lamps and charcoal braziers stood in the main hall, in the centre of which there was a hearth and that low benches were arranged along the walls of the porches.

Returning to the Lion Gate, one follows the course of the

original zigzag ramp, up which the chariots climbed to the western extremity of the hill crowned by the Palace buildings. It is rough-going, steep and shadeless, the rocky ground overgrown with prickly shrubs. The ramp is narrow and can never have been very imposing. In spite of the gigantic slabs of masonry employed by prehistoric architects, Mycenaean houses and streets were very constricted, with none of the spaciousness associated with Hellenic buildings.

Though the foundations of the **Palace** indicate a complex of rather poky chambers, the royal terrace commands a dizzy view of the ravine and the lovely patchwork plain below, at the end of which lies the fortified Larissa of Argos, a 300-metre-high cone of rock rising sheer out of the plain. The mountains of Arcadia - grim, slashed with tremendous precipices - form a seemingly impenetrable barrier in the west. There is an airy splendour about this impregnable position.

One turns first into the Great Court, which had a cemented floor with painted squares and a dado in the form of a split-rosette frieze running along the base of painted walls. It was approached from the south by a flight of steps, of which one remains. The marks of burning on the floor are presumed to be traces of the great fire that destroyed Mycenae around 1100 BC. West of the court is a small throne room, the throne probably having been placed in a sunken part of the floor against the north wall. East of the court one passes through a porch and vestibule into the *megaron*, the largest chamber in the palace, part of which has now fallen into the ravine. Painted designs of circles and other geometric patterns created a blaze of colour on the floor; the walls, judging from fragments in the National Museum, were covered with frescoes depicting warriors, horses and chariots.

The *megaron* was where the court assembled; the barbaric monarch surrounded by his olive-skinned attendants armed with axes and Homer's 'lovely' Argive women in their 'long robes'. Three of the four column-bases surrounding the hearth, which was in the shape of a shallow circular trough, are preserved, as are many door-sills in the chambers.

It is difficult, if not impossible, to identify the maze of small rooms north of the *megaron*. One is believed to have been a bathroom, because its sunken floor reveals signs of red plaster within a raised surround. Some guides like to say it is the bath in which Agamemnon was hacked to pieces.

East of the wind-swept summit one dips down to the so-called 'House of the Columns', near a watchtower overhanging the desolate ravine. There are two interesting points about the foundations of this house: first, the design corresponds with Homeric descriptions of the palace of Odysseus in Ithaca, and second, it possessed a court surrounded by a colonnade aligned with the *megaron* walls - a feature that foreshadowed the houses and *prostyle* temples of the Classical period, with columns at each corner, forward of the side walls.

Following the line of walls, one reaches the **Secret Cistern**, an underground chamber dated to the thirteenth century BC, with a corbelled roof in the form of an inverted V. An initial flight of sixteen steps is followed by a sharp turn and a claustrophobic descent of a further eighty-three steps into the limestone bowels of the citadel. At the bottom, where there is a square stone shaft brimming with water, a feeling of constriction grips the throat. Death is omnipresent at Mycenae; in this fetid chamber it makes an almost palpable impact. The Spring of Perseus, which lay outside the perimeter of the citadel, was connected by terracotta conduits with this cistern; the water supply of the fortress was thus assured in times of siege. Back in the open, where nothing seems to disturb the solitude of the bleak slopes of Mount Zara and the surrounding scrub-covered hills, one welcomes the thyme-scented air and the chirping of cicadas.

A westerly course completes the circuit of the citadel after passing the Postern Gate, a small but formidable gateway with an enormous lintel, through the double doors of which Orestes fled after the murder of Clytemnestra. The area between the Postern and the Lion Gate is littered with debris from the short-lived Hellenistic township.

The descent from the Lion Gate to the lower town is honeycombed with foundations of prehistoric dwellings and *tholos* tombs. Across the road from the ticket office lies the **Second Royal Grave Circle**, first excavated in 1952, and believed to be considerably older (c.2000-1600 BC) than the one discovered by Schliemann - in other words about half a millennium before the polygonal wall was built round the citadel. The epithet 'royal' is again inspired by the quantity of precious objects discovered in the graves (jewellery, vases, swords and a lovely rock-crystal bowl in the shape of a duck, all now in the National Museum). In one grave, the skeleton of a young woman, a 'Mycenaean princess', was found richly bedecked with gold and silver clasps and necklaces; crystal-headed bronze pins on her shoulders were obviously intended to hold up a garment, the fabric of which had perished. In another grave two male skeletons were buried with their weapons: a lance, a knife and an ivory-pommelled sword, all of bronze. In yet another, a little girl of about ten was adorned with miniature ornaments. Beside the little skeleton lay a baby's rattle of gold.

The large modern building beyond and below the entrance is to be a Museum of Archaeology. Down the road, beyond the Second Grave Circle, are the remains of houses, including the foundations of the House of the Oil Merchant, once a large building containing a store-room with oil-jars ranged in a row against the wall and clay tablets inscribed with Linear B script; daggers, shields and bronze implements were also excavated. We thus have visual evidence of the weapons used by Homer's heroes, of the ornaments worn by their women and of the layout of the houses in which they dwelt. The archaeologists might be said, therefore, to have performed a notable service to literature, by raising Homer above the level of a mere mythographer with an incomparable talent for story-telling; after visiting Mycenae one returns to the *Iliad* and the *Odyssey* with a sense of increased intimacy.

The **tholos tombs** come next. They are unquestionably the most astonishing monuments of the prehistoric age in Greece. Believed to be an entirely Mycenaean concept, they combined various characteristics of prehistoric Aegean architecture into symbolic representations of man's eternal awe of death. The circular chambers were subterranean, preceded by a *dromos*, or paved way, cut out of the rock. Earth covered the apex of the conical chamber, thus creating the effect of a tumulus. The most impressive is the so-called **Tomb of Agamemnon** or **Treasury of Atreus** (to the right of the descending road), a huge sepulchre dated, by means of pottery fragments, to the fourteenth century BC. The *dromos* is walled with square-cut blocks of dark grey rock set in regular courses. At the end of this thirty-six-metre passage stands the doorway, its sides slanting inwards as they rise, flanked by column bases and covered by triangular stonework which probably contained a sculptured block similar to the one above the Lion Gate. The door-sill of reddish rock is perfectly preserved. Passing under the massive, six-metre-wide lintel, one enters the dark, empty, beehive-shaped tomb, the diameter of which is nearly fifteen metres and the height only slightly less. A few bronze nails in the uppermost of the thirty-three courses of stonework indicate the original existence of some form of decoration, probably metal rosettes. To the right is a small rock-hewn chamber, where lay the corpse of the royal personage, encased in gold leaf. It cannot have been that of Agamemnon however, since the building precedes the Trojan Wars by over a century.

Some visitors tend to poke their noses in, sniff the dank air, think it all looks rather gloomy and return to the *dromos* with a sigh of relief. But it is wise to stay a little longer, to get used to the dark and to run your eye slowly up, course after contracting course, to the towering cone. It is not difficult then to comprehend that this primitive monument must have been designed by an architect who not only knew how to deal with the technicalities of thrusts and stresses, but who was also inspired by creative imagination.

There are eight more tholos tombs, far less well-preserved, scattered about the surrounding countryside. One, the so-called **Tomb of Clytemnestra**, just below the citadel, next to the Second Royal Grave Circle, is interesting insofar as the beehive chamber is taller and slightly narrower, with the upper courses ascending more sharply; the design gains thereby in refinement. Beside it is the Tomb of Aigisthos. All these names are, of course, designed purely for classification; they possess no historical significance.

Mycenae is a haunted place, peopled by figures inflated by legend and literature into creatures of demonic stature, as sinister as the natural boulders and slabs of Cyclopean masonry raised to protect them, in death, from the hatreds engendered by their own tragic actions. But the treasure of gold, silver, ivory and alabaster, wrought by the Mycenaeans with such unerring skill and taste, remains a priceless testimony to the degree of civilization achieved by an otherwise cruel and barbaric people.

From the village of Mykines a road skirts the base of Mount Evvia to the **Heraion of Argos**. (One can also approach it from Argos itself, passing through Honika, where there is a restored twelfth-century Church of the *Koimesis*.) The Heraion is situated on a ledge overlooking the plain, to the west of which the wall of Arcadian mountains is gashed by a broad, winding gorge that penetrates into the heart of the massif. The worship of Hera, the national deity of the Argives, was centred here. Throughout the area known as the Argolid all myths are dominated by the Queen of the Heavens, twin sister of Zeus, who was courted by her brother in the form of a cuckoo. They spent their wedding night at Samos and it lasted three hundred years. After this prolonged ecstasy, Zeus, surfeited with his sister's charms, began to look elsewhere for amorous distraction; his infidelities drove Hera insane with jealousy.

The ruins of the Heraion are not very impressive, but the prospect is spacious, and the utter loneliness of the site unique in the populous plain. It was, for all its religious significance, a small sanctuary, but nevertheless one to which pilgrims flocked along dusty paths, on foot and in chariots, from the various citadels in the plain. A stepped wall leads to the remains of the mid-fifth century BC south *stoa*, with its interior colonnade. From this level, a monumental stairway climbs to a higher terrace, across which spreads the stylobate of the Doric temple of Hera, also fifth-century. Although built of limestone, the temple had marble decoration and within the *cella* stood the great gold and ivory statue of the goddess by Polykleitos. Hera was depicted in the full panoply of her rank, a pomegranate in one hand and her royal sceptre in the other.

One then climbs to the third terrace, to look at the scanty vestiges of the stylobate of the old seventh-century BC temple and to stand on the deserted ledge where the Achaean leaders swore allegiance to Agamemnon before embarking for Troy. South-west of the terrace are the remains of Roman baths, with mosaic-floored rooms under which there were hollow spaces heated by a furnace. To the south of the baths is the very ruined L-shaped *stoa* of an ancient gymnasium.

The road from Mykines goes on through dense orange groves to Honika, from where one can turn right to Argos or take a road to Tiryns and Nafplion via Merbaka (Ayia Triada) with its twelfth-century church of the Panayia. Cross-in-square with a single dome, its combination of brickwork and faience decoration on the exterior walls creates a charming effect.

Argos itself is a busy market town devoid of distinction, sprawling beneath its picturesque acropolis. However, few Greek towns have such a rich legendary and historical past. Danaos, father of fifty daughters, took refuge here after quarrelling with his brother, Aigyptos, father of fifty lusty sons, who pursued their uncle from Egypt in order to marry their cousins and fulfil an obligation incumbent on all bachelors with unmarried female relations. Girls in ancient Greece were considered a liability, having to be married off to their closest relations if other suitors were not forthcoming. Danaos, who had a vindictive nature, seized the opportunity presented by the family loyalty shown by his nephews to revenge himself against his brother and the latter's progeny. He consented to the multiple marriage, but secretly instructed his daughters to kill their husbands on the wedding night by stabbing them in the heart with long pins. The girls dutifully obeyed and, as a punishment for their crime, were condemned to pour water eternally into a bottomless well.

At the time of the Trojan Wars, Argos was governed by Diomedes, the famous horse-tamer, with Hera, worshipped as the goddess of fecundity and symbolized as a cow, being revered above all other deities. In the seventh century BC the city reached the height of its power under King Pheidon, who defeated the Spartans, and who introduced coinage and a new scale of weights and measures. Though the Argive ascendency in the Peloponnese was later eclipsed by the rise of Corinth and Sparta, in classical times Argos remained a commercial and artistic centre, situated at an important junction of roads, five kilometres from the sea.

The modern town spreads across the ancient site, dominated by the **Larissa**: gaunt, beige and cone-shaped, rising out of the surrounding fields and orchards. It takes just under an hour to climb to the castle on the summit, its double circuit of medieval ramparts studded with ruined towers. It was built by the Byzantines and Franks, with Turkish additions, and proved a more enduring piece of masonry than the Temple of Zeus which once stood above the town. From the castle, or even from the whitewashed chapel in a cypress grove less than halfway up, one can view the plain from a new angle. Cornfields and orchards spread northward beyond the gravelly, oleander-bordered bed of the Xerias - the ancient Charadros - which flows (when there is any water) into the Inahos. To the east, citrus groves fringe the coastal strip as far as Nafplion. The lower hill to the east is the *Aspis*, so-called because its shape resembles that of a shield. There are some Bronze Age remains and shaft tombs, and a rectangular terrace on the south-west slope is believed to be the Sanctuary of *Athena Oxyderkes* (The Sharp-Sighted).

South of the centre of the town and to the left of the road to Tripolis are some fragmentary remains of the *agora*. A great school of sculpture flourished here in the fifth century BC under Agelados, and ancient writers repeatedly refer to the quantity of statues that embellished the city. It was also a musical centre and Herodotos calls the Argives the best musicians in Greece.

Opposite the *agora* are more important ruins: first the red-brick shell of part of the Roman baths; then the crypt of an apsidal hall containing three sarcophagi, fragments of mosaic floors and marble paving stones. Behind the hall rise the tiers of the theatre, more unusual for its size and its unusually steep *cavea* than its state of preservation. Dated to the late fourth century BC, it had eighty-one tiers and could seat twenty thousand spectators. Between the theatre and the baths, an aqueduct leads to a first century AD Roman *odeion* - a small concert hall - of whose *cavea* fourteen tiers survive.

The museum in Vasilissis Sofias Street possesses Proto-Geometric and Geometric vases and Neolithic finds from neighbouring Lerna which include a gruesome female terracotta statuette with sharply pointed breasts, stunted, childish arms and a mouth in the shape of a beak. From these primitive objects one turns to the sumptuous elegance of the large fifth century AD mosaic floors depicting hunting scenes, with startlingly life-like portraits, removed from the Roman baths. There is also a head, allegedly of Sophocles, fished out of a nearby stream. Fifth century BC writers describe the dramatist as one of the most handsome young men of his generation. The head in the Argos museum does little to indicate that he retained his looks in maturity.

Between Argos and Nafplion the low, oblong hump of 'wall-girt' **Tiryns** rises above the alluvial plain, beside the trimly-kept garden of a local prison. At first sight unimpressive, it soon makes an impact; for the entire circumference is made up of massive walls, six to seven metres thick, the oldest dating from the fourteenth century BC, and composed of huge limestone blocks, grey or reddish in colour, two and a half metres long and a metre wide. Strabo says the walls were built by the Cyclops, who came from Lycia and were called 'bellyhands' because they were paid in food for their manual labour. Here dwelt Herakles, generally represented in mythology as amiable and chivalrous, though somewhat prone to excesses of lechery and gluttony and occasional bouts of violence.

To view this pile of monstrous stones strung out on three levels it is best to take the path from the ticket office up to the ramp leading to the main east gate. At the ramp turn in through the outer walls to the upper terrace, where the palace was encircled by an inner rampart, until another gate is reached. Judging from its dimensions, it may have resembled the Lion Gate at Mycenae. Cuttings for pivots and jambs, where an enormous bar was drawn back into the wall, are still identifiable. Beyond the gate is a **stone gallery** (thirteenth century BC) in a remarkable state of preservation and of a singular vaulted construction, with doorways overlooking the orange groves. The endless rubbing of sheep against the walls -

for centuries the gallery was a sheep-pen - has given the huge stones an extraordinarily smooth, shining patina.

One then turns right to enter the larger of two *propylaia*, the formal entrance to the palace, whose interior was built of sun-dried bricks. Only the foundations of the palace exist; below them, fragmentary remains of a circular building (c. 2000 BC) have been excavated. The *propylaia* led into the great court, at whose southern end there is another covered stone gallery with five doorways. To visit a confusing labyrinth of foundations of small chambers one turns right from the large court, passes through a smaller *propylaia* and enters the *megaron*, preceded by a porch and vestibule. In the centre there was a hearth, surrounded by four wooden columns with stone bases which supported the roof. The floors were stuccoed and painted with designs of sea monsters. Adjoining the *megaron* were the private royal apartments. To the west of the palace a secret passage, with a well-preserved flight of steps, tunnels through the western rampart to a postern, whence one descends towards the main road.

Tiryns has little to offer in the way of architectural refinements - nothing but the sheer bulk of its masonry. The size of the stones, hewn by men of whom we know next to nothing, haunts the imagination. The architecture was purely military in concept, execution and function. Tiryns was inhabited in the third millennium BC - a thousand years before these stupendous walls were raised. Unlike Mycenae, to which it was probably subject, it had no Homer, Sophocles or Euripides to recount the bloody deeds of its ruling house. No royal tombs have revealed the treasure that astounded the eyes of Schliemann at Mycenae although, like Mycenae, it suffered a violent end and the palace was gutted by fire long before the classical era. Today the suburbs and factories of Nafplion encroach on the barbaric site.

Illustrations: *Sithonia peninsula; Halkidiki*
Karyes; Mount Athos
Corinth Canal
Nafplion
Turkish Bridge; Arta
Mount Tomaros and the ancient Theatre; Dodona
Grigoriou Monastery; Mount Athos

22

The Argolid: The Periphery

AFTER THE PREHISTORIC NIGHTMARE of Tiryns it is a relief to enter **Nafplion**, a charming little port sheltering below a fortified rocky headland. It has plenty of hotels and is an obvious centre from which to visit all the sites in this part of the Peloponnese, but it tends to be overcrowded in summer. There is a hint of Italian architectural distinction in the town and, though it would be a mistake to expect palazzi, Renaissance order or Baroque extravagance, there are tall, colour-washed houses with corbelled balconies and walled gardens filled with hibiscus and Bougainvillea, mandarin and rubber trees.

In itself, Nafplion has no ancient history to speak of. The days of affluence and of heroic sieges belong to the Venetian era. It first emerged from obscurity in the thirteenth century as the domain of Leon Sgouros, a venal, violent and blood-thirsty tyrant who went so far as to murder a page for breaking a glass in his presence. On another occasion he invited the Bishop of Corinth, with whom he was on bad terms, to dinner; after feasting the prelate, Sgouros gouged out his eyes and cast his body over the cliff.

The French Crusaders made Nafplion the capital of a duchy. Later they sold it to Venice and the whole area of the kingdom of the House of Atreus came under Venetian rule. In the prolonged struggle between Venice and Turkey for possession of the maritime stations of the Peloponnese, Nafplion underwent some great sieges and its inhabitants suffered terrible privations; the peasants too, in the surrounding countryside, were almost exterminated and had to be replaced by Albanian settlers.

The town was finally captured by the Turks in 1715. A bold attack by the Janissaries secured for the besiegers a foothold on the covered way leading to the summit of the rock. The next day the Ottoman fleet opened a devastating bombardment and the Venetians were routed. There were 25,000 casualties and, to the accompaniment of wailing fifes and beating drums, another 1000 Italian soldiers were beheaded outside the Grand Vizier's tent, which

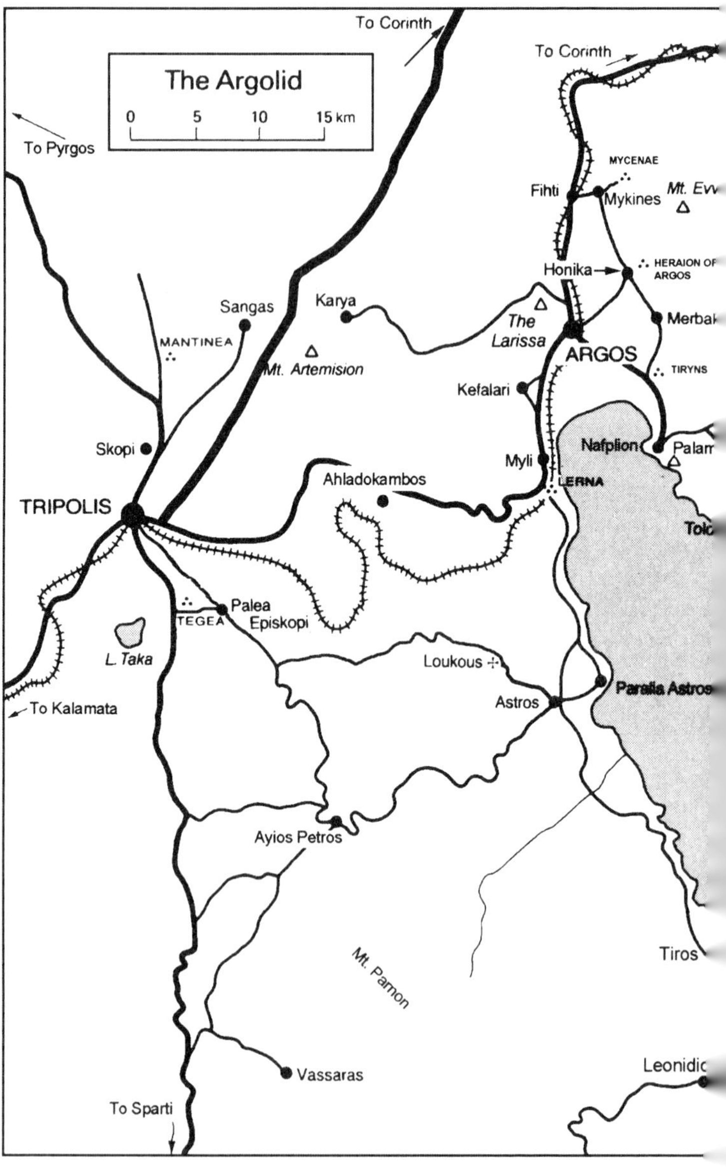
The Argolid
0 5 10 15 km
To Corinth
To Corinth
To Pyrgos
MYCENAE
Fihti
Mykines
Honika
HERAION OF ARGOS
Sangas
Karya
MANTINEA
Mt. Artemision
The Larissa
ARGOS
TIRYNS
Kefalari
Skopi
Nafplion
Myli
LERNA
Ahladokambos
TRIPOLIS
Palea Episkopi
TEGEA
L. Taka
Loukous
Astros
Paralia Astros
To Kalamata
Ayios Petros
Mt. Pamon
Tiros
Vassaras
To Sparti

To Corinth
N
Agnoundos
Nea Epidavros
Palea Epidavros
Ligourio
EPIDAUROS
Ano Fanari
Anghistri
Eyina
Methana Pen.
Poros
TROEZEN
Galatas
Didyma
Ermioni
Kranidion
Portoheli
Kosta
Gulf of Argolis
Hydra
Spetses

was bedecked with Damascus silks and Bokhara rugs and surrounded by fluttering pennons. For the next hundred years the Crescent flew unchallenged on the highest battery of the fortress.

Nafplion was wrested from the Turks early in the War of Independence and from 1829 to 1834 was the official capital of the country which, at that time, only included the Peloponnese and the mainland as far north as Arta in the west and Volos in the east. But political machinations and personal rivalries sabotaged all attempts at a proper administration of the liberated areas. Ten years of bitter campaigns against the Turks brought out most of the qualities and the shortcomings of the Greek character: the stubborn bravery and the unquenchable patriotism; the passion for political intrigue; the incurable envy of the man at the top. Administrative anarchy and exaggerated reports of burning villages and civilian massacres by self-styled patriots heightened the tension in the overcrowded little capital and culminated in the assassination of Count Capodistria, who had been elected President of Greece by the National Assembly in 1827. In 1832 Greece was declared an independent kingdom and Prince Otto of Bavaria was elected King. In the following year he arrived as King Othon at Nafplion, the first capital of his tiny, turbulent kingdom. The nineteen-year-old Bavarian boy landed from an English frigate, escorted into the Gulf of Argos by the fleets of the three Protecting Powers; he rode between ranks of English, French and Russian sailors, followed by a train of Bavarian officers in plumed hats and brightly-coloured uniforms. Massed bands played martial tunes; they must have rung strangely in the ears of Greek peasants accustomed to '*kleftic*' ballads.

The notable buildings include the seventeenth-century Venetian upper fortress of Palamidi, the lower fortress surmounting the headland of Acronafplion and the Cathedral, which was originally Roman Catholic. There is a small beach which can be reached along a path, starting at the West Mole, which rounds the rocky promontory below Acronafplion. 500 metres offshore is Bourdzi, a miniature Chateau d'If, which was built by the Venetians; crenellations and a pretty octagonal tower were added by the Turks and, more recently, it has been used as an hotel. There is a typically Greek provincial public garden - wispy, with an equestrian statue of the ubiquitous Kolokotronis, a large main square, an old upper town with winding stairways and alleys and a waterfront looking out across the pellucid water of the bay towards the Arcadian mountains. The situation is perhaps unrivalled - even in the Peloponnese.

Travellers should not miss the **Museum**, housed in a handsome eighteenth-century Venetian building (formerly an arsenal) in Syndagma Square. Here are displayed prehistoric pottery, Mycenaean *stelae* and, more important, an almost complete and indeed unique suit of Mycenaean armour, as well as the only inscription and some fragments of frescoes from Tiryns, a mould for gold jewellery found at Mycenae, seventh-century BC votive discs, figurines and *amphorae*. Also of considerable interest is the collection of Folk Art at the Peloponnese Folklore Foundation in a fine old house in Alexandrou Street.

Acronafplion, the lower of the two fortresses, is reached through an arched gateway surmounted by a Venetian lion: a welcome reminder of the advantages enjoyed by maritime Greece under the colonial administration of the Serene Republic, at a time when the rest of the country was being reduced to desolation by corrupt and rapacious pashas. The fortress walls now enclose the only luxury hotel in the Peloponnese.

The much higher **Palamidi**, a gleaming pile of rock towering above the town, is one of the finest fortresses in the Morea, the name often used for the Peloponnese when speaking of the medieval and later periods. To reach the summit by car one follows 25 Martiou Avenue in an easterly direction passing, on the way, the Church of the *Evanghelistria*, surrounded by cypresses, which crowns a rock in the suburb of Pronia. This is where the National Assembly met in 1832 and ratified the election of Prince Otto as King of Greece. The citadel of Palamidi is entered through a gateway consisting of a five-sided fort. Within the enclosure, which is on an incline, five distinct forts are discernible (there were seven originally), all built by the Venetians at the beginning of the eighteenth century. Each fort had its own cistern, thus enabling the garrison to withstand long sieges, and the highest battery, dominating the entire defence system, was furnished with shell-proof shelters. From the southern side of the summit there is a sheer drop of over 200 metres to the base of the cliffs, which run eastward in an unbroken line. Westward, across the crescent-shaped bay fringed with mud-flats, the mass of Mount Artemision rises above the Lernean Marsh.

From the north-western end of the fortress a stairway of 857 steps zigzags down the perpendicular face of the cliff, passing under four arched gateways. It was down this dizzy flight of hairpin bends that the Janissaries poured into the town in pursuit of the routed

Venetians in 1715. The stairway leads into the path which winds round the great cliff to the harbour.

Just outside the old town, the road to Epidauros forks to the right off the Argos road. After little more than a kilometre a turning to the right leads to a pretty twelfth century convent church, that of *Zoodohos Piyi* (The Source of Life), situated near a spring commonly identified as the Kanathos, in which Hera bathed once a year in order to renew her virginity. Remains of an ancient wall and aqueduct add charm to the rustic setting.

After the next village, another turning to the right leads to **Tolon**, a busy holiday resort with many small and medium-sized hotels strung out along a strip of sandy beach often packed with holidaymakers from Northern Europe. Tolon is still a fishing village and occasionally a caique chugs in and netfuls of slithering silver-grey *marides* (the nearest Greek equivalent to whitebait) are unloaded. There are several open-air tavernas, where the freshly-caught fish is apt to be expensive. At weekends the village is crowded with Argives anxious to escape the oppressive heat of the plain. At the eastern end of the bay, a little promontory crowned by a prehistoric acropolis has been identified as Asine, mentioned by Homer in the Iliad. East of Asine there is a long stretch of sandy beach; inland the country is flat and featureless.

The road to **Epidauros** then leaves the plain and continues through citrus groves and farmland, which contrasts with the scrub-covered, rocky hills on either side. After passing through the village of Ligourio a turning to the left leads to the **Sanctuary of Asclepios**, which spreads across a gentle slope studded with pine trees. It is surrounded by barren grey mountains, the highest of which, Mount Titthion, dominates the scene and has a forbidding aspect.

Asclepios, child of Apollo and Koronis, his semi-divine nature proclaimed by the lightning flashing from his head, was, in infancy, suckled by a goat on the slopes of the mountain. Asclepios studied medicine under Cheiron and then travelled about Greece, healing the sick, devising new remedies and even raising the dead. Zeus was so angry with Asclepios for restoring Hippolytos to life and thus reversing the laws of nature (with which he alone had the right to tamper), that he cast a thunderbolt at him and sent him to dwell in the Underworld. Despite this, the cult of the god of healing flourished and had its centre at Epidauros, which became famous for the growth of plants with medicinal properties.

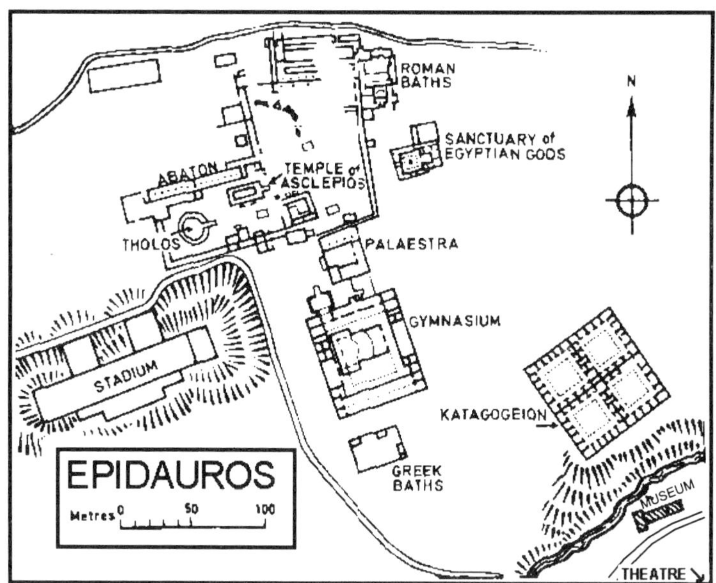

The sacred enclosure was called the **Alsos**, which means grove, and must have been thickly wooded with tall pine trees. A few pines still cast their shade over the foundations of temples, ancient hostels and dormitories, for Epidauros was equipped with all the amenities of a spa and invalids flocked to it from the furthest corners of the Hellenic world. The place swarmed with persons afflicted with paralytic, dropsical and renal ailments. Miraculous cures were worked by the ministrations of tame yellow serpents - peculiar to Epidauros and symbolic of the act of renewal (because they slough off their old skin every year) - which licked the patients in their sleep until recovery was complete. The curative rites were a closely-guarded secret, to which only priests had access: the restoration of life was apparently effected by the administration of Medusa's blood stored in a holy phial. However, the miraculous cures did not preclude the application of conventional remedies, such as baths, poultices and therapeutic unguents. In some cases the god recommended exercise and a strict diet.

Convalescents were able to applaud the most popular athletes of the day on the track or find distraction at the theatre. The whole place was fragrant with resinous pine and surrounded by shrub-covered hills, from whose slopes the breeze still carries the scent of thyme and sage. It is nice to know that nobody has ever died here, for no deaths were allowed to occur in the sacred enclosure.

The ruins, apart from the astonishing theatre, which is the greatest single classical ruin in Greece outside Athens, are little more than foundations. However, it is pleasant to wander under the trees, among the marble slabs and limestone bases, to breathe the pure air and yield to the serenity of the place.

The outline of the stadium is among trees just north of the large car park. Unlike the course at Delphi, perched on a high ledge, this stadium is hollowed out of a depression, so that one climbs down, not up, to it. On the grassy south embankment there are a few well-preserved tiers, which must once have accommodated querulous patients, exchanging news about their latest symptoms whilst burly wrestlers and swift-footed runners performed spectacular feats on the track. Broken pillars beside the starting point at the eastern end probably formed part of a formal gateway, although the athletes entered the stadium through the passage between the tiers on the north embankment.

At this end of the main site there are the remains of temples, baths, *stoas* and fountains. First come the circular foundations of the **Tholos,** designed in the mid-fourth century by Polykleitos the Younger: an unimpressive ruin, but once a very holy building and the show-piece of the sanctuary. The exterior colonnade of twenty-six Doric columns screened the *cella*, which was paved with a chequer-board of coloured marbles and surrounded by fourteen Corinthian columns. The roof was conical, the stuccoed walls painted with frescoes; the marble gutter was lavishly carved with acanthus-leaf designs and the frieze decorated with large rosettes in the centre of the *metopes*. An idea of the opulent decoration is obtained from the sculpted fragments in the museum. Originally there were six concentric inner walls and the architectural design was so labyrinthine that in order to approach the centre of the building one had to proceed in serpentine windings round each of the six rings. At the centre was the altar, where sacrifices and offerings were made to Asclepios' yellow snakes, which dwelt in a subterranean pit. The curiously sinuous approach was deliberately devised as a symbolic allusion to the movements of the sacred reptiles.

North of the *tholos* are vestiges of a *stoa*, known as the *abaton*, where the supplicants slept and were visited in dreams by the god, who diagnosed their ailments and prescribed a treatment. At the east end of the *abaton* was the Temple of Asclepios, the foundations of which are clearly outlined. Built in the second half of the fourth century BC of Corinthian tufa, it was of the Doric order, though somewhat foreshortened, having the usual six columns at either end but only eleven instead of twelve side columns. This was the centre of the worship of Asclepios and his effigy in gold and ivory towered above a pit into which the supplicants descended with offerings. The god was depicted enthroned, touching the head of a snake with one hand, holding a staff in the other. Strabo describes the temple as crowded with the sick and full of votive gifts, on which the names of grateful supplicants and a full description of their treatment, were recorded. A forest of votive monuments surrounded the temple.

South-east of the temple lies the site of the *palaestra* (a court surrounded by chambers), followed by what may have been the gymnasium, with ruins of Roman buildings within it. East of the gymnasium is the outline of a large square structure, the *katagogeion*, which served as a hostel for visitors. It was built of mud bricks on a stone foundation and consisted of four equal parts, each with a central court, separated from the adjoining rooms by Doric colonnades. In spite of its size, the *katagogeion* cannot have accommodated all the patients who crowded the sanctuary. More modest hostels were probably scattered about the periphery.

Next comes the **museum**. First, there are the inscriptions from the Temple of Asclepios, recording recoveries from diseases ranging from tapeworm to sterility; then statues (some are casts) of Asclepios and Hygeia, goddess of health. These are followed by sculptural pieces from the temple and reconstructions of sections of it, as well as a fragment of the *tholos* pavement. Next to this is the elaborate Corinthian capital, also from the *tholos*, said to have been carved by Polykleitos the Younger. Finally, there are some lovely architectural fragments from the *tholos*, including part of the circular wall and its deeply coffered ceiling.

Near the museum there is a tourist pavilion and a small motel (temporarily closed) where, in summer, it is enchanting to dine under the great pines, the silence of the deserted place broken only by the chirping of a few indefatigable cicadas. From here one climbs a pine-clad slope to the **theatre**. One can see it from a distance as one approaches the sanctuary, its grey stone tiers, framed by dark green shrubs, on a slope of Mount Kynortion. At close quarters its completeness and the beauty of its proportions are impressive. It was built by Polykleitos the Younger about the middle of the fourth century BC in the hollow of the hillside. The forty-one semi-circular tiers of stone, accommodating up to fourteen thousand spectators, are separated by eleven stairways below and by twenty-one above the wide *diazôma*. They are in an admirable state of preservation. The seats in the first two rows and those immediately above and below the *diazôma* have carved backs and were reserved for officials; the remainder are plain. The tiers above the *diazôma* rise more steeply and are completely symmetrical. The acoustics are so perfect that a whisper uttered in the centre of the orchestra, a large circle of white stone, can be heard from the highest tier.

Of the *proskenion* and *skene* only the foundations exist, upon which a stage is constructed and scenery erected for present-day performances. The *skene* consisted of two stories crowned by battlements, adorned with columns and divided by a balcony called a *pluteion*, along which the *theologeion* - a platform surrounded by painted clouds, intended for the appearance of the gods - would be moved backwards and forwards. From this Olympian perch, divine personages conversed with mortals on the stage or with the chorus in the orchestra. The cast was thus ranged on three levels: gods, protagonists and chorus. Sometimes mortals would be snatched up from the stage by a crane-like contrivance called the *yeranos* and raised to the godly level. From behind the *skene*, movable chambers were rolled out on wheels to indicate a change of scene. Then there were devices such as bladders filled with pebbles which were rolled on copper sheets to simulate thunder and a triangular prism of mirrors to represent lightning. Scenery consisted of painted canvases on wooden frames, placed in front of the *skene*. Tragic actors wore thick-soled leather boots to increase their stature; their heads were covered by large masks with wide-open mouths. Comedians, on the other hand, were shod in light-soled buskins and slaves were played by actors wearing masks with deformed mouths. All the actors were well paid by the State, underwent rigorous training and maintained a strict diet. On the stage their movements were confined by the narrow space and gestures were probably abrupt and angular. Their lines, it is believed, were delivered in a sing-song stentorian chant which penetrated every cranny of the immense theatre.

On either side of the stage were the *paradoi*, through which the chorus entered the orchestra, whereas the actors passed through five doors onto the stage. The *paradoi* at Epidauros have been restored, the more complete one is an elegant Hellenistic structure consisting of a double gateway between pilasters supporting a decorated cornice.

A festival of ancient drama is held in the theatre every summer.

The plays are performed in modern Greek except for occasional productions by distinguished visiting companies. Buses for the performance leave from Athens and take the coast road down from Corinth, but it is worth enquiring whether a ship has been laid on (there is no scheduled service) as the trip by sea is delightful. If possible one arrives with an hour or two to spare, to wander among the ruins under the great pines, with the crowds from Athens and neighbouring towns and villages.

At the play, if you choose a seat on one of the highest tiers, you can lean back against the sun-warmed stone without being jabbed in the back by the feet of some restless neighbour. When the sun sets a brief twilight hangs over the valley, and Mount Titthion assumes a less forbidding aspect. Down below in the orchestra the chorus weave stylized, choreographic designs as they invoke the gods and lament the hero's tragic fate. A few cicadas drone on, but never loud enough to prevent a single word uttered on the stage, almost sixty metres below, from being heard.

The coastal road from Corinth to Epidavros turns off shortly after the Canal. It runs along the shore of the Saronic Gulf through pine woods, past an untidy resort and vineyards and orange groves, then climbs amid glorious scenery. Shortly after the turn-off to the right for the village of Sofikon is the small, post-Byzantine Church of the *Odiyitria* (The Virgin Indicator of the Way) with an octagonal drum. After the church, the descent towards the coast again affords glimpses of scrub-covered cliffs rising sheer from deep-water inlets. To the east, Eyina and the islet of Anghistri emerge from the sea-haze.

The road swerves inland again and soon after, on the left, stands the **Monastery of Agnoundos**, surrounded by a defensive wall. The monastery, supposedly founded in the tenth century, flourished in the fourteenth, when it was rebuilt - as it was again during the Turkish occupation. Today it is inhabited by only a handful of nuns and its massive two-storied outer wall is in ruins. On the ground floor were monastic storerooms, the refectory, kitchens and bakery; on the upper, the cells, library and guard-room whose walls are pierced by gun slits. The small court is planted with flowering shrubs. Above the western entrance to the Church of the *Koimesis*, a lion's head (once a gargoyle from a fourth century BC gutter), flanked by a finely-carved meander pattern, is embedded in the masonry. Local peasants believe the leonine effigy is proof of the monastery's foundation by a Byzantine emperor called Leo. The present church is domed, triapsidal, but not cruciform; a mixture of architectural styles resulting from repeated renovations. The conch of the sanctuary has been dated to the eleventh century. Every inch of the interior walls is frescoed; the paintings, which are entirely derivative, reflecting late Paleologos influences. Against blue backgrounds, holy figures jostle each other in the familiar cycles of the lives of Christ and the Virgin and scenes from the Old and New Testaments. According to another local legend, the most venerated icon, that of the Virgin Indicator - a crude piece of post-Byzantine painting - flew from another village in the Argolid and even undertook airborne journeys to the great monastery of Megaspilion. Stories of restless icons flitting, generally by night, across the mountains of the Peloponnese once formed part of the stock-in-trade of post-Byzantine folklore and superstition.

After the monastery the road descends again to the coast. A turn to the right takes one directly to Ligourio, but going straight on the road passes below the village of Nea Epidavros, built on a crag which rises dramatically out of a rocky gully. Here, in 1822, the National Assembly of Epidavros was held, which gave modern Greece its first constitution - at least on paper. The rival chieftains, who had risen so boldly against their Turkish masters, were still unable to place national above personal interests; consequently the constitution proved as ill-starred as any of its successors.

A little further on, where the direct road to the Sanctuary passes above Palea Epidavros, a branch road descends through lemon, orange, and pomegranate orchards to a crescent-shaped bay, site of the ancient port of Epidauros. Traces of polygonal masonry can be identified - with difficulty - and some fragmentary ruins of an early Christian basilica are scattered on the hilltop. A small theatre or *odeion*, dating partly from the fourth century BC, has been restored and is used for concerts in summer. The sea has encroached on the coast and there are underwater ruins of classical buildings.

On the northern part of the bay are the hotels and houses of the modern Palea Epidavros, set amidst lanes and small squares lined with scarlet hibiscus: yachts and caiques moor beside the mole. The maritime strip is surrounded by mountains; to the east the volcanic mass of the Methana peninsula is very imposing. The older road to the Sanctuary, via Ligourio, goes up a wooded ravine, with streams running among orchards between banks of agnus castus, ivy, laurel and oleander.

Beyond Palea Epidavros the road continues to the south, climbing the coastal heights and then joining the road from Ligourio to Kranidion. A short way along this road there is a turn-off to the left (for Galata) which takes one to Ano Fanari. This tiny village commands one of the finest views not only in Greece, but in the entire Mediterranean: the jagged peaks of the volcanic mass of the Methana peninsula rise above the broken coastline below you with, to the south-east, the densely green island of Poros, towards which the road descends in hairpin bends.

Five kilometres south of Argos, a side road to the right leads to **Kefalari**, where the waters of the Kefalari River gush out of a rock at the foot of a steep cliff. In ancient times the river, known then as the Erasinos, was believed to have made a long underground journey from Lake Stymfalia. The smaller of two caves contains a chapel dedicated to the Virgin, painted a garish yellow, with a rock-hewn narthex. Water plants grow in the pool below the cave and the stream divides into willow-lined rivulets which water the fields, uniting again to flow to the sea through the Lernean Marsh. It is a shady place, and the Kefalari is the only Argive stream that is not dry in summer.

Beyond the turn-off to Kefalari the road continues between the mountains and the sea. The village of Myli is the site of ancient Lerna, where Herakles slew the Hydra, a creature with a dog-like body, a breath so venomous that one exhalation was enough to destroy life and, according to different myths, anything between ten and ten thousand heads, one of which was immortal. Between the sea and the road, amid the rushes and long grass, a prehistoric site (mainly c. 2000 BC) has been excavated by the American School of Classical Studies. It includes the foundations of a two-storied palace called the House of Tiles, because of the large number of roof tiles found here. To the west rises Mount Pondinos, topped by the ruins of a Frankish castle.

Just beyond Myli there is a fork. The main road climbs west into Arcadia. The traveller taking the south-bound road passes through the desolate splendour of Kynouria, where the mountains rise sheer from the sea, broken occasionally by narrow strips of fertility. Patches of sea stained a turbid shade of red suggest the outflow of subterranean streams, pouring out the silt and sludge accumulated in the course of their underground meanderings.

The first large fertile area is the Thyreatic Plain, where the road forks. On the coast to the left is **Paralia Astros**, a fishing village turned resort, situated on a spit of land, with the insignificant ruins of a Frankish fortress. On the north side of the headland there are fragments of ancient walls, part of a site that has not been identified.

Inland to the right is the village of Astros, whence a road, leading eventually to Tegea and Tripolis, passes the whitewashed buildings of the **Monastery of Loukous** in the corner of a small plain. To the left of the entrance to the monastery the ruined arch of a Roman aqueduct, strung with stalactites, spans a brook.

Entering the court of the monastery on an autumn morning I have seen the walls ablaze with morning glory and well-tended flower-beds filled with salvias, chrysanthemums and multi-coloured dahlias. Slabs of sculpted marble, including a headless statue of Athena, were ranged around the court and benches were placed in shady corners. Out of the middle of this charming garden rises a sturdy, yet elegant, little twelfth century Byzantine Church of the *Metamorphosis*, with a tall octagonal drum and three-sided apses. Faience plates are inlaid in the exterior wall and blocks of ancient sculpture have been built into the south wall, at the east end of which there is a fragment of mosaic paving. Two fine Corinthian columns flank the west doorway. The lavish use of materials from ancient pagan buildings is a fairly common feature of rural churches in Greece. It creates an agreeable sense of continuity. Undoubtedly stone to build the church was taken from the nearby country house of Herodes Atticus - it has recently been excavated, cleared and opened. Within the church, which has an extended east end, four old marble columns form the inner square supporting the dome, and there is a fine decorated pavement with marble slabs arranged in geometric designs of cubes, diamonds and rectangles, with a double-headed eagle in the central medallion. The post-Byzantine frescoes are not outstanding, but some of the icons of the same period on the carved walnut-wood *iconostasis* are worth looking at.

In the garden, nuns in black habits go about their daily chores. The order and serenity of the place make a striking contrast with the picturesque untidiness and slapdash friendliness typical of male monastic establishments. During the War of Independence the monastery provided the rough chieftains with money and shelter, most of its relics being sold in order to contribute to the war effort.

The coastal road continues south past deserted coves shut in by crags and cliffs seamed with bright red mineral deposits. In autumn the hills are covered with heather.

Beyond the little harbour of Tyrou, surrounded by a crescent-shaped expanse of olive trees below great cliffs, a row of ruined windmills stretches along the spine of a hill. Cypress groves increase in number and the coves are fringed with shingle. Soon the mountains withdraw sufficiently to make room for a small estuary surrounded by olive and fruit trees, enclosed, except at the seaward end, by conical peaks and rugged cliffs of tremendous height looming over **Leonidion**, one of the most beautiful small towns in the Peloponnese. The whitewashed houses, square and low, are splayed out across the mouth of a dramatic gorge which recedes, in a succession of curiously-stepped cliffs of a fantastic flame-like colour, into the heart of the wild Tsakonian country. Streets, alleys and little squares, built on different levels, form a charming architectural pile within the great arena of refulgent cliffs.

The road turns inland, climbing past the Monastery of Elona, clinging vertiginously to the cliff, and over the Parnon massif to the Yeraki crossroads, south-east to Monemvassia, south to Yithion and west to Sparti.

After turning inland beyond Myli, the main road from Argos into Arcadia climbs a series of hairpin bends between fierce escarpments. There are entrancing backward views of the bay of Nafplion and Palamidi. Passing high above the village of Ahladokambos, terraced on the side of a cup-shaped valley, the road mounts between slate-grey mountains until it reaches the Arcadian plateau, scattered with little oases of poplar and morello cherry trees. One senses a highland climate, barely sixty five kilometres from the stifling heat of the Argolid. The road cuts across the plain and is joined by the new National Road from Corinth just before Tripolis, the modern capital of Arcadia.

23

The Arcadian Scene

IN HIS FAMOUS PICTURE in the Louvre, Poussin depicts a group of shepherds reading an inscription - *Et in Arcadia ego* - on a Roman tomb. In the background there is a leafy landscape with wooded mountains; pink fleecy clouds sail across the indigo sky. The atmosphere is elegiac. Nothing, however, could be more different from the Arcadian scene of today - or from the one described by ancient Greek writers. 'Leafy' is the last adjective one would associate with Arcadia, though some of the highland valleys are dotted with stunted oaks and the mountain slopes with spruce and other conifers.

Arcadia is a scrub-covered massif, dominating the centre of the Peloponnese, from which the sea is seldom visible. In antiquity the inhabitants, reputed to be the most boorish people in Greece, tended flocks of sheep and goats and hunted bears and wild boar. For all their uncouthness, however, they were said to be a musical people with Hermes, an Arcadian deity born in a cave on Mount Kyllini, making the first pipes from reeds and the first lyre from cow-gut and tortoise-shell on the banks of the Ladon torrent.

Why then has the adjective 'Arcadian' been so long associated with a pastoral landscape traversed by limpid streams, inhabited by rosy-cheeked shepherds and shepherdesses basking in an eternal summer? 'Shepherds' is the operative word. These bare, shut-in valleys were, and still are in some places, the preserve of shepherds and goatherds - solitary figures, clad in heavy sheepskin cloaks, perched on dizzy ledges and surrounded by their flocks of sheep and mountain-goats, scrabbling among the prickly shrubs and jagged boulders. Apparently Roman poets, particularly Virgil, took the word 'shepherds' as a cue, probably because of Pindar's reference to Arcadia as 'a land of flocks'. They imagined a rural landscape inhabited by flock-tenders who had nothing better to do than recline in flowery meadows and play their reed pipes, under the dappled shade of elms and planes. The legacy was handed down through the centuries and great works of art were inspired by a wholly false image of Arcadia which reached its apotheosis in the paintings of Poussin and the poetry of Milton.

Local myths and history go a long way back. Pelasgos was the first king of Arcadia and is reputed to have devised shelters and sheepskin coats to protect his subjects from the inclement mountain weather. Later the Arcadians took part in the Trojan war though, being a mountain people, without ships or sailors, they embarked for Troy in Agamemnon's vessels. In the Peloponnesian War they were allied, under duress, to Sparta, but after the Theban victory over Sparta at Leuktra, they became enthusiastic members of the Arcadian confederacy, the brain-child of Epaminondas, which aimed at breaking Sparta's stranglehold over the Peloponnese. They were equally enthusiastic members of the Achaean League, one of the many abortive Greek attempts at political unity, designed to resist the tyrannical encroachments of the Macedonian Diadochi, Alexander's heirs. No Arcadian state ever became a great power; but the rugged inhabitants seem on the whole to have been on the side of democracy against autocracy, except when under the pressure exercised by the formidable Spartans.

Modern Arcadia has, so far, escaped excessive urbanization and industrialization. The chief town, **Tripolis**, first heard of during the Turkish occupation when it was the residence of the Pasha of the Morea, lies near the site of Pallantion, an ancient Arcadian city of which nothing remains. There is little to recommend the modern town except that it has some hotels and a large arcaded public square with cafés. However it is the hub of Peloponnesian travel, with roads radiating to north, south, east and west to modern towns as well as ancient and medieval sites.

In the mountainous north the first objective is Mantinea, where Spartan militarism repeatedly pitted its strength and near-invincibility against the democratic city states of Greece. The narrow plain, north of Tripolis, is flat and rather featureless. The sky, except at the height of summer, is often overcast, and drifting clouds cast their shadows on the dun-grey mountains whose conical peaks surround the elliptical plateau like the rim of a vast crater. At Skopi a line of rocky hills projects into the plain which contracts to less than two kilometres in width. In 418 BC the **Battle of Mantinea**, one of the decisive engagements of the Peloponnesian War, was fought here, when the Spartans, ten thousand strong, led by King Agis, inflicted

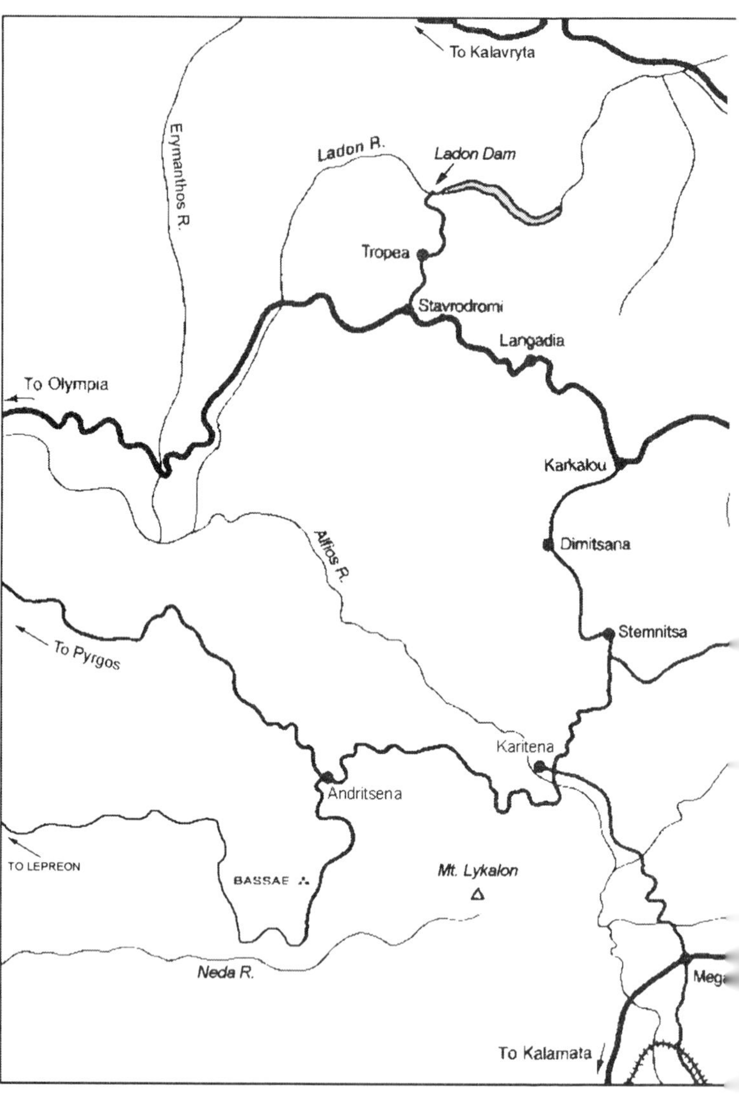
To Kalavryta
Erymanthos R.
Ladon R.
Ladon Dam
Tropea
Stavrodromi
Langadia
To Olympia
Karkalou
Dimitsana
Alfios R.
Stemnitsa
To Pyrgos
Karitena
Andritsena
TO LEPREON
BASSAE
Mt. Lykaion
Neda R.
To Kalamata

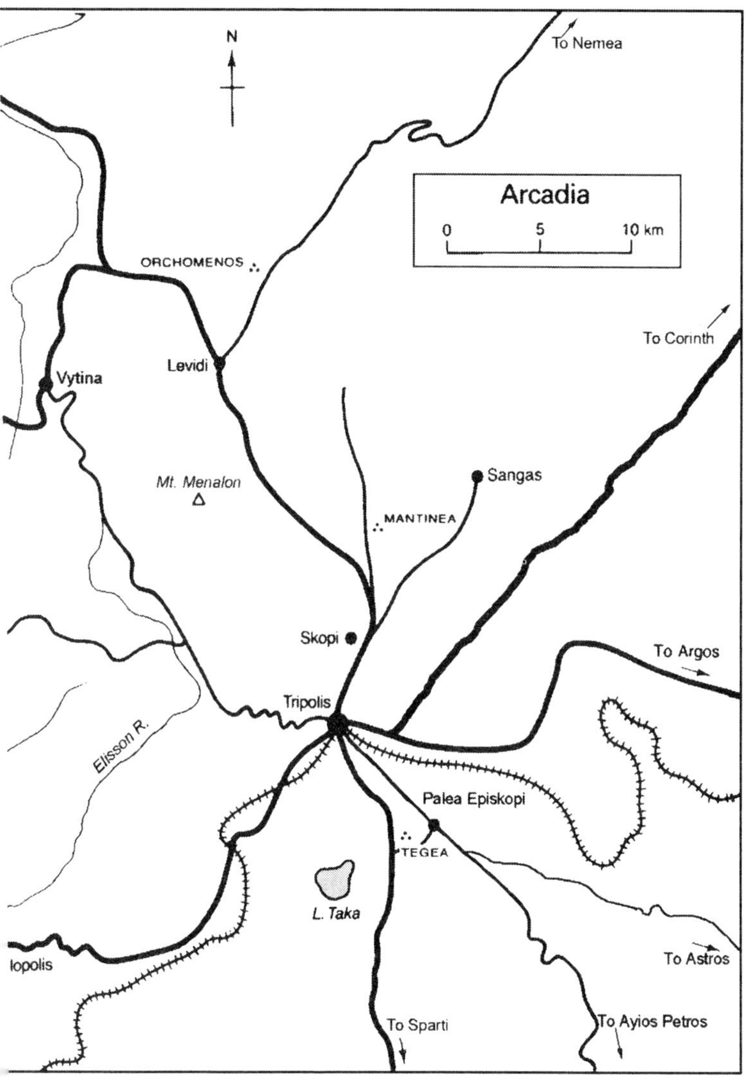
N
To Nemea
Arcadia
0
5
10 km
ORCHOMENOS
To Corinth
Levidi
Vytina
Sangas
Mt. Menalon
MANTINEA
Skopi
To Argos
Tripolis
Elisson R.
Palea Episkopi
TEGEA
L. Taka
lopolis
To Astros
To Sparti
To Ayios Petros

a major defeat on the allied armies of Athens, Argos, Elis and Mantinea. The victory was a classic example of the triumph of Spartan discipline and its 'chain of command' system, unknown in other Greek armies, whose generals relied on impassioned rhetoric, exhorting their troops to rush at the enemy in impulsive and sometimes foolhardy charges.

Although the field of Mantinea, in the shadow of its amphitheatre of grey mountains, witnessed the Spartan victory in the Peloponnesian War, it was also the setting, sixty years later, of one of the most violent convulsions in the long-drawn-out death agony of Spartan militarism. From a rocky projection, Epaminondas, most brilliant of Theban statesmen and generals, watched the second battle of Mantinea in 362 BC. Only when the irresistible charge of the Theban Sacred Band, clad in shining helmets and armed with burnished shields and spears, had broken the brute mass of Spartan helots did the wounded Epaminondas remove his hand from his breast, which had been pierced by an enemy arrow, and let the blood drain from his body. The loss of this noble man robbed the Thebans of the fruits of victory. The army, horror-struck by his death, remained as though paralysed and allowed the defeated Spartans to stream southward and escape unmolested.

North of the Skopi turn-off, the main Olympia road bears left; the road ahead, which is signposted, leads to the site of the city of **Mantinea**, built, contrary to the general rule, on level ground, without an acropolis. The city was surrounded by walls, with ten gates and many watchtowers, of which there is now very little visible evidence. What little remains is now fenced in, the entrance being opposite an extraordinary church. The theatre, however, is easily identified on a low knoll: two tiers are preserved and some slabs of the *proskenion* litter the empty field; the stage was placed at a slightly oblique angle to the orchestra and the *cavea* is greater than the usual semi-circle.

All this part of the plain was swampy ground, crossed by unsuspected streams, one of which enabled the Spartan King Agesilaos to crush Mantinea in 385 BC. Raising an embankment across the River Ophis, which flowed through the town, he blocked its efflux. The stream overflowed, the low walls made of sun-dried brick collapsed and the town was inundated; the inhabitants were obliged to disperse to neighbouring villages. The reduction of Mantinea into scattered settlements is a typical example of Spartan policy, aimed at breaking up those civilized states on which

Hellenism was founded. With the ascendancy of Thebes and the consequent decline of Spartan power, Mantinea was rebuilt on a plan that excluded the streams from its midst. The problem raised by the constant flooding of this level ground, however, remained unresolved, for in spring the water of the swollen streams was unable to run into the *katavothres*, the subterranean channels with which the Arcadian massif is riddled. Polybios says the Mantineans finally took to cutting trenches, through which the waters were directed into the *katavothres* and thence to the coast.

The extraordinary church was built in the early 1970's in a mixture of styles, mainly Byzantine, classical and Minoan; there are also pastiche classical temples in the grounds - the whole constitutes the most remarkable architectural folly in Greece. There is a melancholy beauty about Mantinea. In summer the mountains have a forbidding, metallic quality; kestrels fly over the barren slopes and frogs plop in the marshy pools.

Beyond the turning for Mantinea, the main road runs over a saddle between the arid hills that divide the Mantinean from the Orchomenian plain. At the large village of Levidi a road to the right descends into a bowl-shaped valley surrounded by craggy peaks. Climbing out of the valley you come, on the left, to the sign for ancient **Orchomenos**. Above the village of Kalpaki, at an altitude of 900 metres on a hillside facing the summit of Mount Menalon, is the site of the acropolis. From here Orchomenian kings ruled over Arcadia in the earliest times. Beside the chapel of *Ayios Ioannis* and a circular threshing-floor, there are three well-preserved column bases of a temple of Artemis overlooking the sparsely-cultivated plain. A steep climb to the summit (a poor road goes most of the way) brings one to the fragmentary ruins of a little temple of Athena and some ancient foundations. To the right, the terrace of the Bouleuterion overlooks the valley and the peaks to the east. The hollow of the theatre, its tiers buried in the soil, is discernible. The place has a wintry air: bleak, desolate and grand.

From Levidi the road skirts the northern slopes of Mount Menalon, passes through fir forests and then comes to a fork. The road to the right leads indirectly to Patras, while the left-hand fork goes southwards to the popular alpine resort of Vytina and then on to Olympia. From Karkalou a branch road leads to **Dimitsana**, on a terrace above a deep chasm through which the stream of the Lousios flows in a wide loop. The mountains slope gradually down to the upper valley of the Alfios and the plain of Megalopolis, bounded in the west by Mount Lykaion and in the south by the Lakonian ranges. During the Turkish occupation, Dimitsana was a centre of learning and possessed a school and a famous library. Much smaller today, it is mainly visited for its lovely view. However, antiquarians may search for some very fragmentary remains of Cyclopean and Classical walls. Partly-abandoned villages - inhabited by perhaps half a dozen families, a few sheepdogs and some scraggy hens - clinging to the mountain-sides like petrified sentinels with nothing left to guard, are a melancholy feature of the Arcadian scene. In the gorge below Dimitsana, the Monastery of *Ayios Ioannis Prodromos*, originally an imperial Komnenos foundation of the twelfth century, is tucked away in a shady ravine.

From Dimitsana the road continues past Stemnitsa, where there is a simple but good hotel, and then descends into the plain of Megalopolis.

North-west of Karkalou, the long winding descent to Olympia begins. It is one of the loveliest in the Peloponnese. A bend in the road soon affords an astonishing view of the large village of **Langadia**, its red-roofed houses climbing a steep mountain-side. Here one can stop for lunch on a terrace overlooking the gorge. There are tourist shops filled with sheepskin rugs, woollen bags, modern imitations of peasant embroideries, striped bedspreads and sheep bells.

Further down the descent, at Stavrodromi, a turning to the right leads to Tropea, another strikingly-situated village, beyond which the road winds between slopes dyed crimson by manganese deposits. Soon a precipice falls sheer into a deserted valley through which flows the **River Ladon**, an important tributary of the Alfios. It is a savage setting: beetling crags tower above the gorge, at the bottom of which lies a sheet of pale green, crystal-clear water - the artificial lake formed by a dam.

Beyond Stavrodromi, the main road descends into more pastoral country as it follows the course of the Ladon, its banks lush with planes and poplars, the rolling foothills thickly wooded with tall, feathery pines and the gullies bright with gorse and broom in late spring. On these banks, Demeter was found by her brother, Poseidon, who was suddenly seized by an uncontrollable passion to possess her. In order to escape his attentions she changed herself into a mare, whereupon Poseidon changed himself into a stallion and ravished her on the spot. Demeter then cleansed herself by bathing in the waters of the Ladon.

After diverging from the Ladon, the road reaches another river, the swiftly-flowing Erymanthos, which marks the boundary between Arcadia and Elis. Green rolling hills enclose the lower valley of the Alfios, as it winds serenely between sand-banks towards Olympia.

Travellers heading towards Kalamata take the south-western route from Tripolis which zigzags across a spine of featureless hills separating the plain of Tripolis from the wide valley of Megalopolis. In a fold of one of these hills a monument marks the spot where three hundred Resistance fighters were made to dig their own graves before they were shot by the Germans in 1944. Ten of them refused. The Nazi commander was so impressed that he commuted their sentence to life imprisonment.

The descent into the plain, which is traversed by the upper Alfios and studded with copses, hillocks and little oases of vegetation, reveals a new aspect of Arcadia. The altitude is lower and the atmosphere warmer and more humid, the vistas wider, the mountains less austere. The range of Mount Lykaion, a series of broken ridges running roughly north to south, forms a barrier in the west. In the disastrous earthquake of 1965 the whole mountain is said to have shifted slightly and the villages on its slopes were reduced to heaps of rubble. Featureless modern Megalopolis (whence the main road continues to Kalamata and the Messenian plains in the south) is badly polluted by a lignite-burning power station supplied from open-cast mines near the road. However, the site of the ancient city a short way to the north is worth visiting.

Megalopolis, the 'Great City', founded by Epaminondas during the heyday of Theban supremacy, was the headquarters of the Arcadian Confederacy which aimed to contain Sparta and prevent her from repeating her hitherto all-too-successful attempts to divide the Peloponnese into small units under her domination. Politically, Epaminondas' idea was a good one, but somehow Megalopolis did not quite come off. The 'Great City', meeting place of the Council of the Ten Thousand (composed of representatives of all the federated states), was great in name only. Laid out on either side of the River Elisson and encircled by a wall five and a half miles in circumference, its size was out of proportion to its small population. Polybios, who was a native of the city, says its power quickly declined, and in the late Hellenistic age a comic poet facetiously described the 'great city' as a 'great desert'. When visited by Pausanias it was abandoned and largely in ruins.

However the city possessed the largest **theatre** in Greece, capable of accommodating twenty thousand spectators. Hollowed out of a small hill shaded by large pines, its beautifully-proportioned *cavea* is turned towards the north and the wide bed of the Elisson, with the earthquake-shattered hills of Mount Lykaion in the background. Only the front row of seats is intact, with another six rows fairly well preserved. This is one of the few ancient theatres not yet restored for regular summer performances - but some do take place in spite of the acrid smoke of the nearby power station.

Beyond the *proskenion* are some bases of the numerous columns of the Thersileion, a great assembly hall seating six thousand people - a kind of ancient prototype of the Palais des Nations in Geneva: equally fleeting, equally ineffectual. But with the passing of time the historical stage came to be set on infinitely wider dimensions and the endemic rivalries of the Greek city states, often little more than border quarrels, were destined to pale before the imperial ambitions of Macedonia and, much later, of Rome. The site of the *agora*, which was built on a magnificent scale, has been identified on the north-west bank of the Elisson.

North-west of Megalopolis the undulating plain is dominated by the fortress of **Karitena**, most splendidly situated of Frankish castles. The more deeply one penetrates into the Peloponnese, the more one is impressed by this succession of ruined medieval castles. Compared to Venetian military architects, the Franks were amateurs, but the sites on which they raised their strategic redoubts cannot be matched for wild and romantic beauty. The sojourn of the northern knights in this sun-drenched land of dusty olive groves and vine-clad valleys was not a long one. Internecine strife and sporadic wars with the conquered Greeks took their toll. Only two generations after the Crusaders had overrun the Morea many of the great feudal names were extinct.

Karitena is built on twin heights, dominating the passes leading into the heart of the Morea. The village is on the eastern hill, the castle on the western, which is higher and has a flat top. Village houses extend across the saddle between the two. A sloping ledge at the foot of the castle suddenly falls away sheer: hundreds of feet below, the shining streak of the Alfios winds through a narrow chasm between russet-coloured cliffs. On the left of the road up to the village, a little Church of the *Panayia* (originally of the eleventh century) clings to the side of a steep declivity beside a pretty brickwork Frankish belfry. It possesses an elaborate *iconostasis*, brightly painted with birds and other ornamental patterns. A maze of increasingly narrow alleys between dilapidated, often uninhabited, houses, some with projecting balconies, ascends towards the saddle. Huge slabs of masonry, which have fallen from the medieval keep, lie smothered in brambles and spurge. The younger generation has packed up and gone to Athens, America or Australia, though recently the exodus has been stemmed somewhat, as even mountainous Arcadia benefits from EU agricultural handouts and the tourist boom.

North of the saddle, the Byzantine Church of *Ayios Nikolaos* overlooks a cemetery and a grove of cypresses. Four small, very low domes surmount the corners, with a larger central one on a squat drum in the centre: the gabled roofs form an agreeable intersection of planes. The proportions of the interior are strictly Byzantine and give an impression of loftiness in spite of the church's relatively small size. The frescoes (probably post-Byzantine) are too damaged to give one a chance to judge their quality, although the general effect is of a lovely roseate glow.

The visit to the castle is strenuous, for the going is steep. In spring the path is bordered with bee-orchids and long-stalked, mauve-pink *Anemone hortensis*, with elliptical petals and three bracts well below the flower. Two-thirds of the way up, clinging to the rock, is a chapel of unusual structural design: Greek Cross plan with a small extended nave on the west. The little ruined house beside it is called the house of Kolokotronis, who probably stayed here during the campaign of 1821.

The castle is entered through the barbican. Although it was the seat of one of the great baronies of the Morea, it is disappointing within - very ruined and with little of the splendid military architecture evident in the Venetian fortifications of Acro-Corinth and Nafplion. Founded in the thirteenth century by Hughes de Bruyeres, father of Geoffroy, most famous representative of French chivalry in the Morea, it conveys a greater impression of impregnability than any other medieval castle in Southern Greece, with the exception of Monemvassia. Purely strategic in purpose, its history is uneventful. With the decline of the Frankish ascendency in the Morea, it was sold to the Greeks in 1320 and became a dependency of one of the monasteries of Mystra. In 1460 it was captured by the Turks. It served a final military purpose in the Second World War, when the German army of occupation, constantly harassed by guerrillas, installed gun emplacements on the summit. From the barbican the path turns left to the main arched gate, which is set in the curtain wall, flanked by a square tower to the north. The gate leads to a vaulted passage into the triangular keep, with a square tower at its apex (north) and a ruined hall at the base (south).

Hundreds of feet below lies a circular threshing-floor, with the foothills of Mount Lykaion rising abruptly on the other side of the gorge. In the foreground, to the north, the Church of *Ayios Nikolaos* stands securely above the chasm. In the south-east the river winds across the undulations of the plain from its source in the distant hills north of Taiyetos.

Back on the road to Andritsena and the west, one crosses a modern bridge beside an old Frankish construction with six arches, of which four remain. A somewhat dotty effect is created by the tiny chapel crowning the middle pier, from which a stone stairway leads down to the bed of the Alfios. Karitena, seen from across the gorge, is strikingly beautiful. The road climbs the foothills of Mount Lykaion, and the chasm is lost to sight. At the end of the highland stretch one reaches **Andritsena**, its houses banked up on the abrupt slope amid gnarled, shady planes, some of whose trunks are so large that they have been hollowed out in order to form reservoirs from which water flows through metal pipes. The library has a large collection of books donated by a native of the village who had literary interests ranging from the ancient writers to masterpieces of nineteenth-century French fiction.

From Andritsena the main road descends into the lower valley of the Alfios towards Olympia (turn off at Krestena) and the coast. Another road climbs up to **Bassae** through a scene of utter desolation: not a dwelling, barely a tree. In the late spring, wild flowers relieve the austerity of the denuded landscape, but in summer there is only scrub and in the long winter, snow on range upon range of mountains. Several circular stone threshing-floors are the sole evidence that men and animals still inhabit, or once inhabited, these friendless uplands.

One's first sight of the impressive **Temple of Epicurean Apollo** used to come as a considerable surprise, but the whole building is now protected from the elements by a huge plastic shelter in which the badly-eroded stone is being treated. There was a proposal to move the entire temple to another site, but this scheme has been abandoned; however it should be possible to remove the shelter in due course. The fluted columns of the temple, grey as the stones from which they sprout and crowned by pieces of architrave, stand on a ledge at the foot of Mount Kotilion. It seems extraordinary that a major temple, designed by Iktinos, the leading architect of the fifth century BC, should have been erected on one of the loneliest sites in the Peloponnese, at an altitude of nearly 1200 metres. Except at the site, there is no house, hamlet or village in sight; and yet outside Athens there is no more complete temple in Greece.

The architectural arrangement is unconventional. It has six columns, front and back, and fifteen, instead of the usual twelve, at either side. The building thus acquires an air of unusual elongation. The *adyton*, the secret chamber from which the public was generally excluded, is not separated from the *cella* by a wall. Since the temple was dedicated to Apollo, the front faces north, towards Delphi, the god's holiest shrine. It would be too much to expect all the subtle curves and refinements of the Parthenon, for Iktinos, no longer working in marble as he did on the Acropolis, was unable to apply these to the hard local limestone. (Some experts believe the temple precedes the Parthenon.) Only part of the architrave remains, but thirty-seven of the Doric columns of the peristyle are still standing. Twenty-three panels of the frieze, depicting battles between Centaurs and Lapiths, Athenians and Amazons, were removed to Corfu in the nineteenth century and bought by the British Government for £15,000; they are now in the British Museum. The almost complete *cella* is unique in having five columns connected to the side walls on each side; seven of these ten engaged columns, with beautiful bases and a smooth grey patina, are well preserved. They were once crowned with Ionic capitals, adding greater variety to the chamber, which also contained the large bronze cult statue of Apollo. At the south end, the base of the earliest-known Corinthian column is discernible. The air up here on the slopes of Mount Kotilion is cool and wonderfully bracing, although the sun burns in summer. There is no shade and the solitude is awe-inspiring, but (with the cover removed) the cluster of slender columns, within the ring of arid mountain peaks, creates a place of worship in perfect harmony with its setting. Like the Acropolis in Athens and the site of Delphi, there is a profound feeling of timelessness.

After Bassae, Western Arcadia contains little of major interest, but the road goes on down to the coast, offering some fine scenery and the opportunity to visit the scanty remains of Phygalia (the Phygalians built the temple at Bassae) and of Lepreon.

From Tripolis the main road to Sparti runs south. At the eighth kilometre a road to the left goes to the site of **Tegea**. Once the most powerful city state in Arcadia, Tegea put up a prolonged resistance to Sparta; but in the Peloponnesian War, its position on the Lacedaimonian border obliged its rulers to ally themselves with the hated neighbour. Of the Temple of Athena Alea, burned in 395 BC and rebuilt by Skopas, little remains above the second drum of the columns (town and temple alike were razed to the ground by Alaric at the end of the fourth century AD). Contemporary writers describe the temple as superior in size and quality to any other in the Peloponnese. The famous cult image of Athena Alea by Skopas was carried off by Augustus after the battle of Actium. Some of the great grey drums, each about four feet high, lie on their sides; others are ranged in rows so that the spacious proportions of the temple are easily perceived. The small, well-arranged museum in the village has copies of several works by Skopas, including one of the lovely head of the Goddess of Health which is in the National Museum in Athens; there are also some slabs of the architectural decoration of the temple and a fragment of cornice.

There are more remains of Tegea at the neighbouring village of Palea-Episkopi, the site of medieval Nikli, a well-walled stronghold commanding all the lines of communication across the Morea, but destroyed in the thirteenth century. Some of the warlike people from here settled as refugees in the southern part of the Mani; helping to build its reputation for fierce feuds between neighbouring villages. The fine church incorporates some elements of a much older building.

After the fork to Tegea, the main Sparti road skirts what is left of marshy Lake Taka, once abounding in wild fowl, now mostly cultivated land. To the south is a range of grim-looking hills, followed by a bleak, featureless mountain stretch. Then the slow, winding descent begins. The air loses some of its highland quality; vestiges of vegetation appear in the gullies. Suddenly the road emerges from the hills and a view of immeasurable grandeur opens up: the Taiyetos Mountains, highest of the Peloponnesian ranges and snow-capped for more than half the year, raise their many peaks above the plain of olives. Below the mountains extends 'Hollow Lacedaimon': a wide and fertile valley traversed by the oleander-bordered stream of the Evrotas. In the middle of it lies the modern town of Sparti.

24

Sparta

THE NAME ALONE - SPARTA - recalls the fear and hatred it once inspired in those Greek city states whose relatively enlightened civilizations were extinguished by the will of this 'master race'. Striking out from their capital city, the Spartans expanded their control throughout Lakonia and much of the rest of the Peloponnese. Yet the landscape has a radiance and a fertility that make an instant appeal to the senses. Homer says that Lakonia - or Lacedaimon - was 'full of hollows', and indeed the red earth of the valley, now covered with olive trees, is broken up by escarpments and gullies thick with evergreens and aromatic shrubs. Streams flow down from Taiyetos through groves of oranges and mulberries into the swift, muddy currents of the Evrotas. The river banks are bordered with luxuriant oleanders and the orchards are studded with dwarf palms, from whose fronds rope was made in the Bronze Age. Over it all looms Taiyetos. The result of some prodigious primeval convulsion, its spurs, rent with chasms and precipices, are crowned by a series of jagged summits, on the highest of which horses were sacrificed to the sun. From certain angles the range has a savage, even cruel, aspect; it is not difficult to associate it with the austere militaristic community that dwelt in its shadow.

Lakonia is a traveller's paradise. Landscape, mythology, history, primitive sculpture, Byzantine churches, medieval castles - it has them all. With Sparti, its modern name, as a base, the traveller could spend three days pleasantly: one day for the sites of ancient Sparta, including the Museum and Therapne, at least half a day for Mystra, a day for Monemvassia, visiting the churches of Hryssafa and Yeraki on the way.

The usual approach is to go south from Tripolis, with side-trips to the east and west. One begins, in fact, at the end of the story. Just as the final descent to the Lakonian plain starts, there is a turning to the right which leads, after two kilometres, to the village of Sellassia; nearby is the site of the battle of Sellassia. Here, in 222 BC, the

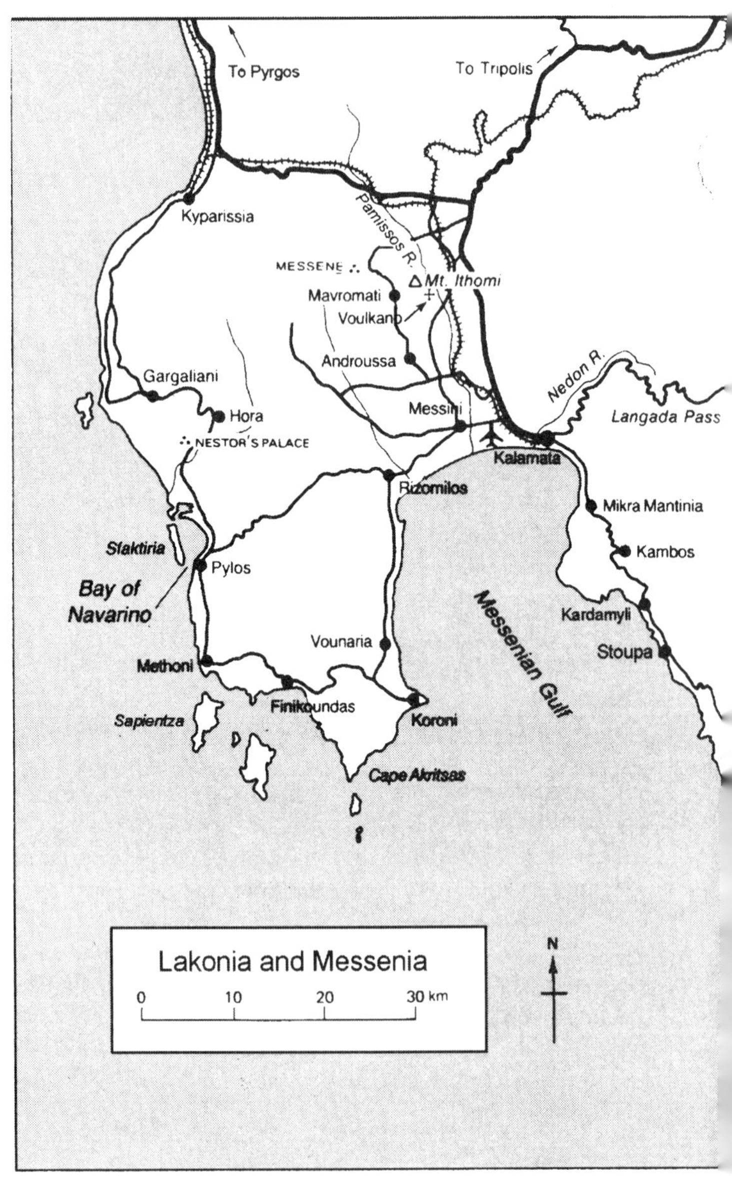
To Pyrgos
To Tripolis
Kyparissia
Pamissos R.
MESSENE
Mt. Ithomi
Mavromati
Voulkano
Androussa
Gargaliani
Hora
NESTOR'S PALACE
Messini
Nedon R.
Langada Pass
Kalamata
Rizomilos
Mikra Mantinia
Kambos
Sfaktiria
Pylos
Bay of Navarino
Kardamyli
Messenian Gulf
Stoupa
Vounaria
Methoni
Finikoundas
Koroni
Sapientza
Cape Akritsas
Lakonia and Messenia
0
10
20
30 km
N

To Tripolis
Astros
Ayios Petros
Gulf of Argolis
Tyrou
Mt Parnon
Leonidion
SELLASSIA
Elona
SPARTA
Hryssafa
THERAPNE
Kosmas
Mystra
Sparti
AMYKLAI
Evrotas R.
Yeraki
Taiyetos Mts.
Platsa
Nomitsis
Yithion
Sykia
Itylo
Limoni
Passava
Ayeranos
Vahos
Areopolis
Monemvassia
Pyrgos Dirou
Kotronas
CASTLE OF MAINA
Lakonian Gulf
Kita
Yerolimena
Neapolis
Vathia
Cape Tenaro (Matapan)
Cape Maleas

prolonged struggle which the Spartans had waged so stubbornly and courageously against the overwhelming forces of the Macedonian king, now allied to the Peloponnesian states, came to a calamitous end when repeated charges of Macedonian heavy cavalry broke the Spartan line and put their king to flight. For the first time in history a hostile army entered Sparta.

Today, Spartans, enjoying the produce from their rich soil, emigrate less than their neighbours, the Arcadians. Traditionally right-wing, they have inherited the love of order of their ancestors.

The modern town, called **Sparti**, was built in the nineteenth century on the site of the sprawling communes of antiquity. Intersecting parallel streets are surrounded by gardens filled with magnolia trees and semi-tropical plants. There are several good hotels.

The ancient ruins are not impressive but the setting is bucolic - the hilly ground, shaded by olive trees, is covered with vetch and mullein. The relative insignificance of the site, compared with the brilliance of the Athenian Acropolis, underlines the difference of outlook, character and way of life between the two states. The Spartans, having confidence both in their military pre-eminence and in the ring of mountains that defended their land from invaders, did not feel the need to huddle round a fortified citadel. Their temples and public buildings were few and, though scattered amid gardens and orchards, were remarkable neither for beauty of form nor for sculptural embellishment. Thucydides, in a famous passage, was forced to conclude: 'For I suppose, if Lacedaimon were to become desolate and the temples and the foundations of the public buildings were left, that as time went on there would be a strong disposition with posterity to refuse to accept her fame as a true exponent of her power.' Prophetic words. Even at that magical moment when the late afternoon sun turns the snow-capped peaks of Taiyetos to flame, the most romantic of travellers is unlikely to find the verdict of Thucydides exaggerated.

Not only was architectural distinction lacking. Rare among ancient Greeks, the Spartans were indifferent to the arts and literature, music and verse serving only as a means of extolling the martial virtues. Ignorant of international commerce and unmoved by social graces, they were also devoid of any talent for philosophy, rhetoric or dialectics. Conquest, regimentation and observance of the law were deemed worthier goals. Citizens were divided into three classes: Spartans proper, claiming unmixed Dorian descent, who dwelt in the city and constituted the ruling class; *perioiki*, freedmen, who lived in neighbouring townships but were not allowed any share in government; and *helots*, who were bound in serfdom to the soil, performed military service and farmed the royal estates. The spirit of heredity was ingrained and it applied, says Herodotos, to all professions - even cooks, flute-players and town-criers; a man with a fine, loud voice, eager to prove his talent as a herald, could not do so unless his father had been one before him. At the summit of the oligarchical chain were the two kings, that curious dual monarchy peculiar to Sparta which, as Herodotos relates, had its origins in the birth of male twins to the reigning monarch - an event that placed the Spartans in a dilemma and even perplexed the Delphic oracle. As there was no way of telling which was the elder, both sons ascended the throne and the dual monarchy became a permanent institution; the system prevented either monarch from gaining preponderant power. Since the kings led the army into battle, they were more closely identified by the people with conquest than with government; administration and policy-making were in the hands of a body of *ephors* (literally 'overseers') who were elected annually and protected the people from royal abuse. This election, democratic in essence, is paradoxical in an otherwise wholly dictatorial system. The *ephors* wielded immense power and had the authority to recall a monarch from the wars, even to try him and punish him if his conduct of a campaign was questionable. Behind the *ephors* lurked the *Krypteia*, an unsavoury secret service, as all-pervading as any modern totalitarian institution of its kind. Its agents consisted largely of young thugs, fully armed, who roamed the countryside terrorizing insubordinate *helots*.

The position of women was curiously anomalous. Spartan maidens did not lead as joyless or secluded an existence as their sisters in other Greek states. Clad in short tunics and those famous slit skirts that scandalized the rest of Greece, they underwent as rigorous a physical training as the youths, taking part in foot races, wrestling and boxing matches. In order to toughen the women, Lykurgos ordered them to go naked in processions and, Plutarch adds, to 'dance too, in that condition, at certain solemn feasts, while the young men stood around, seeing and hearing them'. These exhibitions were intended as incitements to matrimony, i.e. procreation, sole Spartan object of union between men and women. At the same time homosexuality between men was not only condoned but encouraged, particularly in the army, where high-ranking pederasts trained their protégés in the science of war and the principles of Spartan discipline. Bachelors, however, were so heartily despised for failing to produce male children that they were disenfranchised and obliged to march naked round the market place on the coldest winter day as a mark of their disgrace. Married men only approached their wives at night and, after spending an hour with them in total darkness and silence, returned to the men's quarters. Often a man did not see his wife's face by daylight until after the birth of their first child. From the age of seven all healthy male children led a barrack-like life. If they showed any physical disability they were left to die on Taiyetos. A mother's final exhortation to her son going to the wars was a blunt command to return alive if victorious, dead if defeated. Everything - education, diet, love and recreation - was geared to the single aim of military efficiency.

That the ideals of regimentation and militarism alone should have sustained a whole people, and made them the great power which played a dominating rôle in the civilised Hellenic world for nearly five hundred years, remains a tribute to their staying-power, selflessness - and stupidity. To realize how such a 'civilization' was possible, one has only to glance at the map. With the Arcadian massif to the north and the sprawling bulk of Parnon in the east, the sea (with its paucity of anchorages) in the south and the impassable barrier of Taiyetos in the west, the 'iron curtain' was complete. There was hardly a chink through which the new currents of thought galvanizing the rest of Greece could penetrate. Moreover, all the records indicate that Sparta's attitude to her victims was one of arrogance and high-handedness. She was, in fact, thoroughly hated by everyone.

From the town centre it is a quarter of an hour's walk northwards up the main street to the long, low hill of the principal ancient site, excavated by the British School of Archaeology at Athens. First to be seen is a rectangular substructure with two or three well-preserved courses of square stone slabs, which is all that remains of a small Hellenistic temple. Next comes a low Roman wall and, beyond it, the centre of **ancient Sparta**, undefended by walls until the second century BC. Silence now reigns over the exiguous ruins of the 'hated' city. Beyond the Roman wall there is evidence of some stone-built 'ovens' or 'bakeries', also Roman. Nearby was a spacious *agora*, of which little remains. Various very solid foundations, exposed in deep cavities, are difficult to interpret, and higher up are the substantial remains of a large circular or elliptical building, the purpose of which is unclear. To the west, cutting into the hillside, is the *cavea* of the Hellenistic theatre, one of the largest in Greece. A few tiers are preserved, but excavations continue, and more, especially of the extensive stage area, is revealed each year. The building was used mainly for public assemblies, but a movable stage was available for dramatic presentations - the grooves for the wheels can be seen to the right. Above the theatre at the north end of the hill is a grove of eucalyptus and pine trees, and foundations of the most famous building in Sparta, the **Temple of Athena Chalkioikos** (The Brazen House of Athena), so-called because its walls were entirely covered with bronze shields depicting the exploits of the Dioscuri and the Labours of Herakles. It stood in a sacred enclosure surrounded by colonnades, with the tomb of the Homeric king, Tyndareos, at the southern end. It was outside the Brazen House that Lykurgos, fleeing one day from his enemies, was attacked by a hot-headed youth, who blinded him in one eye. He took the disfigurement very philosophically and promptly ordered a temple of Ophthalmitis to be raised within the enclosure to commemorate the event.

In the middle of the flat hill-top above the theatre is the distinct outline, with column bases and apses, of the tenth-century basilica of St. Nikon Metanoitis ('The Repenter'), a nomadic missionary. Across the Evrotas the undulating red ground ascends gradually towards the foothills of Parnon, which lies further from Sparti than Taiyetos, giving a feeling of spaciousness which is absent in the west, where the immense range rises like a wall.

At the point where the northbound road that passes through the centre of the town meets the road that bypasses the centre, a track leads down to the **Sanctuary of Artemis Orthia** ('The Upright') on the bank of the river, among the reeds and croaking frogs. This was the religious centre of the sprawling city, where ferocious 'coming of age' rites were performed, including the flagellation ordeal, in which boys were whipped on an altar in front of the temple until their flesh was torn to bleeding ribbons. Those who endured the ordeal without crying out were awarded the title of altar-winner and the prize of a sickle blade. The excavations have revealed a series of substructures of altars one below the other, dating from the eighth century BC to the third AD, the earlier ones consisting of unworked stones and rough slabs. The walls were of unbaked bricks. In Roman times a horse-shoe shaped theatre was built looking down on the temple to accommodate the numerous visitors for the re-enactment of some of the ancient rites. In fact the Spartans, showing for once some business acumen, invented more rites to satisfy the customers, and increase their revenues from tourism. Now the site has little to offer, except gruesome memories, the sound of running water and the sight of farm workers tending fruit trees.

The **museum**, in Lykourgou Street, though rather in need of reorganisation, should not be missed. The exhibits, found mostly around the acropolis and sanctuary of Artemis, are the only existing relics of creative art in ancient Sparta. Lakonian Archaic sculpture is crude but arresting. The best fragments - more vigorous than elegant, symbolic than idealistic - belong to the sixth and fifth centuries BC. After that the curtain comes down and all art withers and dies.

The entrance hall contains *stelae* dedicated to Artemis Orthia by winners in the whipping ordeal. Some are inscribed with the names of youths trained to bear the most atrocious physical pain in the service of a puritanical goddess.

Taking the right wing first, one enters Room 1, notable mainly for sections of mosaic pavement, which once adorned the floors of sumptuous Roman villas. Thousands of fragments of coloured stone form compositions of mythological scenes and personages. They are evocative of wealth and a patrician way of life - Roman, spacious, luxurious. Life in Roman Sparta was uneventful and probably very agreeable, for the conquest of Flaminius had banished all thoughts of further military aggression from the inhabitants.

One mosaic has the story of **Europa and the Bull**, rather coarsely rendered, in which the pretty daughter of the King of Tyre is borne away on the back of Zeus, transformed into a bull maddened with lust. Another represents **Orpheus playing to the animals** - the figure with the lyre is conventional and the poet-musician's features lack the spirited expression of the flirtatious Europa. Others include a headless Aphrodite, Perseus decapitating Medusa, and the scene, inferior in quality, of Achilles dressed as a girl among the daughters of Lykomedes.

Sculptures here and in the second room include several related to the Dioscuri, Helen's twin brothers, all offspring of Leda. These are the most ubiquitous characters in Spartan mythology and appear repeatedly in Lakonian art. Two sides of a **pyramidal stele** (c. 600 BC) are carved with snakes, symbol of the Dioscuri. On the third side we see a helmeted Agamemnon beseeching Clytemnestra, the Spartan princess, to marry him. Both figures are very squat.

Clytemnestra's hair hangs in tight curls down to her shoulders and she holds the mysterious sickle in her left hand. An early fifth-century *stele*, in the very flat relief typical of Lakonian sculpture, depicts an unknown bearded man in profile, seated on a throne, the legs of which terminate in lions' feet. The elegant throne, the self-assured pose of the seated figure and the details of a dog and horse combine to produce a minor masterpiece. An earlier sixth-century *stele* in the same flat relief represents a seated man and woman. The man's face is missing, but the woman's, with large almond-shaped eyes and a firm chin, has an Egyptian impassivity.

Further on are *stelae* of the Dioscuri: **stele No. 575** (early sixth-century BC) depicts the immortal twins armed with spears, facing each other on either side of two large *amphorae* with slender necks. Above them, two snakes flank the egg of Leda, from which their lovely sister was hatched. Executed in grey marble in the shallowest possible relief, crude and primitive in technique, it nevertheless possesses remarkable symmetry and formality. Two other *stelae* are worth looking at: one of Pentelic marble representing the brothers frontally, their spears resting on their horses' manes; and a smaller one of red Taiyetos marble, in which they are mounted, facing each other.

An unusual and very fine painted capital from the throne of Apollo at Amyklai is a good example of the polished workmanship of late sixth-century BC Ionian sculpture, with its blending of Doric vigour and Ionic grace. In the third room we move into a more classical atmosphere: No. 468 is a fifth-century *stele* of the Attic school, of Artemis pouring a libation into a vase extended by Apollo, who holds a lyre. The richness of the drapery, the flowing line and graceful design seem extraordinarily effortless after the harsh austerity of the stylized Lakonian reliefs. The same room contains a bust of a **helmeted warrior** in Parian marble, found on the site of the Brazen House and immediately called 'Leonidas' by the workmen on the dig. An early fifth-century work, it was probably executed shortly after the death of the hero of Thermopylae. The warrior is depicted at maturity, the half-smiling mouth full-lipped, the neck short and thickset. It is obviously the work of an accomplished artist. More beautiful is the headless **torso of an athlete** (No. 94), without legs or forearms, sometimes ascribed to Polykleitos. In its economy and perfection of modelling, with the torso growing so beautifully out of the slender waist, it recalls an earlier and greater masterpiece: the Kritios Boy in the Acropolis Museum.

The left wing of the museum is less interesting. Room 4 possesses a collection of tiny metal figures, in very flat relief, of warriors, animals and winged creatures as well as several striking terracotta theatrical masks. In Room 5 there are more mosaics, including heads of Apollo, the poetess Sappho and, the most effective, Alcibiades, as well as torsos of headless youths, mostly less than life-size - eternal glorification of the self-centred Spartan male. Providing some variety are: a clay model of a Roman galley, a life-size black wild boar, the very pretty head of Ptolemy III (third century BC) and part of a sarcophagus with *putti*, very fine Roman Imperial work.

One tends to leave the museum with mixed feelings: admiration for the vigour of execution of the totem-like *stelae*; nostalgia for the purity and perfection of Attic sculpture, and a sense of relief that a tiny chink of light has illumined the strange, sullen character of Xenophon's 'master race'. The Spartans may have been militaristic bullies, but they were not unmoved by the desire to create an aesthetic image, crude but sincere, of their religious aspirations. In the final analysis, however, Lakonian sculpture is a blind alley. Like Sparta's citizens, it was incapable of evolution.

Just south of Sparti, along the main road to Yithion, a road to the left runs through orange groves to a hillock with a chapel of Ayia Kyriaki. This, and not the modern village of Amyklai through which the main road passes, is the site of flowery **Amyklai**, where, in pre-Hellenic times, the cult of Apollo was practised. Later Amyklai was linked with Sparta by a sacred way, and the *Hyacinthia*, a national festival with melancholy associations, was celebrated there at the height of summer, a season of torrid heat and wilting flowers. The festival was in commemoration of one of the god's ill-starred love affairs: practising discus-throwing at Amyklai one day, Apollo inadvertently killed his favourite, Hyacinthos, when Zephyros, the jealous West Wind, who was also enamoured of the youth, deliberately blew Apollo's discus in the wrong direction so that it struck Hyacinthos on the head. The flower that grew from the soil watered by his blood was the first hyacinth, emblem of death. Now, in early spring, purplish-blue grape-hyacinths grow in clusters among the asphodel at Amyklai. A colossal Archaic statue of Apollo, seated on an ornate throne, the foundations of which lie under the present chapel, was famous throughout Greece. All that remains now is a Roman inscription, part of a votive gift offered by the Emperor Tiberius in memory of Hyacinthos, and a semi-circle of supporting wall running in an arc round the north-eastern side of the hill.

Therapne, probably of equal antiquity, is even more evocative in its commanding position. Just after the bridge over the Evrotas on the Tripolis road is the turn-off to the right for Yeraki. About four kilometres along that road, a track to the left mounts an escarpment covered with tall grass, brushwood and fruit trees, passes a chapel, and then climbs between gorse and broom interlaced with honeysuckle. The **Menelaion** is perched on a precipitous bluff above the orange groves bordering the gravelly bed of the Evrotas. The view is magnificent. To the north extends the upper valley of the river, powdery blue in the afternoon sun, its main stream of ice-cold water winding down from the saddle between Taiyetos and the Arcadian massif where it has its source. In the east roll the bleak Tsakonian hills, seamed with shallow ravines.

Ruined masonry from the shrine of Menelaos and Helen stands on three platforms, crowning the hill. Extending over the two lower terraces are Mycenaean remains, dating back to the fifteenth century BC, which were excavated by the British School of Archaeology in 1910 and in several recent years. The palace, similar to (although smaller than) the Palace of Nestor at Pylos, was destroyed by fire in 1200 BC. The site is dominated by the massive Menelaion itself, with a stylobate: a stepped, rectangular structure with three courses of enormous stone blocks. Tradition - confirmed by Pausanias - holds that it is the site of a temple of Menelaos which contained both his and Helen's tombs. Suppliants used to flock here: the men to implore Menelaos to grant them victory in battle, the women to beseech Helen to endow them with beauty.

Close by lay the Phoebaion (the site has not been identified), which contained a temple of the Dioscuri. Sacrifices were held here before the ceremonial fights designed by Lykurgos to harden the young men of Sparta. The nocturnal ceremony involved all-in wrestling fights between youths, with the contestants kicking, biting and gouging each other's eyes out. When the ceremony was over, the winners hurled the battered bodies of their opponents into the river; there were no half-measures in Lykurgos' toughening programme.

West of Sparti, on the Langada Pass road to Kalamata, the village of Tripi overhangs the plain on a buttress of Taiyetos. Onto one of these spiky rocks the Spartans used to hurl criminals and political prisoners. The only survivor was Aristomenes, the Messenian national hero, who had a miraculous escape. His fall was broken by a projecting ledge and he reached the bottom alive; clinging to the tail of a fox, he found his way out of the gloomy canyon and rejoined the Messenian patriots.

The **Langada Pass**, which crosses the spine of Taiyetos and descends towards Messenia through the most splendid mountain scenery in the Peloponnese, starts at Tripi. Beyond the village the road winds above a torrent between vertical cliffs; passing through a tunnel of rock, it weaves round towering bluffs and along narrow platforms blasted out of the limestone. Landslides and avalanches are common. In antiquity, Pausanias says all this country was 'well-stocked' with deer, boar and wild-goats - the black mountain-goat is still here, hopping from one dizzily perched ledge to another. After reaching the conifer belt and crossing from Lakonia into Messenia, the road enters a densely wooded valley, bowl-shaped, majestic in its proportions. The ground is covered with thick bracken and the air, even at the height of summer, is cool and bracing. On one occasion I remember that storm clouds suddenly blotted out the peaks, the rain pelted down and thunder ricocheted across the crater-shaped arena which is the heart of the Taiyetos range. Equally suddenly it was all over. The tiled roofs of two hamlets flashed like garnets; a pale rainbow in the west formed a tenuous arc from one pinnacled summit to another and the chestnut forests turned gold as shafts of sunlight pierced the scudding clouds.

The road then funnels into another narrow gorge and the descent begins, winding interminably between imprisoning heights. Slowly the walls of rock yawn open, the horizon widens and there are glimpses of green lowlands and a distant range of mountains crowned by a perfect 'Japanese' peak. The descent becomes more abrupt; hundreds of feet below, the town of Kalamata, dominated by the ruins of William de Villehardouin's castle, sprawls across the edge of the shimmering plain.

25

Medieval Cities.

IN THE THIRTEENTH CENTURY William de Villehardouin, most sympathetic and philhellenic of Frankish Princes of Achaea, built a strong fortress at **Mystra,** a spur of Mount Taiyetos. Although not his capital, it was William's favourite residence, from which he could dominate the Slav settlers in the valley of the Evrotas and the tribesmen of the Taiyetos range. (After the Slav invasions of the seventh century, the Lakonians had fled either south to the Mani or into the mountains; Slav blood is assumed to run in the veins of most present-day Spartans.) Looking down from the summit of the keep onto these fertile domains, enclosed by ranges of purple mountains, one understands why William felt so deeply about it and was heart-broken when, after his capture at the battle of Pelagonia by the forces of a renascent Byzantium, he was obliged to surrender Mystra as part of his ransom. The hill-town's brief but glorious history began at that moment. Today, unlike any other Byzantine site, it is an entire medieval walled city, where the main churches have been expertly restored and steep, narrow stairways climb between ruined chapels and roofless houses.

After William de Villehardouin's cession of the castle to the Emperor Michael VIII, Mystra began to grow in importance as a haven of Byzantine civilization in a rapidly dwindling empire. High-ranking officers came from Constantinople to command its garrison and, by the early fourteenth century, eminent architects were building lavishly-decorated churches. In 1348 the Emperor John VI appointed his son, Manuel Kantakouzenos, as governor of Mystra, with the title of Despot. During the thirty years of his Despotate, Manuel not only improved the living conditions of the Lakonian population but also encouraged church-building, created facilities for scholars, engaged book-illuminators to copy valuable manuscripts and promoted the collection and study of books. By the first half of the fifteenth century the city was a recognized seat of learning, frequented by scholars, sophists and courtiers; the analogy with an

Italian city of the Renaissance is not too far-fetched. Politically too, as the Turks drew the ring tighter round Constantinople, Mystra grew in importance to the Empire. Furthermore, never in its short heyday of fame was Mystra's history debased by the catalogue of political crime and assassination which punctuated that of Constantinople with such depressing regularity.

In 1449, when the end was near, Constantine XI Paleologos (Dragases), last and most heroic of Byzantine emperors, was crowned at Mystra. But it was all over by 1459 - six years after the fall of Constantinople. Under Turkish rule the town continued to be inhabited and, at one time, local pashas resided in the Palace of the Despots. They do not, however, appear to have turned any of the arcaded churches or princely mansions into harems or *hammams*.

Mystra was a brief flowering of the best qualities of Byzantine civilization, a last refuge of sanity and scholarship in a dying world. Today its fame rests mainly on its church frescoes, some of which are among the finest examples of late Byzantine painting. The Mystra frescoes are claimed by enthusiastic connoisseurs to be the purest reflection of the Hellenistic tradition continued in terms of Christian art (with additions of eastern mysticism and Oriental splendour), and to have influenced Giotto directly. Greek iconographers had certainly begun to emigrate to Italy by the fourteenth century and Giotto may well have been influenced by Byzantine models; but he never saw the Mystra frescoes, which were executed between 1330 and 1430 - that is to say, in the century following his death. The frescoes also possess undeniable evidence of Western influence and it was probably a case of two-way traffic, with Byzantine scholars visiting Italy in increasing numbers and, on returning to Constantinople and Mystra, passing on the lessons they had learnt in the West to local artists and architects.

At its worst, late Byzantine (or Paleologos) painting is illustrative and fussy; at its best, as in Mystra, it reveals the development of the twelfth-century desire to introduce a more naturalistic element into the representation of the Divine. Poses, gestures and attitudes are more relaxed, the manipulation of colours fresher and more subtle, attention to detail greater and the treatment of crowd scenes more dramatic. But what Paleologos painting gains in richness and variety, it loses in economy and sturdiness. The later trends, for all their exhilarating effect, sap the monumental vigour which is the glory of Dafni and Ossios Loukas. After Mystra, true Byzantine painting - whose inspiration had lasted a thousand years - died.

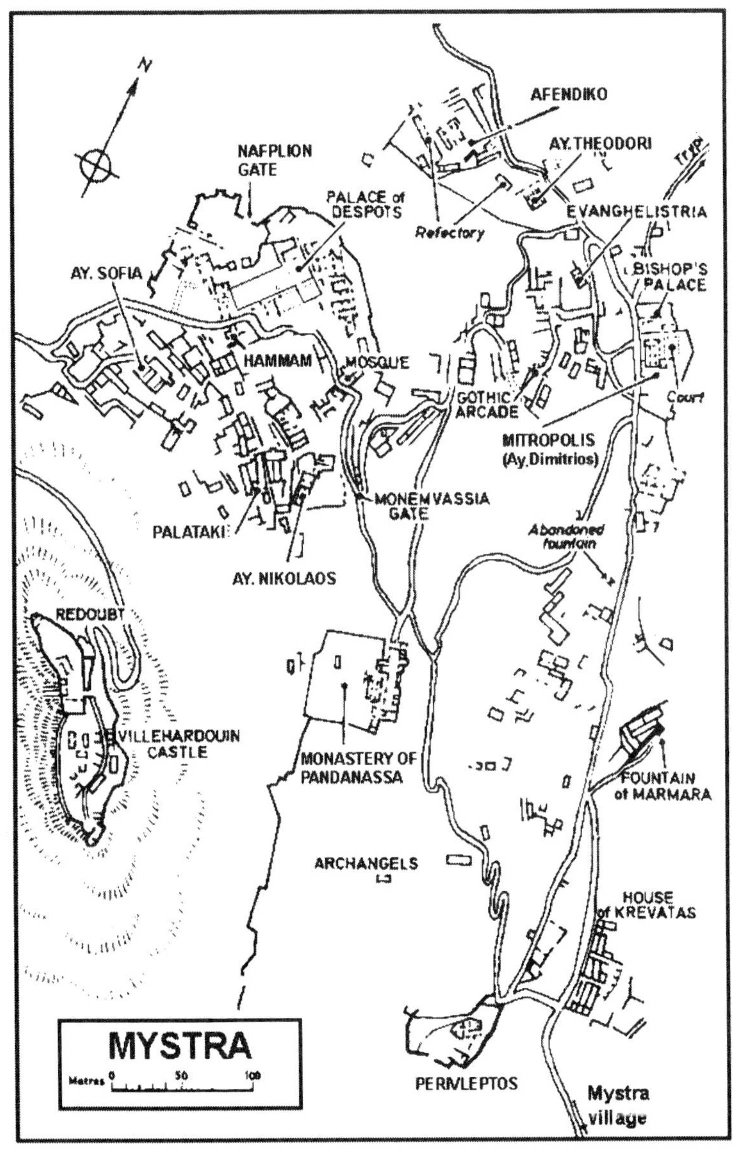
AFENDIKO
AY.THEODORI
NAFPLION GATE
PALACE of DESPOTS
EVANGHELISTRIA
Refectory
AY. SOFIA
BISHOP'S PALACE
HAMMAM
MOSQUE
GOTHIC ARCADE
Court
MITROPOLIS (Ay.Dimitrios)
MONEMVASSIA GATE
PALATAKI
Abandoned fountain
AY. NIKOLAOS
REDOUBT
VILLEHARDOUIN CASTLE
MONASTERY OF PANDANASSA
FOUNTAIN of MARMARA
ARCHANGELS
HOUSE of KREVATAS
MYSTRA
Metres 0 50 100
PERIVLEPTOS
Mystra village

Post-Byzantine art continued the tradition in other parts of the country, notably on Mount Athos, in Crete and the Ionian islands; but it is always a requiem - splendid, solemn and rather redundant.

The road from Sparti goes as far as the upper gate of the city from where a path leads to the Frankish castle. The usual entrance, however, is by the restored gate into the lower city, which is a warren of dereliction, with the empty shells of churches, houses and shops. A steep north-bound path leads to the **Mitropolis**, dedicated to St Dimitrios and first in rank, though not in artistic quality, among the churches of Mystra. A short, Roman-inspired three-aisled basilica, it is surmounted, as a result of later transformation, by a cross-in-square upper storey with five cupolas and a gallery on either side of the basilica aisles. This unusual plan, very rare elsewhere, derives from two other Mystra churches: the *Afendiko* and *Pandanassa.* It causes the churches, small as they are, to seem overcrowded and complex. The upper level, the Greek Cross, creates an air of loftiness within, which is absent from the outside. Here the celestial hierarchy is depicted in frescoes set out in strict conformity with the liturgical canons, and the whole is crowned by the central cupola where Christ reigns over the world. The lower level consists of aisles, side chapels, porches, arches and screens, all possessing a symbolic significance. These break up the main body of the church into different compartments and heighten the impression of complexity. This is deliberate, for Byzantine church-builders sought thereby to create a sense of mystery and religious awe.

The *Mitropolis* was built in the early fourteenth century and considerably altered in the fifteenth. The frescoes, some severely damaged, are rather stereotyped in style, but recent cleaning has disclosed the brilliance of the colours, as well as fresh details formerly overlaid by inferior works of later periods. The Last Judgement in the narthex is full of the usual horrors, including naked figures around which snakes are coiled. The marble columns on either side of the central nave support capitals, possibly taken from the debris of ancient Sparta, and a marble slab carved with the Byzantine double-headed eagle is popularly believed to indicate the spot where the last emperor stood during his coronation. The small adjacent episcopal palace houses a museum of local finds; the courtyard, surrounded by arcades, is a lovely, quiet place overlooking the plain, with the billowing foothills of Parnon forming a bluish barrier, full of shadows, in the east.

The next two churches, dependencies of the Monastery of the

Vrontohion, are small: overlooking the buildings adjoining the *Mitropolis* is the **Evanghelistria**'s high apse and octagonal drum, its four windows alternating with arched niches. In the simplicity of its single dome and inclined roofs, it seems almost out of place at Mystra. **Ayii Theodori**, the oldest church in Mystra (late thirteenth-century), is conspicuous for its large squat dome, perched, like a vast tea-cosy, above the confusion of planes created by various roof-levels and three three-sided apses with elaborate brickwork decoration around arched windows. The frescoes are very damaged.

To the north of *Ayii Theodori* is the rather showy **Afendiko**, dedicated to the Virgin *Odiyitria*: a mass of rounded forms, almost concentric in effect. Once the main church of the *Vrontohion* Monastery, the *Afendiko* is a sumptuous affair, with tall supporting buttresses, toy cupolas, barrel vaults, billowing apses, a succession of inclined roofs and a little loggia composed of three slender columns on the north side.

The interior plan is similar to that of the *Mitropolis*, which derives from it, but is grander. The frescoes are of better quality with the accent on movement, narration and dramatic incident. In the narthex, generally reserved for miracles, the Woman of Samaria stands between figures grouped on either side of the well where she is drawing water. The figures are relaxed and naturalistic, the drapery of their garments subtly shaded. In the north chapel of the narthex, nine martyrs of varying ages, their expressions devoid of the usual rigid tension, screen a host of other martyrs, whose haloes recede into an opaque haze. The chapel contains the tombs of the Despot Theodore II Paleologos and the Abbot Pahomios, founder of the church; the Abbot is portrayed in a fresco as a small and humble monk offering his foundation to an upright Virgin. The walls of the sombre south chapel, the so-called 'Chamber of the Chrysobulls', are lined with copies of the imperial charters listing the monastery's assets, which included entire villages and great tracts of the Peloponnese.

In the main nave a beautiful capital crowns the first column of the south colonnade and, in a diminutive south cupola, a portrait of the **Prophet Melchizedek** is framed within rolled leaves. It is a venerable head, with an expression of fierce intensity, the flesh standing out ivory-smooth against green and brown shading. He holds a golden scroll and the drapery of his garment is the colour of faded rose. A new and subtle use of colour is apparent in this portrait. One of the objects in using a wider range of colours was to heighten the human quality of the faces; the head of Melchizedek is a landmark in this process.

In the centre of the Greek Cross, Christ reigns in glory, worshipped by apostles with conventional expressions of awe. Below the celestial plane, figures of saints and prophets in garments of brown and old gold are scattered across vaults and outer aisles.

Leaving the lower town, you now take the steep path which winds up through the double-arched Monemvassia Gate to the aristocratic quarter, where the Despot dwelt. The size alone of the **Palace of the Despots** is proof of the splendour and solemnity with which the Despots surrounded themselves. The L-shaped palace occupies a wide ledge of the mountainside and looks down towards the valley through which the Evrotas flows between ranges of foothills. A mass of ruined chambers dating from the mid-thirteenth century to the late fourteenth, mostly built by the first Despot, Manuel Kantakouzenos, are ranged along the east wing, where the remains of a little Turkish mosque strike a somewhat incongruous note in a setting which could not be less Oriental.

The west wing of the palace (built later by the Paleologos Despots and now handsomely restored) is more impressive, with its superimposed storeys: first a vaulted ground floor, then a low-ceilinged first floor with eight chambers which do not intercommunicate and finally a long, rectangular top storey consisting of a throne-room with shallow apses in the walls and stone seats for dignitaries under arched windows; here were held large public gatherings, attended by the social and intellectual élite of Mystra. Higher still are successive rows of square and round windows through which diagonal shafts of light fell upon the assembled court. On the outer façade of the east wing, a narrow projecting balcony, supported by six great arches, overlooks the Evrotas valley. It is rare in Greece to find such a finely-preserved piece of lay architecture.

South of the palace, near the small Church of *Ayios Nikolaos*, is the shell of a large mansion known as the *Palataki* (the Little Palace), residence of one of the leading local families and once having numerous arcades, balconies and interior stairways. The tower on the south side is rich in brickwork decoration and even in its present state, as a jumble of insecure masonry, the *Palataki* succeeds in conveying the impression of a great town residence, where the good life was led and where rich men and women dwelt in cultivated ease, waited on by well-trained attendants.

Higher up from the *Palataki*, the attractive little Church of *Ayia*

Sofia crowns a ledge below the castle. It was a palace chapel built in the mid-fourteenth century by the Despot Manuel, whose coat-of-arms is carved on a marble slab. The entrance is through an unusually large domed narthex and the historiated pavement is the most lavish in Mystra. The architectural arrangement is the usual maze of naves, chapels and galleries; the frescoes are negligible. The charming belfry above the north gallery was transformed into a minaret during the Turkish occupation.

A steep, twisting path leads up to the keep of the **Castle** built by William de Villehardouin in the mid-thirteenth century. Born in Greece, he loved the country and governed his part of it, the Morea, better than any other Frankish prince. But his education, outlook and way of life were French. At Mystra, where he established a school of chivalry famous throughout Europe, he was protected by a bodyguard of a thousand horsemen, who must have presented an alien spectacle to the inhabitants of the plain when they rode out with the Prince to visit some neighbouring vassal, their lances crowned with pennons fluttering above the dusty olive branches.

The outer gate of the Castle is on the north-west side. A vaulted passage leads through the curtain wall into the outer bailey. The path ascends again to the inner bailey. To the left is a vaulted cistern; used in times of siege, it still contains a pool of slimy water. Beyond the cistern, a round tower commands an immense prospect of the plain. Higher up still extends the rubble of the irregular, oval keep. Its rounded bastions are all Frankish, with a few Byzantine and Turkish additions. On the wind-swept summit, between stone slabs eroded into strange pock-marked forms, wild flowers grow. To the west, the rock falls away sheer into a deep and wild ravine.

Back down at the Monemvassia Gate, another path slants to the south towards a narrow terrace where the **Monastery of the Pandanassa**, with its pretty bell-tower, is flanked by cypresses. The *Pandanassa* is the most homely place in Mystra and it is still inhabited - by nuns. Films, colour slides, post-cards and guidebooks are on sale in the guest house. The courtyard is full of flowers.

The *Pandanassa* may be small but there is a great deal to see; an hour is well spent. Take the exterior first. Founded in 1428 by the Despot's first minister, the church is architecturally a replica of the *Afendiko* but on a smaller scale, with very high two-storey apses. Both levels are arcaded, with windows and blind arches, and they are separated by a frieze in the form of a garland, painted blue and red. Even the belfry at the extremity of the east façade has arched porticoes on its two upper storeys and is crowned by an elliptical dome. The whole thing is a riot of warm, red-brick curves.

Passing through a doorway ornamented with Cufic designs, one enters the church, a basilica with a cross-in-square upper storey, a plan peculiar to Mystra. The six marble columns which divide the aisles are crowned by capitals with floral designs, combining the Ionic and Corinthian orders. The light is dim and the space confined - the anonymous painters of the *Pandanassa* must have had an agonizing task trying to condense the whole of Heaven and Earth into this maze of little cupolas, shallow pendentives and slender barrel vaults. The most important compositions are high up on the cross-in-square level and it is not always easy to view them from a satisfactory angle.

These frescoes are roughly contemporary with the foundation of the Monastery. In the variety and treatment of costume, drapery and facial expression, in the lavish architectural backgrounds and, above all, in the startling range of colour, the artists of these crowded compositions seem to have turned their backs on the majestic severity of the eleventh and twelfth centuries. The perspective is still halting, the drawing often awkward, but the artists who worked here (like those of the Cretan school) were clearly trying to achieve a new liveliness and animation. In so doing they were, in a sense, precursors to the religious art destined to flourish on Mount Athos, in Serbia, in Russia and in Crete itself, during the sixteenth century. If the frescoes of the *Pandanassa* are the swan-song of strictly Byzantine fresco art, they are also an important stage in the evolution of religious painting in Eastern Europe.

The greatest compositions are those from the *Dodekaorton*. Take the **Ascension** first, in the vault above the altar. Two groups of apostles, centred round the figures of the Virgin and Archangel respectively, gaze upwards in awe. The Archangel, one of the most idealized portraits in Byzantine painting, might almost be a forerunner to the celestial beings that swirl across the roof of the Sistine Chapel.

The acknowledged masterpiece is the **Raising of Lazarus**, in the vault of the north arm of the cross. The scene is dominated by the tragic corpse; it is flanked by a moving and naturalistic weeping figure and by a man vigorously unwinding the opaque and mouldering shroud; within the limits imposed on him by tradition and convention, the artist has succeeded in conveying the dramatic anticipation inherent in the situation. The **Entry into Jerusalem**, in the vault of the eastern arm, is another favourite. Although the composition suffers from excessive overcrowding, the range of its hues is incomparable: amid a riot of colour, Christ rides into the city on a snow-white donkey, while the children play along the path before him and the elders of the city advance to meet him.

The very damaged **Nativity** in the vault of the south arm of the cross recalls in its detail more than one Giottoesque representation of the same scene: the crib, the animals, the dashing yet stylized horses on which the Magi, in green and yellow cloaks, are mounted. As a composition, it is more quaint than moving; but the figure pouring water from the pitcher is very compelling. In the **Annunciation** (also in the south vault), against an opulent, palatial background broken by porphyry columns, the angel, whose face is damaged beyond repair, is borne on outstretched wings painted in metallic greens and yellows tinged with a softening grey; the marble floor is deep pink, and at the angel's feet a striped quail drinks from a pool fed by a pineapple-shaped fountain. In a little north-west cupola there is a particularly impressive head of a bishop: a dark mass painted entirely in green and purple, the light provided (in the Byzantine manner) by a series of white brush-strokes which follow the wrinkles of the brow and the matted strands of the beard.

From the *Pandanassa* the path zigzags down the hill. This must have been a populous residential quarter; now scattered with the ruins of private houses, it includes that of Ioannis Frangopoulos, the founder of the *Pandanassa*, which has a balcony supported by arches, a vaulted basement and a water cistern.

At the end of the incline, the small, early fourteenth-century **Church of the Perivleptos** (The Resplendent One), shelters in a pine wood. It is a plain cross-in-square edifice with architectural adaptations necessitated by the sharp declivity of the ground. Like the *Pandanassa*, it once formed part of a monastic establishment, but there is none of the prettiness of the *Pandanassa*, and more Byzantine austerity. The apses are not arched and they have no brick-work decoration. The frescoes, some of the most important in Mystra, are probably the work of two artists and those of the inferior one are easily distinguished by their oleograph-like quality; but the good frescoes are very good indeed, radiating sobriety and dignity in the best traditions of Constantinopolitan taste. At the *Pandanassa* the artists' *joie de vivre* and their desire to express the beauty of the physical world are uppermost; at the *Perivleptos* their predecessor blurred his colour tones, making his transitions less clearly defined, thus achieving a greater idealism. The artist's predilection for a luminous dark blue sets the tone immediately - a cool, solemn grandeur. The best-preserved frescoes are in the aisles and apses. In the sanctuary vault a tight-lipped, shrewish Virgin *Orans* stands between two archangels with tender expressions, while the apostles in bold, contorted attitudes gaze up at the wonder of the **Ascension**, and four angels in flowing drapery support the portrait of Christ. In the central apse the Virgin, in a more tender mood, sits enthroned holding the Child, painted in gold, flanked again by archangels. In the north apse, unfortunately very badly lit, unfolds the superb **Divine Liturgy**, a masterpiece of hieraticism, in which russet-haired angels with green wings, clad in long white vestments, carry the bread and wine for the Eucharist against a background of intense dark blue; in spite of the solemnity of the procession, the attitudes of the angels are natural and relaxed. Equally impressive is the figure of St John Chrysostom with a gentle, sensitive expression, wearing ceremonial vestments and unfolding a scroll.

Next come the scenes from the *Dodekaorton*: the **Transfiguration** in the western arm of the cross, with its red-headed Christ in a white robe with orange tints; the **Crucifixion** in the south arm of the cross, with its variety of costumes; the tragic Virgin in the **Descent from the Cross**, which betrays Sienese influences; the Virgin again, this time a reclining figure, in the **Nativity** (south arm), brooding and sullen, as though stunned by the momentous event that has just befallen her, watched by angels with expressions of wonderment.

The *Perivleptos* frescoes remain among the great masterpieces of Byzantine art; thereafter, the feeling of elegance and elaboration, so pronounced at the *Pandanassa*, increases; but in the process the inspiration has become blurred.

Descending from the *Perivleptos* to the road, one passes the ruined mansion of Krevatas, a local dignitary of the eighteenth century; Mystra, or at least the lower city, was thus still inhabited by people of consequence only two centuries ago. Below it, as the hill slopes more gently into the plain, extended the Turkish quarter of Mufteika where Ottoman officials dwelt. It is only a few minutes' walk from here to the hotel in the modern village of Mystra.

After Mystra, the churches at Hryssafa and Yeraki are an anticlimax, though the setting, among the scrub-covered hills of Parnon, presents a new aspect of Lakonia, more rugged and remote. The sturdy churches and country chapels with their interior walls covered with frescoes, some painted by local iconographers, seem to sprout out of the stones of the Parnon country. Like Taiyetos, Parnon is a range rather than a mountain. The two ranges run parallel to each other but Parnon, unlike Taiyetos, is composed of detached, amorphous masses. Stony, covered in brushwood and sparsely populated, much of it is dotted with wild almond trees, twisted into contorted shapes by the north wind that blows across the plateau in winter.

Just to the north of Sparti, after crossing the Evrotas on the Tripolis road, there is a turning to the right for Yeraki. Very shortly the **Hryssafa** road turns off to the left, mounting slowly between escarpments of red Lakonian earth. Looking back, Taiyetos recedes and the whole splendour of the range, as it tapers southward into the final extremity, the Mani, is seen in proper perspective - a great bluish, snow-capped spine severing the Southern Peloponnese. In front, the folds of Parnon run in irregular seams towards the Lakonian Gulf. On reaching the village it is essential to ask at the café who has the keys of the churches - usually the priest, who may be able to take you round. The straggling village and the fields below it are dotted with churches dating from the fourteenth century onwards; in late medieval times Hryssafa must have been a prosperous community. The four main churches are typical of Lakonian provincial art in the late Byzantine period. The first two are in the village itself: on the top of the hill *Ayios Dimitrios*, the usual domed cross-in-square, with a seventeenth-century narthex, its blackened frescoes creating a sombre effect, possessing a good post-Byzantine icon of Christ *Elkomenos* (Christ being dragged); and lower down the fourteenth-century *Koimesis*, smaller and less elegant than *Ayios Dimitrios*, with a hideous modern *iconostasis* and frescoes that have been restored as far as possible but are still difficult to make out - a big torch would be handy. The two most important outlying churches - half an hour's walk across the undulating upland - are *Ayios Ioannis Prodromos*, where there is a fine Transfiguration, with Christ clad in dull yellow garments ascending to Heaven in a pink cloud, and the *Hryssafiotissa* which was once a small monastery.

The road on to Yeraki can be reached from Hryssafa. To the north is the high-lying plateau of Tsakonia, with hardly a village worthy of the name; the few inhabitants are called Tsakonians, a race of which little is known, probably Slav in origin, wild and independent, some still speaking a dialect of their own.

Yeraki lies at the foot of a bare hill, near the site of ancient Geronthrai, a Spartan township, where an annual festival was held in honour of the god of war. Its Frankish castle formed part of the string of fortresses, running in a rough horseshoe (west-north-east), that protected the fertile Lakonian valley. *Yeraki* in Greek means falcon: a legacy of the days when French knights, hawks perched on their gloved hands, cantered across the bleak countryside to hunt woodcock and pigeon. It is essential to find the *fylakas*, for the churches are scattered among almond orchards around the village and up the castle hill. If the *fylakas* is already taking people round you might have a long wait, unless someone can tell you approximately where to catch up with him. When the castle of Yeraki passed from the Franks to the Byzantines after the battle of Pelagonia, it obviously remained a strategic stronghold; a small town grew up around it and a number of churches were built. Unlike Mystra, however, Yeraki was no cosmopolitan centre, no seat of learning. The churches are very small, their architecture and faded wall-paintings mostly provincial. First is *Ayios Ioannis Hryssostomos*, a barrel-vaulted church with a single nave and apse. The south exterior has some haphazardly-arranged decoration - bricks mixed with inlaid stone slabs - which creates an odd but not unattractive effect. More slabs round the main doorway form an impressive frame for this modest entrance to an even more modest interior. The exterior walls of *Ayios Sostis* (The Saviour) are decorated with the same inlaid slabs. In the fields below the village lies *Ayii Theodori* - its walls again inlaid with inscribed slabs - and *Ayios Nikolaos*, now inhabited by bats, with faint traces of painting (probably rather good late thirteenth-century work).

Returning to the village along paths between stone walls, there is the *Evanghelistria*, a little cruciform church in a cypress grove. Although the cylindrical drum is disproportionately tall, it is balanced by still-taller cypresses. Some of the frescoes are in a fair state of preservation: in the cupola, a Pantocrator with glowing eyes; a Transfiguration in the barrel vault above the sanctuary.

From the *Evanghelistria* the road continues and then there is a climb up the steep hill, covered with prickly holm-oaks, to the castle, one of the hundred and twenty-two that once crowned the strategic heights of the Morea. A whole side of the hill is scattered with interesting small churches and the ruins of Byzantine buildings, though these were never, unlike those at Mystra, the dwellings of an aristocracy, either of class or of wealth. The castle ramparts are poorly preserved, except on the south side. The thyme-scented keep is entered from the south-west through an arch. At the north end of the enceinte is a postern. More interesting is the triple Church of *Ayios Yeoryios*, near the main gateway; Frankish in origin - one of the few that remain in Greece - it bears a coat-of-arms over the arched entrance: a shield decorated with chequers. Within the church, and framing a modern icon, there is a little stone shrine with two knotted columns supporting a Gothic arch carved with stars, fleur-de-lys and a coat-of-arms. Nothing could seem more incongruous than this crude piece of Gothic sculpture in the ruined chapel overlooking the sun-scorched Tsakonian wilderness.

The road from Sparti to Monemvassia, which can easily be joined from Yeraki, is the Yithion road for 28 kilometres. Running first through flat, then undulating, country, it then crosses the rush-bordered Evrotas and the plain of Sikia, covered with dense orchards of fig trees. After climbing a range of lonely hills the road then descends abruptly to the barren east coast of Lakonia, with the rock of **Monemvassia** squatting elephantine at the southern extremity of a crescent-shaped bay (where Pausanias found the prettiest-coloured pebbles he had ever seen).

From Monemvassia came Malmsey wine and the first, the inevitable, association is with the butt of Malmsey in which the Duke of Clarence was drowned in 1478. Today, however, there is no sign of the grapes from which the most highly-prized wine in medieval Europe was pressed. When, in 1540, the Venetians surrendered the keys of Monemvassia, the last Christian fortress to hold out against the Turks, they removed not only their garrison and artillery, but also many of the inhabitants, who wished to settle in other Venetian colonies: in Crete, Santorini, Corfu and Dalmatia. As they left, the Monemvassians dug up the vines, which they replanted in their new homes; a sweet, amber-coloured wine, now produced on the volcanic island of Santorini, is said to be the nearest thing to medieval Malmsey.

The situation is remarkable, with the walled town lying at the foot of a formidable, reddish-coloured rock which turns violet in the afternoon sun. It is joined to the mainland by a narrow causeway - *i moni emvasis* ('the only entrance'): hence its name, Monemvassia. Lying on the main trade route between Italy and the Levant, its strategic value was once considerable. Wisely governed under

Komnenos rule in the eleventh and twelfth centuries, the inhabitants enjoyed rights and privileges unknown elsewhere in Greece, and were renowned for their sense of civic responsibility. Monemvassia's trading vessels ranged all over the Eastern Mediterranean and its sailors were among the most experienced in the imperial fleet.

As the Frankish conquest swept over Greece, Monemvassia was a formidable obstacle in the way of William de Villehardouin's domination of the Morea. The siege lasted three years and the garrison was reduced to a diet of cats and mice. To effect the final reduction, William had to invoke the aid of the Dukes of Athens and Naxos, the Baron of Evvia and Count Orsini of Kefallinia, as well as the Venetian fleet - an impressive force. But the French did not stay long. Eleven years after Monemvassia's capture, William suffered his humiliating defeat at Pelagonia and was forced to cede it as part of his ransom to the Byzantine emperor.

Once under Byzantine rule, Monemvassia became an important bishopric and again a flourishing commercial centre. The Emperor Michael VIII was so impressed that he granted the merchants fiscal exemptions and the great squat rock, with its impregnable fortress, now towered above a port filled with vessels flying the flags of Byzantium, Venice, Genoa and Amalfi.

After the fall of Constantinople, when Sultan Mehmet II was overrunning the Morea, his greatest ambition was to reduce the 'violet rock' as the Turks called Monemvassia; yet even he, brilliant tactician that he was, refrained from attacking it, having a profound respect for the tradition of courage and endurance established by its inhabitants. While he was hesitating, the Monemvassians sought the protection of the Pope, whose local representative was a Catalan corsair. Soon growing resentful, however, of Pius II's attempts to extend his spiritual sway over this stronghold of Orthodoxy, they turned out the papal agents, including the Spanish corsair, and placed their fate in the hands of a less bigoted Catholic power, the Serene Republic. The Venetians ruled wisely and tolerantly. Affluence and the special privileges enjoyed by the merchants under Byzantine rule returned. The rock, isolated, remained a bastion of Christianity on a Moslem shore. By 1540, with Ottoman power reaching its zenith, Venice was no longer able to supply and maintain her maritime forces and Monemvassia, like Nafplion, surrendered to the army of Suleiman the Magnificent. The loss of the two fortresses marked the end of Venetian colonial influence in mainland Greece and the banner of the Lion of St Mark disappeared from the mainland. There was a respite in 1690 when, following Morosini's expedition, the Venetians recaptured Monemvassia, to the joy of the inhabitants; but in 1715 the Turks returned and the curtain came down on Monemvassia. The buildings fell into ruin, the inhabitants lapsed into illiteracy, the birth-rate dropped and commerce languished. When the War of Independence broke out in 1821, Monemvassia was the first fortress in the Morea to be liberated by the Greeks.

The remains of the once-flourishing port are strung out along a narrow ledge between the 'violet rock' and the sea. A small town with several hotels has grown up on the mainland, where the vineyards once extended. Across the causeway, under the perpendicular cliff, the old town faces seaward and is approached through a vaulted passage forming part of a triangular bastion. To the left of the passage a stairway leads up to the parapet. Parallel walls run down to the sea, enclosing the town on its east and west sides. The rectangle is completed by the vertical cliff to the north and by a sea-wall, along which one can stroll, to the south. Within the walled enclosure there is no wheeled traffic. In summer, boats and hydrofoils from Piraeus call regularly at the port.

A narrow alley, which is the main street, ends in a small square, from where a Turkish cannon points out to sea. To the south, the last spurs of Parnon run into Cape Maleas, whose wild and rocky coast was the terror of ancient sailors. On the east side of the square is the seventeenth-century Church of Christ *Elkomenos*, restored and whitewashed, built on the site of a more ancient foundation. The church was once the home of a famous icon of 'Christ being dragged', which was considered so holy and so beautiful that Emperor Isaac II Angelos removed it to Constantinople. The church has lost another icon more recently: following the theft and recovery of a number of artistic treasures, the Byzantine Museum in Athens has retained a fine icon of the Crucifixion - supposedly until the church makes better security arrangements. Two pilasters with Corinthian-style capitals frame the main doorway and, above the lintel, there is a cornice with a decorative design in which two peacocks, facing outwards, perform an awkward but animated dance. Above the *Elkomenos* is the more severe pile of the fourteenth century Church of the *Myrtiotissa*, with its shapely dome. The interior is as bare as the exterior, whose stonework presents a blotchy, grey-brown surface - very forbidding after the extravagance of Mystra.

Further east is the Church of *Ayios Nikolaos*, austere and

structurally almost identical to the *Myrtiotissa*, mud-grey in colour and with the same sturdy architectural lines. The *Hryssafiotissa* (The Virgin of Hryssafa) near the sea, is more modern (early seventeenth-century), ugly and whitewashed, with a huge tea-cosy dome; in the minds of Lakonian peasants, however, to whom the dividing line between religion, superstition and folklore is often tenuous, this church holds a special place, for it contains a chapel in which the famous flying icon of Hryssafa was found. The Virgin herself indicated the spot - a water-well, which still exists - in a dream to an old woman. The icon, it was said, had flown of its own volition from Hryssafa to Monemvassia at the Virgin's command. The inhabitants of Hryssafa had doubts, however, about the mechanics of the miraculous flight. Suspecting foul play, they came to Monemvassia on some specious pretext and stole back the icon. Again it flew, like a homing pigeon, across the Tsakonian mountains to its new abode. In the end the people of Hryssafa accepted a substitute icon presented by the triumphant Monemvassians, who kept the disputed one. The holy image's nocturnal flights ceased forthwith.

Below the *Hryssafiotissa*, the south rampart is well-preserved and it is possible to walk along the entire length of the sea-wall, which is slit with gun embrasures. Equally well-preserved is the long, descending line of the east wall (from the cliff face to the sea). Beyond it there is nothing but rocks, waves and a lighthouse, with the crenellated fortress towering three hundred metres above.

The **Fortress** or upper town is approached by a path which zigzags up the cliff, passing under a large arched gatehouse with a sentry post commanding a lofty view of the domed churches and houses below. At intervals the parapet is cut with arrow slits, but it is difficult to imagine how an invader could have contemplated scaling the perpendicular rock. One passes through a second arched passage to enter the upper town. Above the main arch is a plaque inscribed with the words 'Christ reigns here'. The iron-plated doors are studded with nails and prison cells line one side of the vaulted passage. Emerging into the open, you face a slope covered with the debris of barracks, cisterns and guardrooms. A crenellated wall encircles the summit, except on the north side where the cliff is sheer. The bastions and a square fort are Byzantine structures. The shell of one house bears a Venetian coat-of-arms and the Lion of St Mark is carved on a well-head. The rest of the fortifications, choked with thistles, spurge and thyme, are Turkish; in summer the scent of scorched herbs is overpowering. A wild fig tree points the way to the **Church of Ayia Sofia** on a final crowning terrace. Previously believed to have been founded at the end of the thirteenth century by the Emperor Andronikos II, an untiring patron of religious art, it is now thought to be much older. It was built on a similar plan to that of the church at Dafni, an elaboration of the cross-in-square plan - the east end is considerably narrowed by the creation of small apsed chapels on either side. The other three arms of the Greek cross are narrowed to conform, with rectangular spaces at the four corners of the enclosing square. *Ayia Sofia* is lofty in conception and majestic in its proportions. Above the entrance, a marble slab depicts two lambs and two doves. The interior is very bare: some fragmentary frescoes on the squinches and in the narthex; Christ, rather better-preserved, holding an open Book of Gospels above the main apse; a cornice with carvings along the divisions separating the narthex and nave. In its adornment *Ayia Sofia* is negligible, in its proportions it is in the best traditions of Byzantine architecture.

To the north, the crescent-shaped bay with its long ribbon of sand is dominated by the heights on which the Argives founded the colony of Epidauros Limera. Immediately below, the cliff is fringed with black spiky rocks flecked with the spray of breaking waves.

Monemvassia has an excellent anchorage for yachts and the mainland beach, two kilometres from the modern town, is superb. Recently, new life has been brought into the dereliction of the old town by Athenians and foreigners who have restored many of the narrow three-storied houses. Some of the once-abandoned towers have been transformed into shops and little bars, their Venetian stonework self-consciously festooned with fishing-nets and strung with conches, but at least the place is alive again.

26

The Mani.

THE MANI OFFERS NO ANTIQUITIES and little mythology; Pausanias scrabbled among some ruined shrines, but they failed to arouse his enthusiasm. The peninsula, the southernmost point of mainland Europe after Spanish Tarifa, projects like a misshapen fang, flanked by two others, into the Eastern Mediterranean. Its history is that of a small, but important, section of the Greek people: descendants of the ancient Spartans, with a strong dash of Slav blood. Fiercely independent, their warlike virtues inspired considerable dread in the Sultan's armies and their passion for fratricidal strife persuaded the Sublime Porte that costly operations to subdue them were quite unnecessary. For centuries the treeless plateaux and boulder-strewn ravines echoed to the crack of pistol shots fired by feuding families. Swathed in bandoliers and armed with *yataghans*, axes and muskets, they rode out of their towers - all houses worthy of the name possessed their protective towers: tall, rectangular obelisks of grey stone - not to till the fields or tend the vines but to kill their neighbours in the next village; the great Maniot families lived by the rule of blood and iron. In the eighteenth century they were granted official autonomy, thus securing a privileged status in the Ottoman Empire. The Mani may not be in the mainstream of Greek history, but for anyone anxious to peep through a little chink into the fascinating enigma of the Greek character, it is immensely rewarding.

For the lover of landscape, the Mani is one of the most exciting experiences in Greece. Geographically, it divides into two distinct regions: the Outer Mani (or Messenian Mani), its deep, fertile gullies overhung by precipitous crags, lying north of a line running from the Bay of Itylo in the west to Ayeranos in the east; and the Inner or Deep Mani, the southern part of the peninsula which, right down to the tip of Cape Tenaro (also known as Cape Matapan), is a scorched land of rocky plateaux, shaded only by ferocious, barren slopes - bold, angular and in the grand style.

Starting from Sparti in the morning, one can drive across the central spine, down to the southernmost part of the mainland and then up along the spectacular west coast, reaching Kalamata in the evening, but a little more time would be well spent.

The Mani begins at **Yithion**, once the naval base of Sparta, terraced on a hill overlooking the bay. The houses are colour-washed cream, pink and lemon-yellow. To the south of the once-busy harbour, a causeway joins the waterfront to a flattish, pine-covered islet, now called Marathonisi (Fennel Island), with a chapel built on the foundations of an ancient temple. It is not in the least striking, yet this is Homer's **Kranai**, where Helen and Paris spent the first night of their journey from Sparta to Troy. Everything else about Yithion pales before the thought of that delirious night under the stars at Kranai.

From Yithion the road winds inland through vineyards, olive groves and fields of maize bordered by agaves and cypresses. The sea disappears behind a screen of hills. The spine of Taiyetos draws nearer and the road enters a canyon of reddish rock with vestiges of crenellations lining the ridge to the left. At the exit from the canyon the scene comes properly into focus: the crenellated ridge forms part of a hill, fringed by vineyards and crowned by the remains of the Frankish castle of **Passava** (so-called from the French war-cry '*passe avant*'). The castle, thirteenth century stronghold of Jean de Neuilly, hereditary marshal of the principality of Achaea, commanded the Lakonian Gulf in the east and the route over southern Taiyetos in the west. It takes half an hour to climb up to the ruins through dense bushes of arbutus and brushwood - the path starts to the south-west of the hill. The centre of the *enceinte* is empty, except for the roofless shell of a chapel choked with prickly shrubs; but there is a spectacular walk along the west battlements, with narrow slits in alternate embrasures overlooking the chasm which the fortress was intended to defend against unruly Maniots.

In the mid-fourteenth century Passava fell to the Byzantines, later to the Turks and to the Venetians. The latter abandoned the castle, believing they could guard the pass equally well from Yithion. Passava is one of the few strictly historical sites in the Mani. Seen in the afternoon light, with the woods and vineyards reflecting a lambent serenity, it is an idyllic place. Ahead lies little that can be so described.

The road now follows a narrow valley. In summer feathery branches of agnus castus, flecked with pale blue blooms, straggle among bright pink oleanders along the banks of dried-up torrent beds, where the heat seems trapped in an almost palpable stillness. The valley alternately widens and narrows. Beyond the village of Vahos the aridity becomes more pronounced. The saddle has been crossed. The Messenian Gulf opens up in the west, Taiyetos is to the north, and a chain of slate-grey mountains - angular, geometric and desiccated - extends southward. The road dips and bends between low stone walls, enclosing plots of red earth from which stunted trees sprout in twisted, dwarf-like shapes; finally it reaches the town of **Areopolis**, spreading across a small plain high above the sea. The road up the western coast turns off just before the town.

Originally called Tsimova, it was renamed Areopolis (the city of Ares, the god of war) in the early nineteenth century by the head of the most bellicose clan in the Mani, the Mavromihalis (the 'Black Michaels'), later destined to provide Greek cabinets with eminent ministers. The Mavromihalis and their exploits have passed into Greek folklore. The men, armed to the teeth with knives, *yataghans* and finely chased carbines, were said to possess a virile, god-like beauty, with bushy eyebrows and huge black moustaches. One of them, Petrobey, brought the greatest lustre to the name of Black Michael during the War of Independence: having managed, in the national interest, to effect a truce between the warring clans, he was able to lead three thousand united Maniots to enforce the surrender of the Turkish camp at Kalamata. During the war he fought in forty-nine battles and was regarded as a reincarnation of Ares. However, when peace came, he succumbed to the heady delights of political intrigue, fell out with Capodistria, whose rank of head of state he coveted, and was thrown into prison. For this intolerable insult to Maniot honour, his nephews assassinated Capodistria at Nafplion and the entire population of the Mani rose in revolt against the first government of the new Greek state.

Areopolis is the provincial capital of the Mani, a busy, sun-drenched little town; but a hush seems to have fallen on the place. The hoarse shouts, the orders and the blasphemies, the neighing of prancing horses and the shots fired in the air now echo only in the imagination. Although one sees here the first examples of one of its distinctive features - the tower-houses - the Mani is no longer very different from the rest of the Peloponnese.

The centre of Areopolis is a minute square distinguished by the **Church of the Taxiarhi** (The Archangels), a domed, single-nave basilica with a tall, tapering belfry of dazzling white, and exterior decoration which is a masterpiece of local, traditional fantasy; the general effect of whiteness is heightened too by the lime-washed trunks of acacia trees on the raised platform of the church. The decoration of the apse starts with a course of pink rosettes from which rise five pilasters in shallow relief, their capitals joined by arches. Above these runs a fairy-tale frieze of seraphim and grinning, beady-eyed suns with rays like hedgehog prickles. The signs of the zodiac are represented by prancing animals.

The bas-relief above the main doorway has, in the centre, a shield resting on the breast of a Byzantine double-headed eagle, with rich plumage and outstretched claws, flanked by two lions rampant; below the eagle, a scroll between two large rosettes bears the date 1798 and above the bird, two sun-disks stare with enormous round eyes; on either side stand the Archangels, one holding a sword, the other a cross. The frieze of rosettes is crowned by a sphinx-like face emerging from a crescent moon; on either side, two perky birds with staring faces are almost Archaic in their tense immobility of expression. Folk art, applied to church architecture, is sometimes monotonous, even boring. Not so at Areopolis. The mind that conceived the exterior church decoration had a sense of both humour and fantasy; the whole composition is an extraordinary, if crude, example of vigour, imagination and expressive force. But what does it all mean?

No less striking is the bas-relief above the south doorway. Again we have the Archangels with the military saints, George and Theodore, on either side. Above the frieze of rosettes, the Dove and the Hand of God are framed within more rosettes. Throughout, the emphasis is on the warlike character of the Archangels, patrons of the main church of a town which was an arsenal dedicated to the god of war. The interior of the church is without special interest.

A few minutes' walk from the Church of the Archangels lies the more conventional Church of *Ayios Ioannis Prodromos*. The interior walls of this small, barrel-vaulted, single-chamber chapel are covered with monkish frescoes. The figures have enormous faces with bulging eyes, out of all proportion to their puny bodies. There is no lack of animation in the scenes of miracles and martyrdoms (for instance, St Peter being crucified upside down) and a charming effect is created by the decorative stars and rosettes on the dark blue robes of a rather plebeian-looking Christ on the *iconostasis*.

South of Areopolis the Deep Mani begins. The last formidable spurs of Taiyetos plunge through a series of wild ravines into the sea. These are the **Kakovounia (The Evil Mountains)** - dramatic in their forms and stark in their aridity, their pyramidal peaks, sudden vertical declivities and huge sheets of limestone belonging to a nightmare world. In the middle of the day their colour is that of molten lead; in the afternoon they turn beige, in the evening mauve. The Evil Mountains are well-named.

Near **Pyrgos Dirou**, at Triandafyllia, is the church of *Ayios Petros,* pre-twelfth century. Maniot church-builders, though working far from the centres of culture, were quick to pick up the latest trends. In the dry, stony country between Pyrgos Dirou and Yerolimena there are a number of Byzantine chapels and churches, mostly dating from the eleventh to the thirteenth century, some decorated with the exterior brickwork revetments that had, by then, come into fashion. Apart from a few exceptions these churches are of interest to the specialist, rather than to the average traveller, but they emphasise the power exercised by the Byzantine Church over the remotest regions of the Empire. They also indicate that the country must have been relatively thickly populated before the great vendettas of the Turkish occupation. Some of the churches have interesting wall paintings, but most of these are locked. For information about the keys, contact the *Eforia* of Byzantine antiqities in Sparti (Lakonia) or Kalamata (Messenia).

A winding descent leads to the Bay of Dirou and the famous caves. A short way down, a sign to the left indicates 'Fortified Settlement', in fact a very small village, Fourniati, with a number of fort-like houses. Just beyond the lower end of the village is the little church of *Ayios Ionannis*, dated to the early twelfth century, but not domed, though this period is generally associated with the widespread adoption of the dome.

Down at the Bay of Dirou, once a port, the beach is strewn with large pebbles and the cliffs are honeycombed with small caves. In summer, trippers queue to visit the large, spectacular caves discovered in 1958: several kilometres of the complex, some with spacious chambers and galleries above water-level, have now been lit and opened up to boats. Narrow in parts, the caves occasionally widen out and there are large expanses of water which is fresh on the surface but salty at the bottom. The stalactites vary in colour, and there are some striking ones seamed with red Taiyetos subsoil. In another cave, rather grudgingly open to the public, anthropologists are examining palaeolithic paintings, stone implements and the remains of a primitive pottery workshop.

The Bay of Dirou is a dead end and one has to return to the

village of Pyrgos Dirou to continue southward. From here the tower-houses become more frequent; this is the **country of the Niklians**, a hybrid Franco-Greek people with Slav blood, who fled southward from Arcadia after the Frankish defeat at Nikli in the thirteenth century. They populated the villages of the barren plateau between the Evil Mountains and the sea and soon acquired the reputation of being the fiercest and most warlike community in the Mani. The desert-like region in which they settled became the heart of the Deep Mani, epitome of every association that the word 'Mani' conjures up - vendettas, killings, death-laments. During the period of the vendettas, the ritual wail of the death-lament - the haunting dirge often sung to the accompaniment of a lute or clarinet - would echo from one warring village to another. As time passed, the Niklians developed into a powerful aristocracy. They possessed arms, owned land and towers, and were skilled in the arts of piracy and pillage. Their tower-houses dominated the countryside, their minions - subservient families of non-Niklian stock - inhabiting the lower parts of the villages.

Just above the small village of Vamvaka is the Church of *Ayios Theodoros*, a fine, domed cross-in-square church with interesting brickwork and carvings, dating back to 1075. It is normally kept locked. Several of the other villages around here also have notable churches, especially Kato Gardenitsa (*Sotiras*) and Erimos (*Ayia Varvara*).

To the west extends the long southern arm of the Bay of Tigani, where the villagers used to gather salt from rock pools. The peninsula ends in a rocky hump, the site of the castle of Maina, which, with Mystra and Monemvassia, composed the strategic triangle guarding the Southern Morea. The shadeless plateau at the foot of the Kakovounia has an infernal quality: boulders are strewn across walled fields in frantic confusion; there are stunted olive trees, and occasionally a couple of needle-like cypresses flanking a crumbling tower; on the hilltops, grim-looking towers stand among piles of rubble. One is struck by what must once have been the density of the population. Sometimes less than two kilometres separated one warring village from another.

On a rugged hillside above the bay of Tigani is one of the finest of all the Mani churches, known as *Episkopi*. The church is not easy to find (ask at Ayios Yeoryios or at Stavri for directions - also for the nearby church at Vlaherna) and, as it is locked, one must have found out in advance who holds the keys. The church is of the familiar domed cross-in-square type with a narthex. The principal interest, however, is in the very extensive wallpaintings of the twelfth century, in particular the scenes from the life of St George. Two other churches of the same period as *Episkopi*, but rather less interesting, are nearby: one within sight, the other at Vlaherna.

If the Niklian country was the heart of the Deep Mani, the village of **Kita** was the nerve-centre. Today, Kita is a shattered monument to this self-contained community, whose habits and pursuits had the primitive quality of the granite on which their embattled dwellings stood. It is a maze of ruined towers, their surfaces broken by no visible doorway, portcullis or window below the top storey - thus creating an illusion of exaggerated height. The roofs are flat, with occasional gun-slits. Niklian wars were generally provoked by some infringement of property or quail-shooting rights. To trespass on one's neighbour's property meant war, formally declared by a family council and proclaimed throughout the village by a herald and the ringing of church bells. Victory was only complete when the enemy's tower was captured and destroyed. Running battles were a routine occupation and Maniot children grew up to the accompaniment of day-long fusillades. The Niklian wars only came to an end after the War of Independence, when the inhabitants of Kita and neighbouring villages were despatched to quell disorders in other parts of the Morea.

In summer the sun burns down with a North African intensity and the heat is thrown back in refractory waves from the scorched boulders. Kita is now largely deserted and in the walled lanes, goats munch dried-up weeds. The jagged wilderness of grey rock is only relieved by the dust-coated branches of the occasional almond tree trailing over a wall. With good reason, Kita has been used as the setting for films portraying the grimness of village life in the past.

Above the road, a short way before Kita and easy to find, is the beautifully restored twelfth-century Church known as *Tourloti*; actually St Sergius and St Bacchus: rather tall for its size and with the usual cross-in-square plan. The exterior of the three-sided apse has some brickwork decoration, and a step-pattern frieze - an obvious importation from the north - surrounds the little edifice. The wall-paintings of the interior are hopelessly damaged, but the acanthus-leaf capitals are in the best tradition.

To the west, two miles away, is the village of Nomia, chequered with labyrinthine stone walls bordered by prickly pear trees, its towers ranged like ninepins across a ridge behind the village.

After Kita, the road descends from the plateau to **Yerolimena**, a handful of houses strung out round a semi-circular harbour, where there has now been some unattractive modern building. The bay is small and to the west a massive rocky bluff, Cape Grosso, juts out into the sea; the mountainside above the village has been terraced into strips by low, parallel walls. For centuries Yerolimena, the most southerly inhabited part of the Greek mainland, was a notorious pirates' lair and its inhabitants, like those of other maritime villages of the Mani, had a bad reputation. A French traveller describes priests and children joining gleefully in shipwrecking forays. Today the fishermen and their families are friendly, peaceable people. The harbour, with caiques rocking in the swell, is littered with coils of twine with which the men and boys make nets. There is a feeling of relaxation after the tension and ferocity of the plateau, with its clusters of forbidding grey sentinels. Yachts and sailing boats now lie peacefully at anchor where once, to the accompaniment of beating drums and blood-curdling yells, the corsairs used to moor their galleys when they returned from their buccaneering expeditions.

The villages on the plateau west of Yerolimena are more alive than most of those in the Inner Mani; there are also several churches with interesting exteriors, notably *Ayios Nikolaos* at Ohia and *Ayios Ioannis* at Keria, whose exterior is a jumble of ancient panels and carved stones.

Above Yerolimena, at the foot of the mountains, is the village of Ano Boulari, at the top of which is the very humble-looking church of *Ayios Stratigos* (St Michael), with an even more complete, and possibly finer, set of frescoes than *Episkopi* at Tigani. The church is kept locked - there should be a key at Yerolimena.

The road continues south-east to Vathia, where several of the characteristic tower-houses have been restored to make a pleasant hotel. They overlook the sea and the last of Taiyetos' terrible spurs: the convulsion which is **Cape Tenaro (Matapan)**, one of the several Gates of Hell through which Herakles descended into the Underworld and seized the three-headed dog Cerberus by the throat. Protected by his lion pelt from the furious lashings of the hound's barbed tail, he brought it back to the light of day.

The sea is generally rough near the Cape, whose only historic association is of more recent date, for it was in these waters that the Battle of Cape Matapan was fought between the British and Italian fleets in the Second World War.

The return to Areopolis can be made along the increasingly busy east coast by way of Kotronas (to return to Yithion, one can keep to the west coast by taking a new road north of Kotronas). North of Areopolis the road winds along the shore of the Messenian Gulf, climbs and descends in hairpin bends, crosses whale-back humps and skirts pebbly bays bordered with rushes and agnus castus. The first of these is the Bay of Itylo. On the south side, a few fishermen's houses mark the site of Limeni, where the Mavromihalis dwelt in state and Petrobey entertained foreign travellers in oriental style. The surprisingly small tower and house have now been beautifully restored. The little anchorage is protected by a headland rising sheer from the sea, like a huge curtain of grey stone. High up on the cliff there is a cluster of holiday houses and apartments built to look like a Mani village.

In 1770 a Russian expedition under Feodor Orloff, ordered by Catherine the Great to liberate the Greeks, landed in the Bay of Itylo. The Maniots received the Russians with open arms; but the first tumultuous acclamations had barely subsided when distrust of the liberators' intentions began to poison relations. First, the expeditionary force was too small to be effective. Secondly, the Greeks were expected to become loyal citizens of the Empress. It was soon manifest that the expedition was no more than a diversion, though led by a sincere philhellene, in the course of Russia's long struggle with the Ottoman Empire. At first, the Turkish first line of defence was overrun but, as the shock wore off, the Turks threw into battle increasing numbers of Albanian troops who behaved with their usual atrocious brutality. Invaders and native patriots alike were thrown back and the Russian fleet sailed ignominiously out of the Bay of Itylo, not to reappear in Greek waters for over half a century. For the Greeks the 'diversion' brought nothing but disillusionment and cruel reprisals.

The coastal strip is fringed with olive trees; beyond the anchorage of Nea Itylo the road climbs up to the prosperous village of **Itylo**, whose houses, some of which are castellated, overlook the calm, unruffled bay. The contrast between Itylo and Kita is striking. Here are pergolas of climbing roses and gardens filled with hibiscus and pomegranate trees; cannas grow in pots on the balconies; domed chapels nestle amid terraced groves of cypresses. Women wearing enormous umbrella-like straw hats (a feature of the Mani) wander along serpentine paths between low walls. Itylo was once the most important place in the Mani, the centre of a slave market, crowded with corsairs from North Africa, not to mention local pirates from the Inner Mani. In 1675 one of the leading families, the Stefanopouli, crippled by Turkish exactions, invoked the aid of the Republic of Genoa. The Genoese duly came and removed nearly a thousand members of the clan to Corsica. There they remained, proudly speaking Greek, preserving Maniot customs. One of their descendants, the Duchesse d'Abrantès, wife of Napoleon's marshal, Junot, claimed that Napoleon himself was of Maniot origin - Buonaparte, being a literal translation of the Greek name Kalomeris ('the good part').

South-east of Itylo, across the ravine, a series of escarpments rise to a natural platform surrounded by a low wall: the vast *enceinte* of the Turkish fort of **Kelefa**, reached from the Areopolis-Yithion road. This boulder-strewn enclosure, treeless and dull beige, represents the limit of Turkish penetration into the Mani. From its commanding position, the inhabitants of Itylo could be carefully watched and the exaction of tribute backed up by force, with guns trained on the bay and its good anchorage. It also served as a defensive bastion against violent eruptions of Niklians from the south.

North of Itylo the landscape is much less fierce and cows graze in green fields shelving down to the sea. At Langada, opposite a Byzantine church with attractive brick and tile decoration, there is the Folklore Museum of the Mani. Just before **Nomitsis**, the road runs through a little group of minuscule churches. They are of the Middle Byzantine period, charming in their bucolic setting. To the right of the road is the Church of *Ayii Anaryiri*, with a little squat dome. The *iconostasis* is built into the main structure and on the left there is a well-preserved fresco of the two philanthropic doctors - St Kosmas and St Damian - to whom the church is dedicated. *Ayios Sostis*, also on the right, contains vestiges of frescoes and four marble columns. To the left of the road, where the orchards dip down towards the sea, is the tiny domed *Ypapandi* (Presentation at the Temple).

From Nomitsis it is only a short distance to **Platsa**, where the sturdy Byzantine **Church of Ayios Nikolaos Kambinari** stands on its own, high above the sea a little to the south-west of the village. The church, which is a tenth-century foundation, has no narthex, but a rather awkward dome of a much later date. From an inscription in the nave, we learn that the church was renovated in the fourteenth century by Constantine Spanis, the military governor of a tribe of Slav origin dwelling on Mount Taiyetos. However, there is nothing 'provincial' about the painted decoration of the interior. Spanis must have commissioned artists from neighbouring Mystra to carry out his ambitious scheme; it is astonishing to find frescoes of such an evolved style in a humble church in one of the remotest parts of the country. Look first at the *Deisis* in the apse of the sanctuary: a great stocky Christ seated on a heavy throne, flanked by the Virgin and St John the Baptist. Among the frescoes in the nave I would pick out the Baptism, full of picturesque detail, the Transfiguration and the Ascension. These are certainly not frescoes by a local Maniot artist.

The south arm contains the best preserved frescoes: the cycle of scenes from the life of St Nicholas. The style is quite different from that in the nave; less solemn, more illustrative with astonishingly lively colours. The church has been partly restored and is now kept locked.

After Platsa the road winds down through olive groves separated by lines of cypresses; it scales brush-covered hills and descends into coves which are popular with holiday-makers. Stoupa, with its excellent beaches, is a burgeoning resort. It is Mediterranean country *par excellence*. The best-situated place is **Kardamyli**, where a dramatic gorge opens out into a wide, gravelly river-bed. In the little harbour there is a rocky islet, on which Neoptolemos is supposed to have landed on his way to the court of Menelaos to woo Hermione. Nearby, another islet is referred to in Spartan mythology as the birthplace of the Dioscuri. Before the bridge spanning the river-bed, a track to the upper village ascends through orchards towards a wooded hill, topped by the remains of a Venetian castle; an eighteenth-century church with a tall, pointed *campanile* adds an Italianate touch. To the east, the valley contracts into a rugged defile of Taiyetos, with the familiar jagged peaks towering above a belt of black spruce; just to the south of Kardamyli a road leads up to Exohori on the edge of this dramatic gorge.

After Kardamyli the scenery remains grand and wooded, with thickets of cypress concealed in gullies of red Taiyetos rock; but the spirit of the Mani - its towers, vendettas and lunar wastelands - recedes. The village of Kambos is dominated by a conical hill, covered with the ruins of the fifteenth- and seventeenth-century forts of Zarnata. The coastline is very steep as the road descends to Mikra Mantinea and Kalamata. Sometimes a tower, shorter and squatter than the grim obelisks of the Inner Mani, is silhouetted against the skyline.

27

Messenia.

THE NUMEROUS SITES scattered around the Messenian plain cover the whole range of Greek history. There is a great deal to see and there are admirable beaches. Taking Kalamata as the starting-point, all the important sites can be visited comfortably in two to three days as part of a circular tour of the Peloponnese. A logical progression would be: ancient Messene and Mount Ithomi, then down to Koroni; across to Methoni and then up to Pylos, a good place to stay for one or two nights. From Pylos take the boat trip round the Bay of Navarino to Sfaktiria, Koryfassion, Paleokastro and walk to Neokastro. Finally, on the way northwards, visit the Palace of Nestor, the museum in Hora and then on to Kyparissia and Olympia.

More hurried travellers could omit Messene, the Bay of Navarino and Hora, visiting only the Palace of Nestor and the three castles: Koroni, Methoni and Neokastro.

In a comprehensive clockwise tour of the Peloponnese, one would reach Kalamata from the Mani, but it can also be approached from Sparti over the Langada Pass. The direct route from Athens is through Tripolis: after passing through Megalopolis, the road crosses the upper course of the Alfios and descends in hairpin bends, which are slowly being straightened out, into the Messenian lowlands, a shimmering canopy of olive trees, streaked with cypresses. Vineyards are hedged round with spiky agaves and waving banana trees; palm-trees shade whitewashed farmhouses. The groves are succeeded by cotton and wheat fields; there are mulberries everywhere. In winter there is the fluff of mimosa, in summer the blaze of sunflowers. North to south flows the stream of the Pamissos where, in antiquity, ailing children were brought to bathe in the curative waters. In summer the sun burns so fiercely on this dazzling expanse of fertility that it acquires an almost tropical quality.

Kalamata was very badly damaged in the disastrous earthquake of 1986, but the work of reconstruction has long since been completed. It is linked by bus, rail and air with Athens, and is famous for its large purple olives, its olive oil - the best in Greece - and the *kalamatianos*, a dance performed by men and women in chain formation, the leader waving a handkerchief and executing great turning leaps in the air.

The town lies at the foot of a spur of Taiyetos, a little way inland from its port. There is a good beach with hotels, fish restaurants and a fine view of the Mani. In two adjoining former private houses near the post-Byzantine Church of *Ayii Apostoli*, striking for its exterior brickwork decoration, is the museum. The buildings and some items in the collection were badly damaged in the earthquake, and the museum, whose collection includes ancient fragments from nearby sites, did not reopen until 1995.

The riverbed of the Nedon runs through the town, the stream - which is often dry - issues from a gorge of Taiyetos and continues round two sides of a fortified hill: this is the Villehardouin castle; Kalamata was the hereditary fief of the family for a hundred years. After them, however, the castle was bandied about between Burgundian dukes and Florentine bankers until 1387, when it was acquired by Marie de Bourbon, titular Empress of Constantinople. Marie had a mania for collecting baronies on behalf of her son, the Prince of Galilee; at one time she was mistress of sixteen castles in the Principality of Achaea alone. (Throughout the Frankish chronicles of Greece, the figures of proud, strong-minded women stand out, ancestors of future crowned heads of Europe and quite as ambitious and power-hungry as any of the grasping barons.) In the fifteenth century, the Venetians, trying to impede the Ottoman invasion, set fire to the castle rather than let it fall intact into Turkish hands.

Little is left now of the vaulted chambers in which Villehardouin and Anjou, Savoy and Bourbon hatched plots, drew up marriage settlements and drafted acts of restitution. Two oval enclosures can be discerned, the inner one on a higher level. The outer gate, overgrown with moss, was the best-preserved: a square tower with an arched entrance, but the earthquake brought down much of what was left. Below the very ruined keep is the ancient theatre.

Leaving Kalamata, the road to the west runs a short distance inland from the seaward end of the plain - once a malarial marsh, now a chequer-board of farmland and small factories - and crosses the Pamissos, up which, says Pausanias, deep-water fish used to swim '...especially in the spring, as they do up the Rhine and the Meander'. From the town of Messini (not to be confused with ancient Messene) one makes a diversion to the north, along roads which wind up into the hills. After skirting the walls and ruined towers of the Frankish castle of Androussa, the road reaches Mavromati, a village surrounded by trees, and continues up to the north gate of the fortifications of Messene, on a slope of Mount Ithomi.

There are three things to do at Mavromati: climb to the summit of Mount Ithomi, walk along the line of fourth-century BC fortifications, and visit the ruins of ancient Messene. First, the ascent of **Mount Ithomi** where, the Messenians claim, Zeus was born beside a spring below the summit and was nursed by two nymphs, Ithome and Neda. There are no ruins here but it is, in a sense, a pilgrimage. The mountain, its flat top rising like a lofty watchtower above the fertile plain, was a vital stronghold in the long and tragic wars waged by the Messenians in the defence of their country against the Spartans. The First Messenian War (eighth century BC) was provoked by the Spartans, who introduced a group of armed youths dressed as girls into a chamber where some eminent Messenian men were resting. Ostensibly provided for the pleasure of the Messenians, the Spartan 'maidens' promptly whipped out daggers and swords. In the ensuing scuffle, however, the 'maidens' were killed and Sparta was provided with a pretext to conquer the fertile lands of Messenia by force.

Although the Messenians performed prodigious deeds of valour, exhaustion and pestilence drove them to abandon their unfortified towns and settle on Mount Ithomi. The portents were consistently unfavourable: when their king was about to sacrifice to Zeus, the sacrificial rams broke loose and dashed their horns against the altar with such violence that they were instantly killed; at night dogs howled around the stronghold and fled to the Spartan camp; a shield fell from the statue of Artemis and the Delphic oracle predicted a harsh fate for 'the dwellers in the circle of the dancing-ground'. After the suicide of their king the last defenders surrendered.

In the seventh century the oppressed Messenians revolted, provoking the Second Messenian War. This conflict was celebrated for the exploits of Aristomenes, an intrepid leader who carried out daring raids into Spartan territory, even penetrating the Brazen House of Athena, where he left a shield inscribed with the words 'The Gift of Aristomenes to the Goddess'. In the Second War the Messenians chose Mount Eira, north of Ithomi, as their stronghold and it fell only when the Spartans, well informed by spies, scaled the walls during a torrential rainstorm and surprised the defenders. The country was reduced to serfdom and a large number of Messenians emigrated to Sicily, where they founded Messina. A final revolt broke out in 464 BC (the Third Messenian War) and Ithomi was again the last stronghold to surrender.

On the summit (800 metres) nothing is left of the sanctuary of Zeus or of the citadel which held out so courageously and for so long; now there are only tortoises and lizards. The zigzag path, bordered by vetch and spiky thistles, is steep, but not as painful as Homer implies when he calls it 'ladder-like'. The view is prodigious, with the Arcadian highlands rising abruptly to the north, Taiyetos to the east, gashed by the Langada Pass, tapering off southward into the Mani and a chain of low mountains, dominated by a high peak, separating the plain from the Bay of Navarino in the west. On the eastern slope of Mount Ithomi, below the saddle linking it with Mount Eva, and among cypress and oak trees, the monastery buildings of Voulkano form a quadrangle round a church. Apart from its airy position, the monastery has little to offer.

The **fourth-century fortifications**, the best-preserved and the most extensive in Greece, once guarded the city of Messene from Spartan, and later Macedonian, aggression. Like Megalopolis, Messene was built after the Theban defeat of Sparta at Leuktra, for protection against a possible Spartan recovery. Epaminondas, the Theban leader and founder of the Arcadian League against Sparta, chose the site, which could be stoutly defended. Needless to say, his choice was deeply resented by the Spartans who, alone among the Greek states, abstained from guaranteeing the autonomy of the city.

A ten-kilometre circumference of walls, broken at intervals by watchtowers, can still be traced almost in its entirety, straggling across the scrub-land around Mount Ithomi. The *enceinte* is best-preserved in the north, where the road from Mavromati goes through the **Arcadian Gate**, a round court with niches for statues and double gates facing each other. Nine courses of stone-work are preserved, the blocks expertly cut so that each course diminishes in height as the masonry rises. The gateway's massive lintel is propped against the inner wall of the court. A considerable garrison was probably stationed here, and the towers must have commanded such a wide prospect of the hilly countryside that any approaching army would quickly have been spotted by sentinels. One can stroll in either direction along the sentry-walk. To the east, the chain of redoubts climbs the slope of Ithomi; to the south, the fortified line vanishes into a more domesticated landscape. Clusters of cyclamen sprout from crannies in walls which once enclosed a vast area of cornfields intended to save the Messenians, when besieged, from starvation. The superb finish of the stone courses, built entirely of ashlar, makes the rough masonry of Crusader castles, constructed 1500 years later, look very shoddy. The fortifications underwent their severest test when the Messenians withstood a massive siege by a Macedonian army under the young Demetrios, son of Philip V; Demetrios' phalanx was so fiercely bombarded with boulders - and tiles hurled by female warriors - that it was almost entirely wiped out.

Halfway back to the village from the north gate, a path to the right goes down to the main site of ancient **Messene**, on gently shelving ground. Epaminondas attended the foundation ceremony of the city and offered the first sacrifices, mindful of a Boeotian oracle predicting that: 'The bright bloom of Sparta shall perish and Messene shall be inhabited for all time.' Less pretentious than Megalopolis, Messene seems to have been more durable. Leading architects of the day were commissioned to design the temples and public buildings, and statues by Damophon, the only Messenian artist of note (who repaired Phidias' great statue of Zeus at Olympia), adorned the temples and courts. The memorial to Aristomenes, the national hero, was one of the principal sights. The remains of a large theatre are among the olive trees on one's right, but the main part of the site is occupied by the spacious **Asclepeion**, with the temple in the centre. On the north-western side are the ruins of four chambers, the first of which was a shrine to Artemis Orthia. A fine stairway leads up between truncated columns to the north-east and, in the eastern corner, there is a small theatre or *Odeion* - an extremely elegant ruin: at least ten tiers of grey limestone are intact and the floor of the orchestra is composed of red, white and blue paving-stones. Adjoining it to the south are the foundations of two buildings, one of which is the *Bouleuterion*, a large square hall with a stone seat running round the four walls. To the south of the *Asclepeion* extends the rubble of what is thought to have been a temple dedicated to all the gods. A few slabs from the tiers of the stadium lie among the olive groves to the south-west. Excavation continues on the site.

From modern Messini the main road goes to the south-west as far as

Rizomilos, a well-watered village, where there is a fork. The turning to the left (south) leads down the third prong of the Peloponnese which has an essentially mellow character, with none of the ferocity of the Mani or the ruggedness of Cape Maleas. At Vounaria, large oil and wine jars were, until recently, made by methods handed down from antiquity and this fine craft is being revived at the nearby village of Kombi; in medieval times the jars were filled with oil and loaded onto Venetian merchantmen bound for the Levant. Further south, the town of **Koroni** climbs up the side of a headland crowned by one of the finest Venetian castles in the country. Below the bastions, where galleys used to anchor, fishing caiques chug across the pellucid water.

Koroni and Methoni, with their twin castles, were the first Venetian colonies on the Greek mainland. A provisioning station for merchantmen, Koroni was celebrated for the export of cochineal and olive oil. With their usual religious tolerance, the Venetians allowed Greek bishops complete spiritual authority over their Orthodox flock, and prosperity grew as increasingly large numbers of Catholic pilgrims broke their journey to the Holy Land at one or other of the two stations. The Venetians fraternized with the natives and were only insistent upon one thing: they forbade their troops to grow beards, which the Greeks, like good Byzantines, favoured. In 1500, Koroni fell to the Turkish army and the Sultan made a spectacular entry into the port, to the accompaniment of thunderous drum-beats and wailing fifes. During the reign of Suleiman II the Magnificent, the Genoese admiral, Andrea Doria, temporarily wrested Koroni from the Turks; but he was unable to hold it and the inhabitants, who had received him with open arms, suffered appalling reprisals when he sailed away.

Koroni's waterfront is pleasant and the houses on the cliff-side are painted in bright colours. Massive walls and bastions defend the eastern projection of the headland. The **Castle** is in the shape of a quadrangle, divided by a north-south wall into two separate enclosures of unequal size. One approaches the main entrance, on the north side, from a cobbled, ramp-like street. The gate, a beautifully-shaped Gothic arch framing an entrancing prospect of the port and the mountains beyond, forms part of a tower-like structure leading into a vaulted passage. It is one of the most impressive castle gates in Greece and leads to a plateau dotted with tiny houses set among almond trees; at the right of the Gothic gateway is the Convent of *Ayios Ioannis*, which is inhabited by nuns. It has black-painted gates, five domes on slender but awkward-looking cylindrical drums and a crypt. There is also a cemetery. The whole plateau is surrounded by crumbling Venetian and Turkish masonry. To the east of the entrance gate, two large round bastions, one higher than the other, rise perpendicularly from the rock-fringed shore; most impressive when seen from the harbour, the bastions exhibit a soaring expanse of smooth, perfect stone-work, like a natural cliff, which turns gold in the afternoon light. The bastion at the south-east end has a domed roof supported by embrasures, with a gun-platform reached by a spiral stairway. On all sides, except the west, the vista is one of open sea. At right-angles to the south curtain wall stretches a long sandy beach. A modern stairway descends from the plateau to a shaded terrace with a church and a small museum which contains little of interest.

A good road links Koroni with Methoni, crossing the olive groves of Cape Akritas and touching the sea at the fishing village and resort of Finikoundas. If you do not take this road you return to the Messini-Pylos road at Rizomilos.

The main road from Messini continues westward from Rizomilos to Pylos, affording splendid backward views of the Messenian Gulf and plains, with Taiyetos vanishing southward into the haze of the Evil Mountains. The road descends towards the west coast and the Ionian Sea where there is a new, much softer, climate. Below lies the landlocked **Bay of Navarino**, with the cream-coloured houses of **Pylos** at its southern end. To understand all that has happened here it is essential to grasp the configuration of land and sea, which is very complex, with the semi-circular bay (five kilometres long and three kilometres wide), the island of Sfaktiria enclosing it like a huge reef from one mainland promontory to another, the small islands, the three channels to the sea, the reed-fringed lagoon and the elegant peak above the town.

The Bay is, of course, best known for the battle of 1827 between Turkey and the allies of Greece; but the port of Pylos, the island and the two castles (Neokastro and Paleokastro) have a much earlier history. The medieval town grew up round the castle hill at the southern end of the Bay and was originally called Avarino, after the tribes of Avars who overran the country in the sixth century, and this became Navarino. With the Greek passion for reviving classical names, it has become Pylos, although the ancient city of the same name was further north.

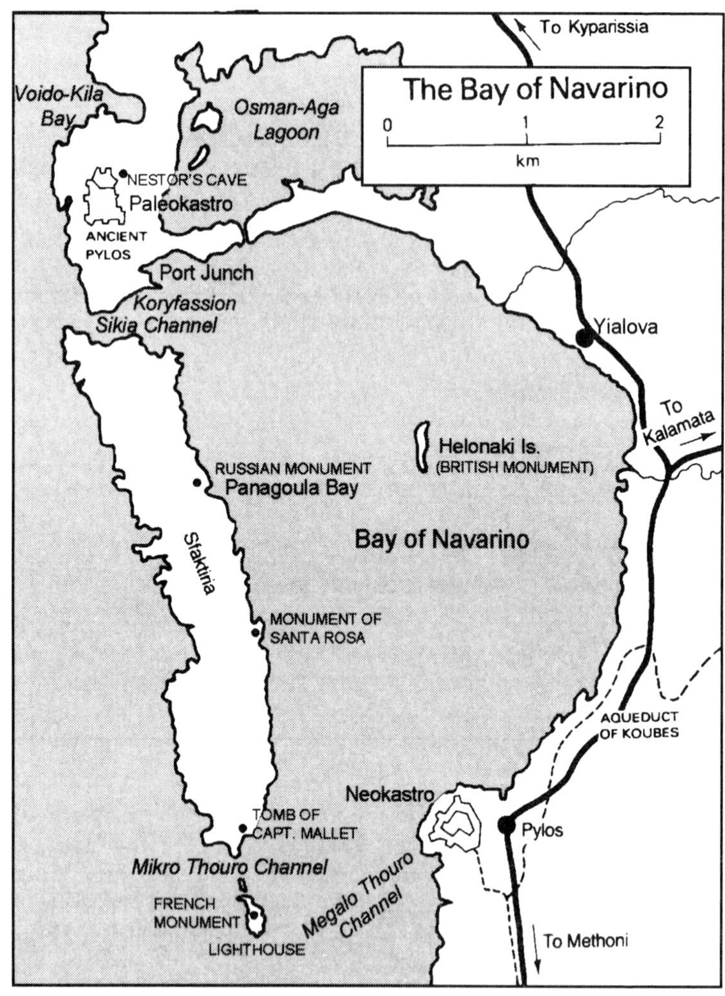

It was here, at Pylos, in the fourteenth century, that Marie de Bourbon took refuge from her rival in castle-collecting, the Venetian Carlo Zeno, who was Canon of Patras but had more taste for soldiering than for theology. Later, in the tragic twilight years of Byzantium, when the Emperor John VIII travelled to Florence in a vain attempt to enlist Western aid against the Turks, it was from

Navarino, then a flourishing maritime station, that he sailed in one of the Doge's vessels. During the War of Independence Greek patriots seized Navarino, but when Ibrahim Pasha, the scourge of the Morea, laid siege to the castle in 1825, it was found that the untrained Greek irregulars were no match for the better-equipped Turkish army.

In the arcaded square there is a monument to the three Allied admirals who were victorious in the battle of 1827 and it is pleasant to sit here in an open-air café and pore over maps and try to work out the movements of the fleets on that day. It seems incredible that four major fleets should not only have been able to penetrate this landlocked stretch of water, but also to have engaged in actual combat. In a sense, the battle was a mistake. In 1827 the Greek effort against the Turks was waning; six years after it had begun, the crusade for liberation had degenerated into a squalid civil war between self-styled generals. On the international level, Russia alone championed Greek independence. Austria and Prussia were openly inimical to Greek aspirations and England and France, while sympathizing with the Greeks, had no wish to be engaged in a war with the Turks.

The brief of Admiral Codrington, Commander-in-Chief of the Allied fleets of Britain, France and Russia, was to avoid a war with the Turks but to ensure that they did not commit any more atrocities, like the wholesale deportation of the inhabitants of the Morea, which had so shocked European public opinion. In October 1827 the entire Turco-Egyptian fleet was concentrated in the Bay of Navarino. Fearing it was about to break out in order to perpetrate some further enormity, Codrington sailed into the Bay to stage a warning demonstration. The Turco-Egyptian fleet, disposed in a wide semi-circle, consisted of eighty-two ships, the Allied of only twenty-seven, although they had more battleships than the Turks. Codrington, on his flagship *Asia*, was the first to pass between the southern tip of Sfaktiria and the Turkish castle; his squadron was followed by the French and the Russians came last. Twenty thousand Turkish troops encamped on the slope below the castle watched breathlessly as ship after ship nosed its way through the narrow channel. It was just past noon. The first shot was fired by the Turks - probably in panic, certainly without their commanders' orders. *Dartmouth* and *Sirène*, the French flagship, replied. In a few minutes the action was general. The vessels were stationary - for there was no room to manoeuvre - and the range point-blank. Skilfully avoiding the Turkish fire-ships, Codrington and the French concentrated their guns on the enemy's battleships, while the Russian squadron destroyed the rest of the enemy's frigates and sloops. The conflagration must have been appalling; by the evening the whole Bay seemed to be ablaze, as one Ottoman ship after another exploded, sending myriads of sparks flying through the smoke-laden sky. The rocks of Sfaktiria reflected the fiery lights and the heat was intolerable. Wreckage of masts, poops and yards floated in the lurid sea, with Turkish sailors clinging to them. Allied crews had to fight all night to prevent their own vessels catching fire. By morning only twenty-nine of the eighty-two enemy ships remained afloat.

After Navarino the Turks lost command of the sea. Never again would the Sultan or his Egyptian vassal, the hideous, pock-marked Ibrahim Pasha, be able to supply and reinforce their mainland troops. Greek independence had virtually been gained, but no Greek fought in the battle. It was won by British, French and Russian sailors in a remarkable demonstration of international co-operation. Navarino, the last major engagement to be fought before the steamship revolutionized naval warfare, was one of the decisive battles of the nineteenth century. By making Greek independence possible, it altered the map of Eastern Europe and ushered in the long period of sickness from which the Ottoman Empire was ultimately to perish. It is also ironical that, exactly twenty-two years after Trafalgar, British and French admirals should have been able to operate in such perfect accord and with so successful an outcome.

Motorboats, in which you can make a round trip of the Bay - a more than worthwhile experience - are moored alongside the jetty at Pylos. It is wise to start early if you want to see the hulks of the Turkish vessels lying at the bottom of the sea, before the water is ruffled by mid-morning breezes. The minimum time for the trip is a long half-day. The boat bears south-west towards the islet on either side of which Codrington's squadrons entered the Bay; a rock-hewn stairway leads to the summit, which is topped by a lighthouse and a monument to the French sailors who fell in the Battle. The channel is dotted with curious flat-topped rocks, one of which is pierced by a natural arch through which the water swirls into the strait. You then chug northward under the lee of the rugged coast of **Sfaktiria**, an uninhabited island five kilometres long and only one kilometre wide; cliffs speckled with evergreens rise sheer from the water, seeming to form an immense breakwater protecting the Bay. The boat pulls in at the little cove of **Panagoula**, where the fiercest fighting took place and the wrecks of the Ottoman vessels sunk by the Russians can be seen through the translucent water. It is the only anchorage on the island. There is a white chapel and a cypress-shaded memorial to the Russian dead, which has been refurbished by the Russian Government.

Panagoula was also the site of a Spartan defeat in the seventh year of the Peloponnesian War (425 BC). The Athenians, with great audacity, had entrenched themselves in enemy territory on the mainland at Koryfassion, guarding the northern entrance to the Bay; the Spartans countered by landing on Sfaktiria. However, the Athenian triremes, entering the Bay from north and south, inflicted a severe defeat on the Spartan fleet and the garrison on Sfaktiria was cut off. The Spartan *ephors* sent envoys to Athens to sue for peace but the Athenians refused to parley. Quick to react to adversity, the Spartans made every effort to break the blockade. *Helots* were promised freedom and large sums of money in return for landing provisions secretly on the island. 'Divers' says Thucydides 'swam in underwater, dragging skins filled with poppy-seeds mixed with honey and bruised linseed.'

As winter approached, the Athenians, controlling all sea communications, decided to risk an all-out assault. The attack seems to have taken the Spartans by surprise and they retreated up the cliff, where they were taken in the rear by another enemy detachment. A brief parley was followed by total surrender. The Athenians triumphantly carried off their prisoners, the *corps d'élite* of the Spartan army, to Athens. The siege had lasted seventy-two days. The blow to Spartan prestige was enormous and the victorious Athenians became even more intractable. So the long and tragic war went on.

The line of cliffs, their bases eroded into caves and fissures by the endless lapping of waves, continues northwards; then suddenly Sfaktiria ends in a soaring hump. The Sikia channel, between the tip of the island and the mainland promontory of **Koryfassion**, is only a hundred metres wide and too shallow to allow passage for vessels other than caiques. The width and depth of the channel must have altered since the time of Thucydides, who speaks of several triremes sailing abreast through it. Vestiges of a fourth-century BC mole are visible beside the landing stage at Koryfassion, site of the Athenian camp and probably of the classical city of Messenian Pylos. Otherwise there are no traces of the 'fortress situated on the sea' mentioned by Strabo, who suggests that it was founded by the inhabitants of Nestor's Pylos who, when overwhelmed, possibly by

Dorians, fled southward from their burning citadel, some time in the twelfth century BC. In the Middle Ages the harbour at Koryfassion was used by the Franks and was known as Port Junch.

A sandy, reed-fringed beach borders the shallow sea and from here, abandoning the motorboat for a while, it is a good half-hour's climb to the castle of **Paleokastro** on the summit of the hill. Outgrowths of rock thrust jagged edges through a mist of blue-grey thistles; lizards and snakes keep up a continuous rustling in the brushwood. The castle was built on this imposing site by Nicholas de St Omer, a thirteenth-century baron of Flemish origin who married into wealth and, though renowned for his arrogance, was respected for his expenditure on the construction and preservation of fortifications - he also built the castle at Thebes. The quadrangular castle spreads across the crest. To the right of the arched entrance a passage leads into the *enceinte*. There are round bastions at either end of the south wall and the battlements and part of the wall-walk are well preserved; the redoubt at the north end of the plateau, identified by the remains of four towers, may be the site of the classical acropolis. St Omer's castle went through all the usual vicissitudes: after the decline of Frankish power it was occupied successively by Venetians, Turks, Morosini's Venetians and Turks again, as evidenced by the ruins of the inner *enceinte*, which are Frankish, and the outer, which are Venetian or Turkish. There is probably no wall-walk in the Morea along which it is so fascinating to stroll: going round clockwise, starting from the east, you see first the rush-bordered Lagoon of Osman-Aga, then the crescent-shaped Bay of Navarino sweeping southward towards modern Pylos; Port Junch was at the foot of the south-west slope, with the cliffs of Sfaktiria behind it; westward lies the expanse of the Ionian Sea, with the little, almost circular, Bay of Voido-Kila biting deep into the coast just to the north. To complete the circle, hazy green hills ascend towards the north-east, with Mount Egaleon vanishing behind them into the horizon.

On the northern slope of the hill, concealed among rocks and brushwood, is the entrance to Nestor's Cave (the descent from the keep is frighteningly steep). Pausanias calls it 'the stables of the oxen of Neleos and Nestor'. According to another myth, the cave served as a cow-shed for the oxen stolen by the infant Hermes from his half-brother Apollo.

On the return journey to Pylos, the motorboat passes the island of Helonaki ('Little Tortoise') in the middle of the Bay. It was around here that Codrington's squadron destroyed some of the Turkish ships; a low flat rock bears an unassuming monument to the British sailors who fell at Navarino.

It is a few minutes' walk from Pylos to **Neokastro**, the restored sixteenth-century Turkish castle which guards the entrance to the Bay, where an Institute of Underwater Archaeology is planned. The hexagonal fortress with bastions on each corner is entered through the west gate. From the wall-walk, which overlooks barrel-vaulted prison cells, a curtain wall supported by recessed arches descends towards the shore where two quadrangular bastions command the channel. A post-Byzantine church, *Ayios Sotiras*, lies within the enclosure, where the Turkish population dwelt in pestilential conditions before the capture of the fortress in 1821 by Greek peasant patriots. Frantzis, a Greek cleric, has left a lurid eye-witness account of the fearful blood-bath which followed the fall of the castle: of Turkish women, their flesh hanging in ribbons from sabre-cuts, felled as they ran dementedly towards the sea; of babies torn from their screaming mothers' arms and hurled against walls bespattered with human brains; of children thrown into the sea where they were left to drown; of piles of hacked corpses littering the blood-soaked shore. The Greeks held the fortress and the area around until 1825 when Ottoman forces recaptured it and retained it until 1828. Subsequently the French garrison, commanded by General Maison, demolished all the squalid Turkish hovels and built the modern town below the castle. Now thyme-scented scrubland has replaced the putrefying slum.

South of Pylos, lies **Methoni**, formerly Modon, where a semi-circular beach of fine sand ends at the battlements of the Venetian fortress, which sprawls across a land's end facing the island of Sapientza. The beach is bordered with small hotels and tavernas.

Methoni's origins are more ancient than those of Koroni: it was one of the seven cities offered by Agamemnon as a bribe to induce Achilles to stop sulking and resume the fight against the Trojans. In the Roman era it was strongly fortified by Antony, who placed his ally, King Bogud of Mauretania, in command of the garrison. In the Middle Ages it was a nest of corsairs who preyed on merchantmen returning from the east. After the Latin sack of Constantinople, Geoffroy I de Villehardouin, hurrying to secure his share of the spoils, was carried, he writes, 'by wind and chance ... to the port of

Modon'. The future Villehardouin supremacy in the Morea stems from this fortuitous visit, for it was whilst waiting at Methoni for the storm to abate that he realized with what ease a relatively small number of knights would be able to overcome the ill-equipped Greeks; indeed, with his compatriot, William de Champlitte, he did later conquer the Morea. At this time, the port of Methoni, noted for its wine and its cochineal, was filled with the vessels of so many nations that one historian calls it 'the Port Said of Frankish Greece'. A few years later, however, the French sold Methoni to Dandolo, the blind Doge, and it became the first Venetian station on the Greek mainland. On the landward side of the citadel there were orange groves and a busy market where the peasants sold pigs to the Venetians. Another fifteenth-century pilgrim says that all the bacon sold in Venice came from Methoni, where sausages were also made.

A bridge, supported by a succession of arches, built by the French after Navarino, spans a wide moat which bisects the promontory from sea to sea. The **Castle**, at the western end of the beach, possesses some of the finest Venetian military architecture in Southern Greece. Walls and bastions are well-preserved and their unbroken line gives an air of formidable impregnability to the land approach. The arched entrance, flanked by two bastions, is succeeded by a second and a third gateway. Entering the huge enclosure, one is faced with a squat, granite pillar crowned by a carved capital, known as the Morosini capital. In the seventeenth-century Turco-Venetian War, Francesco Morosini was the commander of the besieging army; whilst he was inspecting an advanced position, and accompanied by a retinue of ostentatiously-dressed Venetian dignitaries, the Turks spotted him and opened fire. The noblemen ran in all directions; only Morosini stood immobile, unflinching, the embodiment of Venetian *bella figura*. His behaviour greatly impressed the Turks who subsequently surrendered.

The entire enclosure, surrounded by the upper walls and a parapet punctuated with ruined towers, was once a congested urban quarter, first Venetian, then Turkish. The only surviving edifice within is a little domed *hammam*. The east walls, with Venetian and Turkish gun emplacements, overhang the beach. The west side, facing the open sea, is the oldest part of the castle - perhaps thirteenth-century - its ruined ramparts overlooking savage rocks, against which the waves break with showers of spray. The paths are choked with thistles and it is wise to stick to the wall-walks, although these are often on different levels and involve a great deal of scrambling up and down. In this confined enclosure a Venetian garrison of seven thousand defenders endured a terrible siege by a hundred thousand Turks under Sultan Bayazit II who, throughout the sweltering August of 1500, pounded the garrison with five hundred cannon. When the Janissaries finally scaled the walls, the buildings were set on fire, the Latin bishop was immolated whilst praying with his flock and every male over twelve was decapitated. In Venice the fall of Methoni was regarded as a national disaster.

At the southern end of the enclosure are the ruins of the Sea Gate, flanked by two towers, which leads to a landing-stage protected by a parapet with battlements. A causeway connects the Sea Gate - the tip of the headland - with a **Turkish fort** on a rocky shoal, where the Venetian garrison made its last heroic stand against Bayazit's Janissaries. The fort is the most picturesque ruin at Methoni: an octagonal tower in two sections, the higher one smaller and domed, and surrounded by a crenellated parapet.

Littered with the ruins of artillery bastions, look-out posts and ravelins, Methoni is one of the most evocative Venetian sites in Greece. The Lion of St. Mark smirks down from pointed arches and the escutcheons of famous Venetian families crown blocked-up gateways; however, neither art nor literature flourished here.

Methoni is one of the southernmost tips of the Greek mainland. The traveller now returns northward - through Pylos. All the way up the west coast the country has a mellow, domesticated quality, but the softness never degenerates into formlessness. The chain of Mount Egaleon runs parallel to the sea in a line of rocky saddlebacks, which repeat the humps of Sfaktiria on a larger scale. North of Pylos the road skirts the bay and winds up into a region of wooded hills and lush ravines. Eighteen kilometres from modern Pylos a signpost indicates the site of the so-called **Palace of Nestor** and the Mycenaean city of Pylos, which extended across a wide hilltop against a background of rugged hills.

Ancient writers do not agree about the locality of Nestor's capital. Some imply that it was in Elis, others in Messenia. Homer is rather contradictory: in the *Iliad* he says that the palace crowns a 'steep hill overlooking the Alfios, on the borders of sandy Pylos' (at no point does the Alfios flow through Messenian territory; it winds through Arcadia and Elis, well to the north) and in the *Odyssey* he says that Telemachos found the inhabitants of Pylos 'on the foreshore' (this palace is situated well inland). However, when

Telemachos mounted his chariot and drove through 'the echoing porch', the horses 'glad to be loosed, flew down from the steep crag of the citadel of Pylos out onto the plain'. Here the relationship between citadel and plain fits the present site, although 'crag' is an overstatement.

The excavations, since 1952 conducted by Professor Blegen at the head of a Greek-American team, have cast fresh light on Homeric topography. This palace (1300-1200 BC), in size and arrangement, is comparable to that of Mycenae and must therefore have been the residence of a great king. As Professor Blegen says: 'The only royal dynasty strong enough and rich enough, in the thirteenth century BC in western Messenia, to build and maintain such a palace was that of the Neleids'. Nestor was the son of Neleos, founder of the dynasty, and his contribution in ships to the Greek expedition against Troy was second only to that of Agamemnon.

Where all ancient writers and poets are in agreement is on the bucolic character of the land over which Nestor ruled. Homer says it was rich in sheep and horses and Strabo mentions flocks of sheep browsing in olive groves and describes the cattle raids carried out by Nestor. The poets also agree on the character of the king: although a confirmed cattle-thief, he was also apparently wise, just, cautious, a generous host - and a bore without much sense of humour. More fortunate than Agamemnon or Odysseus, he returned from Troy to enjoy a happy old age in the bosom of his family.

It is fascinating to form an idea of how this man and his court lived, over three thousand years ago. There is, admittedly, none of the drama of the citadel at Mycenae, in spite of architectural features in common and the fact that both palaces were gutted by fire in the twelfth century BC. There are no encircling Cyclopean walls, no gateways supporting huge lintels, no circular royal graveyards. This, as far as we know, was not a blood-drenched palace. Nothing standing is more than waist-high, but, being built on a level hill-top without the declivities of ground that add such complexity to the layout of Mycenae, its architectural disposition and domestic arrangements are more quickly grasped than those of Agamemnon's palace. The huge metal roof does not improve the general effect, but it does protect the prehistoric foundations and walls of clay from drenching rain and scorching sun.

The main building was the royal residence, with apartments of state and storerooms grouped round it. The king and his household lived well. The residential part of the palace was two-storied, with

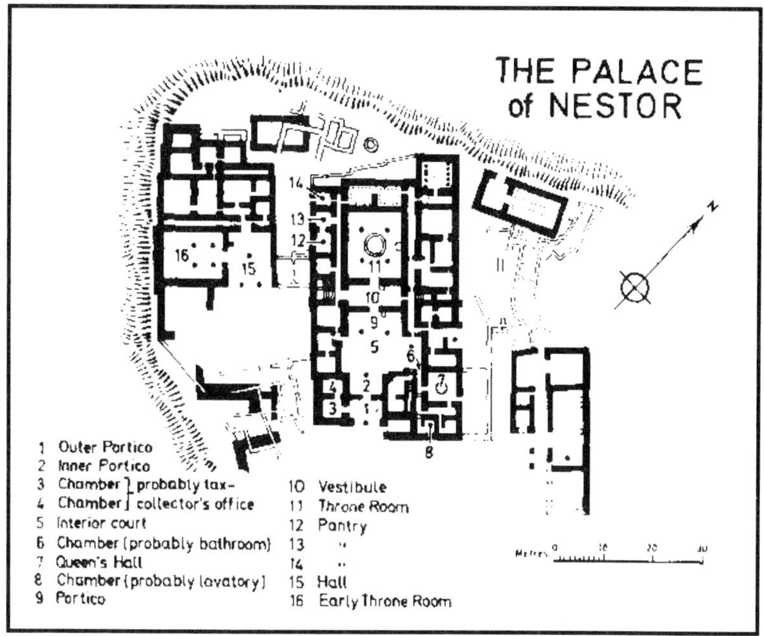

flat roofs on different levels. In the centre of each of the outer and inner porches is a stone base which once supported a fluted wooden column; to the left of the outer porch there are two small chambers, believed to have been the tax-collector's offices, in which the palace accounts, recorded on tablet, were kept. The inner porch leads to a courtyard open to the sky where, to the right, a stairway (three steps are preserved) mounted to a tower, thought to have been a look-out post; from here sentinels commanded a view of the rolling, wooded hills.

On the left of the courtyard were waiting rooms with benches, where visitors sat and were offered wine by servants. In the 1939 excavations a large quantity of clay tablets, inscribed with the signs of a hitherto-undeciphered language, were found in the palace. More were excavated in 1952. At this point, Michael Ventris, an architect and linguist, began the decipherment of the script which had, until then, baffled scholars and which, it was thought, might even be unrelated to any known Greek dialect. Ventris and his philologist collaborator, John Chadwick, soon recognized an interrelationship of phonetic values that corresponded with the Archaic declensions used by Homer. The grammatical structure of the language gradually emerged and the script, known as Linear B, used by the Minoans and Mycenaeans of the Bronze Age, was revealed to be a form of Archaic Greek. The only disappointment was that the Pylos tablets were inscribed with nothing more important than household inventories and accounts.

A long, narrow chamber to the right of the interior court contains, against its south-east wall, a painted terracotta bath-tub set on a clay base; vessels found nearby were probably used for pouring water into the tub. To the south-east of the bathroom lies the so-called Queen's Hall, with a hearth in the centre and walls, judging from the fragments remaining, once stuccoed and decorated with frescoes of griffons and wild beasts. The Hall and bathroom are believed to have been gutted by the flames from the burning oil which fell from jars stored on the upper floor when the great fire swept the palace. Another chamber, separated from the Queen's Hall by a corridor to the south-west, is thought to have been a lavatory, for there are indications that water could be flushed through an aperture in a stone slab in the east corner, flowing thence into a subterranean drain.

It is now best to return to the court and proceed through a portico into what must have been a brightly-frescoed vestibule; from here a stairway to the right, of which eight steps are preserved, once led to an upper storey, where the royal ladies probably dwelt. The vestibule leads directly into the large Throne Room, a hall of state and the most sumptuous apartment in the palace. In the centre is the great ceremonial hearth of clay, once surrounded by four wooden columns supporting a broad gallery. Impressions of the columns' shallow flutes can be discerned on the floor. The smoke from the hearth, which was the holiest place in the palace, is believed to have escaped through a terracotta chimney in the roof. The wooden throne, decorated with ivory and other inlays, was placed against the right wall. The shallow depression, probably a basin, to the right of the seated king, may have enabled Neleos, Nestor and their royal descendants to pour out libations without descending from the throne.

The grooves in the wall of the Throne Room were intended to receive the ends of upper floor beams, which Professor Blegen thinks may have been left exposed. The whole room was bright with dazzling decoration: frescoes of leopards, lions and other wild beasts covered the walls; linear designs within squares covered the floor. The colours used were red, blue, yellow, black and white, all of the gaudiest. It seems clear, from the fragments assembled in the neighbouring museum at Hora and the National Museum in Athens, that the scene must have been one of barbaric splendour.

There are corridors on either side of the Throne Room which separate it from a maze of little storerooms. The ones on the south-west side are believed to have been the main pantries, because of the mass of crushed pottery (over six thousand pieces) found here. Tablets stacked in two large storerooms directly behind the Throne Room bore inscriptions describing the different qualities and flavours of olive oil.

To the south-west of the palace, a complex of more devastated buildings rises above the sloping olive grove, where the lower city once descended in terraces. The walls of a large entrance hall, preceded by two stone bases for wooden columns, were decorated with an elegant frieze of pink griffons, fragments of which were found scattered about the floor. The hall led into a large reception chamber of an earlier period than the Throne Room.

North-east of the main palace is another complex of storerooms where raw materials were kept; tablets referring to repairs in leather and bronze indicate that this may have been the main workshop of the city. To the north is the large wine store, where many cracked and broken jars of different sizes still stand as they were found.

Tholos tombs, possibly burial places of kings, have been excavated in the vicinity. The most important is in an olive grove about a hundred metres north-east of the palace. Its contents included gold and jewellery - amethysts, amber necklaces, rings - votive offerings, effigies of little owls and a royal seal on which the image of a winged griffon was stamped. The other tombs lie south of the palace hill.

A few kilometres to the north is Hora, where the museum possesses fragments of pottery, frescoes and stucco flooring from the palace. From Hora the road continues northward, between the sea and the range of Mount Egaleon, whose rocky fingers thrust upwards in a succession of strange nodular peaks. At **Kyparissia**, founded by Epaminondas in the fourth century BC at the same time as Messene and Megalopolis, and later to become a flourishing Byzantine port, one can drive up to the picturesque upper town, Ano-Kyparissia: a maze of rock-hewn stairways and village houses, with the ruins of a medieval castle built on the site of a Hellènic tower so ancient that it was supposed to have been raised by the giants when they were at war with the gods.

28

Olympia.

OLYMPIA IS IN ELIS, which Homer calls 'goodly' - not without reason. When the treacherous Oxylos, an outlawed prince from Kalydon in Etolia, led the Dorians across the Peloponnese in search of rich pasture lands, he deliberately conducted them through the rugged Arcadian defiles so that they should not observe the fertility of Elis, which he coveted for himself. Apparently pleased with his services, the Dorians made him king of the country that he had not shown them. According to a local legend, it was Oxylos who subsequently founded the Olympic Games.

The lower valley of the Alfios, which flows past Olympia and through the ancient country called Pisatis, is one of the most gracious landscapes in Greece: pine-clad hills, covered with wild flowers in spring, overlook gullies filled with ilex and arbutus; streams bordered by oleanders and agnus castus wind through humid, hidden valleys and the walls of village houses are bright with flowering creepers. In antiquity, however, the lagoons were infested with mosquitoes and the inhabitants had to appeal to Zeus and Herakles, two very Elean deities, to rid them of these pests.

Olympia can be approached either direct from Athens via Corinth and Patras, or from Tripolis, or from the south - the route normally taken by travellers making a full circular tour of the Peloponnese.

The previous chapter described the route from Pylos up the west coast to Kyparissia. The first part of the direct route to Olympia and Patras from Kalamata goes up the valley of the Pamissos, either by the main road or by a quieter road through Messini, and then, before reaching the Arcadian foothills, branches left for the west coast. The coastal road to the north enters the territory of Elis at the river Neda, crosses the densely olive-clad Triphyllian Plain, and approaches Olympia.

About fifteen kilometres north of the Neda, below Mount Lapithas, lies the pine-fringed lagoon of Kaiafa with a spa situated on a wooded island. The road then leaves the coast and ascends gently through pine trees, which become larger and more luxuriant. Five kilometres beyond Kaiafa, a track to the right leads to the fine, fourth-century BC walls of Samikon, a fortress which commanded one of the passes into Arcadia and was built by the Eleans as a bulwark against Spartan aggression. The main road skirts another lagoon, from the east side of which a road to the right climbs to Andritsena and Bassae (this road provides a short cut to Olympia via Krestena). The road then enters the flat, alluvial plain of the Alfios; after crossing the river one reaches Pyrgos, which is notorious for earthquakes. For Olympia you take the main Tripolis road to the east through an undulating woodland country. The landscape has retained its idyllic beauty but modern Olymbia is, however, a sad anti-climax; the better hotels are well situated, but the cheaper establishments and restaurants, as well as the gaudy tourist shops, give the main street an unpleasantly commercial atmosphere. There is now a Museum of the Olympic Games, just off the main street, which contains historical information about the modern Games.

After Athens and Delphi this is the most important classical site in the country. In one day it is possible to visit the Altis (the sacred enclosure) and the museum in relative leisure. However, it requires a rather longer stay to experience that charmed moment when the astonishing harmony between the ruins and their setting suddenly comes into focus, bringing to life the historical associations within their own landscape and topography.

The sanctuary, scene of the most dazzling assembly of celebrities in the ancient world, was sacred to Zeus; every fourth year, for century after century, during the period of the full moon following the summer solstice, men flocked to the sanctuary to praise the benefits of peace and to watch Greek youth display its prowess in the stadium. The festival was primarily an occasion for athletic contests, for the winning of the cherished olive crown - considered the greatest honour to which a young man could aspire. Mythographers say the first games were instituted by Herakles and that Apollo vanquished his half-brothers, Hermes and Ares, in a foot-race and a boxing match. The first recorded festival was in the year 776 BC and henceforward Greek chronology was based on Olympiads, the periods of four years between festivals. The Games began as a series of foot-races, to which more elaborate events were added. It was organized by a confederacy of Western Greek states and gradually acquired panhellenic proportions under the aegis of the

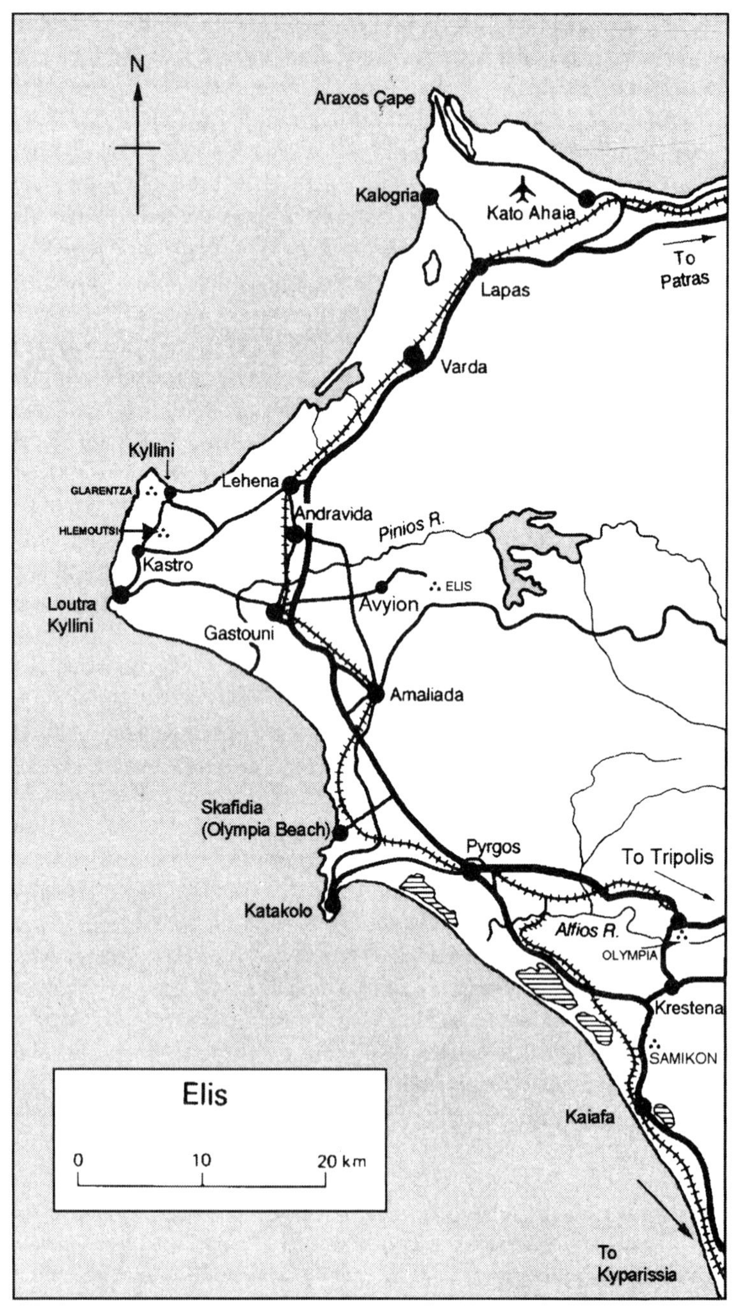
N
Araxos Cape
Kalogria
Kato Ahaia
To
Patras
Lapas
Varda
Kyllini
GLARENTZA
Lehena
Andravida
HLEMOUTSI
Pinios R.
Kastro
ELIS
Loutra
Kyllini
Avyion
Gastouni
Amaliada
Skafidia
(Olympia Beach)
Pyrgos
To Tripolis
Katakolo
Alfios R.
OLYMPIA
Krestena
SAMIKON
Elis
0
10
20 km
Kaiafa
To
Kyparissia

Eleans. Throughout the country heralds would announce a Sacred Truce between all warring states for the period of the celebrations; thus peace became the symbol and keynote of the Games, and Hellenic unity, if only for a few days every four years, a reality. (On one occasion, Elis, a comparatively weak state, had the audacity to impose a fine on Sparta, the mightiest power in Greece, for violating the truce.)

The actual rules were never, according to Aristotle, codified; athletes knew them by tradition and instinct. The sacred element attached to the athletics was illustrated by the sacrifices preceding the events and the number of altars raised in the precinct. The Olympian festival soon became a paean of worship to the father of the gods, every athlete offering a solemn sacrifice to Olympian Zeus, Lord of the Lightning, before entering an event.

The sanctuary was not only the haunt of priests and sports fans, but the resort of men of fashion and eminent politicians. The latter went to the Games as diplomats go to cocktail parties, hoping to make new contacts and pick up useful information. Discreet discussions, held in the shady recesses of the Echo Colonnade, paved the way for new alliances, new alignments, new betrayals.

The place swarmed with temperamental athletes, surrounded by their trainers, admirers and publicity agents; and a vast fly-infested encampment, teeming with beggars and pedlars, spread across the neighbouring fields and vineyards. Roofed accommodation was reserved for athletes, while the crowds slept under canvas or in the open. At night, after the victorious athletes had marched in procession in the light of the full moon, chanting praises to Zeus the All-Seeing, the great concourse was transformed into a vast sexual playground: although women were not allowed to attend the Games, they could - and did - approach the periphery of the sanctuary.

During Roman times Olympia did not decline in importance, but the ideal was tarnished, the standards lowered. Hadrian, as might be expected, did much for the embellishment of the sanctuary but, in 392 AD, Theodosios the Great, anxious to extirpate every trace of paganism in the empire generally, decreed a series of proscriptions which temporarily banished all light and gaiety from the civilized world. Thus the Olympic Games came to an end and with them perished a great Hellenic ideal. Thirty years later Theodosios II ordered the destruction of the principal buildings.

The main street of the village leads to the bridge - a gift from Kaiser Wilhelm II, who financed the first excavations - across the

Kladeos, just before its confluence with the Alfios. The prospect is one of great serenity, the Alfios flowing through the wide valley with rolling, wooded country on either side. Across the bridge is the entrance to the **Altis**. At first it is difficult to associate all this rubble of grey limestone with the brilliant panhellenic sanctuary where sport was born and statesmen and philosophers assembled to preach political unity. The setting however is idyllic, with olive trees now added to the dark pines planted by the nineteenth-century German archaeologists. In spring the paths between the ruins are bordered with irises and gladioli, and the furry, scalloped leaves of golden henbane peep out of cracks in broken slabs of masonry; in summer the bitter-sweet fragrance of agnus castus is overpowering and in autumn the air is balmy with the scent of resin from the pines around and on Mount Kronion, whose slopes are covered with deep pink cyclamen. Gradually the spaciousness of the grove and the sheer volume of the surviving stonework - the huge drums, the imposing stylobate of the Temple of Zeus, the ample proportions of the buildings where the athletes trained, ate and slept - begin to make an impact. One is conscious of a sense of grandeur, of immeasurable peace.

The devastation is not wholly the work of Theodosios II. The Alfios is a capricious river: constantly changing its course and flooding its banks, it has buried many monuments under the porous soil. Earthquakes, to which Elis is very prone, have also taken their toll. It required the patient work of the team of German archaeologists to bring the foundations to light and reveal the ground-plan of the various edifices, which grew up without any architectural or chronological relation to each other. Visitors can choose their own course. One of the most practical is to follow a more-or-less straight line from the Gymnasium to the Leonidaion, then left to the Bouleuterion (strictly-speaking these three buildings lay outside the enclosure of the Altis), turn north to the Temple of Zeus and the Pelopeion, visiting also the important buildings west and north of it, and finally east to the Stadium; with minor detours to right and left, the ground is then covered.

The **Gymnasium**, its walls once inscribed with the names of victors of the olive crown, was famous for the excellence of its running tracks. It is identified by a double row of truncated columns. The **Palaestra**, immediately after the Gymnasium, is a more attractive ruin: a forest of short, slender Doric columns with plain capitals; trees grow in the central court. Seen from the south, with

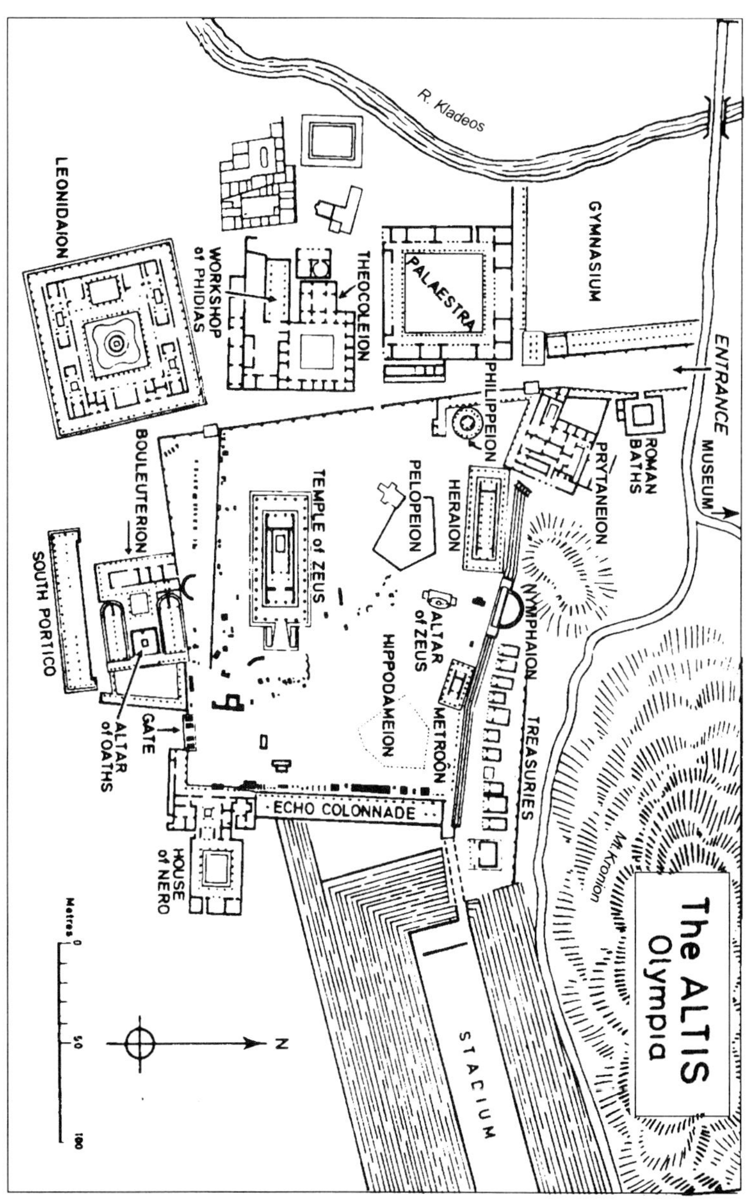
The ALTIS
Olympia
R. Kladeos
GYMNASIUM
PALAESTRA
THEOCOLEION
WORKSHOP of PHIDIAS
LEONIDAION
ENTRANCE
MUSEUM
ROMAN BATHS
PRYTANEION
PHILIPPEION
HERAION
PELOPEION
TEMPLE of ZEUS
BOULEUTERION
SOUTH PORTICO
ALTAR of ZEUS
NYMPHAION
HIPPODAMEION
METROÔN
TREASURIES
GATE
ALTAR of OATHS
ECHO COLONNADE
HOUSE of NERO
Mt. Kronion
STADIUM
N
Metres 0
50
100

the colonnade silhouetted against a line of cypress-clad hills, the scene is one of extraordinary harmony. The building was square, with chambers opening onto the colonnaded courts: a club room; a hall where *ephebes* were anointed with oil; pools for bathers and drying rooms. There were also *exedrae* where retired athletes lectured, and seats where spectators sat and gossiped while wrestlers trained and practised. The athletes considered themselves a race apart and were generally very conceited: though usually of the upper classes, working-class boys with a talent for sport were not debarred from participating. Professionalism was unknown until Hellenistic times, when the festival became a spectacle provided by highly-paid competitors for a noisy rabble. The Palaestra was also thronged with trainers, who lived in a special enclosure and were extremely important people. They were fussy about their athletes' diets, forbidding them starch, but not cheese, and encouraging fish as a suitable diet for muscle-building. Plutarch says they would not even let the young men talk at dinner, lest conversation should give them a headache.

After the Palaestra comes the **Theokoleion**, of which only the outline is now traceable. Built around two courts, it was the headquarters of the priests in charge of the sacrificial rites. Then comes the shell of an early Christian basilica, site of an ancient workshop much venerated by the Eleans because the great Phidias and his pupils worked there on the huge ivory and gold statue of Zeus; during the excavations, some of the clay moulds that were used to form the draperies of the god's gold *himation* were found on the site. Fluted columns with foliate designs frame the ruined Christian altar. South of the basilica, and near the processional entrance to the Altis, the foundations of a large, square building have been identified as the **Leonidaion**, which served as a hostel for high-ranking officials and later for Roman governors. The chambers were ranged round a court with ponds and flower-beds, and there was an exterior colonnade consisting of one hundred and thirty-eight columns. Most of their bases, on some of which their Ionic capitals have been placed, survive on the north and east sides. From this shaded *stoa*, visitors obtained a close-up view of the procession of priests and athletes with which the festival opened. A shallow moat surrounds a circular area in the centre of the court. Large rectangular and smaller square chambers (probably bedrooms) are outlined on the west and south sides. In spring wild larkspur grows among the debris in the former flower-beds.

East of the Leonidaion, across a waste of Greek and Roman foundations, two apsidal halls, joined later by a Hellenistic edifice, formed part of the **Bouleuterion**, where the officials responsible for the administration of the festival assembled. The committee room contained a statue of Zeus, the Oath-God, holding a thunderbolt in each hand. These deadly missiles were intended to strike terror into the hearts of athletes, who swore on pieces of boar's flesh to observe the rules. All that remains of the fourth-century BC South Portico - possibly a market hall - is a row of column bases crowned with Corinthian columns.

We now enter the Altis, the Sacred Area. To the north-east a ramp ascends to the stylobate of the **Temple of Zeus**, at once the heart of the sanctuary and its holiest place. Between them, Theodosios, the Alfios and earthquakes have left nothing standing above the level of the lowest drum; but the huge platform, with formidable column bases on the north colonnade, still dominates the grove in a most majestic way. It was built of local shell-conglomerate by Libon, an Elean architect, in the mid-fifth century BC and the fluted Doric columns, six at each end, thirteen on either side, were equal in height to those of the Parthenon, but considerably thicker. The superb sculptures of the *metopes* and pediments are, happily, in the museum, few having found their way to foreign collections; hidden from sight for hundreds of years under a protective layer of loam and clay mixed with pine needles, the marbles were at least preserved from the attentions of Western antiquity-plunderers. The general impression made by the temple is thought to have been massive yet uninspiring - probably not unlike the Theseion in Athens - but as a ruin it could not be more imposing. All round the high stylobate lie gigantic drums: some neatly sliced in rows, others a mass of contorted rubble as though blown sky-high by some demonic force before crashing down in a pile of shattered masonry.

The mass of the exterior colonnade was only a foretaste of what awaited the spectator in the *cella*, which was entered through massive bronze doors. Here, between two more rows of Doric columns, the base of Phidias' Zeus, most celebrated of ancient statues, occupied a third of the inner chamber. Thanks to Pausanias we have a minute description of this mammoth effigy, which stood twelve metres high and must have looked like some fifth-century BC version of the Albert Memorial: the god was depicted seated on a throne, his head - almost touching the ceiling - crowned with a garland of olive branches. In his right hand he held an effigy of Niké and in his left, an ornamented sceptre surmounted by an eagle. The flesh was of ivory, the drapery of gold, worked with designs of animals and lilies. The finished product, of the greatest sculptor of his age, probably owed much to the popular notion of the god as a kind of implacable Nemesis: Zeus' thunderbolts and Poseidon's trident are instruments intended to strike terror into men's hearts. In Byzantine times the Dafni Pantocrator scowled threateningly down at the faithful from his celestial cupola. The continuity is obvious.

Screens, intended to keep curious spectators at a respectful distance, were decorated with panels painted by Panainos, a nephew of Phidias. In front of the statue, the floor was paved with black tiles within a circular marble rim intended for the retention of olive oil which, says Pausanias, was 'beneficial to the image', and prevented the statue 'from being harmed by the marshiness of the Altis'. One day Caligula decided to take the head of the statue to Rome and substitute his own effigy. However each time the imperial executioners approached the statue with the intention of decapitating it, the image - it is said - roared with laughter and frightened them away. In the fifth century the temple was destroyed and the statue removed *in toto* by Theodosios II to Constantinople, where it perished in a fire.

Around the temple extended a forest of votive statues known as *Zanes*, mostly of Zeus, but also of distinguished athletes. Paionios' great Niké, now in the museum, stood near the east façade of the temple. Pliny estimates the number of statues at three thousand, many of which were removed to Rome and Constantinople.

There were also over fifty altars scattered about the Altis, including one to Zeus - a huge mound of ashes, piled up from innumerable sacrifices. Around the statues and altars well-known actors declaimed to groups of theatrical students, and great public figures were surrounded by admirers: Themistocles, at the height of his fame; Herodotos, followed by the boy Thucydides who burst into tears from emotion when listening to a public reading of the *Histories*; the ranting, boastful Sophists.

North-west of the temple is a grassy mound surrounded by stone slabs: the only surviving trace of the **Pelopeion**, a pentagonal enclosure dedicated to Pelops, Poseidon's cup-bearer, who gave his name to the peninsula and to whom the Eleans annually sacrificed a black ram on a fire piled with white poplar-wood. To the west of the Pelopeion lies the stylobate of the **Philippeion**, which was a circular edifice with an external colonnade and Corinthian engaged half-columns on the walls of the *cella*. Commissioned by Philip II of Macedon after his victory over the united Greeks at Chaironeia and later adorned with statues of the Macedonian dynasty, it was from here that Nikanor proclaimed Alexander the Great's divinity in 324 BC. The beams of its bronze roof were held together by a boss in the form of a carved poppy. All that now remain are the inner and outer circular walls up to knee level, two courses of a stepped wall and a ring of column bases.

To the north of the Philippeion are the remains of the shattered Prytaneion, where the magistrates resided, and to the east extends the impressive stylobate of the seventh-century BC **Heraion** (sufficiently well-preserved for the outline of the *cella* to emerge clearly). It is the oldest extant temple in the country, Doric and peripteral, and was an enlargement of an older temple originally built of limestone and sun-dried bricks, with wooden columns and a tiled roof. Dedicated to the worship of Hera, the Queen of the Heavens, it ranked second to the shrine of Zeus in religious importance and contained the ivory and gold table, carved by a pupil of Phidias, on which rested the victors' olive crowns. Squat and bulky, but with all the dignified self-assurance of Archaic art, the Heraion, although the most ancient, is the best-preserved building at Olympia. The stone-work of the truncated columns of the north colonnade has acquired a light, almost honey-coloured hue and in spring the shady paths around the stylobate are dotted with cistus - pink, white and mauve. Two short columns, complete with flat Archaic capitals, rise intact at the west end of the stylobate. An elongated base, which once supported a statue of Hera enthroned with a helmeted Zeus beside her, is still visible. Pausanias found the statues 'crude works of art', but he admired the Hermes of Praxiteles (now in the museum) which was found lying across the floor of the *cella* at the time of the excavations.

On a bank to the east rises the second-century, semi-circular **Exedra of Herodes Atticus** (or Nymphaion), with two unbroken fluted columns and a large basin, its cornice decorated with lions' heads as spouts. This once-imposing enclosure is followed by a row of ruined treasuries belonging to the principal states, ranged along a narrow ledge supported by a stepped base. The first of these, the **Treasury of Sikyon**, is the best-preserved (indeed better than its more famous namesake at Delphi) and is easily identified by a single short Doric column, with a complete capital, raised on a stone parapet.

Opposite the ledge are three courses of the stone wall of the **Metroön**, a small Doric temple dedicated to the Mother of the Gods. Fragments of broken columns lie lop-sided among the pine needles, and volutes of Ionic capitals are framed in straggling weeds.

Beyond the treasuries is the tunnel of the **Krypte**, 'The Hidden Entrance', a vaulted passage of Roman construction leading to the Stadium. Before it stood some of the numerous *Zanes* which dotted the Altis. The cost of these statues was defrayed from fines imposed on athletes who broke the rules. There is no evidence of large-scale cheating at Olympia but, after the Hellenistic period, when professionalism vitiated the religious nature of the festival, bribery was not unknown; the *Zanes*, strategically placed at the entrance to the stadium, were probably meant to serve as a warning.

From the Krypte, the Echo Colonnade, one of the finest in Greece, ran along the east wall of the Altis. It is now unfortunately completely destroyed. Built in the mid-fourth century BC and famous for its sevenfold echo, it was designed to offer shade to spectators waiting to enter the stadium. Here, during Roman times, were held the musical competitions which Nero, with his passion for singing, inaugurated and took part in.

At the southern extremity of the one-time colonnade there is another group of foundations and ruins which are believed to have been the residence of the judges and umpires. To the east, where the main stream of the Alfios used to flow below the Altis, are the remains of the villa where Nero dwelt during the summer of AD 67 when, hoping to impress his Greek subjects with his magnanimity, he declared all northern Peloponnesians free men. However, the expense involved in surrounding the licentious emperor with the trappings due to a divine personage caused prices to rise astronomically, and the Greeks had to pay dearly for the imperial condescension.

One returns to the Krypte, through which athletes entered the **Stadium**. Ahead extends a rectangular running-track between grassy embankments. Unlike other Greek stadia it never possessed marble, stone or even wooden seats; the spectators, some forty thousand, sat or stood on the ground, which was probably covered with dry grass at the time of the festival. The simplest, most unadorned Greek stadium, it nevertheless ranked first. Assured of attracting the largest assembly, the governing body preferred to spend money on the architectural and sculptural adornment of the sanctuary. Strabo says the stadium was situated in an olive grove, and this has now been replanted. The surroundings - the exquisite contours of the wooded hills, the streams flowing through the valley - cannot have altered much.

An initial feeling of anti-climax at the absence of any major visible ruin soon wears off. The length of the track, from start to finish, is 193 metres. At the west and east ends respectively are the *aphesis* and the *terma*, the starting line and the finishing post, consisting of narrow rectangular slabs, with grooves for the toes of the athletes in the slabs of the *aphesis*. Water conduits have survived and halfway along the south embankment are the vestiges of a tribune for the judges; opposite, on the north embankment, are the remains of an altar of white marble, over which presided a priestess of Demeter, the only woman permitted to enter the arena.

Here then, at the height of the summer, athletes assembled from all over the Greek (and later Roman) worlds to take part in an unchanging programme of events which lasted for a thousand years and whose ideals were handed down to posterity, like an unwritten Magna Carta of sport. The festival lasted five days, beginning with a procession and sacrificial rites and ending with feasts. The track accommodated twenty runners and Lucian speaks of sprinters running in deep, fine sand. All athletes were naked after an incident, it is said, in 720 BC when a sprinter's shorts accidentally slipped off during a race, whereupon the Hellenodikai - the judges - decided that even the skimpiest garment hindered the athletes' movements and forbade the wearing of any clothing whatsoever. To the Greeks there was nothing immodest in nakedness, worship of the human body being strongly ingrained in their aesthetic traditions. It is unlikely that the presence of naked athletes in the Olympic stadium was the cause of the exclusion of women from the Games. In Greek society women held a subservient position; they stayed at home and did not aspire to the pleasures and entertainments provided for men; at Olympia, women who tried to enter the stadium were cast off the neighbouring Typaean rock. One woman, however, succeeded in slipping through the Krypte. Disguised as a trainer, she accompanied her son, a competitor, to the Games; but she was found out and, as a consequence, all trainers were also obliged to enter the Stadium naked.

The foot-races began at dawn, so that the runners could benefit from the cool air of early morning. Other events were held in the middle of the day: wrestling and boxing matches (boxers wore thongs bound round their hands instead of gloves) were followed by the pentathlon, introduced in 708 BC, a composite event - long jump, discus-throwing, javelin-throwing, foot-race and wrestling match. Finally, most popular of all, came the *pancration*, a form of all-in wrestling, with boxing thrown in to make it an even more severe test of physical endurance. In the blinding August sunshine, the audience excitedly followed the punching, kicking and throttling as the tanned and muscular bodies, powdered with fine sand, grappled amid the clouds of dust raised by their straining feet.

Victorious athletes, clad in purple garments, returned to their native cities at the head of enormous processions - in one case, three hundred chariots drawn by white horses - and laid their olive crowns on temple altars; sometimes the city walls were torn down to make the victor's entrance more spectacular. Poets and writers of all ages (with the exceptions of Plato and Euripides, who doubted the wisdom of such extravagant hero-worship) never ceased to laud the athletes. Cicero claims that no victorious general entering Rome was ever received with such manifestations of homage.

After the stadium there are no more ruins. No vestige remains of the theatre mentioned by Xenophon, who lived in retirement in neighbouring Skillos, where he owned a large estate with woods, orchards and pastures, and spent his time riding, hunting and writing his memoirs.

Near the entrance to the Altis a path winds up the slope of Mount Kronion, a conical hill thickly wooded with the tallest, most luxuriant pine trees in Greece - the scent of resin is intoxicating. The summit, where sacrifices were held at the spring equinox in honour of Kronos, father of Zeus, overlooks the Altis and the stadium. From there, on summer evenings, you may see village boys running races in the stadium. Beyond it, where the hippodrome is supposed to lie under ages-old layers of silt, the streams of the Alfios wind between sandbanks. The heat-haze extends across the vista of vineyards and corn-fields, though a breeze sometimes blows through the branches of the pines.

The new, earthquake-proof **Museum**, which is set back, across the road from the site, contains all the most important statuary, the old neo-classical building now being used as a store. It possesses one of the finest collections of ancient sculpture (Archaic to Roman) in the country. The exhibits are arranged chronologically in eight rooms surrounding a central hall dominated by Paionios' **Niké**, back on show after many years' restoration work. She floats down to earth from Olympos in an ecstasy of sheer movement, her wings (now gone) outstretched, her gossamer garments, fastened to her right shoulder with a clasp, clinging to her rounded form as they are blown back by the wind. The statue, raised during the Peloponnesian War to commemorate the abortive Peace of Nikia, stood on a pillar in front of the eastern entrance to the Temple of Zeus.

The remains of the **pediments and metopes of the Temple of Zeus** are ranged majestically along the walls. The huge figures of the pediment, some headless or limbless, monumental in their simplicity of conception and execution, are slightly later in date than the *metopes*. Executed in the finest Parian marble by an anonymous Elean sculptor, they are from that exciting transitional period in the mid-fifth century BC, when Archaic rigidity and tension have relaxed and the liberating breath of classical art begins to galvanise the static figures, rendering them mobile and articulate, without depriving them of the poise and grandeur of the earlier models.

The east pediment depicts the last-minute preparations for the fateful chariot race between Oenomaos, the Pisatan king, and Pelops, suitor to the king's daughter, Hippodameia. The king's assent to their union is dependent upon his own defeat in the chariot race, a matter in fact already settled by the infatuated Hippodameia in collusion with Pelops: she has bribed her father's charioteers to remove the nails from the hubs of the royal chariot wheels. The race is run, the accident occurs according to plan and the king meets his death. In the centre of the composition is a colossal headless Zeus, umpire of the race, holding a thunderbolt, flanked by the two contestants. All the figures, whether erect, crouching or reclining, seem to be filled with an awareness of impending disaster, which heightens the unity and dramatic quality of the composition.

The west pediment, a group of twenty-one statues, is even more exciting. Here the feeling of expectancy is replaced by the confusion of battle. It depicts the climax of the struggle between the Centaurs and the Lapiths at the wedding of Pirithoös and the Lapith Deidameia, celebrated in a cave on Mount Pelion in Thessaly. The Centaurs, guests at the wedding, became so inflamed with wine and desire that they sought to rape the Lapith women, until the Lapith men, led by Theseus, came to the rescue. Stylistically, the west pediment is more evolved than the east. In both, however, the respective moods, tension and conflict, are conveyed by a surprising economy of line. Over it all broods the figure of Apollo. For sheer style - the curve of the neck, the powerful but graceful modelling of the arms, the expression on the imperious mouth with the full, slightly parted lips - there is no finer statue in early classical sculpture; the personification of order and spirit over lust and chaos, austere yet serene, the perfect combination of god and man, he dominates the conflict. The figures of the combatants flanking him are no less striking. Among the finest are the beautiful Lapith bride, very unwillingly submitting to the violent attentions of the Centaur leader; an enraged Centaur preparing to kick a Lapith woman whose nails are dug deep into his cheek, and a Lapith youth strangling a Centaur who bites his arm viciously.

While admiration for the east pediment is universal, this astonishing assembly of primitive creatures depicted in a frenzy of unbridled passion is not without certain blemishes. The modelling of some of the figures is rough, there is an awkward disproportion between the human and equine parts of the Centaurs' bodies and the drapery of the Lapith women's *chitons* is heavy and tubular. Although the pediment was meant to be viewed from fifteen metres below, no Athenian sculptor of the fifth century would have tolerated such imperfections.

Paionios' wonderfully graceful Niké offers a contrast and an antidote. On either side of the entrance are four *metopes*, depicting the Labours of Herakles. Left to right: Herakles bringing the Stymfalian Birds to Athena - it is a relief to find her in a relaxed mood and without her ungainly helmet; Herakles, his head resting on his right hand, reflecting for a moment in the midst of his fight with the Nemean Lion; Herakles, a lithe, vigorous figure cleansing the Augean Stables, assisted by Athena (who has lost her chin and has consequently acquired a rather fatuous expression); and Herakles dragging the dog Cerberus, its jaws open ready to snap, from the Underworld. There are two more *metopes* at this end of the hall: Herakles capturing the Bull of Knossos and **Herakles supporting the heavens** - the acknowledged masterpiece - with the aid of Athena, while Atlas brings him the Golden Apples of the Hesperides, fruits of the Tree of Life. The vertical symmetry of the composition - the strictly linear folds of Athena's garment and the erect postures of the male figures - is broken only by the horizontal projection of Herakles' forearms. The head of Herakles is identical throughout the series - an indication that the *metopes* were executed by a single artist.

Among the most important items in the surrounding rooms is the large **head of Hera** in the room devoted to the Archaic period. The late sixth-century BC effigy was probably part of the cult statue in the Heraion. The Queen of the Heavens has an air of authority and majesty and the half-smiling, autocratic mouth gives remarkable distinction to the broad, flat face under the stylized head-dress.

In a room to himself, the famous **Hermes** - supposedly one of the few extant statues of Praxiteles, the most distinguished sculptor of the late Attic school - stands proudly alone on his pedestal against a sky-blue apsidal background. Chiselled out of Parian marble, which has acquired an astonishingly white patina, the Messenger of the Gods carries his baby brother, Dionysos, on one arm. The infant god of wine, who has a very knowing look, stretches out a hand to grasp what is believed to have been a bunch of grapes, teasingly held at a distance by his elder brother. The modelling of the god's figure is masterly: neck, diaphragm, buttocks, thighs and calves forming a unity of separate but interrelated volumes. The god is leaning on a tree-trunk, draped with his cloak, which forms an integral part of the composition. His expression is calm and aloof; some critics have described it as 'icy' and the small mouth does almost look mean. The statue is perhaps rather self-consciously graceful, the artfully-arranged locks suggestive of curling-tongs, but the work is an outstanding example of the consummate technique of the late fourth century BC: that smooth perfectionism which produced a series of polished masterpieces whose lack of dynamism often matched their spiritual emptiness. In the fourth century BC the sculptural scene was dominated by Skopas and Praxiteles. Temperamentally Skopas was attracted by the harsher, more violent aspects of beauty, Praxiteles by the gentler, tenderer sentiments that it inspired. Modern scholars believe that if the Hermes at Olympia, described by Pausanias as standing at the west end of the Heraion, is not the original, it must at least be a masterly copy by a Graeco-Roman sculptor of the original work by Praxiteles.

29

Frankish Elis and the Achaean Coast.

THE ROUTE BACK TO CORINTH from Olympia goes via Pyrgos and Patras, where one can join the National Road; it is more interesting, however, to use the old road from Patras, which keeps closer to the coast. Most of the main sights, which lie along this route or just off it, can be seen in one day, but the side-trip to Megaspilion and Kalavryta may entail spending a night at either place. The most important sights are Hlemoutsi and the monastery of Megaspilion; the visit to Glarentza can be omitted by the less leisurely traveller. The highlight of the journey is the lovely Achaean coast: steep, wooded and washed by the inland sea of the Corinthian Gulf.

North-west of Pyrgos the road enters a flat plain. The mountains recede to the east and the prospect is less shut-in than elsewhere in the Peloponnese. The landscape, which is treeless except for some orchards, is richly agricultural and, it has been said, recalls Champagne and Flanders; perhaps that is why the French knights felt so strongly about it. From Gastouni (the Frankish Gastogne) a branch road to the east for Avyion leads to the site of the ancient city of Elis, where Herakles cleansed the stables of King Augeias by diverting the course of the Pinios into the royal yards. The ruins are mostly Roman, the theatre and much of the *agora* having, so far, been revealed by excavation. There is also a small museum.

Just off the highway to the north of Gastouni is **Andravida**, the Andreville of the Franks. It is difficult to associate this unprepossessing town, once a Turkish market centre, with the flourishing medieval city and seat of successive princes - Champlitte, Villehardouin, Anjou, Savoy, Valois, Bourbon - who ruled from here over the whole principality of the Morea. Its historical buildings are gone: the palace in which the Villehardouins dwelt in princely state and the chapel in which they were buried; the hostelries of the religious orders - Teutonic, Carmelite, Knights Templar. There is just one Gothic ruin, which is not without charm: to the north of the main square, the third turning to the left leads to the honey-coloured stone shell of the Latin Church of Ayia Sofia. After Olympia, with its glut of classical associations, this diffident little medieval relic with its pointed arches - choir, apse and rib-vaulted side chapels - fascinates by sheer contrast.

Just north of Andravida, whether you are on the main road or the road to Lehena, a turning to the left will take you to Neohorio where a road to the right leads to the small port of Kyllini. A short drive to the south then takes you to a low, flat-topped sandstone mountain, surmounted by **Hlemoutsi**, one of the grandest medieval castles in the Morea and a landmark for miles around. The castle looks north to Kyllini. (The traveller should note that the name Kyllini is used to refer to the village and port, the headland, the stretch of sand-dunes to the south and the spa, as well as to the site of the ancient port of Kyllene to the north.)

Hlemoutsi can also be approached from the village of Kastro to the south; indeed, the castle is at its most impressive when seen from the wheatfields surrounding it on this side. Built by the Franks in the thirteenth century, it was originally known as Clermont; later the Venetians called it Castel Tornese. The castle's history begins with a quarrel between the Pope and Geoffroy I Villehardouin, an Achaean Prince who had no qualms about financing the construction of his new citadel out of revenues from sequestered ecclesiastical fiefs. Geoffroy refused to abandon his project and the Pope excommunicated him. More interested in military defence than in Holy Communion, the Prince of Achaea paid little attention to the fulminations of Rome and completed his castle, whose strategic position helped to make the Morea safe against any possible Byzantine threat.

Geoffroy's successor, William, increased the importance of the castle by establishing a mint. The coins, known as *tournois* (having originally been minted at Tours), were stamped with the prince's title and an image of the Church of St Martin de Tours. It was from these *tournois* that the castle afterwards acquired the Italianized name of Tornese. Here Marguerite, William's daughter and heir, was caught up in a web of intrigue spun by false claimants: a typically strong-minded Frankish princess, she refused to surrender her hereditary rights and, seeking support from a foreign power, arranged a marriage between her fourteen-year-old daughter and the Infante Ferdinand of Majorca. The Burgundian barons, fearing that the principality might pass into Spanish hands, seized Marguerite and

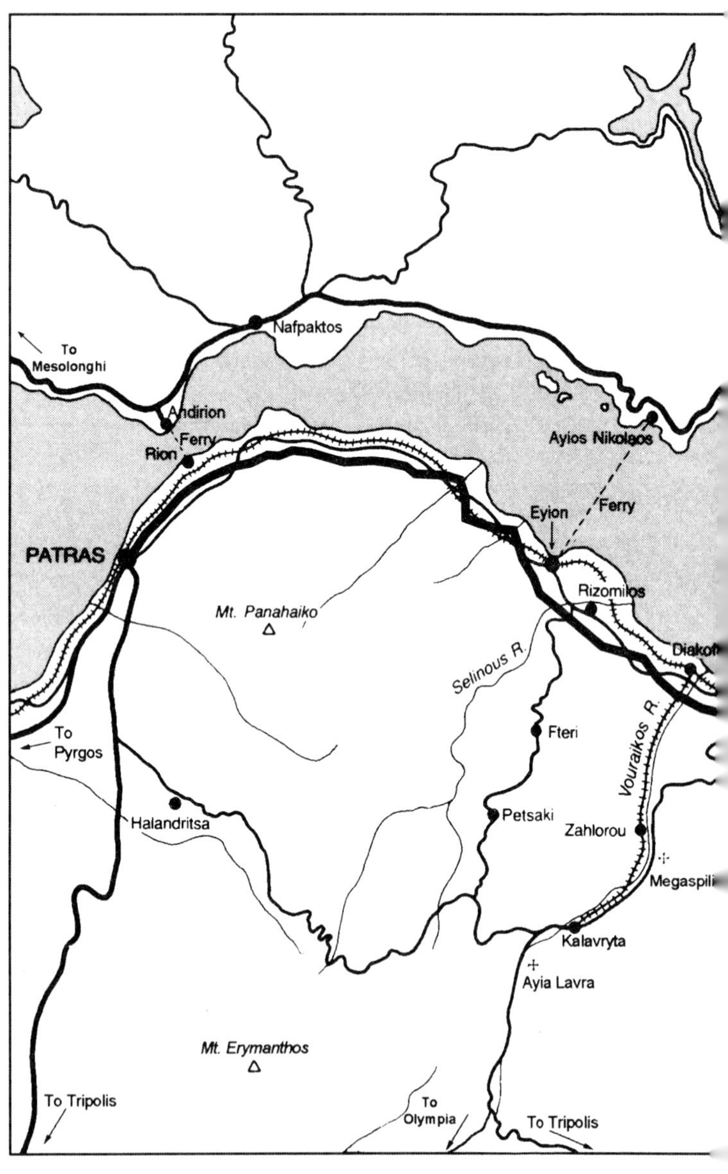
Nafpaktos
To
Mesolonghi
Andirion
Ferry
Rion
Ayios Nikolaos
Eyion
Ferry
PATRAS
Rizomilos
Mt. Panahaiko
Selinous R.
To
Pyrgos
Fteri
Vouraikos R.
Halandritsa
Petsaki
Zahlorou
Megaspili
Kalavryta
Ayia Lavra
Mt. Erymanthos
To Tripolis
To
Olympia
To Tripolis

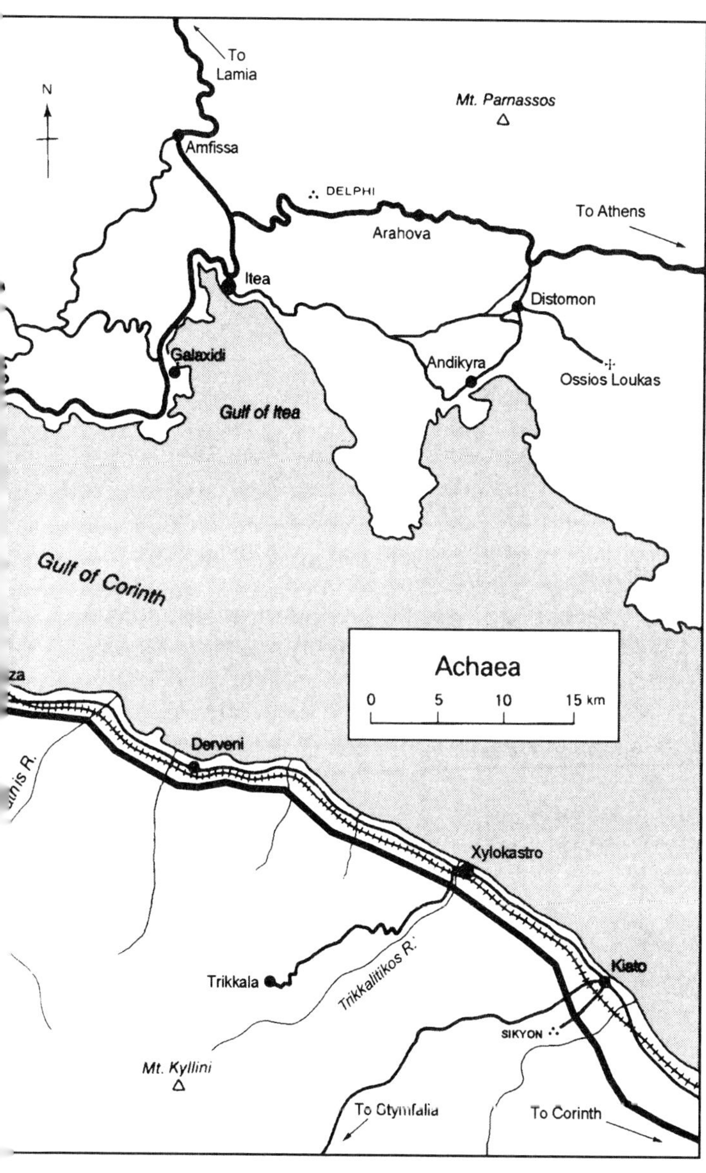

To
Lamia
N
Mt. Parnassos
Amfissa
DELPHI
To Athens
Arahova
Itea
Distomon
Galaxidi
Andikyra
Ossios Loukas
Gulf of Itea
Gulf of Corinth
Achaea
0
5
10
15 km
Derveni
Xylokastro
Kiato
Trikkala
Trikkalitikos R.
SIKYON
Mt. Kyllini
To Corinth

cast her into a dungeon of the castle, where she died, the last of the Villehardouins, proud and courageous to the end, in 1315. The castle was later captured by Ferdinand and held for a short period until 1316 when he was defeated by an alliance of French and Greek troops.

In the fifteenth century, Constantine Dragases, soon to become the last Byzantine Emperor, resided here whilst conducting a brilliant campaign against the Italian buccaneer-overlords of the Morea. Finally, some four hundred years later in 1825, when Ibrahim's Egyptian army swept across the Morea leaving a largely deserted wasteland in its wake, the castle was blown up.

Most of the ruins date from the original thirteenth-century construction. The great outer curtain wall, its original height defined by crenellations, sweeps majestically round the north, north-west and west sides, enclosing a hexagonal court with a bailey. The outer gate at the north-west angle of the wall penetrates a mass of masonry nearly fifteen metres high. Two domed archways lead into an open space, followed by a vaulted passage and an enclosure with the remains of houses. The inner gate of the keep is at the north angle of the hexagon, flanked to the right by a round tower. A vaulted passage opens into the north gallery - the best-preserved of six halls strung around the keep like a chaplet. Now empty except for nesting swallows, its barrel-vaulted roof partly open to the sky, the north gallery still has seven arched windows on the south side. Although the other five galleries are not so well-preserved, they contain traces of fireplaces; enormous logs must have been required to heat the lofty stone halls when winter gales blew across the Ionian Sea. From all the galleries doors opened onto balconies, supported by arches, which commanded wide prospects of the dunes and surf-fringed beaches of the Zakynthos channel. In this cluster of spacious galleries, the Villehardouins often took up their official residence.

To walk from Hlemoutsi to the site of **Glarentza** will take an hour, across the fields bordering the coast. The country is flat or faintly rolling, green but never wooded. White-crested waves break on a shoreline alternately rocky or sandy and seaweed-covered; gulls squawk overhead. Here, too, was the ancient port of Kyllene, with its sanctuaries of Aphrodite and Asclepios and, Pausanias says, 'a statue of Hermes that the people there worship so devoutly, which is just an erect penis on a pedestal'. Across the sea loom island shapes: mountainous Kefallinia and Homeric Ithaki; to the west the low outline of Zakynthos (Zante) is crowned by its pyramidal peak.

What is left of Glarentza, in medieval times the busiest port in the Morea, is a little to the west of modern Kyllini harbour and village. The site has no history before the Fourth Crusade, and none after its destruction in the fifteenth century. The harbour, with its artificial defences, was once full of Italian trading galleys and amongst its buildings was a great Franciscan monastery. The only traces now left of its medieval architecture are some fragments of ramparts and moles scattered about the shingly beach. Tufts of arbutus and heather cover the sandstone undulations of the deserted site, once so thriving a trading centre that, to the Florentine banking firm of Acciajuoli, their Glarentza office equalled the London one in importance.

The few blocks of heavy masonry still to be seen are the substructures of edifices dating back to the ancient Hellenic Kyllene. There is nothing else. For the city's total destruction - more complete than any caused by Goths or earthquakes - Constantine Dragases was responsible. Having acquired Patras for his main port and afraid that Glarentza might fall into the hands of those who would use it as a strategic base for a Latin re-conquest of the Morea, he ordered it to be razed to the ground. Its banks, trading houses, shops and churches were flattened, its bankers, merchants and seamen sent into exile. The Byzantine destruction of Glarentza - ironically enough on the eve of the Turkish conquest - marks the end of the Latin period, that strange elusive interlude in the history of Greece when its sunny plains and rocky defiles became the hunting-ground of successive generations of dashing Western adventurers. Of the Latin colonizers of Greece, only the Venetians now remained in their maritime strongholds.

The featureless coast to the north of Kyllini extends up to the flat, dreary outline of Cape Araxos, near which there is an important Greek Air Force base and civil airport. The main road, some way inland, goes north-east through flat, fertile country to Patras: an extensive area of vineyards, producing some of the best wines in the country, succeeded by orchards of orange, lemon and other citrus fruit.

Crossing into Achaea one reaches **Patras**, a town of almost two hundred thousand inhabitants and departure point for the car ferries to Italy, which has a number of arcaded streets and an air of having known better days. The town livens up enormously during Carnival, when spectacular processions are staged and masqueraders and decorated floats are pelted with flowers and confetti. Its position is impressive, the town being strung out, behind the harbour, below a spur of Mount Panahaiko; higher up are wooded foothills with curiously convulsed shapes.

Patras played no important part in ancient history and was devastated during the wars between Rome and the Achaean League, after which it was re-populated by order of Augustus.

After Augustus, Patras' most distinguished visitor was St Andrew (its patron saint) who converted the Roman governor and, it is believed, suffered his martyrdom here, when he was crucified on an X-shaped cross of olive wood. The relics of no other saint have undergone so wide a dispersal: some went to Amalfi; a tooth, a knee-bone and three fingers went to St Andrews in Scotland, and the head, after being bandied back and forth between Patras and Constantinople, was carried by the Despot of the Morea, fleeing from the advancing Turks, to Rome, where the Pope organized a great ceremony for its reception on the Mulvian Bridge. Pope Paul VI returned the head to Patras and it has come to rest - let us hope, permanently - in the large new cathedral. In spite of the far-flung dispersal of his mortal remains, the first-called of Christ's disciples did not forget his flock at Patras even after his death; his intervention, relates the chronicles, saved the town from being sacked by the Sclavonians in the ninth century when, in the form of a shining apparition, he personally hurled the invaders back from the battlements. After the Frankish conquest in the thirteenth century, Patras became a strategically important barony, guarding the Corinthian Gulf from westerly invasion, until taken by Constantine Paleologos (Dragases) in 1429..

Patras re-enters the limelight in 1821, when it was a hot-bed of Greek patriots. Whether the initial call to arms against the Turks - which led to the outbreak of the War of Independence - was made at Patras or Kalavryta remains debatable. In his picaresque memoirs, Makriyannis, one of the most colourful leaders of the insurrection - brave and honest, though foul-mouthed - has left, a vivid account of the first days of the war in Patras: pursued by Turkish agents, he sought refuge in the Russian Consul's house (where, incidentally, he was upbraided for his insanitary personal habits). Venturing out later he witnessed the fighting, which was very fierce, with the Turks holding the castle while the Greeks drew up their ranks along the shore.

In the upper town there is the unimportant, though charming, partly-restored Roman **Odeion**, with red brick walls, white marble tiers and fragments of mosaic pavement. A little to the east, one must climb nearly a hundred steps to reach the summit of the acropolis, scene of the savage annual festival of Artemis Laphria. The method of sacrifice to the goddess of the chase was unusual: the festival opened with a procession in honour of the goddess winding up the hill, with the officiating maiden-priestesses riding in a chariot drawn by deer. Logs of fresh wood were then placed in a circle round the altar. The next day the logs were ignited and the worshippers cast birds, wild boar, deer and gazelles into the flames, together with the choicest fruit.

The **Castle**, on the site of the ancient acropolis, is worth visiting, if only for the magnificent view of the screen of mountains rising abruptly from the Lokrian shore, with the channel fanning out into the Corinthian Gulf which cuts deep into a mass of mountain ranges for another hundred and fifty kilometres to the east; to the west spreads the town and the fertile Achaean plain. The ruins of the castle are a hotchpotch of Byzantine, Frankish, Venetian and Turkish work. The approach by car is from the south side (Papadiamandopoulou Street) and then through a Frankish arch within a Byzantine structure. On the left (the south-west angle) rises a well-preserved Turkish octagonal bastion. The north curtain wall is ninth-century Byzantine - one of the points from which the Greeks (with the aid of St Andrew) threw back the Sclavonians. The enclosure is in the form of a triangle, with the quadrangular keep at the north-east base and a tower at each corner, reached along a causeway over a shallow moat and then through a ruined archway bearing the effigy of an heraldic lion. A walk along alleys of oleander, bordered with arbours of honeysuckle and flower-beds shaded by cypress and quince trees, brings one to a round Venetian bastion which marks the apex of the triangle.

Eight kilometres east of Patras a turning off the road to Athens leads to **Rion**, whence a car-ferry sails every twenty minutes to Andirion on the opposite coast; this is the main route between Athens and Western Greece. The narrow channel (called 'the little Dardanelles') between the Peloponnese and continental Greece is one of the most important crossroads of sea and land communication in the country and is to be bridged. East and west of the two kilometre-wide waterway extend the two deep gulfs - of Corinth and Patras. Two low circular forts with outworks, built by Sultan Bayazit II on the site of two ancient shrines of Poseidon, face each other across the narrows. Known as the castles of the Morea and of

Roumeli, they look oddly toy-like, sprawling across the flat shore. At the end of the War of Independence the castle of the Morea was the last Turkish fortress to hold out - against the French: after the Battle of Navarino, the mutual rivalries of Britain and Russia having delayed the pacification of the Morea, the French Government sent an army of fourteen thousand men under General Maison to sweep across the Morea, clearing up pockets of Turkish resistance. The only serious opposition he encountered was at Rion, where the French army delivered the *coup de grâce*. Maison was accompanied by a mission of engineers and welfare officers who built roads and cleared up the shambles left by the Turks.

Beyond Rion, wooded coves alternate with reed-fringed strands and bushy promontories, but the beaches of this inland sea are not particularly attractive, though there are numerous hotels and holiday apartment developments. Everywhere there are flowering hedgerows and vineyards, for this is currant-producing country - *raisins de Corinthe*. The mountains to the south are still well inland, but the convulsed nature of their earthquake-rent forms is already apparent. **Eyion,** built on three levels, is backed by terraced cliffs. Cafés, shaded by plane trees, spread across a square overlooking the railway station and harbour, whence a car-ferry sails for Ayios Nikolaos on the north shore of the Corinthian Gulf. Gone now is every trace of the sanctuary of Eileithyia, goddess of childbirth, and of ancient Aigion, the headquarters of the Achaean League, where the federal assembly, one of the few serious attempts to achieve Hellenic unity, met twice a year to establish a common policy in resisting Macedonian and later Roman aggression.

East of Eyion, the village of **Rizomilos** is near the site of ancient Helike, an important Achaean city which, as the result of a violent earthquake, sank into the sea one night during the fourth century BC, drowning the entire population. In antiquity the Achaean coast - a mountainous land-mass rising precipitously from the Corinthian Gulf - was, as it still is, a country of earthquakes, then regarded as manifestations of the anger of the gods. The menace of earthquakes is ever-present and always near the surface of Greek consciousness; the inhabitants have had to come to terms with it and a whole lore of superstition has grown up around the manner and place in which 'the Earth-shaker' will strike next. In ancient times earthquakes were said to be preceded by portents: the sun would be screened by a red or black haze, trees would be uprooted by whirlwinds, springs dry up and flames dart across the sky. These manifestations would be followed by the roar of winds below the earth's crust - 'the Earth-shaker' working himself up into one of his tantrums; this ominous premonitory rumbling is as familiar to the present inhabitants of Achaea as it was to those of antiquity.

Around Rizomilos the coastal strip is at its widest, but soon the first spurs of the Arcadian limestone mass advance dramatically towards the sea, the chalky soil of their scarred and ravaged precipices sprinkled with pines. South of Diakofto, which lies slightly inland, a huge wooded cleft cuts the mountain wall in two. This is the opening of the **Vouraikos Gorge**, so narrow that the road to Megaspilion and Kalavryta has to climb indirectly from Trapeza, further to the east.

If one does not intend to drive beyond Kalavryta, the ascent through the beautiful gorge can be made from Diakofto by a miniature railway which is partly rack and pinion. The toy carriages sway and clatter as the wheels grind up the narrow track on an alarmingly steep gradient between walls of rock, then descend into little verdant glens, where pools of ice-green water surrounded by large, smooth boulders are shaded by stunted plane trees. In autumn the imposing cliffs blaze with the orange, amber and coral of dying leaves. Sheets of maidenhair and other luxuriant ferns fringe the turbulent stream and bright pink cyclamen grow beside the rail-track. There are no dwellings and the sun only lights up the chasm with the briefest of shafts at noon.

As the altitude increases, the gorge widens out and the train stops at Zahlorou, a mountain hamlet on the road up from the coast, which is the station for **Megaspilion**. It takes half an hour to walk to the monastery, along a path which mounts the scrub-covered hillside above the mountain valley of the Vouraikos River. Along this path once came two Early Christian fathers from Jerusalem; the Virgin had appeared in a vision and ordered them to travel to Achaea, where they would find her image in a cave in a mountain recess. When they reached the Achaean coast, the Virgin appeared before them again and directed their steps up the gorge to the foot of a great cliff, where St Euphrosyne, a shepherdess of royal blood, stood perched upon a rock and hailed them. Imperiously striking the ground with her crook, she caused a spring to gush forth and commanded them to proceed to a cave where a dragon had its lair. A sudden flash of lightning fortunately caused the monster to drop dead and the pilgrims then found not only the holy icon of the Virgin but also the table upon which St Luke had copied out his

Gospel.

The *Mega Spilion*, or Great Cave, subsequently became a place of pilgrimage and a monastery grew up around it. The present monastic buildings date only from 1934, fire having destroyed the older edifice and its fine library. They cling strikingly, storey upon storey, to the surface of a vertical cliff with a large cross on its flat summit. In the fissures of the rock the shapes of three crosses are said to be discernible - to devout Orthodox eyes only. In Byzantine times the monastery was one of the most prosperous in Greece and monks fleeing southward after the fall of Constantinople further enriched the library with valuable manuscripts.

The interior of the monastery is worth visiting, if only to stroll along the gallery overlooking the mountain-girt valley with the orchards and kitchen-gardens of the monks terraced on the slope below. The church is dedicated to the *Panayia Hryssospiliotissa* (The Virgin of the Golden Cave) and its most revered object is the icon discovered, with the help of St Euphrosyne, by the two holy fathers; miraculously this has escaped destruction in successive fires. It is a primitive image on wax, attributed to that most prolific of iconographers, St Luke. Amongst the relics that survived the 1934 conflagration are St Euphrosyne's skull in a silver reliquary, one of her hands in a silver sheath, a fine twelfth-century *cloisonné* Gospel book-cover and the skulls of two military saints - Theodore the Tyro and Theodore Stratelates.

Visitors may spend the night here, accommodation being provided in a guest-house for which there is a charge. The air is wonderfully clear and there are beautiful walks along paths bordered by cyclamen in autumn, by primroses and wild violets in spring.

From Zahlorou the railway and road continue through more open country to **Kalavryta**, which is both a mountain resort on the rugged Helmos range and a national memorial. Streams course through the town and the waters of one, the Alyssos, were supposed to cure men and dogs of rabies. In the thirteenth century the great French family of La Trémouille dwelt in a castle on the table mountain that towers three hundred metres above the town, guarding the Frankish-held coastline of Achaea against incursions by Arcadian mountain-dwellers; the ruins of the castle, known, like the mountain, as Tremola, are hardly worth the climb however.

Above the town, on the north slope of Tremola, stands a large cross commemorating the wholesale massacre of the male population by the Germans in 1943, as a reprisal against local guerilla activity.

It was December and freezing; men and boys were led up the snow-covered slope and machine-gunned; the principal buildings were gutted by fire. The hands of the clock on the main church, the *Mitropolis*, still stand at the time, 2.34, at which the massacre took place. That is what 'Kalavryta' means to the Greeks.

The **Monastery of Ayia Lavra**, is situated seven kilometres south-west of the town, amongst ilex woods and cypresses. Here Yermanos, Metropolitan Bishop of Patras, a prelate inspired by the most patriotic of motives, raised the standard of revolt against the Turks, supposedly beside the large plane tree in front of the main church on 25th March, 1821, thus beginning the eleven year War of Independence. The monastery, burnt by Ibrahim Pasha in 1826, rebuilt and burnt again by the Germans in 1943, has, in its post-war transformation, the air of a Western Roman Catholic convent: neat, well-ordered and colonnaded. The adjacent small, seventeenth-century, cross-in-square Church of the Dormition, more evocative of the Byzantine heritage, escaped both fires; in it was held the service which preceded the start of the revolution. The treasury contains sacerdotal vestments worn by local prelates at the historic service and also the banner, unfurled by the martial bishop, representing the Dormition of the Virgin. The hole in the face of the angel in the top left-hand corner was made by a bullet. There are also manuscripts dating from the eleventh to the fourteenth centuries and a hideous Gospel-cover presented by Catherine the Great.

From Kalavryta the main road goes westward before branching a few kilometres outside the town. From the junction, one branch goes south and, after passing below *Ayia Lavra*, divides: right for Olympia via Tripotama, left to join the Tripolis road south of Klitoria. Another branch road from the junction leads back to the coast; it climbs into the mountains, passing through the bleak village of Fteri and crossing the watershed, before descending through oak forests into the majestic Selinous Gorge; here, towering buttresses of rock overhang a winding torrent which runs parallel to the Vouraikos and is of equal natural beauty. This road reaches the coast at Eyion.

Continuing to the west from this junction near Kalavryta the road for Patras goes through magnificent scenery between Mount Panahaiko and, to the south, Mount Erymanthos; a half-moon of craggy mountains points skywards in a series of ever-changing forms of naked limestone, their bases thickly wooded with spruce. Below the slopes of Panahaiko - a relatively featureless mountain compared with the splendid peaks and crags of Erymanthos - a path to the right leads through fields of pink garlic, blood-red adonis, funnel-shaped arums and Serapias orchids, to the little **Church of the Panayia**. This minor detour is not recommended for the architectural beauty of the church - it has none - but it is the oldest extant Byzantine church in the Peloponnese, possibly ninth-century. The dilapidated, roofless little chapel lies half-buried in a flowery field and you have to descend steps to enter it. Two marble columns with sculpted capitals, preserved intact, separate each of the tiny aisles.

Beyond Halandritsa, once a Frankish barony forming part of the ring of strongholds encircling the Arcadian plateau, the road descends into the north-eastern corner of the olive-covered plain of Achaea. The rest of the way to Patras is through flat, mostly agricultural, country.

East of Diakofto, on the road to Corinth, the coastline is very splendid and the Corinthian Gulf widens to its greatest extent. Across the water towers Parnassos, its bluish summit often wreathed in cloud. Somewhere on the mountainside is Delphi. The gorge of the Pleistos, below the sanctuary, is just visible in clear weather. On the Peloponnesian shore, the Achaean mountains approach so close to the sea that there is nothing but the narrowest coastal strip left, along which the old road and the railway wind below pine forests (the new National Road is a little further inland). Along this old road once came the first Crusaders, Champlitte and Villehardouin, from Corinth to Patras to found the Principality of Achaea, which was to include the whole of the Morea and was to last over two hundred years.

The chalky surface of the crags and escarpments is scarred with ravines and precipices. There are two more great gorges, the Krathis (into which flows the trickle of the Styx) and the Sythas, which opens out fanwise to reveal terraces of whitish soil thick with cypresses. The inlets are bordered with vines, myrtles, orange trees and willows.

Xylokastro, a popular beach resort, was probably the port of ancient Pellene, one of the twelve Achaean cities, and said to have been founded by a giant. The shingly beach is bordered by dark umbrella pines. A branch road climbs to Trikkala (Corinthia) on the slopes of Mount Kyllini, the main skiing centre of the Peloponnese.

One is soon at Kiato, below the plateau of Sikyon, with the familiar hump of Acrocorinth, key to all the treasures of the Peloponnese, squatting above the vineyards.

30

The Approaches to the West

WESTERN GREECE is a series of formidable massifs, more or less parallel to, and west of, the Pindos spine, fringed by fertile coastal strips and washed by the Ionian Sea and the Gulf of Corinth. Variety in landscape is matched by the immense chronological span of the historical sites: ancient, medieval and Ottoman. There are four main approaches.

- Corinth - Rion - Andirion -

The direct way to Western Greece is, perhaps surprisingly, via Corinth and along the northern shore of the Peloponnese as far as Rion. The coastline covered by this route was described in Chapter Twenty-nine. From Rion there are frequent ferries to Andirion on the mainland coast and a bridge is under construction.

- Galaxidi - Nafpaktos - Andirion -

From Athens to Galaxidi via Delphi is a four-hour drive (see page 78). After Galaxidi the road runs along the northern shore of the Gulf of Corinth to Eratini, spreading across a green maritime strip; the Delphi Beach hotel, gaunt and barrack-like, rises incongruously from a shore of spiky rocks. From nearby Ayios Nikolaos ferries ply across the Gulf to the Peloponnesian port of Eyion. Fishing hamlets are surrounded by cypress groves, and low islands are dotted about the crescent-shaped bays. Soon the austere mountains recede, making room for the river Mornos to flow through an alluvial valley into the sea; then they advance again and the road reaches **Nafpaktos**, cramped between the reed-fringed coast and the mountains.

After the Third Messenian War (464-459 BC), in which the Messenians were routed by the formidable Spartans, the Athenians established Messenian exiles here. Filled with hatred for the Spartans, who were also the Athenians' chief rivals in the struggle for

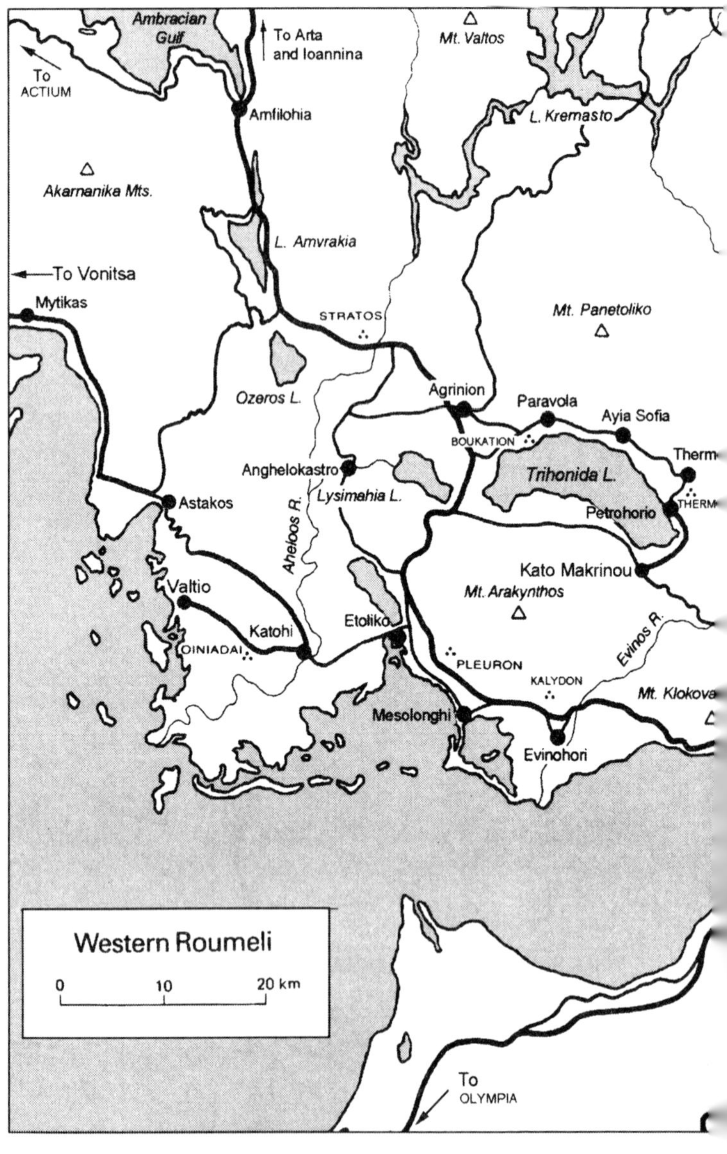
Ambracian Gulf
To Arta and Ioannina
Mt. Valtos
To ACTIUM
Amfilohia
L. Kremasto
Akarnanika Mts.
L. Amvrakia
To Vonitsa
Mytikas
STRATOS
Mt. Panetoliko
Ozeros L.
Agrinion
Paravola
Ayia Sofia
BOUKATION
Anghelokastro
Trihonida L.
Lysimahia L.
Astakos
Aheloos R.
Petrohorio
Kato Makrinou
Mt. Arakynthos
Valtio
Katohi
Etoliko
OINIADAI
PLEURON
Evinos R.
KALYDON
Mesolonghi
Evinohori
Western Roumeli
0
10
20 km
To OLYMPIA

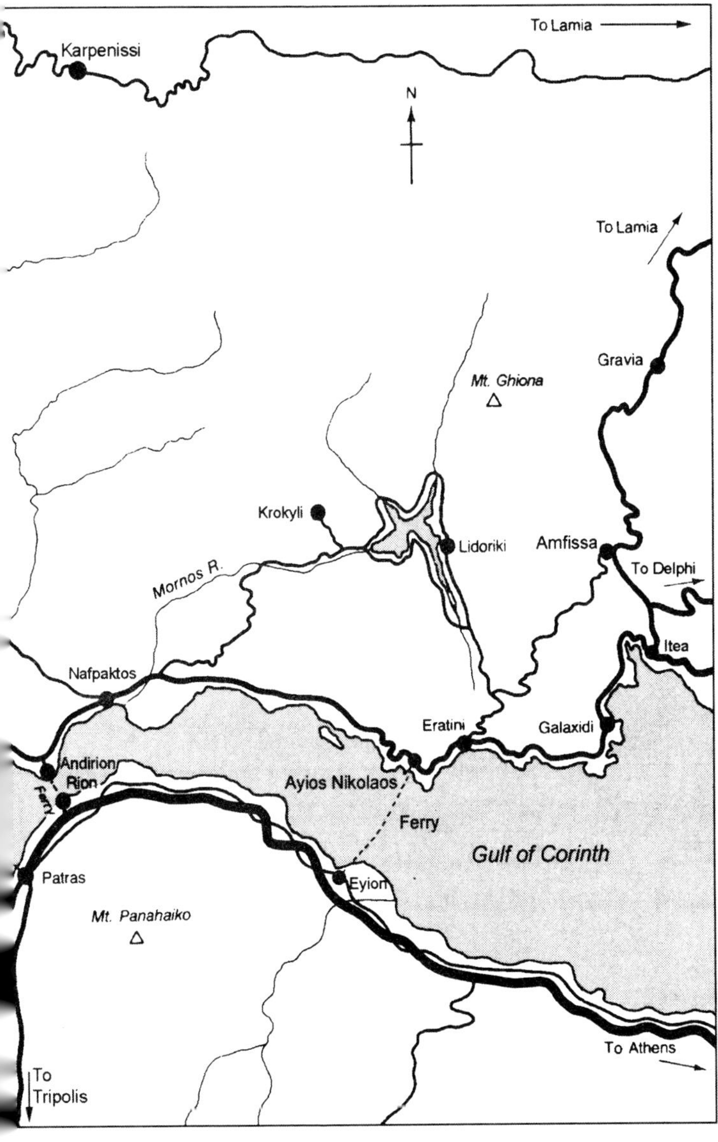
To Lamia
Karpenissi
N
To Lamia
Gravia
Mt. Ghiona
Krokyli
Lidoriki
Amfissa
To Delphi
Mornos R.
Itea
Nafpaktos
Eratini
Galaxidi
Andirion
Rion
Ferry
Ayios Nikolaos
Ferry
Gulf of Corinth
Patras
Eyion
Mt. Panahaiko
To Athens
To
Tripolis

leadership of the Greek world, the Messenians gladly manned this strategic naval station which commanded the approach through the narrows into the Gulf of Corinth from the west. It was in these confined waters in 429 BC that Phormio, the Athenian admiral, engaged the entire Spartan-led Peloponnesian fleet. Commanding twenty swift triremes, he boldly encircled the larger enemy fleet, constricting it, so that many Peloponnesian vessels fell foul of each other. Then he attacked, forcing the enemy to retire; but they were unwilling to admit defeat and at one point succeeded in driving the Athenians so close inshore that Phormio was forced to deploy his vessels in a dangerously attenuated line. However, handling his small, fast squadron with dash and discipline, he broke through the more cumbersome Peloponnesian triremes and routed them. There was no second round. Timokrates, the disgraced Spartan admiral, threw himself overboard and was drowned in the harbour.

In medieval times the town, then called Lepanto, was ruled by the Venetians, who built the great castle, made it 'the strongest bulwark of the Christian people' and stayed for nearly a hundred years. A Christian island in a Turkish sea, the wall-girt city suffered violent siege, with Turkish cannon-balls raining down for weeks on end. It fell in 1499: the last Venetian stronghold on the Greek mainland. Its loss was such a blow to Venetian pride that Grimani, the surrendering admiral, was lampooned in Venice as 'Antonio Grimani, the ruin of the Christians'.

From here, one October morning in 1571, set sail the Turkish fleet of Sultan Selim the Sot (who preferred women and wine to battle); they were to engage the combined Papal, Spanish and Venetian squadrons consisting of two hundred galleys commanded by Don John of Austria - the Battle of Lepanto. Within hours the Turkish defeat was total: over a hundred galleys and thousands of men were lost. Christendom, it was proclaimed, was saved, the invincibility of Ottoman power proven a myth. However the battle was not decisive; the allies fell out among themselves and Venice made a separate peace with the Sultan. Turkish dockyards, working overtime, made good the losses and by the seventeenth century the Crescent once more fluttered unchallenged throughout the Eastern Mediterranean.

The little Venetian port of Nafpaktos, as it now is, with its painted caiques, is oval in shape and is defended by two towers at either extremity of the breakwater - a perfect stage-set. A steep cone-shaped hill, girdled with a triple line of walls, overlooks the port and a road, passing below the line of well-preserved fortifications, winds up to the **Venetian Castle**. Passing on foot through a series of arched gateways overlooked by a crenellated bastion, one enters the bailey, now a shady pine-wood. A slippery path, thick with pine needles, mounts to the chapel of *Profitis Ilias*, once the site of a pagan sanctuary. Fragments of watch-towers, built on ancient Hellenic foundations, form belvederes. A wall-walk north of the chapel commands a view of a steep, pine-clad slope falling away into a ravine. The outer line of the defences makes a fine sweep to meet a transverse wall. Further down, another transverse wall runs impressively along the entire width of the *enceinte*. From here it is easy to perceive the general design of the castle, which is divided into five successive wards on different levels. Below, the little town clings to the side of the hill, with the harbour, guarded by its two diminutive bastions, in the exact centre of the picture; on either side extend sandy, reed-fringed beaches. Across the strait rise the Peloponnesian ranges.

Beyond Nafpaktos, the road runs westward along a well-irrigated coastal plain. **Andirion**, terminal of the ferry service from Rion, is little more than an agglomeration of port installations, distinguished by a low fort; known as the Castle of Roumeli, it was built by the Turks on the site of a medieval defensive position and topped with a lighthouse. A new bridge will eventually cross to Rion but, until then, the wash from ferry boats, crammed with vehicles, will streak the blue channel. The sea is often choppy, for the wind is funnelled into the narrow channel between high mountain ranges. Eastward extends the Gulf of Corinth; westward the Peloponnesian and mainland shores open out, the mass of Kefallinia, with Ithaki in front of it, emerging out of the Ionian Sea. In the south, the eroded hills of Mount Panahaiko pile up towards the Peloponnesian heights.

- Delphi - Lidoriki - Nafpaktos -

A longer, more devious, route from Delphi goes through the mountains and into the Mornos valley leading down to Nafpaktos. From Amfissa the road climbs the bare, elephantine flanks of Mount Ghiona, providing stupendous views of the ring of mountains enclosing the Sacred Plain. Starting off in a south-westerly direction, the road curls round the mountain and ends up at **Lidoriki**, only fifteen kilometres west of Amfissa, after a journey of almost fifty kilometres. Situated at an altitude of nearly 600 metres, in an unproductive, sparsely-populated wilderness whose desolation is only relieved by a rash of battery chicken farms, the village was a famous guerrilla hide-out in the Second World War. It is pleasant to break the journey for refreshment in the village; the air is crystalline, the inhabitants blond, ruddy and friendly. Thence begins the grand, meandering descent to the coast. The mountain configuration acquires an increasingly intricate character, with canyons, sunless valleys and hollow gorges; an isolated crag is crowned by a white chapel. The road follows the northern shore of the lake formed by the damming up of the Mornos River to augment the water-supply of Athens; only a thin trickle now flows below the dam among great cliffs and fir-clad slopes.

A road to the right leading to Krokyli (a minor detour of ten kilometres) ascends steeply above the confluence of the Mornos and one of its tributaries. With the increasing altitude, the vistas become more awe-inspiring, especially in autumn when the lower forest belt is ablaze with colour. Beside a plane tree at Krya Vryssi (The Cold Spring) there is a monument raised to the memory of Makriyannis, one of the ablest and most extrovert generals of the War of Independence. Less than one kilometre beyond the monument is the abandoned village of Isvora, where Makriyannis spent his childhood and youth fostering his flamboyant patriotism and hatred of the Turkish oppressor. More striking than Isvora is the red-roofed village of Krokyli, below a fearsome peak. The terrace of the village church overlooks a narrow wooded valley, beyond and around which rise successive ranges, capped by nodular peaks and crags.

The main road to the south-west continues through the Mornos valley; after a final descent through a valley of orchards and vineyards, planted with lines of dwarf cypresses, it approaches the northern shore of the Gulf of Corinth. The road turns westward, crosses a bridge spanning the Mornos and enters Nafpaktos.

- *The Pindos spine - Metsovo - Ioannina* -

Finally, further north, there is the route from Kalambaka, which you would take if you were already in Central or Northern Greece. It is perhaps the most spectacular of all; scaling the Pindos range at a tremendous altitude, the road leads to Ioannina, capital of Epirus. From the Kalambaka-Grevena fork it ascends in wide loops; to the east, below and behind you, the Pinios winds through a wide wooded valley, with the tusks and obelisks of the Meteora forming a grotesque gateway into the plain beyond. Ahead, westward, loom range upon range of mountains. Occasional villages, with ugly corrugated-iron roofed houses, spread across hillsides of apple and fig orchards. The deeper one penetrates into the massif - into the actual spine of the whole country - the grander the 'Alpine' landscape becomes, with wooded heights pressing in on all sides. The holm-oak belt is succeeded by the stone pine - a Christmas tree scene, with the watershed dominated by a beetling crag. At the top of the formidable pass - the Katara (the Damned One) - a large hollow arena opens up to the south-west. The road gradually descends the slopes of fir, box and beech into the heart of the bowl, where the twin villages that make up **Metsovo** (Prosilio and Anilio), cling to the sides of precipitous cliffs. Their names mean 'with' and 'without' the sun - the one in bright light, the other condemned to eternal shade.

Metsovo, one of the show villages of Greece is, by the very nature of its position, claustrophobic (the mountain makes walking an exhausting recreation but favours skiing in this rudimentary winter sports resort). It remains a centre for Rumanian-speaking Vlachs who, it has been suggested, may be the descendants of Roman legions stationed in the bleak, but strategic, passes of the Pindos mountains. The village was always populous in spite of its remoteness and under the Turks the inhabitants did not suffer the worst of depredations. A seventeenth-century vizier, fleeing from the Sultan's displeasure, took refuge here. When pardoned, he became Grand Vizier and, in recognition of the hospitality offered him by the inhabitants, he granted them special privileges in the form of grazing rights and tax exemptions. The prosperity of the village never diminished and today it is famed for its wood-carvers, its gold and silversmiths, its trade in tourist souvenirs (bedspreads and fleecy sheepskin rugs) and its excellent smoked cheese.

Narrow, cobbled alleys descend between tourist shops and tall houses (the older ones roofed with grey slate) to a large, poplar-shaded square where, in summer, as the sun sets over the mountains to the west, the inhabitants mix with the increasing numbers of tourists. On feast days, round dances are performed here: the men, their weather-beaten faces set in stony expressions, wearing black kilts and black *tsarouhia*, the women in flower-embroidered dresses and black cloaks, with pigtails hanging down their backs from under black kerchiefs - this is one place where traditions are assiduously kept up. Adjoining the square is the Church of *Ayia*

Paraskevi, a sixteenth-century foundation in basilica form, with a clock-tower surmounted by a cross. The departing Turks, after their defeat in the First Balkan War (1912), tried to shoot the cross down and carry it off as loot, believing it to be made of gold. The church's main interest lies in its wooden *iconostasis*, dated to c. 1730, in which the Epirot craftsman has carved representations of God and the Expulsion from the Garden of Eden. South-east of the square is a playground, perched dizzily over the bowl-like valley across which the great peak of Peristeri, towering over the whole central mass of the Pindos, casts its shadow.

The **Tossitsa House**, which serves as a museum of local popular art - it is signposted - has been restored as a typical grand old Metsovo house. The layout is similar to that of the mansions of the Turkish period at Ambelakia, Siatista and Kastoria: armoury and wash-house on the ground floor; bedrooms on the first; reception rooms with wide, low divans and banquettes all round on the second. The floors are carpeted with fine, locally-woven *kilims* and the bedroom cupboards are filled with the elegant cloaks worn by the gentlemen and the bridal dresses worn by their ladies.

Another agreeable visit is to the Monastery of *Ayios Nikolaos*. A branch road descends into the ravine of the Metsovitikos stream at the bottom of the sombre mountain bowl. To the south, across the cliff-face, spreads Anilio, in its allegedly permanent shade. The short ascent to the monastery is along a path bordered by ferns. Hens peck among dead leaves under an arbour of walnut trees; pansies, snapdragons and geraniums create a blaze of colour in the monastic courtyard. Here all is serenity; the ring of awesome mountains is out of sight. The church, restored in 1960, is in basilica form. The post-Byzantine frescoes, also restored, cover every inch of wall space: small panels, rather than the usual grand compositions. A band of saints' heads amid vine tendrils round three sides of the interior is attractive, but the carved wooden *iconostasis* must surely be too fussy for even the most enthusiastic admirer of this form of Epirot church decoration. In the narthex, converted into a miniature museum, are displayed icons, the most striking of which is one of St Matthew, a dark figure depicted in the act of composing his Gospel, while an angel in red garments stands beside him.

Glad as one is to have visited Metsovo and penetrated the heart of the lonely central Pindos massif, it is agreeable to escape from its claustrophobic atmosphere and to be on the road again. The westbound way into Epirus continues to offer an impressive spectacle, as one ascends and descends slopes of scrub-oak and crosses torrent beds strewn with huge boulders. It was in this rather desolate country, at the locality called Peristeri, that General Tsolakoglou signed an armistice with the Axis forces in April 1941 which paved the way for the occupation of Greece by German and Italian forces.

After spanning a bridge, the road climbs the foothills of the barren limestone barrier of Mount Mitsikeli and descends one of its southern flanks, passing the Monastery of *Panayia Dourahan*. This was founded by an infidel Turkish pasha as a token of gratitude to the Virgin for protecting him during a nocturnal ride across the frozen lake of Ioannina. A panoramic view then opens up: the opaque lake with its wooded islet, the mosque crowning the citadel of the city of Ioannina, all surrounded by hazy, beige hills.

31

Western Roumeli

BEYOND NAFPAKTOS and Andirion variety is the keynote: mountain ranges rise on the north side of the gulf separating the Peloponnese from the mainland; from the gorges between the mountains flow streams, which swell into rivers and wind across the plains into lagoons. The plains are scattered with rocky knolls and ridges; some of these were once the sites of well-fortified Hellenic cities and extant walls recall their military importance. All this country is known as Western Roumeli.

Three days (with two nights at Agrinion, an unattractive hot town, but central and with suitable hotels) is the minimum time required to see all the places described in this chapter. Going by the direct route, without detours, the traveller can visit the scanty ruins of Kalydon and the Heroes' Garden at Mesolonghi; the ramparts of Pleuron too can be identified from the highway, which also runs below the walls of Stratos in the Aheloös valley. The two most rewarding sites, however, Oiniadai and Thermon, lie well off the main road.

Beyond Andirion the road loops westward round the formidable mass of Mount Klokova, which rises 1000 metres sheer above the sea. After overhanging the sea at a great height, the road winds through a wooded valley filled with Judas trees, and crosses the shingly bed of the Evinos, which flows in serpentine loops between steep, shrub-covered banks. Water from this river now supplements the water supply of Athens.

This was always wild country, its mountains scarred with rugged ravines and once inhabited by warlike tribes dwelling in scattered and unprotected settlements, unlike most of the Greeks, who were basically a gregarious people, concentrated in fortified cities. The inhabitants of today seem to have inherited few of the characteristics of their turbulent ancestors: a staid, provincial people, they take little part in shaping the destiny of modern Greece.

The road crosses the Evinos and climbs a little above the wide, intensively-cultivated plain of Mesolonghi. About three kilometres past the river, and after a line of eucalyptus trees on the right, there is the small car park for **Kalydon**. On the great hump of Mount Varasova opposite, and commanding the complex prospect of land and sea, there are still fragments of the towers from which sentinels signalled the approach of hostile vessels. The city which was founded, according to legend, by Aetolos and named after his son, Kalydon, was the home of many famous mythological figures: of Oeneus, who received the first vine from Dionysos; of Thoas, who went to the Trojan War in a fleet of forty black ships; of Oxylos, king of Elis, who, some say, founded the Olympic Games; and of the fearsome Kalydonian Boar.

A stony path leads up through olive trees into the low, dry foothills. A short way up on the left are the remains of the tiered seating of the Council House, and a few hundred metres further up a signpost points (right) to the Heroön, the Heroes' Sanctuary. Ancient slabs litter a straggly olive grove where vestiges of chambers constructed of rectangular blocks (only a course or two survive) are grouped around what must have been a peristyle court surrounded by a colonnade. Beside an adjacent wall, steps descend into a vaulted passage leading to a burial chamber (c. 100 BC) directly under the court. The path to the left, also signposted, leads to the remains of the sanctuary of Artemis Laphria, goddess of the chase who, in a land of huntsmen, was worshipped above all other deities at Kalydon. The outline of the stylobate of the fourth-century BC temple, with *cella*, colonnades and porch, buttressed with the rectangular blocks of an earlier retaining wall, are clearly identifiable; the temple once contained the famous statue of Artemis Laphria, afterwards removed to Patras. Nearby is the site of the sixth-century BC Temple of Apollo: to the unprofessional eye a mass of unidentifiable outlines.

A few kilometres beyond Kalydon is the turn-off for **Mesolonghi**, its undistinguished modern houses surrounded by shallow water - sea and lagoon. With flourishing fisheries and a good trade in *avgotaraho* (an expensive delicacy: fish-roe pressed into cylinders and coated in a rind of yellow wax), the historic little town remains mosquito-infested, smelling of marsh and salt; rain-lashed in winter, burning hot in summer. At sunset, the lagoon, across which flat-bottomed boats skim between rows of piles, reflects an impressionist blend of colours that recall Turner's (rather than Canaletto's) Venice: bands of amethyst, grey and lavender, speckled with coils of green, yellow and pink. A reef separates the lagoon from the sea.

During the War of Independence leading figures, headed by Alexander Mavrocordatos, first President of the National Assembly, chose this melancholy place for their headquarters because, strategically, it occupied a position similar to that of Kalydon in antiquity, controlling both the entrance to the Gulf of Corinth and all communications between the mainland and the Peloponnese from the west. It was also the first place in Western Greece to be liberated (and the first in which the Moslem population was exterminated to a man). To it flocked patriots and it seemed the best place for Byron, as representative of the London Committee formed to help the Greeks in their struggle for liberty, to try to unite the rival factions and persuade them to fight the enemy rather than each other. He arrived on 2nd January, 1824, wearing the scarlet uniform of the Eighth Regiment of Foot and surrounded by kilted Souliot guards; guns fired salvoes and wailing *kleftic* tunes were played on lutes and clarinets as he was received by the assembled dignitaries: the *banditti*-turned-politicians, the gorgeously-robed clerics and the sallow, aquiline-faced aristocrats.

Byron showed unaccustomed patience, endeavouring to instil some notion of constructive patriotism into the vain and mercenary men who paid lip-service to him because he had gold to give away and a title which impressed them. But his greatest contribution to the cause of Greece was his death, which occurred, aptly enough, in the course of a violent thunderstorm, after a ten-day bout of malarial fever. The drama of the end matched the record of the past. Not only Greece and England were moved by the circumstances of his death; all Europe suddenly became conscious of the Greek struggle for liberty. The flow of volunteers from France, Italy and Russia increased. In the minds of the ordinary Greek people he was - and indeed still is - not only the greatest Englishman who ever lived, but also a symbol of all those qualities that their own leaders sometimes lacked: altruism, reliability and authority, enveloped in an aura of aristocratic and eccentric glamour. When his body was taken back to Newstead, the inhabitants of Mesolonghi pleaded that some part of his body should remain with them. So his intestines were enshrined in four jars and placed in the church of St Spyridon. They were later interred, but there is no record of exactly where. The house in which he lived and died is no longer standing.

The **Heroes' Garden** lies at the north-west end of the town, shaded by dusty pines, palms and eucalyptus trees; the muzzles of old cannon project from gun-slits in the Turkish walls which run along two sides of it. The monuments to the heroes of the war - Byron's occupies the place of honour - are outstandingly ugly, the palm going to that of the Anonymous Philhellenes: a pile of rock and cannon balls crowned by an urn. However, it is pleasant to sit on a shady bench where the fresh smells of pine and eucalyptus drive away the saline odours rising from the lagoon.

After Byron's death, the siege of Mesolonghi began in earnest, and it was from the landward side that the famous sortie was made. The town, which was defended by a garrison of five thousand Greek soldiers, peasants and boatmen, was surrounded by a Turkish army under Reshid Pasha; after nearly a year's siege, Ibrahim Pasha brought up his Egyptian army from the Morea and launched flotillas of flat-bottomed boats across the lagoon to attack with musketry and fiery missiles. Every attack was thwarted by the Greeks. The heroism of the defenders was indeed prodigious but, with the Turks in command of the lagoon, it was no longer possible to supply the garrison; so in April 1826 the decision was taken to make a mass sortie through the labyrinth of ditches, dykes and pools surrounding the town. As the Greek soldiers sprang forward, writes Finlay, 'neither the *yataghan* of Reshid's Albanians, nor the bayonet of Ibrahim's Arabs, could arrest their impetuous attack.' However a traitor warned the Turks, and the Greeks found the roads blocked with Turkish cavalry; hunger, wounds and fever took their toll of the surviving groups which straggled away from Mesolonghi up the mountain paths. As the Turks entered the shattered town, the few remaining Greeks blew themselves up. Mesolonghi is justifiably a national shrine.

After Mesolonghi, you can either take the old road along the lagoon to Etoliko in order to visit Oiniadai, or follow the main road and, after three kilometres, you will see, high up on the hills to the right, the walls of **Pleuron**. A tarmac road climbs Mount Arakynthos and leads up to the site, high above the plain: it is well worth visiting. The early Archaic city was destroyed by Demetrios II of Macedonia in the third century BC and a new Hellenistic city rose up shortly afterwards during the wars between the Macedonian kings and the Aetolian League. This later city was built on the higher, more inaccessible site where the main ruins can be seen today. By the early first century AD Strabo reported that the site was deserted.

Below the walls can be seen one of several tombs which form an extra-mural necropolis. Descending through a hole in the ground, one enters a vault consisting of two chambers, one containing a stone bench decorated with a volute; the well-preserved stone wall has a lovely smooth patina. It may have been the tomb of some senior garrison officer, for Hellenistic Pleuron was a military stronghold, ruled by no great kings and claiming no distinguished citizens.

The entry into the *enceinte* is from the south-west - the visit is made easier by a raised boardwalk leading up over the very rough terrain and entering the main gate. Huge rectangular blocks of limestone litter the ground which is carpeted in autumn with pale pink crocuses; a massive lintel, almost four metres long and one metre wide, is propped against the wall. From here it is best to go roughly northwards across the windswept ledge; first, to the vestigial remains of a theatre, the smallest in Greece, built into the western rampart, where the garrison troops were probably entertained with the farces of Aristophanes and Menander; it had only eight tiers and was entirely unornamented. Next comes a strange sunken structure, believed to have been a huge cistern containing the main water supply for this barren, inaccessible place. The pit is approximately 30 metres by 20, its sides are overgrown with ivy and it is divided by four parallel walls which may have supported a roof. Each of the oblong chambers formed by these walls is connected with the next by a curious triangular aperture.

To the east extends the site of the *agora*. The outlines of the foundations are almost incomprehensible and the strictly military nature of the citadel, a formidable observation post dominating the plain, may account for the fact that there is not a fragment of a capital, or a column or decorative moulding. A parapet surrounds the east side; immediately below it, the well-preserved eastern gate, with clearly discernible holes in which the door pivoted, overlooks the bleak slopes of the Arakynthos range.

Turning south-east in order to complete the circuit, one passes the base of an apsidal edifice and the sunken foundations of a square chamber into which a stairway descends; one then skirts the line of the eastern walls, two metres thick and in a good state of preservation: as impressive an example of third-century BC military architecture as any in the country. Composed of massive stone blocks and crowned at intervals by low, rectangular towers (originally there were over thirty), the line extends unbroken, generally six courses high - sometimes as many as fifteen. Vestiges of steps, by means of which sentinels mounted the *terreplein*, are discernible. In a wide arc running from east to west one can see the cliff of Varasova like a huge beast crouching above the plain, the lagoon of Mesolonghi intersected with causeways, the fields and cypresses of the coastal plain, and a shoal of islets - the Ehinades, off which the Battle of Lepanto was fought - strung out along the shore where the Aheloös winds through sandbanks to the sea.

The old road from Mesolonghi to the north passes through a well irrigated plain with a complex of lagoons and salt-pans on the left. A very wide, shallow inlet runs north alongside the road, until a causeway to the left forms a narrow inner lagoon which bites deep into the land, with the colour-washed houses of Etoliko, on its island, reflected in the motionless water.

After Etoliko the road to Astakos passes through an idyllic domesticated countryside of maize fields and olive groves. After crossing the reed-fringed Aheloös and passing through the market town of Katohi, a turning to the left leads through rich alluvial farmlands towards Valtio. This reclaimed marshland was originally Lake Melita and was connected with the sea by a channel. Now the isolated hills rise out of maize fields, their bases fringed with reeds and luxuriant thistles; all evidence of the lake has vanished. After about five kilometres there is a low, flat-topped hill, running north to south, which is locally known as Trikardo: the site of ancient **Oiniadai**.

The city acquired considerable fame for its impregnability. An Athenian army, commanded by Pericles, was unable to scale its well-defended sides in 453 BC, and in the Peloponnesian war, in 428 BC, Oiniadai having sided with Sparta, twelve Athenian triremes sailed up the estuary of the Aheloös but were unable to capture the citadel. In Hellenistic times the hill was encircled with strong new fortifications, and the arsenal and harbour on Lake Melita were joined to the citadel by ramparts. Thus fortified by nature and by man, it occupied a strategic position dominating the Akarnanian lowlands but, like other Hellenistic cities of the western littoral, it contributed little to the evolution of Hellenistic civilization.

The whole eminence, obviously once an island, is peppered with fragments of walls (originally a circuit of five kilometres), with gates, posterns, sally-ports, cisterns and foundations of houses the site has been completely fenced in and is kept fairly clear of undergrowth. The entrance to the site is on the left of the road and, past the gates, the track continues within the precinct. The contours of the port - once a sinuous creek biting deep into the limestone cliff-side - are discernible, enclosed within parallel ramparts running

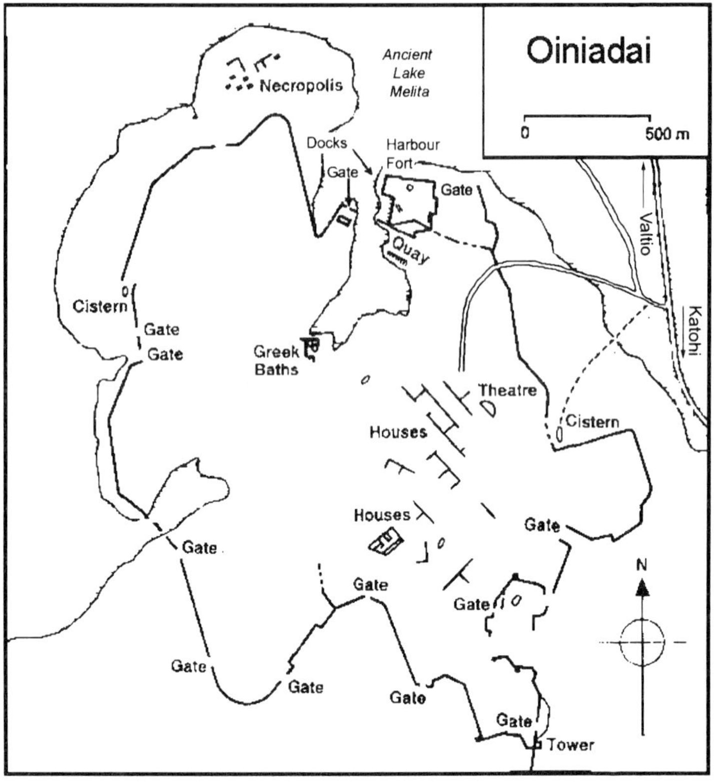

south to north. A fine polygonal wall and a prominent tower overlook the former lake. The track passes close to the tower and ends just before the Theatre, which is completely fenced in. (The guardian is not usually at the site but can be found at Katohi if you want to see the site properly.) The **Theatre** consists of fragments of more than twenty tiers and part of the orchestra. The *cavea* was divided into eleven sections and there were twenty-five rock-hewn seats in the front row for notables; from the highest tier there is a memorable view through a tracery of oak branches. The southern extremity of the hill slopes towards the serpentine estuary of the Aheloös, flowing through green fields and shoals of silt. East of the river mouth, a group of hills with craggy crests complete the

Poussin-like composition: serene, classical and pastoral. Only the heroic figures are absent - Oiniadai today is a very deserted place; there are few views in Greece which approximate more closely to the seventeenth-century French concept of a classical landscape.

To the east of the theatre is a large cistern, followed (south-east) by the remains of what could have been an important gateway. Returning to the entrance, a rough track leads north-west to the **Port**. The narrow bottleneck of the creek opens out into the harbour in which triremes once anchored. At the southern extremity of the creek are the ruins of the second-century BC baths: a rectangular edifice with a stone bathing pool and two circular rooms containing basin-like hollows, where bathers stood as hot water was poured over them from cauldrons.

The **Docks** are at the foot of the hill, beneath the prominent tower. This area is also fenced in and the gate kept locked. The site is unique in Greece: below a massive wall, tall parallel buttresses, between which ships were berthed, are easily identifiable; traces of the slipways, once latticed with wood to protect the keels of the triremes, are just discernible. There is an uncanny feeling of unreality, of something one cannot quite believe in, about these ancient port installations, barely distinguishable from the rock out of which they were hewn, and with no visible sign of the sea for miles around.

Back in Katohi one can either take the road left to Astakos and then the coastal road up to Mytikas and on to Vonitsa, or return to Etoliko and take the main road to Agrinion. The latter route follows the eastern shore of the inner lagoon, goes through a dramatic defile and passes between the two main Akarnanian lakes: Lysimahia and Trihonida. An alternative is to turn left before the defile and go north west into the valley of the Aheloös, between the ranges of the Akarnanika and the Arakynthos chains: a country of scrub-covered, sometimes olive-clad, hills. The village of Anghelokastro, once the second capital of the Despots of Epirus, is crowned by a ruined Byzantine tower. After crossing a saddle of hills, the road descends into the green bowl of the Akarnanian plains, dotted with lakes and traversed by the streams of the Aheloös, with the jagged spurs of Mount Panetoliko massing up behind Agrinion.

Agrinion, an important market town and one-time centre of the tobacco trade, is linked by a mountain road with Lamia in the east via Karpenissi. It is also the starting-point for a visit to Thermon and a tour of Lake Trihonida. Stiflingly hot in summer, the plain of Agrinion is subject to violent earthquakes (the town was completely destroyed in 1887 and subsequently rebuilt). There is a lively public square, lined with hotels, restaurants and the usual confectioners' shops. Distant hills and mountains, blue or gunmetal according to the time of day, form an imposing ring round the well-watered plain; the two lakes lie to the south.

To visit Thermon you take the road along the north shore of **Trihonida**, the larger, crescent-shaped and more beautiful of the two lakes, once believed to be unfathomable at its eastern end. In antiquity, all this shore was densely populated. Now, cypress thickets and plantations of pomegranates mount in terraces above the lake; the route is lined by a succession of prosperous villages and mulberry trees with whitewashed trunks surround open-air wayside cafés. The first place of importance is **Paravola**, where, scattered across a steep hill between the village and the lake, are the ruins of the large, ancient fortress of **Boukation**, of whose history little is known. Hellenistic walls radiate in all directions from the small, oval summit of the citadel. Climbing the north-west side, one skirts defence works composed of rectangular blocks, twelve courses high. The entrance to the summit is guarded by two round, medieval towers from which sentinels could spot hostile armies debouching from the defiles of Mount Panetoliko. From this platform, studded with wild almond trees and stunted oaks and girdled by fragments of the acropolis wall which follows the irregular configuration of the eminence, one gets a good idea of the fortifications: acropolis walls, inner and outer, with steps leading down to the lower town, also defended by inner and outer defence works. Three fortified salients radiate from a striking semi-circular tower. The north-east side of the terrace, where there are two more very ruined semi-circular towers, is buttressed by a fine wall made from polygonal blocks. A rampart descends in a north-westerly direction to the village school, whence another line of less well-preserved walls runs southward in the direction of the lake. The *enceinte* is one and a half kilometres in circumference.

Further east, streams cascade through the pretty village of Ayia Sofia under arbours of plane trees, the ice-cold water gurgling round huge, contorted tree-trunks. On the hillside, amid pines and cypresses, there is the curious, barn-like Church of *Ayios Nikolaos*, built entirely of ancient materials - pilasters, columns, capitals and cornices - plundered from a temple of Aphrodite at Thermon. North of the church, the shell of a little Byzantine basilica nestles in the shade of prickly oaks; south of it, a minuscule Turkish mosque raises its shallow dome above the tombstones - one of those numerous examples of the juxtaposition of antiquity, Byzantium and Islam which constantly diversify the Greek landscape. To the north, the spurs of Mount Panetoliko are dotted with fragments of Hellenistic watch-towers and walls, part of a vast, crescent-shaped defensive system protecting the prosperous settlements of the lake district.

The important site of **Thermon** lies just beyond the village of the same name. It was the spiritual centre of the Aetolians - to these rough people Thermon held the same meaning as the Acropolis to the Athenians or as Delphi and Olympia to all Greeks. Its ruins are embedded in marshy ground surrounded by cultivated fields and the spruce-covered sides of the Panetoliko massif, rising to bare, beautifully-proportioned peaks, form a semi-circle round the sanctuary.

In spite of the presence of prehistoric buildings and Archaic temples, we know that the sanctuary did not acquire nationwide renown until the third century BC, when it became the headquarters of the Aetolian League, a loose federation of states which tried to dispute the mastery of Greece with Macedonia. All the treasure of the Aetolians was stored at Thermon. In 218 BC Philip V of Macedon, unwilling to tolerate Aetolian pretensions any longer, set out to punish the League. He sacked Thermon, smashed two thousand statues and hurried off with much treasure. Twelve years later, infuriated by the Aetolians' provocative alliance with Rome, Philip returned and, according to Polybios, 'once more defaced all the sacred objects that he had spared in his former occupation of the place'. Henceforth Thermon ceased to exist.

A tour of the ruins - which are fragmentary, though not unimpressive - follows a roughly straight line, north to south, within what was a rectangular enclosure once flanked by third-century towers. The barbaric note, associated with the character of the Aetolians, is struck from the outset: several lopsided slabs of porous stone, projecting from the soil like a miniature Stonehenge, mark the site of a very early temple. Following the side of the embankment, one reaches the foundations of the Temple of Apollo, originally of the seventh century BC, but later refashioned. This, the holiest shrine of the Aetolians, extended across a stepless stylobate. Its most unusual feature was its length in relation to its width: fifteen columns on each side and only five at each end, as opposed to the

Parthenon's seventeen and eight. A row of twelve columns ran along the centre of the *cella*, supporting the roof. There was no front porch at the south end, and the wooden entablature was crudely decorated with painted terracotta *metopes*. The massive limestone drums of the north façade give some idea of the heaviness which must have characterized the building. Primitive in conception and execution, it expresses the backwardness of the people whose shrine it was.

Beside the temple are the outlines of two early pre-Hellenic structures known as Megarons A and B, which may have served as palaces. South of the temple's front entrance, a pile of stones indicates the site of the altar, once heaped with the ashes of sacrificial animals, around which pilgrims, priests and savage tribesmen gathered at the Panaetolian celebrations every autumn.

Continuing southward past a square reservoir, one reaches three successive *stoas*, which form a long rectangle, now choked with weeds; landcrabs, on which the local inhabitants fed during the German occupation of 1941-44, crawl among the damp, mossy deposits. Here were situated the shops and stores from which Aetolian merchants sold their wares during the annual assemblies. Well-preserved statue-bases extend in a long line, shorn of the stone and marble effigies which were hacked to pieces by Philip V's soldiers. The brambles grow thicker, the ground more swampy: it is not easy to explore the site. Across the fields, west of the *stoas*, lay the *agora*, in which an annual market was held during the Panaetolian festival.

The **Museum** (a modest building) should not be missed. There is a collection of *acroteria* with heads, gargoyles and grotesque masks, many with their paint still preserved, which were originally placed on the edge of the roof of the Temple of Apollo to screen the tile ends. The execution, though not refined, is robust and not without a hint of coarse peasant humour. There are also figures and emblems of anatomical features.

At this point the traveller who does not want to return to Agrinion can take an interesting, little-used road to the coast at Nafpaktos. The road descends from Thermon to the lake at Petrohorio, goes along the lake-shore, and then ascends to Kato Makrinou, where it joins a road from the north-west. There are superb views back to Lake Trihonida and of the mountains to the north. Going on to the south-east, there is a high saddle looking down into the deep valley of the Evinos which emerges from rugged, bare mountains. There are no villages; scrub-covered slopes drop down on all sides. The drifting scents of sun-scorched thyme and *agnus castus* possess an almost medicinal quality. A feeling of claustrophobia is inevitable and the absence of human beings adds to it. The winding descent affords sudden glimpses, tantalizingly interrupted by the emergence of barren eminences, of the bed of the Evinos: a streak of silver water flowing between tree-lined sandbanks. Soon after a bridge over the Evinos, there are a few old houses where there was once a roadside inn; one has the feeling that this is not a place in which to tarry. After another climb into scrubby hills (with two turn-offs to a remote village that one never even glimpses), there is a long, pleasant descent to Nafpaktos.

The less adventurous traveller, anxious to complete the circuit of Lake Trihonida and return to Agrinion, ignores the left turn to Nafpaktos at Kato Makrinou and drives north-west, through a string of villages set in a lush countryside of mulberry trees and olive groves. In the evening old men sit in rustic roadside cafés, playing with their worry-beads as they exchange the latest agricultural gossip. In places the road fringes the southern shore of the lake and, through clusters of reeds, one catches glimpses of its flat, calm water in which Mount Panetoliko is reflected. In due course one joins the main road a short distance to the south of Agrinion.

North-west of Agrinion, the road crosses the barrage over the wide Aheloös, whose turbid streams flow from their torrent sources in the Pindos between reed-fringed sandbanks until they unite above the barrage. In antiquity the river, symbolic of all fresh water in Greece and infinitely perplexing in its innumerable and erratic changes of course, constantly overflowed its banks and flooded the countryside. Strabo says the river was likened to a bull because of the roaring of its waters, and to a serpent because of its endless sinuosities.

After crossing the Aheloös signposts to the right direct one to the site of **Stratos**, which is scattered over a low hill overlooking the river. Thucydides and Xenophon called it the chief city of Akarnania. Its inhabitants were a tough, disciplined people. In the Peloponnesian War they sided with Athens and when the unruly Ambracians from the north were incited by Sparta to attack Stratos in 429 BC, they were ignominiously routed by the intrepid Akarnanian slingshooters. In the third century BC neither Philip V of Macedon, the sacker of Thermon, nor his more temperate successor, Perseus, were able to capture it.

The ruins are scanty. The fifth-century BC main gate, which consists of two large, curved slabs covering a postern, leads through the thick walls into a bleak, shadeless plateau, broken up into low eminences. To the north are traces of the *agora*; eastward lie the remains of the **Theatre** which has been excavated and is used for occasional performances, although large sections of seating are missing and other are badly broken up. Continuing northward, one reaches the site of the acropolis. A more satisfying ruin is the fourth-century BC Temple of Zeus at the western extremity; limestone drums of Doric columns and pieces of architrave are scattered around the foundations. Stratos has little to offer but its walls and a view of the curiously cream-coloured streams of the Aheloös, flowing below the barrage through a bed nearly one kilometre wide, along which Strabo says vessels used to sail up from Oiniadai.

The road continues northward through domesticated country where modern agricultural methods are now employed. To the west lies the little lake of Ozeros at the foot of the Akarnanika Mountains. Soon another lake, Amvrakia, comes into view, its pale blue waters compressed within a narrow basin fringed with farmlands. To the north-east, the advancing mountains of the Valtos are bare and forbidding. A causeway crosses the lake which tapers off into a slender channel. A short climb between arid hills is followed by a descent towards the Ambracian Gulf, where Amfilohia huddles round a narrow inlet.

32

The Ambracian Gulf

THE GULF, entered from the sea by a channel no more than a kilometre wide, is broken up by bluffs and spits of land, the mirror-like surface of its shallow waters scattered with shoals and reefs. Lagoons, crossed by causeways, fringe the northern shore and many of the creeks are inaccessible to anything but flat-bottomed boats. Two rivers which have risen in the Epirot highlands, the Louros and the Arahthos, wind through orange groves, forming wide shingly beds, before pouring their waters into the inland sea. Beautiful mountains rise on three sides: the peaks of the ancient Epirot kingdom of Thesprotia to the north, the Valtos spurs of the Pindos to the east and the abrupt slopes of the Akarnanika Mountains to the south. There is a pale, mirage-like quality about the scene which is grandiose yet serene.

A circular tour of the Gulf, taking in the medieval fortress of Vonitsa, the thirteenth-century churches of Arta hidden among orange groves, the ruined Byzantine Castle of Rogoi and the extensive Roman ruins of Nikopolis is easily accomplished in two days - of ancient Actium little remains but the name and the memory. The most pleasant place to stay is the Xenias Hotel in Arta, if it is open. The drive up the valley of the Arahthos to see the 'Red Church', overlooking one of the most spectacular mountain prospects in Western Greece, also starts from Arta.

Amfilohia serves as a curtain-raiser to the new scene: it has a lively waterfront at the head of a narrow creek and, away from the main road, whitewashed houses with red roofs cling to a steep hillside among mulberry and eucalyptus trees. On the hill to the east, vestiges of ancient walls, probably those of Limnaia, are discernible. The port, where it is pleasant to stop for coffee or a drink, was founded by Ali Pasha in the early nineteenth century as a military outpost, when the Albanian tyrant's dominions extended all over Epirus and beyond.

Before taking the northbound road to Arta, a short westerly diversion can be made to Vonitsa and the isle of Lefkada. Successive

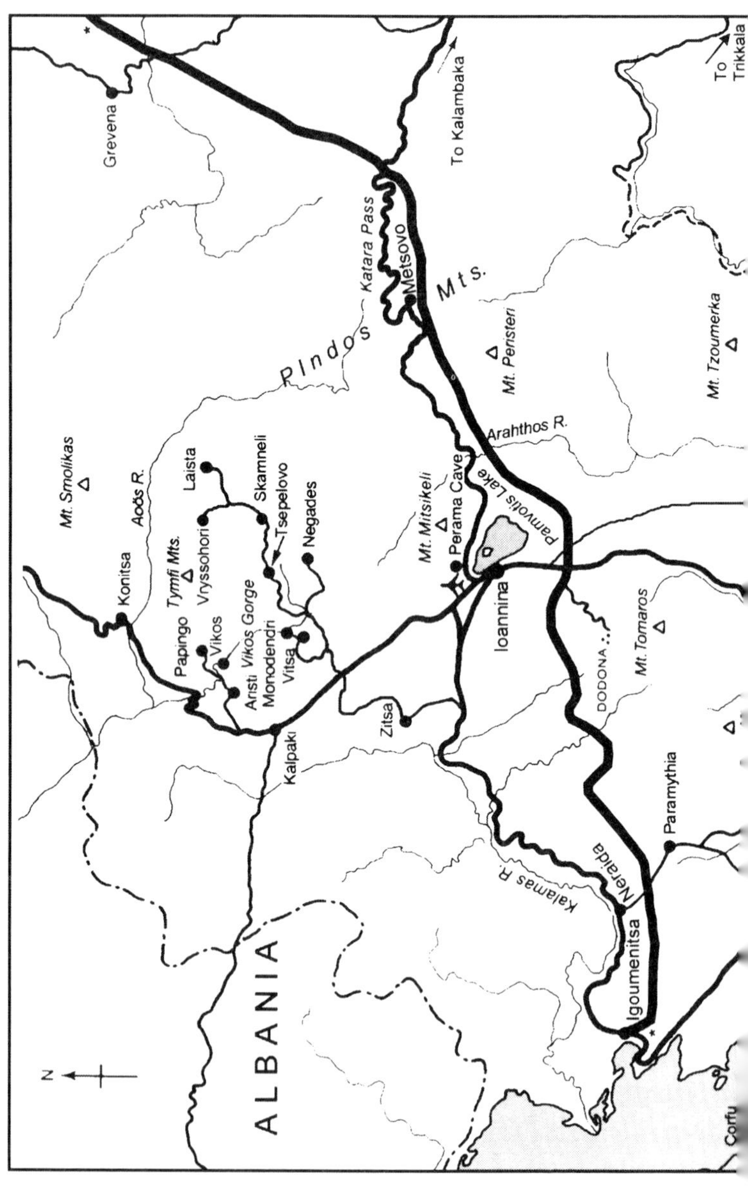
Grevena
To Kalambaka
To Trikkala
Katara Pass
Metsovo
Pindos Mts.
Mt. Peristeri
Mt. Tzoumerka
Mt. Smolikas
Aoös R.
Arahthos R.
Laista
Skamneli
Tsepelovo
Negades
Vryssohori
Tymfi Mts.
Konitsa
Papingo
Vikos
Vikos Gorge
Aristi
Monodendri
Vitsa
Mt. Mitsikeli
Perama Cave
Pamvotis Lake
Ioannina
Mt. Tomaros
DODONA
Zitsa
Kalpaki
Paramythia
Neraida
Kalamas R.
Igoumenitsa
ALBANIA
N
Corfu

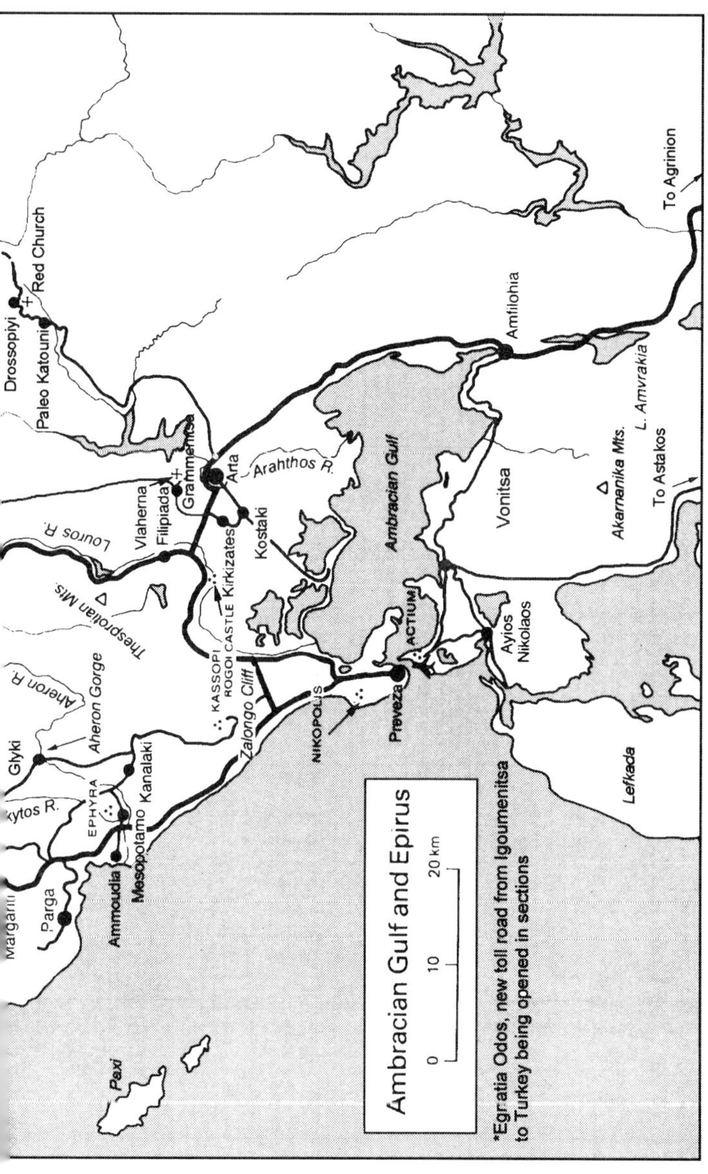

Ambracian Gulf and Epirus
0
10
20 km
*Egratia Odos, new toll road from Igoumenitsa to Turkey being opened in sections
Drossopiyi
Paleo Katouni
Red Church
Grammenitsa
Arta
Arahthos R.
Vlaherna
Filipiada
Louros R.
Kirkizates
Kostaki
Thesprotian Mts.
KASSOPI
ROGOI CASTLE
Zalongo Cliff
Aheron R.
Aheron Gorge
Glyki
EPHYRA
Kanalaki
Mesopotamo
Ammoudia
Parga
Paxi
NIKOPOLIS
Preveza
ACTIUM
Ambracian Gulf
Ayios Nikolaos
Lefkada
Vonitsa
Akarnanika Mts.
L. Amvrakia
Amfilohia
To Astakos
To Agrinion

creeks to the west of Amfilohia afford views of small, flat islands strung out across the motionless gulf. After climbing for a while into the formidable Akarnanika, the road dips down to a wide bay backed by a green plain, with the town of **Vonitsa** (a good place for an overnight stop) spreading along the shore, its medieval castle crowning a bluff above its small port.

On the way to the castle there are two picturesque churches: the small Basilica of the *Ayii Apostoli* has a wooden *iconostasis*, more Italianate than Byzantine in style and execution, decorated with coloured designs of rosettes and tendrils; the money-box, into which one drops twenty drachmas for a candle, is painted with figures of St Peter and St Paul holding a model of the church. In the larger Basilica of *Ayios Nikolaos* (just below the castle) the effigies of two lions with human faces and curling moustaches support the Cross on the summit of the screen.

The **Castle** was originally a Byzantine fortress guarding the approaches to the inland sea. It passed in 1294 into the hands of Philip of Taranto as part of the extravagant dowry brought to him on his marriage to the beautiful Thamar, daughter of the Despot of Arta. In turn Frankish and Venetian, it was seized in 1362 by Leonardo Tocco of Corfu, whose descendants held it for over a century. In the fifteenth century Carlo Tocco bequeathed Vonitsa to his widow, the Duchess Francesca, a formidable lady of much ability and vigour, and divided the rest of Akarnania among his five bastard sons. Even after the Turkish conquest the fortress remained an Italian outpost in Ottoman territory but, during the War of Independence, it fell into ruins. After the establishment of the modern kingdom in 1833, a Greek garrison was stationed in the crumbling keep and the military insurrection which led to the abdication of King Othon and his headstrong queen had its genesis here in 1862. (There are few changes of Greek political regime in which the military does not have the first word.)

The ruins are mostly Venetian with Turkish additions. You enter through a large gateway in the massive outer walls and then go up into the inner precinct, surrounded with pine trees. In the centre are the remains of a two-storied building, probably the residence of the Turkish commander, whose windows look out over a prospect of sea, mountains, islets and headlands. On the left is a long, low chapel and beside it (to the east) steps lead down to a deep, vaulted cistern. Hardly anyone comes here; only insects hum in the evergreen shrubs and the wind whistles through the windows of ruined buildings. In the triangular keep were the vaulted halls and chambers to which Philip of Taranto brought the seductive Thamar from Arta, together with all the gold of her fabulous dowry.

From Vonitsa there is a fine scenic road south to Astakos, while the main road goes west and then divides: the road straight on leads to the village of Ayios Nikolaos and the opening bridge which crosses the narrow channel to the island of Lefkada, guarded by impressive remains of Turkish fortifications. The road to the right leads to the headland of Aktion, whence one can cross by tunnel to Preveza.

The main road from Amfilohia to Arta runs along the eastern side of the Gulf. Cliffs, thickly wooded with ilex, overhang a rocky shore, and the pastel-shaded gulf is so extensive that it is sometimes difficult to grasp its configuration. Soon the borderline between Akarnania and Epirus is reached: not the craggy northern Epirus of the mountain redoubt, but the lowland fringe, a country of orange groves, stretching for miles around Arta - indeed, in spring the scent of orange blossom is intoxicating, all-pervasive. On the left side of the road, gullies filled with parallel rows of fruit trees, debouch into shallow shingly coves. Avenues of dwarf cypresses form wind-breaks and huge fig trees provide luxuriant shade.

Six kilometres before reaching Arta a lane to the right, bordered by honeysuckle, dog-rose and wild gladioli leads, in less than half a kilometre, to the **Church of the Panayia tou Vrioni**, least important of Arta's countryside Byzantine churches. The church's exterior walls are decorated with lavish brick inlay, inferior in design and execution to that which distinguishes most of the churches of the plain; but the setting - a cypress grove and a cemetery full of rose bushes and flowering Judas trees, their trunks entwined with periwinkle - is charming and the detour is short enough to be worthwhile.

Arta, undistinguished though lively, spreads across a saddleback eminence, with the Arahthos winding in an arc round the northern side of the town. The people are friendly and among the best-looking in Greece, but the place is not famous for its food. The **Xenia Hotel** in the Castle is approached through a medieval gateway. The modern hotel building dominates the Castle precincts (now public gardens) which are still encircled by the well-preserved thirteenth-century Byzantine ramparts, with a castellated bastion overlooking the plain to the north. No hotel in Greece is more attractively situated:

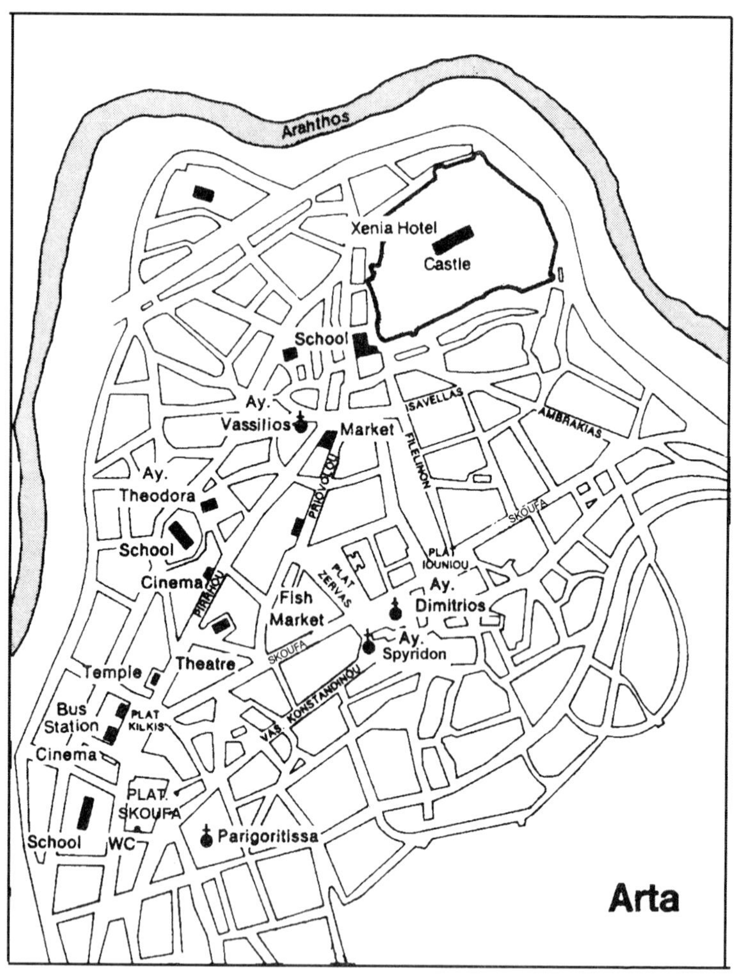

bedroom balconies overlook the streams of the Arahthos estuary where, beyond the sand-banks, groves of orange and lemon trees stretch out in a softly-coloured haze; lines of poplars climb green foothills against the back-drop of the grey and lonely Epirot mountains. In summer frogs croak on the banks of the streams and the sandflies, which swarm into the damp gardens and orchards, are a pest.

It was in the third century BC that fame and lustre were conferred on Arta (known then as Ambracia) by Pyrrhos, the Molossian king. He adorned and fortified the city, made it his capital and fought so staunchly against the Roman Republic that Hannibal considered him the greatest of all generals. In the late second century BC it fell into the hands of the then all-powerful Aetolians. However the sun had virtually set on the power of Hellenistic Greece - whether Macedonian, Aetolian or Spartan - and Ambracia declined in importance. After the battle of Actium in 31 BC, the Roman victor, Augustus Caesar removed all the inhabitants to nearby Nikopolis.

Arta's renown, as reflected in the visible remains of its remarkable churches, belongs to the Middle Ages. As capital of the Despotate of Epirus, it was, after Thessaloniki, the most important city in Mainland Greece during the thirteenth and fourteenth centuries. The rugged nature of the mountains surrounding the plain and Gulf formed a natural protection against the Crusaders who, in 1204, sacked Constantinople and split the Byzantine Empire into a number of Latin kingdoms. Michael Angelos lost no time, while the Crusaders were sweeping Greece, in making Arta the military and political headquarters of his Despotate. He formed a militia of Ambracian natives, hired mercenaries and soon turned to the offensive; playing one Latin state off against the other, he maintained Byzantine administration within his Despotate, whose boundaries he extended from Ioannina in the north to Nafpaktos in the south. While feeble Flemish Counts tottered uneasily on the great golden throne in Constantinople, Michael and his successors created in Western Greece a Byzantine state, with Arta as its capital, which not only became a political force, but rivalled in importance the other, more 'legitimate', Byzantine empire in exile at Nicaea in Asia Minor. In 1215, while campaigning in Northern Epirus, Michael was murdered in his sleep by one of his slaves.

With Michael's successors - Theodore and Michael II - the Despots of Arta reached the zenith of their dynastic ambitions. Theodore captured the Latin Emperor in an ambush in the mountains and crowned himself Emperor at Thessaloniki in 1227. Michael II, an eccentric character no less violent than his predecessors, made Arta a brilliant capital, and it was touch-and-go whether an Angelos of Arta or a Lascarid of Nicaea would re-enter Constantinople as Emperor when the ridiculous Latin creation crumbled and the 'God-Guarded city' was restored to its legitimate Greek masters.

It was, in fact, the Nicaean Emperor who recaptured Constantinople in 1261, though a measure of autonomy was granted to the Despotate of Arta: the history of its vigorous defence of the ideal of Hellenism during the half-century of Latin depredation had taken too strong a hold on the minds of the population of mainland Greece to be lightly dismissed. The subsequent Despots, however, were men of less mettlesome character and, by the middle of the fourteenth century, Arta succumbed to the Serbian flail. But the Serb empire was also a passing phase and in 1417 Carlo Tocco, Lord of Vonitsa, moved into the citadel. The curtain came down in 1499 with the Turkish conquest; Ali Pasha, the sultan's turbulent viceroy of Epirus and Albania, was the last notable personage to stay in Arta's ancient fortress.

The number of churches in and around the city bears witness to its one-time importance. Descending from the castle, we come first to the little **Church of Ayios Vasileios**. A rectangular church of the fourteenth century, it is outstanding for its exterior ornamentation, with two courses of inlaid glazed tiles which offer a sharp but pleasing contrast to the brickwork decoration on the north and east sides. In each of the windows there is a single unfluted colonnette crowned by an Ionic capital. The church could hardly be smaller - the side apses are positively diminutive - and the interior is now without interest, but this is not dull provincial architecture; one is immediately aware that the Despotate, insulated from the rest of Greece by geopolitics was, like the far-away empire of Trebizond on the Black Sea, a centre of artistic creativity.

More important, in a nearby square, is the **Church of Ayia Theodora**, approached through a gabled arch decorated with brick inlay. The church is dedicated to the pious Theodora, a strait-laced aristocrat, who came from Servia in Western Macedonia as the bride of the despot Michael II Angelos. In spite of her estimable character, Theodora did not enjoy a happy married life. Her husband, infatuated by a notorious courtesan who was also a sorceress and went by the extraordinary name of Lady Gangrene, not only dismissed his wife from the palace but drove her into exile. This saintly woman kept body and soul together by living on the roots of wild plants, occasionally accepting hospitality from remote mountain monasteries. Eventually, however, Michael had a traumatic vision: Christ appeared to him and denounced him roundly for succumbing to the wiles of Satan's agent, the Lady Gangrene, and threatened to destroy him with fire and thunderbolts. Terrified and conscience-stricken, Michael scoured the country for his victimized wife, found her and restored her to her rightful place in the palace. Thanks to Theodora's merciful intercession, the Lady Gangrene, instead of being strapped to an ass, as ordered by the remorseful Michael, and exposed to the ribaldry of the inhabitants prior to her execution, was allowed to leave Arta unmolested.

The exterior of *Ayia Theodora* is charming. The building, which is of the fourteenth century, is low, irregular and architecturally eccentric. In spring the garden beside it is a mass of lilac and the snowball blooms of the guelder rose. Two very dark green cypresses of considerable age, one of which serves as a bell-tower, add proportion and perspective to the scene. The west front, through which the narthex, crowned by a small low drum, used to be entered, is decorated with lavish brickwork bands: zig-zag, dog-tooth and herringbone. The *naos* is well-proportioned, with four old columns disposed in a square and crowned with acanthus leaf Theodosian capitals, plundered from a nearby Early Christian basilica. The central aisle, higher than the others, is lit by a clerestory. The *narthex* is distinguished by the nineteenth-century reconstruction of the tomb of St Theodora, including a large marble slab sculpted in low relief: it depicts the pious lady who, though crowned and robed as befits a Despot's consort, wears the veil of a nun. The diminutive figure beside her represents her infant son, Nikeforos, who succeeded his father as Despot. Flanked by two Archangels, both figures stand under a canopy supported by knotted columns, while the hand of God points at Theodora.

Next comes the **Church of the Parigoritissa** (The Virgin of Consolation), Arta's most imposing monument, now a museum of Christian antiquities; it stands on higher ground above Skoufa Square, overlooking the orange groves beyond the river. Founded at the end of the thirteenth century by the Despot Nikeforos and his wife Anna Paleologaina, it is one of the most important Byzantine churches in Greece. Three-storeyed, it is in the shape of a tall Greek Cross within a square (the cross is only perceptible in the interior). The drums and cupolas, six in all, seem puny, ill-proportioned affairs without any relation to the barrack-like cube of stone and brick which they crown.

The interior, however, is impressive, if unusual. The sombre, lofty *naos* is an extraordinary structure, height being achieved by a cumbersome architectural disposition which was never repeated, presumably because of its impracticability: at each corner of the central square three superimposed courses of columns support high squinch arches, forming an octagon on which the drum rests; the columns of the highest course are more slender and decorative in effect than structural in purpose. Between each course of vertical columns there are granite column sections which have been laid horizontally, projecting into the church. The vertical columns stand on the projecting part of the horizontal sections - cantilevered over the *naos* - and have become cracked in many places by the stresses within the structure. The column-courses are capped by a system of vaults and arches that fails to cohere aesthetically. Admittedly there is no absence of height and spaciousness - even perhaps of grandeur.

Turning from architecture to decoration, one's attention is automatically drawn to the dome crowning the lofty square in which a thirteenth-century **Christ Pantocrator** of colossal dimensions is depicted in mosaic, gorgeously robed and holding an ornamented Book of Gospels. Below are ranged prophets and cherubim in beautiful draperies. Most remarkable is the imposing figure of St Sophronios, boldly modelled, with violent contrasts in the colour scheme, which is unique for a mosaic of this period. Another fragment worth looking at is the rather crude but charming Nativity, full of bucolic serenity, on the topmost north vault. The fourteenth-century frescoes of the apse are hopelessly damaged.

From the gallery, reached by a modern staircase, there is a good close-up view of the amazing architectural intricacies of the Gothic tracery in one of the squinches and also of the fine carving on the north and west arches. One can also examine the beautiful mosaics of the prophets around and below the Pantocrator at approximately eye-level.

A little out of town on the Kommenon road to the south is the **Monastery of Kato Panayia**. The Monastery is set in a garden filled with oleander, pine, olive and orange trees interlaced with creeping vines; the garden extends across a slope overlooking the Arahthos, where an enormous plane tree dips its branches into the water. The cloistered courtyard and domeless church, with its cross-roofs, gables, transverse vault and tall belfry (a later addition), create a complex of subtly-graded planes on different levels. The frescoes of the exterior west wall, shaded by a wide projecting gable, which has replaced a destroyed narthex, are of no particular merit. To the left of the doorway, however, there is a lively panel showing God swirling across the heavens as He creates the world, and another in which the Almighty, now crowned, creates man in the garden of Eden. On the right there is a further representation of the Creator: this time He is warning Adam and Eve against evil, while Satan, in the form of the Serpent, writhes at His feet and angels prepare to expel Adam and Eve from the garden.

The church was founded in the thirteenth century by Michael II Angelos (his monogram is inscribed on the south wall) as a token of penance for his shameful treatment of Theodora. The interior is of little interest, although in some places the overlay of eighteenth-century frescoes has flaked off to reveal earlier paintings. Capitals of different orders crown the unattractive mud-coloured columns in the *naos*.

Other churches, of considerable interest to Byzantine enthusiasts, are scattered around the countryside and it is enchanting to walk to them along the flowery lanes. Unfortunately, however, most of the churches lie in different directions, and the smaller ones are not easy to find; it is wiser to drive through the maze of orchards, vineyards and straggling hamlets rather than to try to find them on foot.

One starts by descending to the west from the *Parigoritissa*, away from the centre of the town. Here the Arahthos, flowing in a series of loops towards the gulf, is spanned by the famous **Turkish Bridge of Arta**, the largest and most striking of all those elegant half-moon structures that bridge the rivers and torrents of Epirus and Albania. This one, built by the Despots on Hellenic foundations and entirely refashioned by the Turks for packhorses, has four graceful, crescent-shaped arches of different dimensions, through which there are lovely views up the river from the lower, modern road bridge. The fact that the highest point (above the largest arch) is not in the centre of the bridge adds further diversity to the construction. According to a legend, immortalized in Greek folk-song, the thousand Greek masons who built the bridge, under the direction of Turkish engineers in the seventeenth century, found that the middle pier, at which they would toil all day, was repeatedly swept away in the evening by the waters of the Arahthos. Finally, a little bird perched itself on the middle pier, twittered in a human voice and delivered the sinister message that, until the master-mason's wife was buried in the foundations, the bridge would never be completed. So the unfortunate woman was induced by a ruse to descend inside the pier, ostensibly to recover her husband's ring which had fallen inside. Stone and rubble were quickly heaped over her, and the masons set to work to strengthen the pier. Since then the bridge has stood intact.

Crossing the modern bridge, from which there is a fine view of the Turkish one, you turn off into an olive grove where a tall poplar screens the little Byzantine **Church of Ayios Vasileios tis Yefiras** (St Basil at the Bridge), a charming little extravaganza. The church is minute, crowned by a cylindrical drum which is taller than the main body of the church. The frieze below the cornice and the brickwork decoration on the drum are crude but picturesque. The interior is without interest.

Continue a short distance on the Ioannina road and then take the first turning to the left. This road runs through flat, lush countryside to the village of Kostakii. At each of two successive forks turn to the left, until you come (just outside the hamlet of Plisous) to the **Church of Ayios Dimitrios Katsouris**, which is surrounded by olive and orange trees, their trunks entwined with ivy. Originally a tenth-century dependency of a Patriarchal monastery, it was restored under the Despots and finally abandoned in the eighteenth century. *Ayios Dimitrios* has no exterior decoration, but the tall drum, the planes of slanting roofs and the three apses create a pleasing effect; small, but well-proportioned, this country church has an air of relative loftiness which raises it above the level of a rural chapel. In the middle of the sanctuary of the deserted cross-in-square interior there is a fine painting of three saints: typical portraits of old men with serene, expressive faces; assigned to the twelfth century, this fresco is older than any other in the Arta region and also reflects the relatively high level of artistic creativeness that existed here even before the time of the Despots. In the side conch on the right, we see St Basil and St John Chrysostomos and, in the apse, the Virgin and Child, the former distinguished by an acid and spiteful expression that would do credit to Medea in one of her nastiest moods. The rest of the frescoes - of little interest - are of the seventeenth and eighteenth centuries.

From *Ayios Dimitrios Katsouris* one drives along lanes bordered by mulberry trees and hedgerows of flowering brambles to the hamlet of Kirkizates, which is hidden among orange groves and shaded by huge fig trees. A boy from the café will fetch a key from the local priest and conduct you to the thirteenth-century **Church of Ayios Nikolaos tis Rodias** (St Nicholas of the Pomegranate Orchard), now standing impressively isolated in the sunken field which has replaced the original orchard. The exterior of the church is distinguished by a tall drum and brick inlay decoration on the higher courses of the walls. In the *naos* are two squat marble columns without bases, crowned with well-preserved capitals carved with the device of the double-headed eagle. The frescoes, very damaged, are stylistically of the thirteenth century. A panel on the right side of the *iconostasis* contains a fine icon of the Dormition of the Virgin, remarkable for the vividness of its red tints. Though provincial in execution, it is nevertheless elegant and sophisticated.

The most important of Arta's outlying churches is at the **Monastery of Vlaherna**. A road to the right from the Arta-Ioannina road (beyond the bridge), winds through fruit orchards and olive groves between the Epirot foothills to Grammenitsa, from where a minor road goes to the Monastery, which was founded at the end of the twelfth century. Originally a single-nave church, later with central dome and domed cross-aisles added, has irregular vaults and three apses of different shapes - one rounded, one three-sided, one five-sided - the whole creating an architecturally complex effect: varied and asymmetrical, but not without harmony. There is much brick inlay decoration in the window surrounds of the central dome and apses, where the different designs embellishing each of the irregular projections create a decorative ensemble full of fantasy and ingenuity. Sculptural fragments, which originally formed part of a marble screen, decorate the exterior walls and add to the general air of diversity.

In the interior, part of the floor is covered with boards which the custodian will remove on request to reveal marble paving-stones decorated with stone *tesserae*. The high central octagonal dome, painted with a Christ Pantocrator in a bluish-grey mantle, surrounded by prophets and apostles, is flanked by secondary domes north and south. In the south aisle lies the tomb of Michael II Angelos, decorated with crosses, rosettes and stylized foliate bands. Morbidly-minded visitors with small hands may slip them through a hole in the east end of the sarcophagus and finger the bones of this violent man, whose lust, ambition and ability combined to make him one of the most colourful personalities of thirteenth-century Greece. In the north aisle a second royal tomb is said to contain the remains of his sons, Dimitrios and John, who were quietly put away by their younger brother Nikeforos I. I have not succeeded in tracing the subterranean passage that led under the river from the Despot's palace. It is said to have been used constantly by Theodora when, heavily veiled as a nun, she came to worship at Vlaherna, her favourite church.

The **Church of the Nativity of the Virgin**, commonly known as the '**Red Church**' is the ostensible objective of an expedition up the valley of the Arahthos to Drossopiyi. North-east of Arta the road climbs successive spurs of the Tzoumerka massif: precipitous grey cliffs have been sliced by erosion and now show the patterns and folds of the rock strata; this is earthquake country. The road climbs and dips, affording entrancing views of the ice-cold Arahthos and the lake formed by the building of the Pournari Dam. Among orchards of quince and almond, houses with slate-grey roofs are scattered throughout the little green valleys. Ever nearer, more imposing, looms Mount Tzoumerka itself, cloud-capped, gashed with forbidding ravines filled with snow, its lower slopes dark with evergreens and scrub. Occasionally a shepherd is seen, standing on the summit of a ridge; invariably he waves. Epirots are among the friendliest of Greeks.

Beyond the hamlet of Paleo Katouni, which lies in a valley, the road mounts steeply between groves of almond and Judas trees. Suddenly, on the right, one catches sight of the crimson-tiled roofs of the 'Red Church': as sophisticated a piece of Byzantine ecclesiastical architecture as one is likely to encounter in a remote highland region. It was founded in 1281 by the *Protostrator* Theodore (the imperial Master of the Horse). Why here in this mountain wilderness? We do not know. A saddleback roof has replaced the broken dome of the cruciform church. The walls are elaborately decorated with bands of ceramic tiles and there are rich brick patterns around the windows. All the bricks are of a bright red which makes the walls glow with an extraordinary refulgence - especially striking when seen in springtime against a background of pink and white blossom. On the apse, shaded by the plane tree which serves as a bell-tower, more brick inlay outlines the elliptical arches of the windows. The interior, now abandoned, is without interest.

A few kilometres from the 'Red Church', the grey houses of Voulgarelli, now called **Drossopiyi** ascend a precipitous mountainside on the fringe of the fir belt, above which towers the sombre summit of Tzoumerka. One can sit at a café halfway up the terraced village and admire the panorama of the Agrafa range extending southwards, with the elegant cone of Tymfristos just visible on the horizon. In the last war this mountain redoubt was the headquarters of EDES, the right-wing resistance organization, whose members spent much of their time (as well as much of the gold and arms supplied to them by the British Government) in fighting the Communist-controlled

ELAS liberation army, instead of the Germans. Today, two unexploded bombs flank the doorway of the main church.

A little further up the mountainside one can cross into central Greece by joining the road to Porta Panayia in Thessaly, which follows the route taken by the Despots when they set out from Arta to extend their dominions in Thessaly and Macedonia.

Leaving Arta for the west one takes the main Ioannina road but, immediately after crossing the Louros bridge, turns left for Preveza. The road runs along the fringe of the Ambracian Plain, some way in from the Gulf. A few kilometres along this road one sees an elegant limestone hill rising above the marshy fields on the north bank of the river; the hill was once crowned by the **Castle of Rogoi**, a stronghold built by the Despots to guard Arta against hostile armies advancing from the coast. After 1204 and the Latin sack of Constantinople, Rogoi acquired a curious notoriety: after making off with the remains of St Luke from the imperial capital, a Frankish adventurer sold them to the Duke of Kefallinia who placed them in a shrine at Rogoi, which lay within his domain. Later, after the Turkish conquest, the Evangelist's remains were smuggled to a Danubian fortress.

It takes no more than ten minutes to climb up to the keep, where the remains of strong walls, which sometimes reach a height of twenty-three courses, stand out impressively. The foundations reveal Hellenic masonry, and part of the ancient circuit of walls is discernible to the north-west. The towers and crenellated battlements, from whose crannies sprout wild olive trees and thick shoots of dark green ivy, dominate a fine sweep of the Louros river winding round the base of the hill. On the north side of the keep there is a single-naved chapel, repaired in the seventeenth century, with moderately well-preserved frescoes of the Virgin, the Archangels and the Dormition.

The road turns south onto the promontory which encloses the Ambracian Gulf from the north-west and, shortly after passing a complex network of lagoons, one reaches an isthmus of rolling meadows and tall grass. Straddling the isthmus are the ruins of **Nikopolis** (the City of Victory), the most extensive Roman site in Greece. Built by Augustus to commemorate the battle of Actium, it was forcibly populated by immigrants from the towns of Ambracia, Akarnania and Aetolia, whose treasures of marble ornaments and statues were removed to adorn the new city. In conception Nikopolis is Roman and illustrates the importance attached by Rome to the memory of a decisive battle fought entirely between Romans in the land of Plato and Aristotle. It is a perplexing site, with the remains of Roman and Early Christian walls and foundations scattered over the whole isthmus. Two or three hours are needed to identify the main ruins, most of which lie at a considerable walking distance from each other.

For two centuries it was the chief city of Western Greece. St Paul spent a winter here, and from it he addressed his moving exhortation to his companion, Titus. By the fourth century, however, it had declined in importance and it was left to the Emperor Julian the Apostate, in one of his transports of pagan fervour, to renovate the city and restore the Actian festival (founded originally by Augustus in commemoration of his victory). In the fifth century Alaric and his Goths left little but the debris of broken walls and smashed statues, but in the sixth century Justinian restored many of the walls, although he diminished the size of the city by reducing their compass; several very fine churches were also built.

The **Theatre**, the first monument encountered by the traveller driving from Arta to Preveza, looks out over the pale waters of the Gulf. It has been completely cleared and partly restored for performances in the summer, but storks still nest in the niches of the upper portico, a semi-circular gallery from which there are views of the meadows sloping down to a lagoon. An ancient geographer says of the lagoon that the fish were so plentiful 'to be almost disgusting'.

Just to the west of the Theatre lies the outline of the **Stadium**, overgrown with brambles and asphodel, and with snakes making sinister rustling noises among the bushes of wild artichoke that grow between the scattered remains. Unlike other stadia in Greece this one was semi-circular at both ends. Here was celebrated the Actia, the quinquennial festival founded by the victorious Augustus. Sacred to Apollo, the festival consisted of the usual athletic and musical contests, chariot races and gladiatorial shows, while mock sea-fights re-enacting the Battle of Actium were staged in the bay. North of the Stadium, just beyond the hamlet of Smyrtoula, rises the hill on which the future Emperor's army was encamped on the day of the battle. After it was all over, he built a temple of Neptune on the spot where his tent had been pitched. Only fragments remain, including those of a frieze inscribed with huge letters - part of a description of the battle.

To the south of the Stadium excavations have uncovered Baths and the remains of two cemeteries. Mounds of rubble indicate the site of Roman brick houses and beyond them extend stretches of low Roman walls. The road then runs through the Byzantine precinct, parallel to a fine stretch of massive Byzantine walls, the walls nearer the sea having largely disappeared. On the left-hand side, against a background of ferns and long grass descending to the sea, are the extensive ruins of the early sixth-century **Basilica of Alkyson**, (a local bishop). This must have been a very impressive complex; more like a whole Roman Forum than a church. A very large colonnaded stoa with no apparent purpose crosses the site, and is followed by an equally Roman courtyard with a portico all round. The huge main entrance to the church itself is still standing. The church too is far more Roman than Byzantine, in spite of its date, resembling those of Nea Anhialos. The nave is partly enclosed from the double side aisles by a line of carved *transennae* and the tiered seating for the clergy is in place at the east end. An exceptionally fine mosaic floor is usually covered.

On the right, beyond the Basilica, is an imposing gate in the well-preserved Byzantine walls which then form a massive right-angle. The other really important church, the sixth-century **Basilica of Ayios Doumetios**, is reached up a path from where the road meets the walls, passing the remains of Baths and of the Bishop's Palace. This Basilica too is an elaborate establishment, with many courts and side rooms, in some of which there are beautiful floor mosaics, masterpieces of elegant design, the work of artists who, if early Byzantine, were clearly influenced by Roman mosaic work. In one we see two swans floating under fruit-laden pear trees, with an inscription dedicated to Doumetios, the Persian monk who was stoned to death for his faith. There are also representations of seagulls and young fishermen spearing tuna, with here and there an ambiguous nude. In another, men savagely hunt animals among plane trees, all surprisingly pagan.

The **Museum** is nearby: small, nicely arranged, and with several outstanding pieces, including a fine Hellenistic Symposium scene, and a superb circular statue base with third-century BC reliefs of the Battle of the Amazons. This was brought to Nikopolis by the Romans and placed later in the Basilica of Alkyson.

After going through the gate and scrambling over fragments of Byzantine walls, you come to another Roman building, the **Odeion**, built of grey stone on a massive substructure. The *cavea*, almost wholly restored, is one of the most impressive monuments on the site. The position dominates the whole of the tapering peninsula. To the north rise the hills from which Octavian (later Augustus), now confident of victory, watched the rout of Antony's and Cleopatra's fleets. Northward too, beyond the fragments of the Roman aqueduct which probably traversed the whole of the hilly isthmus, the Epirot mountains rise steeply. To the east, beyond the Byzantine walls and the road, the lagoon, where herons wade, is separated from the main bay by a thread of land.

The main road goes southwards under shady poplars, past the remains of small arched buildings, probably sepulchres, which are scattered about the meadows. Below the road the lagoon is broken up by reed-bordered creeks, where the water lies motionless until stirred by the incoming waters of the Ionian Sea at the waterfront of **Preveza**, the little port on the tip of the promontory which has recently made its appearance on the tourist map. There is a saline, fishy smell about the place, but there are some pleasant side-streets bordered with whitewashed houses, and geraniums, hibiscus and bougainvillea blaze in fragrant courtyards.

The site is that of an ancient city, founded in the third century BC by Pyrrhos. In the Middle Ages it was occupied in turn by Venetians and Turks, until 1797, when it was ceded to France. However, Ali Pasha, the Sultan's Albanian satrap, quickly descended upon Preveza and his executioner, a man of formidable stamina, beheaded every member of the French garrison; their heads were crated and despatched as trophies to the Sultan in Constantinople. There are no ancient monuments in the town: only some outcrops of Venetian walls on the periphery, with the ruined citadel (west of the town) overlooking the Ionian Sea. Open-air cafés, restaurants and modest fish tavernas overlook the strait - no more than a kilometre wide - which connects the vast, lake-like Gulf with the open sea. A car-ferry still plies the to the opposite point of Aktion, but most traffic uses the new tunnel. A few sun-tanned children splash about in a shallow inlet; in the background rise the Akarnanika mountains and, westward, the majestic outlines of the island of Lefkada.

Scenically, the promontory of Aktion is no more prepossessing than that of Preveza and there are few tangible remains of **Actium**, but it is pleasant to cross the strait in the evening, when the waters turn from light blue to mauve and finally to a deep purple-grey. A spit of land, flat and sandy, all but closing the entrance to the Ambracian Gulf from the sea, the point bears few visible marks of its fame. Slightly to the north of the ferry landing point are the minimal vestiges of the fifth-century BC Temple of Apollo Actios, which was restored and enlarged by Augustus. On the eminence of Anaktorion, to the east, overlooking the shore, Augustus built a commemorative temple in the Roman style. Strabo says it dominated a sacred grove and harbour where some of Anthony's captured vessels were preserved in boathouses. A kind of naval museum, probably.

But the temptation to ponder on the actual course of the engagement, the third and last Roman conflict fought in Greek territory, is irresistible. Upon the tactics and strategy displayed by the commanders on 2nd September, 31 BC, few historians disagree. Antony, whose larger and more cumbersome vessels were crammed bow to stern into the bay of Preveza, is thought to have been encamped with the élite of his army, on the point of Actium, whereas Octavian's lighter and faster galleys were anchored well within the Ambracian Gulf. More impetuous than his rival, Antony decided to risk all - mastery of the empire - in a battle at sea; the attempt proved to be a failure of massive dimensions. The engagement, in which Octavian's smaller vessels displayed greater manoeuvrability in these confined waters, was fought in the Bay of Preveza, which serves as a kind of ante-chamber to the Ambracian Gulf. It is said that Cleopatra's unexplained defection with sixty Egyptian galleys, at the height of the engagement, turned the scales. Peevish and petulant - as described by Shakespeare thus: 'The ribald-rid nag of Egypt' with 'the breese* upon her, like a cow in June' - she hoisted her sail and fled, abandoning her infatuated lover, whose 'lust and sleep and feeding' had sapped 'his honour even till a Lethe'd dullness'. Then 'like a doting mallard, leaving the flight in height', he flew ignominiously after the purple sails of the royal vessel speeding towards Egypt.

Abandoned by their eccentric, somewhat hysterical, leaders, Antony's captains were pounced upon by Octavian's more manageable galleys which, says Plutarch, sailed 'round and round' and annihilated 'these huge vessels, which their size and their want of men made slow to move and difficult to manage'; Octavian, heretofore trapped in the shallow Ambracian Gulf, was at last able to break out into the open sea. After the naval battle, the land troops were too dispirited to carry on the fight, and Antony's leaderless legions deserted in droves. The last of the great Roman civil wars

* Shakespeare is referring to a fly that irritates horses and cattle.

was over. In this narrow strait between the Ionian Sea and the lagoon-like Gulf, skimmed by wild fowl and ringed by mountains, the sickly Octavian won the battle of Actium and became Augustus Caesar.

33

Epirus

SEAMED BY NARROW VALLEYS funnelling out of forbidding gorges, Epirus is abundantly supplied with water by several major rivers. Apart from the Aherousian plain, there are few open stretches. Slate-coloured mountains, bare or wooded and sometimes reaching impressive altitudes, achieve a structural perfection, with peaks, screes and ravines composing an organic architectural whole: highly compressed though never claustrophobic. In Epirus one has the feeling of sitting on top of the whole of Greece, of being perched on the final crown of this incomparable convulsion of schist, limestone and marble.

In Homeric times, Neoptolemos, the son of Achilles, settled in Epirus with Andromache, the widow of Hector. He was succeeded by his son Molossos, who gave his name to the future kings of the country, a land famous for its dogs, its oxen and its torrents, which wind through sunless canyons. The nature of the country gave Achilles' descendants little opportunity to indulge in royal trappings, with the absence of coastal plains retarding, if not actually precluding, the process of Hellenic cultural colonization. After defeating the Macedonians at the battle of Pydna in 168 BC, the Romans, under Aemilius Paulus, occupied the whole of Epirus and razed some seventy towns to the ground, condemning the inhabitants to slavery. In medieval times the mountain redoubt of Epirus remained out of the main current of events but, during the Turkish occupation, its inaccessibility made it a stronghold of Hellenism and its chief city, Ioannina, a centre of scholarship. In the War of Independence its bandoliered brigand-patriots fought ferocious battles in mountain passes of incredible grandeur. During the Second World War a tiny Greek army and air force checked and routed a numerically vastly superior Italian expeditionary force which had set out from the Albanian border; Mussolini's illusions were rudely shattered in the Epirot snowdrifts.

The configuration of the province renders a circular tour

impracticable. Two routes, which include all the main sites, are feasible. (i) Starting at Preveza, visiting Kassopi and Zalongo; then across the Aherousian plain, taking in the Aheron gorge, to Parga and on to Igoumenitsa. (ii) Starting at Arta, to the classical site of Dodona, on to Ioannina, the Epirot capital, then north to the Zagori villages and Konitsa on the Albanian border; back to Ioannina, then to Zitsa and down to Igoumenitsa.

The first journey could include a worthwhile overnight stop in Parga; the second two or three nights with Ioannina, where there are plenty of hotels, as a base.

From Preveza, the main road to the north follows the coast as far as the River Aheron; this route has little of interest except good beaches and scenery. One can, therefore, make a detour inland which takes in several interesting places. Eighteen kilometres north of Preveza the main road to Arta turns east and, after following this road for two kilometres, there is a left turn onto a road which leads through the mountains to Paramythia in the north. After a short distance, a country road to the right, signposted Zalongo, climbs the Thesprotian foothills. Towards the end of a steep climb, a signpost points west to a bramble-bordered path leading to the remains of ancient **Kassopi**, on a broad mountain shelf. Both in respect of altitude and the extent of the stone debris - there is no marble here - the site is one of the most striking in Western Greece.

Originally colonized during the Bronze Age, it was the tribal capital of the Kassopeans, an Epirot people who dwelt in the country lying between the Ambracian Gulf and the river Aheron. During the fourth century BC, Aphrodite was worshipped here in a large temple, and her symbols of a dove and serpent, together with her bust, are found on Kassopean coins.

The first inhabitants raised strong walls on three sides of the plateau. In Hellenistic times towers were added to an *enceinte* of some three kilometres in circumference, and the central city plan was laid out in the traditional geometric style perfected by Hippodamos, the fifth-century BC Ionian town-planner. A wide arterial paved way, forming an east-west axis, followed the line of the great ledge across which the buildings spread. To the north, the city was protected by tawny-coloured limestone cliffs and the situation, one of great dominance, enabled the inhabitants to enjoy a bird's-eye view of sea, gulf, lagoons and promontories.

The ruined city can be traced in its entirety within the fortified *enceinte*, though most of the walls overlooking the formidable southern declivity have unfortunately been destroyed. Immediately to the left of the main street, in the area of the *agora*, there are traces of a long *stoa*, consisting of an outer Doric colonnade and an inner one of square columns; another *stoa* ran north to south on the west side of the *agora*. To the east are the remains of an *odeion*, with over twenty tiers carved out of the rock; from here politicians harangued the people massed in the quadrilateral market place.

Across the main street from the north *stoa* is the finest extant ruin: the **prytaneion** or town hall, residence of the city elders and hostel for distinguished visitors. The main walls are of polygonal masonry, the diagonal interior ones at the four corners of the building constituting a novel feature, probably intended to provide extra support to the upper storey. A large central court was surrounded by Doric colonnades, behind which there were seventeen chambers in which the town councillors transacted their business. The upper storey, whose roof was decorated with *acroteria* carved with lotus flowers and palmettes, stopped short on the south side, thus giving the building the shape of a Greek letter π and enabling the dwellers to enjoy the benefits of the mountain breezes. This building, the layout of which is perfectly clear to the naked eye, was destroyed during the Roman occupation of Epirus in the second century BC.

Further evidence of the importance - in this instance not military or strategic - of Hellenistic Kassopi is provided by the ruin of a large third-century BC **Theatre**, where ancient drama was taught. Carved out of the cliff-face to the north-west of the *prytaneion* and reached after a stiff climb, it was capable of accommodating six thousand spectators. The gradient is terrifyingly steep; two huge rocks lying in the centre of the orchestra remind us of the repeated landslides which have buried the foundations of Kassopi under successive strata of boulders.

At the north-west end of the plateau there is an underground burial chamber. Stone steps lead to a vaulted passage, terminating in a square chamber which was plundered in the early nineteenth century. Ancient graffiti are identifiable on the walls of the passageway which, like those of the chamber, were surfaced with marble dust and sand to give the impression of fine marble panels; situated within the city walls, the chamber may well have been the funerary sanctuary of some Kassopean military hero. For all its size, and the robust architectural features of its scattered civic buildings, Kassopi remains an enigma. Many large edifices, whose function is unknown, have still to be cleared.

Immediately east of the signpost to Kassopi, the country road dips down to the little eighteenth-century Monastery of *Ayios*

Dimitrios. Above it towers the cliff of **Zalongo**, a national shrine, dominated by a huge modern sculpture of a group of white figures. The shrine commemorates a rather over-romanticized incident from the long campaign by Ali Pasha against the Souliots: after the fall of the Souli forts in 1803, a number of Souliots fled southwards and took refuge from the pursuing Turks below this prominent eminence. One day, children playing outside the church spied a detachment of Ali Pasha's Albanians approaching from the south-east. The women and children scrambled up the cliff, but the men were ambushed by another Moslem detachment approaching from the north and, caught in the cross-fire, were all killed. About sixty of the women, fearing rape and captivity, reached the summit, whence they hurled themselves, with their children, into the abyss below. It is said that the women performed a slow, circular folk-dance on the rocky eminence before falling off one by one, at the end of each revolution, as though in execution of some solemn sacrificial rite. A zig-zag stairway climbs the cliff-face. Halfway up, a little chapel contains the bones of the women whose corpses were found among the boulders. The summit is razor-sharp and one is tempted to wonder whether the dance could ever have taken place in such a confined space; nevertheless the story remains sacrosanct. To the south, undulating grasslands shelve down past Nikopolis to the Ambracian Gulf; to the north roll the Thesprotian mountains, compressed into mysterious billowing forms.

Beyond the turn-off to Kassopi and Zalongo, the northbound road to Paramythia enters a lush, wooded valley which contracts into a defile and descends into the Aherousian plain, across which the Aheron flows sluggishly through a series of swamps. Yellow irises border rivulets which criss-cross fields of maize and rice-paddies; buffaloes graze in meadows shaded by poplar, fig and plane trees; in summer the heat is intense. To the north-east the mountain-wall of Souli rises sheer to a height of over a thousand metres: arid, forbidding, with razor-sharp crests sliced by vertical crevices.

The Paramythia road leads to **Glyki**, at the foot of the mountains. A detour to the village is worthwhile: the streams of the Aheron form meres of sun-dazzled water and cafés spread under immense plane trees.

East of the village a track climbs to the entrance of the **Aheron Gorge**, through which flowed one of the mythical rivers of the Underworld. Thence a path penetrates the 'Defile of the Dead', which is deep, dark and narrow, with a stream of aquamarine water flowing swiftly between banks of ilex. It was in this sinister setting that Charon, squatting on one of those contorted, cream-coloured boulders, waited to ferry the souls of the dead across to the world of shades. If the souls, still in the form of corpses, did not have a coin placed behind their ears or laid under their tongues, the avaricious boatman refused to ferry them across to the Asphodel Fields; they were then doomed to wait on the banks of the lugubrious river throughout eternity. Rugged cliffs rise to barren summits, dominated by the strange bulbous pinnacle above Mount Kiafa; behind it is a higher peak and, to the south, the box-like fort of Kounghi. Rocky bluffs create a zig-zag formation as the defile deepens. No gorge in Greece is more macabre. The silence is total, except for the flow of ice-cold water between the dipping branches of plane trees. Occasionally one hears the tinkle of a bell, hanging from the neck of a black mountain-goat perched on a jagged rock, like some infernal herald pointing the way to Hell. Once the entrance to the Gorge is lost sight of, a feeling of constriction, even near-panic, is unavoidable.

Only the deserted forts on the ledges above the path remind us that the Gorge was once inhabited by the turbulent people who gave their name to the whole mountain range of **Souli**. The Souliots settled here in the fifteenth century, retaining their Albanian mother tongue and Christian faith. During the early centuries of Ottoman occupation they enjoyed a measure of autonomy, unconquered by the Sultan's soldiers; they lived by plunder, descending on the farms of Turkish pashas and Greek peasants alike. Towards the end of the eighteenth century, their militaristic activities aroused the interest of the Russian Government and Czarist agents penetrated the Aheron Gorge to encourage and support the Souliots with gold and arms. Ali Pasha's riposte was a full-scale attack in 1792; but the campaign was a failure and most of Ali's soldiers fell to the shots of Souliot snipers posted in hidden crannies overlooking the Gorge.

Ali Pasha could not allow this state of affairs to go on indefinitely; the siege was renewed. It went on for years, the Souliot women fighting alongside the men in defence of the forts. However, the Souliot stocks of arms and provisions diminished as the Turkish ring of pennon-crowned tents tightened round the entrance to the Gorge. Eventually the brigands surrendered, but not until after their leader, the priest Samuel, had blown himself up in the powder magazine of Fort Kounghi. Survivors migrated to other parts of Greece but, after the outbreak of the War of Independence, they returned to the mountains and once more took up arms against the Turks. However, the Ottoman forces under Omar Vrioni (successor to Ali Pasha) proved too strong for them and, when offered honourable terms of capitulation in September 1822, they accepted and emigrated to the Ionian Islands; only Markos Botsaris remained in Western Greece to carry on the fight. The Souliot exploits, probably over-dramatized, remain engraved in the national consciousness, immortalized in poem, folk-song and history book.

Returning south from Glyki and turning west, through Kanalaki, on the road which crosses the rush-bordered streams of the Aherousian plain, one reaches the hill-top village of **Kastri**. Site of ancient Pandossia, founded in the seventh century BC, its *enceinte* once included twenty-two square towers and rough, fourth-century BC polygonal walling on the east side. The modern village, past which the Aheron flows towards the sea, is green and pleasant.

Five kilometres to the west is the village of Mesopotamo, where **Ephyra**, site of a celebrated *nekromanteion* (oracle of the dead), crowns a rocky knoll above the Kokytos, a tributary of the 'infernal' Aheron. The excavations lie beneath the eighteenth-century church of *Ayios Ioannis*. The site, among the most important of its kind in the country, has much in common topographically with the one described by Homer in the eleventh book of the *Odyssey*, in which Odysseus performs the greatest of his feats: the descent into Hell. Archaeologists have indeed demonstrated that Ephyra has a Bronze Age history, and it was here that Neoptolemos settled after the Trojan War and ruled as the first of the Molossian kings.

The ancient Greeks believed that all hollows and fissures in the earth's crust led to the Underworld, where dwelt the souls of the dead who uttered prophecies to enquiring mortals bold enough to search them out. At Ephyra, pilgrims had to undergo purification rites, as at all oracles: diet, prayers, ablutions and total silence were among the regulations. Sacrifices too, for the dead liked to be propitiated with honey, milk, wine and, above all, the blood of sacrificial animals.

The site is an extremely complex one, and the custodian's assistance is indispensable. Walls of thick polygonal masonry - five massive courses of the east wall are preserved - enclose a labyrinth of corridors and ancillary chambers where some heavy lintels and doors have survived in good condition. In these chambers, which include a bathroom and dormitories, we can still see the famous jars which used to contain lupin seeds and Egyptian jonquil given to pilgrims in order to produce hallucinations, flatulence and giddiness. At the end of the maze of corridors, in which the pilgrims submitted to further unusual rites - including the eating of oysters - which caused them to be worked up into an hysterical and receptive state, was the central apartment flanked by three chambers on each side. Here one may still descend through an arched entrance into a gloomy, vaulted pit where it was believed that Hades, Lord of the Underworld, and his wife Persephone reigned in their infernal 'palace'. Iron wheels and pulleys, by means of which the shades of the dead were raised in order to gabble their oracles to the open-mouthed pilgrims, lie in the central court, but the windlass mechanism itself is in the Ioannina Museum. It is worth noting the thickness of the walls, which allowed the priests' movements and 'preparations' to be carried out inaudibly. It is the survival of the props, as well as the pleasant, almost pastoral, setting of the oracle, that tend to produce such an impression of ambivalence in the modern visitor: frankly, there is nothing in the least infernal about the place. How unlike the Gorge of the Aheron.

Before joining the coastal road at Mesopotamo, a short and pleasant diversion can be made along a minor road, bordered by sea lavender and agnus castus, which crosses the plain to Ammoudia and the mouth of the Aheron. This area was referred to by mythographers as the 'Forest of Persephone', but the trees that filled the sacred wood of the goddess have gone, replaced now by a dusty village and small resort. The harbour has become so extensively silted up that it is difficult to believe that this was once the anchorage for an entire Corinthian fleet before an attack on the Corcyraian flotillas in one of the early moves of the Peloponnesian War (433 BC).

The main coastal road crosses the north-western corner of the Aherousian plain, the awful crags of the Souliot mountains no longer dominating the landscape. The road then leaves the lowlands, which are scattered with walnut, fig and mulberry trees, and climbs into bare hills. To reach Parga, one turns off to the west and drives above a steep, wooded coast of brick-red cliffs, passing a branch road down to the lovely Lyhnos beach. Finally the road descends through olive groves to a beautiful bay. Here, nature and vernacular architecture have combined to make the little port of **Parga**, which is in the shape of an amphitheatre, one of the most attractive on the mainland: paved alleys and stairways mount steeply between slate-roofed, whitewashed houses and courtyards filled with orange trees, roses and jasmine. Unfortunately tourism has added its contribution: nondescript hotels, caravans, camping sites, a plethora of shoddy tavernas; but the crescent-shaped waterfront is animated (in the evenings at the height of summer the animation can be overpowering), resounding with the chug and splutter of caiques and the polyglot chatter of crowds of holidaymakers at the cafés and tourist shops which spread across the paving-stones. One looks out across the harbour, with its picturesque pine-covered rocky islets, one of which is topped with a whitewashed chapel, to the Ionian Sea and the low, flat shape of the island of Paxi. At the western end of the bay the ruins of a Venetian castle are spread over the headland. Beyond the castle the golden sands of Valtos Beach sweep westward around another crescent-shaped bay: this is one of the finest beaches in Greece. Thence, paths mount through terraced orchards and olive groves dotted with whitewashed chapels and farmhouses surrounded by fig trees. The lower levels are the preserve of campers; overcrowding is now the lot of Parga.

We do not hear much of Parga before the fourteenth century, when it was included in the domains of the Despots of Arta and was famous for its sugar plantations. Under Venetian rule, most of its inhabitants were pirates, and the Doge's architects transformed its rocky little fortress into a maritime bulwark against further Turkish expansion. After the Napoleonic Wars it was ceded to Britain with the Ionian Islands and should have been administered as part of the Protectorate, but the Sultan persuaded Britain to renounce its claim and the little port reverted to Moslem rule. This surrender was considered an act of betrayal by the inhabitants, who dug up the bones of their ancestors as a precaution against desecration and publicly burnt them amid loud lamentations. The majority then took off to Corfu in rowing-boats, hugging their children and little else, for Ali Pasha's cavalry had already descended the steep paths, occupied the port and sequestered all Greek belongings. This pusillanimous act of British foreign policy is often recalled in lurid oleographs entitled 'The Exodus to Corfu'.

There is no sightseeing. The Venetian castle is very ruined. On the crest of the ridge between the two scythe-like bays there is a whitewashed square with pleasant cafés under shady plane trees. Sea-bathing, fishing and walking in the shade of olive and fruit trees, against a screen of rugged hills, constitute the attractions of Parga.

Returning eastwards from Parga to the main Igoumenitsa road, you climb again into the rugged hinterland; sea and islands disappear from view. The road crosses a saddleback range and enters the **Valley of Margariti**, scene of much guerrilla activity in 1944, an elliptical crater with mountain peaks forming a kind of lunar rim round it. The road then runs northwards down to the sea and follows the coast around a beautiful bay to Igoumenitsa.

The second suggested route to Igoumenitsa starts by going northwards from Arta to Ioannina. Beyond the village of Filipiada, the road forces a way through the slate-grey mountains which form a semicircle to the north of Arta. Ambracian softness is succeeded by Thesprotian ruggedness. The narrow, claustrophobic valley of the Louros, whose sources lie high up in the heart of the Thesprotian massif, winds northwards. Just before reaching the Louros dam, which retains a sheet of pale water surrounded by bare crags, there are vestiges of an ancient water conduit: part of the great aqueduct which supplied Nikopolis with water. Further on, the knotted branches of plane trees form an arbour over the stream as the valley contracts. After passing through a tunnel at the narrowest part of the gorge, the road climbs into the deserted country where Crown Prince Constantine (soon to be King Constantine I) had his headquarters during the First Balkan War, when his forces were besieging Ioannina. The encircling peaks become higher, more desolate, dominated to the west by the summit of Mount Tomaros. Eight kilometres before reaching Ioannina, a turning to the left leads to Dodona. The road winds up a spur of Tomaros, affording stupendous views of the cruel crevices of the Pindos to the east and the Mitsikeli massif soaring above the lake of Ioannina. The zigzag road ends in an elliptical valley, with three hamlets straggling across the lower slopes of Tomaros. The mountain is speckled with firs and crowned with an elegant snow-capped peak; its slopes are scarred with screes and russet-coloured crevices, down which icy torrents must once have flowed.

In the valley, immediately facing the backcloth of Tomaros, are scattered the ruins of **Dodona**, one of the most evocative classical sites in Greece, almost Delphic in its solitude and grandeur. It is not a smiling scene. 'Wintry Dodona', Homer calls it. The Dodonian oracle, dedicated to Zeus, is the oldest in Greece and was consulted by pilgrims long before Apollo took up his abode at Delphi. It is to Herodotos that we owe the story of the oracle's foundation: two black doves took flight one day from Thebes in Egypt. One alighted on an oak tree at Dodona and spoke with a human voice, instructing the inhabitants to found an oracle of Zeus; the second flew west into the desert to establish another at Siwa. Gods and heroes travelled across the Epirot wilderness to consult the oracle, whose pronouncements were revealed by the rustling of oak leaves in the wind.

As Delphi gained international fame and attracted increasing numbers of consultants, Dodona, more inaccessible, declined in importance. Nevertheless, poets and writers continued to hold it in high esteem. By the fifth century BC, the priests had been succeeded by old women (whom Herodotos and Sophocles called 'dove-priestesses') who went into transports of ecstasy before making their extremely ambiguously-worded pronouncements.

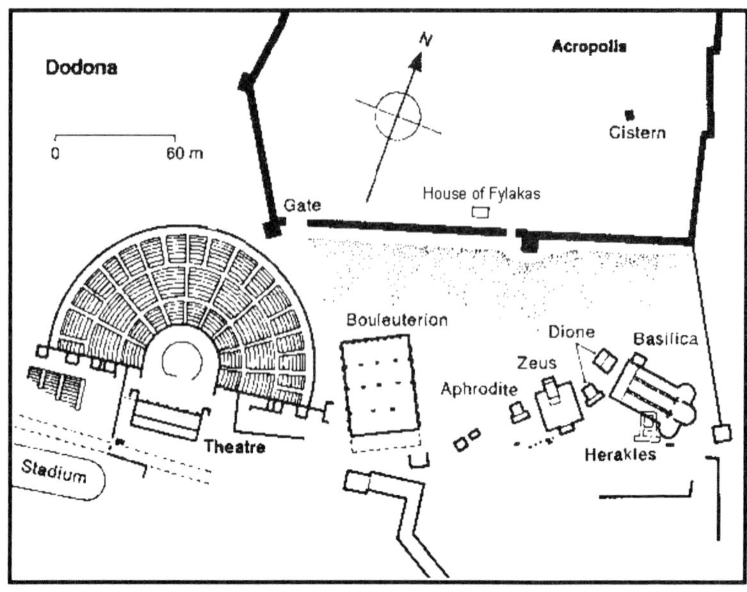

Sections of ancient walls stand out prominently and a few holm-oaks are dotted about the valley. Beyond the outline of the stadium rises the magnificent semicircle of the **Theatre**, built in the reign of Pyrrhos (third century BC) and recently sufficiently restored to constitute one of the major monuments of its kind in the country. The Theatre has no ornamentation left - no statues, friezes, pediments or carved seats for notables - only the harmony and simplicity of the concentric tiers of grey stone. The *skene* is a muddle of chambers which are difficult to identify. The west *parados* (side entrance), preceded by a double gate with three fluted Ionic half-columns, leads into the circular orchestra, where the horseshoe-shaped drainage conduit is remarkably well-preserved. The large *cavea*, supported (where it is not recessed into the hill, like most Greek theatres) by a sturdy retaining wall, is intersected by two *diazômas*, its ten stairways forming nine sections, each with forty-five tiers. Eighteen thousand spectators could be accommodated and one wonders how so vast an auditorium, concealed in a mountain hollow on the virtual roof of the country, could ever have been filled to capacity.

A gateway behind the Theatre leads to the acropolis, where extant substructures are mostly of the Hellenistic period. From there a path descends to the sanctuary: scattered heaps of stones, among fields where sheep browse, do not form an easily comprehensible layout. Three courses of well-fitted rectangular slabs indicate the site of the *Bouleuterion*, where the Epirot confederacy assembled, and a complex of outlines has been identified as the Temple of Zeus, beside which the mantic oak rustled its sacred leaves. The Temple was surrounded by cauldrons resting on tripods; these were placed close together, so that when one was struck, the echo reverberated through the others. Here too, also on a tripod, was a statue of a boy holding a bronze whip which, when blown by the wind, hit the cauldron next to it, setting off a clang that vibrated through all the brazen ornaments. Pyrrhos surrounded the sacred enclosure with Ionic colonnades but, in 219 BC, the Aetolians, at war with the Macedonians, destroyed the Temple, as well as the Theatre, and burnt the sacred grove of oak trees. The Temple of Zeus was subsequently rebuilt and enlarged with an Ionic propylaia; Philip V of Macedon repaired the Theatre and added the Stadium.

The last substructure is that of the small temple of Dione, which retains some evidence of column bases and calcified shafts. To the right, the outline of an apse and a marble slab carved with a cross are the only vestiges of a Christian basilica: an indication that Dodona, unlike Delphi, became a Christian sanctuary after the Edict of Theodosios (392) banned all pagan worship.

The short stretch of highway from the Dodona turn-off to **Ioannina**, capital of Epirus, is without interest. This mountain-girt seat of Ali Pasha, once considered sufficiently important for the British, French and Russian governments to have appointed fully-accredited Consuls, remains one of the busiest provincial towns in Greece with a large choice of hotels. A garrison and university town, most of the public buildings - whether administrative, cultural or military - are painfully plain; only Ali Pasha's Citadel retains an air of nineteenth-century picturesqueness and arouses memories of the semi-oriental city about which Byron enthused. From the large central square, the town shelves down to a bluff dominated by the Citadel; a few ruined minarets and domes are outlined against the pale waters of the lake. On the opposite shore Mount Mitsikeli, a bleak wall of grey limestone, rises sheer. To the east, the perspectives are more intriguing, with mysterious, uninhabited valleys winding steeply into the wilderness of the Pindos.

The city's history is largely medieval. Named after a lakeside monastery of St John the Baptist, it enters the limelight in the late eleventh century, when Bohemond, an uncouth but astute Norman, invaded and made it his winter quarters, strengthening the walls and plundering the surrounding countryside. During the brief Serb domination in the fourteenth century it was ruled by Thomas Preljubovic, who impoverished the inhabitants by creating monopolies so that all their agricultural produce was traded exclusively by his bailiffs. Given, we are told, to 'unnatural vices', he was murdered by one of his own bodyguard, and his widow (and successor), the delightful Maria Angelina, took as her consort a civilized Florentine of the Buondelmonti family. Ioannina settled down to happier days. In the fifteenth century, however, the Turks came. In 1611 an irresponsible and unsuccessful revolt, led by a drunken prelate, hardened the mood of the conquerors and the dead hand of the Turks settled on all Epirus. The inhabitants, however, were more active than other Greeks in keeping the ideal of Hellenism alive by founding schools, some secret, some open. In no other part of the country was the standard of education so high. The schools of Ioannina and their teachers - historians, geographers, theologians - provided much of the patriotic fervour, and a little of the learning, that would make the War of Independence a possibility and modern Greece a reality.

In the early nineteenth century Ioannina became the capital of Ali Pasha, the cruel, astute and capricious Albanian tyrant who ruled over the pashalik of Southern Albania, which included the whole of Western Greece. Then Ioannina, a miniature metropolis, knew its palmiest days, with its Oriental court, its foreign diplomatic representatives and its prosperous trading-houses, visited by merchants, adventurers and travellers from the west.

The focal point of the modern town is the central square (Kentriki Platia) and the adjoining public gardens, where some remains of the fortress palace of Ali's son, Muchtar Pasha, can be seen below the modern Cultural Centre; from the café, there is a fine view of the eastern shore of the lake, backed by snow-capped peaks. On the other side of the gardens is the **Museum**, whose exhibits range from antique finds to a collection of nineteenth-century paintings. The antiquities come from various Epirot sites: there is a fine Roman sarcophagus from Paramythia, carved with a procession of nude male figures and clothed women in Bacchanalian attitudes, their drapery blown back by the wind. There are small lead tablets, inscribed with the questions asked by pilgrims consulting the Dodonian oracle; also prehistoric pottery, weapons from Dodona and two gold icons, of St John the Baptist and the Raising of Lazarus.

A few eighteenth-century houses, homes of the grand old families of Ioannina, are scattered about the eastern urban slope. From Kentriki Platia, Averoff Street descends towards the citadel and the lake, between antique shops and silversmiths filled with buckles, clasps and boxes inlaid with filigree, for which the craftsmen of Ioannina have long been famous. One passes the plane tree from whose branches Ali Pasha's victims - both Christian and Moslem - used to hang until the stench of their decomposing bodies proved too much even for the local Janissaries. The **Citadel**, enclosed within walls of the Turkish period, is a warren of clean, whitewashed cottages and some small, gaudily-painted modern houses; it is crowned by the seventeenth-century hexagonal **Mosque of Aslan Aga**, now the Municipal Museum of Popular Art.

The walled-in area of the Citadel can be entered at several points and arrows indicate the way to the Mosque, with its well-preserved minaret. The Mosque is entered through a glass exo-narthex supported by six columns. The exhibits, of varying quality, constitute a somewhat eccentric miscellany from different periods; it is like wandering through a rather superior Oriental junk-shop. Exhibits include Epirot costumes and silverware, relics of the War of Independence, Turkish carved wooden chairs with mother-of-pearl inlay, some beautiful Turkish rugs and embroideries. The whole strange hotchpotch is crowned by an oleograph of Lady Hamilton.

After a short walk above the lake, you approach the **Fetiye Mosque** through an arched gateway. The tea-cosy dome and minaret overlook the whole citadel area, from whose fortified parapet the muzzles of old Turkish cannon are still trained across the lake. The plain tomb in front of the Mosque is that of Ali himself. The Seraglio, where the old Lion of Ioannina kept his countless wives, was demolished after his death.

At this point it is best to leave the Citadel and descend to the café-lined landing stage, from which the tree-shaded lakeside road follows the fortifications round the promontory. A ferry takes about ten minutes to cross the green waters of **Lake Pamvotis** to the island (Nissi), whose reed-fringed shore is surrounded by eel-traps. The island's Byzantine churches can be seen in a single morning or afternoon, but there is no more agreeable way of spending a whole day than by roaming along Nissi's herb-scented paths and cobbled alleys. One can lunch on eels, frogs, trout or cray-fish at the tree-shaded taverna of *Kyra Vasiliki*, on the landing stage. The taverna is named after Ali's beautiful Greek concubine who entered his harem at the age of twelve and later used her influence over the ferocious old pasha with such astuteness that she was often able to intercede successfully on behalf of her oppressed compatriots.

The sightseer's itinerary, which includes five monasteries, begins at the jetty. One crosses the village, its paved alleys bordered by whitewashed cottages bright with flowering creepers, in order to reach the first church on the west shore. The little **Monastery of Ayios Nikolaos of the Filanthropini** spreads across a rocky slope where sheep graze among the asphodel. In the courtyard there is a ruined refectory. The single-nave church, the most interesting on the island, has a saddleback roof: as well as the narthex it has an exo-narthex with side chapels, of a later date, providing the rustic edifice with architectural unity. It was founded in 1292 by Michael Filanthropinos, who came to Ioannina from Constantinople. Michael was the first abbot, in which office he was succeeded by four members of his family. The frescoes, restored in 1963, were painted in the sixteenth century by the brothers Dikotaris of Thebes. There are no masterpieces, but the work is animated - in spite of the awkward attitudes of the saints. In the south chapel, to the left of the entrance, there are paintings of some of the great figures of antiquity, including Solon, Aristotle and Plutarch. In this side chapel too there is an horrific rendering of the Last Judgement. In an arched niche (left) in the narthex we see the benefactors, the five abbots of the Filanthropini, waiting on St Nicholas; above him, at the apex of the arch, reigns Christ, with an open Book of Gospels before him. In the north side chapel, believed to be the site of one of the secret schools of Ioannina, the walls are painted with lively scenes of martyrdom: blood spurting from severed heads, truncated limbs lying about in contorted attitudes. On the south wall there is a charming if naïve Creation, full of birds and animals and stylized trees.

To the south of the Filanthropini we come to the **Monastery of Ayios Nikolaos of Dilios**, overlooking a grove of poplars, with rushes full of croaking frogs and the lake beyond. The church, dating from the early days of the Despotate, is basilica-shaped, with a large narthex and half-cylinder apse showing traces of exterior brickwork decoration. The frescoes are of the mid-sixteenth century and the artists are believed to have been influenced by the work of Theofanes of Crete, who painted more ambitious murals on Mount Athos. The Apocalypse, above the narthex door, is distinguished by a nice blend of colours: yellows, browns and golds. On the wooden *iconostasis*, said to be the work of the woodcarver responsible for the far more elaborate screen in the Monastery of *Ayios Stefanos* at Meteora, animals browse in a complex foliate setting.

From here, one descends to the grove of poplars and follows a shady path in a south-easterly direction, whence there is an unbroken view across the lake to the mosques, minarets and fortifications of the Citadel. The path ends up at the **Monastery of the Eleoussa**: named after a miraculous icon of the *Panayia Eleoussa* (The Virgin of Mercy), it too is dedicated to St Nicholas, patron saint of sailors.

The architectural arrangement is similar to that of St Nicholas of Dilios, but on a smaller scale. The uncleaned frescoes are too damaged to merit detailed attention.

The Eleoussa is a dead end. Returning, one skirts the swampy shore back to the landing-stage and crosses the village again - but in an easterly direction - as far as the **Monastery of Ayios Pandeleimon**, which nestles below a cliff, shaded by enormous plane trees, overlooking the north-east part of the lake. An aisled basilica of the sixteenth century, it is of little interest except for the architectural oddity of the women's gallery, shaped like the dress circle of a theatre. Beside the church is a ramshackle wooden house, rather pretentiously called the **Museum of Ali Pasha**, scene of the old Lion's dramatic end in 1822. For years Ali's obdurate insubordination had been a cause of growing anxiety in Constantinople. After abortive negotiations with Kurschid, Sultan Mahmud II's military envoy, Ali retired to his kiosk on the island; there he hoped to gain time in which to manoeuvre the Sultan into granting him a pardon, before taking up arms again in defence of his quasi-independent little Albanian empire. Kurschid, suspicious of the old wizard's intentions, sent an armed detachment to spy on his movements. Determined not to submit to intimidation, Ali fired on Kurschid's men from the window; in a moment the peace of the soporific little island was shattered by the crack of musketry. Ali, though wounded in the arm, organized resistance among his bodyguard, but the regular troops soon penetrated the ground floor and fired through the frail ceiling; a bullet pierced the old pasha's groin. It was a fatal wound. Resistance collapsed. Ali's head was severed and carried in state to the citadel. Thus ended the long and turbulent reign of the Albanian adventurer, the stories of whose amorous and military exploits had thrilled all Europe. The chamber in which Ali was shot has been furnished in the Turkish style, with broad divans ranged against the walls, on which hang nineteenth-century prints illustrating the story of Ali and the War of Independence.

From the museum you pass through a tunnelled passage onto a little terrace overlooking the lake. Here the diminutive sixteenth-century **Church of Ayios Ioannis Prodromos** (St John the Baptist) is built picturesquely against a small rocky cliff. The consequent architectural arrangement is therefore somewhat eccentric, with the sanctuary facing north, a saddleback transept replacing the usual dome, and two side apses at the east and west ends. The tasteless frescoes are of the eighteenth century.

Four kilometres north-west of Ioannina a hump-like eminence rises out of the plain near the airport, its base pierced by the entrance to the **Cave of Perama**. One of the most remarkable in Greece, it was accidentally discovered by villagers seeking refuge from Italian bombers in 1940-41 when, beyond the recess in which they huddled, they caught glimpses of vast caverns and galleries. After the war the speleologists came and electricity was installed; today, guides conduct visitors through a complex of fetid chambers, pools of water and twisting tunnels lined with stalactites and stalagmites. Some of the more fragile stalactites, grouped in organ-pipe formations, produce an audible tintinnabulation when struck.

The journey from Ioannina to the Albanian frontier should include a diversion to **Zagoria**, an area of forty-six villages scattered across upland meadows or perched on crags overlooking the Stygian gorges of the Zagori massif. Remains of cyclopean walls testify to the antiquity of occupation, but the elegant fifteenth-century stone bridges spanning an abundance of green torrents, are the outstanding features of the Vikos-Aoös National Park, which extends to the east of the road. A day's drive from Ioannina gives one time to visit a few of the most strikingly-situated villages.

From Ioannina the road to Konitsa, near the Albanian frontier, runs north-west below the flank of Mitsikeli. After about twenty kilometres a branch road to the right ascends a rocky wasteland, speckled with poplars and wild pear trees, to the village of **Vitsa** (keep left twice, and then right once, after leaving the main road). Its well-preserved grey stone houses, roofed with tiles - lozenge-shaped, elliptical, polygonal - cling to the mountain-side. Arched windows in the middle of the ground floor enliven the otherwise unrelieved austerity of these grim, rectangular buildings intended to protect their inmates from the harsh elements and to keep wolves and brigands at bay.

The villages of Zagoria are little heard-of before the Turkish occupation, when their inhabitants emerge as Christian communities to whom the Turks granted special privileges. By the eighteenth century they had formed a confederacy, dwelling in a state of semi-independence, exempt from the fiscal extortion that crippled the more prosperous lowland communities. Many villagers, hard-working and ambitious, emigrated to metropolitan centres within the Ottoman Empire and became members of the professional classes. However they always came back to Zagoria, to bestow wealth and to build sturdy houses furnished with fine carpets and furs. After the First World War emigration increased and many of the dwellings now remain firmly shuttered.

Beyond Vitsa the road climbs steeply to **Monodendri**. Architecturally the village differs little from Vitsa, for throughout the Zagori massif Epirot stonemasons adopted a uniform plan for dwelling-houses and made use of identical materials. Cobbled mule-tracks are bordered by primitive pavements; they run between stone walls and roofed gates, over which branches of almond trees scatter their blossom in spring. In the paved square is the Church of *Ayios Minas* (1630), as typical of the local basilica style as *Ayios Athanassios* (1830), both richly decorated with frescoes and elaborate gilt carvings. One of the fine old houses has been converted into an original, if somewhat rustic, guesthouse.

A ten minute walk along a lane from the village square of Monodendri leads to a shelf of rock from which one stares down into the immensity of the **Vikos Gorge**, at the point where the River Voidomatis and a torrent unite, their confluence forming three mighty chasms. The cliff-walls, dotted with clusters of evergreens, are absolutely vertical, the stratification of the crevices and shelves as symmetrical as Hellenic masonry. An abandoned threshing-floor forms a kind of belvedere, and the hum of thousands of bees echoes up from the boulder-strewn ravines. The little refurbished Monastery of *Ayia Paraskevi*, built of grey stone, with its slate roofs almost indistinguishable from the rock to whose sides it clings, is suspended like an Athonite eyrie above space. To the north the gorge widens out and below the path some horse-chestnut trees are scattered across vertiginous ledges.

From Monodendri one can continue along the road to the north; it climbs above the village into an uninhabited lunar landscape of strange rock formations. Groups of boulders, like dolmens, have been weathered into horizontal, parallel and angular folds of such regularity and finish that one has the impression of gazing at a forest of man-made structures. The feeling of hallucination provoked by this geological phenomenon is haunting: I recall my relief at seeing a few poppies growing amid the misshapen rocks, and some beehives, although I wondered who ever climbed to this dizzy altitude to tend them. The road passes another point overlooking the Vikos Gorge, about midway along its course to the north from Monodendri. From here one looks across the whole massif, which resembles an uneven tableland slashed by multitudinous chasms, where lynxes still have their lairs. The road comes to an end here but will eventually be continued to the village of Vikos.

To visit the easterly Zagoria villages, one has to go back from Monodendri to Vitsa. After turning left at the next two intersections, the road crosses the Vikos. The outstanding painted church is a few miles east at **Negades**, where the basilica is triply dedicated: to the Holy Trinity, *Ayios Yeoryios* and *Ayios Dimitrios*, each with a separate altar, at the head of the nave and the two aisles. The vivid frescoes include Aristotle and Plutarch among the saints, while the stream of hell sweeps Judas, bishops and priests, followed by lesser sinners, into the devil's mouth. Surrounded on all sides by cloisters, the church is a fine example of the highly original Epirot architecture, which differs radically from the Byzantine ecclesiastical style.

The road to the north from the bridge over the Vikos goes to Tsepelovo, near which is the Rongovou Monastery, rebuilt in 1749. The road continues to Skamneli, with its Monasteries of *Ayia Paraskevi* (1697) and *Ayios Nikolaos* (1683). The vegetation becomes lusher round the villages of Laista and Vryssohori, below the snowy peaks of Mount Tymfi.

Much of this mountain area is within the Vikos-Aoös National Park and is of considerable botanical and zoological interest. Black pine and oak give way to the Rombola tree - a pine peculiar to the Balkans - on the higher peaks; among the innumerable wild flowers are many varieties of lily and narcissus. Although there are few, if any, bears left, wild boar, wild cats and mountain goats abound, not to mention birds of prey and wildfowl. To the south extend the summits of the Mitsikeli range: strange shapes, like petrified giants caught in the act of executing the most elaborate acrobatics.

Returning to the Ioannina-Konitsa road, one continues north-west through undulating scrubland, with Mount Tymfi to the north-east. On the left of the road a memorial marks the furthest point reached by Mussolini's army on Greek territory in the autumn of 1940. After Kalpaki, from where there is a road to the principal Albanian border crossing, the main road turns north, then north-east, with the Albanian foothills away to the left. Four kilometres after Kalpaki, one can take a road to the east and climb through grassland slopes shaded by holm-oaks, horse-chestnuts and Judas trees. At the top of the pass, the colossal cirque of the valley of the Voidomatis is suddenly revealed, against a wide, crescent-shaped screen of summits shaped like fangs. A dizzy descent in hairpin bends leads to the village of **Aristi**, architecturally similar to Monodendri, but with more of its houses occupied. At the bottom of the bowl, a modern arched bridge spans the stream of the Voidomatis, where it flows out of the Vikos Gorge. Plane trees line the river banks, the peace and serenity of the scene providing a strange contrast to the immensity of the scale. The road then climbs the east side of the bowl and follows a spine of foothills, their stratifications of schist resembling regular courses of masonry. To the south, the jaws of the Vikos Gorge yawn: cliffs, screes, crags and dolomites, all peppered with caves and arched recesses, disappearing into a tunnel of profound gloom. On a bluff opposite is the village of Vikos - like a last human outpost before the gates of Hades.

The road ends at the village of **Papingo**, a sheep village and winter refuge of the Sarakatsanis, the once-migrant people with no occupation other than grazing their flocks, whose wooden huts used to be scattered throughout the valleys of upland Greece. The stone village houses, with their squat, barn-like roofs and cobbled passages, spread among almond trees under castellated cliffs which taper off into six monstrous tusks, eroded into shapes as weird as the rock formations of Meteora. The highest peak of Mount Tymfi is called Gamila, the Camel.

The Church of *Ayios Vlassios*, a basilica with a wooden gallery at the west end reserved for the female congregation, stands beside its pretty, octagonal, three-storeyed campanile - a typical addition to Zagoria churches. There are several traditional-style *pensions* to stay at in the village.

Back on the main Konitsa road, one should not omit to take a last look at the heights above Papingo, which now acquire the semblance of distorted organ-pipes, and at the northern outlet of the macabre Vikos Gorge: the savagery of the scene is equal only to its perfection. We descend into a cultivated plain traversed by the Aoös, which rises in the heights of Smolikas, the highest peak of the Pindos mountains, looming majestically in the north-east. At the point where the river forces its way through the pinnacles and pyramids of rock, a packhorse bridge - a single wide arch of the utmost elegance - spans the translucent green stream flowing between the sandbanks. Here, near the Albanian frontier, as elsewhere in the Zagoria, one has the impression that the deities who presided over the architectural landscape of Greece must have decided to complete their task freehand, putting away their rulers, dividers and compasses. They certainly ended with a flourish.

At no distance from the bridge, **Konitsa**, whose inhabitants suffered horribly in battles between the Communists and the Greek national army in 1947-49, looks out from the lower slopes of Smolikas across the plain to the Albanian foothills. One of Greece's loneliest, yet loveliest, roads continues north-east between the Smolikas and Grammos massifs, then east to the Neapolis junction in Western Macedonia.

Back in Ioannina, one now turns to the west on the Igoumenitsa road. About twenty kilometres from Ioannina a branch road to the right leads to **Zitsa**. Slate roofs spread among Judas trees across the mountain-side. At the inn you may try the local Zitsa wine - much commended throughout Epirus: a naturally sparkling *rosé*, it is sweet and rather sickly. A more rewarding way of spending half an hour is to visit the Monastery of *Profitis Ilias*, situated on a windy platform surrounded by oaks and pines. The exterior of the church is barn-like, with a slate roof crowned by three shallow domes - hardly perceptible from outside - ranged in a straight line, one above the narthex and two above the *naos*. The frescoes are late post-Byzantine and in no way remarkable. The elaborate *iconostasis* is a good piece of Epirot woodcarving, with gilded floral designs surmounted by double colonnades, each with seventeen columns terminating in pointed arches. A commemorative plaque informs us that Byron stayed here in October 1809. From the plateau, along which the poet strolled with the monks, there is a wide view of the valley of the Kalamas, one of the four great rivers of Epirus. Byron fell in love with Zitsa; it was his first experience of the impact of the Greek landscape.

From the turn-off to Zitsa, the main road continues its sinuous descent to the Ionian coast, following the course of the Kalamas above a narrow gorge. Clusters of Judas trees are dotted among pines and ilex, and slate-roofed villages perch on bluffs below the level of the mountain road. There is an exhilarating feeling of lightness of spirit as one aerial view succeeds another. Emerging from the gorge, the road enters an enormous mountain-girt basin where the right flank of Mussolini's army was decisively defeated in 1940. There are glimpses of the sea and of Corfu.

Just after the village of Neraida, a branch road climbs to the south and descends into the northern part of the Aherousian plain, passing through the valley of the Kokytos. **Paramythia**, a big village loud with the din of coppersmiths, sprawls across the lower slope of Mount Korillas, which merges into the Souli range. The village was always famous for the olives cultivated in its green valley, and the discovery of coins, inscriptions and some exiguous Roman remains has confirmed that it was an ancient site. During the Venetian era Paramythia was known as Castel Donato and there are fragmentary remains of a castle, with Turkish additions, above the village. The branch road continues south and descends to meet the main coastal road at Morfi.

Along the Igoumenitsa road beyond Neraida, the shells of roadside houses and ugly white monuments commemorate skirmishes between Greek guerillas and German troops during the Second World War.

The journey ends at the busy port of **Igoumenitsa**, which has little in common with the rest of Epirus - or indeed Greece. A port of embarkation for Italy, it is distinguished by nothing but its bus terminal and the bustle of ferry-boats and chugging caiques. A string of hotels and tavernas lines the waterfront. Islets, like sprawling porpoises, form a garland round the crescent-shaped bay, beyond which flows the Corfu channel. Igoumenitsa has the impersonality of a frontier town: the traveller's main business is to get himself, his belongings and his car onto the right ship, and the mind's eye is already projected westward - towards Italy, beyond the horizon.

Soon, however, memories begin to crystallize: flashes of the tremendous architectural landscape of Zagoria; pale reflections of Moslem Ioannina and its lakeside Byzantine chapels; perspectives of the 'wintry' valley of classical Dodona; visions of the infernal Aheron gorge, with the heat-haze hanging over the mythological Aherousian swamp; the Souliot range with its grim forts - and of all the Hellenic lands that lie beyond, with their marble silhouettes and red-brick domes and medieval bastions; columns, pediments, tombs; *amphorae*, figurines and Attic profiles; icons, frescoes, floor-mosaics; asphodel waving on windswept slopes and dust lying thick in potholed village streets lined with wispy acacias; the inland seas ringed round by mountains with legendary names; the smell of pine resin and burning incense, of scorched herbs and frying mutton-fat; nostalgia for the demise of past genius; affection for an ebullient, contentious people always ready to be won over by a compliment, a joke or a wink of complicity. The impressions resolve into imperishable, deeply-felt experiences.

Appendices

General Information

Seasons

January and February can be cold and wet, with intervals of brilliant sunshine. A period of cloudless skies and calm seas in early January corresponds to the ancient Halcyon Days - breeding time of the mythological halcyon birds. Brief falls of snow are not uncommon in Attica and Boeotia (the high mountains are snow-covered from November to April). In northern Greece snowfalls and cold spells are of longer duration. Fog is not unknown in Thessaloniki. Almond blossom and the first wild flowers (anemones). Woodcock shooting.

March, unpredictable, as everywhere. Hillsides covered with wild flowers. Mid-March to Mid-April is the ideal time for botanists.

April can be showery or idyllic. Good season for travelling, with lengthening days. Dirt roads sometimes impassable after spring rains. Scent of lemon and orange blossom is intoxicating in the orchard country.

May, generally fine and warm. Occasional rain. Flowers in profusion.

June, still a good time for travelling. Not too hot. Sometimes cloudy in the middle of the day.

July-August, very hot. Hordes of tourists. Season of fruits. Crystalline light emphasises the quality of the landscape. Barren mountains, the colour of gun-metal, turn a glowing purple in the late afternoon. Cooling Etesian winds. Macedonia is sometimes intensely humid. Athens area subject to more severe atmospheric pollution than in other seasons.

September, still full summer but not as hot as July-August. Fewer tourists; fewer local trippers. Quail shooting.

October, in spite of the first rains, generally lives up to the tradition of a 'golden autumn'. Hillsides covered with cyclamen and autumn crocus.

November, unpredictable. Can be a prolongation of the 'golden autumn' or a foretaste of December. Dirt roads often impassable after autumn rains.

December, inclined to be cloudy; raw, but not very cold, with some fine spells and magnificent winter sunsets.

Museums

Archaeological sites and museums are usually open from 8 or 9 a.m. to 3 p.m. or later on weekdays and Saturdays, Sundays and holidays. Nearly all state-controlled sites and museums are closed on Mondays, but the very important ones open towards noon. A few sites and museums are closed on Tuesdays.

Hours of opening should be checked as they are liable to alter and are certainly not uniform throughout the country. Hotel receptionists generally have up-to-date information and for the Athens area the *Athens Daily News* publishes a reliable list.

All museums and archaeological sites throughout the country are shut on 1 January, 25 March (Independence Day), Good Friday (Orthodox), Easter Sunday (Orthodox) and Christmas Day.

Churches and Chapels

Some of the churches of architectural or artistic importance no longer function as places of worship and are in effect museums, with regular visiting hours and admission tickets, e.g. Dafni and at Mystra. Many others are functioning parish churches and in consequence are open all day (at least in the towns) except for two or three hours at midday. Village churches, however, are likely to be open only for services. The priest, or a church functionary, usually lives nearby and will have the key. If one feels that a tip would be unsuitable, one should put something in the church box. Churches or chapels out in the country which are only used occasionally are more of a problem, but someone in the nearest village will know who has the key.

The most difficult are churches and chapels that do not function at all, in the country or even in a town (e.g. Kastoria), especially those in the care of the Ministry, for which it may be necessary to find the official custodian (*fylákas*). Arrangements change, and it is not possible to give specific up-to-date information for each church.

Communications

Olympic Airways provides regular services to Alexandroupolis, Ioannina, Kalamata, Kastoria, Kavalla, Kozani, Preveza and Thessaloniki on the mainland and to many of the islands. Buses are plentiful; even remote mountain villages are connected with the nearest town by a daily service.

It is not always easy to get a taxi in Athens unless one uses one of the excellent Radio Taxi services. A passing taxi driver with spare seats will often pick up passengers if their destination is convenient - if a taxi slows down at your signal, shout the name of your destination. Taxis are parked in the main squares of small provincial towns. For long trips the price should be fixed in advance. A shared-taxi system operates to and from Athens.

The railway network does not cover the whole country. One can go from Athens to Thessaloniki, and thence to Yugoslavia, Bulgaria or Turkey (passing through the depths of the Nestos Gorge), but one cannot cross the Pindos spine which runs from north to south down the length of mainland Greece. A circuit of the Peloponnese is possible with stops at Corinth, Argos, Tripolis, Kalamata, Olympia, Pyrgos and Patras.

ELPA (the Automobile and Touring Club of Greece) affords free assistance to members of affiliated associations. It issues maps, leaflets on parking, etc. Its offices in Athens are in the Athens Tower, 2 Mesoyion, at Ambelokipi (Tel: 01.748.8800); in Thessaloniki at 228 Vasilissis Olgas (Tel: 031.426319). There are also offices in all the important towns and centres. For assistance in Attica, Tel. 104. For Tourist information Tel. 174 (in Athens), 01-174 (elsewhere).

For anyone using public transport and staying any length of time, the monthly *Greek Travel Pages* and the similar *Hellenic Travelling*, sold in foreign-language bookshops, are extremely useful.

Transliteration of Place Names

In Athens and some other towns, street names are given in Roman as well as Greek lettering, and motorists will find this also with road signs generally. In an attempt to make names comprehensible to speakers of foreign languages, the authorities have tried to adopt a phonetic rendering of the modern Greek, e.g. *Imitos* rather than *Hymettos*. However different authorities and organisations have produced different versions, especially on maps, and the lack of uniformity is complicated by two things: many Greek names have two forms - an official one and an everyday one; and secondly, one can put a name in the nominative (e.g. *Delfi*) or in the accusative (*Delfous*).

Throughout this book the transliterations are intended to provide the nearest equivalent in English to the Greek sounds, disregarding in some cases the versions produced by the authorities (thus: *Ymittos, Psyhiko, Nafplion*). The traditional forms for the most important places have been retained - *Athens, Piraeus, Patras.* The best-known classical sites are also given in the traditional form, sometimes slightly amended - *Epidauros, Delphi, Olympia, Mycenae*. Where the modern town or village has the same name, pronounced differently, it is transliterated according to the pronunciation - *Epidavros*. However a phonetic spelling, approximating to modern Greek usage has been adopted for the less well-known sites: *Hlemoutsi* (previously spelt Chlemoutsi), *Perahora* (Perachora), *Veryina* (Vergina).

In the past, names from the ancient Greek were transliterated into English in the Latinised form (Asclepius, Demetrius, Plataea) but over the last forty years many of these forms have gradually been abandoned in favour of spellings more consistent with the ancient Greek (*Asclepios, Demetrios*), which are used in this book. However some Latin-based spellings are still in normal use (*Aeschylus, Pericles, Plato*) as are some nouns (*stadium, stelae*).

One thing is certain: there is no absolutely correct spelling, using Roman letters, for any Greek name and it is therefore likely that most names will have a wide variety of forms in use for many years to come. Everyone will have their favourites and will be offended by either old-fashioned or modern forms; it is hoped that in this book we have been able to help travellers to recognise and pronounce, reasonably correctly, the alternative spellings that they will encounter in maps, road signs and other Guide Books!

Hotels

There are plenty of modern hotels in all towns and tourist resorts. Their most remarkable feature is, on the whole, their lack of distinction: of three or four hotels in a provincial town, it is often pointless to recommend any particular one in preference to the others. The names of a few hotels are mentioned in the text, largely because of their outstanding positions.

Hotel standards are liable to sudden fluctuation, particularly regarding furnishings and facilities. Promised services sometimes don't exist, especially out of season, and indeed, some hotels may even close altogether without warning. The official rating of hotels (de Luxe, A,B,C,D,E) is not a completely reliable guide - in Athens in particular; a hotel's charges often give one a better idea of its standing.

It is advisable to reserve accommodation in Athens during the summer months, as also for Delphi, Nafplion, Olympia and for all seaside resorts. Thessaloniki can be a problem from late August to early October, owing to the International Fair. In the resorts there are also apartments and self-catering establishments and comfortable rooms in houses, usually with their own shower, etc. Most of these are good value, as are the modest, family-run hotels in the C and D categories.

Greek Travel Pages and *Hellenic Travelling*, give lists of hotels, with prices, numbers of rooms and facilities - sometimes with photographs. Local Tourist Information Bureaux always have current information about hotels in their areas.

Restaurants, Tavernas, Cafés

Greeks generally have never been fastidious gastronomes and the works of ancient authors contain few references to their repasts. Homeric kings lived on bread, wine, olive oil and roast kid. No elaborate dishes are mentioned by the great dramatists, or by Plato when Socrates and his companions conversed round the dining table. The same applies to Byzantium: no Byzantine chronicler has left any record of meals served in the imperial palace or the houses of the Byzantine aristocracy.

The main ingredients in modern Greek cooking are olive oil, tomatoes, onions and garlic. Most dishes are of Eastern (romantics say Byzantine) origin and in private houses, where the quality of the materials is good, the food can be delicious: *pilafi*, *mousaka*,(minced meat between layers of fried aubergines and onions, a crust of béchamel) and vegetables (tomatoes, peppers, aubergines, marrows) stuffed with rice and herbs or minced meat.

A relative lack of discrimination as to quality, temperature and presentation of food is not conducive to a demand for a wide range of really good restaurants and the traveller may be surprised at the paucity of choice in a city the size of Athens. Most of the more expensive restaurants, usually with foreign names, meet local requirements ideally, but are not of great interest to foreign visitors. With a few exceptions it is the tavernas which provide occasions, often delightful, for dining in a relaxed, informal atmosphere, but the food (at which Greeks tend to peck at in a leisurely fashion and without strict adherence to the Western concept of an ordered sequence of dishes) is seldom memorable - veal, pork or lamb chops, *souvlakia* (small pieces of meat skewered and grilled), *moussaka* (seldom hot) and other cooked meat dishes, fried potatoes, *horiatiki salata* (sliced tomatoes, peppers, onions, with olives and chunks of *feta* - goat's milk cheese). With luck there will be a selection of *mezedes* (starters) including the delicious smoky-flavoured *melitzanosalata* (aubergines worked with oil - occasionally with *yoghourt* - into a pulp and flavoured with onions).

Travellers with queasy stomachs had best keep to grilled meat (and fish, where available). Most restaurants (but not tavernas) are indoor, even at the height of summer. Service may be slap-dash, but waiters are usually friendly - they often lose their heads, but seldom their sense of humour.

Wines have improved considerably in recent years, and now, apart from the products of the big wineries, there are some excellent and rather expensive estate wines, although these are not usually on wine-lists. Most Boutari wines are good, and reasonably unchanging from year to year, especially the reds. Tsandali and Porto Carras white wines are very drinkable, and, best value of all, the remarkably cheap Kourtaki wines.

Cheeses can be good; apart from the popular *feta* there are several *Gruyère* (*Graviera*) types, which tend to vary in quality according to the season, the year, and as to what animal the milk comes from. Corfu and Naxos *Graviera* are excellent. *Kasseri* is the Turkish *Kaskeval*, *Manouri* is like *Mozzarella* and is good when fresh (winter and spring) and seasoned with pepper and salt, smoked *Metsovo* (*Metsovone*) is very good.

The summer fruits (May to September) - strawberries, cherries, plums, yellow and white peaches, nectarines, grapes, figs and melons - are outstandingly good, as are the citrus fruits and pears in winter.

A selective list of restaurants and tavernas is published in the daily English language newspaper, *Athens News*, and in the weekly pamphlet, *The Week in Athens*, which can be bought in most kiosks that sell newspapers and periodicals.

Cafés, both indoor and open-air, are plentiful in Athens and the provincial towns. Confectionery is popular with the older Greeks, who have a very sweet tooth; the range of cream cakes is staggering. The ices are generally good. Many open-air cafés are open until the small hours, especially in summer.

As in many Mediterranean countries, café life has always played a large role in shaping the people's and the country's destinies. In many an Athens city-centre café of the older type (*kafenion*) contracts are drafted, debts contracted and settled, dowries discussed, important new contacts made and plots to overthrow the government hatched.

Shops

In central Athens the principal shopping areas are Ermou Street (women's wear and accessories, household goods, materials) and Stadiou Street (shoes, men's clothes). Branches of leading fashion houses are to be found in the Kolonaki to Syndagma Square area and in innumerable boutiques in the luxury hotels.

Antiques and local handicrafts are more likely to interest the traveller. Antique shops of varying quality proliferate in Plaka, Monastiraki (Pandrossou Street) and Kolonaki areas.

If you buy any museum-worthy (and therefore inevitably expensive) item, whether ancient Greek, Roman or Byzantine, it is advisable to get an official clearance from the seller. It is possible that your luggage will be looked into when you leave Greece (this is now uncommon), and you would not want to be accused of illegally carrying off the country's antiquities.

International jewellers are represented on their homeground by LALAOUNIS, 6 Panepistimou and ZOLOTAS, 9 Stadiou and 10 Penepistimou, who sell original jewellery based on antique and Byzantine designs. Less expensive hand-made jewellery, traditional or otherwise, and some of it very attractive, can be found at many small jewellery and gift shops.

Tourist shops, filled with plaster casts of famous statues, reproductions of classic vases and modern icons, are numerous in the Syndagma/Plaka area. Here are also displayed *tagaria* (woolen bags) and tablecloths, etc. woven or embroidered with peasant designs. Some of the modern icons (copies of old Byzantine ones) are of a high standard.

The only real department stores in Athens are LAMBROPOULOS and MINION, both near Omonia. Supermarket chains are SKLAVENITIS and (up-market) VASILOPOULOS. Most useful are the MARINOPOULOS shops combining a supermarket and a store, with toiletries, cosmetics, haberdashery, stationery, casual beach clothes, shoes, underwear, etc. There is one fairly near Syndagma in Kanari Street, Kolonaki.

The traveller will be impressed by the number of English language bookshops, well stocked with standard works and all the latest publications. English and other foreign newspapers are usually on sale by lunch-time at most kiosks in the Syndagma, Kolonaki and Omonia areas as well as in the shops of leading hotels.

Visiting Mount Athos

Formalities

Only men, not even 'beardless boys', are allowed to cross the frontier which runs across the neck of the peninsula. A recommendation for a permit of four days is issued to non-orthodox laymen for religious or scientific reasons only (if supported by a testimonial from their Consulate) by the Ministry of Foreign Affairs in Athens or the Ministry for Northern Greece in Thessaloniki. At Ouranopolis or Karyes, the capital of the republic, the document issued by the Ministry of Foreign Affairs is exchanged for a residence permit signed and countersigned by the Holy Synod and the Nomarch, the local civil authority. This permit must be presented to the guest-master of every monastery at which the traveller wishes to stay. Control of passports is effected at the port of Dafni.

Method of Travel

Caiques leave daily from Ouranoupolis and Ierissos. They put in at the landing place of every monastery - and at any *skiti* or hermitage on request. Private caiques can be chartered at Ierissos, Ouranoupolis, Dafni and some of the larger monasteries. Transport is available to Karyes from Dafni, but there is sometimes a steep climb up to the monasteries from their landing places. One has to carry one's own baggage so it is essential to travel light.

Accommodation

Monastery gates are shut at sunset, after which it is possible to gain admittance only under exceptional circumstances. It is important to make friends with the guest-master (*archontaris*), a vital personage, who will accept a gratuity. He allocates beds (often in a dormitory) and regulates hours of meals. Applications to visit the library, treasury and various chapels should be made to the librarian through the guest-master.

Organization

The Julian calendar (thirteen days behind the Gregorian) is kept throughout Mount Athos. Except at Vatopedi, which keeps standard or 'western' time, the monasteries keep Byzantine time, but in two forms: either sunset is at 12, and you work back from that, or dawn is at 12. In the cenobitic (communal) foundations travellers share their meals with the monks in the refectory. Lunch is usually at 9 a.m., dinner at 5 p.m. In the idiorrhythmic establishments, where discipline is milder, meals for visitors are served in the guest-house (*archontariki*) at more conventional hours. During fasts (which are frequent) food is likely to consist of boiled vegetables. At other times it can be more varied - and perhaps nastier. Visitors would do well, while travelling light, to take a supply of tinned food, biscuits, cheese, etc. At the Monasteries of Vatopedi and Grand Lavra, biscuits, cigarettes and *loukoumi* (Turkish delight) are sold. There are grocers at Karyes and Dafni.

Itinerary

Foreign tourists are admitted to Mount Athos at the rate of ten a day. The residence permit obtained at Ouranopolis or Karyes is now valid for only four days but one can go back to renew it. The journey described in Chapter 17 was an eight-day tour by caique. This would therefore be possible with one renewal of the permit. A one-day visit is possible from cruise ships.

Feasts and Holidays

1 January. Public Holiday. Feast of St Basil (Ayios Vasilios, popularly known as Ay. Vasili), one of the most distinguished Early-Christian Fathers of the Church. *Vasilopitta* (St Basil's Cake), a kind of large, round brioche, is cut just after midnight in every Greek house, it contains a coin which brings good luck to the finder.

6 January. Epiphany ('*Ton Foton*'). Public Holiday. Blessing of the waters. An official ceremony is held at Piraeus and also at Dexameni in Athens, attended by high-ranking prelates flanked by acolytes bearing banners, and also by cabinet ministers and representatives of the armed forces. Ships' sirens hoot as the officiating priest throws the Cross into the sea and the waters are blessed. Throughout the country wells and springs are blessed.

At Epiphany the earth is rid of *Kallikantzari*, puckish demons with red eyes, monkeys' arms and cloven hooves, who run amok during the twelve days after Christmas and are probably a Christian version of the boisterous and equally grotesque Satyrs and Sileni, who danced attendance on Dionysos. Some of the favourite pranks of the *Kallikantzari* include riding piggy-back on frightened mortals, flinging pitch at front doors, dousing fires and polluting food.

February-March-April

Carnival (the three weeks before Lent). During the three Carnival weekends of the period, children in fancy dress roam the streets; gipsies, accompanied by performing monkeys, bang on tambourines (into which pedestrians drop coins) at street corners. In Athens, the tavernas of Plaka are crowded. Streamers and confetti litter the pavements. The biggest and most lively Carnival procession takes place in Patras during the third week-end.

Kathari Deftera ('Clean Monday') - the day after the last Sunday of Carnival. A public holiday. So-called because it is the first day of Lent. There is a general exodus into the country and the occasion is one for picnics. Kite-flying begins. At Thiva there is a lively parody of a peasant wedding, a thinly veiled spring fertility rite, at which the 'relatives' arrive riding donkeys backwards. The 'bride' (sometimes a man crudely got up as a woman) is bedecked with clanging bronze bells round her neck, and the whole thing becomes a bit riotous.

Traditional 'Clean Monday' food (meatless and served cold) consists of *fasolia piaz* (beans dressed with vinegar and sprinkled with slivers of onion), *tarama*, (a pinkish purée made of cod's roe and breadcrumbs), *galantzi dolmades* (rice, currants and pine-nuts, flavoured with onion, cooked in olive oil and wrapped in vine leaves) and *lagana*, flat loaves of unleavened bread. Octopus, prawns and other seafood are also permitted, but not fish.

25 March. Independence Day and the Feast of the Annunciation. Public holiday. Anniversary of the day when Bishop Yermanos raised the standard of revolt against the Turks at Kalavryta in 1821. Military parades are held in all towns and villages.

The Easter Cycle. Orthodox Easter, which rarely coincides with that of the Western churches (they are sometimes as much as five weeks apart), generally falls within the second half of April, seldom before, occasionally in early May. The weather can be showery, but the flowers are at their most prolific, the gardens heavy with the scent of lilac, wisteria, Banksian roses and stocks. Holy Week is known as *Megali Evdomada* (Great Week), and each day has the epithet *Megali*.

Maundy Thursday (Megali Pempti). The red eggs which will be cracked and eaten on Easter Day are dyed. In some places the first egg placed in the dye belongs to the Virgin; it is regarded as a talisman and must not be eaten. The colour red is supposed to have protective powers. Interiors of churches are decorated with black, purple and white shrouds and church bells toll throughout the evening.

Good Friday (Megali Paraskevi). A day of complete fast kept by very many Greeks. Brown wax candles are sold at street corners. Church bells toll, and until midday solemn music is broadcast by the state radio and TV network. Many people like to visit cemeteries to put flowers on the graves of their loved ones.

At about nine in the evening (earlier in the villages), the *Epitafios*, the funeral of Christ, the most moving and beautiful ceremony in the Orthodox calendar, begins. Behind the Cross, the body of Christ, in the form of a gold embroidered pall, smothered with wreaths woven out of scented flowers, is borne under a gilded canopy through the main streets of towns and villages. Priests, ranging from mitred bishops in lavish vestments to black-frocked deacons, walk slowly behind it, flanked by acolytes in coloured shifts, carrying banners. Then come the officials (civil and military) followed by a crowd of silent, dark-clothed worshippers, lighted candles cupped in their hands. The procession halts from time to time and prayers are said. By about ten o'clock the beflowered bier has been borne back to the church and the pall has been kissed by the more devout. Many cafés and restaurants are closed on Good Friday, those that are open are likely to close earlier than usual.

Easter Saturday. Nothing could be more striking than the contrast between the solemnity of the *Epitafios* and the liveliness of the *Anastasis*, the Resurrection service, the greatest feast in the Orthodox Church. Throughout the afternoon funeral drapings are removed from churches and replaced with branches of laurel and myrtle, while sprigs of rosemary are strewn across the floor of the *naos*. White (no longer brown) candles, decorated with white or blue ribbons (the national colours) are sold at open-air booths.

The service begins in a dim incense-laden atmosphere. Gradually more lights are turned on until the whole church is brilliantly illuminated. Towards midnight the service moves out to an open stage in front of the church to enable all to participate in the Resurrection. On the stroke of midnight the priest, in a soaring triumphant tone, chants the words '*Christos Anesti*' ('Christ is risen!'). The doors of the sanctuary open amid a blaze of light and the bier, only yesterday borne to the grave, is seen to be empty: Christ has risen. Church bells ring, children shout and let off firecrackers in the street. Members of the congregation shake hands or exchange the kiss of Resurrection, with the greeting 'Christ is risen!' and the reply 'In truth he is risen.' All personal quarrels are (supposed to be) forgiven and forgotten.

The crowds then disperse homeward-bound, holding their candles - it is a good omen to reach the house with the taper alight - and break their fast with a dish of *mayiritsa* (a thick soup made of chopped lambs' offal with egg, lemon and rice, seasoned with dill - rich but delicious) and red-dyed hard-boiled eggs.

Easter Sunday. A day of national rejoicing. In Athens, while the Head of State and Cabinet attend the doxology in the Cathedral, the cannons on Mount Lykavittos fire thunderous salvoes. The paschal lamb is roasted on a spit in gardens and open spaces and red eggs are cracked one against the other. Homes are decorated with lilac - *paschalia* - the flower of Easter.

Easter Monday. Public holiday.

Friday after Easter. Feast of the Virgin Mary, who is represented as *Zoödohos Piyi*, 'The Source of Life'. In villages where the church is dedicated to the Life-Bearing Spring, a procession headed by a priest carrying an icon of the Virgin winds through the streets in the late afternoon, as at Aharne (Menidi), twelve kilometres north of Athens.

23 April. St George's Day. When the date falls within Holy Week, the feast of St George is moved to a later date. The martyr is one of the most popular saints in the Orthodox calendar. Like the equally venerated Dimitrios, he represents a Christian reincarnation of the noble *ephebe* of antiquity.

At Arahova, near Delphi, St George's Day is celebrated with a religious procession, followed by folk-dances with drums and bagpipes, and athletic contests.

30 April. On the eve of May Day, wreaths of flowers - stocks, roses, lilies, pansies - symbolizing the advent of summer, are hung above the doors of houses, where they remain, brown and withered, until the feast of St John the Baptist.

Athenians flock to the suburbs of Ano Patissia and Nea Filadelfia, where fireworks crackle and much wine is drunk in tavernas. As at Easter, lamb is roasted on the spit in the open. The streets are lined with booths where wreaths of flowers are sold and, late at night, the pavements are littered with bruised blooms.

May Day is an official public holiday.

21 May. Feast of St Constantine and St Helena. The feast's importance derives from the aura of veneration attached to the figures of Constantine the Great, founder of the Byzantine Empire, and his pious mother, Helena.

Whit Monday. Public Holiday

June-August. Festival of ancient drama at Epidavros.

24 June. Birth of St John the Baptist. Bonfires are lit in villages and the suburbs of Athens on the eve of St John's Day. The inhabitants cast their May wreaths onto the pyre and dance round it, leaping over the embers, thus purifying themselves of their sins. The ashes, which possess protective and divinatory properties, are collected by housewives.

Sea-bathing and the eating of water-melon (cheapest and most popular of summer fruits) begin 'officially' on St John's Day, and the proverb runs 'Do not swim before you see water melon peel floating on the sea'.

17 July. St Marina's Feast. The saint was martyred in Antioch in the third century and her feast ushers in the season of grapes. Peasants flock to the vineyards to cut the first bunches and bear offerings of fruit to the churches.

A fair is held outside the church of Ayia Marina near the Theseion in Athens, where the saint is worshipped as protectress against smallpox. She is also the scourge of all insects.

20 July. Feast of the Prophet Elijah, patron saint of rain, thunder, and lightning. Worshipped on hilltops crowned with whitewashed chapels where bonfires are sometimes lit (as on Mount Taiyetos) and associated with the prophet's ascent to Heaven. As Lord of the Thunder (the thunderclaps being attributed to the rolling of his chariot wheels), he represents a Christian counterpart of Zeus.

15 August. Assumption of the Virgin. Public holiday. After Easter and Christmas the most important religious holiday in the Greek calendar, a symbol of the Orthodox veneration of the Virgin. 1-15 August is a period of fast, which Greeks keep with varying degrees of strictness.

Two great religious pilgrimages are made on this day: to the Aegean islands of Tinos and Paros.

29 August. Feast of St John the Baptist (Beheading). The malarial fevers that until recently ravaged many of the plains, especially during the torrid month of August, were supposed to be the manifestations of the shock or spasm suffered by the Baptist when he was beheaded to please Salome (a scene much favoured for reproduction in rustic icons). Fairs (*paniyiria*) are held in villages where the main church is dedicated to St John the Baptist.

14 September. The Exaltation of the Cross. An important Orthodox feast. In churches a priest presents the congregation with sprigs of basil as a token of the herb that sprouted at the foot of the Cross.

26 October. Feast of St Dimitrios, one of the most popular saints in the calendar. All churches dedicated to St Dimitrios, a gallant young convert martyred by Galerius in a public bath at Thessaloniki, are brilliantly illuminated on the nights of 25 and 26 October.

The weather is usually fine and the last week in October is referred to as 'the summer of St Dimitrios' - the Greek Indian summer (if it comes earlier it is known as the 'donkey's summer'). The saint's name day is the occasion for the tasting of new wine.

28 October. Public holiday to commemorate the Italian invasion of Greece in 1940. In the course of the invasion a small Greek army routed Mussolini's numerically superior but ill-equipped divisions. Commonly known as '*Ohi*' Day, from the simple negative uttered by the Prime Minister, Ioannis Metaxas, when presented with the Fascist ultimatum by the Italian Ambassador.

6 December. St Nicholas' Day. Commonly regarded as the first day of winter. The saint, patron of sailors, is occasionally represented in popular hagiography dressed in clothes covered with brine, seawater dripping from his long white beard, after rescuing sailors from sinking ships in winter storms. His affinity with Poseidon is obvious, but he is more benign, less violent, than the Lord of the Trident. He prefers to pacify tempests rather than to rouse them.

Every Greek ship, from the largest cruise liner or super-tanker to the smallest caique, possesses an icon of the saint covered with votive trinkets in the shape of vessels.

Chapels dedicated to St Nicholas abound in the islands and maritime districts of the mainland.

12 December. Feast of St Spyridon. The embalmed remains of the Cypriot bishop, martyred during Diocletian's reign, and borne overland from Constantinople to Corfu after 1453 in order to escape Ottoman desecration, are now displayed in an elaborate silver coffin in the church of St Spyridon at Corfu. The saint, patron of Corfu, is greatly venerated throughout the country.

The name Spyridon derives from the word *spyri*, a grain, which can also mean a pimple, and according to popular superstition, the wonder-making properties of the saint's relics act as an antidote against smallpox, rashes and skin diseases.

24 December. Little boys and girls ring doorbells and ask: '*Na ta poúme?*' ('Shall we say them?'). In other words, should they sing the *kalanda* (the Greek equivalent of Christmas carols) while they beat a miniature hammer on a little metal triangle, in return for a small gratuity.

25-26 December. Public holidays

31 December. Singing of *kalanda* as on Christmas Eve. In the evening most Greeks play cards. It is traditional to try one's luck at the gaming-table on the threshold of the New Year.

Glossary

Abacus - slab crowning the capital of a column
Acroteria - ornamental effigies or mouldings placed at either end of pediment in ancient Greek architecture
Adyton - inner sanctuary and holiest chamber of a temple where oracles were delivered
Agora - a Greek market place. Equivalent to Roman forum
Ambo - pulpit in an Orthodox church
Amphora - a two-handled Greek or Roman jar with narrow neck and base
Apse - a projection, usually semi-circular, on the east end of a church
Archon - magistrate in ancient Athens. A notable during the Turkish occupation
Aryballos - ancient flask (swollen in the centre) with a round base, used as a perfume container
Ashlar - masonry of square-hewn stone - often used as facing to a rubble wall
Basilica - a large Roman public building, or a similar Romanesque or Byzantine Christian church, essentially rectangular with a semi-circular or polygonal apse. Colonnades or piers on either side separate the nave from the side aisles
Bouleuterion - senate house
Bouzouki - a large mandolin with a particularly plangent tone
Cantharos - a tall two-handled drinking cup
Cavea - the part of an ancient theatre used by for spectators
Cella - enclosed inner room of a temple, often containing the cult statue
Cenobite - monk living with others in a community
Chiton - sleeveless tunic, fastened over the shoulder by clasps and round the waist with a girdle, worn by men and women in ancient Greece
Chlamys - oblong outer garment, smaller than the himation and even more ornamented, hung from the neck
Choregic - pertaining to a choregos, administrator and financier of a chorus
Chrysobull - Byzantine imperial charter

Clerestory - the upper part of a church with windows above the side aisle roof

Conch - the concave surface of the vault of an apse

Cross-in-square or Greek Cross - form of Byzantine church architecture in which the dome over the central square area of the naos is supported by four columns at the corners, or by two columns and two sections of wall on either side of the apse

Deisis - representation of Christ between the Virgin and St John the Baptist

Deme - geographical unit for local government purposes in ancient Attica

Diazoma - horizontal passage, between the tiers of an ancient theatre, which served as a foyer

Dodekaorton - the Twelve Feasts, the principal scenes from the lives of Christ and the Virgin, which (either in fresco or mosaic) decorate the walls of all Byzantine churches

Dormition - the death and laying-out of holy personages, particularly the Virgin

Dromos - a public way, often lined with statues, temples, etc.

Entablature - the part of a building - such as a temple - above the columns, including the architrave, frieze and cornice

Entasis - a convexity in the shaft of a column: an intentional distortion designed to eliminate the optical illusion whereby a straight column appears thinner in the centre than at the top or bottom

Ephebe - a youth just entering manhood or just enrolled as a citizen in ancient Greece

Ephoros - inspector, curator

Epitafios - flower-decked bier of Christ borne in procession in towns and villages throughout the country on the evening of Good Friday

Eremite - a hermit

Exedra - apsidal (sometimes rectangular-shaped) recess with seats

Ex-Voto - a gift or offering made as a consequence of a vow

Faience - glazed earthenware

Firman - an administrative order issued by an Ottoman sultan

Fylakas - guard, custodian

Gigantomachia - a battle between the gods and giants depicted on the friezes of temples

Glykofiloussa - a type of icon of the Virgin and Child (The Sweetly Kissing One) in which the Child is depicted resting his cheek against the Virgin's

Hammam - Turkish bath

Helot - serf who formed the backbone of the Spartan army

Hetaira - a courtesan in ancient Greece

Himation - a cloak of varying texture, colour and embroidered decoration, worn by both men and women in ancient Greece

Hoplite - heavily armed ancient Greek infantryman

Iconoclasts - those who took part in the movement, of the eighth and ninth centuries, to stamp out the use of icons in Byzantine churches.

Iconostasis - screen adorned with icons separating the sanctuary from the remainder of an Orthodox church

Idiorrythmic - a monastery in which each monk maintains himself independently

Imaret - hospice for pilgrims and travellers in Turkey

Impost - the projecting part at the top of a column

In antis - two porch columns between two prolongations (antae) of the side walls of the cella of a temple

Katavothra - subterranean stream flowing under the hard limestone rock of many Greek mountains

Kelim - a woven carpet

Kellia - retreats of hermits

Kioshk - Turkish palace or pavilion

Koimesis - 'falling asleep', used for the death of the Virgin

Kokkinelli - slightly resinated rosé wine

Koré - an ancient Greek maiden. Term commonly applied to statues of young women of the Archaic period

Kouros - an ancient Greek youth. Term commonly applied to statues of young men of the Archaic period

Krater - a vessel with a wide mouth in which liquids, chiefly wine and water, were mixed

Lekythos - a slender vessel (derived from the domestic oil-flask) with long spout-like mouth, used at fifth-century BC funerals. The base is sometimes rounded

Linear B - syllabic script used for writing the Mycenean Greek language from c.1400 to c.1150 BC.
Loukoumi - Turkish delight
Loutrophoros - a tall ancient Greek vessel used to bring water for the bath
Mandorla - almond-shaped aureole surrounding depictions of holy personages in Christian art
Megaron - the great hall of an ancient palace
Metope - one of the square stone panels, either decorated or plain, between triglyphs in a Doric frieze
Metroön - temple of the Mother of the Gods
Mihrab - prayer niche indicating the direction of Mecca in a mosque
Naos - the main chamber, or inner shrine, of a Greek temple, in which the effigy of the deity was kept. Also the main body of a Byzantine cruciform church, entered though the narthex
Narghile - synonym for hookah
Narthex - vestibule across the west end of an Orthodox church
Necropolis - cemetery or burial-ground
Nome - administrative division in ancient Attica
Odeion - a small theatre for music
Oinoche - an ancient jug, with a handle, for pouring
Opisthodomos - an enclosed space at the back of a Greek temple, corresponding to the pronaos at the front
Orans - representation of the Virgin or a saint with arms outstretched in an attitude of prayer
Orchestra - circular space below the lowest tier of an ancient theatre where the chorus chanted and performed dance patterns. A small segment of the orchestra was generally occupied by the narrow stage (see proskenion)
Palaestra - an open space for wrestling or athletics in ancient Greece, especially the forecourt of a gymnasium
Panayia - the Virgin
Pantocrator - The All-Ruler (Christ), of whom there is an effigy in the central cupola of most Byzantine churches
Parados - one of the two side entrances into the orchestra of a Greek theatre originally used by the chorus only. The paradoi often had architectural embellishments

Patera - a broad, shallow dish used for pouring libations at sacrifices

Pendentive - a concave section of vaulting in the angle of two walls or arches leading up to, and supporting, one quarter of the circular base of a dome

Peplos - fifth-century BC dress (ankle length, belted) worn by women on ceremonial occasions. Often elaborately embroidered

Peribolos - an ancient precinct, or the wall around it

Peripteral - a Greek temple surrounded by a single row of pillars

Peristyle - colonnade surrounding a temple or court

Phiale - holy water basin

Podium - low platform or continuous base carrying a colonnade or building

Pronaos - outer chamber (sometimes a portico) of a temple, in front of the naos

Propylaia - entrance way (generally a monumental gateway) to a sacred enclosure

Proskenion - narrow stage of an ancient theatre on which the protagonists, but not the chorus, performed

Prostyle - colonnaded portico in front of an ancient building

Protome - sculpture of head and shoulders (bust)

Quadriga - chariot drawn by four horses

Ravelin - an outwork or salient projecting from the main fortifications of a castle

Satrap - a local ruler, the Governor of a province

Simandron - oblong wooden board outside an Orthodox monastic church which is banged to summon monks to prayer

Skene - back wall of an ancient Greek theatre. Sometimes used loosely to mean the whole stage and its embellishments

Skiti - dependency of a monastery

Soffit - the under surface of an arch or beam

Souvlakia - pieces of lamb, veal or pork grilled on a skewer

Squinch - section of vaulting arched across an angle used in reducing a square to an octagon to support the dome

Steatite - soapstone

Stele - upright stone or marble, often sculptured, placed above ancient graves

Stoa - a roofed colonnade

Stylobate - continuous base or substructure from which the columns of a temple rise

Sublime Porte - the Ottoman Government

Telesterion - a place of initiation

Terma - finishing post of an ancient Greek race-track

Tholos - a circular building, generally a temple

Tholos tomb - circular mausoleum with a monumental approach and a conical beehive roof, covered with earth so as to form a tumulus

Thrysos - a staff borne by Dionysos

Triglyph - a block of stone or marble carved with three vertical bars used in the entablature of temples of the Doric order

Trireme - ancient Greek galley rowed by three banks of oars

Tsarouhia - Turkish-style red or black slippers with pompoms

Volute - spiral ornament, especially the distinctive corner feature of an Ionic capital

Yataghan - a Turkish sabre with a curved blade, an eared pommel and no guard

Chronological Table

Neolithic Period (6000-3000 BC)

Early inhabitants, using stone tools and weapons, lived in relatively advanced agricultural communities in Thessaly, and more primitive ones in many other parts of Greece.

Early Helladic Period (3200-1900 BC)

Further migration from the East brought the use of metal (copper and bronze) to Greece. Development of the Minoan civilization in Crete. The Helladic civilisation flourished in the Cyclades, and in mainland Greece was centred in the North-East Peloponnese, Attica and Boeotia.

Middle Helladic Period (1900-1550 BC)

The Achaeans migrated from Asia Minor and settled throughout Greece. Their civilisation, centred in the Peloponnese and Central Greece, was less advanced than the Minoan of Crete, with its great palaces at Knossos and Phaistos.

Late Helladic Period (1550-1100 BC)

c.1550-1450 Minoan ascendancy

c.1450-1200 Mycenean ascendancy on the mainland and in Crete. Destruction of Cretan palaces. Building of palaces at Mycenae, Tiryns and Pylos. Use of Linear B script.

c.1250-1200 Trojan War - the extended, and ultimately successful, Mycenean expedition to capture Troy which, at the entrance to the Hellespont, was the key to Black Sea trade. Destruction of Thebes (c.1200)

c.1200-1050 Decline of the Mycenean civilisation and destruction of palaces

Early Iron Age (1100-700 BC)

c.1100-750	Dorian infiltration from Epirus and Macedonia ended the Mycenean civilization - the cities were destroyed and the 'dark Ages' descended
c.750-700	Rise of the Greek city states with Athens dominant in Attica, Thebes in Boeotia and Argos, Corinth and Sparta in the Peloponnese. Greek colonies established in Italy and Sicily
c.800-700	Fame of Delphic oracle established
776	First panhellenic games held at Olympia

Archaic Period (700-480 BC)

c.750-700	Homer
c.600	Byzantium founded by Megarian colonists
c.680-650	Dominance of Argos under King Pheidon
c.657	Rulers of Corinth overthrown by Kypselos, first of the tyrants
c.730-710	First Messenian War - Messenians finally surrendered to the Spartans on Mount Ithomi
c.635-620	Second Messenian War. Messenians again defeated - this time on Mount Eira - by the Spartans. Many Messenians emigrated to Sicily and founded Messina
c.594-593	Solon's social reforms in Athens
582	Pythian festival at Delphi transformed into panhellenic festival
560-510	Tyranny of Peisistratos and his sons in Athens
530-515	Temple of Apollo at Delphi rebuilt by the Alkmaionids, an Athenian family in exile
507	Reforms of Kleisthenes introduced a democratic constitution in Athens
490	Seaborne Persian expedition sent by Darius against Athens as punishment for support of Greek colonies in Asia Minor. Battle of Marathon in which the Persians were routed
480	Second Persian expedition under Xerxes. Athenians defeated by Persian fleet at the Battle of Artemesion. Persian army, advancing overland,

	overcomes Leonidas and the Spartans at Thermopylae and takes Athens; buildings on the Acropolis destroyed. Battle of Salamis at which Athenians, led by Themistocles, regain command of the sea - Xerxes and his fleet return to Persia
479	Battle of Plataia: Persian army under Mardonius defeated by confederate Greek army and forced to return home

Classical Period (480-323 BC)

5th Century	Building of Erechtheion and Theseion in Athens, Temples at Bassae and Sounion and Tholos at Delphi. Plays of Aeschylus, Sophocles, Euripedes and Aristophanes written
476-460	Growth of Athenian confederacy around the Aegean under the leadership of Kimon abroad and Aristides at home.
468-456	Building of Temple of Zeus at Olympia
464-459	Third Messenian War; ends when Messenians surrender to Spartans on Mount Ithomi for the second time
460-430	Athens dominant in the Greek world - the 'Age of Pericles'
447-432	Building of Parthenon and Propylaia on the Acropolis
431	Outbreak of Peloponnesian War - chronicled by Thucydides - between Athens and confederacy of other states led by Sparta
429-427	Plataia - garrisoned by the Athenians - besieged and reduced by Peloponnesian army
425	Siege of Sfaktiria - Spartans surrender to the Athenians
421	Peace of Nikias emporarily halts hostilities between Athens and Sparta. Dedication of Temple of Niké Apteros in Athens
419	Resumption of hostilities between Athens and Peloponnesians

405	Spartan fleet, commanded by Lysander, destroys the Athenian fleet at Aegospotami in the Hellespont; ends Athenian naval supremacy
404	Athens blockaded and forced to surrender; destruction of the Long Walls. End of Peloponnesian War
403	Thrasyboulos overthrows the Thirty Tyrants. Restoration of democracy in Athens
401	March of the Ten Thousand under Xenophon
4th Century	Building of new Temple of Apollo at Olympia, Temple at Tegea and Theatre at Epidauros
399	Birth of Aristotle (tutor to Alexander the Great) who settled in Athens in 335 and founded the Lykeion
371	Battle of Leuktra: Thebans commanded by Epaminondas, drive Spartans out of Central Greece; ascendency of Thebes follows
371-369	Foundation of Megalopolis and Messene
362	Second battle of Mantinea - Spartans defeated by Boeotians. Death of Epaminondas in battle
359-336	Growth of Macedonian Empire under Philip II
356	Birth of Alexander the Great
338	Battle of Chaironeia - Philip II defeats the Athenians and Thebans; becomes master of Greece. End of Greek democracy
336	Assassination of Philip II. Accession of Alexander the Great
334	Alexander crosses into Asia to conquer Persian Empire. Macedonian Empire extended from Egypt to India
324	Alexander's divinity proclaimed at Olympia
323	Death of Alexander at Babylon, followed by disintegration of Macedonian Empire outside Greece

Hellenistic Period (323-146 BC)

323	Outbreak of war between the Diadochi (successors to Alexander). Foundation of the Aetolian League - guardians of the Sanctuary at Delphi
323-2	Lamian War. Greeks revolt against Macedonian tyranny
307	Demetrios Poliorketes master of Athens
281	Formation of Achaean League
226	War between Sparta and Achaean League
222	Battle of Sellassia - Sparta defeated by armies of Macedonia and Achaean League
220-217	War between Aetolian League and Achaeans, supported by the Macedonians
215	Second Punic War between Rome and Carthage: Macedonia under Philip V allied to Hannibal, Aetolians and Spartans side with Romans
197	Second Macedonian War: Philip V defeated by Romans. The Consul, Flaminius, declares Rome 'the Protector of Greek Freedom'
168	Third Macedonian War ends with Battle of Pydna. Defeat of Perseus, son of Philip V, by Aemilius Paulus. End of Macedonian Monarchy
148	Macedonia becomes Roman province
146	Sack of Corinth by Mummius. Suppression of Achaean League. Southern Greece added to Roman Empire as dependency of Macedonia

Roman Period (146 BC - 330 AD)

88-87	War in Greece between Rome and Mithridates, King of Pontos (Asia Minor)
86	Athens, in alliance with Mithridates, sacked by Sulla
48	Battle of Pharsalus - Pompey defeated by Julius Caesar
44	Corinth refounded by the Romans; later becomes capital of province of Achaea after separation from Macedonia by Octavian

42	Battle of Philippi - Cassius and Brutus defeated by Mark Antony
31	Battle of Actium - Mark Antony defeated by Octavian
50-53 AD	St Paul's mission to Greece
66-67	Nero visits Greece
125-129	Hadrian visits Greece
132	Completion of Temple of Olympian Zeus at Athens
250	First invasion by Goths
267	Athens captured by the Goths who were subsequently driven back to the Danube by the Romans
313	Edict of Milan. Toleration of Christian worship
325	First Council of Nicaea. Adoption of Christianity as the religion of the Empire
330	Constantine the Great transfers capital of the Roman Empire from Rome to Byzantium, and renames it Constantinople

Early Byzantine Period (330-843)

392	Edict of Theodosios the Great proscribing paganism. Sanctuaries at Delphi and Olympia closed down
395	Visigoths invade Greece but move on towards Spain
467-488	Ostrogoths invade Greece, then move on towards Italy
6th Century	Slavs invade Greece; they do not capture main cities but settle, nevertheless, in the countryside
726-780	First Iconoclast period
802-842	Second Iconoclast period
843	Proscription of Iconoclasm by seventh Council of Nicaea

Middle Byzantine Period (843-1261)

10th Century	Bulgar expansion into Northern Greece
1018	Byzantine victory over Bulgars. Emperor Basil II makes triumphal tour of Greece and visits Athens
1054	Schism between Roman and Eastern Churches
1081-1084	Normans under Robert Guiscard invade Greece
1146	Normans invade again and sack Thebes and Corinth
1185	Normans loot Thessaloniki, then return home
1186-1258	Second Bulgarian Empire including parts of Northern Greece
1204	Fourth Crusade. Capture and sack of Constantinople by Crusaders. Division of Byzantine Empire between the Crusaders (the Latin Dukedom of Athens, the Kingdom of Thessaloniki), Venice (Dukedom of The Archipelago, most of the other islands, some outposts on the mainland) and the remaining Byzantine rulers (Despotate of Epirus, the Greek Empire of Nicaea). Geoffrey de Villehardouin lands at Methoni
1204-1261	Expansion of Greek Empire under Laskarid and Paleologos dynasties to cover much of Northern Greece and western Asia Minor
1205	Othon de la Roche first Latin Duke of Athens. Conquest of the Morea by Geoffrey de Villehardouin and William de Champlitte
1248	Siege of Monemvassia by William de Villehardouin
1259	Battle of Pelagonia. Decisive defeat of Franks by Greek army
1261	Greeks recapture Constantinople. End of Latin Empire of Constantinople - re-establishment of Byzantine Empire

Late Byzantine Period (1261-1453)

1262	Byzantine Empire recovers Mystra, Maina and Monemvassia from Franks
14th Century	Rise of Ottoman Empire; Byzantine Empire confined to Constantinople, Thessaloniki and Peloponnese
1311	Battle of Kifissos. Frankish Dukes of Athens routed by Grand Company of Catalans
1311-1387	Catalan rule in Athens
1348	Manuel Kantakouzenos first Despot of Mystra
1388	Athens occupied by Florentines
1388-1456	Acciajuoli family (bankers from Florence) were Dukes of Athens
1393-1414	Turkish conquest of Central Greece
1427-1432	Byzantine campaign drives Latins out of the Peloponnese
1453	Fall of Constantinople

Turkish Period (1453-1832)

1459	Fall of Mystra and end of Despotate
1499-1500	Venetians surrender maritime stations on Greek mainland to Turks
1685-1687	Venetians, commanded by Morosini, conquer the Peloponnese
1687	Destruction of Parthenon during Venetian siege of Athens
1715	Venetians driven out of Greece by Turks
1801	Lord Elgin receives permission from Turks to remove sculptures from Acropolis
1809-1811	Byron in Athens
1821	Standard of revolt raised against Turks by Bishop Yermanos at Kalavryta
1824	Arrival of Byron at Mesolonghi. Death of Byron
1825	Ibrahim Pasha devastates the Morea
1827	Battle of Navarino. Destruction of Turkish fleet by British, French and Russians
1828	French army under General Maison liberates the Morea

1832	Protocol of London. Greece declared an independent kingdom. National Assembly at Nafplion ratifies election of Prince Otto of Bavaria as King Othon of Greece

Modern Greece (1833-)

1833	Arrival of King Othon at Nafplion, capital of new kingdom
1834	Capital transferred to Athens
1875-1881	German archaeologists excavate Olympia
1876	Schliemann excavates Mycenae
1892-1903	Site of Delphi excavated by French School of Archaeology
1896	First revived Olympic Games held in Athens
1900	Sir Arthur Evans excavates Knossos in Crete
1912-1913	First and Second Balkan Wars
1916	Venizelos proclaims provisional government at Thessaloniki. Greece enters War against Central Powers
1919-1922	Graeco-Turkish campaign in Asia Minor
1923	Expulsion of Greek population from Asia Minor
1924	Establishment of Greek republic
1935	Restoration of Monarchy
1940	Italian invasion of Greece
1941	Landing and evacuation of British Expeditionary Force
1941-1944	German-Italian-Bulgar occupation of Greece
1944-1945	First Communist uprising
1946-1949	Second Communist uprising
1967	Establishment of military dictatorship. King Constantine II leaves Greece
1973	Re-establishment of Greek republic
1974	Parliamentary democracy replaces military dictatorship. Referendum goes against restoration of monarchy
1981	Greece joins the European Economic Community

Greek History: Biographical Details

The following brief notes are intended to introduce the reader to the principal characters in Greek history referred to in this book. There is only a fine line between Greek mythology and ancient history; predominantly mythological characters are shown thus: (M).

Abderos; (M) Friend of Herakles; the city of Abdera was founded by Herakles to commemorate his death.

Abdul Hamid II; (1842-1918) Sultan of Turkey. Autocratic ruler who cruelly suppressed revolts and massacred the Armenians. Deposed and exiled in 1909.

Achilles; (M) The son of Peleos and Thetis. His exploits as a Greek hero of the Trojan War were related by Homer in the *Iliad*.

Aemilius Paulus; (2nd c. BC) Roman Consul (182). He ended the third Macedonian War by routing Perseus at Pydna (168).

Aeschylus; (525-456 BC) Athenian tragedian. Born at Eleusis. Wrote over 60 plays including *Prometheus* and the *Orestia* trilogy.

Aetolos; (M) Third son of Endymion, King of Elis. Founder of Aetolia in the south-west of mainland Greece.

Agamemnon; (M) King of Mycenae. Son of Atreus. Commanded the Greek expedition to Troy but quarrelled with Achilles (described in the *Iliad*). Murdered by Aigisthos, lover of his wife Clytemnestra.

Agis II; King of Sparta from 427 to 399 BC. Restored Spartan authority in the Peloponnese by victory over the Argives and their allies at the Battle of Mantinea in 418 BC.

Alaric (370-410); Visigoth King from 395, when he invaded Greece. Fought with and against the Eastern and Western Roman Emperors; finally sacking Rome in 410.

Alexander the Great; (356-323 BC) King of Macedonia from 336 to 323 BC. Son of Philip II and Olympias. Born at Pella in 356. Sacked Thebes (335), defeated the Persians (333), founded Alexandria (331), invaded India (326), died at Babylon (323).

Ali Pasha; (1741-1822) An Albanian brigand who became Turkish Viceroy of Epirus, maintaining a barbarous court at Ioannina.

Andrew, St; (1st c.) Apostle who preached in Asia Minor and Greece. Crucified by the Romans in Achaea.

Andronikos I Komnenos; (1122-85) Byzantine Emperor from 1183, his rule was marked by murder and tyranny. Overthrown 1185.

Andronikos, Manolis; (1919-1992) Professor of Archaeology at Thessaloniki University who discovered the Royal Tomb of Philip II at Veryina in 1977.

Antony, Mark; (83-30 BC) Roman general, relative and supporter of Julius Caesar. After Caesar's death he joined with Augustus and defeated Brutus and Cassius at Philippi (42). Captivated by Cleopatra. Ruled the Eastern part of the Empire but fell out with Augustus and, with Cleopatra, was defeated at Actium (31). Fled to Egypt, committed suicide (30).

Apelles; 4th c. BC painter. Friend of Alexander the Great.

Apollo; (M) Greek God. Son of Leto; born on Delos; his sister was Artemis. His chief oracular shrine was at Delphi.

Aratos; (271-213 BC) Sikyonian statesman and national hero.

Archelaos; King of Macedonia 413-399 BC. Built up Macedonia's military strength, fostered trade and the arts. Moved the court from Aigai to Pella.

Aristomenes; Messenian hero in wars with Spartans in 650 BC. After the fall of his stronghold at Mt Eira he was expelled to Rhodes.

Aristotle; Athenian philosopher and scientist. Born 384 BC at Stageira. Studied under Plato in Athens. Taught Alexander at Pella. Founded a school and library in Athens. Died 322 BC.

Arkadios; Eastern Roman Emperor 395-401. Son of Theodosios I.

Asclepios; (M) God of Healing. Son of Apollo and Koronis. Born at Epidauros, educated by Cheiron.

Ataturk, Mustafa Kemal; (1881-1938) Turkish statesman, born in Thessaloniki. Leader of Turkish Nationalist movement. President (1923-38). Responsible for modernization of Turkey.

Athanassios, St; A monk from Trebizond who became the first Abbot of the Grand Lavra, the first Athonite Monastery (963).

Attalos; (2nd c. BC) King of Pergamum (a city in western Asia Minor which was allied to Rome in 133 BC).

Augustus Caesar, Octavian; (63 BC-14 AD) First Roman Emperor. An ally of Mark Antony after Julius Caesar's death. Overcame opposition from Brutus and Cassius; triumphed over Mark Antony at Actium (31 BC) and became sole ruler.

Basil II; Byzantine Emperor (976-1025). One of the most successful Byzantine military rulers; known as the '**B**ulgar-slayer' from his campaign in 1018-19.

Bayazit II; (1448-1512) Sultan of the Ottoman Empire for 32 years from 1481. Fought many wars to expand the Empire.

Blegen, Carl; Archaeologist who carried out excavations at the Palace of Nestor from 1952.

Bohemond; (1056-1111) Son of Robert Guiscard. Fought against Byzantine Emperor (1081-85) and in the First Crusade (1096) after which he became Prince of Antioch.

Brasidas; 5th c. BC Spartan leader. Captured Amphipolis (424). Killed at second battle of Amphipolis (422) in which Spartans defeated Athenians under Kleon.

Brutus, Marcus Junius; (85-42 BC) Roman general. Allied to Pompey in the Civil War. Pardoned by Caesar after Pharsalus. Governor of Cisalpine Gaul (46). Conspired against Caesar with Cassius (44). Raised an army in Greece, defeated by Augustus and Mark Antony at Philippi (42). Committed suicide.

Byron, Lord; (1788-1824) Philhellenic British Poet. Joined the Greek insurgents against the Turks at Mesolonghi, where he died of fever in 1824.

Cadmos; (M) Founder of Thebes

Caesar, Gaius Julius; (100-44 BC) Roman general and statesman, formed the first Triumvirate with Pompey and Crassus. Extended Roman frontiers to the north and west, including Gaul and Britain. Caesar quarrelled with Pompey who withdrew to Greece. Appointed Dictator and defeated Pompey at Pharsalus (48). Wars and insurrections continued and Caesar was assasinated by conspirators led by Brutus and Cassius (44).

Caligula; (12-41). Became Roman Emperor after the death of Tiberius (37). His reign was renowned for murder, despotism and extravagence. Assassinated in 41.

Callas, Maria; (1923-1977). Opera singer, born in New York of Greek parents.

Capodistria, Count; (1776-1831) Elected President of Greece in 1828, his autocratic behaviour (learnt in Tsarist Russia) aroused discontent. Assassinated at Nafplion by Mavromihalis from Mani.

Cassius, Gaius; Roman ally of Brutus; committed suicide after his defeat by Mark Antony at Battle of Philippi in 42 BC.

Cheiron; (M) One of the Centaurs who lived in the mountains of Thessaly. Their upper parts were human and lower were equine. Generally a wild beast-like tribe, known for their rape of the Lapith women. Cheiron was a wise, old medicine-man who educated Achilles, Asclepios and Jason.

Cleopatra; (69-30 BC). Became Queen of Egypt with support of Julius Caesar. After the Battle of Philippi she joined Mark Antony at Tarsus. Antony and Cleopatra were defeated by Augustus at Actium (31). Committed suicide (30).

Clytemnestra; (M) Wife of Agamemnon. Murdered for infidelity by her son Orestes.

Codrington, Sir Edward; (1770-1851) English Admiral. As C-in-C Mediterranean Squadron he joined with French and Russian ships to annihilate the Turkish fleet at Navarino 1827.

Constantine I; (1863-1923) Led the Greeks to victory in the Balkan War of 1912-13. Succeeded his father, George I, as King of Greece (1913). Abdicated 1922.

Constantine XI Paleologos; last Byzantine Emperor 1449-53

Curzon, Robert Lord; (1810-73) English diplomat and scholar. Travelled widely in Greece and the Middle East; wrote about his experiences and visits to monasteries.

Damophon; (2nd c. BC) Messenian sculptor. Repaired Phidias' Zeus at Olympia. Worked at Messene, Aigion and Megalopolis.

Dandolo; (1108-1205) Venetian statesman and soldier. Elected Doge (1201). Led the 4th Crusade; occupied Constantinople (1204) and established Baldwin I as the first Latin Emperor.

Darius; (548-486 BC) King of Persia (521), expanded the Empire to the Indus and Caucasus, subdued Thrace and Macedonia. Defeated by Athenians at Marathon (490). Succeeded by Xerxes before he could mount another expedition against Athens.

de Champlitte, William; Joined with Geoffrey de Villhardouin in the conquest of the Morea (1205) and became Prince of Achaea (1205). Returned to France in 1208.

de Villehardouin, Geoffroy I (1160-1228) French nobleman and historian. Took part in Fourth Crusade but was diverted to Greece where he made substantial conquests with William de Champlitte, whom he succeeded as Prince of Achaea 1208-28.

de Villehardouin, Geoffroy II; Prince of Achaea 1228-1246

de Villehardouin, Marguerite; Younger daughter of William II de Villehardouin. Died in captivity at Hlemoutsi in 1315.

de Villehardouin, William II; Prince of Achaea 1246-78

Demeter; (M) Goddess identified with the 'fruits of the earth', especially corn.

Demetrios Poliorketes; (336-283 BC) Son of Antigonas I of Macedonia. Fought from 317 to 301 to rebuild Alexander's empire. A period of instability and murder followed his father's death; he became King in 297. Tried to reconquer Asia but lost the support of the Greeks and drank himself to death.

Dimitrios, St; (4th c) Patron saint of Thessaloniki. Christian convert executed by order of Galerius.

Demosthenes; (384-322 BC) Athenian orator, statesman and lawyer. Champion of the Athenian cause against Macedonia.

Deukalion; (M) The Greek Noah, son of Prometheus. When Zeus flooded the earth he built an ark with his wife, Pyrrha, and floated until the waters subsided. Their son was Hellen, founder of the Hellenes.

Diogenes; (410-320 BC) Philosopher from Pontos who settled in Athens. Founded the Cynic Set and lived an austere, ascetic existence with ostentatious disregard for personal comfort.

Dionysos; (M) Son of Semele (daughter of Cadmos) and Zeus. The God of wine, also known as Bacchus, whose cult originated in Thrace. Festivals, which included dramatic performances, known as Dionysia, were held thoughout Greece.

Dionysios the Areopagite (1st century) Athenian converted by St Paul. Believed to be first Bishop of Athens.

Dioscuri; (M) Castor and Polydeuces (Pollux), the twin sons of Zeus, brothers of Helen of Troy.

Doria, Andrea; (1466-1560) Genoese statesman and admiral who fought the Turks in Greece and the Eastern Mediterranean.

Dusan, Stephen; (1308-1355) Serbian Tsar and national hero. Conquered Bulgaria, Macedonia and Albania.

El Greco; Domenikos Theotokopoulos (1541-1614). Painter, born in Crete. Studied in Italy and settled in Toledo.

Elgin, Lord; (1766-1841) British diplomat. As Ambassador to the Ottoman Empire he arranged for the Parthenon sculptures to be sent to England for safety. They were later purchased for the nation and are displayed in the British Museum.

Epaminondas; (418-362 BC) Theban statesman and general. Became famous for his defeat of the Spartans at Leuktra (370). Continued the war against Sparta in the Peloponnese and founded the city of Megalopolis.

Epeios; (M) Builder, with Athena, of the Trojan horse.

Euripides; (485-406 BC) Tragedian, born at Salamis. Wrote over 90 plays, of which 18 have survived. Left Athens in 408 for the court of King Archelaos of Macedonia where he died (406).

Evans, Sir Arthur; (1851-1941) English Archaeologist who excavated the palace at Knossos in Crete.

Fokas, Nikeforos; (547-610) Byzantine Emperor from 602-610. Reputation for vice, tyranny and incompetence.

Galerius; (250-311) Emperor of the Eastern Roman Empire from 305. Led the persecution of the Christians from 304.

George I; (1845-1913). Became King of Greece in 1863, after the deposition of King Othon. Son of King Christian IX of Denmark. His long reign saw the consolidation of Thessaly and Epirus into modern Greece. Assasinated at Thessaloniki and succeeded by his son Constantine I.

Gorgias; (483-376 BC) Sicilian sophist and teacher of rhetoric.

Hadrian; (76-138) Roman Emperor (117). Stabilised the boundaries of the Empire. Reorganized the army, ruled justly and was a patron of the arts. Visited Greece in 125 and 128.

Hera; (M) Ancient pre-Hellenic goddess. The wife of Zeus. Widely worshipped, but especially at Argos and Samos.

Herakles; (M) Greek Hero, possibly a Prince of Tiryns. Reputation for strength and valour. Performed the 12 Labours, which were recorded in the metopes of the Temple of Zeus at Olympia, and had many adventures. Six of the Labours were in the Peloponnese. Death by burning on a pyre on Mt Iti.

Herodes Atticus; (101-177) Wealthy Athenian. Consul at Rome. Benefactor who paid to have the Stadium in Athens clad in marble.

Herodotos; (482-425 BC) Greek historian born in Asia Minor. Travelled widely throughout the Greek and Roman world. Wrote the nine books of his *History* which started with the conquest of Asia Minor by Croesus and continued through the subsequent wars with the Persians.

Heuzey, Leon; French archaeologist who discovered the first Macedonian tomb at Veryina in 1861.

Hippocrates; (5th c. BC) The most famous Greek Physician. Little is known of his life except that he was born on Kos, travelled widely and died at Larissa.

Horace; (65-8 BC) Roman poet from Apulia who went to school in Rome and University in Athens. Served under Brutus in Greece until the defeat at Philippi. Returned to Rome where he worked in the civil service. His success as a poet - the *Satires, Epodes, Odes,* and *Epistles* - brought him wealth and the post of Poet Laureate.

Hyacinthos; (M) Pre-Hellenic god, worshipped at Amyklai. Beloved of Apollo and accidentally killed by a discus thrown by him. After his death the hyacinth sprang up in his memory.

Ibrahim Pasha; (1789-1848) Viceroy of Egypt and successor to Mehmet Ali. Landed at Methoni in 1825 to reconquer Greece. By 1825 he controlled most of the Morea, except Nafplion. Defeated by Codrington at Navarino (1827), subsequently his forces were cleared from the Morea by a French army.

Iktinos; (5th c. BC) Architect. Worked with Kallikrates on the design of the Parthenon. Also responsible for the Temple of Apollo at Bassae and the Telesterion at Eleusis.

Ioannis Doukas; (13th c.) Rebellious, illegitimate son of the Epirot Despot, Michael II. Built a castle at Ypati in Thessaly; known as Duke of Neopatras. Founded the Church of Porta Panayia.

Jason; Tyrant of Pherai (385 BC), gained control of Thessaly (374). Allied with Thebans and friendly with Athens. Assassinated (370).

Jason; (M) Leader of the Argonauts. Brought up by Cheiron after fleeing from Iolchus as a boy. Returned to claim his throne but was induced to set off in the *Argo* to fetch the Golden Fleece from Colchis and had many adventures on the voyage.

John II, Kantakouzenos; (1292-1383) Became Byzantine Emperor (1347), forced to abdicate (1355). Retired to a monastery.

Justinian; (482-565) Emperor of East Roman Empire from 527. Reunited the Empire and restored much of the territory that had been lost. Fortified the frontiers and codified Roman law.

Kallikrates; (5th c. BC) Architect, worked with Iktinos under the direction of Phidias on the design of the Parthenon.

Kleon; (5th c. BC) Athenian politician. Succeeded Pericles as ruler of Athens during the war with Sparta. Took over command during the Siege of Sfaktiria and defeated the Spartans (425).

Kolokotronis, Theodoros; (1770-1843) Patriot leader who fought to overthrow the Turks in the War of Independence. Led the assault on Nafplion in 1822. Supported the appointment of Prince Otto of Bavaria as King.

Konon; (444-392 BC) Athenian admiral, defeated the Spartan fleet at Cnidos (394). Returned to Athens and completed the construction of the Long Walls between Athens and Piraeus.

Korais, Adamantios; (1748-1833). Linguistic reformer and humanist scholar; the 'father' of modern Greek literature. He laid the intellectual foundations of the struggle for independence with his advocacy of revived classicism.

Leake, William; (1777-1860) British army topographer. Travelled in Greece and wrote about the country and its antiqities.

Leonidas; (5th c. BC) King of Sparta from 491. Died at Thermopylae defending the Pass against army of Xerxes (480).

Lykurgos; (M) Semi-legendary law-maker and founder of the Spartan civil and military systems.

Lykurgos; (390-325 BC) Athenian orator and statesman who controlled the city finances and raised money for major public building works.

Lysippos; (4th c. BC) Sculptor born in Sikyon. Produced over 1500 bronzes including several busts of Alexander the Great.

Mahmud II; (1785-1839) Ottoman Sultan from 1808, worked to modernise the Empire but during his reign Bessarabia, Serbia, Egypt and much of Greece were lost.

Manuel Kantakouzenos; First Despot of Mystra 1348-80. Builder of the Church of Ayia Sofia at Mystra.

Mardonius; (5th c. BC) Nephew of Darius. According to Herodotos he was the moving spirit behind Xerxes' invasion of Greece. Taking over command of the army after the battle of Salamis he retreated from Attica and was defeated and killed at Plataia in 479 BC.

Mavrocordatos, Alexander; (1791-1865) First President of the National Assembly (1821).

Mehmet Ali; (1769-1849) Pasha of Egypt. From 1821 his troops under Ibrahim Pasha occupied parts of the Morea to assist the Turks against the rebelling Greeks. After Navarino the Egyptian forces were forced by the French to leave Greece.

Mehmet II; (1432-81) Sultan of Turkey 1451-81 and founder of the Ottoman Empire. Captured Constantinople (1453) and extinguished the Byzantine Empire. Added Serbia and Greece to his Empire, visited Athens where he turned the Parthenon into a mosque. Died in a campaign against Persia (1481).

Michael I Angelos; Despot of Epirus 1204-15

Michael II Angelos; Despot of Epirus 1237-71

Mithridates VI, the Great; (132-63 BC) Became King of Pontos as a boy (120), ruled the kingdom in Asia Minor which he expanded; came into conflict with the Romans. Invaded Greece, was defeated and made peace with Sulla (75). Wars with Rome continued; Pompey defeated him at Nikopolis in Pontos (66).

Mnesikles; (5th c. BC) Architect; Designer of the Propylaia and possibly the Erechtheion.

Molossos; (M) Son of Neoptolemos, King of Epirus. His name was taken by the kings who ruled part of Epirus in the 4th century BC.

Morosini, Francesco; (1618-94) Venetian admiral and statesman. Commanded the Venetian fleet in wars with the Turks (1657). Reconquered the Morea and Athens (1685). Doge (1688).

Mummius; (2th c. BC) Roman consul and general. Crushed uprising of Achaean League against Rome. Captured and destroyed Corinth.

Mussolini, Benito; (1883-1945) Italian Fascist Dictator. His forces invaded Greece in 1940 from Albania but were defeated and driven back, subsequently Greece was occupied by German armies advancing from Yugoslavia.

Neoptolemos; (M) Also known as Pyrrhos. Son of Achilles. In the Trojan War he was one of those who manned the Wooden Horse. He went to Epirus, where the kings claim descent from his son Molossos. Pindar says he was killed in a quarrel at Delphi.

Nero; (37-68) Roman Emperor 54-68. The adopted son of Claudius, his rule is noted for debauchery, murder and tyranny. In Greece (66-7) he collected works of art, competed in the Games at Olympia and started to dig a canal across the Isthmus.

Nestor; (M) King of Pylos. Son of Neleos. He lived to a great age giving rather ineffectual advice to Achilles and others. The Mycenean palace north of Navarino is reputed to be the home of Nestor and Neleos.

Nikeforos I Doukas; Despot of Epirus 1271-96.

Octavian; see Augustus Caesar.

Olympias; Daughter of King Neoptolemos of Epirus. Married Philip II (357 BC). Mother of Alexander (356). Played a major part in the struggle for power after death of Alexander. Responsible for many murders, she was eventually assassinated.

Opheltes; (M) The infant son, either of the King of Nemea or of a priest of Zeus, who was killed by a snake-bite. According to legend the Nemean Games were founded in his memory.

Orestes; (M) Son of Agamemnon and Clytemnestra. Avenged the murder of his father by Aigisthos and murdered his mother.

Orloff, Feodor; (1786-1861) Russian commander in war with Turkey (1828-9). C-in-C Russian Black Sea Fleet (1833).

Othon; (1815-1867) First King of Modern Greece. Second son of King Louis I of Bavaria. Chosen as King by the Great Powers; governed autocratically until forced to become constitutional monarch (1843). Failed to win more territory, deposed (1862).

Oxylos; (M) According to one legend, Oxylos from Kalydon was a King of Elis who founded the Games at Olympia.

Paionios; (5th c. BC) Greek sculptor from Mende in Macedonia. His statue of Winged Victory (Niké) is in the Museum at Olympia.

Paul, St; (1st c.) Apostle, his second missionary journey took him through Greece where he preached at Thessaloniki, Athens and Corinth.

Pausanias; (2nd c.) Greek geographer who travelled widely and recorded his impressions of the history and topography of the cities, ancient sites and countryside. He covered Greece thoroughly; his books are readily available.

Peisistratids; (6th c. BC) Rulers of Athens. Peisistratos and his sons were popular rulers of Athens from 546 BC. Internal peace enforced and the peasants favoured over the aristocracy.

Pelasgos; (M) Pre-Hellenic King of Arcadia

Periander; Ruler of Corinth 625-585 BC. Repressive ruler who built-up Corinth's trade and power in Greece. The arts flourished (Temple of Apollo & Peirene Fountain at Corinth), he built the Diolchos (roadway for ships) across the Isthmus.

Pericles; (490-429 BC) Athenian statesman. Tried to form a Hellenic confederation; thwarted by the Spartans. Ruled Athens during the years in which two of the temples and the Propylaia on the Acropolis were built. The city flourished until war broke out with Sparta in 431.

Perseus; (213-165 BC) Last King of Macedonia. From 179 he consolidated his kingdom after the Roman defeat of his father, Philip V. Finally defeated at Pydna in 168. Died in captivity in Italy. Monarchy abolished.

Pheidon; (7th c. BC) King of Argos. Made Argos an important power in the Peloponnese; Seized Olympia (670). Instituted a system of standard measurements.

Phidias; (5th c. BC) One of the greatest sculptors of the Classical Period. Commissioned by Pericles to oversee the design of the buildings on the Acropolis and make the sculptures for the Propylaia and Parthenon. He also made the great statue of Zeus at Olympia.

Philip II; (382-336 BC) Born at Pella. Became King of Macedonia 359. Built up the army and expanded the kingdom by force of arms. Founded Philippi. Organized the Greek states into a federal league and prepared to invade Persia. Assassinated in 336 and succeeded by his son, Alexander.

Philip V; (238-179 BC) Followed Antigonos Doson as King of Macedonia in 221. He took over a strong kingdom but came into conflict with the growing power of Rome and was eventually defeated in 197. Succeeded by his son, Perseus.

Philip of Taranto; Prince of Achaea 1307-13. Married Thamar, daughter of the Despot Nikeforos I of Epirus.

Phormio; (5th c. BC) Athenian admiral. Blockaded Corinth (430) restored Athenian prestige by defeating Spartan fleets (431).

Pindar; (522-440 BC) Poet, born near Thebes in Boeotia. His triumphal odes celebrating victories in the games at Olympia, Delphi and Nemea have survived.

Plastiras, Nicholas; 20th c. Soldier and Politician. Army officer who forced abdication of King Constantine (1922). Supported Venizelos' Republican movement (1932). After the liberation of Greece (1944) he succeeded George Papandreou as Prime Minister for a few months in 1945.

Plutarch; (46-120) Greek historian, born at Chaironeia. Best known for his biographies of important Greek and Roman figures, he also wrote moral and political treatises.

Polykleitos; (5th c. BC) Sculptor from Argos. He worked at Olympia and Argos, specialising in athletic subjects in bronze.

Pompey; (106-48 BC), Roman statesman and general. Although he was initially allied to Julius Caesar they later became enemies and Pompey's army was routed at Pharsalus (48). He fled to Egypt where he was assassinated.

Poseidon; (M) Greek god of earthquakes and the sea.

Poussin, Nicolas; (1594-1665) French painter who specialised in mythological and landscape subjects.

Praxiteles; (4th c. BC) Athenian sculptor. His statue of Hermes with Dionysos was found in the Temple of Hera at Olympia.

Pyrrhos; (319-272 BC) King of Epirus. Tried to expand his kingdom in all directions. Fought: Romans, advancing almost to Rome; Carthaginians in Sicily; Macedonians under Antigonos Gonatas; Spartans in the Peloponnese. Killed at Argos.

Samuel; Bulgarian Tsar who invaded N. Greece in 10th century. Occupied Kastoria (990) until defeat by Emperor Basil II.

Schleimann, Heinrich; (1822-1890) German archaeologist who excavated the ancient sites at Troy, Mycenae and Tiryns.

Skopas; (4th c. BC) Sculptor from Paros who settled in Athens. Worked at Tegea and Sikyon.

Selim II; (1524-1574) Ottoman Emperor (1566). Son of Suleyman the Magnificent. He proved to be an idle drunkard (Selim the Sot). Defeated at Lepanto by Don John of Austria in 1571.

Sophocles; (496-405 BC) Athenian tragedian born at Kolonos. Wrote over 100 plays, best known for *Oedipus Tyrannos* and his version of *Elektra*.

Telemachos; (M) Son of Odysseus and Penelope. His exploits, recorded in the *Odyssey*, include his visit to Nestor at Pylos.

Thamar; Daughter of the Despot Nikeforos I. Married Philip of Taranto (1294); the Castle at Vonitsa was part of her dowry.

Themistocles; (528-462 BC) Athenian statesman who built up the fleet which triumphed over the Persians at Salamis (480). Strengthened the walls of Athens and Piraeus. His downfall was plotted by Sparta; banished to Argos and, later, Asia.

Theodora Angelos; wife of Michael II (Despot of Epirus 1237-71). Known for her piety and virtue; buried at Arta where the Church of Ayia Theodora is dedicated to her.

Theodore Angelos; Despot of Epirus 1215-1230, half-brother of Michael I. Expanded the area under his control eastwards, taking Thessaloniki (1224) where he was crowned Greek Emperor in 1227.

Theodosios I (the Great); (346-395) Became Eastern Roman Emperor in 379. In 390 he ordered the massacre at Thessaloniki. Became sole Roman Emperor in 394.

Theodosios II; (401-450) Grandson of Theodosios I, son of Arkadios, Eastern Roman Emperor from 408.

Theofanes; 16th Century Cretan painter who worked at the Grand Lavra, Mount Athos and Ayios Nikolaos, Meteora.

Theseus; (M) Son of Poseidon and National hero of Athens. Plutarch tells of his many adventures with monsters, brigands and Amazons. As King of Athens he united Attica.

Thucydides; (460-400 BC) Athenian historian. Exiled in Thrace after he commanded a naval engagement which failed to relieve Amphipolis. Wrote a history of the Peloponnesian War.

Venizelos, Eleftherios; (1864-1936) Greek Statesman. Born in Crete. He was Prime Minister four times between 1910 and 1933 during which time he extended Greek boundaries to the north and east. Clashed with Constantine I and set up a rival government in Thessaloniki in 1916.

Ventris, Michael; (1922-56) English architect and code expert. Deciphered (with John Chadwick), the Linear B tablets from Knossos and mainland Greece; proved the language to be an early form of Greek.

Xenophon; (435-354 BC) Athenian commander and historian. Fought in Asia Minor with Greek mercenaries for the Persian Prince Cyrus. Joined the Spartans against Athens. He was presented with an estate by the Spartans and retired to write.

Xerxes; (519-465 BC) King of Persia 486-465 BC. Succeeded his father Darius. Gathered a huge army to invade Greece. Bridged the Hellespont with boats and dug a canal across Athos peninsula. At Thermopylae (480) he overcame Leonidas and then sacked Athens. Defeated at sea by the Greeks at Salamis; withdrew after his general, Màrdonius, lost at Plataia (479).

Yermanos; Bishop of Patras who raised the flag of revolt against the Turks on 25th March 1821 at the Ayia Lavra, Kalavryta.

Zeus; (M) Father of the Gods. Athena, Artemis, Apollo, Ares and Dionysos were his children. Identified with weather and fire.

Some Books on Greece

There are plenty of books on the country and its people. This selective bibliography relies heavily on books which have been published or reprinted since 1990.

Travel Guides

Blue Guide, Greece and *Blue Guide, Athens* by Robin Barber. Indispensible to the serious traveller who needs detailed information about the country and its archaeological sites.

Greece - The Rough Guide by Mark Ellingham. Penguin. An excellent practical guide, packed with accurate and up to date information.

Specialist Guides

Guide to Greece, Pausanias. Penguin. Fascinating description of a tour of Greece in the fourth century with plenty of footnotes to help one identify the sites as they are today.

Literary Guide to Travel in Greece, Richard Stoneman. Oxford.

Travel Books

Mani, Patrick Leigh Fermor. Penguin. First published in 1958 this account of the author's first visit to the Southern Peloponnese will always be a classic description of Greece and the Greeks.

Roumeli, Patrick Leigh Fermor. Penguin. Published in 1966, the companion volume to '*Mani*' covers Leigh Fermor's travels in Northern Greece from the Turkish border to the Ambracian Gulf via the Monasteries of Meteora.

History

Alexander the Great, Robin Lane Fox. Penguin. Very readable account of the life of Alexander.

A Concise History of Greece, Richard Clogg. Cambridge. Useful introduction to Greek history from the late 18th century.

History of the Peloponnesian War, Thucydides. Penguin. Classic account of the wars between Athens and Sparta.

Inventing Paradise: the Greek Journey, Edmund Keeley. Farrar Straus. Greece as seen by poets and painters such as Sefaris and Ghika, and its impact on their friends Miller and Durrell.

Modern Greece: a Short History, C.M. Woodhouse. Cambridge. History of Greece from the third century to the present day.

Miscellaneous

The Alexander Trilogy, Mary Renault. Penguin. Now published in one volume, the trilogy covering Alexander's life is as readable as Mary Renault's other books covering Greek history such as *The Bull from the Sea* and *The King Must Die.*

Art of the Byzantine Era, David Talbot Rice. Thames and Hudson. Excellent introduction to the subject with plenty of good colour pictures to whet one's appetite before a visit to the churches and museums of Greece.

Attic in Greece, Austen Kark. Warner. Retirement to a beautiful, old house in Nafplion gave the author and his wife every opportunity to get to know modern Greece.

The Decipherment of Linear B, John Chadwick. Cambridge. Chadwick tells the story of his involvement with Michael Ventris in solving the riddle of Linear B.

A Luminous Land: Artists Discover Greece, Richard Stoneman. Oxford. Paintings, watercolours and engravings by European artists who visited Greece from the 15th to the 20th century.

Index

Ancient cities and sites are shown thus: *Epidauros*